CULTURE AND INTERNATIONAL LAW

PROCEEDINGS OF THE INTERNATIONAL CONFERENCE OF THE CENTRE FOR INTERNATIONAL LAW STUDIES (CILS 2018), OCTOBER 2-3, 2018, MALANG, INDONESIA

Culture and International Law

Editors

Hikmahanto Juwana, Jeffrey Thomas, Mohd Hazmi Mohd Rusli &
Dhiana Puspitawati

CRC Press
Taylor & Francis Group
Boca Raton London New York

CRC Press is an imprint of the
Taylor & Francis Group, an **informa** business
A BALKEMA BOOK

CRC Press
Taylor & Francis Group
6000 Broken Sound Parkway NW, Suite 300
Boca Raton, FL 33487-2742

First issued in paperback 2020

Typeset by Integra Software Services Pvt. Ltd., Pondicherry, India

ISBN-13: 978-1-138-38766-9 (hbk)
ISBN-13: 978-0-367-77662-6 (pbk)
DOI: https://doi.org/10.1201/9780429426032

Visit the Taylor & Francis Web site at
http://www.taylorandfrancis.com

and the CRC Press Web site at
http://www.crcpress.com

Culture and International Law - Juwana et al. (Eds)
© 2019 Taylor & Francis Group, London, ISBN 978-1-138-38766-9

Table of contents

Culture and International Law - Juwana et al. (Eds)
© 2019 Taylor & Francis Group, London, ISBN 978-1-138-38766-9

Preface

The 9th CILS International Conference on Culture & International Law was held in Malang, East Java, Indonesia, October 2-3, 2018. It was organized at the regional law faculty of the CILS FHUI collaboration partner. For 2018, the 9th CILS was held in collaboration with the Faculty of Law, University of Brawijaya, Malang with the theme "Culture and International Law". The subthemes are (1) Cultural heritage; (2) Cultural rights; (3) Culture and economic activity; (4) Culture and armed conflict and (5) General Topics.

The 9th CILS 2018 aims to become a forum for scientific meetings of academics focusing on the field of international law and providing a forum for the development of international legal science, especially on the topic of International Law and Culture for both Indonesian and international circles. This meeting took two days with the pattern of implementing two types of sessions, namely a Plenary Session (Session Main) and Panel Sessions (Session Panels). Also, the conference provided an excellent venue to present projects and receive quality feedback. Keynotes speakers and presenters shared new concepts, best practices, knowledge, experience, strategies and solutions, with a focus on promoting the significant influence of culture on international law. This starts with the stage of formation to embodiment, encouraging the need for comprehensive and in-depth legal discussions by relevant experts and practitioners.

All papers have undergone careful peer review by expert referees to professional and scientific standards before being selected for publication in these proceeding. The total number of submitted papers was 66 and 45 were accepted.

Culture and International Law - Juwana et al. (Eds)
© 2019 Taylor & Francis Group, London, ISBN 978-1-138-38766-9

Acknowledgments

The 9th CILS International Conference on Culture & International Law was generously supported by The CILS Faculty of Law University of Indonesia and Faculty of Law, University of Brawijaya.

The Organizing Committee was very pleased with the success of the conference and wishes to acknowledge the contribution of the many members of the Programme Committee who helped ensure the high quality of the papers this year. The Programme Co-chairs would also like to acknowledge the efforts of the local organizers in ensuring the smooth running of the conference and the warm welcome extended to delegates which helped create a collegial atmosphere throughout the event.

Finally, we would like to acknowledge the Dean from the Faculty of Law, University of Indonesia and Faculty of Law, University of Brawijaya undertaking so much to support and made these proceedings so successful. We extend our warmest welcome to all our conferences delegates.

Chairman Committee of 9th CILS 2018
Dr. Adi Kusumaningrum, SH.MH.

Culture and International Law - Juwana et al. (Eds)
© 2019 Taylor & Francis Group, London, ISBN 978-1-138-38766-9

Committees

SCIENTIFIC COMMITTEE

Hikmahanto Juwana (Indonesia)
Dhiana Puspitawati (Indonesia)
Jeffrey Thomas (US)
Lucas Lixinski (Australia)
Eric De Brabandere (The Natherland)
Mohd Hazmi bin Mohd Rusli (Malaysia)
Rohimi Shapiee (Malaysia)

ORGANIZING COMMITTEE

Chairman	:	Adi Kusumaningrum
Vice Chairman	:	Dhiana Puspitawati
Secretary	:	Ach Murtadho
		AAA. Nanda Saraswati
Treasurer	:	Hikmatul Ula
		Meiliana
Event section	:	Fransiska Ayulistya Susanto
		Ladito Risang
		Prischa Listiningrum
		Kartika Dian Ningtyas
Secretarial section	:	Yasniar Rachmawati
		Yolanda Kumalasari
		Ach. Eko Syarifudin
Liason Officer	:	Agis Ardhiansyah
		Dony Aditya Prasetyo
		Setiawan Wicaksono
		Syahrul Sajidin

Culture and International Law - Juwana et al. (Eds)
© 2019 Taylor & Francis Group, London, ISBN 978-1-138-38766-9

Culture and armed conflict: Destruction of cultural heritage as method of ethnic cleansing

Helga Špadina
Assistant Professor, Faculty of Law Osijek, University J.J. Strossmayer Osijek, Croatia

ABSTRACT: Deliberate damage of historical monuments and buildings dedicated to art, culture, religion or science was forbidden by the international humanitarian law (or law of armed conflict) and subject to legal proceedings as early as from 1907 when the Hague Regulation IV explicitly prohibited destruction of cultural treasures and religious shrines. In different times of history, protection of cultural property during conflicts was regarded unimportant when compared to military targeting and goals of the warfare. Wars in former Yugoslavia brought in new dimension of armed conflict – historical monuments were deliberately targeted to destroy cultural identity of a nation. This was supposed to lead to ethnic cleansing of a certain area. Further development of international humanitarian law resulted in formation of international criminal tribunals and adoption of their viewpoint that deliberate targeting of cultural heritage constitutes war crimes. The most recently, UN Security Council Resolution 2347 from 2017 condemns unlawful destruction of cultural heritage.

This paper will analyze legal arguments and assessment of used by International Tribunal for former Yugoslavia related to the destruction of cultural heritage as method of ethnic cleansing. It will explore whether awareness of the status of UNESCO World Heritage Site demonstrated perpetrators willingly strived to inflict longer-reaching damage to the nation and whether this should be used as aggravating circumstance. Finally, we will analyze whether destruction of monuments indeed obstructs post-conflict recovery.

KEYWORDS: destruction of cultural property, international humanitarian law, ethnic cleansing

1 INTRODUCTION

Destruction of cultural heritage, particularly if under the protection of UNESCO and in the category of world cultural site is crime *per se*. As such, it is punishable according to Article 1 of The Convention on the Protection of Cultural Property in the Event of Armed Conflict (further: the Hague Convention) of 1954[1]. The Hague Convention of 1954 is considered to

1. Art. 1, Definition of Cultural Property: 'For the purposes of the present Convention, the term "cultural property" shall cover, irrespective of origin or ownership: (a) movable or immovable property of great importance to the cultural heritage of every people, such as monuments of architecture, art or history, whether religious or secular; archaeological sites; groups of buildings which, as a whole, are of historical or artistic interest; works of art; manuscripts, books and other objects of artistic, historical or archaeological interest; as well as scientific collections and important collections of books or archives or of reproductions of the property defined above; (b) buildings whose main and effective purpose is to preserve or exhibit the movable cultural property defined in sub-paragraph (a) such as museums, large libraries and depositories of archives, and refuges intended to shelter, in the event of armed conflict, the movable cultural property defined in subparagraph (a); (c) centers containing a large amount of cultural property as defined in sub-paragraphs (a) and (b), to be known as "centers containing monuments".' The Convention is available at: http://portal.

form an integral part of customary international law. Furthermore, after the Hague Convention and following some legal gaps stemming from the provisions of the Convention, several other legal instruments were introduced among which its First Protocol from 1954 dealing with protection of cultural property during times of occupation which was part removed from Convention and placed into Protocol due to its controversial nature.[2] Second Protocol was also drafted out of necessity to regulate better questions of application of the Hague Convention to the conflicts of internal character and to fill the legal gap in State Party's obligation to create a criminal offense for destruction of cultural property under its domestic law. The Protocol came to force in 1999. Prohibition of destruction of cultural property is also regulated in Article 53 of the 1977 Additional Protocol I to the Geneva Conventions is entitled 'Protection of cultural objects and of places of worship'[3], as well as in Statues of international criminal tribunals.[4]

In landmark ICTY case *Blaskic*, for the first time Tribunal provided a definition of crime of destruction of property when the Trial Chamber found that

> "[a]n Occupying Power is prohibited from destroying movable and non-movable property except where such destruction is made absolutely necessary by military operations . To constitute a grave breach, the destruction unjustified by military necessity must be extensive, unlawful and wanton. The notion of "extensive" is evaluated according to the facts

---

unesco.org/en/ev.php-URL_ID=13637&URL_DO=DO_TOPIC&URL_SECTION=201.html, accessed on 1 July 2018.

2. Patty Gerstenblith, 'Protecting Cultural Heritage in Armed Conflict, Looking Back, Looking Forward', (2009) 677, 7 *Cardozo Pub. L. Poly'&Ethics, J.*
3. "Any destruction by the Occupying Power of real or personal property belonging individually or collectively to private persons, or to the State, or to other public authorities, or to social or co-operative organizations, is prohibited, except where such destruction is rendered absolutely necessary by military operations," Geneva Convention.
4. ICC Statute Articles expressly prohibiting acts against cultural property in Art. 8(2)(a)(iv): 'extensive destruction and appropriation of property not justified by military necessity and carried out unlawfully and wantonly'; Art. 8(2)(b)(xiii): "destroying or seizing the enemy's property unless such destruction or seizure be imperatively demanded by the necessities of war"; Art. 8(2)(e)(xii): "destroying or seizing the property of an adversary unless such destruction or seizure be imperatively demanded by the necessities of the conflict".

   'Article 6 of the Nuremberg Charter establishing the International Military Tribunal prohibited "plunder of public and private property, wanton destruction of cities, towns or villages, or devastation not justified by military necessity" among war crimes." Art. 3(d) of the ICTY Statute reads: 'd) seizure of, destruction or willful damage done to institutions dedicated to religion, charity and education, the arts and sciences, historic monuments and works of art and science", available at: www.icty.org/sid/135, accessed on 7 July 2018.

   Rome Statute of International Criminal Court in Art. 8.2. among war crimes, lists '(iv) Extensive destruction and appropriation of property, not justified by military necessity and carried out unlawfully and wantonly.' 'Other serious violations of the laws and customs applicable in international armed conflict, within the established framework of international law, for ICC include (ix) Intentionally directing attacks against buildings dedicated to religion, education, art, science or charitable purposes, historic monuments, hospitals and places where the sick and wounded are collected, provided they are not military objectives' both of international and not international character, available at: https://www.icc-cpi.int/resource-library/Documents/RS-Eng.pdf, accessed on 7 July 2018.

   Art. 7 of the Law on the Extraordinary Chambers of Cambodia, available at: www.eccc.gov.kh/english/law.list.aspx, accessed on 7 July 2018, which is the only criminal provision which is directly linked to the provision of the 1954 HC, reads: "[t]he Extraordinary Chambers shall have the power to bring to trial all Suspects responsible for the destruction of cultural property during armed conflict pursuant to the 1954 Hague Convention for Protection of Cultural Property in the Event of Armed Conflict, and which were committed during the period from 17 April 1975 to 6 January 1979". On the other hand, the ICTR Statute (Art. 4(f)), available at: www.un.org/ictr/statute.html, accessed on 7 July 2018, and the Statute of the Special Court for Sierra Leone (Art. 3(f)) explicitly mention only pillage as a war crime related to cultural property.' Micaela Frulli, "The Criminalization of Offences against Cultural Heritage in Times of Armed Conflict: The Quest for Consistency", (2011) 22(1) *The European Journal of International Law*, 203–217.

of the case – a single act, such as the destruction of a hospital, may suffice to characterise an offence under this count."[5]

In the final report of the UN Commission on crimes in former Yugoslavia, destruction of historical monuments, works of art or places of worship which constitute the cultural or spiritual heritage of peoples and to which special protection has been given by special arrangement, got qualified as grave breach of Additional Protocol I (Article 85, paragraph 4)d).[6]

International Law Commission in 1991 emphasised persecution may take the form of the systematic destruction of monuments or buildings representative of a particular social, religious, cultural or other group *inter alia*, have all singled out the destruction of religious buildings as a clear case of persecution as a crime against humanity.[7]

In this paper, we argue that destruction of cultural property often has another aspect that is not closely linked to the willingness to destroy property of great importance to the world. This second aspect is intention to remove one ethnical or religious group from certain territory through destruction of cultural property of particular importance for cultural identity of that group. Most commonly, this is done through destruction of religious sites or monuments that have significant importance only for one ethnical or religious group. We will look into the ethnical cleansing definitions under the international law in order to establish the legal argument that destruction of cultural property is actually aimed at ethnic cleansing and when committed with the intention to achieve ethnical cleansing should be qualified as a grave breach of international law. This is due to its double consequences – loss of cultural property of great importance and removal of specific certain ethnic or religious group from certain geographic areas.

2 ETHNIC *CLEANSING* AS CRIME UNDER INTERNATIONAL LAW

Ethnic cleansing was not defined neither in international humanitarian law, nor in human rights law as such. Today, we can find term ethnic cleansing in judgements and indictments of the International Tribunal for ex-Yugoslavia (further: ICTY) where it has been acknowledged, although it did not constitute one of the counts for prosecution, but instead was used as explanation of widespread practice in conflicts on territories on countries of ex-Yugoslavia. United Nations introduced its definition in 1990's through their report published in 1993[8] in which they reported on violations of Geneva Conventions with particular emphasis on the practice of ethnical cleansing committed in the territory of former Yugoslavia. UN Secretary General. The Commission reported on violation of international humanitarian law among which are ethnic cleansing and destruction of religious and cultural property.

Landmark Report defined 'ethnic cleansing' as following:

> "*... rendering an area ethnically homogeneous by using force or intimidation to remove persons of given groups from the area.*"

5. Available at: http://www.icty.org/x/cases/kordic_cerkez/tjug/en/kor-tj010226e-2.htm, accessed on 7 July 2018, p. 340, accessed on 2 August 2018.
6. United Nations, Security Council, Final Report of the Commission of Experts established pursuant to Security Council Resolution 780 (1992), S/1994/674, 27 May 1994.
7. "Persecution may take many forms, for example, a prohibition on practising certain kinds of religious worship; prolonged and systematic detention of individuals who represent a political, religious or cultural group; a prohibition on the use of a national language even in private; systematic destruction of monuments or buildings representative of a particular social, religious, cultural or other group. Such acts could come within the scope of this article when committed in a systematic manner or on a mass scale." Yearbook of the International Law Commission, 1991, p.294. Available at: http://legal.un.org/ilc/publications/yearbooks/english/ilc_1991_v1.pdf, accessed on 17 July 2018.
8. UN, Interim Report of the Commission of Experts established pursuant to the Security Council Resolution 780 (1992). Available at: https://undocs.org/S/25274, accessed on 7 July 2018.

At the end of investigation, final Report broadened definition of ethnic cleansing to include:

> "... *a purposeful policy designed by one ethnic or religious group to remove by violent and terror-inspiring means the civilian population of another ethnic or religious group from certain geographic areas.*"

For the UN Commission, ethnic cleansing in the territory of former Yugoslavia was aimed at the removal of the civilian population and can include murder, torture, arbitrary arrest and detention, extrajudicial executions, rape and sexual assaults, severe physical injury to civilians, confinement of civilian population in ghetto areas, forcible removal, displacement and deportation of civilian population, deliberate military attacks or threats of attacks on civilians and civilian areas, use of civilians as human shields, wanton destruction of property, robbery of personal property, attacks on hospitals, medical personnel, and locations with the Red Cross/ Red Crescent emblem. Ethnic cleansing has not been recognized as an independent crime under international law although Commission expressively noted that "those crimes constitute crimes against humanity and can be assimilated to the specific war crimes' and fall into the scope of the Genocide Convention."[9] The term "ethnic cleansing" has been used in resolutions of the Security Council and the General Assembly.

3 DESTRUCTION OF CULTURAL HERITAGE AS A METHOD OF ETHNIC CLEANSING THROUGH THE JURISPRUDENCE OF THE ICTY

3.1 *Prlic et. al. (IT-04-74)*

ICTY was extremely instrumental in 'cementing the legal foundation for accountability for the destruction of cultural heritage.'[10] Several judgements are of particular importance in legal discussion on link between destruction of cultural property as a method of ethnical cleansing. Among them, here we will look into the Milosevic indictment and judgments in cases of Prlic et al., Strugar and Kordic and Cerkez cases.

In judgement Prlic et al. ICTY clearly established existence of:

> "a joint criminal enterprise with an ultimate goal to establish Croatian territorial entity with part of the borders of the Croatian Banovina of 1939 to enable a reunification of the Croatian people. In order to achieve that, it was necessary to modify the ethnic composition of the territories claimed to be part of the Croatian Community of Herceg-Bosna and perform wilful and intentional ethnic cleansing of Muslim population in Bosnia and Hercegovina during 1993 with the purpose to have either a majority, or an exclusively Croatian population."[11]

Indictment against Prlic and others included count on destruction or willful damage done to institutions dedicated to religion or education (p.171) as a serious violation of the laws or customs of war punishable under Article 3(d) of the ICTY Statute. 172. The Tribunal emphasized double legal protection for buildings of a cultural, historic and/or religious nature: broad protection afforded to civilian objects of property by Article 52 of Additional Protocol I. as long as the edifice makes no actual contribution to military action and its destruction or capture does not offer a specific military advantage at the moment of attack. Other type of protection is special protection granted under Article 53 of Additional Protocol I. This provision prohibits the commission of "any acts of hostility directed against the historic monuments,

9. Ibid.
10. Statement of ICTY Registrar Mr. John Hocking at a high-level UNESCO conference "Cultural diversity under attack: Protecting heritage for peace", available at: http://www.icty.org/en/press/icty-paved-way-for-accountability-for-attacks-on-cultural-heritage, accessed on 9 July 2018.
11. ICTY Judgement Summary for Jadranko Prlić and others, The Hague, 29 May 2013, available at: http://www.icty.org/x/cases/prlic/tjug/en/130529_summary_en.pdf, accessed on 9 July 2018.

works of art or places of worship which constitute the cultural or spiritual heritage of peoples." The Chamber found that for Article 3(d) of the Statute to apply, the perpetrator of the crime must act with intent to destroy the protected property and points out that omission to not using such a visible sign does not in any event withdraw protection from the property provided that the property has not been transformed into a military objective. The Chamber concludes that the 'crime of destruction or willful damage done to institutions dedicated to religion or education comprises the following elements: (1) an intentional act or omission; (2) causing destruction or damage to a cultural or religious object of property; (3) the property did not constitute a military objective within the meaning of Article 52 of Additional Protocol I and (4) the act or omission is perpetrated with intent to destroy the cultural or religious property' (p.178).

Indictment, later confirmed by the ICTY judgement, includes destruction of ten mosques in East Sarajevo[12] in East Mostar, destructions of two mosques in West Mostar[13] and the destruction of the Old Bridge (a World Heritage Site included in the UN list of worldwide cultural heritage monuments") on 9 November 1993 by Croatian Military Forces (HVO). Old bridge was an international landmark crossing the Neretva River between East and West Mostar built by architect Hairudin almost 500 years old. Old Bridge was one of the major symbols of the Balkan region, but of particular value to the Muslim community in Mostar. The ICTY Chamber established that the bridge had great symbolic importance, primarily for the Muslims (p.1364.) and that collapse of the Old Bridge also condemned the residents of the Muslim enclave on the right bank of the Neretva to almost complete isolation (p. 1365.) The Chamber heard testimony and admitted documents specifically indicating that the HVO was fully responsible for the destruction of or damage to mosques in East Mostar in 1993. The Chamber finds that because of the constant shooting on and shelling of East Mostar by the HVO from the direction of West Mostar, Hum mountain and Stotina hill, there is no doubt that the HVO further damaged or destroyed the ten mosques (p. 1375). The Mufti of Mostar from 1992 to 1994, specified that in 1994, there were no mosques left in the town of Mostar where believers could go to pray because they had all been destroyed (p.1372), stating that the HVO had destroyed religious property "in a systematic way" and deliberately, by adopting a modus operandi necessarily aimed at destroying the mosques targeted. Therefore, ICTY Chamber finds that the ten mosques listed in the Indictment were destroyed or significantly damaged by the constant shooting and shelling of East Mostar by the HVO. All six convicted were found guilty and sentenced to between 10 and 25 years imprisonment.

If we look closely into the ICTY legal arguments, it is very clear that ethnic cleansing and crimes against population were very much intertwined with destruction of cultural property (in this case, destruction of mosques and Old Bridge). Exact figures of destroyed number of religious monuments (Catholic and Orthodox churches and mosques) in Bosnia and Herzegovina are very difficult to find and estimates range between 60% and 90% of religious objects were destroyed or damaged during the conflict in Bosnia and Herzegovina.

3.2 *Strugar (IT-01-42) 'DUBROVNIK'*

Indictment for Strugar in this case was based, inter alia, on counts for unjustified devastation, unlawful attacks on civilian objects, destruction or wilful damage to institutions dedicated to religion, charity and education, the arts and sciences, historic monuments and works of art and science for destruction of UNESCO protected World Heritage List Old Town of Dubrovnik in 1991 despite 'a number of the buildings in the Old Town and the towers on the city walls being marked with the symbols mandated by the Hague Convention on the Protection

12. The Sultan Selim Javuz Mosque, the Hadži Mehmed-Beg Karadjoz Mosque, the Koski Mehmed-Paša mosque, the Nesuh Aga Vučjaković Mosque, the Ćejvan Ćehaja Mosque, the Hadži Ahmed Aga Lakišić Mosque, the Roznamedžija Ibrahim Efendija Mosque, the Ćosa Jahja Hodža Mosque, the Hadži Kurto or Tabačica Mosque and the Hadži Memija Cernica Mosque.
13. Baba Bešir and Hadži Ali-Beg Lafo mosque.

of Cultural Property in the Event of Armed Conflict' (violations of the laws or customs of war, Article 3 of the ICTY Statute).[14]

> "As a result of the unlawful shelling of the Old Town of Dubrovnik on 6 December 1991, 824 buildings in the Old Town, 563 (or 68.33 per cent) had been hit by projectiles in 1991 and 1992. 438 roofs had been damaged by direct hits and 262 by fragments of projectiles. 314 direct hits were recorded on building facades and on the paving of streets and squares. Six medieval palaces were completely destroyed by fire and hundreds more suffered damage.' (p. 24. of the judgement). The Chamber found that of these buildings and structures, it has been established that 52 were damaged and six of them being destroyed, during the 6 December shelling of the Old Town by the JNA."

It was further established that there were no military objectives in the immediate vicinity of the 52 buildings and structures destroyed or damaged on 6 December 1991, or in the Old Town, or in its immediate vicinity, so that the destruction or damage of property in the Old Town on 6 December 1991 was not justified by military necessity.[15] Strugar was fully responsible for failing to stop the attack on 6 December 1991 when he could and should have done so, and afterwards for failing to ensure the perpetrators were punished was proved under Article 7(3) of the Statute, as the superior commander of the JNA forces who perpetrated the unlawful shelling of the Old Town on 6 December 1991 and sentenced him to 8 years' imprisonment.

3.3 *Kordic and Cerkez (IT-95-14/2) 'LASVA VALLEY'*

In Kordic and Cerkez case, ICTY took the whole matter of destruction or wilful damage done to institutions dedicated to religion (from Article 3(d) of the Statute) a step further by proclaiming that 'this act, when perpetrated with the requisite discriminatory intent, amounts to an attack on the very religious identity of a people. As such, it manifests a nearly pure expression of the notion of "crimes against humanity", for all of humanity is injured by the destruction of a unique religious culture and its concomitant cultural objects. The Trial Chamber therefore finds that the destruction and wilful damage of institutions dedicated to Muslim religion or education, coupled with the requisite discriminatory intent, may amount to an act of persecution.'[16]

In this landmark case, ICTY actually established following elements of this offence:

"(1) institutions dedicated to religion or education were destroyed; (2) the destruction or damage was committed wilfully; (3) the institutions destroyed or wilfully damaged were protected under international humanitarian law; (4) there was a nexus between the destruction or wilful damage and an armed conflict; and (5) the accused bears individual criminal responsibility for the attack under either Article 7(1) or 7 (3) of the Statute."[17]

The ICTY Trial Chamber notes that 'educational institutions are undoubtedly immovable property of great importance to the cultural heritage of peoples (Article 1 of the Cultural Property Convention) in that they are without exception centres of learning, arts, and sciences, with their valuable collections of books and works of arts and science. This offence overlaps to a certain extent with the offence of unlawful attacks on civilian objects except that the object of this offence is more specific: the cultural heritage of a certain population. Educational institutions are certainly civilian objects. The offence this section is concerned with is the *lex specialis* as far as acts against cultural heritage are concerned.'[18]

---

14. Summary of Strugar case, ICTY, available at: http://www.icty.org/x/cases/strugar/cis/en/cis_strugar_en.pdf, accessed on 10 July 2018.
15. Ibid.
16. Kordic and Cerkez Summary of Judgement, available at: http://www.icty.org/x/cases/kordic_cerkez/tjug/en/kor-tj010226e-2.htm, accessed on 15 July 2018.
17. Ibid.
18. Ibid.

3.4 *Milosevic (IT-O2-54) 'KOSOVO, CROATIA AND BOSNIA'*

Indictment against Slobodan Milosevic was, inter alia, based on the count for destruction or wilful damage done to institutions dedicated to education or religion, as violation of the laws or customs of war, punishable under Articles 3(d) and 7(1) and 7(3) of the Statute of the ICTY. Milosevic participated in a joint criminal enterprise established with a purpose to forcibly remove the majority of the Croat and other non-Serb population from the approximately one-third of the territory of the Republic of Croatia that he planned to become part of a new Serb-dominated state through the commission of crimes in violation of Articles 2, 3, and 5 of the Statute of the Tribunal. Thus, from 1 October 1991 until 7 December 1991, during this same shelling attack, he acting alone or in concert with other known and unknown members of the joint criminal enterprise, planned, instigated, ordered, committed, or otherwise aided and abetted the planning, preparation and execution of the wanton destruction or wilful damage and plunder of the public and private property of the Croat and other non-Serb population within the area of the Dubrovnik Republic. This campaign included the destruction, damage or plunder of homes, religious, historical and cultural buildings and other civilian public or private buildings, not justified by military necessity.[19] During this shelling campaign, approximately 1000 shells fired by the Serb forces impacted in the Old Town area of the city. The Old Town district of Dubrovnik was an UNESCO World Cultural Heritage Site in its entirety. A number of the buildings in the Old Town and the towers on the city walls were marked with the symbols mandated by the Hague Convention on the Protection of Cultural Property in the Event of Armed Conflict (1954). No military targets were located on or within the walls of the Old Town.[20] By these acts and omissions, he committed extensive destruction and appropriation of property, not justified by military necessity and carried out unlawfully and wantonly, a grave breach of the Geneva Conventions of 1949, punishable under Articles 2(d) and 7(1) and 7(3) of the Statute of the Tribunal; wanton destruction of villages, or devastation not justified by military necessity, a violation of the laws or customs of war, punishable under Articles 3(b) and 7(1) and 7(3) of the Statute of the Tribunal and destruction or wilful damage done to historic monuments and institutions dedicated to education or religion, as violation of the laws or customs of war, punishable under Articles 3(d) and 7(1) and 7(3) of the Statute of the Tribunal.[21] Proceedings against Milosevic were terminated and he was never sentenced for his crimes because he died in ICTY prison in 2006 prior to the end of the trial.

If we look into the judgements in Prlic et. al, Strugar and Kordic and Cerkez cases, as well as indictment for Milosevic, ICTY had no major difficulties in proving that criminal enterprises made a clear-cut plan for ethnical cleansing of members of minority communities not only through systematic killing, rape, detention and forced removal of local population, but also through well planned and meticulously executed destruction of important religious sites, UNESCO World Heritage Site of Dubrovnik and a landmark Mostar bridge which left Muslim population in total isolation for prolonged period of time. Deliberate destruction of those cultural properties resulted in inability of minority population to perform their religious rituals for example in 1994 in Sarajevo, but also in other parts of Bosnia and Herzegovina, Croatia and Kosovo. Due to the extent of damage of religious cultural property, in todays' countries of former Yugoslavia, ethnic cleansing proved to be successful and very sustainable as it decreased interest in return to locations where it took place. Therefore, cases before the ICTY perpetrated in former Yugoslavia are model examples of destruction of cultural property as a method of ethnic cleansing.

---

19. Second amended indictment Croatia, p. 77 of the indictment, available at: http://www.icty.org/x/cases/slobodan_milosevic/ind/en/mil-2ai020728e.htm, accessed on 18 July 2018.
20. Ibid 78.
21. Ibid, 83.

4 ELEMENTS OF DESTRUCTION OF CULTURAL PROPERTY AS A METHOD OF ETHNIC CLEANSING

In order to test hypothesis of this paper that destruction of cultural property is a method of ethnic cleansing, we need to look into the specific elements of two UN definitions on ethnic cleansing and put them into the context of the destruction of cultural property:

1. "... rendering an area ethnically homogeneous by using force or intimidation to remove persons of given groups from the area."

<u>Rendering an area ethnically homogeneous</u>

This element is present because the main reason why military commanders choose to target cultural, educational, or religious object without military importance is attempt to delete history of one ethnical group and to force them to leave to places where they can practice their religion or conviction. Destruction of places of worship leads to inability to practice religion actually harms tangible cultural property (churches, mosques, shrines), as well as intangible cultural property (customs, habits, freedom of religion).[22] By destroying specific cultural heritage, affected minority population is more inclined to move out of that area which then can become ethnically homogenous. ICTY judgments have demonstrated that destruction of cultural and religious property have in fact rendered the whole areas or even countries ethnically homogenous because in parts of the world where religion has almost a central point in determining cultural identity, destruction of places of worship also destructs ethnical identity and fulfils the main purpose of ethnical cleansing.

<u>Use of force or intimidation</u>

Cultural heritage is most frequently destroyed by the use of force (Old Town Dubrovnik, Old Bridge Mostar, almost all churches and mosques in countries of former Yugoslavia, city of Timbuktu in Mali, two Budha statutes in the Bamiyan valley in Afghanistan, the shrine of Abdel Salam al Asmar in Libya, the church of Virgin Mary in Mosul, Eliyahu Hanhavi synagogue in Damascus, prophet's Jonah's tomb in Iraaq, etc.). Use of force in destruction of cultural property has a goal to ensure that targeted objects would not be reparable and often, use of force also jeopardizes lives of civilian population since target objects are usually in residential areas.

Intimidation is done through high publicizing of destruction of cultural property through mass media or Internet it in order to achieve a terror-inspiring effect on others and cause them to flee.[23]

<u>Removal of persons of given groups from the area - To remove by violent and terror-inspiring means the civilian population of another ethnic or religious group from certain geographic areas</u>

The final goal of destruction of internationally protected UNESCO World Heritage Sites is message to the part of the population that since their cultural links physically do not exist anymore, their cultural identity is lost and they should move out of that area. [24] Or as Johannot-Gradis wrote:

22. Christiane Johannot-Gradis, 'Protecting the past from the future: How does law protect tangible and intangible cultural heriate in armed conflict?', 97 (2015) *Int't Rev. Red Cross.*
23. Point 135, United Nations, Security Council, Final Report of the Commission of Experts established pursuant to Security Council Resolution 780 (1992), S/1994/674 from 27 May 1994.
24. "Other noteworthy practices are widespread destruction of villages by systematically burning them to the ground and blowing up all the houses and structures in a given area. This includes cultural and religious monuments and symbols. The purpose of this destruction is to eradicate cultural, social and religious traces that identify the ethnic and religious groups. In the cases where the practices described above do not occur, these groups are forced to leave under duress by reason of a well-founded fear for their personal security."

"Such acts (destruction of cultural property) seem to reflect its' members intention not only to erase forever these vestiges of the region's past, but in so doing also to obliterate all traces of the cultural and spiritual identity of the population concerned."[25]

2. "... a purposeful policy designed by one ethnic or religious group to remove by violent and terror-inspiring means the civilian population of another ethnic or religious group from certain geographic areas."

Purposeful policy

Destruction of culturally important objects cannot be performed without particular preparation and purposeful policy by the military commanders. In order to execute purposeful policy of ethnical cleansing through, *inter alia*, destruction of cultural property, perpetrators of war crimes in former Yugoslavia formed so called criminal enterprises with the purpose to carefully plan sequence of ethnical cleansing.

Designed by one ethnic or religious group

Destruction of cultural heritage is usually designed by the majority group in the conflict. In cases before the ICTY court in The Hague, Croatians were planning to execute destruction of cultural property in Bosnia and Herzegovina and parts of Croatia inhabited by Serbian national minority, while Serbs did it in Kosovo, Bosnia and Herzegovina and Croatia in areas inhabited by members of non-Serb ethnical groups.

From all above, we can conclude that destruction of cultural property indeed easily falls within the scope of the definition of ethnic cleansing and may be classified as a form of ethnic cleansing.

5 CONCLUSION

Wars in former Yugoslavia brought in new dimension of armed conflict – historical monuments were deliberately targeted to destroy cultural identity of a nation with the far reaching consequences through destruction of most significant and irreplaceable monuments. This was done with a very clear purpose to achieve ethnic cleansing of a certain area of country or even the whole country. Taking examples of ICTY judgements and indictments, it is evident that international law is continuously developing and evolving to encompass new forms of war crime or genocide. Intention to accelerate forced removal of population by destroying their places of worship, important bridges, or simply the most remarkable monuments has been recognized by the ICTY and punished in all cases where it was proved that criminal enterprises were formed with the aim to force out members of either minority group or religion other than perpetrators' through destruction of important cultural property.

In testing elements of destruction of cultural property against definitions of ethnic cleansing, we came to the conclusion that destruction of cultural property does fulfill all requirements for qualification as ethnic cleansing. As such, destruction of cultural property with the aim to achieve ethnic cleansing should be grave forms of violation of international humanitarian and human rights law and aggravating circumstance when deciding on the sentence for perpetrators. Attack on cultural property of specific religious or ethnical group is not so much linked to the cultural value of the property, as much it is linked to the emotional center point of a certain culture with a goal to eradicate the specific culture.

Destruction of cultural heritage of certain religion or (usually minority) ethnic group can happen in all phases of forced removal or displacement i.e. prior, during or after the conflict and it is equally detrimental in all of those phases.

United Nations, Security Council, Final Report of the Commission of Experts established pursuant to Security Council Resolution 780 (1992), S/1994/674. p.136 from 27 May 1994.

25. Christiane Johannot-Gradi, above n 22.

Deliberate attack on cultural property that is violation of both tangible and intangible cultural heritage of a certain nation or ethic group. While tangible cultural heritage could be repaired (example for it is Old Mostar Bridge), intangible cultural property is either irreparable or reparable through significant period after the armed conflict. Destruction of religious and cultural monuments significantly obstructs post-conflict recovery because it delays return and reintegration of displaced population whose cultural property has been destroyed prior or during displacement.

Finally, destruction of cultural and religious property as a method of ethnic cleansing is being extensively covered in ICTY jurisprudence which established that destruction of cultural heritage can and often is, a new method of ethnic cleansing.

REFERENCES

Frulli, Micaela, 'The Criminalization of Offences against Cultural Heritage in Times of Armed Conflict: The Quest for Consistency', (2011) 22(1) *The European Journal of International Law*.

Gerstenblith, Patty, 'Protecting Cultural Heritage in Armed Conflict, Looking Back, Looking Forward', (2009) 677, 7 *Cardozo Pub. L. Poly'&Ethics, J.*

Johannot-Gradis, Christiane Johannot-Gradis, 'Protecting the past from the future: How does law protect tangible and intangible cultural heriate in armed conflict?' (2015) 97 *Int't Rev. Red Cross*.

United Nations, Security Council, Final Report of the Commission of Experts established pursuant to Security Council Resolution 780 (1992), S/1994/674. p.136 from 27 May 1994.

UN, Interim Report of the Commission of Experts established pursuant to the Security Council Resolution 780 (1992). Available at: https://undocs.org/S/25274, accessed on 7 July 2018.

Kordic and Cerkez Summary of Judgement, available at: http://www.icty.org/x/cases/kordic_cerkez/tjug/en/kor-tj010226e-2.htm, accessed on 15 July 2018.

Milosevic indictment Second amended indictment Croatia, p. 77 of the indictment, available at: http://www.icty.org/x/cases/slobodan_milosevic/ind/en/mil-2ai020728e.htm, accessed on 18 July 2018.

Judgement Summary for Jadranko Prlić and others, The Hague, 29 May 2013, available at: http://www.icty.org/x/cases/prlic/tjug/en/130529_summary_en.pdf, accessed on 9 July 2018.

Summary of Strugar case, ICTY, available at: http://www.icty.org/x/cases/strugar/cis/en/cis_strugar_en.pdf, accessed on 10 July 2018.

Statement of ICTY Registrar Mr. John Hocking at a high-level UNESCO conference "Cultural diversity under attack: Protecting heritage for peace", available at: http://www.icty.org/en/press/icty-paved-way-for-accountability-for-attacks-on-cultural-heritage, accessed on 9 July 2018.

Yearbook of the International Law Commission, 1991, p.294. Available at: http://legal.un.org/ilc/publications/yearbooks/english/ilc_1991_v1.pdf, accessed on 17 July 2018.

Culture and International Law - Juwana et al. (Eds)
© 2019 Taylor & Francis Group, London, ISBN 978-1-138-38766-9

The objectives of Indonesian private international law

Tiurma M. Pitta Allagan
Member of the Conflict of Laws and Private International Law Teaching Team, Faculty of Law, University of Indonesia, Indonesia
Ph.D. Candidate, Faculty of Law, University of Groningen, The Netherlands

ABSTRACT: The academic bill of Indonesian Private International Law (PIL) is in discussion. It covers the important objectives of PIL, namely legal certainty and decisional harmony. This paper discusses this issue in terms of basic thoughts about an Academic Bill of Indonesian PIL. By applying library research to the basic thoughts of Indonesian scholars and judges on the objectives of the Indonesian PIL, the author seeks to revisit and reconfirm the objectives of Indonesian PIL.

KEYWORDS: Indonesian private international law, Indonesian decisional harmony, harmonization of law

1 INTRODUCTION

The draft of the Indonesian Private International Law (PIL) and the academic text of the law have recently been discussed. This discussion was raised when the PIL bill was re-drafted by the National Law Development Agency (*Badan Pembinaan Hukum Nasional*/BPHN). The discussion focused on the preparation of academic texts and the development of PIL in Indonesia and their influences on existing articles.

From the discussions, which were held in Bandung, there were interesting recommendations and arguments regarding the authority of judges from an appeal court judge. The judge suggested giving judges the freedom to consider and create laws when the regulations or laws do not exist.

This discussion raised the idea of why judges needed to be given the freedom in the trial of PIL cases, as well as how far the freedom could be granted by law. This question is closely related to the aims and purpose of PIL, and it is important to rethink the basic principles of PIL so that the rules that are being drafted remain in the PIL realm.

Discussing this particular topic is challenging. The Indonesian literature is limited and very classical because the objective of PIL was already in discussion when Indonesia was still the Dutch East Indies. Therefore, in obtaining precise answers, observation of the Indonesian PIL history and basic understanding is necessary.

1.1 *The research questions*

The focus of this paper is to answer the question: what is the target or goal of PIL?

1.2 *The methodology of research*

To answer the above question, this paper uses library research methods. Research into the basic thoughts of PIL scholars and judges is the main focus and consideration. These thoughts were obtained by examining PIL dissertations and writings in Indonesia, as well as examining existing court decisions.

1.3 *The purposes of the research*

This study aims to examine what the goals of PIL are and how these objectives influence PIL rules in Indonesia

1.4 *Outline of writing*

This paper consists of three major parts. The first part covers the history and background of PIL in Indonesia before its independence. The second part considers the thoughts of scholars of PIL in Indonesia after its independence. This section includes the results of research into PIL in terms of court decisions and dissertations. Finally, I draw conclusions obtained from the discussion of PIL thoughts and recommendations for the academic text and drafting of a PIL bill, if appropriate.

2 THE HERITANCE: *INTERGENTILESRECHT* AND PIL

Indonesia inherits PIL rules as stated in Articles 16, 17 and 18 AB, respectively, regarding *statuta persona, statuta realia*, and *statute mixta* or *locus rigit actum*. These articles show the influences of classical Italian *statuta* from Bartolo Saxoverato.[1]

These articles were developed in Indonesia with influence from several Indonesian scholars and experts of PIL. One of them was Kollewijn, the expert on the Conflict of Laws in Indonesia. At that time, PIL rules were developed concurrently with the Conflict of Laws.

Kollewijn had an opinion that in determining the applicable law in a case of Conflict of Laws, the consideration should not be based on the substantive rules between the involved legal systems. The choice of the applicable law must be based on the closest connection between the respective case and the 'chosen' law because the involved legal systems are in equal position to one another. Kollewijn stated that the legal system that has the closest connection to the respective case should be the proper applicable law to result in the best settlement for the involved parties. His statement was an encounter with the idea of Conflict of Law, which developed in France and tends to apply the French legal system in all such cases.[2]

He stated that the consideration of 'better substantive rules' shall have no place in the Conflict of Laws. Such consideration is irrelevant, and it could turn down the Conflict of Laws. Therefore, the Conflict of Laws must be based on the basic notion of the equality of every legal system.[3]

---

1. In addition to those articles, there was Article 3 AB in relation to foreigners within the territory of the Republic of Indonesia, and Articles 100 RV and 436 RV regarding foreign courts awards.
2. "*Hukum yang paling erat hubungannya dengan hubungan hukum bersangkutan adalah hukum yang paling tepat sebagai hukum yang berlaku, karena dari hukum demikian dapatlah diharapkan penyelesaian yang baik kiranya* [The law that is most closely related to the relevant legal relationship is the most appropriate law as applicable law, because from such law it can be expected that a good settlement will be done]". This statement was the idea of H. Solus of France who preferred to give priority to French law as the applicable law in conflict of law cases whenever it was involved. It seems there was an assumption that French law was superior to others. Yet, H. Solus denied this; he argued that the local law was either silent or offered no solution, and therefore French law must intervene for the sake of legal certainty and a simple solution (see Prodjodikoro, 1976, pp. 19–20, 235–236).
3. "*Pertimbangan berdasarkan isi materiil dari sistem hukum yang tersangkut tidak dapat diberikan tempat dalam ilmu HAG (Hukum Antar Golongan), oleh karena pertimbangan yang demikian akan menghapuskan ilmu HAG. Dalam ilmu HAG, maka isi materiil dari sistem hukum adalah irrelevant, atau dengan perkataan lain dapat dikatakan bahwa: HAG harus berpokok pangkal pada persamarataan semua hukum.* [Consideration based on the material content of the involved legal system cannot be recognised by the interlegal law (*intergentiel rechts*), because such considerations will eliminate the knowledge of interlegal law. In the knowledge of interlegal law, the material content of the legal system is irrelevant, or in other words, it can be said that: interlegal law must base itself on the equality of all laws.]" (see Prodjodikoro, 1976, pp. 235–236).

In the development of the Conflict of Laws in the Dutch East Indies, there were some cases and exceptions whereby Netherlands law was applied. For instance, the voluntary submission (*penundukkan sukarela*) of the local people to Netherlands law, which then developed and could be divided into the partly voluntary submission (*penundukkan sukarela terhadap perbuatan hukum tertentu*) and the comprehensive voluntary submission (*penundukkan sukarela terhadap seluruh hukum*) (Gautama, 1991a). The application of Netherlands law based on those submissions was acceptable due to the ease or simplicity of daily activities in trading and business at that time. Such cases did not override or set aside the main approach in determining the applicable law in Conflict of Laws cases. Kollewijn remained devoted to the main principle in cases of the Conflict of Laws, as stated before; the closest connection that influenced the thought of Sudargo Gautama in relation to Indonesian PIL, as will be further described below.

3 *POST* INDONESIAN INDEPENDENCE

3.1 *Wirjono Prodjodikoro: the justice*

Wirjojo Prodjodikoro[4] stated that the Conflict of Laws, as well as PIL, must put forward justice as its objective. He mentioned that the rules of the Conflict of Laws and the PIL must be invented in such a manner as to fulfill the sense of justice of involved parties of the cases, or even in the broader scope, the society. The judges are entitled to found substantive rules according to their discretion or prudence (*rechtsvinding*) for the sake of justice. He mentioned that the ultimate framework and main objective of the PIL rules are to provide justice to the society. The justice must be placed at the center of gravity and becomes the basis of the entire rules and system of PIL (Prodjodikoro, 1979, p. 49).[5]

Wirjono Prodjodikoro mentioned that it was too rigid if the Conflict of Laws is only to determine the applicable law in a case. According to him, the Conflict of Laws has a broader task in that it must find another rule as a possibility for settling a case for the sake of justice. Another such possibility could be, for instance, another rule beyond the legal systems of the defendant and the claimant, or international conventions.[6] He mentioned that the application of the rules of international conventions should be according to *lex fori* (Prodjodikoro, 1979, p. 13). Prodjodikoro argued that this is acceptable as long as the rules fulfill the sense of justice of the parties, or in other words, justice remains the main purpose (Prodjodikoro, 1976, p. 11).

In line with the above consideration, Prodjodikoro argued similarly about the PIL rules. He mentioned that the objective of PIL is achieving justice for those in society who are subject to the respective legal systems. For such purposes, he supported any effort of the unification of substantive rules, though, to some extent, he believed that such unification might not provide any guarantee that justice could, in the end, be found. Along with this purpose, the principle of the equality of all legal systems must be respected (Prodjodikoro, 1976, p. 19).

4. Wirjono Prodjodikoro was the Chairman of the Indonesian Supreme Court from 1952–1966. His court decisions were appreciated by and became the models and illustrations in the lectures by Mr B. Ter Haar. He was awarded *Doctoris Honoris Causa* by the Faculty of Law, University of Airlangga in 1964; before this inauguration he wrote at least 14 books about Indonesian law, besides articles and annotations of court decisions, which became guidelines for other judges.
5. *"Pada permulaan buku ini saya sudah mengemukakan, bahwa tujuan dari hukum perdata internasional adalah untuk memenuhi rasa keadilan baik dari masyarakat nasional, maupun dari masyarakat negeri lain yang bersangkut paut dalam suatu peristiwa yang mengandung unsur-unsur asing.* [At the beginning of this book, I have stated that the aim of international civil law is to fulfill a sense of justice both from the national community, as well as from international communities that are related to an event that contains foreign elements.]". The legal opinion of Wirjono Prodjodikoro is mentioned and quoted by Sudargo Gautama (Gautama, 1988, pp. 156–157).
6. Yet, Prodjodikoro mentioned that the application of rules shall be interpreted according to *the lex fori* (see Prodjodikoro, 1976, pp. 30–36).

In addition to the above statement, he mentioned that the provision described in Articles 16, 17 and 18 AB is decent, yet it is not perfect for the entire PIL caseload in Indonesia. In particular cases, those skeleton keys might require a legal innovation or a legal reform or even the establishment of another rule for the sake of justice (Prodjodikoro, 1976, pp. 25–26).

Prodjodikoro stated that the Conflict of Laws, as well as PIL, must put forward justice as its objective. He mentioned that the rules of the Conflict of Laws and PIL must be invented in such a manner as to fulfill the sense of justice of involved parties of the cases or even, in the broader scope, society. Judges are entitled to found substantive rules according to their own discretion or prudence (*rechtsvinding*) for the sake of justice. He mentioned that the ultimate framework and main objective of the PIL rules are to provide justice to society. This justice must be placed at the center of gravity, and become the basis of the entire rules and system, of PIL (Prodjodikoro, 1979, p. 49).[7]

It could be imagined that if Prodjodikoro was still present, he could support what is nowadays called the 'better law approach as a content-based method'. With this approach, the court consciously is looking at the content of the laws involved. This law selecting method is not blind to what the respective rules say. Before its appliance, the courts will observe first as to whether or not this law could provide the correct legal solution to the parties involved. The goal of this approach is the right outcome between the parties, or materially the best solution, which he believed to be 'justice'. However, in his writings he did not further explain the method he preferred to use or his approach to finding 'the justice' (Reimann, 2017, pp. 179–180).[8]

3.2 *Sudargo Gautama: the green paper of Indonesian PIL*

Sudargo Gautama, the prominent Indonesian PIL scholar, consigned the Indonesian PIL in his eight PIL book series and further added to it with more than a hundred related books. His pivotal contribution was also the landmark decision book series about PIL cases awarded by the Indonesian courts. It is not surprising that Hartono asserted him to be the father of the Indonesian PIL (Hartono, 1976, p. vii). Kollewijn, in his letter to Sudargo Gautama, appreciated his effort in collecting the Indonesian landmark decisions as a dynamic legal source for the Conflict of Laws (Gautama, 2010b, pp. 82–83).[9]

Gautama started his works when *Integentielrecht* was developed side by side with the Indonesian PIL. In his systematic approach to the Indonesian PIL, he elaborated each of the PIL's general theories and carried out comparisons with several states before converting them into Indonesian context at the end of each discussion. The similar approach was applied to the particular PIL theories, the personal status or family law and the civil procedural law (*hukum acara internasional*), respectively, in his seventh and eighth Indonesian PIL book series. In the discussion of the principles of personal status, he discussed, among others, the relationship between parents and children, adoption, marriage, and so on (Gautama, 2010a). Gautama developed the Indonesian PIL by elaborating the intellectual property rights and confiscation and nationalization in Indonesia in the Tobacco Bremen case (Gautama, 1975).

The summary of the Indonesian PIL, the so-called Introduction of Indonesian Private International Law, was published after his PIL book series was completed. In this book, he offered his suggestion that Indonesia could adopt the Principle of Domicile for foreigners who have their domicile within Indonesia after more than two years, or another number of years as

7. See footnote 5.
8. In the development of this 'better approach', there are three methods, namely judicial selectivism, legislative selectivism, and substantivism.
9. In his inaguration speech as a professor of Conflict of Law in FHUI, Sudargo Gautama mentioned the letter dated 24 August 1957, wherein Kollewijn wrote to him, "*In de stroom van rechtspraak woordt de wijsheid van Jaren meegevoerd van mannen, die oog in oog met de praktijk van het leven stonden. In hun juridische fouten weerspiegeken zich niet zelden de eisen der gerechtigheid. Wie niet naar de rechtspraak wil omzien, omdaat daarin ook subjectieve dwaasheid en onverstand zich wertoont – zeker maar de stroom voert ze niet mee, ze verzinken – snijdt zich zeld af van de maatschappij, die hij moet dienen.*"

designated by the immigration law.[10] His suggestion is based on several reasons, including the most connecting factors between the people and their surroundings, and the comparison with *intergentielrecht* mentioned by Kollewijn, whereby the applicable law shall be the most connected law. He remains attached to particular principles in specific cases, for instance, what is in the best interests of the child up for adoption.

He compiled his thoughts about the Indonesian PIL in the academic bill of the Indonesian PIL.[11] His immense influence is undeniable, although the bill was revised several times. He mentioned that justice is the objective of any legal system, including the Conflict of Laws and the PIL. Yet, the justice in these fields differs slightly, which is reflected in the principle of equality of any connected legal systems in a case of Conflict of Laws or PIL.

He supported the Indonesian PIL to pursue the decisional harmony or so-called *Entscheidungsharmonie*, whereby the differences between legal systems shall not handicap any relationships even if such relationships were established across national boundaries. Gautama adopted the idea from Von Savigny that the Conflict of Laws should create legal certainty in international legal intercourse by creating the decisional harmony, '*Entscheidungsharmonie*'.[12] This objective was discussed by Gautama to encourage Indonesia to participate in international conventions and to support *renvoi*. He also mentioned the necessity for flexibility in the PIL in order to absorb the development of the PIL, referred to as *pelembutan hukum* (law softening) (Gautama, 1998, pp. 145–146, 184–186)[13], or *rechtsverfijning* by Lemaire and Wertheim (Gautama, 1998, pp. 156–157).[14]

---

10. This advice was resubmitted by his apprentice, Zulfa Djoko Basuki, as five years after the respective person has had his domicile in Indonesia. See the Proposal of the Bill of Indonesian PIL of 2015.
11. The Bill of Indonesian PIL was first drafted in 1983. This draft was revised several times and became the Bill of 1997, which acted as the starting point for the discussions about drafting (again) a new bill of Indonesian PIL in 2014. The new team was chaired by I.B.R. Suprancana and introduced the new bill on PIL in 2015. This bill was issued by the National Law Development Agency (*Badan Pembinaan Hukum Nasional*) under the Department of Law and Human Rights of the Republic of Indonesia, and should be evaluated by a public hearing. After the process of a public hearing, the bill of 2014 will be sent by the Indonesian Government to the House of Representatives for approval. This will be further discussed in the next sub-chapter.
12. Th. M. de Boer, as quoted in ten Wolde et al. (2011, pp. 10). See also Symeonides (2017, pp. 48–50).
13. Sudargo Gautama mentioned one example in a tort case, which absorbed the *pelembutan hokum* [softenings law]. The classic principle in the tort cases mentions that the applicable law shall be the local law where the tort happened (*lex loci delicti*). Yet, the classic principle is softened by considering the relevant or surrounding factors of the respective case. The same approach is applied in the principles of 'the proper law of contracts' by Morris, '*Zociale Umwelt*' by Binder, or '*milieu social*' by Bourel and Stromholm. Gautama mentioned that such a tendency was happening in Indonesia in the internal Conflict of Laws. In tort cases, the classic principle was shifted to consider the law of the victim. Gautama stated "*Sudah berulang-ulang harus diperhatikan 'social surroundings' dari peristiwa hukum yang dihadapi. Misalnya saja pada saat menelaah persoalan: percampuran dengan suku bangsa asli (vermenging met de autochtone bevolking), persekutuan dengan masyarakat hukum setempat (deelgenootschap van locale rechtsgemeenschap), peralihan agama, atau penyelundupan hukum (wetsontduiking) yang selalu menekankan pada segi-segi social ini, peralihan social (maatschappelijke overgang), dan sebagainya* [The 'social surroundings' of the existing legal events have been repeatedly taken into account. For example, when examining problems such as: mixing with indigenous tribes (vermenging met de autochtone bevolking), fellowship with the local legal community (deelgenootschap van locale rechtsgemeenschap), religious conversion, or legal smuggling (wetsontduiking), which always emphasizes social aspects, social transition (maatschappelijke overgang), and so on]". In another example, Gautama mentioned that the Principle of Nationality should be softened whereby the Indonesian law should be applicable to foreigners who have had domicile in Indonesia for more than two years. In this case, Zulfa Djoko Basuki offers it after five years.
14. "*Rechtsverfijning terjadi bilamana suatu kejadian pada umumnya terang termasuk karena disebut dalam suatu peraturan hukum, tetapi karena beberapa hal dianggap bahwa kejadian itu dikecualikan saja dari berlakunya itu. Jadi lembaga ini mengakibatkan bahwa luas berlakunya kaidah hukum tertentu dipersempit. Pasal 16 AB menentukan bawa peraturan hukum nasional mengenai status personal mengikuti kaula negara Belanda (kini Warga Negara Indonesia) di mana pun mereka berada di luar negeri. Secara analogy dianggap pula bahwa orang-orang asing yang berdiam di Indonesia tetap takluk kepada hukum nasional mereka di bidang status personal ini. Setelah Pasal 16 AB ini secara analogis dilebarkan lingkungan berlakunya, maka pasal itu harus*

Based on the above facts, Gautama supported the appliance of foreign law because it indicated that the judge also respects it. He also agreed with Prodjodikoro that the appliance of foreign law and of international convention rules must be according to *lex fori.* In this sense, he addressed that foreign law could be set aside by public policy if the application is manifestly incompatible with the values of the judge. In the Indonesian context, it is the Indonesian Constitution of 1945 and Pancasila.

The above thought was comparable to that of Koesnoe (1965), who also contributed valuable thought to the development of PIL. He mentioned in his dissertation that the development of the Indonesian legal system, and PIL in particular, shall be based on or must be in line with the Indonesian Constitution of 1945 and Pancasila. On the other hand, Indonesia must also be ready to make an adjustment and adaptation to international regulations and international cooperation.[15] Gautama also mentioned that the *rechtsidee* or basic Indonesian values must become the basis of the Indonesian legal system as contained in the Indonesian Constitution of 1945.[16]

3.3 *Sunaryati Hartono, the development of economic law*

CFG Sunaryati Hartono is one of the influential scholars of the Conflict of Laws in Indonesia. Together with Mochtar Kusuma Atmadja, she argued that the Indonesian legal system should be developed according to the functionalist approach. Atmadja claimed that both scholars offered pragmatic legal realism. By adopting the thoughts of Roscoe Pound from the United States, Hartono stated that a legal system is a tool of the social engineer that must be developed according to its function to develop social welfare in the future. Through regulation and legislation, the creation of an atmosphere conducive to the support of trading and business activities could be accomplished. Therefore, this field could be developed pragmatically. This idea was about supporting the Indonesian development that was beginning to grow.[17]

According to Hartono, the development of PIL, in particular, the economic aspects such as investment and international trading, was no longer sufficient with the approach of PIL only. Such cases and relations transformed into transnational aspects, therefore, it needs another field of law, for instance, the administrative law for international public, known as the 'transnational aspects' (Hartono, 1976, pp. 165–167). She also mentioned that PIL should be hand

diperhalus (verfijnd) lagi sehingga perluasan secara analogis tidak dilakukan lagi, apabila peristiwanya berasal berkenaan dengan orang-orang asing di Indonesia yang berasal dari suatu negara dengan prinsip domisili [Rechtsverfijning occurs when an event is generally bright, including because when it is referred to in a legal regulation, but because some things are considered that the incident is excluded from the enactment. So this institution resulted in the extent of the validity of certain legal rules being narrowed. Article 16 AB determines that the national law regarding personal status follows the Dutch state (now Indonesian) state wherever they are abroad. Analogically, it is also considered that foreigners who reside in Indonesia remain subject to their national law in this area of personal status. After this, Article 16 AB has been broadly analogous to its enactment; the article must be refined (verfijnd) again so that the analogical expansion is not repeated, in the event with respect to foreigners in Indonesia originating from a country with the principle of domicile]".

15. This idea was also supported by Sunaryati Hartono as one of the bedrocks of Indonesian development (see Hartono, 1976, pp. 67—68).
16. "*Nilai-nilai dasar tata hukum Indonesia menurut UUD 1945 antara lain: hukum harus berwatak melindungi daripada memerintah, mewujudkan keadilan sosial bagi seluruh rakyat, hukum itu dari rakyat dan mengandung sifat kerakyatan, hukum adalah pernyataan kesusilaan dan moralitas yang tinggi, baik dalam peraturan maupun dalam pelaksanaannya sebagaimana diajarkan dalam agama dan adat rakyat Indonesia* [The basic values of the Indonesian legal system according to the 1945 Constitution include: the law must have a character of protecting rather than governing, realizing social justice for all people, the law is from the people and contains a democratic nature, the law is a statement of morality and high morality, both in regulation and in the implementation as taught in the religion and customs of the Indonesian people]". See Dimyati (2004).
17. Hartono emphasized that the legal system must be developed and orientated to the future. It has human invention in its formation (see Hartono, 1976, pp. 58–68). See also her ideas about the 'transnational approach' in her dissertation (Hartono, 1973).

in hand with other fields of law; for instance, PIL should be hand in hand with Comparative Law because the comparison will show the best settlement that is suitable, appropriate and convenient for the Indonesian situation (Hartono, 1976, p. 47).

3.4 *'Sporadic' development of Indonesian PIL*

Besides the influence of the main thoughts described above, there are also some of the works on PIL that mentioned and discussed the PIL's basic thoughts and theories. In a sub-chapter in her dissertation, Sumampouw (1968) quoted Gautama in mentioning that justice in PIL is different from justice in the substantive law of the civil law. The basic principle in achieving justice in the PIL is the equivalence of all legal systems.[18] In determining the applicable law, the content or substantive of the law shall not be considered, but instead which law has the closest connection with the case and/or the relation. The connection shall be evaluated objectively and not necessary by territorial means (Sumampouw, 1968, pp. 7–8). Concerning the applicable law of a contract, the applicable law shall be determined by the law that dominates the agreement. In looking at the most suitable applicable law, the choice of law between the parties is acceptable. Such freedom is limited by the public policy if the contract must be connected to the state's interest whereby the consideration of the same must consider the legal certainty and justice.[19]

In relation to public policy, particularly in the context of the enforcement of foreign arbitration awards, it was found that Indonesia tends to prioritize internal public policy over external public policy, because the public policy was interpreted closely with the national interest and conditions, as commonly found in developing countries (Longdong, 1998, pp. 253–258). The tension to interpret according to *lex fori* and national values is delicate. The researchers of the enforcement of the foreign arbitration awards in Indonesia also resulted analogous in relation to the Convention on Recognition and Enforcement on Foreign Arbitral Awards of 1958 (New York Convention), the Convention on the International Centre for Investment Settlement Dispute (ICSID), and Indonesian Arbitration Law.[20] Each of the set-aside, refusal, annulment and/or cancellation of foreign arbitration awards are interpreted according to *lex fori*; in other words, it is performed according to the prevailing Indonesian rules and regulations.

The free-personal-values areas, for instance, the contract laws or agreements about trading and international business, as well as international arbitration, are developing rapidly in Indonesia. The development of those rules is according to the situation and in support of the daily business activities in Indonesia, and at the same time it is supported by the values of the 1945 Indonesian Constitution and Pancasila. This shows that the suggestions of Sunaryati Hartono and Muhammad Koesnoe are delicate.

In the same field, Hardjowahono states that the development could be directed to the unification of the substantive rules and not the choice of law rules, either through the regional or international conventions or law restatements. The expected result at the end of the process is an independent and autonomous commercial law system (Hardjowahono, 2006, p. 319).[21] The author appreciates this thought, while emphasizing that the implementation of those

18. "*Keadilan dalam hubungan HPI adalah berlainan dengan keadilan yang dicapai oleh hukum materiil intern, pokok pangkal untuk mencapai keadilan HPI ialah persamarataan semua sistem hukum* [Justice in PIL relationship is different from the justice achieved by internal material law; the main point in achieving PIL justice is the equality of all legal systems.]". See Siong (1960, pp. 170–171).
19. "*Dalam hal ini pencarian hukum yang berlaku ini, pencarian bergerak dengan dua pola tujuan: kepastian hukum dan keadilan.* (In the case of searching for the prevailing law, the search moves with two patterns of purpose: legal certainty and justice.]". See Sumampouw (1968, pp. 358–360).
20. See the thoughts as described and argued in the writings of, among others, in chronological order, Gautama (1989, 1991b, 1996a), Adolf (1994), Radjagukguk (2000), Latip (2002), Abdurrasyid (2002), Suparman (2004), Wibowo (2007), and Zuraida (2009).
21. He also states that personal status or the field that closely attaches personal values is better regulated by the principles of PIL as part of national law, with harmonization or coordination of the common choice-of-law, either regionally or internationally through relevant and proper regional/international conventions for the sake of legal certainty in international relations.

rules, as both Prodjodikoro and Gautama stated, must be interpreted according to *lex fori*, the Indonesian values. In addition, PIL is basically part of the national law.[22]

In terms of the field of family law, development also occurs, although the number of researchers is not as many as in the free-personal-values field.[23] The protection of women and children is developed in the perspective of human rights and equality of gender, due to Indonesia's participation in the international conventions (see subsection 6.2).

The fundamental development of family law or personal status occurred in the protection of children from mixed marriages due to Indonesian participation in the UN Convention on the Elimination of all Forms of Discrimination Against Women (CEDAW). Basuki (2005, 2007) made the suggestion that Indonesia could participate more in the international conventions of the Hague Conference, particularly the conventions in relation to child protection. She argued that the law applicable to the cases of child maintenance should be the local law where the children have habitual residence, and, in the cases of dual or multi- nationalities of children, she added a reference to the active nationality of the children. In her other writings, she mentioned that the 'habitual residence' and the principle of the best interest of the child should be at the heart of considerations. In addition, she also considers that the applicable law for foreigners who have domicile in Indonesia should be under Indonesian law after five years, due to the period of immigration regulation. It is obvious that the closest-connections principle plays the main role.

4 WHICH WAY FORWARD?

These main thoughts from prominent Indonesian scholars provided the fundamental principles in the development of PIL in Indonesia. Some of the principles remain relevant and could be the basis of references to go further. The equivalence of legal systems and Indonesian values, as described in the Indonesian Constitution and Pancasila, remain necessary in the consideration of Indonesian PIL.

The author agrees with the opinion that the equivalence of legal systems remains the basis of Indonesian PIL because it is a reflection of justice in PIL in achieving decisional harmony. The other objective should be legal certainty, to ensure that the relationship should not be handicapped by the differences existing between legal systems when a legal dispute crosses national borders. Nevertheless, it shall be flexible. The author supports these thoughts because they are significant and the author has no other reason to opine otherwise. Therefore, the author encourages the mention of these objectives in both the proposal for and the bill for Indonesian PIL of 2015 itself, along with the necessity to reflect the ASEAN 'One Community'.

This decisional harmony is so important that this idea became the background of the existence of conventions (Gautama, 1997, pp. 2–5).[24] These conventions color the existence of PIL regulations and influence the development of PIL.

5 CONCLUSIONS

From the discussion above, we can conclude the following:

a. PIL has goals and objectives in regulating and completing a legal relationship for cases containing foreign elements.

22. See further, ten Wolde et al. (2011, p. 11). See in Indonesian context, Sudargo Gautama.
23. Other recent research is about interfaith and/or international mixed marriage that took place abroad; see Wahyuni (2016). One of the stated conclusions is that the registration of such marriage of the return of the couple is the silent recognition of the same. This is confirming the principle of *lex loci celebrationis* in Indonesia. In addition, the research suggested that MA 1974 should facilitate interfaith marriages due to the pluralism of Indonesian society. This suggestion is analogous to the judge's consideration of the Andy Vony Gany case.
24. Also see Gautama (1996b, Ch. 1) and Soenandar (2004, pp. 2–5).

b. PIL has a goal of justice in determining the applicable law when two or more legal systems meet. In this case, the equality of the legal systems emerge and become a priority, rather than substantive justice considerations.
c. In applying or implementing foreign law as a valid law, the judge can consider making adjustments if there are things that are in conflict with *lex fori.*
d. The opinions and thoughts mentioned above are still the main objectives and considerations in PIL. Therefore, it is very good and useful to be mentioned in the academic text and as a record for the PIL bill (*memory an toelichting*) as a record for PIL judges and observers.

ACKNOWLEDGMENTS

The author would like to thank the editors for their input and comments for this writing, while any mistakes are solely the responsibility of the author.

REFERENCES

Abdurrasyid, P. (2002). *Arbitrase & Alternatif Penyelesaian Sengketa.* Jakarta, Indonesia: PT. Fikahati Aneska dan Badan Arbitrase Nasional Indonesia.

Adolf, H. (1994). *Hukum Arbitrase Komersial Internasional.* Jakarta, Indonesia: Radjagrafindo.

Basuki, Z.D. (2005). *Dampak Perkawinan Campuran terhadap Pemeliharaan Anak (Child Custody), Tinjauan dari Segi Hukum Perdata Internasional* (Dissertation, Yarsif Watampone, Jakarta, Indonesia).

Basuki, Z.D. (2007). *Bunga Rampai Kewarganegaraan Dalam Persoalan Perkawinan Campuran.* Depok, Indonesia: Fakultas Hukum, Universitas Indonesia.

Dimyati, K. (2004). *Teorisasi Hukum, Studi Tentang Perkembangan Pemikiran Hukum di Indonesia 1945–1990.* Surakarta: Indonesia: Muhammadiyah University Press.

Gautama, S. (1975). *Segi-segi Hukum Internasional pada Nasionalisasi di Indonesia.* Bandung, Indonesia: PT. Alumni.

Gautama, S. (1988). *Hukum Perdata Internasional Indonesia Buku Ketiga Jilid Kedua (Bagian Kedua)* (3rd ed.). Bandung, Indonesia: PT. Eresco.

Gautama, S. (1989). *Perkembangan Arbitrase Dagang Internasional di Indonesia.* Bandung, Indonesia: PT. Eresco.

Gautama, S. (1991a). *Pengantar Hukum Antar Golongan.* Jakarta, Indonesia: PT. Ichtiar Baru-Van Hoeve.

Gautama, S. (1991b). *Hukum Dagang dan Arbitrase Internasional.* Bandung, Indonesia: Citra Aditya Bakti.

Gautama, S. (1996a). *Aneka Hukum Arbitrase (Ke Arah Hukum Arbitrase Indonesia Yang Baru).* Bandung, Indonesia: Citra Aditya Bakti.

Gautama, S. (1996b). *Indonesia dan Konvensi-Konvensi Hukum Perdata Internasional* (2nd ed.). Bandung, Indonesia: PT. Alumni.

Gautama, S. (1997). *Hukum Dagang Internasional.* Bandung, Indonesia: PT. Alumni.

Gautama, S. (1998). *Hukum Perdata Internasional Indonesia Jilid III Bagian 2 Buku ke-8.* Bandung, Indonesia: PT. Alumni.

Gautama, S. (2010a). *Hukum Perdata Internasional Indonesia Jilid III Bagian I, Buku ke-7* (3rd ed.). Bandung, Indonesia: PT. Alumni.

Gautama, S. (2010b). *Hukum Antar Tata Hukum (Kumpulan Karangan)* [Interlegal Law (An Anthology)]. Bandung, Indonesia: PT. Alumni.

Hardjowahono, B.S. (2006). *Dasar-Dasar Hukum Perdata Internasional Buku Kesatu* (4th ed.). Bandung, Indonesia: Citra Aditya Bakti.

Hartono, C.F.G.S. (1973). *Beberapa Masalah Transnasional dalam Penanaman Modal Asing di Indonesia* (Dissertation). Bandung, Indonesia: Binacipta.

Hartono, C.F.G.S. (1976). *Pokok-Pokok Hukum Perdata Internasional* [Principles of private international law]. Bandung, Indonesia: Binacipta.

Koesnoe, M. (1965). *Perkembangan dari Pemikiran Cara-Cara Penyelesaian Masalah Hukum AntarGolongan di Indonesia* [The development of thinking about ways to resolve intergroup legal problems in Indonesia] (Dissertation, FH Universitas Airlangga, Surabaya, Indonesia).

Latip, Y.D. (2002). *Pilihan Hukum dan Pilihan Forum Dalam Kontrak Internasional,* (Dissertation, Fakultas Hukum, Universitas Indonesia, Jakarta, Indonesia).

Longdong, T.L.T. (1998). *Asas Ketertiban Umum dan Konvensi New York 1958, Sebuah Tinjauan atas Pelaksanaan Konvensi New York 1958 pada Putusan-putusan Mahkamah Agung RI dan Pengadilan Asing* (Dissertation). Bandung, Indonesia: Citra Aditya Bakti.
Prodjodikoro, W. (1976). *Hukum Antar-Golongan di Indonesia*. Bandung, Indonesia: Sumur Bandung.
Prodjodikoro, W. (1979). *Asas-asas Hukum Perdata Internasional* (5th ed.). Bandung, Indonesia: Sumur Bandung.
Radjagukguk, E. (2000). *Arbitrase Dalam Putusan Pengadilan*. Jakarta, Indonesia: Chandra Pratama.
Reimann, M.W. (2017). Better law approach. In B. Jürgen, R. Giesela, F. Franco & A. Pedro de Miguel (Eds.), *Encyclopedia of private international law*. Cheltenham, UK: Edward Elgar Publishing.
Siong, G.G. [Gautama, S.] (1960). *Hukum Antar Golongan* (2nd ed.). Jakarta, Indonesia: Ichtiar.
Soenandar, T. (2004). *Prinsip-prinsip UNIDROIT*. Jakarta, Indonesia: Sinar Grafika.
Sumampouw, M. (1968). *Pilihan Hukum Sebagai Pertalian Dalam Perjanjian Internasional* (Dissertation, Faculty of Law, University of Indonesia).
Suparman, E. (2004). *Pilihan Forum Arbitrase dalam Sengketa Komersial Untuk Penegakkan Keadilan* (Dissertation). Jakarta, Indonesia: Tatanusa.
Symeonides, S.C. (2017). *Private international law: Idealism, pragmatism, ecleticsm, general course on private international law*. The Hague, The Netherlands: The Hague Academy of International Law.
Wahyuni, S. (2016). *Nikah Beda Agama Kenapa ke Luar Negeri?* (Dissertation). Yogyakarta, Indonesia: Alfabet.
Wibowo, B.R. (2007). *Arbitrase Sebagai Alternatif Penyelesaian Sengketa Perdagangan di Indonesia* (Dissertation, FH Universitas Airlangga, Surabaya, Indonesia).
ten Wolde, M.H., Henckel, K.C. & de Haan, J. (2011). *European private international law: A comparative perspective in contracts, torts and corporations*. Groningen, The Netherlands: Hephaestus Publishers.
Zuraida, T. (2009). *Prinsip Eksekusi Putusan Arbitrase Internasional di Indonesia, Teori dan Praktek Yang Berkembang* (Dissertation). Surabaya, Indonesia: PT. Wastu Lanas Grafika.

Culture and International Law - Juwana et al. (Eds)
© 2019 Taylor & Francis Group, London, ISBN 978-1-138-38766-9

Restricted right to employment among refugees and asylum seekers in Indonesia and its consequences

Yanuar Sumarlan
Mahidol University, Bangkok, Thailand

Naparat Kranrattanasuit
Lecturer, Institute of Human Rights and Peace Studies, Mahidol University, Bangkok, Thailand

ABSTRACT: Millions of refugees and asylum-seekers have been known to suffer from four major reactions of the locals to these "new minorities" in their residing places: prejudice, discrimination, political opposition, and violence. Restriction of employment is the primary discriminatory practice that stops the refugees and asylum-seekers to survive with dignity. This paper thus questions the reasons for such discriminatory practices around restrictions or limitations of employment opportunities for the refugees and asylum-seekers in Indonesia. After a research visit in Indonesia (Jakarta and Bogor) to the refugees and asylum-seekers as well as the NGOs, Academics, and Government Officials who have been working with them, the researchers collect some primary data (interviews, Focus Group Discussion, etc) that is mixed with publically published sources (Journals, Reports, News, etc) to answer this question. Rather similar to the concept of Deliberate Destitution offered by Nessel (2015) to explain the function of work restrictions to refugees and asylum-seekers both in Europe and the US as [failed] "deterrent", the restrictions to work among refugees and asylum-seekers in Indonesia function as well as political gags to prevent exploded feelings of unfairness among the poor local communities. The anti-refugee discrimination in labor market, as the same thing found in Europe, further the marginalization of refugees and asylum-seekers during both the application and return phases. For this enlarged function of job restrictions to refugees and their negative impact, the challenges for the Indonesian authority to solve lack of livelihood opportunities for surviving refugees and asylum-seekers waiting for [unlikely] resettlement are growing exponentially.

KEYWORDS: refugees, asylum-seekers, restrictions on employment, deliberate destitution, immigration deterrent

1 INTRODUCTION

In the recent past, the fate of asylum-seekers and refugees in finding a job was not as hard as now. For example, in the mid-1980s most of European countries experience fairly low numbers of asylum requests; asylum-seekers were given access to the labor market and negative aspects of this right were not debated so much.[1] In the 1990s, several countries began to face large flows of asylum-seekers, and these groups' access to welfare rights and the labor market

1. Marko Valenta and Kristin Thorshaug, 'Restrictions on Right to Work for Asylum Seeker: The Case of the Scandinavian Countries, Great Britain and the Netherlands.' (2013) 20 *International Journal on Minority and Group Rights* 459, 460.

began to be questioned; the right to work was withdrawn in many countries.[2] Both supporters of right to work and restriction to right to work have their arguments. The supporters of right to work would claim that access to work (1) prevents exclusion from society and then facilitates integration, (2) prevents them from exploitation in illegal labor market, (3) promotes self-sufficiency among asylum-seekers.[3] Immigration authorities, however, would claim back that access to work (1) attracts potential asylum-seekers as a "pull factor" to large influxes that will become threats, (2) increases competition for jobs that worsens conditions for native workforces, (3) undermines attempts with voluntary and forced return, and (4) reduces the attraction of ideas of returning homes.[4]

Theorists and analysts of migration offer their own analysis for asylum-seekers and refugees to go to certain countries. Variations in influx of refugees could be influenced by background factors such as changes in the situation in sending countries and changes in the asylum policies of other countries. For example, conflicts in Bosnia and Kosovo in the 1990s and Afghanistan and Iraq (in the 2000s) mixed with Denmark's restrictive asylum policies suddenly increased influx of refugees o Norway and Sweden.[5] Some researchers claimed that migration is influenced by historical factors and previous ethnic networks.[6] Other researchers argue that the main concern of asylum-seekers are chances of attaining safety and being granted residence rights as well as the long-term possibilities of integration into the new country.[7]

Using these literatures as well as those from the US, this research tries to understand the reasons behind the restriction of asylum-seekers and refugees' right to employment in Indonesia while they are waiting for their refugee and asylum-seeker statuses. Applying some historical facts and events in the past related to actual practices and policy evolution, the authors of this paper seek also the consequences of such restrictions to the fate of asylum-seekers and refugees in Indonesia. The literature on refugees' and asylum-seekers' in Indonesia obviously has pictured the grim situation as the Indonesian authorities strictly disallow access to local labor market for them. The concept of Deliberate Destitution by Nessel (2015) looks familiar and "close" to the phenomenon of refugees and asylum-seekers in Indonesia for its both deliberate and suffering-inducing nature. However, the true nature of Indonesia's share of the stories appears to be different from the forms of the original concept.

This paper is divided into five parts: Introduction (to research methods), Literature Review, Conceptual Framework, Findings, and Conclusion. The Introduction would cover important parts of research methodologies, and the Literature Review looks back through previous research and studies on issues surrounding restrictions on refugees and asylum-seekers' access to local labor market or jobs. After showing and explaining the conceptual framework of the study, the paper would also reveal the Findings into some parts. The Conclusion would end the discussion with some answers and explanation for the phenomenon of interests.

1.1 *Research questions*

1. Why has the Indonesian government constrained the right to work of refugees/asylum-seekers?
2. What are the consequences of the restricted right to employment of refugees/asylum-seekers?

---

2. Valenta and Thorshaug, above n 1.
3. Ibid.
4. Ibid.
5. Ibid.
6. V Robinson and J Segrott, *Understanding the Decision Making of Asylum Seekers* (London: Home Office Research Study, 2002).
7. Marko Valenta and Kristin Thorshaug, '"Asylum Seekers" Perspectives on Work and Proof of Identity: The Norwegian Experience" [2002] *Refugee Survey Quarterly*.

1.2 *Research objectives*

1. To scrutinize the Indonesian government's reasons of constraining the right to work of refugees/asylum-seekers.
2. To examine the consequences of the restriction of the right to work of refugees/asylum-seekers.

1.3 *Research methodology*

For this research, the authors conducted both documentary and field research in Jakarta and Bogor, Indonesia. They reviewed academic articles of local and international scholars on Indonesia and others such as reports of local and international non-government organizations, as well as the UNHCR-based reports to study the laws/policies related to the urban refugees/asylum-seekers in Indonesia and their real implementation. Moreover, the authors conducted interviews and focus group discussions with diverse groups of participants in Jakarta and Bogor, Indonesia between 5 and 9 March 2018. The informants were classified into four groups: Group 1 (refugees/asylum-seekers from Afghanistan, Pakistan, and Iraq, i.e. four children and four adults, Group 2 (scholars: one Indonesian academic researcher specializing in refugees/asylum-seekers, Group 3 (NGOs, United Nations, ASEAN, SUAKA, Human Rights Working Group (HRWG) and UNHCR, and Group 4 (Government Officials: Immigration officer).

2 LITERATURE REVIEW

This section explores the existing research papers pertaining to the right to employment of refugee/asylum seekers. It emphasizes the reasons for restriction to employment for refugees/asylum seekers, possibilities for employment in some countries, and impact of employment restrictions on refugees/asylum-seekers.

2.1 *Reasons for restriction to employment for refugees/asylum seekers*

Immigration authorities in Europe mentioned at least four negative consequences when right to employment to refugees and asylum-seekers is given.[8] First, the right to work would set a 'pull effect' on potential asylum-seekers by setting an attraction for individuals without a real protection need (threats, persecution, etc) to come to the country with the intention to work until they are sent back. Second, there is an assumption that the large influxes of asylum-seekers will also constitute a potential threat to a country's welfare system. Third, giving asylum-seekers access to the labor market means one could create competition for jobs, with worse conditions for the native labor force of countries undergoing economic crises. Fourth, by giving asylum-seekers, especially those with a rejection, the possibility to work, one might strengthen the ties to the country of asylum, setting the thoughts of return less attractive.

However, some potential positive consequences of asylum-seekers' access to the labor market have been stated as well. For example, access to labor market could prevent exclusion from society and facilitate integration both for short-term during the application phase and long-term. Furthermore, the right to work could prevent them from turning to the illegal labor market; this case is true in countries where asylum-seekers get very low welfare assistance. The European Commission states that employment is beneficial for both asylum applicants and receiving countries as "access to employment could prevent exclusion from the host society and promote self-sufficiency among asylum-seekers.[9]

8. Valenta and Thorshaug, above n 1.
9. Ibid 462.

In the United States, denial of work authorization and public benefits to asylum-seekers functions to deter "economic migrants" from filing fraudulent asylum applications to work lawfully.[10] This ban to work is a part of bigger effort to deter asylum-seekers from coming to the United States.[11] The more humane regime—coupling asylum and employment authorization—that existed in the United States until 1995 was finally replaced by the more restrictive "Illegal Immigration Reform and Immigrant Responsibility Act (IIRIRA) in 1996[12]. However, this change into a more restrictive regime of work authorization to asylum-seekers was criticized as a violation of the spirit of the Refugee Convention and the very right to seek asylum (Universal Declaration of Human Rights, G.A. Res. 217 (III), A, U.N. Doc. A/RES/ 217/(III) (Dec. 10, 1948)), an anomaly against other humanitarian immigration relief existing in the United States immigration law, a difficult push for asylum-seekers to return home to persecution, and obstacle to restore dignity to refugees and re-alignation of U.S. immigration policy with important international law norms.[13]

2.2 *Possibilities for employment in some countries*

Like other countries that fall under former-colony countries, Ireland inherited the Immigration Law of British with some necessary modifications; the first legislation was the Aliens Act of 1935.[14] This legislation, like the original one, limited the rights of residency and work among those who were not Irish nationals; the Act allowed the Minister of Justice discretionary powers to decide who could enter Irish space by immigration, where immigrants could live, to have aliens deported, and to make other regulations (or "orders") to apply to immigrant rights and entitlements. However, the Celtic Tiger phenomenon beginning in the 1960s that moved Ireland into a new economic power had opened Irish economy.[15] Although unemployment was persistent there, the labor shortage appeared in some occupations. The ESRI (1999) reported not only labor shortages in low paid service jobs but also in other high-skills areas such as scientific and technical areas, software and computing. The long processing times of applications (around 3 years for a decision) meant that many asylum-seekers were

10. Lori A Nessel, 'Deliberate Destitution as Deterrent: Withholding the Right to Work and Undermining Asylum Protection' (2015) 52 *San Diego Law Review* 313, 316–37. This argument is based on the distinction between "deserving" true refugees and undeserving "economic migrant". However, this distinction fails to capture the nuances in immigration and the mix of persecution and economic harm that may be the impetus for fleeing (Kahn 2000). In Kahn's own words (2000), "The poverty people are escaping is often tied in with the political and social malaise a country is experiencing: 'by suggesting that there are "genuine" people that are forced out of their homes by persecution and war, on the one hand, and those who simply seek a better life, on the other, the simplistic and unhelpful dichotomy between an asylum-seeker and an economic migrant ... is perpetuated. In reality, "the same situations of societal transformations and crisis linked to war, poverty, and nation-state formation" contribute to a mixed flow of asylum-seeker and economic migrants." In this context, to question whether people leave out of desperation or aspiration is irrelevant. They seek to escape from social, economic and/or political insecurity to a more secure future."
11. Lori A Nessel, 'Externalized Borders and the Invisible Refugees' (2009) 40 *Colum. Hum. Rts. L. Rev* 625.
12. Ibid above n 10, 323. The Clinton administration reacted to decouple the process of asylum and employment authorization for some reasons given by immigrant scholar and former counsel to Immigration and Naturalization Service David Martin (Nessel 2015, p. 321). For example, a week into the Clinton administration, a lone gunman who fired and killed two outside the CIA headquarters in Northern Virginia was identified as a Pakistani national who allegedly entered the United States illegally and got an extension to stay with work authorization as an asylum applicant. Some of those charged in the World Trade Center bombing a month later also turned out to be asylum applicants who had stayed in the United States as part of the backlog [delayed processes of asylum authorization].
13. Nessel, above n 10.
14. Steven Loyal and Ciaran Staunton, 'The Dynamics of Political Economy in Ireland: The Case of Asylum Seekers and the Right to Work' (2001) 10(2) *Irish Journal of Sociology* 33.
15. K Allen, *The Celtic Tiger* (Manchester: Manchester University Press, 2000); D O'Hearn, *Inside the Celtic Tiger* (London: Pluto, 1997).

sitting idle when they could be given the opportunity to work.[16] In this context, the current right to work scheme for asylum-seekers to work in Ireland was constructed.

Under the umbrella of the Asylum Rights Alliance (ARA), some groups campaigned since November 1998 for asylum-seekers to be given the right to work. This pressure group consisted of NGOs and employer associations such as Irish Small and Medium Enterprises (ISME), Irish Business and Economic Confederation (IBEC), and the Small Firms Association (SFA).[17] Under this pressure, the Irish Government allowed right to work to asylum-seekers who applied in Ireland 12 months before 27 July 1999[18]; this right would be extended to those who applied for asylum in Ireland on or before 27 July 1999. By 27 July 2000, this right to work amnesty produced 3,536 work permits. The jobs were non-transferable, and the employers must pay a monthly salary of IRP25 or a one-off annual fee of IRP125 to the Department of Enterprise Trade and Employment (DoETE); furthermore, the employer must prove that an Irish or other EU national could not have filled the vacancy.[19] This restriction limited the number of work permits given (67 permits) between 27 July and 15 December 1999.[20] The non-transferable nature of the work permit also produced exploitation by the employers who knew that the work permit holders could not change jobs easily.

The Department of Justice, Equality and Law Reform (DJELR) later allowed some flexibility to apply for a broader range of jobs; however, at the end of the right to work amnesty, about half of the eligible asylum-seekers were still jobless. The official figures gave only 1,787 asylum-seekers out of 3,353 entitled to work either found job or ceased to claim social welfare payments for other reasons.[21] Fanning, Loyal and Staunton[22] analyzed that this low take-up was a result of the fact that the right to work was not accompanied by the necessary supporting rights and social mechanisms which would aid asylum-seekers to find and adjust to jobs.

This case of Ireland's policy on right to work to asylum-seekers reveals two arguments: human rights and economic arguments. The Asylum Rights Alliance that covered around 100 NGOs, trade unions and employer organizations including Irish Refugee Council and church organizations campaigned for the right to work since November 1988 with human rights arguments. Their general argument was that the right to work offered a means for the asylum-seekers to gain dignity and to aid integration into Irish society, especially when claims for asylum took a long time. The case for a more relaxed immigration policy emphasized the right to work as an economic principle.[23] The groups such as Irish Business and Economic Confederation (IBEC) and Irish Small and Medium Enterprises (ISME) focused mainly on the needs of the economy and employers more than the rights of non-citizens. For these groups, including some political parties like Progressive Democrat (PD), integration and social rights were irrelevant to the acceptance of asylum-seekers; their sole concern was the ability of individuals to sell labor power as a commodity on the market.[24] Thus, these groups tended to advocate a selective immigration policy aimed at preventing a general inflow of low-skilled refugees or asylum-seekers. Irish Small and Medium Enterprises (ISME) and Goodbody Stockbrokers, for example, proposed the establishment of a quota system based on the skills needs of the Irish economy, an immigration policy similar to rather corporatist models of Australia and Canada.[25]

16. Loyal and Staunton, above n 14.
17. B Fanning, S Loyal and C Staunton, *Asylum Seekers and the Right to Work in Ireland* (Dublin: Irish Refugee Council, 2000).
18. Loyal and Staunton, above n 14.
19. Ibid.
20. Ibid 38.
21. Ibid 39.
22. Fanning, Loyal and Staunton, above n 17.
23. B Fanning and S Loyal, 'Asylum Seekers and the Right to Work' (Understanding Class in Ireland, Dublin, December, 1999).
24. Ibid.
25. Fanning, Loyal and Staunton, above n 17, 59.

These two arguments underpin the case for the asylum-seekers to be given the right to work.[26] Presupposing a broad social distinction between polity and the economy, these groups did not use these two arguments in mutually exclusive or in a binary opposition. Nevertheless, an analytical distinction on which group emphasized or prioritized which argument—or by the Irish Government—is important. The policy of barring asylum-seekers from jobs was based on Minister of Justice's belief that the access to jobs would act as a 'pull' factor to more asylum-seekers.[27] When Progressive Democrats explicitly criticized Minister of Justice in media and implicitly threatened to pull their support for the Government, the Government issued the right to work amnesty out of economic principles and not humanitarian one.[28] Therefore, the lack of social and material support for these asylum-seekers—despite the access to jobs—continued undisturbed.

When the Irish Government faced the need of having an expanding economy that required skilled labor, 18,500 work permits issued by Department of Enterprise, Trade and Employment by the end of 2000 was a three-fold increase from 1999. Simultaneously and contradictorily, the Government found itself deporting asylum-seekers as "bogus" because they are 'really' economic migrants; in a way, the basic binary division between the sphere of the polity and the sphere of economy had to be re-qualified because the division were threefold among 'genuine' asylum-seekers, 'bogus' asylum-seekers (or economic migrants) and 'genuine' economic migrants.[29]

2.3 *Impact of employment restrictions on refugees/asylum seekers*

Employment restrictions against asylum-seekers and refugees appear in largely three methods. The *first* method involves legal terms and regulated practices through which asylum-seekers and refugees are selectively denied right to work. The *second* method involves a set of less obvious "improvement" in a set of rather relaxed terms into a more restrictive or harsher term that reduce the chances of asylum-seekers to access to works to survive while waiting for the decision for the application and after the decision (likely refusal). The *third* method typically involves a brutal and non-negotiable refusal to access to work for asylum-seekers or refugees as the countries applying this refusal assume that there are not giving asylum to anyone.

Some European countries have since the 1990s emphasized the restrictive regulations to the refused asylum-seekers.[30] The combination of motivation and compulsion in the work of those who have received a final refusal (to be asylum-seekers) can be regarded as a form of indirect compulsion intended to reduce the person's standard of living[31]; the stay in the country should be terminated and the persons should return to their home countries.[32]

Sweden, for example, went against the trend of most European countries to reduce asylum-seekers' access to the national labor markets by extending access to work to asylum-seekers.[33] Swedish authorities emphasize that asylum-seekers should support themselves during the application period; the group can obtain an authorization to be able to access the labor market after providing certain requirements to get such authorization. After 2009, Norway authorities decided that only asylum-seekers who present a passport or national identity card can be given a temporary work permit.[34] In the Norwegian government's White Paper No. 9,

26. Fanning and Loyal, above n 23.
27. Loyal and Staunton, above n 14, 49.
28. Ibid.
29. Loyal and Staunton, above n 14.
30. Valenta and Thorshaug, above n 1, 464.
31. Ibid.
32. A Strand and Et Al., *Return in Dignity, Return to What? Review of the Voluntary Return Programme to Afghanistan* (Oslo: Chr. Michelsen Institute, 2008).
33. Valenta and Thorshaug, above n 1, 467.
34. Ibid 468.

2009-2010, the changes were intended to "make it less attractive for asylum-seekers who do not need protection to come to Norway with the primary intention of working." Denmark's center-right government during 2001-2011 restricted access to work in the asylum policies; only two exceptions were given to a very small group of asylum-seekers.[35] The first group is asylum-seekers who have a work contract or an actual job offer within a specialist field with a great need for workers (in the so-called "*Positive List*"). The second group is asylum-seekers under the Pay Limit Scheme or individuals with written offer of a well-paid job with income not lower than a limit set by the Danish authorities.[36]

In Great Britain up until 2002, asylum-seekers who had been waiting for six months for an initial decision on their asylum application could apply for a work permit (called employment concession).[37] Since autumn 2010, however, asylum-seekers with a work permit could only work on occupations listed on Great Britain's official list of jobs with shortages of workers.[38] In the Netherlands, with some exceptions in long application periods, asylum-seekers cannot work during the application phase. Currently, if an asylum procedure has lasted for six months, the applicant can work for 24 weeks in the course of a 52-week period[39]; this person also needs to hold a leave to remain (*W-document*) card issued to asylum-seekers who do not document their identity, or asylum-seekers who have not provided proof of identity may work.

When asylum-seekers have been given a final refusal and asked to leave the country (Sweden), they could retain jobs that have been held during the period as an asylum seeker.[40] Furthermore, Swedish law allowed a grant of temporary residence permit with a right to work to refused asylum-seekers if temporary barriers to return existed; in fact, the Swedish government in 2006 allowed around 17,000 formerly-refused asylum-seekers to remain in the country with an accompanying right to work.[41] In Norway, since 2008 the regulations regarding refused asylum-seekers' rights to work were tightened and at present asylum-seekers in Norway have no right to work; exception is made if the authorities recognize that the individuals cannot be removed due to external circumstances.[42] In Denmark, refused asylum-seekers do not have access to the labor market; the failed asylum-seekers will have to leave Denmark and apply for a residence and work permit via a Danish diplomatic mission (more on this regulation is available on www.nyidanmark.dk, visited last 6 March 2012). In Great Britain, the restrictive asylum policies have not allowed a right of work to refused asylum-seekers. Even if refused asylum-seekers can apply for permission to work if they have waited more than 12 months for a decision on the new asylum application, it is not known how many of around 45,000 refused asylum-seekers have managed to put this new right into practice.[43]

In conclusion, there are clear differences in immigration regimes within the same welfare regime; even in the Scandinavian countries, Denmark and Norway have been more reluctant to give "amnesties" to rejected asylum-seekers due to a fear that such measures may contribute to soften up asylum policy and to increase the influx of asylum-seekers.[44] Sweden may be associated more than any other countries surveyed (Sweden, Denmark, Norway, the Netherlands, Great Britain) with an inclusive migration regime.[45]

---

35. Ibid.
36. Ibid.
37. Valenta and Thorshaug, above n 1.
38. Ibid 469.
39. Ibid 470.
40. H Andersson and S Nilsson, '"Asylum Seekers and Undocumented Migrants" Increased Social Rights in Sweden" (2011) 49(4) *International Migration* 167.
41. Valenta and Thorshaug, above n 1; B Parousel, 'Sweden' in *Focus Migration* (2009).
42. Valenta and Thorshaug, above n 1, 475.
43. Ibid 476.
44. Ibid 478.
45. Ibid.

3 CONCEPTUAL FRAMEWORK

This paper applies "deliberate destitution" for conceptual framework. It comes from Nessel's article (2015) that divides the immigration rules of the United States into "pre-1995" and "post-1995" regimes as well as argues that the restriction to job market among asylum-seekers brings so many negative impacts on them. The following parts will be discussing on the reform that took place in the United States and some events behind the reform in 1995. The more humane regime that existed in the United States until 1995 permitted asylum-seekers with bona fide claims to work while their claims proceeded.[46] The Refugee Act was implemented in 1980, and Congress's intention was to harmonize United States law with its obligations under the U.N. Refugee Convention.[47] From 1980 to 1987, the Immigration and Naturalization Service (INS) held discretion to grant or refuse employment authorization to asylum-seekers (Employment Authorization, 45 Fed. Reg. 19, 563 (Mar. 26, 1980) (to be codified at 8 C.F.R. pt. 109). In 1987, the INS promulgated new regulations guaranteeing a right to employment authorization in all non-frivolous cases after a judge in a class action case found a livelihood of irreparable harm if the district director of INS was allowed to continue to deny employment authorizations to asylum-seekers[48]. For the next 8 years from 1987 to 1995, a refugee in need of protection could apply for asylum and the right to work simultaneously (Control of Employment of Aliens, 52 Fed. Reg. 16, 216, 16, 226 (May 1, 1987) (to be codified at 8 C.F.R. pt. 274a). If the government did not find the application for asylum to be frivolous, it granted employment authorization that the asylum-seeker could pay for their basic necessities of life and survive while the claim was processed (Control of Employment of Aliens, 52 Fed. Reg. 16, 216, 16, 226 (May 1, 1987) (to be codified at 8 C.F.R. pt. 274a).[49] However, long processes to adjudicate asylum claims created a growing backlog.[50] The Asylum Corps that was expecting to process 70,000 claims a year received 103,000 filed claims in 1992 and 150,000 claims in 1993 (History of the United States Asylum Officer Corps, AM. IMMIGR. L. CENTER, in http://www.ailc.com/services/asylum/history.htm#F [http://perma.cc/26ME-YRW9]). As the backlog continued to mount without myriad of enforcement and deterrent mechanisms that exist today, asylum-seekers who held employment authorization could evade removal [out of the country] if the asylum claim was finally denied[51]. Later, some exaggerated accounts of rampant abuse picked up parts in the media, including allegations that any asylum-seeker could get a work permit by uttering the word "political asylum"[52].

In the flurry of activity in Congress like hearings on asylum reform, some asylum applications were characterized as a "torrent" and as a "giant cascade" (Asylum and Inspections Reform: Hearing on H.R. 1153, H.R. 1355, and H.R. 1679 Before the Subcomm. On Int'l

46. Nessel, above n 10, 317.
47. Ibid.
48. Diaz v. INS, 648 F. Supp. 638, 65 (E.D. Cal. 1986) (granting a preliminary injunction prohibiting denial and revocation of work authorization until adjudication process for asylum claim had been completed). The judge found, "I am hard pressed to see how placing a refugee in a position where he or she must break the law to survive during the years it may take for a decision on a political asylum *cannot* be considered an irreparable hardship."
49. Nessel, above n 10, 320.
50. Ibid.
51. Asylum and Inspections Reform: Hearing on H.R. 1153, H.R. 1355, and H.R. 1679 Before the Subcomm. On Int'l Law, Immigration, and Refugees of the H. Comm. On the Judiciary, 103d Cong. 1-3 (1993) (statement of Romano L. Mazzoli, Chairman, Subcomm. On Int'l Law, Immigration and Refugees).
52. Ira H Mehlman, 'The New Jet Set: Think the Rio Grande Is a Porous Border? Try New York's JFK, Where Anyone Can Enter Through the Magic of Political Asylum' (1993) March 15 *Nat'l Rev.* 40, Referring to a Liberian asylum-seeker in the JFK Airport, one officer asserted that "...once he utters 'political asylum' his chances of remaining in the United States are 93 percent". According to this story, the Asylum Officer at JFK Airport complained, "We're being deluged. It's scandalous ... in a matter of hours he's going to be walking out onto the street joining the ranks of the unemployed. We don't know anything about him. We don't know if he has AIDS. We don't know if he's a murderer.

Law, Immigration, and Refugees of the H. Comm. On the Judiciary, 103d Cong. 1-3 (1993) (statement of Romano L. Mazzoli, Chairman, Subcomm. On Int'l Law, Immigration and Refugees). An immigration scholar and former general counsel to Immigration and Naturalization Service recounted some political factors that began the splitting between asylum grant and employment authorization. For example, just few days after President Clinton was sworn in, a lone gunman who killed two persons outside the CIA Headquarters in Northern Virginia was identified as a Pakistani who was said as entering the United States illegally and got extended stay with work authorization as an asylum applicant.[53] Later, "some charged in the World Trade Center bombing a month later also turned out to be the asylum applicants who had stayed in the United States as part of the backlog.[54] The storms of stories and the widespread media attention finally affected lawmakers.

Bills to revamp the asylum regime began to churn through Congress. Many calls appeared for mandatory detention for all asylum seekers and a requirement that asylum applications be lodged within days of entering the country.[55] The Clinton Administration added more asylum officers and put more provisions in place to reduce the backlog of cases and make asylum processing more efficient.[56] To follow this new regulation, the system set an "asylum clock" that would run once the application submitted a complete asylum application.[57] The new system also separated the process for seeking asylum from that of seeking work authorization.[58] When Congress passed the restrictive Illegal Immigration Reform and Immigrant Responsibility Act (IIRIRA), the new employment authorization regulations for asylum-seekers became official law (Illegal Immigration Reform and Immigration Responsibility Act, Pub. L. No. 104-208, § 401-405, 110 Stat. 3009-546, 3009-655 to -666 (1996).

This immigration regime wreak havoc on asylum-seekers' right to work. Applicants for asylum could no longer secure work authorization for at least 180 days after filing their asylum application, and often much longer if applicants requested an adjournment at any point.[59] This IIRIRA is harsher for applicants who have been denied asylum or asylum-seekers renewing their work authorization; if an asylum officer denies asylum to an applicant previous holding work authorization, the authorization expires 60 days after the denial or upon the expiration of the authorization, whichever time period is longer (8 C.F.R. § 1208.7(b)(2)).

Most of comments received in response to this set of regulatory changes were negative and foresaw some negative impacts to asylum-seekers. In fact, the government statistics revealed that the new regime was not working as it was planned. Between 2007 and 2011, around 285,025 pending cases happened before the administration courts; out of these pending cases, 262,025 (or 91.9 percent) had their employment authorization clocks stopped at some point (Plaintiff's Motion for Class Certification at 1-2, 4, A.B.T v. U.S. Citizenship & Immigration Serv., No. C11-2108-RAJ (W.D. Wash. Nov. 4, 2013, available at http://www.legalactioncenter.org/sites/default/files/docs/lac/AsylumClock-Motion-Exhibit-Order-12-20-2011.pdf). The hardship caused by such delays had been reported. Congress also applied a system of expedited removal to dramatically reducing the backlog of cases.[60] The immigration officer stationed as a

53. David A Martin, 'Making Asylum Policy: The 1994 Reforms' (1995) 70(725) *WASH. L. REV.* 738.
54. Ibid.
55. Nessel, above n 10, 322.
56. Ron Fournier, 'Immigration Curbs Sought—Clinton Seeks to Add Border Agents, Speed Asylum Reviews' *The Seattle Times*, 1993 <http:community.seattletimes.nwsource.com/archive/?data=19930727&slug=1712986>. Accessed 21 May 2015
57. Nessel, above n 10, 322, Once applied for asylum, the asylum-seeker must wait until the "clock" had registered at least 150 days before submitting a request for work authorization. At this point, the government had thirty days to consider the work authorization application. Furthermore, "any delay requested or caused by the applicant" would stop the clock until the proceedings were restarted. An asylum-seeker would not start to accrue time toward work authorization if she or he "failed to appear for a scheduled interview before an asylum officer for a hearing before an immigration judge."
58. Martin, above n 53, 753–754.
59. Nessel, above n 10, 323.
60. Ibid 328.

port of entry is empowered to determine whether to remove quickly a person who has improper or no documentation or to allow them to seek asylum (Ruth Ellen Wasem, Cong. Research Serv, 7-5700, U.S. House of Representatives Committee on the Judiciary Hearing on "Asylum Abuse: Is It Overwhelming Our Borders?" 7 (2013); 8 U.S.C § 1225(b)(1)(A)(ii)(2012)). When enacting IIRIRA, Congress added revisions to existing law that further restricted an asylum-seeker's ability to see protection; for example, Congress imposed a one-year time limit for seeking asylum protection.[61]

If the motive for restricting the right to work was to reduce fraud and provide a disincentive to seeking asylum solely to gain employment authorization, the unintended consequences of this immigration regime appeared as impact of such "deliberate destitution." Human Rights Watch and Setton Hall University School of Law (2013) reported many kinds of negative impact of such destitution to asylum-seekers.

4 FINDINGS

This section reflects the reasons of why the Indonesian government has constrained the right to employment of refugees/asylum-seekers. It is divided into three subsections: 1) policy context of post-Vietnam war, Australia's influence, and post-Suharto's reforms (1999) and President Jokowi's political turn (2017); and 2) refugee status determination and its subsections of policy implementation and impact on employment restriction and hardship.

4.1 *Policy context*

4.1.1 *Post-Vietnam War*

Indonesia first encountered the large exodus of refugees after the fall of Saigon in 1975 when hundreds of thousands of Vietnamese and later Cambodians, asylum seekers fled by boat to Indonesia and its neighbors. Around 19 May 1975, about 92 people passed through the town of Tarempa (Riau Islands) on their way to Singapore[62]; since then until 30 June 1979, more people (reported at 43,000) Vietnamese and Cambodians 'boat people' stayed in Indonesia's territory. After so much reluctance[63] The Government of Republic Indonesia agreed to allow the Galang Island (previously used as a transit site for returning Japanese soldiers on the World War II back to Japan in 1946) in the Riau Archipelago as a temporary home for up to 10,000 refugees at that time.[64] Presidential Decree No. 38 of 1979 (11 September) confirmed that under the coordination of Ministry of Defense, Foreign Affairs, and Interior Affairs, two teams would handle the "Indochinese refugee problem." The refugees would stay there only for a "reasonable period" around three to five years. The reluctance of Indonesia to spend any domestic resources on running the center in Galang Island was compensated by the UNHCR's agreement to bear all costs, estimated at around USD18,562,000 over two years.[65]

61. Besides, anyone who has traveled through a "safe-third country" prior to seeking asylum in the United States is now barred from asylum protection; asylum-seekers who have previously applied for, but were denied, asylum are also ineligible; and if the Attorney General determines that an asylum seekers submitted a frivolous application, the asylum seeker becomes "permanently ineligible for any asylum benefits" (Nessel, above n 10, 330).
62. RM Fandik, 'Penampungan Orang Vietnam Di Pulau Galang 1975-1990′ (1992) 1(1) *Avatara* 164.
63. ("That it would not receive refugees in its territory, but for the sake of humanitarianism it was forced to accept them during transit while they were waiting to move to a third country, as well as actively providing thoughts and concrete support to find solution for this problem"), Indonesia agreed to accept the refugees (Department of Information of the Republic of Indonesia 1989, p. 1).
64. A Missbach, 'Waiting of the Islands of "Stuckedness" Managing Asylum Seekers in Island Detention Camps in Indonesia: From the Late 1970s to the Early 2000s' (2013) 6(2) *Current Research on South-East Asia/ASEAS* 281.
65. Indonesia Department of Foreign Affairs of the Republic of Indonesia, Jakarta, 'Meeting on the Establishment of a Processing Centre for Indochinese Refugees' (1979).

The Indonesian government decided based on the option of restricted control of movement and better efficiency of centralized management and better surveillance mechanisms; besides, the more orderly migration schemes for asylum seekers could be accommodated or controllable. In this very constricted island environment with all kinds of life support supplies given to the refugees, highly restricted access to employment for refugees was natural. Thus, illegal self-organized attempts to cross to Australia would be less likely. Between July 1979 and July 1982, around 623,800 Indochina refugees were resettled from Southeast Asian region to a total of 20 countries like the US, France, and Canada[66]. UNHCR[67] reported the arrivals of around 121,708 Vietnamese in Indonesia from 1975 to 1995.

4.1.2 *Australia's influence*

Following Kneebone (2017), this study divides the evolution of the inter-subjective processes on security between the two countries into three phases: (1) Indonesia's acquiescence with Australian securitization policy (2001-2008), (2) Indonesia's prevarication facing increasingly aggressive Australian policies (2008-2013), and Indonesia's turning to the region (after the Andaman Sea crisis of 2015). With its somewhat ambiguous approach to refugees, ASEAN includes refugees in the ASEAN Political-Security Community (APSC) pillar of the ASEAN Community and provides refugees, through ASEAN Human Rights Declaration, some freedoms like freedom of discrimination, principle of *non-refoulement*; Indonesia is considered as a leader within ASEAN, particularly in APSC areas, for its strategic location in the Malacca Straits and interests in regional and maritime security.[68] After MV Tampa (a Norwegian ship) arrived in Australian waters with a cargo of 433 asylum seekers coming from Indonesia's direction to be refused by the Australian Government in August 2001, the elected PM John Howard enabled the passage of legislation that established offshore processing of refugees (or Australia's Pacific Solution I) to response to increasing boat arrivals from Indonesia. Implying that the asylum seekers were also Indonesia's responsibility by asking the MV Tampa captain to return them to Indonesia, Australia was dealing with 1,550 refugees (per February 2002) held on Nauru and Manus Islands to be processed within six months after their arrival.[69] By May 2005, around 65.5 percent of the asylum seekers under the Pacific Solution I had been resettled in Australia and New Zealand. After the Rudd Labor Government won the election in November 2007, in February 2008 Pacific Solution was stopped.[70] This closing up the Solution did not mean that the acquiescence of Indonesian Government to Australia's securitization policy was reduced; in fact, some new solutions were undergoing in production.

The Regional Cooperative Arrangement (RCA) dating back from the late 1990s was also the bilateral agreement between the two states to involve a non-state actor (the UNHCR) and an intergovernmental actor (International Organization for Migration or IOM). This RCA demands the Indonesian government to intercept and detain "Australia-bound" irregular migrants, to notify the IOM which is to provide advice and assistance, and then the UNHCR will assess the claims. The Indonesian officials will refer asylum seekers to IOM for "case management" and "care", who then refer them to the UNHCR to make asylum claims if they express such a wish. The UNHCR performs Refugee Status Determination (RSD) because Indonesia has not signed the Refugee Convention; the IOM as an intergovernmental body is funded by interested government especially the Australian government and its activities in

66. UNHCR, *The State of the World's Refugees: Fifty Years of Humanitarian Action* (Oxford, UK: Oxford University Press, 2000).
67. Ibid 98.
68. F Heiduk, *Indonesia in ASEAN: Regional Leadership between Ambition and Ambiguity* (SWP Research Paper, Berlin, RP 6, April, 2016).
69. S Kneebone, 'Australia as a Powerbroker on Refugee Protection in Southeast Asia: The Relationship with Indonesia' (2017) 33(1) *Refuge* 29, 31.
70. S Kneebone, 'Migration Control as Sea: The Australian Case' in Bernard Ryan and Valsamis Mitsilegas (eds), *Extraterritorial Immigration Control: Legal Challenge* (Leiden: Martinus Nijhoff, 2010) 349.

Indonesia.[71] The RCA itself gives more roles to the IOM than to the UNHCR; the IOM has more offices than that (only one) of the UNHCR (in Jakarta). After the commencement of the Regional Cooperative Arrangement, the IOM's roles were shifted from a system of Australian-funded accommodation in five designated areas to a system of detention.[72]

The further cooperation that epitomizes the securitized approach to refugee management was the implementation of Enhanced *Cekal* System or ICS (*cekal* is Indonesian acronym for *cegah* or prevent and *tangkal* or stop) to assist Indonesia to detect the movement of terrorists and other transnational criminals.[73] The impact and continuation of the Bali Process (since 2002) produced a law that was signed in 2011 as Law No. 6 of 2011 "Concerning Immigration" in which some new anti-smuggling laws were set. Consistent with the Regional Cooperation Agreement and Indonesian legislative policies that recognize the status of "refugee," the Indonesian Minister for Foreign Affairs made a rare statement acknowledging the protection needs of refugees.[74] The Indonesian 1945 Constitution (the amended version after 1998), in fact, recognizes "asylum seekers" although not in the same terms of the definition of the Refugee Convention; the Constitution splits between political and "foreign" refugees. The refugees are divided into those who have human rights needs and those who need the protection of another country.

Between 2008 and 2013, the Rudd and then the Gillard labor government focused on "breaking the people smugglers' business model"[75]; the Coalition government in 2013 created the Operation Sovereign Border (OSB) in September 2013, the strategy shifted to "stopping the boats." Under this strategy, Australia increasingly became bolder in its unilateral measures to breach international law such as through interdictions, turn-back, and tow-back policies of dubious legality under international law[76] to provoke the anger of the Indonesian counterparts.[77] During this time, Indonesia moved to a rather less tolerant approach, framing asylum seekers as illegal immigrants and acceding to the creation of detention facilities.[78] The IOM has been receiving the increased funding while the NHCR funding has to be stretched further to deal with increasing numbers of asylum seekers stuck in Indonesia. As a result, in November 2014, Australia announced that it would no longer resettle asylum seekers transiting from Indonesia.[79] As the number of asylum seekers arriving in Indonesia was increasing, the UNHCR struggled to keep up the demand for processing of claims with waiting times increasing. During 2008 to 2009, Australia allocated AUD807,727 to the UNHCR for protection capacity-building activities, AUD1,600,000 to the IOM for interpreting services for displaced persons in Indonesia, and AUD386,000 to the IOM for educational and social services for refugees and irregular migrants in Indonesia.[80] In 2014, the 13 Immigration Detention

71. Kneebone, 'Australia as a Powerbroker on Refugee Protection in Southeast Asia: The Relationship with Indonesia', above n 69, 32.
72. Ibid.
73. Australia Australian Government (Department of Immigration and Citizenship), 'Annual Report: 2006-2007' (2007) <http://www.border.gov.au/ReportsandPublications/Documents/annual-reports/annual-report-2006-07-complete.pdf>.
74. S Kneebone, 'The Bali Process and Global Refugee Policy in the Asia Pacific Region' (2014) 27(4) *Journal of Refugee Studies* 596.
75. C Barker, 'The People Smugglers' Business Model' in *Parliament of Australia, Department of Parliamentary Services, Research Paper* 37.
76. N Klein, 'Assessing Australia's Push Back the Boats Policy under International Law: Legality and Accountability for Maritime Interceptions of Irregular Migrants' (2014) 15(1) *Melbourne Journal of International Law* 1.
77. Australia Parliament of Australia (The Senate, Foreign Affairs, Defence and Trade References Committee), 'Breaches of Indonesian Territorial Waters' (2014).
78. A Nethery, B Rafferty-Brown and S Taylor, 'Exporting Detention: Australia-Funded Immigration Detention in Indonesia' (2013) 26(1) *Journal of Refugee Studies* 95.
79. Kneebone, 'Australia as a Powerbroker on Refugee Protection in Southeast Asia: The Relationship with Indonesia', above n 69, 34.
80. Australian Government (Department of Immigration and Citizenship), above n 73.

Centers in 13 provinces were running under "arbitrary rule"[81]; in 2015, the UNHCR added around 20 temporary detention facilities and 4,511 detainees.

From about 2008, there was a surge of departures of the Rohingya from Myanmar and push-backs by the Thai Navy, which led to the revival of the Bali Process in 2009. As the crises increased, in 2013 Indonesia convened with the UNHCR a special Conference on Addressing Irregular Movement of People outside the Bali Process. The ensuing Jakarta Declaration on Addressing Irregular Movement of Persons pledged the countries of origin, transit, and destination to work together to address irregular migration. After the Andaman Sea Crisis in 2015, the three most affected states (Malaysia, Indonesia, and Thailand) worked cooperatively to find a solution to the crisis. The Ministers of Foreign Affairs of these countries met on 20 May 2015 and announced on the same that "... necessary measures ... on humanitarian grounds, beyond their international obligations, as the issue cannot be addressed solely by these three countries" ("Joint Statement: Ministerial Meeting on Irregular Movement of People in Southeast Asia" from https://kln.gov.my/archive/content.php?t=3&articleId=5202813).

In every phase of these three stages of the relationship between Indonesia and Australia (acquiescence, prevarication, and regional solution), the discrepancies—as every agency is playing its own particular games—appear at least at three levels: at the strategic issues, regulatory, and infrastructure. In the Acquiescence Stage, for example, the Indonesian government's jobs were to "intercept and detain" Australian-bound irregular migrants; to launch this strategy, the government needs regulations, infrastructure (detaining systems and personnel), and other requirements (like social components). The detention strategy would produce certain impact to the refugees and asylum seekers or other kinds of migrants as they will likely to lose their rights of movement (the prohibition for refugees and asylum seekers to perform occupations is already in local regulations) and the rights to education (either for basic knowledge or vocational skills). In the next stage of "Prevarication," the Indonesian government became less tolerant and added a campaign to portray irregular migration as "illegal migration" both in building more detention centers and creating regulations to set the term of "illegal immigration" as official jargon. However, after some incidents[82], the cooperation between Indonesia and Australia grew sour.

When Indonesia decided to turn to its neighbors (Malaysia and Thailand) for a solution, it could only pledge for a "humanitarian" solution for "one year"; the recommendations offered by the Joint Statement only focused upon preventing irregular migration and responding to the issues of "human trafficking" and "people smuggling" rather than a set of lasting plan. Just like the other phases, this phase is obviously marked by lack of sustainable strategy, temporary and arbitrary nature of regulations used by the state or non-state authorities, and lack of proper infrastructure or personnel to sustain the solution. Most of the rights of refugees and asylum seekers, especially the rights of movement, rights to employment and rights to education have never been secured and sustained.

---

81. Indonesia IOM (International Organization for Migration), *Alternative to Detention* (2014) <https://www.iom.int/files/live/sites/iom/files/Country/docs/IOM-Indonesia-Alternatives-to-Detention-September-2014.pdf>.
82. In September 2009, a boat named "Jaya Lestari 5" with 255 Sri Lankans was intercepted and returned to the Indonesian port of Merak (north side of West Java) by the Australian authorities after an arrangement between the Australian PM and Indonesian President. The asylum seekers remained on board of the ship for six months because they were afraid to be detained by the Indonesian authorities. The Australian government promised AUD50 million to fund policing and processing of asylum seekers in Indonesia, but the Indonesian officials refused to intervene to forcibly remove the "Jaya Lestari 5" refugees. Only later, the asylum seekers were forcibly removed into a detention center. Some voluntarily returned to Sri Lanka (and get arrested), while others stayed on in Indonesia (IOM and UNHCR advice). (Full story is available in https://www.greenleft.org.au/node/45634.) The other incident involved another boat with 78 Sri Lankans in a boat that was intercepted and sent to Indonesia's Bintan Island for processing in an IOM-managed detention center. The diplomatic incident happened when the Sri Lankans refused to disembark until getting an assurance that their claims for refugee status would be processed and the province's governor refused to accept the asylum seekers on the Island. After a stalemate for weeks, the asylum seekers disembarked and were processed rapidly amid protests (of other asylum seekers) of unfairly favored treatment (Kneebone 2017, p. 35).

4.1.3 *Post-Suharto's reforms (1999) and President Jokowi's political turn (2017)*

Shortly after Gen. Suharto was forced to step down from presidency in 1998, some changes at the level of 1945 Constitution appeared to accommodate the new "democratic" government under President Habibie the protégé of Gen. Suharto. Under the pressure of a demand for a better Constitution in post-Suharto era, the majority of MPR (*Majelis Permusyawaratan Rakyat* of People's Consultative Assembly) or the highest body in Indonesia's state structure tired of rather powerful Presidential institution in the structure that allows dictator at government helm—insisted to build a more democratic, modern, comprehensive, and responsive Constitution.[83] Despite the resistance of the "old guards" who wanted to keep the status quo, the People's Consultative Assembly finally launched a series of amendments of the 1945 Constitution in four steps. The first step took place in 1999 to amend the Presidential power and authority as well as the power and authority of People's Representative Council or *Dewan Perwakilan Daerah* (DPD). In the amended 1945 Constitution, for example, President has only the right to propose draft of law to *Dewan Perwakilan Rakyat* (People's Representative Board) and to stipulate government regulation to carry out the laws.[84]

The second step took place in 2000 to reformat the structure of local governance units, the positions of citizens, the better respect to human rights, state defense and security, etc. The third and fourth steps happened in 2001 and 2002, respectively, to omit the *Dewan Pertimbangan Agung* (Supreme Advisory Council) from the state structure, to create the People Representative Council (DPD or *Dewan Perwakilan Daerah*), national education, etc. In the older 1945 Constitution, for example, only Articles 27 (1, 2) and 28 mentioned the principle of equality before law, freedom of occupation, freedom of life, humanism, freedom of assembly, freedom of speech, etc. In the amended 1945 Constitution, at least 10 Articles have been amended/added to follow and adopt the spirit of the Universal Declaration of Human Rights (Sarsito 2007, p. 10). Below is the list of the amended Articles of the 1945 related to human rights that might be relevant to refugees and asylum-seekers.

Generally, only a handful of Indonesia's regulations or laws are relevant to refugees and asylum-seekers living in Indonesia right now. These are (1) The Amended 1945 Constitution, (2) The Human Rights Law of 39 of 1999, (3) The Immigration Law of 2011 "Concerning Immigration", (4) President Regulation No. 125 of 2016 (*Perpres*), and (5) Regulation of Directorate General Immigration Number IMI-0352.GR.02.07 on "Procedures for Illegal Immigrants who Claim themselves as Asylum-Seekers or Refugees". These regulations follow the hierarchy principle which means that the lower regulations are not supposed to violate the highest regulations in the hierarchy, with state philosophy of *Pancasila* (Five Fundamentals) and the 1945 Constitution as "highest" regulations. The lowest regulation in this hierarchy is the Directorate General Immigration Regulation as the actual "guide" for the immigration officials to do their tasks.

The Indonesian laws related to the right to employment are consistent with the international legal framework. For instance, Article 3 of the Human Rights Law No. 39 of 1999 signed by President Habibie in September 1999 prohibits non-discrimination because everyone is entitled to fundamental human rights in accordance with the ICCPR and the ICESCR.[85]

83. Totok Sarsito, *The Indonesian Constitution 1945: Why Was It Amended?* <https://www.researchgate.net/publication/235665343_The_Indonesian_Constitution_1945_Why_was_it_amended?enrichId=rgreq-db20e60a96b820a04b3ac0566f7ab42b-XXX&enrichSource=Y292ZXJQYWdlOzIzNTY2NTM0MztBUzo5NzIwMDg3Mjg4NjI3NUAxNDAwMTg1OTA0NDgz&el=1_x_2&_esc=publicationCoverPdf>.
84. Sekjen MPR RI, 'Persandingan Undang Undang Dasar Negara Republik Indonesia Tahun 1945' (Jakarta: Sekretariat Jendral MPR RI, 2001); Sarsito, above n 83, 6.
85. Article 2 of International Covenant on Civil and Political Rights (ICCPR) articulates that "1. Each State Party to the present Covenant undertakes to respect and to ensure to all individuals within its territory and subject to its jurisdiction the rights recognized in the present Covenant, without distinction of any kind, such as race, colour, sex, language, religion, political or other opinion, national or social origin, property, birth or other status." And Article 2 of International Covenant on Economic, Social and Cultural Rights (ICESCR) also imposes that "2. The States Parties to the present Covenant undertake to guarantee that the rights enunciated in the present Covenant will be exercised without discrimination of any kind as to race, color, sex, language, religion, political or other opinion, national or social origin, property, birth or other status."

Article 28D[86] of the Constitution; Articles 5,[87] 18,[88] and 66[89] of the Human Rights Law of 1999 on Legal Aid No.16 of 2011 recognize and protect everyone as a person before the law, guarantee the right to access to court and legal assistance, as well as prohibit torture or inhumane punishment against children prescribed in Article 14 of the ICCPR.[90] However, there are several provisions of national Indonesian laws that may not be applicable for refugee/

86. Article 28D of the 1945 Constitution of the Republic of Indonesia states that "(1) every person shall have the right of recognition, guarantees, protection and certainty before a just law, and of equal treatment before the law. (2) Every person shall have the right to work and to receive fair and proper remuneration and treatment in employment. (3) Every citizen shall have the right to obtain equal opportunities in government. (4) Every person shall have the right to citizenship status."
87. Article 5 of the Human Rights Law of 1999 provides that "(1) everyone is recognized as an individual who has the right to demand and obtain equal treatment and protection before the law as befits his or her human dignity. (2) Everyone has the right to truly just support and protection from an objective, impartial judiciary. (3) All members of disadvantaged groups in society, such as children, the poor, and the disabled, are entitled to greater protection of human rights."
88. Article 18 of Human Rights Law of 1999 imposes that "(1) everyone arrested, detained, or charged for a penal offence has the right to be presumed innocent until proven guilty according to law in a trial at which he has had all the guarantees necessary for his defense, according to prevailing law. (2) No one shall be charged or held guilty of a penal offence for any act or omission which did not constitute a penal offence under prevailing law, at the time when it was committed. (3) Should any changes be made to law, the provisions most advantageous to the person held guilty shall apply. (4) Everyone brought before a tribunal has the right to legal aid from the start of the hearing until a legally binding decision is made by the tribunal. (5) No one shall be charged more than once for an action or omission concerning which a tribunal has previously made a legally binding decision."
89. Article 66 of Human Rights Law of 1999 explains that "(1) every child has the right not to be the object of oppression, torture, or inhuman legal punishment. (2) Sentence of death or life imprisonment shall not be handed down child offenders. (3) Every child has the right not to have his freedom unlawfully taken from him. (4) Children may be arrested, detained, or jailed only in accordance with prevailing legislation and only as a measure of last resort. (5) Every child whose freedom is taken from him has the right to humane treatment, as befits the personal development needs of his age, and shall not be separated from his parents unless this is in his own interest. (6) Every child whose freedom is taken from him has the right to access effective legal or other aid at every stage of ongoing legal proceedings. (7) Every child whose freedom is taken from him has the right to defend himself and to access to a private hearing before an objective and impartial Child Tribunal."
90. Article 14 of ICCPR identifies that "1. All persons shall be equal before the courts and tribunals. In the determination of any criminal charge against him, or of his rights and obligations in a suit at law, everyone shall be entitled to a fair and public hearing by a competent, independent and impartial tribunal established by law. The press and the public may be excluded from all or part of a trial for reasons of morals, public order (order public) or national security in a democratic society, or when the interest of the private lives of the parties so requires, or to the extent strictly necessary in the opinion of the court in special circumstances where publicity would prejudice the interests of justice; but any judgment rendered in a criminal case or in a suit at law shall be made public except where the interest of juvenile persons otherwise requires or the proceedings concern matrimonial disputes or the guardianship of children. 2. Everyone charged with a criminal offence shall have the right to be presumed innocent until proved guilty according to law. 3. In the determination of any criminal charge against him, everyone shall be entitled to the following minimum guarantees, in full equality: (a) To be informed promptly and in detail in a language which he understands of the nature and cause of the charge against him; (b) To have adequate time and facilities for the preparation of his defense and to communicate with counsel of his own choosing; (c) To be tried without undue delay; (d) To be tried in his presence, and to defend himself in person or through legal assistance of his own choosing; to be informed, if he does not have legal assistance, of this right; and to have legal assistance assigned to him, in any case where the interests of justice so require, and without payment by him in any such case if he does not have sufficient means to pay for it; (e) To examine, or have examined, the witnesses against him and to obtain the attendance and examination of witnesses on his behalf under the same conditions as witnesses against him; (f) To have the free assistance of an interpreter if he cannot understand or speak the language used in court; (g) Not to be compelled to testify against himself or to confess guilt. 4. In the case of juvenile persons, the procedure shall be such as will take account of their age and the desirability of promoting their rehabilitation. 5. Everyone convicted of a crime shall have the right to his conviction and

asylum seeker. For instance, Article 28E[91] of the Constitution and Article 38[92] of the Human Rights Law of 1999 explicitly permit his own citizens to have the right to choose the work nature, fair and equal pay and work conditions as stated in Article 6 of the ICESCR.[93]

From about 2008, there was a surge of departures of the Rohingyas from Myanmar and pushbacks by the Thai Navy, which led to the revival of the Bali Process in 2009. As the crises increased, in 2013 Indonesia convened with the UNHCR a special Conference on Addressing Irregular Movement of People outside the Bali Process. The ensuing Jakarta Declaration on Addressing Irregular Movement of Persons pledged the countries of origin, transit, and destination to work together to address irregular migration. After the Andaman Sea Crisis in 2015, the three most affected states (Malaysia, Indonesia, and Thailand) worked cooperatively to find a solution to the crisis. The Ministers of Foreign Affairs of these countries met on 20 May 2015 and announced on the same that "... necessary measures ... on humanitarian grounds, beyond their international obligations, as the issue cannot be addressed solely by these three countries" ("Joint Statement: Ministerial Meeting on Irregular Movement of People in Southeast Asia" from https://kln.gov.my/archive/content.php?t=3&articleId=5202813).

The Jokowi administration quickly responded with this set of crises with a Presidential Regulation (*Peraturan Presiden* or *PERPRES*) No. 125 of 2016 (signed on 31 December 2016). The significance change of this Regulation No. 125 of 2016 is the adoption of the term of "refugee" according to the definition of the Refugee Convention of 1951. An NGO named SUAKA quickly[94] hailed this adoption of the refugee definition as "confirmation of the definition of refugees contained in the 1951 Refugee Convention and discontinuation of the practice to label asylum-seekers as illegal immigrants." SUAKA the most prominent Indonesian NGO that works on refugee and asylum-seeker hailed and welcomed this Presidential Regulation as the "confirmation" of Article 28G of the Indonesia Constitution and Articles 25 to 27 of Law No. 37 of 1999 on Foreign Relations.[95] SUAKA's Chair Febi Yonesta insisted that

sentence being reviewed by a higher tribunal according to law. 6. When a person has by a final decision been convicted of a criminal offence and when subsequently his conviction has been reversed or he has been pardoned on the ground that a new or newly discovered fact shows conclusively that there has been a miscarriage of justice, the person who has suffered punishment as a result of such conviction shall be compensated according to law, unless it is proved that the non-disclosure of the unknown fact in time is wholly or partly attributable to him. 7. No one shall be liable to be tried or punished again for an offence for which he has already been finally convicted or acquitted in accordance with the law and penal procedure of each country."

91. Article 28E of the 1945 Constitution of the Republic of Indonesia enumerates that "(1) Every person shall be free to choose and to practice the religion of his/her choice, to choose one's education, to choose one's employment, to choose one's citizenship, and to choose one's place of residence within the state territory, to leave it and to subsequently return to it."
92. Article 38 of Human Rights Law of 1999 describes that "(1) all citizens have the right to work as befits a human being, in line with his or her ability and capacity. (2) Everyone has the right to free choice of employment and the right to just conditions of work. (3) Everyone, both men and women, who works has the right to equal pay for equal work, and the right to equal work conditions. (4) Everyone, both men and women, who works has the right to fair and adequate remuneration, ensuring for himself and his family an existence worthy of human dignity."
93. Article 6 of ICESCR imposes that "1. The States Parties to the present Covenant recognize the right to work, which includes the right of everyone to the opportunity to gain his living by work which he freely chooses or accepts, and will take appropriate steps to safeguard this right. 2. The steps to be taken by a State Party to the present Covenant to achieve the full realization of this right shall include technical and vocational guidance and training programs, policies and techniques to achieve steady economic, social and cultural development and full and productive employment under conditions safeguarding fundamental political and economic freedoms to the individual."
94. SUAKA Secretariat, *Press Release Suaka: Perpres RI No. 125/2016 Tentang Penanganan Pengungsi Dari Luar Negeri*, (2017) <https://suaka.or.id/2017/01/18/press-release-suaka-perpres-ri-no-1252016-tentang-penanganan-pengungsi-dari-luar-negeri/>.
95. Ibid.

this Presidential Regulation must become the guideline of all immigration or other officers in Indonesia in managing asylum-seekers and refugees; for so long the approach used by the Indonesian officials has been security approach that actually increases the multiplied vulnerabilities of asylum-seekers and refugees.[96]

4.2 *Refugee status determination*

The first step in UNHCR's dealing with asylum-seekers in Indonesia is "registration"[97] through which asylum-seekers complete a Refugee Status Determination (RSD) on the details of their asylum claims to be forwarded to UNHCR. Pulih, UNHCR's implementing partner from 2004 to 2007, assigned its social workers to interview asylum-seekers to complete their RSD Forms at their offices and sent these Forms to UNHCR to assess the application.[98] The typical problem is this step is the reported case of a couple of Sri Lankans interviewed at a penal facility far from Jakarta in 2009 and had been waiting for months for UNHCR to visit and help them to fill the RSD Form.[99] The delay between interception of asylum-seekers and first contact with UNCHR is the Indonesian authorities' preference to finish their own investigations and processing before giving UNHCR access to intercepted person.[100]

The second step is "***interview***." This interview usually takes place about six months after initial registration; in case of asylum-seeker families, husband and wife are interviewed separately but children are not interviewed at all.[101] According to UNHCR, it used 'qualified' interpreters; however, in several cases a reasonably bilingual person who happened to be at hand has been used as an interpreter rather than a professionally accredited person.[102] This amateur interpreter might become source of concern because their language skills may not sufficient to the task as well as their failure to differentiate between the functions of a conduit not a filter.[103] There are no easy solutions to the challenge of finding qualified and impartial interpreters whenever required.

The third step is the "*assessment of protection claims*". After the interview is done, the officer sets a refugee status determination based on the interview and the information from all available sources to UNHCR on conditions of the countries to which protection is sought by the refugee/asylum-seeker. UNHCR would first assess the applicants against the definition of 'refugee' as in Article 1A(2) of the Refugee Convention. If this definition is not found, the officer will check the "other international protection needs" (UNHCR 'Procedural Standards for refugee Status Determination under UNHCR Mandate' or Procedural Standards, 1 September 2005 [2-17]-[2-18]). Persons found to meet the Article 1A(2) definition of 'refugee' or to have 'other international protection needs' are assessed against any exclusion clauses in Article 1F of the Refugee Convention; if they are fit into any of these clauses, their application would be rejected.[104]

The fourth step is the "*notification of initial decision*" that should be, according to UNHCR's Procedural Standards, announced within a month of the interview. This requirement of the

96. Ibid.
97. The reason why Indonesian authorities have no authority to assign refugee status in its own turf is the Directive from the Director General of Immigration re. Procedures Regarding Aliens Expressing Their Desire to Seek Asylum or Refugee Status to: (1) Coordinators of Immigration Affairs/Head of Immigration Affairs, (2) Head of Immigration Offices in Indonesia (or Directive No: F-IL.01.10-1297, 30 September 2002) (Taylor and Rafferty-Brown 2010, p. 145).
98. Brynna Taylor, Savitri, and Rafferty-Brown, 'Difficult Journeys: Accessing Refugee Protection in Indonesia' (2010) 36(3) *Monash University Law Review* 138, 151.
99. Taylor, Savitri, and Rafferty-Brown, above n 98.
100. Ibid.
101. Ibid.
102. Ibid.
103. Ibid 153.
104. Taylor, Savitri, and Rafferty-Brown, above n 98.

Procedural Standards, however, is ranging in reality from 2 weeks to 104 weeks.[105] This decision of UNHCR is conveyed to asylum-seekers in a letter written in English with the reasons for the decision in a very general nature; in case of rejection, this letter advises the applicants that they have 21 days to seek review or appeal of the decision.[106]

The fifth step after the "notification of initial decision" is the "*review*" which is an important safeguard against incorrect decisions. Whenever an asylum-seeker seeks review of the initial decision, UNHCR conducts another round of interview—usually by different officer who made the initial decision—to finalize the case. If the decision is second rejection, then UNHCR must notify asylum-seekers of a review decision in a letter in English to explain the reasons for decision in very generic term. In such letter, sometimes the asylum officer wrote "please note that this decision is final and your case is therefore closed".[107] Nevertheless, Taylor and Rafferty-Brown (2010) reported many twice rejected asylum approached UNHCR to seek a re-opening of their cases; in some few cases, asylum-seekers got lucky. For example, a group of rejected Afghan asylum-seekers who lived in Indonesia since 2011 had their cases re-assessed for the fourth time in 2009 and they got accepted as asylum-seekers to Australia.[108] The fact that UNHCR's processes in Indonesia are not standardized and fair in procedures such as the use of qualified, unbiased interpreters, the provision in languages understood easily by asylum-seekers, and the provision of independent review might mean that some mistakes had taken place in the reviews.[109]

4.3 *Policy implementation*

Reports of each on general nature of things that happen when someone asked for asylum show some stages in this process.[110]

Many refugee/asylum seekers in Indonesia have depended on the financial support of one of their family members, who live in Australia or other destination countries like Canada. Here are their reflections on this issue:

Arian Mameelawi described the fact that living in Indonesia is hard without the right to education, the right to employment, and freedom of movement. Ahmad Surooh shared his opinion that the refugees really rely on the support of money from family members in Australia. Moreover, Hania Nemati described the followings.

> "It will be very hard for us: lack of money, health, food. It's hard to get food. No free food. Nothing free is provided here. If I had to be here, we had to accept it, trying to be happy like others. We can support them emotionally. I will not lose hope to help others. Many old people are here; they're in poor health. We will try to survive like we stay in Indonesia. We could make the same team if I were in Australia. We should not be divided by nationality. If we have to be here for over 10 years, we will try to help other children because education is important. I should not leave hope. I would like to open a charity to help refugees."

105. Ibid 155–156.
106. Ibid 156.
107. Ibid 157.
108. Ibid.
109. Ibid.
110. When the duration of "transit" in Indonesia was growing longer since 2013, more refugees reported themselves to the Indonesia Immigration authorities to renew their depleted financial resources as "unregistered". In 2014 alone, more than 2,600 asylum seekers reported themselves to the authorities although the latter had limited space to accommodate the asylum seekers and showed the unwillingness to spend indefinitely (10 years is the maximum time for the IOM to support the refugees financially). Local Indonesian laws forbid foreigners to work, and the Indonesia Immigration was not ready to give the refugees work permits for (1) language barriers, (2) high unemployment for the locals, and (3) likely opposition from the local population. The refugees who work clandestinely in bakeries and restaurants face risks of detection and exploitation (Missbach 2015).

Arzoo Naderi explained what he would do if he and his family have to be here in Indonesia for over 10 years: he will never give them hope no matter 10 years, but he will be patient. He believes that he would try to enjoy himself (themselves) here in Indonesia. Sadness, for him, will not help; but only happiness will. He will never leave hope afloat. The Australian government might change or create some new rules in every July of the year. He still has a hope that the Australian government will change to better rules. He would like to talk to Australian people that he and other refugees would like them to be in the refugees' shoes. Refugees will work as much as they could. Refugees will not get help easily from the Australian government. Nevertheless, he would provide help for all others as human beings."

4.4 *Policy impact on employment restriction and hardship*

For many asylum seekers and recognized refugees in Indonesia, right to employment is just one of many other issues. The UNHCR noted that 'formal legal and social rights and related benefits, including access to employment, are not accessible to refugees or asylum seekers in Indonesia, and as such, they are entirely dependent on support from the UNHCR and its partners or relatives abroad" (2015, p. 176). The worrying trends of refugees and asylum seekers reporting themselves to immigration authorities preferring to be placed in detention with the provision of food and shelter have been highlighted by the UNHCR and some NGOs to the Indonesian government.[111] Some reports (Sampson, Gifford, and Taylor 2016) showed that many of the refugees interviewed were able to build meaningful lives despite the serious suffering and challenges they faced.

The aforementioned information reflects the strategic status quo with tactical hiccups and no hope of education and employment opportunity in Indonesia. It is noteworthy to state that deprivation of the right to employment has affected psychological health of refugees and Asylum seekers in Indonesia. For example, Farahnaz Salehi said that "There is no right to education/work. She volunteered to work at the school for refugees. Refugees, for her, have missed many opportunities: feeling abnormal to be less than a human-being, feeling invisible, and suffering some sorts of travel limitation. She would like to go places somewhere else that have different seasons. With the typical seasons of rain season and hot season in Indonesia, Farahnaz Salehi feels that she stays in a place very different from what she lived at home before. Division or separation from her own people can affect her mental health." Arzoo Naderi told us that his Mom (32 year-old) cannot work. She is just at home. So, he has stried to make her laugh. According to these refugee children's complaints, Avyanthi Azis pointed out the fact that, "Based on the local view, the right to employment is not for the refugees/asylum seekers because of the local needs. Indonesia doesn't demand foreign laborers because many local laborers need a job. I think if the refugees/asylum seekers have the right to employment, it will be good. They are depressed, useless, doing nothing. They may face forced labor, so the government should allow them to work on the proper channel." No refugees/asylum seekers could work in Indonesia. Therefore, all of them have experienced in their financial crisis. Refugees/asylum seekers have never been allowed to work legally. However, they may be able to work in private sphere, not public sphere.

5 CONCLUSION

Human Rights Watch and Seton Hall University College of Law (2013) set a typology of five kinds of impact on refugees and asylum-seekers in the United States: (1) physical and emotional harm, (2) housing and transportation, (3) food, (4) vulnerability to exploitation, (5) difficulty of access to counsel. What happened in the U.S. to asylum-seekers could

111. UNHCR, *No Title* (2015) 176.

be conceptualized squarely as "deliberate destitution" because the new, less humane, immigration regime began in 1995 through IIRIRA. In Indonesia, however, this destitution is less deliberate but more naturally inevitable because until now, Indonesia has not recognized "refugee" in its legal system except the last Presidential Regulation No. 125 of 2016 that merely "defines" refugee along that of the 1951 Refuge Convention's definition without any legal means to apply this 'recognition' in reality. This "defining" act (or this paper would conceptualize as "pseudo-acknowledgment") is not actually followed by real regulations in the field to immigration authorities dealing directly with refugees and asylum-seekers (to third country). The actual guide for the Immigration officers on dealing with asylum-seekers and refugees is the Indonesia Immigration Directorate General's Directive No: F-IL.01.10-1297 (30 September 2002). This Directive ("Re: Procedures Regarding Aliens Expressing Their Desire to Seek Asylum or Refugee Status to (1) Coordinators of Immigration Affairs/ Head of Immigration Affairs (2) Head of Immigration Offices in Indonesia") states that "persons seeking asylum or refugee status are to be referred to UNHCR for refugee determination and that "the status and presence of aliens holding Attestation Letters or identification cards issued by UNHCR as asylum-seeker, refugees, or persons of concern to UNHCR must be respected." This Directive actually violates international law's adage that "one becomes a refugee when the events giving rise to such status take place rather than when the receiving country affords such status".[112]

The destitution done by the Indonesia government begins with the *first* impact, which is the most fundamental refusal to accept refugees and asylum-seekers directly but instead to allow UNHCR singlehandedly to manage them. Therefore, the impact of this destitution in Indonesia begins with the vulnerability to lack of legal status as this status is granted mainly by UNHCR and its operating mechanisms through International Organization of Migration (IOM). As the consequences of total dependency of asylum-seekers and refugees to the procedures (five steps) through UNHCR and IOM involvement appear along these step, this part would explain what are the impact of total restriction in access to job markets while asylum-seekers and refugees undergo these processes/steps. As this refusal is sequential with the handling down the Refugee Determination Status to the only one UNHCR and its operational handler IOM, the *second* impact is the total dependency to status determination, assistance after the status grant, and other treatments later. Usually, the term used for refugees and asylum-seekers after multiple refusals but having nowhere to go and nobody to assist is "stuckedness" or "living in limbo".[113] Since the Indonesian authorities largely rely on UNHCR and IOM to support asylum-seekers and refugees, this full delegation of power would bring the *third* impact: total ignorance by the Indonesia authorities once refugees and asylum-seekers are refused and thus no longer under the status of "persons of concern," "refugee," or "asylum-seeker" acknowledged by UNHCR. After exhausting the supports from family members at home or abroad, asylum-seekers and refugees tend to report themselves back to the Immigration Detention Centers in urban centers. In fact, between 2014 and 2015, almost 4,000 asylum-seekers and refugees surrendered themselves to immigration authorities because they could no longer afford to support themselves independently outside of the detention system (UNHCR, Monthly Update, Jakarta, March 2016 cited by Missbach 2017).

These three impacts alone would be multiplied by the fact that asylum-seekers and refugees are not allowed to access local job markets.

112. James C Hathaway and Amie K Cusick, 'Refugee Rights Are Not Negotiable' (2000) 21 *Geo. Immigr. L.J.* 484., Many refugee scholars have noted that states try to avoid their obligations to refugees by denying them that title, or even that of asylum-seeker, and instead labeling them as "displaced persons," "illegal immigrants," "economic migrants," "quasi-refugees," "aliens," "departees," "boat people," or "stowaways," GS Goldwin-Gill and Jane McAdam, *The Refugee in International Law 50* (New York: Oxford University Press, 3rd ed, 2007). Indonesian officials fall into this avoidance methods as they term the refugees or asylum-seekers "illegal migrants."

113. Missbach, above n 64.

REFERENCES

Allen, K, *The Celtic Tiger* (Manchester: Manchester University Press, 2000)

Andersson, H and S Nilsson, '"Asylum Seekers and Undocumented Migrants" Increased Social Rights in Sweden" (2011) 49(4) *International Migration* 167

Australian Government (Department of Immigration and Citizenship), Australia, 'Annual Report: 2006-2007' (2007) <http://www.border.gov.au/ReportsandPublications/Documents/annual-reports/annual-report-2006-07-complete.pdf>

Barker, C, 'The People Smugglers' Business Model' in *Parliament of Australia, Department of Parliamentary Services, Research Paper* 37

Department of Foreign Affairs of the Republic of Indonesia, Jakarta, Indonesia, 'Meeting on the Establishment of a Processing Centre for Indochinese Refugees' (1979)

Fandik, RM, 'Penampungan Orang Vietnam Di Pulau Galang 1975-1990' (1992) 1(1) *Avatara* 164

Fanning, B and S Loyal, 'Asylum Seekers and the Right to Work' (Understanding Class in Ireland, Dublin, December, 1999)

Fanning, B, S Loyal and C Staunton, *Asylum Seekers and the Right to Work in Ireland* (Dublin: Irish Refugee Council, 2000)

Fournier, Ron, 'Immigration Curbs Sought—Clinton Seeks to Add Border Agents, Speed Asylum Reviews' *The Seattle Times*, 1993 <https://community.seattletimes.nwsource.com/archive/?data=19930727&slug=1712986>

Goldwin-Gill, GS and Jane McAdam, *The Refugee in International* Law *50* (New York: Oxford University Press, 3rd ed, 2007)

Hathaway, James C and Amie K Cusick, 'Refugee Rights Are Not Negotiable' (2000) 21 *Geo. Immigr. L.J.* 484

Heiduk, F, *Indonesia in ASEAN: Regional Leadership between Ambition and Ambiguity* (SWP Research Paper, Berlin, RP 6, April, 2016)

Klein, N, 'Assessing Australia's Push Back the Boats Policy under International Law: Legality and Accountability for Maritime Interceptions of Irregular Migrants' (2014) 15(1) *Melbourne Journal of International Law* 1

Kneebone, S, 'Migration Control as Sea: The Australian Case' in Bernard Ryan and Valsamis Mitsilegas (eds), *Extraterritorial Immigration Control: Legal Challenge* (Leiden: Martinus Nijhoff, 2010) 349

Kneebone, S, 'The Bali Process and Global Refugee Policy in the Asia Pacific Region' (2014) 27(4) *Journal of Refugee Studies* 596

Kneebone, S, 'Australia as a Powerbroker on Refugee Protection in Southeast Asia: The Relationship with Indonesia' (2017) 33(1) *Refuge* 29

Loyal, Steven and Ciaran Staunton, 'The Dynamics of Political Economy in Ireland: The Case of Asylum Seekers and the Right to Work' (2001) 10(2) *Irish Journal of Sociology* 33

Martin, David A, 'Making Asylum Policy: The 1994 Reforms' (1995) 70(725) *WASH. L. REV.* 738

Mehlman, Ira H, 'The New Jet Set: Think the Rio Grande Is a Porous Border? Try New York's JFK, Where Anyone Can Enter Through the Magic of Political Asylum' (1993) March 15 *Nat'l Rev.* 40

Missbach, A, 'Waiting of the Islands of "Stuckedness" Managing Asylum Seekers in Island Detention Camps in Indonesia: From the Late 1970s to the Early 2000s' (2013) 6(2) *Current Research on South-East Asia/ASEAS* 281

Nessel, Lori A, 'Externalized Borders and the Invisible Refugees' (2009) 40 *Colum. Hum. Rts. L. Rev* 625

Nessel, Lori A, 'Deliberate Destitution as Deterrent: Withholding the Right to Work and Undermining Asylum Protection' (2015) 52 *San Diego Law Review* 313

Nethery, A, B Rafferty-Brown and S Taylor, 'Exporting Detention: Australia-Funded Immigration Detention in Indonesia' (2013) 26(1) *Journal of Refugee Studies* 95

O'Hearn, D, *Inside the Celtic Tiger* (London: Pluto, 1997)

Parliament of Australia (The Senate, Foreign Affairs, Defence and Trade References Committee), Australia, 'Breaches of Indonesian Territorial Waters' (2014)

Parousel, B, 'Sweden' in *Focus Migration* (2009)

RI, Sekjen MPR, 'Persandingan Undang Undang Dasar Negara Republik Indonesia Tahun 1945' (Jakarta: Sekretariat Jendral MPR RI, 2001)

Robinson, V and J Segrott, *Understanding the Decision Making of Asylum Seekers* (London: Home Office Research Study, 2002)

Strand, A and Et Al., *Return in Dignity, Return to What? Review of the Voluntary Return Programme to Afghanistan* (Oslo: Chr. Michelsen Institute, 2008)

Taylor, Savitri, and Rafferty-Brown, Brynna, 'Difficult Journeys: Accessing Refugee Protection in Indonesia' (2010) 36(3) *Monash University Law Review* 138

UNHCR, *The State of the World's Refugees: Fifty Years of Humanitarian Action* (Oxford, UK: Oxford University Press, 2000)

UNHCR, *No Title* (2015)

Valenta, Marko and Kristin Thorshaug, '"Asylum Seekers" Perspectives on Work and Proof of Identity: The Norwegian Experience" [2002] *Refugee Survey Quarterly*

Valenta, Marko and Kristin Thorshaug, 'Restrictions on Right to Work for Asylum Seeker: The Case of the Scandinavian Countries, Great Britain and the Netherlands.' (2013) 20 *International Journal on Minority and Group Rights* 459

IOM (International Organization for Migration), Indonesia, *Alternative to Detention* (2014) <https://www.iom.int/files/live/sites/iom/files/Country/docs/IOM-Indonesia-Alternatives-to-Detention-September-2014.pdf>

Sarsito, Totok, *The Indonesian Constitution 1945: Why Was It Amended?* <https://www.researchgate.net/publication/235665343_The_Indonesian_Constitution_1945_Why_was_it_amended?enrichId=rgreq-db20e60a96b820a04b3ac0566f7ab42b-XXX&enrichSource=Y292ZXJQYWdlOzIzNTY2NTM0MztBUzo5NzIwMDg3Mjg4NjI3NUAxNDAwMTg1OTA0NDgz&el=1_x_2&_esc=publicationCoverPdf>

Secretariat, SUAKA, *Press Release Suaka: Perpres RI No. 125/2016 Tentang Penanganan Pengungsi Dari Luar Negeri*, (2017) <https://suaka.or.id/2017/01/18/press-release-suaka-perpres-ri-no-1252016-tentang-penanganan-pengungsi-dari-luar-negeri/>

Culture and International Law - Juwana et al. (Eds)
© 2019 Taylor & Francis Group, London, ISBN 978-1-138-38766-9

Intentional destruction of cultural heritage and reparations

Ana Filipa Vrdoljak
University of Technology, Sydney, Australia

ABSTRACT: The cultural heritage should be protected all the time. None of the high contracting parties in the hostilities could destroy or even use it as their shield. The role of international responsibility – whether it be individual criminal responsibility, State responsibility, and the responsibility of the international organisations – and reparations in addressing and responding to intentional destruction of cultural heritage shall be clear. The overlap between prohibition against the destruction of cultural property, individual criminal responsibility and reparations evolved in lockstep with international humanitarian law and international criminal law generally. Therefore, this paper examines the *Al Mahdi* Judgment, Sentencing and Reparations Order in this broader context, from the IMT, the *ad hoc* Tribunals, to the ICC today, to better understand why and how international law is addressing the intentional destruction of cultural property. The first part of this paper will examines the general rationales for sentencing in international criminal law and how these translate into conduct directed at cultural property from war crimes, crimes against humanity (particularly persecution) and genocide. The second part considers reparations awarded in respect of these crimes, again by considering the rationale for reparations generally and then as it's translates in respect crimes covering cultural property. The concluding part considers the cleavages and cross-purposes that the ICC Judgment reveals in respect of the priorities of the international community and the ability of international law to address them.

KEYWORDS: intentional destruction, cultural heritage, reparation, international court, international humanitarian law

1 INTRODUCTION

The Judgment and related Orders of the International Criminal Court (ICC) in the case of *The Prosecutor v. Ahmad Al Faqi Al Mahdi* delivered in 2016 and 2017 provide an opportunity to reflect upon the role of international responsibility – whether it be individual criminal responsibility, State responsibility, and the responsibility of the international organisations – and reparations in addressing and responding to intentional destruction of cultural heritage.[1] It is the first time the ICC has found a defendant responsible for intentionally attacking protected cultural and religious sites.[2] It is also the first time that an international criminal court (indeed the same court) has delivered an order for reparations pertaining to this international crime. The tensions manifest between the Court's Judgment and Sentence, and Reparations Order represents the intersection between international criminal law, human rights law and

1. Prosecutor v. Ahmad Al Faqi Al Mahdi, Case No. ICC-01/12-01/15, Judgment and Sentence (27 September 2016) (Al Mahdi Judgment and Sentence); and Prosecutor v. Ahmad Al Faqi Al Mahdi, Case No. ICC-01/12-01/15, Reparations Order (17 August 2017) (Al Mahdi Reparations Order).
2. Article 8(2)(e)(iv), Rome Statute of the International Criminal Court, 17 July 1998, in force 1 July 2002, 2187 UNTS 90 (Rome Statute).

international cultural heritage law, highlighting their nascent nature and competing rationales, and exposing the various fault lines within contemporary international law.

In international law, as in domestic law, law and lawyers are understandably focussed on the development of substantive rules in addressing issues and concerns and perceived gaps. What occurs after these rules are implemented, including sentencing and reparations are in practice, comparatively speaking, an afterthought. Yet, these twin initiatives which are inextricably linked, should be mutual self-reinforcing or the very least non-competing or inconsistent. Yet the *Al Mahdi* decision reveals this not to be the case.

The overlap between prohibition against the destruction of cultural property, individual criminal responsibility and reparations evolved in lockstep with international humanitarian law and international criminal law generally. It is contained in the earliest binding formulations of rules of armed conflict in contemporary international law. Regulations of the 1899 Hague II and 1907 Hague IV Convention provide that during belligerent occupation

> *[a]ll seizure of, and destruction, or intentional damage done to [religious, charitable, and educational institutions, and those of arts and science] institutions, to historical monuments, works of art or science, is prohibited, and should be made the subject of proceedings.*[3]

In the mid-twentieth century, the International Military Tribunal (IMT) at Nuremberg found that the Hague Regulations were 'recognised by all civilised nations and were regarded as being declaratory of the laws and customs of war.'[4] The IMT also entered judgment against and passed sentences against several of the major war criminals, who were found to be individually criminally responsible for war crimes and crimes against humanity including acts relating to the systematic and widespread seizure, destruction and intentional damage to cultural property. While the Allied Powers during the Second World War had vowed to institute restitution in response to these acts, the IMT's Charter was silent on the question of reparations, instead reparations were realised through panoply of instruments adopted and implemented by the occupying Allied powers and peace agreements. Half a century after the IMT, the constitutive Statutes of the ad hoc International Criminal Tribunal for Yugoslavia (ICTY) and International Criminal Tribunal for Rwanda (ICTR), empowered these courts to determine individual criminal responsibility in respect of war crimes, crimes against humanity and genocide including in respect of acts directed at cultural property.[5] The ad hoc Tribunals had only a very narrow remit in respect of reparations and never exercised even this restricted authority. This limitation in the jurisdiction of the Tribunals was heavily criticized and attempts to rectify it came to nothing. Only with the coming into force of the Statute of International Criminal Court was a permanent international criminal court finally established with jurisdiction in respect of international crimes committed against cultural property during armed conflict and peacetime, which was also empowered to awarded reparations to victims of these crimes. The *Al Mahdi* trial, Judgment and Orders are the first example of this development, almost two decades after the Court's establishment.

---

3. Art.56, Convention (IV) respecting the Laws and Customs of War on Land and Annex: Regulations concerning the Laws and Customs of War on Land, Oct. 18, 1907, entered into force 26 January 1910, 187 CTS 227 (Hague Regulations). See also Art.8, International Regulations on the Laws and Customs of War, 27 August 1874, not ratified, 1 AJIL (1907) 1(supp.) 96 (Brussels Declaration). The International Court of Justice has interpreted to this obligation on the occupying power to responsibility in respect of its own acts and omissions and failing to prevent violations by others in the territory, while during hostilities they are only responsible for the conduct of their own forces: *Case concerning Armed Activities on the Territory of the Congo (Democratic Republic of the Congo v. Uganda)* Judgment of 19 December 2005, *ICJ Reports 2005*, p.60.
4. International Military Tribunal Nuremberg, Judgment, in 41 AJIL (1947) 172, at 248-249.
5. Statute of the International Criminal Tribunal for the Former Yugoslavia, GA Res.827 of 25 May 1993, amended by GA Res.1166 (1998), 1329 (2000), 1411 (2002), 1431 (2002) 1481 (2003), 1597 (2005) and 1660 (2006) (ICTY Statute); and Statute of the International Criminal Tribunal for Rwanda, SC Res.955 of 8 November 1994 as adopted and amended to SC Res.1717 of 13 October 2006 (ICTR Statute).

Therefore, this paper examines the *Al Mahdi* Judgment, Sentencing and Reparations Order in this broader context, from the IMT, the *ad hoc* Tribunals, to the ICC today, to better understand why and how international law is addressing the intentional destruction of cultural property. The first part examines the general rationales for sentencing in international criminal law and how these translate into conduct directed at cultural property from war crimes, crimes against humanity (particularly persecution) and genocide. The second part considers reparations awarded in respect of these crimes, again by considering the rationale for reparations generally and then as its translates in respect crimes covering cultural property. The concluding part considers the cleavages and cross-purposes that the ICC Judgment reveals in respect of the priorities of the international community and the ability of international law to address them.

2 REPARATIONS

While the principles concerning reparations in international criminal law have been slower to develop and have relied largely on developments in regional and domestic human rights jurisprudence, where victims have been more successful in attaining redress,[6] past practice teaches us that the international community has been deeply cognisant of the relevance and significance of reparations for victims of international crimes against cultural property.

2.1 IMT, Allied restitution scheme and the draft Genocide Convention

The Declaration of the Allied Nations against Acts of Dispossession Committed in Territories under Enemy Occupation or Control (London Declaration) of 1943 reinforced:

> *[T]heir resolution not to accept or tolerate the misdeeds of their enemies in the field of property, however these may be cloaked, just as they have recently emphasized their determination to exact retribution from war criminals for their outrages against persons in the occupied territories.*[7]

There had been no explicit acknowledgement of victims in the Charters of the Nuremberg or Tokyo Tribunals.[8] The London Declaration instead triggered a series of Allied declarations, multilateral agreements and domestic legislation establishing a restitution program to reverse or ameliorate the effects of Axis policies and actions upon occupied peoples and their own inhabitants.[9] The principles developed and applied following the Second World War are distinguishable because of the scale of the program and its implicit driving force transcended return in response to the violation of the laws and customs of war, extending to neutral states and victims within German territory since 1933.[10] Not coincidentally, the wording of these

6. UN Basic Principles and Guidelines on the right to remedy and reparations of victims of gross violations of international human rights and serious violations of international humanitarian law, adopted by the UN Commission on Human Rights on 19 April 2005, UN Doc. E/CN.4/RES/2005/35 and General Assembly, GA Res.60/147 of 21 March 2006 (Reparations Principles).
7. 8 Dep't St. Bull. (1943) 21. UNWCC viewed criminal prosecutions as its role and found restitution was conducted adequately by the British Commission for the Protection and Restitution of Cultural Material and American Commission for Protection and Salvage of Artistic and Historic Monuments in Europe, observing that their objectives 'though different, was supplementary, to its own': Minutes of 68th Meeting, 4 July 1945, 1/33/PAG-3/1.0.0, UNWCC.
8. S. Zappala, *Human Rights in International Criminal Proceedings* (Oxford, Oxford University Press, 2003) 220.
9. A F Vrdoljak 'Gross Violations of Human Rights and Restitution: Learning from Holocaust Claims' in L. V. Prott (ed.), *Realising Cultural Heritage Law: Festschrift for Patrick O'Keefe* (Builth Wells: IAL, 2012) 165-187.
10. Final Act and Annex of the Paris Conference on Reparations, Annex I: Resolution on Subject of Restitution, in J. Howard, *The Paris Agreement on Reparations from Germany*, (1946), p.19; and Military Government for Germany, U.S. Area of Control, Law No.59: 'Restitution of Identifiable Property', *Military Government Gazette* [Germany. U.S. Zone, Issue G] No.10, (November 1947), 42(supp.) AJIL (1948) 11.

provisions reflected the definition of crimes against humanity in the London Charter and the judgments covering genocide, both in its definition of victim groups and the relevant time period.[11] It was described as effectively an act of humanitarian intervention by the international community in the domestic activities of a state.[12]

The multifaceted forms of Nazi confiscations and the nature of the regime meant that the Allied restitution program applied to transactions 'even when they purported to be voluntary in effect'.[13] A presumption was made in favour of the claimant, that any transaction during the relevant period constituted confiscation, if he or she was directly persecuted because of these grounds, or belonged to a group of persons who because of these grounds 'was to be eliminated in its entirety from the cultural and economic life of Germany by measures taken by the State....'[14] A possessor carried the onus of proof that he or she acquired the item through a 'normal transaction', and payment was not sufficient to overcome this burden.[15] The relevant authorities considering restitution were required to give due recognition to difficulties faced by claimants, especially when production of evidence was thwarted through 'the loss of documents, the death or unavailability of witnesses, the residence abroad of the claimant or similar circumstances'.[16] Contrary to international law practice, a successor organisation, and not the State, could be appointed by the military governments of Germany as 'heir' to the entire estate of any persecuted person.[17] Successor organisation was required to use the property to provide 'relief and rehabilitation of surviving members of such groups, organizations and communities' in the relevant state.[18] Allied governments also sanctioned a generalised program of restitution-in-kind and compensation, when restitution was impossible.[19] No time limit was attached to these restitution programs.[20] These laws were so far-reaching in terms of State responsibility it was suggested they represented a new principle of international law.[21]

The interweaving of responsibility and reparations in respect of international crimes was revisited during the drafting of the Genocide Convention adopted in 1948. The draft prepared by Secretariat included the following provision:

> Draft Article XIII
>
> *When genocide is committed in a country by the government in power and by sections of the population, and if the government fails to resist it successfully, the State shall grant to the survivors of the human group that is a victim of genocide redress of a nature and in an amount to be determined by the United Nations.*[22]

---

11. The U.S. Zone Law No.59 — Restitution of Identifiable Property covered property removed because of the 'race, religion, nationality, ideology or political opposition to National Socialism' of its owner during the Nazi incumbency from 1933 to 1945: Art.1, Part II, Law No.59.
12. Bentwich, International Aspects of Restitution and Compensation for Victims of the Nazis, 32 BYIL (1955-56) 204 at 205.
13. 1943 London Declaration.
14. Art.3(1), Part II, Law No.59.
15. Kunstsammlungen Zu Weimar v. Elicofon 536 F.Supp.813 (E.D.N.Y. 24 August 1978) aff'd 678 F.2d 1150 (2nd Cir.(N.Y.) 5 May 1982).
16. Art.49, Part VIII, Law No.59.
17. Art.10, Law No.59. Jewish organisations argued strenuously against the retention of heirless property by states which had persecuted or continued to persecute minorities: M. Kurtz, *Nazi Contraband: American Policy on the Return of European Cultural Treasures, 1945-1955*, (1985) 198 and 208.
18. Art.25(1), Peace Treaty with Romania.
19. For example, Art.25(1), Peace Treaty with Romania, Paris, 10 February 1947, 49 UNTS 3 at 129. See Robinson, Reparations and Restitution in International Law, 1 Jewish YbIL (1949) 186 at 204-205.
20. See Hall, The Recovery of Cultural Objects Dispersed During World War II, 25 *Dep't St. Bull.* (1951) 339.
21. Robinson, n.# at199 and 203; I. Vásárhelyi, *Restitution in International Law*, (1964) 115-17; Martin, Private Property, Rights and Interests in the Paris Peace Treaties, 24 BYIL (1947) 274, at 280.
22. Draft convention on the crime of genocide, prepared by Secretariat at requested by General Assembly, 26 June 1947 UN Doc.E/447, 5-13. This provision was supported by Belgium, France, Syria and United Kingdom. The Secretariat draft distinguished between criminal and civil State responsibility.

The Secretariat in its comments noted that the draft provision represented 'an application of the principle that populations are to a certain extent answerable for crimes committed by their governments which they have condoned or which they have simply allowed their governments to commit.'[23] It suggested that reparations could include compensation to dependants and restitution of seized property. Also, it suggested that groups would benefit from reconstruction of monuments, libraries, universities and churches and compensation for their collective needs.[24] While there was support for recognition of State civil liability for genocide during deliberations in 1948, the issue became entwined with the ultimately unsuccessful attempt to incorporate recognition of State responsibility for an international crime into the Convention.[25] Viewed as part of the jurisdiction of the future international penal tribunal slated to try genocide cases, the question of restitution and compensation was revived during the 1990s with the establishment of the ICTY and later, the permanent International Criminal Court.

2.2 *ICTY and ICTR*

By the end of the twentieth century, the ICTY and ICTR provided the impetus for the restarting of international criminal law jurisprudence; but their respective Statutes failed to provide effective avenue for reparations for victims. The purpose of the ad hoc Tribunals was not explicitly stated in the Security Council resolutions adopting their founding Statutes.[26] SC Resolution 827 of 1993 establishing the ICTY provides that its 'sole purpose [is] prosecuting persons responsible for serious violations' and to 'contribute to ensuring that violations are halted and effectively redressed.'[27] Although the SC Resolution deliberately excluded reparations as part of the future court's remit, it did provide that its work would be carried out 'without prejudice to the rights of victims to seek, through appropriate means, compensation for damages incurred as a result of violations of international humanitarian law.' While the resolution does not define 'appropriate means', the Security Council had canvassed the possibility of establishing another body to consider restitution claims.[28]

In the end, the ICTY and the ICTR were empowered at the judgment and penalties phase to make orders directly against a convicted person in respect of any property or proceeds acquired by criminal conduct even duress.[29] The ICTY provision specifically refers to 'return' 'to rightful owners', which is not subject to the 'rights of bona fide third parties.' They could order the preservation and protection of such property or proceeds until the forfeiture order is made.[30] The power extended to property or proceeds in the hands of third parties unconnected with the crime.[31] The request for restitution could only be initiated by the Prosecutor or the Chamber and not individuals.[32] While these provisions covered all property including

23. UN Doc.E/447, 47.
24. Ibid. See French version of the draft convention, Art.7 covering reparations, presented 9 February 1948, UN Doc.E/623/Add.I. See W. Schabas, *Genocide in International Law, The Crime of Crimes* (Cambridge: Cambridge University Press, 2000), p.400; H. Abtani and P. Webb, *The Genocide Convention: The Travaux Preparatoires*, vol.I (Martinus Nijhoff Publishers, 2008); and Vrdoljak, 'Genocide and Restitution: Ensuring Each Group's Contribution to Humanity', (2011) 22(1) EJIL 17-47.
25. See UN Doc.A/C.6/SR.95 and 96.
26. SC Res.827 of 25 May 1993 concerning the ICTY Statute; and SC Res.995 of 8 November 1994 concerning the ICTR Statute.
27. SC Resolution covering the ICTR adopted in 1994 included similar language with the additional aim of 'contribut[ing] to the process of national reconciliation'.
28. See V. Morris and M. Scharf, *An Insider's Guide to the International Criminal Court for the Former Yugoslavia* (New York: Transnational Publishers, 1995), 288.
29. Art.24(3), ICTY Statute; and Art.23(3), ICTR Statute.
30. Rule 105(A), ICTY Rules of Procedure and Evidence (RPE).
31. Rule 105(B), ICTY RPE.
32. Ibid.

religious and cultural property, no such orders were ever made.[33] Although the ICTY's Rules of Procedure and Evidence (RPE) addressed compensation, it was circumscribed by its Statute which did not directly referenced reparations generally. Rather, the RPE modestly provided that the Registrar would transmit the judgments of the Court to the relevant national authorities who would consider it final and binding as to the individual criminal responsibility of the defendant. Further, it stipulated that it was up to the victims to claim compensation in national courts pursuant to domestic law.[34] Recourse to national courts has been limited.[35] The provision only covered State responsibility as far as States were responsible for the enforcement of orders between individuals. Following the successful adoption of the Rome Statute, the ICTY Prosecutor and its judges raised the need to address reparations for victims before the Security Council.[36] They noted that to 'bring reconciliation in the former Yugoslavia and to ensure the restoration of peace, it is fundamental that persons who were the victims of crimes that fall within the jurisdiction of the Tribunal receive compensation for their injuries.'[37] They advocated rather than the ICTY Statute being amended, that the Security Council establish an international compensation commission. No response was forthcoming from the Security Council.

As noted, the powers of the ICTY did not prejudice other rights that victims may have under international or national laws, like the Human Rights Chamber for Bosnia and Herzegovina (BiH Chamber).[38] Established pursuant to the General Framework Agreement for Peace (GFA), the BiH Chamber was a *sui generis*, mixed national-international court which sat from March 1996 to September 2003.[39] Its remit covered violations of human rights obligations contained in the European Convention of Human Rights and its Protocols, and sixteen other international human rights instruments including the Genocide Convention. Despite its limited jurisdiction, its jurisprudence, particularly on reparations, alleviated the reticence of the ICTY. The BiH Chamber regularly referenced the findings of fact of the ICTY.[40] While it could reject or defer consideration of a matter if it was already before an international or local body,[41] in practice, it did not declined applications. The BiH Chamber could receive applications from individuals, non-governmental organisations or groups of individuals as victims or acting on behalf of victims who were missing or deceased.[42] Applications concerning cultural heritage were almost exclusively brought by religious entities representing the Islamic Community or Catholic Church.

33. See Chiffet, n.# at pp.100-102; and S. Malmström, 'Restitution of Property and Compensation to Victims', in R. May et al (eds), *Essays on ICTY Procedure and Evidence in Honour of Gabrielle Kirk McDonald*, (The Hague: Kluwer Law International, 2001), 373-384. In respect of the Yugoslav conflicts, it has been dealt with as state succession or in peace agreements: see Agreement on Succession Issues between the Five Successor States of the Former Yugoslavia, 29 June 2001, 2262 UNTS 25, Art.3, Annex A; and Comprehensive Proposal, n.#, Annex V, Art.6.
34. A. Cassese, *International Criminal Law* (Oxford: Oxford University Press, 2003), 429.
35. Malmström, n.#.
36. Address of Carla del Ponte, Prosecutor of the ICTY/ICTR to the Security Council, 21 November 2000, ICTY Press Release JL/P.I.S./542-e; and UN Doc.S/2000/1063 (3 November 2000). Cf. UN Compensation Committee established by SC Res.687 of 8 April 1991 and Governing Council Decision 11, UN Doc.S/AC.26/1991/1 (2 August 1991), and see N. Wühler, 'The United Nations Compensation Commission', in A. Randelzhofer and C. Tomuschat (eds), *State Responsibility and Individual Reparations in Instances of Grave Violations of Human Rights* (1999), 213-231.
37. Ibid.
38. SC Res.826, 25 May 1993, para.7; and Art.75(6), Rome Statute.
39. General Framework Agreement for Peace in Bosnia and Herzegovina, signed and entered into force 14 December 1995, 35 ILM (1996) 89, Annex 6: Agreement on Human Rights.
40. For example, The "Srebrenica Cases", Decision on Admissibility and Merits, Case Nos.CH/01/8397 et al, 7 March 2003, paras.15ff.
41. Art.VIII(2)(d), GFA Annex 6.
42. Art.VIII(2), DPA Annex 6.

Restitution, particularly if it involves cultural heritage, is considered the primary remedy.[43] It is only when restitution is impossible or inadequate that other remedies are considered. Indeed, if the obligation which is breached is a peremptory norm or the violation is ongoing, restitution may also involve cessation of the wrongful conduct.[44] In the *Banja Luka Mosques* case, the order sought by the applicant, that is, the respondent reconstruct the mosques on the former sites could not be made because the destruction occurred in 1993. However, the BiH Chamber found there was an ongoing violation of freedom of religion because the relevant authorities had persistently refused permission for reconstruction after the war, and ordered that such permission be granted.[45] While restitution is the 'preferred' remedy, it is often not feasible in cases involving human rights violations.[46] The BiH Chamber declined to sanction the removal of an Orthodox Church constructed on the site of a destroyed mosque. Instead, it ordered restitution-in-kind by requiring Republika Srpska to make a parcel of land available to the Islamic Community and permit reconstruction of the mosque on the alternate site.[47] Compensation can be used to provide full reparations, in so far as the damage cannot be made good by restitution, the damage is 'economically assessable' and that it is 'appropriate and proportional' to the gravity of the violation in each case.[48] Its purpose is corrective and rehabilitative rather than punitive.[49] In the *Srebrenica* cases, the BiH Chamber ordered Republika Srpska pay compensation to the Foundation of the Srebrenica-Potocari Memorial and Cemetery to enable families bury the deceased according to their traditional religious beliefs and facilitate collective memory of the victims of the massacres.[50] The modest quantum awarded collectively was based only on the right of the families to know the truth, as violations of the deceased's rights fell outside the BiH Chamber's jurisdiction. This award could also be viewed as rehabilitation designed to 'address massive trauma that can be life-long or even multigenerational',[51] and 'restore the dignity and reputation of the victims.'[52]

UN Reparations Principles enumerate satisfaction as a mechanism for redress, designed to address moral injury and facilitate the right to know and the right to justice.[53] Satisfaction in accordance with the right to know can include a public apology which acknowledges the facts and accepts responsibility as in the *Srebrenica* cases,[54] search for and return of human remains of disappeared for reburial according to traditional religious practices,[55] and declaration by way of the publication of the Chamber's finding in the official gazette.[56] Satisfaction in accordance with the right to justice would include effective measures aimed at the cessation of

43. Principle 19, Basic Principles and Guidelines on the Right to a Remedy and Reparations of Gross Violations of International Human Rights Law and Serious Violations of International Humanitarian Law (Reparations Principles), GA Res.60/147, 16 December 2005 includes: restoration of liberty, enjoyment of human rights, identity, family life and citizenship, return to one's place of residence, and return of property.
44. Art.30, Articles on Responsibility of States for Internationally Wrongful Acts, UNGA Res.58/83, 12 December 2001, UN Doc.A/56/10/2001 (Articles on State Responsibility).
45. Banja Luka Mosques case, paras.212 and 213. It also ordered Republika Srpska to allow the Islamic Community to erect fencing around the site of the destroyed mosques, refrain from destroying or removing any other objects remaining on the site, or construct any other structure on the site.
46. D. Shelton, *Remedies in International Human Rights Law*, (2nd edn, 2005), 272.
47. Zvornik Mosques case, p.194, and Decision on Review, 9 February 2001, paras.33 and 34, *Digest*, n.#, at p.178.
48. Art.36(1), Articles on State Responsibility; and Principle 20, Reparations Principles.
49. See Crawford, n.#, at p.219; and Shelton, n.#, at p.291.
50. Srebrenica Cases, para.217.
51. Shelton, n.#, at p.275.
52. Study concerning the right to restitution, compensation and rehabilitation for victims of gross violations of human rights and fundamental freedoms, T. Van Boven, 2 July 1993, UN Doc.E/CN.4/Sub.2/1993/8, 57. See Principle 21, Reparations Principles.
53. Principle 22, Reparations Principles.
54. Principle 22(e), Reparations Principles; and Srebrenica Cases, para.219.
55. Principle 22(c), Reparations Principles; and Srebrenica Cases, para.211.
56. Principle 22(d), Reparations Principles; Srebrenica Cases, para.213.

continuing violations,[57] and judicial and administrative sanctions against persons liable for violations.[58]

2.3 *International Criminal Court and Al Mahdi*

The International Criminal Court recognises that it has a restorative as well as a punitive function.[59] The Rome Statute for the first time enables an international criminal court to award reparations, that is, restitution, compensation and rehabilitation, to victims in an order against a convicted person and where appropriate order it be met through the Trust Fund for Victims established under the same instruments.[60] It charges the Court with establishing principles governing reparations to or on behalf of victims.[61] In this respect, the Assembly of States Parties and the Court has repeatedly recalled the leading UN sanctioned Basic Principles and Guidelines on the Right to a Remedy and Reparations of Gross Violations of International Human Rights Law and Serious Violations of International Humanitarian Law.[62] Victims include not only natural persons suffering harm arising from crimes within the Court's jurisdiction but also 'organizations or institutions that have sustained direct harm to any of their property dedicated to religion, education, art, or science or charitable purposes, and to their historic monuments, hospitals and other places and objects of humanitarian purposes.'[63] The Court may award reparations on an individual or collective basis.[64] The victim or their legal representative, the convicted person, or the Court on its own motion, may appoint an appropriate expert to assess the scope and extent of damage, loss or injury and for victims to suggest types and modalities of reparations.[65]

The Trial Chamber's Reparations Order in *Al Mahdi* was the first it rendered in respect of war crimes against cultural and religious property and the first by an international criminal court.[66] While Al Mahdi was indicted and convicted of a crime against protected property and not against civilians, when determining appropriate reparations the Court observed that cultural heritage must be considered in respect of its 'human dimension.'[67] For the Reparations phase, the sites' importance to the local population was brought to the fore, in addition to their universal importance to humanity. The significance of access to cultural heritage for effective enjoyment of human rights has recently been acknowledged by international and regional human rights bodies. The Court found that the attacks on these religious and cultural sites impacted upon the cultural life and identity of local communities and individuals in violation of international human rights norms. It reinforced this by again relying on reparations principles developed by international human rights bodies.[68]

57. Principle 22(a), Reparations Principles; and Srebrenica Cases, para.211.
58. Principle 22(f), Reparations Principles; and Srebrenica Cases, para.212.
59. Report of the Court on the Strategy in Relation to Victims, Doc.ICC-ASP/8/45, 10 November 2009, para.3.
60. Arts 75 and 79, Rome Statute.
61. Art.75, Rome Statute. See UN Doc.A/CONF.183/C.1/WGPM/L.2/Add.7, 5: referring to reparations for victims, victims' families and successors.
62. UN Basic Principles and Guidelines on the right to remedy and reparations of victims of gross violations of international human rights and serious violations of international humanitarian law, adopted by the UN Commission on Human Rights on 19 April 2005, UN Doc. E/CN.4/RES/2005/35 and General Assembly, GA Res.60/147 of 21 March 2006 (Reparations Principles). See Resolution RC/Res.2 on the impact of the Rome Statute system on victims and affected communities, fourth preambular recital, adopted 8 June 2010.
63. Rule 85, Rules of Procedure and Evidence of the International Criminal Court, adopted Assembly of States Parties on and in force 9 September 2002, Doc. ICC-ASP/1/3, Part.II-A.
64. Rule 96, ICC RPE.
65. Rule 97, ICC RPE.
66. It received submissions on reparations from the Prosecutor, Registry, Defence, UNESCO, HRC/Redress, Trust Fund for Victims (TFV), Legal Representative for Victims (LRV) (representing 139 applicants) and reports from three Court appointed experts. Mali chose not to make a submission.
67. Reparations Order, n.#, at p.11.
68. [citation].

The Reparations Order recognised the importance of the cultural loss to the Timbuktu and its inhabitants, Mali, and the international community by addressing property damage to protected sites, consequential economic loss, and moral harm. For each head of reparation, the Court it prioritized the inhabitants of Timbuktu, whom it viewed as disproportionately affected by the acts. In respect of property damage, it ordered collective reparation for the protection and maintenance of the protected sites and measures to ensuring non-repetition, together with translation of Al Mahdi's apology into local languages. For consequential economic loss, it ordered payments to individual victims whose livelihoods was exclusively dependent on the protected sites destroyed,[69] and collective reparations for the community of Timbuktu compensation to ameliorate financial losses suffered. Moral harm was to be covered by individual reparations for the mental pain and anguish suffered by persons whose ancestors were buried at the sites attacked and collective reparations for the mental pain and 'disruption of culture' to Timbuktu as a whole through rehabilitation including public, symbolic measures (e.g. memorial, commemorations). It awarded Mali and UNESCO the symbolic sum of one euro respectively, noting that the collective reparations to the Timbuktu community would have a positive flow-on effect. The Court's guidance to the TFV in implementing the Order sought to reinforce these priorities. Despite its emphasis on the human dimension of these crimes' impact during the reparations phase, the Court rejected submissions for reparations to address loss and harm to civilians and civilian property. This was a flow-on from narrowness of the indictment and resultant conviction.

The Legal Representative for Victims (LRV) appealed the Reparations Order of the Trial Chamber challenging the limitation of individual reparations for economic loss to only those victims whose livelihoods were exclusively dependent on the destroyed protected buildings,[70] delegation of adjudicative power to the Trust Fund for Victims,[71] and breach of confidentiality through the disclosure of identifying information to Al Mahdi. The ICC Appeals Chamber amended the Reparations Order to reflect that the Trial Chamber could review and make a final determination as to reparations and upheld the last ground of appeal finding that the disclosure of the victims' identity to Al Mahdi was 'essentially creating an unnecessary obstacle to certain victims to receive reparations.'[72] The implementation of the Reparations Order in the case has been further complicated by the arrest of Al Hassan Ag Abdoul Aziz Ag Mohamed Ag Mahmoud in respect of the situation in Mali.[73] Trial Chamber VIII overseeing the implementation by the TFV not the repeated applications for extensions of time by the Fund adding it must 'improve its process' and 'act with a degree of diligence commensurate with the importance of its mandate.'[74]

3 CONCLUDING REMARKS

Escalating international condemnation of the intentional destruction of cultural heritage during international and non-international armed conflicts including in Syria, Iraq, Mali, and Libya, by the ICC Prosecutor, UN Security Council, General Assembly and UNESCO is not

69. LRV is appealing the Sentencing Order on the grounds that individual claims for consequential economic loss be so restricted and the determination of who qualifies for such claims be made by the TFV: LRV, Brief in Support of the Appeal (in part and limited) ICC-01/12-01/15-242-Conf (Oc. 17, 2017).
70. Prosecutor v. Ahmad Al Faqi Al Mahdi, Case No.ICC-01/12/-01/15A, Judgment on the appeal of the victims against the Reparations Order (8 March 2018) (Reparations Appeal Judgment), pp.21-22 rejected on the grounds that the Appeals Chamber found that the Trial Chamber had factored in the logistical difficulties to be faced by victims in making the applications for economic loss.
71. Al Mahdi Reparations Appeal Judgment, n.#, at p.35, the Appeals Chamber found Trial Chamber could delegate administrative screening of individual reparations applications to the TFV, provided there was applicants could have the TFV decision reviewed by the Court, which held the final determination.
72. Al Mahdi Reparations Appeal Judgment, n.#, at p.42.
73. Mandat d'arrêt à l'econtre d'Al Hassan Ag Abdoul Aziz Ag Mohamed Ag Mahmoud, Case No.ICC-01/12-01/18-2 (27 March 2018).
74. Prosecutor v. Ahmad Al Faqi Al Mahdi, Case No. ICC-01/12/-01/15, Decision on the Second Trust Fund for Victims' Request for Extension of Time (5 April 2018), p.5.

a recent phenomenon. The adoption of UNESCO Declaration concerning the Intentional Destruction of Cultural Heritage in 2003 which brings together developments in international criminal law, international humanitarian law, international human rights law, and international cultural heritage law was a response to the intentional destruction of the monumental Buddhas in Bamiyan, Afghanistan by the Taliban in 2001 outside the context of an armed conflict.[75] Indeed each development in international law for the protection of cultural property has been a belated response to public outcries arising from acts of deliberate destruction and damage often on a large scale.

In the face of this condemnation of the intentional destruction of cultural property in various armed conflicts, the indictment and conviction by the Trial Chamber was made easier in *Al Mahdi* because of the referral by the State Party, admission of guilty, and most of the sites attacked were inscribed on the World Heritage list. Although the case clearly is a milestone for the International Criminal Court being the first case concerning crimes against cultural property and the first to order reparations for victims of these crimes, it has received wide ranging criticism. There is no doubt that the decision to indict (and convict) Al Mahdi only in respect of war crimes against cultural property gives rises to many of the concerns of its detractors. It is unsurprising that the Prosecutor chose to pursue a war crimes count as the first case brought before the Court for attacks against cultural and religious property. It replicates a pattern set by the IMT and ICTY, where war crimes proved to be an initial stepping stone to subsequent crimes against humanity (persecution) and genocide cases. These latter international crimes' construction lends itself to a clearer link between human rights and cultural heritage. However these earlier indictments and judgments included war crimes against civilians and civilian property. This omission in the *Al Mahdi* case not only prevented the awarding of reparations specifically in respect of death and injury to civilians and damage and destruction of civilian property, it significantly undercut the link the Trial Court itself recognised between the targeted protected cultural and religious property and the local population and the discriminatory intent of Al Mahdi and other perpetrators. The admission of guilt accepted by the Trial Court therefore in many ways represents – two steps forward, one step back – in this area of the law.

Most of the sites attacked recently are inscribed on the World Heritage list or its In Danger list pursuant to the Convention on the Protection of the World Cultural and Natural Heritage.[76] While the Convention itself does not specifically deal with armed conflict or intentional destruction of cultural heritage, it has become an important indicator of cultural, religious and historic objects protected by international criminal law. As noted above, the Trial Chamber in *Al Mahdi* recognised and acknowledged through awarding of reparations the significance of cultural property to the local community, State and international society. However, consistent with its jurisdiction, confined its Judgment only to the question of individual responsibility. The *travaux preparatoires* of the Rome Statute reveal that there was debate about whether reparations orders could be made against not only convicted individuals but also States.[77] States agitated for the exclusion of the recognition State responsibility generally from any reparation provision. In the end, it affirms that 'no provision in this Statute relating to individual criminal responsibility shall affect the responsibility of States under international law.'[78] The World Heritage Convention, international humanitarian law, and recent Security Council resolutions set out a range of international obligations on States and the international community (through international

75. Declaration on the Intentional Destruction of Cultural Heritage, adopted by the UNESCO General Conference at its 32nd session, Resolution 33/32 (2003) Annex, (Declaration on Intentional Destruction).

76. Convention concerning the Protection of World Cultural and Natural Heritage, 16 November 1972, entered in force 17 December 1975, 1037 UNTS 151 (World Heritage Convention)

77. F. McKay, 'Are Reparations Appropriately Addressed in the ICC Statute?' in D. Shelton (ed), *International Crimes, Peace and Human Rights: The Role of the International Criminal Court* (New York: Transnational Publishers, 2000), pp.163-178.

78. Art.25(4), Rome Statute. See A. Nollkaemper, 'Concurrence between Individual Responsibility and State Responsibility in International Law', 2 ICLQ (2003) 615-630.

cooperation) in respect of the protection of cultural heritage under threat. Likewise the International Court of Justice has examined the obligation of States to prevent and punish genocide covering circumstances which included the deliberate destruction of cultural heritage. The disconnect between the Judgment and Sentencing, and the Reparation Order in *Al Mahdi* may also be reflective of this (politically necessary) compromise in the drafting of the Rome Statute which concentrates on individual criminal responsibility, sidelining questions of the international responsibility of States and international organisations.

The preamble of the Rome Statute recognises that the grave crimes falling with the ICC's jurisdiction are a threat to international peace.[79] While the capacity of the permanent International Criminal Court to order reparations and the establishment of Trust Fund for Victims is a welcome development, the early decisions of the Trial Chamber's appear to reflect the priority implicit in the Statute's Preamble, that is, holding perpetrators to account. As indicated above, the international community has in the past both tried and convicted those responsible for the deliberate destruction and damaging of cultural property and instituted reparations schemes through an independent process, often pursuant to a peace agreement. The ICC's reliance on the UN Reparations Principles in defining and awarding reparations provides this broader understanding of the role of reparations as interpreted by human rights bodies and courts, beyond the priorities of international criminal law. However, the decision in *Al Madhi* reveal the tensions between these demands on the Court. It also challenges assertions that work of the Court alone can facilitate peace on the ground.

REFERENCES

Bentwich, International Aspects of Restitution and Compensation for Victims of the Nazis, 32 BYIL (1955-56).

Cassese, A., *International Criminal Law* (Oxford: Oxford University Press, 2003).

Hall, The Recovery of Cultural Objects Dispersed During World War II, 25 *Dep't St. Bull*, 1951.

Malmström, S., 'Restitution of Property and Compensation to Victims', in R. May et al (eds), *Essays on ICTY Procedure and Evidence in Honour of Gabrielle Kirk McDonald*, (The Hague: Kluwer Law International, 2001.

McKay, F., 'Are Reparations Appropriately Addressed in the ICC Statute?' in D. Shelton (ed), *International Crimes, Peace and Human Rights: The Role of the International Criminal Court* (New York: Transnational Publishers, 2000).

Shelton, D., *Remedies in International Human Rights Law*, (2nd edn, 2005).

Vrdoljak, A F 'Gross Violations of Human Rights and Restitution: Learning from Holocaust Claims' in L. V. Prott (ed.), *Realising Cultural Heritage Law: Festschrift for Patrick O'Keefe*, Builth Wells: IAL, 2012.

Wühler, N., 'The United Nations Compensation Commission', in A. Randelzhofer and C. Tomuschat (eds), *State Responsibility and Individual Reparations in Instances of Grave Violations of Human Rights*, 1999.

Zappala, S., *Human Rights in International Criminal Proceedings*, Oxford, Oxford University Press, 2003.

1943 London Declaration.

Art.25(1), Peace Treaty with Romania.

Articles on Responsibility of States for Internationally Wrongful Acts, UNGA Res.58/83, 12 December 2001, UN Doc.A/56/10/2001.

Basic Principles and Guidelines on the Right to a Remedy and Reparations of Gross Violations of International Human Rights Law and Serious Violations of International Humanitarian Law (Reparations Principles), GA Res.60/147, 16 December 2005.

Brussels Declaration

Convention (IV) respecting the Laws and Customs of War on Land and Annex: Regulations concerning the Laws and Customs of War on Land, Oct. 18, 1907, entered into force 26 January 1910, 187 CTS 227 (Hague Regulations).

Convention concerning the Protection of World Cultural and Natural Heritage.

79. Third preambular recital, Rome Statute.

Declaration on the Intentional Destruction of Cultural Heritage, adopted by the UNESCO General Conference at its 32nd session, Resolution 33/32 (2003) Annex.
Draft convention on the crime of genocide, prepared by Secretariat at requested by General Assembly, 26 June 1947 UN Doc.E/447, 5-13. UN Doc.E/447, 47.
Final Act and Annex of the Paris Conference on Reparations, Annex I: Resolution on Subject of Restitution.
General Framework Agreement for Peace in Bosnia and Herzegovina, signed and entered into force 14 December 1995, 35 ILM (1996) 89, Annex 6.
ICTR Statute.
ICTY Statute;
International Military Tribunal Nuremberg, Judgment, in 41 AJIL (1947) 172, at 248-249.
International Regulations on the Laws and Customs of War, 27 August 1874,
Mandat d'arrêt à l'econtre d'Al Hassan Ag Abdoul Aziz Ag Mohamed Ag Mahmoud, Case No.ICC-01/12-01/18-2 (27 March 2018).
Military Government for Germany, U.S. Area of Control, Law No.59, 'Restitution of Identifiable Property', Military Government Gazette [Germany. U.S. Zone, Issue G] No.10, (November 1947), 42 (supp.) AJIL (1948).
Private Property, Rights and Interests in the Paris Peace Treaties
Prosecutor v. Ahmad Al Faqi Al Mahdi, Case No. ICC-01/12/-01/15, Decision on the Second Trust Fund for Victims' Request for Extension of Time (5 April 2018).
Prosecutor v. Ahmad Al Faqi Al Mahdi, Case No.ICC-01/12/-01/15A, Judgment on the appeal of the victims against the Reparations Order (8 March 2018) (Reparations Appeal Judgment).
Prosecutor v. Ahmad Al Faqi Al Mahdi, Case No. ICC-01/12-01/15, Judgment and Sentence (27 September 2016) (Al Mahdi Judgment and Sentence); and Prosecutor v. Ahmad Al Faqi Al Mahdi, Case No. ICC-01/12-01/15, Reparations Order (17 August 2017) (Al Mahdi Reparations Order).
Report of the Court on the Strategy in Relation to Victims, Doc.ICC-ASP/8/45, 10 November 2009, para.3.
Rome Statute of the International Criminal Court, 17 July 1998, in force 1 July 2002, 2187 UNTS 90 (Rome Statute).
Rules of Procedure and Evidence of the International Criminal Court, adopted Assembly of States Parties on and in force 9 September 2002, Doc. ICC-ASP/1/3, Part.II-A.
SC Resolution covering the ICTR adopted in 1994 included similar language with the additional aim of 'contribut[ing] to the process of national reconciliation'.
Statute of the International Criminal Tribunal for Rwanda, SC Res.955 of 8 November 1994 as adopted and amended to SC Res.1717 of 13 October 2006 (ICTR Statute).
Statute of the International Criminal Tribunal for the Former Yugoslavia, GA Res.827 of 25 May 1993, amended by GA Res.1166 (1998), 1329 (2000), 1411 (2002), 1431 (2002) 1481 (2003), 1597 (2005) and 1660 (2006) (ICTY Statute);
The U.S. Zone Law No.59
UN Basic Principles and Guidelines on the right to remedy and reparations of victims of gross violations of international human rights and serious violations of international humanitarian law, adopted by the UN Commission on Human Rights on 19 April 2005, UN Doc. E/CN.4/RES/2005/35 and General Assembly, GA Res.60/147 of 21 March 2006 (Reparations Principles).
UN Basic Principles and Guidelines on the right to remedy and reparations of victims of gross violations of international human rights and serious violations of international humanitarian law, adopted by the UN Commission on Human Rights on 19 April 2005, UN Doc. E/CN.4/RES/2005/35 and General Assembly, GA Res.60/147 of 21 March 2006 (Reparations Principles). See Resolution RC/Res.2 on the impact of the Rome Statute system on victims and affected communities, fourth preambular recital, adopted 8 June 2010.
UN Doc.A/C.6/SR.95 and 96.
V. Morris and M. Scharf, An Insider's Guide to the International Criminal Court for the Former Yugoslavia (New York: Transnational Publishers, 1995), 288.

Culture and International Law - Juwana et al. (Eds)
© 2019 Taylor & Francis Group, London, ISBN 978-1-138-38766-9

Celebrating traditional culture through information science and technology

Dadan Suhandana
General Secretary of Sobat Budaya, Jakarta, Indonesia

Tri Sony Saragih
Research Associate, Bandung Fe Institute, Bandung, Indonesia

Hokky Situngkir
Department of Computational Sociology, Bandung Fe Institute, Bandung, Indonesia

ABSTRACT: Abstract: Indonesia is arguably one of the most culturally and ethnically diverse countries in the world. It may mean there is a wealth of legacy, but there is also stark contrast, which can potentially lead to social conflict and tensions between social identities. Contemporary advancement in computation and information technology revisits this. People with different cultural expressions are no longer separated from each other, and 'budaya-indonesia.org', as a computational platform, helps intercultural exchange grow even stronger. It encourages electronic and digital recording of every aspect of every Indonesian culture. It is vastly participatory, decentralized, distributed, and on top of that, social. Over the years, there have been many things delivered from the vast amount of cultural data available, such as the fractal batik innovation and taxonomical or relational mappings of cultural expressions. Nonetheless, it is also a form of protection. It helps Indonesians against intentional malicious claims that, from time to time, attempt to exploit certain parts of a traditional culture as an exclusive property of an individual, commercial or even national entity from Indonesia.

KEYWORDS: Cultural diversity, digital library, Indonesian traditional culture, legal protection, participatory, traditional cultural expression, traditional knowledge

1 INTRODUCTION

Culture is a form of collective intelligence (Brown & Hugh, 2000), the results of cognitive mental processes and abstractions of human groups about the universe around them. In a country that is built from diverse ethnic and cultural characteristics such as Indonesia, inter-ethnic interaction becomes very important (Situngkir, 2008). The interaction that exists among social identities has made cultural sharing inevitable, be it related to language, habits and other cultural rituals. In its development, cultural assimilation and acculturation is a result of interaction among societies. These various interactions that occur over a long period of time have eventually enriched the high existence of cultural diversity.

Despite the social diversity, the economic explorations and creative use of those cultural elements have not yet been carried out efficiently on a national scale, whereas the potential of it promises increased product diversity. Cultural diversity is creative and a source of knowledge for the people of Indonesia (Situngkir, 2008). For instance, the variety of languages in Indonesia is overwhelming compared to the number of languages spoken on Planet Earth

(Surya & Situngkir, 2008). About 10% of the world's languages, approximately 710 of 7097, are in the archipelago. Moreover, Indonesia is also rich with varieties of rituals, traditional arts, dances, cuisines, ornaments, songs and other expressions.

The cultural diversities may be related to the geographical conditions and terrains in Indonesia, which is hilly, mountainous and separated by rivers and seas. Unconnected for many generations, the different social identities somehow may evoke conflicts and tensions. Even the slightest difference may trigger misunderstandings and disputes if it is not balanced by cohesive interactions among people from different cultural backgrounds. This may happen among villages, languages and ritual that are occasionally capable of triggering tensions, even within the same political administrative regions.

This situation is exacerbated by the implementation of modern laws encouraging communities within regions to register intellectual property for existing traditional cultural expressions. This is quite contrary to the practical tendencies of Indonesian people, who are more likely to be friendly, to share, and conventionally reluctant to claim sole ownership. For a practical example, most people have never known who is the actual creator of the famous Mega Mendung batik motif or the architecture of the great Prambanan Temple, and so on. Thus, the legal tendency for claiming ownership may cause sparks of conflict between regions because, in some conditions, several traditional communities existed within several political and administrative regions.

The quest for traditional culture is now related to the recent advancement of information technology. Technology does not only change the human perspective but also inspires the improvement of human abilities. Specifically, through the acquisition of recent information technology, people today are able to interact with others without being limited by territorial boundaries and time. Due to such communication, the information flows quickly and has removed geographical boundaries. Someone who is across the ocean will be able to interact with someone on land. Moreover, the nature of information technology provides things that record and store data and information.

One other thing that has been witnessed by the development of information technology and sciences is the emerging so called 'creative economy'. The economic shift from the manufacturing economy to a creative economy requires every human being to be able to evaluate information as economic objects. Here the task of economic processes depends more on finding added value in the product by attaching creativity and innovation into it. This brings us into one source of creativity that can be explored, that is traditional culture, as the product of the collective intelligence of people over generations. Specific examples in Indonesia related to this point of view are how culinary business is growing tremendously based on traditional cuisine, that some clothing is using batik motifs as inspiration, and that some alternative medications are based on traditional knowledge.

Table 1. The three simple epochs in our global evolutionary economic system.

	Economy manufacturing center	High-tech economy	Creative economy
Product quantities	Scarce	Medium	Abundance
Information quantities	Scarce	Medium, localized in academic environment	Abundance
Asymmetry to be equilibrate	Political access	Technology access	Information
Landscape	Nations (geopolitics)	Space (borderless)	Digital

The economic shift into a creative economy has led to traditional culture becoming a source of creativity (Situngkir, 2009a). However, this causes a problem in relation to intellectual property rights. Indonesians, having a great tendency to share, must then contemplate the economic value of their culture. So it is no wonder that in 2008 there was a furor in Bali when a traditional silver craftsman, Ibu Desak Suarti, was arrested for being accused of violating intellectual property rights of some jewelry company in North America. The incident was confusing because her design was traditionally derived, over generations. Since then, there have been many cases of violations of intellectual property experienced by craftsmen. There were also cases of detention considered for Jepara craftsmen in violation of intellectual property rights. In addition, there have been many cases of violations committed by individuals, private companies and the foreign states. How long is this element of our culture to be claimed by foreign countries? The increasingly widespread claims by foreigners to Indonesian cultural expressions are due to the increasing awareness of the importance of creative resources in the economy.

Technology and information sciences should be able to develop and encourage mutual cooperation and a spirit of sharing in Indonesia, while protecting the people's rights to their own living cultural heritage. This article discusses the role of science and technology in bridging high cultural diversity in Indonesia and exploring and protecting the traditional culture of Indonesia.

2 METHODOLOGY

As of 2018, the World Intellectual Property Organization (WIPO), as a worldwide institution dealing with arrangement of intellectual property rights, still conducts hearings to discuss how to protect the traditional knowledge, expression of traditional culture and genetic resources by using conventional ownership law. At the moment, there are still differences of opinions. Several discussions were finally submitted for countries to protect their traditional cultural expressions (WIPO, n.d.).

As a country that has a high cultural diversity, Indonesians should think of specific ways to protect their traditional culture. For countries that do not have such diverse ethnic groups, the law of ownership is able to protect the traditional culture of the country. However, it is different for Indonesia: ownership law will lead to tensions because each region has several tribes whose traditional cultural expressions are sometimes interrelated and have similarities. There are even such tribes among several different administrative areas. This condition potentially may lead to disunity because of claims within communities that they are struggling for their traditional cultural expressions and traditional knowledge, while having affinities to their respective political and administrative regions.

The development of information technology is a marker of a new era in society. The Internet, as part of the rapid technological development, makes it possible to exchange information flow more easily. The limited information flow that initially occurred because of the geographical bulkhead is now surpassed with the help of technology. Every individual has the same rights to share and argue without much hierarchy.

Unfortunately, Internet progress has not been implemented optimally in celebrating traditional cultural diversity, especially in Indonesia. Technological development and high cultural diversity have not been able to reduce potential conflicts that arise in the community.

Budaya-indonesia.org, an Internet portal, was formed in 2008 by the initiatives of some citizens of Indonesia who realized the important cultural role of information technology. The portal is now capable of becoming an Indonesian cultural digital library. The existence of 300 tribes along with 710 regional languages owned by Indonesia would certainly be a great cost for 'top-down' cultural data preservation. In Indonesia, cultural expressions are not only diverse, but also still 'alive' among collective groups of ethnicities in our modern era.

The fundamental basis of *budaya-indonesia.org* is Web 2.0, where content of the portal is submitted and managed in a participatory fashion by netizens. The nature of the Internet website was able to accommodate the diversity of cultures and regions of Indonesia in the form of islands. Data collection by *budaya-indonesia.org* invites all communities, especially young people, to participate in collecting traditional cultural data because it has characteristics such as participation, decentralization, connectedness, and emergence (Choate, 2007).

Being participatory means that each user has the same rights to manage the site's content. The *budaya-indonesia.org* website does not restrict users from uploading the data they have to the site. Decentralization means that users do not have to be in the same place to enter cultural data. Being connected means that each user, besides having the same rights to upload data, can also communicate with other users. They can even comment on each other and critique the existing data. Emergence is a characteristic that is generated when users share data and interact with each other. Since being established, *budaya-indonesia.org* has formed an online community, named *Sobat Budaya*, which has the role of inviting people to submit the traditional cultural data that surrounds us.

With these characteristics, the *budaya-indonesia.org* website becomes a digital library that can be accessed by all levels of society, especially younger generations who prefer openness of data and information disclosure (Laughey, 2006).

3 DISCUSSION

A creative economy emerges when information is able to reproduce and spread widely. Previously, the industrial revolution allowed mass replication of products and services. Products and services that are the result of knowledge and already in the form of commodities then develop further when information and knowledge become commodities that can be sold.

Ironically, among Indonesians, traditional cultural diversity is still rarely seen as information. Traditional dance is only seen as part of an artistic performance, traditional food is only considered as menus, batik is merely pieces of cloth, and so on. Cultural elements possessed by Indonesia have not become information that can be processed and stored in digital form.

3.1 *Legal protection efforts*

In 2000, WIPO member countries established the IGC (Inter-Governmental Committee) on Intellectual Property and Genetic Resources, Traditional Knowledge and Folklore, and in 2009 they agreed to establish a legal instrument that was capable of providing protection for traditional knowledge, genetic resources and traditional cultural expression (folklore), and that can bind WIPO members to ratify legislation in their respective countries (WIPO, n.d.). However, until now the negotiations are still ongoing because sometimes the community and the government are not of the same opinion about how to protect, who should protect and what should be protected. Meanwhile, more and more Indonesian cultural elements are claimed by foreign parties. These claims have caused economic losses due to the implementation of a number of regulations on Intellectual Property Rights (IPR) by the World Trade

Table 2. Comparison of systems and format for inventory of intangible cultural heritage in the People's Republic of China (PRC), Japan and the Republic of Korea (N = No; Y = Yes).

Inventory characteristics	PRC	Japan	Rep. Korea
Standard form/format	In process	Y	Y
National-level inventory (number of registered cultural eyes)	1028	80 + 25, Folk 264	114
Provincial inventory	4155	Y	Y
District/city-level inventory	In part	Y	Y
District-level inventory	In part	Y	N
Engaging the community	Y	Y	Y + help
Involving NGOs	2110	Y	Y + help
Using a metadata system	Not yet	Will be	Will be
Survey software	Y	Not yet	Not yet
Distinguished importantly/folk people	N	47	Yes
Best practice also recorded	Not yet	Y	Y
Classification/Domain	Y	Y	Y
Individual/group differentiation	N	Y	Y
HR difficulties	Training	N	N
Fund limitations	Y	Y	-

Organization (WTO). These regulations cause Indonesian citizens who export cultural products abroad to be threatened with sanctions although it is clear that these products come from Indonesian cultural traditions (Dahlan & Situngkir, 2011).

Some countries have developed legal protection instruments by building a digital cultural library. Japan, China and South Korea are three countries that have built a cultural data collection system. Cultural data collection is a form of defensive protection that aims to stop exploitation by outsiders who want to use traditional knowledge without permission by using a database.

Indonesia has been recording its intangible cultural heritage since 1976. In its journey, the record experienced several obstacles. Until now, the recording of intangible cultural heritage has not been successfully carried out comprehensively and continuously; this is due to the lack of involvement of elements of the community, social groups and individuals (Republic of Indonesia, 2009).

Through *budaya-indonesia.org*, the Indonesian cultural digital library, managed by the Sobat Budaya community, started using the Web 2.0 platform in 2008. As of 2018, the data collected in the Indonesian cultural digital library, according to *Perpustakaan Digital Budaya Indonesia* (https://budaya-indonesia.org), is as shown in Table 3.

Table 3. Amount of data artifacts on *budaya-indonesia.org*.

Cultural artifacts	Amount of data
Musical instrument	1,312
Folklore	2,244
Food and drink	20,108
Cloth motif	1,061
Music and songs	1,331
Ancient manuscripts and inscriptions	557
Ornaments	689
Traditional clothing	496

with a total of more than 8,000 participants from all directions, from Aceh to Merauke who were met through cyberspace.

Therefore, performing a cultural revitalization process to encourage the rise of new cultures is necessary. This must begin with a systematic data collection and research process. The process of data collection on Indonesian traditional cultural wealth must be done in ways that are not traditional. Traditional cultural data collection is not only beneficial for cultural protection but also has several other benefits, such as:

- Cultural restoration, an effort to awaken the civilization that exists in Indonesia;
- Economic value by using traditional culture as a field of creativity;
- Add value to travel and cultural businesses;
- Educate young people to understand their cultural roots (Dahlan, 2009).

Table 4. The various challenges Indonesia has in protecting traditional culture can be addressed by building the Indonesian cultural digital library.

Problem	Solution
High diversity of traditional cultural expressions	Indonesian cultural digital library
Debates among cultural experts regarding curation of expressions	Provide facilities to criticize and curate
Low participation of young people in protecting traditional culture	Make media that is able to invite young people to be active in participating
Cultural interactions are difficult because of the islands	Online media that overcomes free restrictions

Traditional cultural data is crucial for Indonesian people to know their true identity as a nation that has cultural diversity, while in terms of humanity, the existence of a cultural data library can provide benefits for civilization because it becomes a research laboratory related to the evolution of human culture.

3.2 *The phylomemetic tree: a direct aspect after digital library*

As a country with high cultural and ethnic diversity, the 'phylomemetic tree' is introduced. From the tree, we can see the social and cultural structure in Indonesia, cultural expression-wise (Situngkir, 2016).

The phylomemetic tree is a technique adopted from (biological) genetic studies to describe the evolutionary relation between one unit and another. If the phylogenetic trees are generated from genetic analysis to see the kinship between organisms, the phylomemetic one is generated by looking at the sequence cultural 'memes', the smallest unit of cultural information, to see the kinship between cultural groups. The meme has the ability to spread from one party to another through replication in the form of imitation and massive propagation in the form of mass communication media.

Like a gene, a meme is hypothesized to be transmitted from one person to another. But it is difficult to build formalism for such fluidity of culture and its respective expression. All scientific studies require data, and the theory of evolution has had 'Galapagos' island for initialization studies since the time of Charles Darwin. Indonesia, with a high cultural diversity, can be imagined as a 'Galapagos' for traditional culture. The memetic approach has been proposed to capture the diversity of Indonesian culture. The formation of phylomemetic trees can help the analysis of sociological and anthropological studies to read the underlying structure of the social and community system by traditional cultural expressions in the archipelago. The phylomemetic tree is an effort to see and define the face of the Indonesian people in terms of their cultural systems.

3.3 *The phylomemetic tree of batik*

One of the very high cultural diversities in the archipelago is batik motifs. Batik is known as traditional Indonesian clothing. Each different tribe has specific batik ornaments, although sometimes there are similarities among them. Another interesting thing from research on batik is that the dimensions of the batik motif are fractional, or in mathematical sciences 'fractals'. Unlike some shapes we know, the dimensions of fractals are not 1, 2 or 3, but fractions, for example, 1.567. This is what makes batik very unique and different from other modern motifs (Situngkir, 2015). Classical geometry teaches us about the understanding of simple forms, namely the dimensions of integers, for example, straight lines (one-dimensional), circles and rectangles (two-dimensional or flat), and cubes, cones and spheres (three-dimensional or geometric).

The pattern of color characteristics of batik motifs is studied through a color computational approach. The color configuration of batik is stated in RGB, or red, green, and blue (color) histograms. Any color can be formed from the combination of these three colors. To see batik as a whole, we cannot consider the shape per se; the color must also be considered. Color is a vital element in a pattern of motifs because it relates to elements of material or dye that existed in nature where the batik was produced, the ecological aspects and the collective preferences of the community. The parameters obtained from computation of thousands of batik motifs recorded in *budaya-indonesia.org* are analyzed through the evolutionary tree approach commonly found in the study of evolutionary biology. Parameters of geometric shapes and color patterns of batik motifs are processed as information sequences, like DNA sequences in biological structures.

Sequences of data obtained from the color parameters and shape of each motif are then processed into a distance matrix among fabric motif expressions. This distance is then transformed into a phylomemetic tree of traditional Indonesian cloth motifs, as shown in Figure 1.

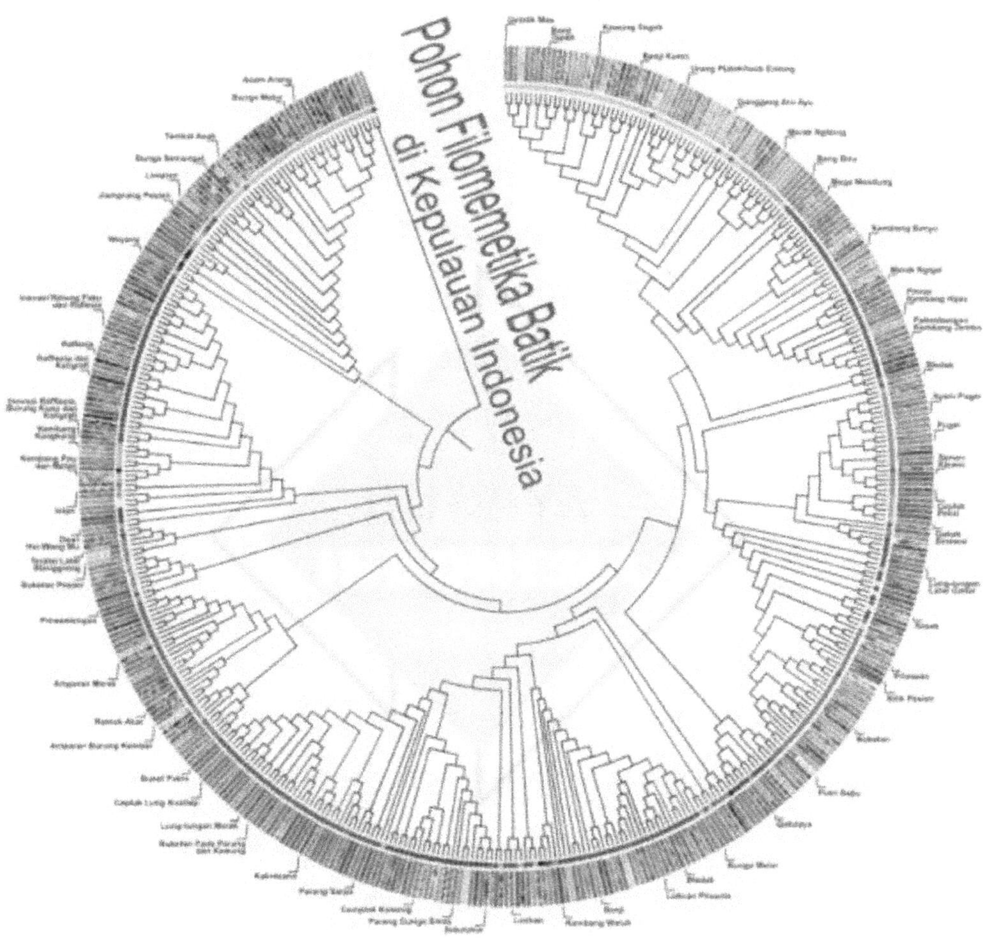

Figure 1. The phylomemetics of Batik.

Moreover, from the batik motif phylomemetics results, there are some interesting findings. Batik motifs are clustered based on the ethno-geographical regions from where the motif originated locally (Situngkir, 2009b). Batik motifs are not grouped merely based on the same basic patterns. *Banji* batik motifs from Yogyakarta are not grouped with the batik motif with a similar title from Garut. However, a sample of batik motifs from Solo are clustered with other Solo motifs. The *banji* motif of Yogyakarta is clustered with other Yogyakarta motifs. Likewise, the motif from Solo is adjacent to the cluster of motifs from Yogyakarta and so on.

Try to imagine you are walking in a market and photographing a particular motif. The motif photo is then inserted into a computer, which had a fabric motif phylomemetic analysis system installed on it. Computers, probabilistically, can find out whether the motif is a batik motif or not, and find out where the motif came from.

Not only that, these batik motifs can be traced further. The evolution of this batik motif turned out to have a connection with the development of the Islamic religion in Java. The Demak Sultanate, which was established at the end of the 15th century, is the first Islamic kingdom in Java. The Demak region continues to expand, covering the Kalinyamat region, which includes Jepara, Kudus, Pati and Rembang.

After going through a series of long conflicts, Demak's influence was replaced by the Mataram sultanate, which was centered more in the interior. Gradually, the influence of the

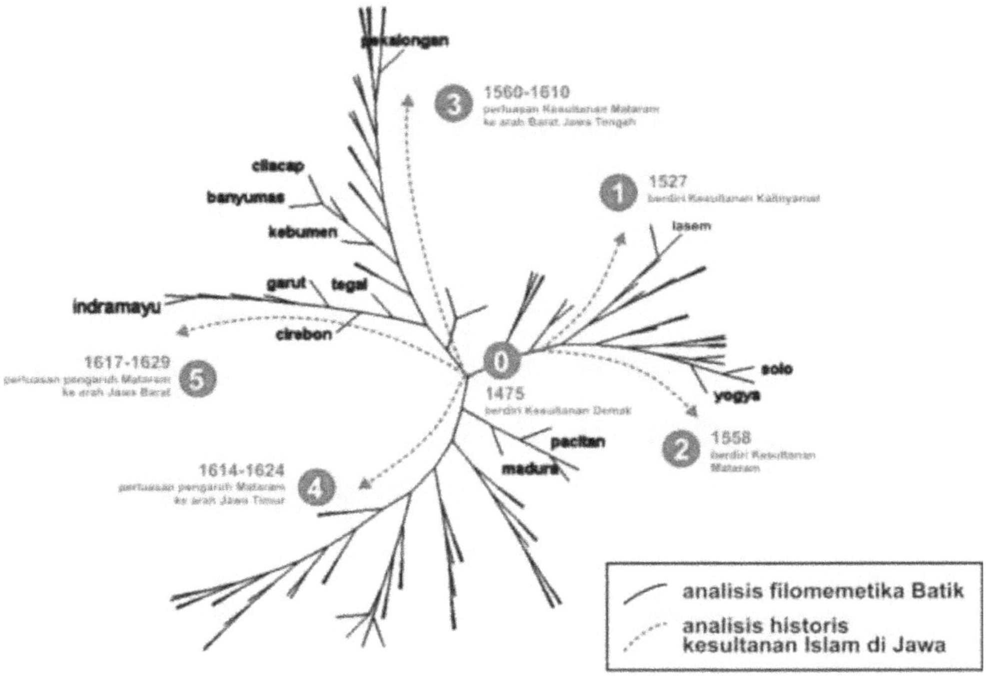

Figure 2. Transmission of Islam in Java.

sultanate extended to the western regions of central Java. In the early 17th century, the influence of the Mataram sultanate continued to expand, reaching the regions of East Java and West Java, as illustrated in Figure 2.

Interestingly, the pattern of evolution of batik motifs has a very high coincidence with the development of the Islamic sultanate in Java. Before Islam entered the island of Java, there might have been batik. But the motifs were very different from what the batik people develop and know now. These ancient batik motifs, however, are thought to resemble in relief the shapes of ancient temples in Java. The motifs are full of depictions of humans and animals as a whole and have a narrative function or tell a certain story.

After Islam entered Java, there was a great acculturation process. The depiction of a human figure is replaced by a symbol that represents certain characters. Animal portrayal is still permissible as long as it is done partially. For example, birds can only be drawn in terms of their wings, like the *sawat* motif. Floral motifs and geometric patterns are thus more dominant, for these are not forbidden at all in Islamic theology.

This process of acculturation finally gave birth to modern batik as we know it today. The batik we wear every day is a result of long mental evolutionary work that is born from the harmonious relationship between religion and culture (Situngkir, 2016).

3.4 *The phylomemetic tree of traditional song*

Traditional Indonesian songs also have high diversity. Each song has lyrics and melodies that have a strong attachment to the characteristics of the area where the song originated. Some traditional songs have ethno-centric themes, some of them illustrate how the dynamic life of the local community in the area of the song originated. Usually, these songs are named according to their cultural areas, such as Javanese folk songs (*Suwe Ora Jamu*), Minang folk songs (*Ayam den Lapeh*), Sundanese folk songs (*Bubuy Bulan*), Maluku folk songs (*Hela Rotan*), and so on (Situngkir, 2007).

More than 500 traditional songs are collected at *budaya-indonesia.org*. The traditional song was converted into a standard digital music format, and then analyzed and computed with the

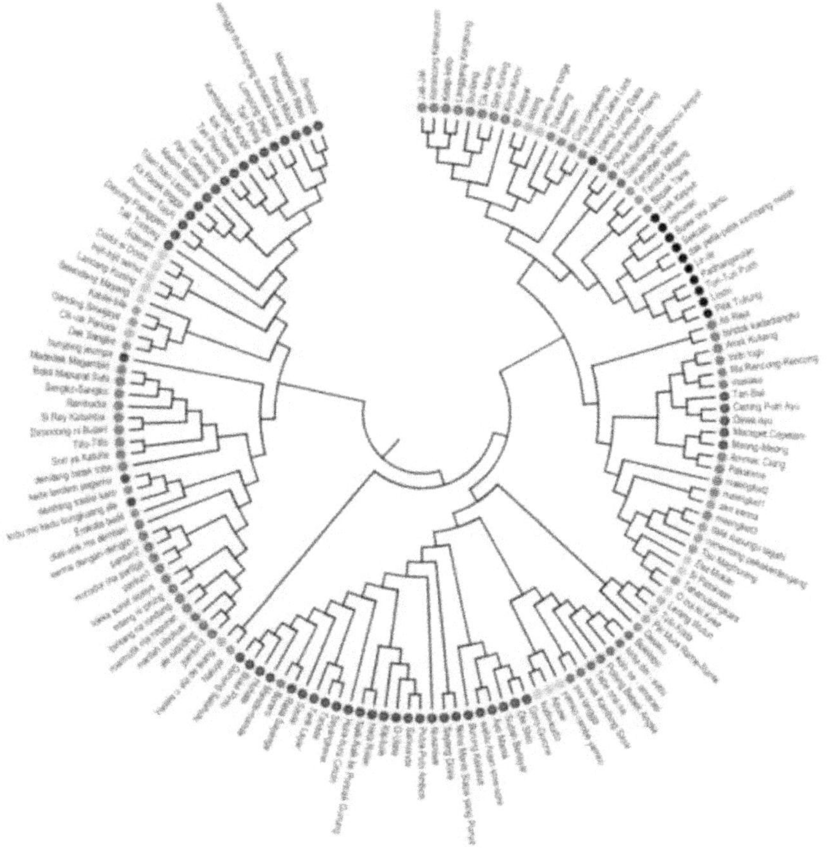

Figure 3. Phylomemetic tree of Indonesian traditional songs.

techniques of mathematical sciences. The computational results then become maps of the traditional archipelago songs (see Figure 3). Interestingly, the songs are clustered accordingly to the ethnicity and geography of a song's origin. From the results of this study, some innovations are awaited. From the collected and compiled data, computer programs can now recognize the mathematical characteristics of traditional Indonesian songs. That way, an application is able to produce new music according to the characteristics of music from a particular area, making it possible to generate a song that is as complex as the traditional song "*O Ina Ni Keke*" from Minahasa, North Sulawesi, with a more modern taste.

3.5 *The phylomemetic tree of traditional cuisine*

As of 2018, the amount of culinary recipe data in the Indonesian Cultural Data Library of *budaya-indonesia.org* involves more than 20,000 entries. You can imagine how many courses are needed for a dinner if all of them are to be served.

For how long can we taste all of these foods and beverages? It takes years of dinners to consume one type of recipe from the Indonesian Cultural Data Library every evening. 'Fried rice' is said to be one of the most delicious cuisines in the world. Furthermore, *rendang* is also stated to be the most delicious food in the world. Both are said to be the most delicious, probably because people have not tried other foods that are also very delicious. Just imagine that from 20,000 recipes, there must be among them the most delicious food that you haven't tasted.

From the collected data, there are at least 50 types of *soto* in various regions in the country and more than 60 types of satay dishes in the archipelago. *Rendang* was not only in the tradition of the West Sumatran cuisine, for *rendang* dishes are also found in Aceh and North Sumatra with different specification. *Rendang*, fried rice and even satay are so delicious and become Indonesian specialties for the historical reality that the tropical islands of Indonesia were once a prima donna of spices and food ingredients.

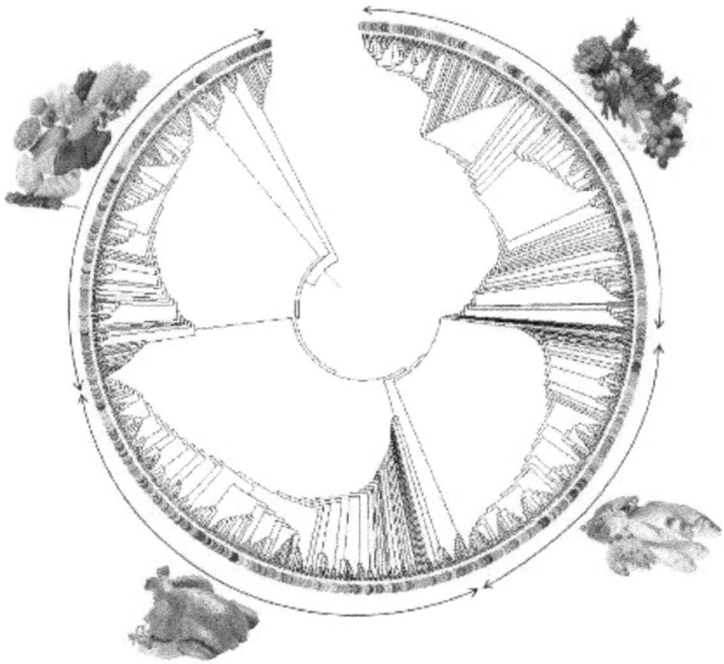

Figure 4. Phylomemetic tree of Indonesian traditional cuisine diversified according to spices used in groups of meat, chicken, fish and vegetable dishes.

The number of spice variations in Indonesia is remarkable. For instance, *Sate Padang* is originally formulated using 70 types of spices and ingredients. Commonly, from the data, to cook one type of food we require only ten spices and ingredients. It is very different from Indonesian traditional cuisine. *Rendang*, for example, requires more than 50 mixes of herbs and ingredients.

Culinary acculturation is a common thing and is a reinforcement of food diversity throughout the archipelago. Most used common ingredients are onion, garlic, chili, lime, ginger, pepper, turmeric, and coconut milk. But the use of unique spice ingredients in each region makes the variation seemingly infinite, not to mention the various types of chili, which numbered more than 100 variations across the archipelago.

From culinary data studies we know of other traditions, such as traditional ceremonies and religious rituals. Many types of food can only be served traditionally during religious rituals, wedding festivals and/or many other rituals that only serve certain foods. Not only that; from the culinary, it can also be seen which foods are useful for medical and healthcare purposes. From thousands of types of recipes available, 1,370 food recipes were mapped in culinary phylomemetics (Situngkir et al., 2016), as illustrated in Figure 5.

Phylomemetics is a family tree of the smallest elements in traditional culture. The way we read it is similar to a family tree. In this study of food phylomemetics, it is generally diversified in spices used in four parts of cooking: meat, chicken, fish and vegetables. The clusters within groups show certain geographic and tribal areas of society.

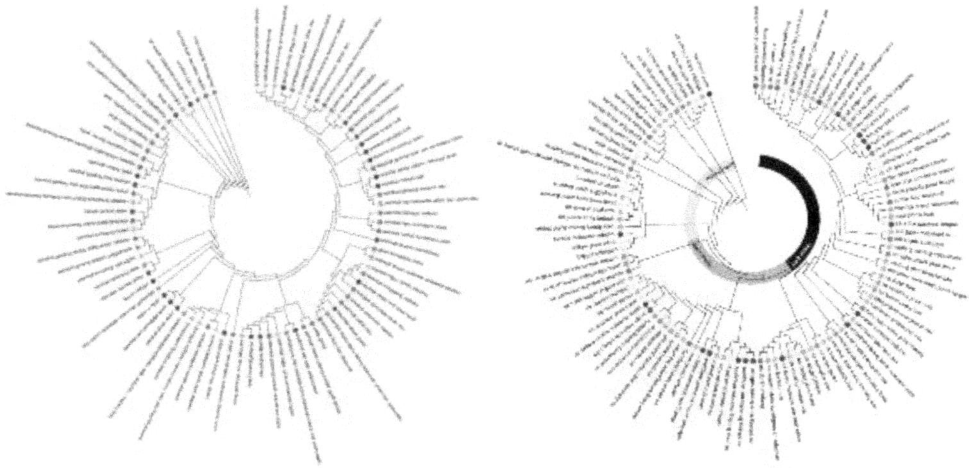

(a) (b)

Figure 5. Phylomemetic trees of: (a) Indonesian traditional sauces; (b) Indonesian traditional drinks.

3.6 *Exploring the greatness of Borobudur Temple*

As a legacy of the glory of the past, Borobudur Temple stands majestically in Magelang, Central Java. The legacy of the Syailendra Dynasty in the 8th century is the largest Mahayana Buddhist temple in Indonesia. Without knowing geometry, mathematics and computation, the building of this structure produces complex architectural patterns.

There are interesting geometric facts when looking at the structure of the Borobudur Temple above the ground, which is shaped like a square. If you look at the Borobudur Temple both vertically and horizontally, Borobudur's body has legs, a body and a head. There is a ratio of 4:6:9 for the size of the legs, body and head of the temple, both vertically and horizontally.

The absence of a standard metric system in the past asked a big question of how they built the Borobudur Temple. Mathematical studies answer the question of how to build Borobudur Temple without using a metric system. The use of three-dimensional cellular automata allows the building of large and complex buildings such as Borobudur without standard models and metrics, as is common in modern architectural concepts. Reconstruction of the Borobudur Temple with cellular automata (see Figure 6) shows how simple rules are able to produce megastructures (Situngkir, 2010).

Cellular automata are computational models that are able to show how complex patterns can be formed from simple rules that keep repeating. Several studies of complexity have introduced many possibilities of art and aesthetics, including traditional artifacts that can be explained using cellular automata.

The geometrical shape of Borobudur Temple, which is different from standard geometry, provides traces of the inhabitants of the archipelago in the mathematics of the past. We, as the generation who inherited the Borobudur Temple, can dig back into stored metaphors with science and technology. Extracting traditional culture through science and technology is possible if massive traditional cultural data collection is carried out.

3.7 *Progress in science and information technology in supporting cultural diversity*

The rise of the nations of Europe, the United States, and Japan began with the revitalization of their cultural heritage. Nations that have a great vision of civilization should follow these steps. Cultural diversity must be seen as an asset to inspire the world. This revitalization is a step toward building the foundation and then building upon this, namely knowledge, technology and public policy (Situngkir, 2010).

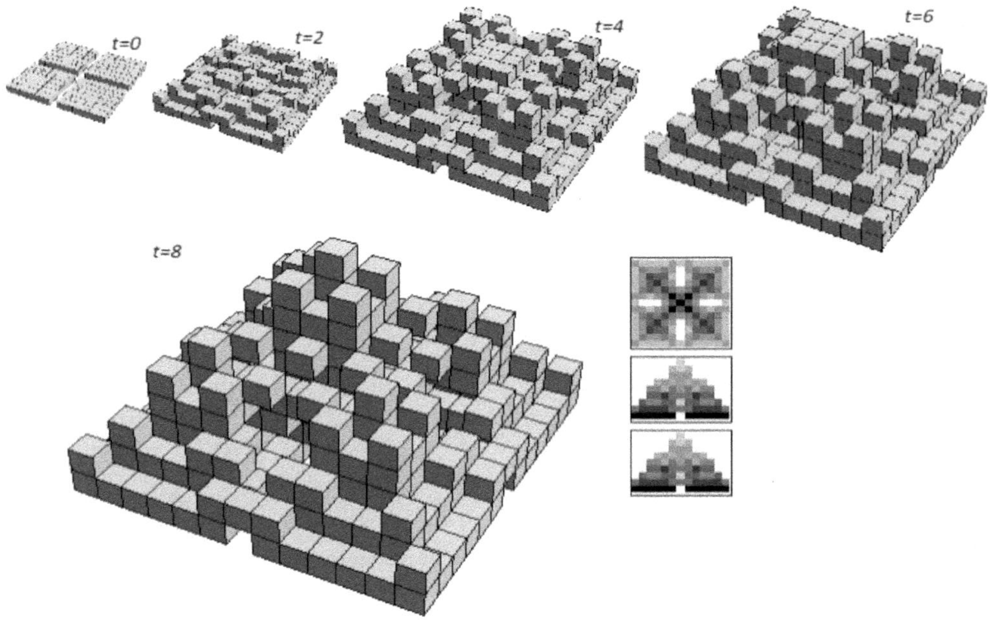

Figure 6. Borobudur Temple development algorithm using cellular automata.

Today, the global community enjoys technological advances in many ways, especially engineering and technology devices. This progress certainly changes the social-ecological landscape of everyday human life, both macro and micro. A life that feels individualistic, pollution everywhere, to the dredging of renewable natural resources. But on the other hand, technological progress is able to answer the problems that have been stored up in society. The advancement of computer technology can be used to study cellular automation, examine the geometric shape of Borobudur Temple and explain the kinship that arises from cultural diversity seen in several phylomemetic trees.

When modern science and technology can uncover the diversity of traditional culture in Indonesia, the excavations will open many interesting opportunities. The Indonesian culture digital library *budaya-indonesia.org* is managed by the community of Sobat Budaya Foundation in an effort to use information technology advances to celebrate cultural diversity. Through data collection, research related to culture can be delivered, information utilized for innovation and cultural protection can be achieved.

4 CONCLUSION AND CLOSING REMARKS

The high cultural diversity of Indonesia can be seen as a double-edged sword. On the one hand, it will create potential conflicts and social tensions if not handled properly, but on the other hand it can be a source of creative economy, a unifying tool of the nation and a source of knowledge in our modern era.

Similarly, the development of acquisitions and the use of computational and information science and technology techniques is currently very demanding. The development of technology accompanied by the heavy spread of information flow may yield a negative side if it is not able to be handled properly by local people. Thus the advancement of information technology, especially for those in rural areas, should be used as a tool to strengthen and protect the richness of Indonesian traditional culture. Cultural data collection in non-traditional and participatory ways is the first step in protecting Indonesian traditional culture.

By utilizing the information revolution, it is time for Indonesia to have a cultural information system. The government needs to create a traditional cultural database system in accordance with the Cultural Advancement Act No. 5 of 2017 that is able to protect human cultural resources (*Undang-Undang Nomor 5 Tahun 2017 Tentang Pemajuan Kebudayaan*). Of course, the government, both central and regional, can work with various cultural stakeholders in order to protect, maintain and develop traditional culture.

The Indonesian cultural digital library, which was built in the spirit of mutual cooperation, has three pillars to be carried. The first is the acquisition of science and technology based on culture. By having a digital library, research related to culture becomes a reality to be developed. We have demonstrated some of the findings and discoveries. Secondly, the emergence of economic innovation from the digital library of Indonesian culture can be a source of creativity and reference for other craftsmen. Thirdly, Indonesia's cultural digital library is a kind of intellectual property protection. Protection can thwart unilateral claims, patents or copyrights made by individuals and companies by using a database.

It is time for us to see Indonesian traditional culture as a source of information. The sound of *gamelan*, singing of Sinden, and even *rendang* food should be treated as information that can be processed scientifically as data. The recorded data is stored digitally and processed into information that in many ways can enrich Indonesian cultural life, embracing the new information age.

ACKNOWLEDGMENTS

We thank colleagues at the Sobat Budaya Foundation and Bandung Fe Institute for their input and assistance.

REFERENCES

Brown, P. & Hugh, L. (2000). Collective intelligence. In S. Baron, J. Field & T. Schuller (Eds.), *Social capital: Critical perspectives*. Oxford, UK: OUP.

Choate, M. (2007). *Professional Wikis*. Indianapolis, IN: Wiley.

Dahlan, R.M. (2009). Menggambar Neksus Tiga Titik: Sebuah Rekomendasi Saintifik Untuk Kebangkitan Indonesia. In *BFI Working Paper Series WP-1-2009*. Bandung, Indonesia: Bandung Fe Institute.

Dahlan, R.M. & Situngkir, H. (2011). Rekomendasi Untuk Rensans Indonesia. In *BFI Working Paper Series WP-III-2011*. Bandung, Indonesia: Bandung Fe Institute.

Laughey, D. (2006). *Music and youth culture*. Edinburgh, UK: Edinburgh University Press.

Republic of Indonesia. (2009). *Practical handbook for inventory of intangible cultural heritage of Indonesia*. Jakarta, Indonesia: Ministry of Culture and Tourism. Retrieved from https://unesdoc.unesco.org/ark:/48223/pf0000186978

Situngkir, H. (2007). Menuju Studi Kompleksitas Musik Indonesia. In *BFI Working Paper Series WPT 2007*. Bandung, Indonesia: Bandung Fe Institute.

Situngkir, H. (2008). Platform Komputasi Untuk Preservasi Budaya Tradisional Secara Partisipatif. In *BFI Working Paper Series WP-XII*. Bandung, Indonesia: Bandung Fe Institute.

Situngkir, H. (2009a). Evolutionary economics celebrates innovation and creativity-based economy. doi:10.2139/ssrn.1272122

Situngkir, H. (2009b). The phylomemetics of batik. In *BFI Working Paper Series WP-8-2009*. Bandung, Indonesia: Bandung Fe Institute.

Situngkir, H. (2010). Exploring ancient architectural designs with cellular automata. In *BFI Working Paper Series WP-9-2010*. Bandung, Indonesia: Bandung Fe Institute.

Situngkir, H. (2015). Indonesia embrace the data science. In *BFI Working Paper Series WP-II-2015*. Bandung, Indonesia: Bandung Fe Institute.

Situngkir, H. (2016). *Kode - Kode Nusantara*. Jakarta, Indonesia: Expose.

Situngkir, H., Maulana, A. & Dahlan, R.M. (2016). A portrait of diversity in Indonesian tradisional cuisine. In *BFI Working Paper Series WP-1-2016*. Bandung, Indonesia: Bandung Fe Institute.

Surya, Y. & Situngkir, H. (2008). *Solusi Untuk Indonesia*. Tangerang, Indonesia: PT. Kandel.

WIPO. (n.d.). Traditional knowledge and intellectual property - Background brief. Geneva, Switzerland: World Intellectual Property Organization. Retrieved from http://www.wipo.int/pressroom/en/briefs/tk_ip.html

Culture and International Law - Juwana et al. (Eds)
© 2019 Taylor & Francis Group, London, ISBN 978-1-138-38766-9

The investment liberalization policy in the ASEAN territory considered in terms of the welfare state concept

Delfiyanti
Lecturer, International Law Department, Andalas University, Padang, Indonesia

M. Jhon
Andalas University, Padang, Indonesia

ABSTRACT: In order to realize the Association of Southeast Asian Nations (ASEAN) single market through free channels for capital investment in ASEAN, the member states have unanimously agreed an ASEAN Comprehensive Investment Agreement (ACIA), which was signed in Cha-Am (Thailand) on 26 February 2009. According to ACIA Article 1(a) in correlation with purpose of formation, the agreement comprises a legal concept for foreign investment, a free-open investment regime in ASEAN to attain the final result of economic integrity in ASEAN economic society. The establishment of economic society will give the chance to member states to expand the scope of economic scale, improve tourist and investor interests, reduce costs of trading transactions, and restore business and trading facilities in accordance with the welfare state concept, Utilitarianism, as initiated by Jeremy Bentham (1748–1832). Historically, the idea of the welfare state is an expansion of classical or liberal legal state concepts, termed *nachtwächterstaat* (night-watchman state) by Immanuel Kant. Utilitarianism is an ideology providing an economic basis to legal thought. The purpose is massive welfare for the majority of people entirely, and the legal evaluation arranged by the consequences of legal implementation process. According to the welfare state concept, the existence of investment liberalization in ASEAN for economic society is an attempt to improve and realize welfare in the member states of ASEAN, through legislation. Finally, as the rules that have been agreed by the states, it must be implemented in tactical phases for the welfare of ASEAN society.

KEYWORDS: Policy, investment liberalization, ASEAN territory, welfare state

1 INTRODUCTION

The member states of the Association of Southeast Asian Nations (ASEAN) have agreed the ASEAN Comprehensive Investment Agreement (ACIA), which was signed in Cha-Am (Thailand) on 26 February 2009. This agreement is the revision and combination of two previous investment agreements agreed by ASEAN: the Framework Agreement on the ASEAN Investment Area (AIA Agreement) of 1998, and the ASEAN Agreement for the Promotion and Protection of Investment of 1987, known as the ASEAN Investment Guarantee Agreements (IGAs) (Thailand Board of Investment, 2016).

ACIA is an investment agreement or comprehensive investment in ASEAN intended to create a free and open investment regime in ASEAN with a final purpose of economic integration according to the blueprint of the ASEAN Economic Community, arranged by phases, such as 'progressive liberalization' or the investment regime of the member states (ASEAN, 2009). Full member states of ASEAN, therefore, will implement liberalization in comprehensive investment based on the concepts in ACIA.

Capital investment is one of many subjects liberalized in the ASEAN Economic Community with the intention of integrating capital flow among the member states of ASEAN, as there is a positive and synergetic relationship between territorial and direct integration to increase investment (te Velde & Bezemer, 2006, p. 41). According to Sornarajah (2010), ACIA is also a combination of the investment liberalization movement in ASEAN and protection of investment in the territory. Thus, the main purpose of the agreement is to provide stability between protection of investment, and protection of investment under the control of the national interest (Sornarajah, 2010).

The ACIA agreement was undersigned and ratified by all ASEAN member states. Indonesia was involved to undersign and ratify this agreement according to the Decree of President No. 49 of 2011 on legalization of the ASEAN Comprehensive Investment Agreement on 8 August 2011. Thus Indonesia was bound to implement the contents of the agreement and be involved in comprehensive investment liberalization in ASEAN. It is a challenge and also an opportunity for Indonesia to improve capital and foreign investments in Indonesia. Another thing that is no less important is the harmonization of the ACIA agreement, which intends to liberalize investment in ASEAN under the regulation of valid investment in Indonesia, especially in relation to Act No. 25 of 2007 on investment.

2 THEORETICAL REVIEW OF THE WELFARE STATE CONCEPT

Welfare state law is the combination of legal and welfare state concepts (Sornarajah, (2010). According to Burkens, the legal state is the state that sets the law as the basis of power and implemented under any circumstances beneath the law power. Meanwhile, the welfare state, according to Manan (1996), is the state or government that acts not only as the guardian of social order but is the main bearer of responsibility to bring into reality comprehensive social justice, common welfare, and social prosperity. The welfare state also attempts to attain social justice for the people, and also provides the opportunity for people to be independent.

Goodin (Nugraha & Mamudji, 2007, p. 19) argues that welfare states do not only attempt to compare the social class living in the state and regulating as well as giving direction of comprehensive economic activity, but also provides goods and services to individuals and families who meet the criteria for distribution of certain rights.

Moreover, it is known the term of social service or an agency of services (Iver, 1950, p. 4) (the state as the service instrument) or in Lemaire it is called *bestuurzorg* (Marbun, 1997, p. 166) (the state implementing common welfare) who concern about welfare state. The state and establishment process could be understood by study and investigating history and the doctrine of scholars at that time. In Logemann, the state is the power organization established by humans: in this case, the human known as nation, and power organization established by purpose to preserve of interest of group thus the organization had authority (*gezag*) and can push the will for people who depending on it (Soehino, 2004, p. 143).

Van Vollenhoven split the phases of state development into three: patrimonial state (*état patrimoine*), authority state (*état puissance*) and national state (*état-nation*) (Sihombing, 2010, p. 83). The principal differences between the three states are based on who held the power. In patrimony, power is in the hands of the king and his family. While the state border determined by power of control can performed by king, thus the borders almost change time to time, especially when new king was defeat the previous one has arisen. It is different in authority state that borders of the state and legal territory has order but people have not aware in comprehensive as the people of kingdom or sense of belonging as people of nation.

In the national state, people has aware on politics as people of nation and the state was already owned by people (Sihombing, 2010, p. 83). In the Middle Ages, Western Europe embraced the government of absolute monarchy. The state power in this model is centralistic in character such that power is in the hands of the king, who determines all decisions and the servant just mede bewind or co-administration (Sihombing, 2010, p. 85). Implementing and maintaining regulations, and trying people who broke the law was in the hands of the king. The absolute power of the king tended to be arbitrary. This total power led to Louis XIV of

France issuing the popular slogan that "the state is me" (*l'état c'est moi*) (Lubis, 2002, p. 55). A state with an absolute system of monarchy is known as an arbiter state, which means that the state is the king. At the time, the conviction arose among the people that when the king is prosperous, so too the people, but actually it is something that never happened, because the characteristic of a king in a state with absolute monarchy is arbitrariness (Sihombing, 2010, p. 85). The subsequent reaction to this situation led to a state with a constitutional monarchy, a state determine of border on power and will of king (no longer as the will of state absolutely) (Sihombing, 2010, p. 85).

In the next decades emerged the development of the basis of people demanding individual freedom from the influence and order of the king, known as the era of liberalism. In the liberal state model the rules are restricted to preserve and protect an economic order based on *laissez faire* and *laissez aller* principles (Utrecht, 1960, p. 21). The state responsibility in the liberalism concept puts stress on regular functions, including political functions, to preserve order and safety, and defense.

Immanuel Kant, as a follower of liberalism, argued that people's welfare must be comprehensively submitted to the people to accomplish the target, because the responsibility of government is only to preserve the order of law. The tenet of law state according to Immanuel Kant called type of liberal legal state (*liberale rechtsstaat*) that provides all over business of social welfare to the public. Kant firmly denied the intervention of the state in social economic living, and maintained the principle of *staatsonthouding* comprehensively; the existence of certain separation between state and people (Utrecht, 1960, p. 86).

Something that must be considered in the liberalism concept is that *staatsonthouding* restricting in firm between role of state and government in politics and economy, which believes the least government is the best government. The concept of a liberal legal state argues that the state is not the instrument of power, but the instrument of law. In Montesquieu, the state is not involved actively in the role of social living as the duty of the government is only to establish and preserve the law, or, in other words, the state only does the job of preserving the safety of the petty-minded, which is identical with a night guardian's duty (*nachtwächterstaat*) (Utrecht, 1960, p. 89). The government in a liberal legal state identic with responsibility in economic thus set the government as a ruling class in public that led to the incapability of government to improve of level of people for better direction (Utrecht, 1960, p. 90). Liberalism by doctrine of the free market only creates the scenario of the rich getting richer and the poor getting poorer.

The concept of a liberal legal state as taught by Immanuel Kant is in fact unable to create equality in social living, and even results in wider social inequity and also the concept of the advantage of a handful of bourgeoisie, while the weak class of the economy will be excluded in free competition (Utrecht, 1960, p. 91). The state do not have the role in correct imbalance of social and economic in common.

For centuries, the principle of the liberal legal state (*liberal rechtsstaat*) has been challenged by other scholars of law, who believe that the state should not be restricted only to preserving the rights and freedoms of the people, which means that they should not only sustain the common order but consider social welfare (Utrecht, 1960, p. 88).

Firstly, Jeremy Bentham, as an adherent of utilitarianism, believed that freedom for business without intervention of the government will finally create equality in the liberal state (Friedman, 1990, p. 273). Freedom just creates happiness for a handful of people without creating happiness for most, as predicted by Bentham. Finally, Bentham came to the understanding that the position of the state should not silence in discern the inequality occurred in common, and the state must also serve to restrain the accumulation of wealth for a handful of people: the state must create togetherness and equality among people.

The disappointed reaction of people to the model of the liberal legal state in Western Europe led to the modern legal state (*moderne rechtsstaat*) that contrasted with the (petty-minded) legal state. The state concept (*moderne rechtsstaat*) attempted to correct the failure existing in the concept of the liberal legal state by creating the social welfare state. The modern legal state called the welfare state refers to the state responsibility for securing the principal welfare of the public. Utrecht (1960, p. 22) argued that the welfare state as follows:

The government of modern legal state active in safety protection comprehensively that the social safety in common. In welfare state the liberal economic society has pass and liberal economic has changed by centralized economy (*centraal geleide economie*). It expected that the government in a welfare state can be active in regulating aspects of social living. The state should not act only as a night-watchman (*nachtwächterstaat*) as arranged by legal state in petty-minded, but must be active in finding out what is needed by the people in order to attain prosperity.

The type of welfare state in Western Europe in the 19th century was established by extensive transition and has great influence on the social values existing in common. The level of social living for those working in industry declined and resulted in social unrest in that period. In fact, the ambition of the revolution in France for independence, equality and fraternity was just a dream, as it was mainly the bourgeoisie who got the benefit of the situation. The emergence of industrial cities resulted in more poor people and at the same time there was an accumulation of wealth in small groups of rich people (Kusnardi & Saragih, 2000, p. 53). Increasingly, the laboring people suffered discrimination as their effort was extracted for employers' interests. The situation led to the struggle of class and power by laborers against the bourgeoisie as the owners of the instruments of production, especially in relation to the power of state (Kusnardi & Saragih, 2000, p. 90).

The opinion of Marx in *Historical Materialism* was certainly opposite to the previous tenet, considering that human awareness determines behavior and that humans with ambition are influenced by material around them. The state is an instrument of power to attain the ambition; meanwhile, the human interest in obtaining freedom could not be obliterated from the earth. The struggle of humans to find freedom is an attempt to be released from slavery and poverty, then in progress influence to the model of state and familiar until present (Kusnardi & Saragih, 2000, p. 91). The state attempted to cope with the situation by providing welfare guarantees for people in order to ensure that the social order was uninterrupted. In the next phase, the guaranteed provision is organized and institutionalized, so that the implementation is orderly. In progress, modern states are almost comprehensively categorized as welfare states by implementing systems to provide better social guarantees (Thane, 1996).

3 AN ASEAN INVESTMENT POLICY IN TERMS OF THE CONCEPT OF THE WELFARE STATE

The ACIA agreement consisting of 49 articles is part of the blueprint implementation of the economic society of ASEAN in order to realize ASEAN as a single market and production base, with the main element being the free flow of investment. In general, the ACIA agreement intends to improve investment activity among the member states of ASEAN and establish the competitive ASEAN territory as a destination for worldwide investors (Penasthika, 2013). Article 3(2) of ACIA states that the "Agreement shall apply to existing investments as at the date of entry into force of this Agreement as well as to investments made after the entry into force of this Agreement" (ASEAN, 2009). The purpose of the establishment of the ACIA agreement, as depicted in Article 1, is as follows:

> *The objective of this Agreement is to create a free and open investment regime in ASEAN in order to achieve the end goal of economic integration under the AEC in accordance with the AEC Blueprint, through the following*:
>
> *(a)* Progressive liberalization of the investment regimes of Member States;
> *(b)* Provision of enhanced protection to investors of all Member States and their investments;
> *(c)* Improvement of transparency and predictability of investment rules, regulations and procedures conducive to increased investment among Member States;
> *(d)* Joint promotion of the region as an integrated investment area; and

(e) Cooperation to create favorable conditions for investment by investors of a Member State in the territory of the other Member State.

Based on Article 1, the objective of the ACIA agreement is to establish a free and open investment regime in ASEAN to attain the final purpose of economic integration in the economic community of ASEAN according to the blueprint. Through this, the arrangement of the law on foreign investment in ACIA embraces a free and open investment regime.

This free and open investment regime is realized by actions such as: the "progressive liberalization on investment regime in member states"; stipulation of protection upgrading for investors of all member states and investments; increasing transparency and predictability of rules, regulation and conducive investment procedures to improve investment in member states; collective promotion of territory as the integrated investment territory; cooperation in creating a profitable situation for investment arranged by investors of member states.

In order to liberalize a free and open investment regime in ASEAN, the ACIA agreement was also reinforced by principles widely used and recognized in international agreements as depicted in Article 2 as follows:

This Agreement shall create a liberal, facilitative, transparent and competitive investment environment in ASEAN by adhering to the following principles:

a. provide for investment liberalization, protection, investment promotion and facilitation;
b. progressive liberalization of investment with a view toward achieving a free and open investment environment in the region;
c. benefit investors and their investments based in ASEAN;
d. maintain and accord preferential treatment among Member States;
e. no back-tracking of commitments made under the AIA Agreement and the ASEAN IGA;
f. grant special and differential treatment and other flexibilities to Member States depending on their level of development and sectorial sensitivities;
g. reciprocal treatment in the enjoyment of concessions among Member States, where appropriate; and
h. accommodate expansion of scope of this Agreement to cover other sectors in the future.

Moreover, the ACIA agreement contains legal stipulations of foreign investment as the basis for all member states of ASEAN to arrange cooperation and investment activity in order to promote liberalization in ASEAN. An arrangement of provision of capital liberalization related to the enactment scope of the ACIA agreement based on Article 3 points (1) and (2) effective toward:

1. This Agreement shall apply to measures adopted or maintained by a Member State relating to:
   a. investors of any other member state; and
   b. investments, in its territory, of investors of any other member state.
2. This Agreement shall apply to existing investments as at the date of entry into force of this Agreement as well as to investments made after the entry into force of this Agreement.

Furthermore, based on Article 3 point (3) of the ACIA agreement, the scope of investment liberalization involves specific sectors:

For the purpose of liberalization and subject to Article 9 (Reservations), this Agreement shall apply to the following sectors:

a. Manufacturing;
b. Agriculture;

c. Fishery;
d. Forestry;
e. Mining and quarrying;
f. Services incidental to manufacturing, agriculture, fishery, forestry, mining and quarrying; and
g. Any other sectors, as may be agreed upon by all Member States.

In addition to the principle above, in order to sustain foreign investment liberalization in ASEAN, the provision of foreign investment law in the ACIA agreement is also sustained by other relevant principles used by the international community (e.g. Most-Favored Nation/ MFN treatment). Thus, the national treatment principles contain provisions as follows (ASEAN, 2009, art. 5):

1. Each Member State shall accord to investors of any other Member State treatment no less favorable than that it accords, in like circumstances, to its own investors with respect to the admission, establishment, acquisition, expansion, management, conduct, operation and sale or other disposition of investments in its territory.
2. Each Member State shall accord to investments of investors of any other Member State treatment no less favorable than that it accords, in like circumstances, to investments in its territory of its own investors with respect to the admission, establishment, acquisition, expansion, management, conduct, operation and sale or other disposition of investments.

Meanwhile, the principle of similar treatment (MFN treatment) contains a provision as follows (ASEAN, 2009, art. 6(1)):

> Each Member State shall accord to investors of another Member State treatment no less favorable than that it accords, in like circumstances, to investors of any other Member State or a non-Member State with respect to the admission, establishment, acquisition, expansion, management, conduct, operation and sale or other disposition of investments.

In MFN treatment, each member state must afford investors of other states a treatment that is at least as profitable as it has given previously, in a similar situation, to investors of the member state, according to the licensing, establishment, takeover, expansion, management, implementation, operational, sales and other investment releases.

The principle of the most-favored nation is also a fundamental principle in international economic legal agreements. Principally, according to Schwarzenberger (1962, p. 230), the MFN clause is a non-discrimination principle among states. The principle requires that the state must provide a right to other states similar to that given to third-party states. However, the principle of MFN contains exceptions, as shown in agreements of international economic law. For example, there is an exception in the General Agreement on Tariffs and Trade (GATT) for the responsibility of MFN to all regional organizations or free trade areas. The exception is permitted in the implementation or provision of Generalized System of Preferences (GSP). It provides treatment of competitive (low) tariff levels to trading products of developing countries (Adolf, 2010, p. 26). Moreover, similar arguments are made by Steger in Davey and Jackson (2008) that the WTO agreement, Article XXIV, provides an exception to implementation of the MFN principle in correlation with trading agreements in the territory.

There exists in the ACIA agreement in Article 23 an exception for special and differential treatment for newer ASEAN member states, as follows:

> *In order to increase the benefits of this Agreement for the newer ASEAN Member States, and in accordance with the objectives and principles set out in the Preamble and Articles 1 (Objective) and 2 (Guiding Principles), Member States recognize the importance of according special and differential treatment to the newer ASEAN Member States, through*:

a. Technical assistance to strengthen their capacity in relation to investment policies and promotion, including in areas such as human resource development;

b. Commitments in areas of interest to the newer ASEAN Member States; and
c. Recognizing that commitments by each newer ASEAN Member State may be made in accordance with its individual stage of development.

Based on ACIA Article 23, ASEAN member states acknowledge the importance of providing special treatment and differentiating the new ASEAN member states such as Cambodia, Laos, Myanmar and Vietnam (CLMV). Such treatment and differentiation is not discrimination but an exclusion to provide an opportunity for new member states to adapt to the new provisions in ASEAN.

Thus, the principles of national treatment and most-favored nation treatment described in ACIA are in essence to forbid the discrimination act (non-discrimination) implemented to the foreign investor or investment arranged among the member states of ASEAN. Thus, each member state must provide fair and balanced treatment and protection, as well as comprehensive safety to investors (Article 11 point 1 of ACIA). Moreover, the discrimination act is also considered as contradictory to the liberalization regime of investment, as described in ACIA: that there is autonomy on investment flow for ASEAN territory.

Finally, the objectives of the investment liberalization policy by the inflow of new investment and reinvestment that in future will increase and give guarantees for the comprehensive economic and social development in ASEAN are described in the preamble of the ACIA Agreement: "...[a] conducive investment environment will enhance freer flow of capital, goods and services, technology and human resource and overall economic and social development in ASEAN".

Moreover, in the ASEAN Charter as the main legal instrument, the establishment of the ACIA agreement in the economic community of ASEAN also contains a welfare state regime as described in the preamble of the ASEAN Charter and Article 1 (points 5, 6, and 11), arguing that the final destination of the establishment of the ASEAN Community is to improve the social welfare of each member state of ASEAN:

- Preamble of ASEAN Charter:

  > To ensure sustainable development for the benefit of present and future generations and to place the well-being, livelihood and welfare of the peoples at the center of the ASEAN community building process;

- Article 1 (point 5):

  > To create a single market and production base which is stable, prosperous, highly competitive and economically integrated with effective facilitation for trade and investment in which there is free flow of goods, services and investment; facilitated movement of business persons, professionals, talents and labor; and free flow of capital;

- Article 1 (point 6):

  > To alleviate poverty and narrow the development gap within ASEAN through mutual assistance and cooperation;

- Article 1 (point 11):

  > To enhance the well-being and livelihood of the peoples of ASEAN by providing them with equitable access to opportunities for human development, social welfare and justice.

In the preamble of ASEAN, it is agreed to guarantee useful sustainable development for the present and next generations and to set decent living and social welfare as the pivotal points of the establishment process of the ASEAN community. Finally, as described in Article 1 Preamble of ASEAN, it is determined that establishment of a single market is intended to improve the welfare and ensure a decent living for the people of ASEAN by providing equal access to human resource development opportunities, social welfare and justice.

4 CONCLUSION

The regulation of foreign investment law in the ACIA agreement embraces that of a free and open investment regime of ASEAN in order to attain the final purpose of economic integration in the economic community of ASEAN. It is arranged by actions such as "progressive liberalization on investment regimes in member state" as described in Article 1 (a) and Article 2 of the ACIA agreement. This agreement also contains the "legal concept of [a] welfare state". It can be seen from the preamble of the ACIA agreement that the establishment of ACIA to liberalize, order and regulate investment regimes in the member states of ASEAN intends to improve of economy and social welfare of the ASEAN territory. Moreover, this is also described in the preamble and Article 1 (points 5, 6 and 11) of the ASEAN Charter. Thus, whether in the ASEAN Charter or the ACIA agreement, the legal instrument contains the welfare state concept.

REFERENCES

Adolf, H. (2010). *Hukum Ekonomi Internasional, Suatu Pengantar* (5th ed.). Bandung, Indonesia: Keni Media.

ASEAN. (2009). *ASEAN Comprehensive Investment Agreement (ACIA)*. Jakarta, Indonesia: Association of Southeast Asian Nations. Retrieved from http://agreement.asean.org/media/download/20140119035519.pdf

Davey, W.J. & Jackson, J. (Eds.). (2008). *The future of international economic law*. New York, NY: Oxford University Press.

Friedman, W. (1990). *Legal theory* (4th ed.). London, UK: Stevens & Sons.

Iver, M. (1950). *The modern state*. Oxford, UK: Oxford University Press.

Kusnardi & Saragih, B. (2000). *Ilmu Negara* (4th ed.). Jakarta, Indonesia: Gaya Media Pratama.

Lubis, M. (2002). *Ilmu Negara* (5th ed.). Bandung, Indonesia: Mandar Maju.

Manan, B. (1996). *Politik Perundang-undangan Dalam Rangka Mengantisipasi Liberalisasi Perekonomian*. FH-UNILA, Bandar Lampung.

Marbun, S.F. (1997). *Peradilan Administrasi Negara dan Upaya Administratif*. Yogyakarta, Indonesia: Liberty.

Nugraha, S. & Mamudji, S. (2007). *Hukum Administrasi Negara*. Jakarta, Indonesia: Center For Law and Good Governance Studies, Universitas Indonesia Law School.

Penasthika, P.P. (2013). The issues on personal status of investor in the ASEAN comprehensive investment agreement from the perspective of private international law. *Indonesian Law Journal, 6*, 67–86.

Schwarzenberger, G. (1962). *The frontiers of international law*. London, UK: Stevens & Sons.

Sihombing, J. (2010). *Peran dan Aspek Hukum dalam Pembangunan Ekonomi*. Bandung, Indonesia: Alumni.

Soehino. (2004). *Ilmu Negara* (6th ed.). Yogyakarta, Indonesia: Liberty.

Sornarajah, M. (2010). *The international law on foreign investment* (3rd ed.). Cambridge, UK: Cambridge University Press.

te Velde, D.W. & Bezemer, D. (2006). Regional integration and foreign direct investment in developing countries. *Transnational Corporations, 15*(2), 41–70.

Thailand Board of Investment. (2016). *Highlights of The ASEAN Comprehensive Investment Agreement*. Retrieved from http://www.boi.go.th

Thane, P. (1996). *Foundations of the welfare state* (2nd ed.). London, UK: Longman.

Utrecht, E. (1960). *Pengantar Hukum Administrasi Negara Indonesia* (4th ed.). Jakarta, Indonesia: Ichtiar.

Culture and International Law - Juwana et al. (Eds)
© 2019 Taylor & Francis Group, London, ISBN 978-1-138-38766-9

Online inventory access of Intangible Cultural Heritages of Indonesia

Zulheri
Faculty of Law, Andalas University, West Sumatra, Indonesia

ABSTRACT: This article aims to describe new laws for the Intangible Cultural Heritage (ICH) of Indonesia and the provision of public access to its inventories. Indonesia consists of various ethnic groups that each generate their own cultures and cultural heritages. Therefore, Indonesia is well-known and recognized as a rich and multicultural country. The problem of ICH is derived from the absence of regulating law to provide public access to its inventory. There are many reasons why a legal framework is urgently required to safeguard ICH. However, one of them is that it is needed to prevent the disappearance of hundreds of verbal languages. This research had been conducted using normative methods and legal terminology, reasoning and theory to present ideas ranging from the problem to the solution. In addition, the problem has also been addressed by using in-depth analysis to find an appropriate solution. From this research, I found that to safeguard Indonesian's ICH, it is necessary to provide a new law to protect, exploit and digitize cultural heritage to create legal certainty in the digital era. I concluded that it is necessary to issue a national policy for safeguarding ICH in a set of regulations, and institutions are required to manage its protection and exploitation. Substantially, such proposed regulations may consist of some of the following points: 1) definition of ICH that has Indonesian character in the form of values, community norms, and traditions; 2) reflection of ICH by ethnic groups; 3) registration of ICH; 4) legal protection (especially through intellectual property regimes, computer law, and other laws); 5) commercial exploitation of ICH; 6) digitalization of ICH; 7) digital access to Indonesia's ICH inventory; 8) infringements of ICH; 9) settlement of disputes; 10) amendments; 11) concluding clauses. From this conclusion, I recommend that a new law should be issued as soon as possible to protect ICH generated by various ethnic groups, and also to reshape and help the establishment of the national identity of Indonesia.

KEYWORDS: Intangible cultural heritage, online inventory access, intellectual property law, commercial exploitation, national identity of Indonesia

1 INTRODUCTION

Phenomenally, the Intangible Cultural Heritage (ICH) of Indonesia is still living, spreading out and developing in at least 300 different ethnic groups, without any safeguarding and protective measures under a specific national legal regime. There is no public access to the inventory of this ICH generated by such multicultural and ethnic groups of people. The problem of accessing ICH is also complicated by the process of liberalization of trade, the advancement of media and communication technology, and rapid social changes globally.

As a consequence, ICH has not yet been fairly exploited nor has it contributed toward the improvement of the lifestyle of the tribes associated with it. Such ICH is difficult for the public to access for commercial and non-commercial purposes. Some of the ICH generated by local people has even been illegally exploited by biopharma corporations. For example, researchers of such corporations have conducted research through biopiracy and bioprospecting measures into the mega-biodiversity resources of Indonesia that could potentially be patented to benefit the welfare of local people.

In addition, the opinion developed in UNESCO/Ministry of Culture (Republic of Indonesia, 2009) emphasized that:

> *The emergence of the process of trade liberalization in goods and services (globalization) is also threatening ICH. Such threats were changing the pattern of consumption, trade in services, massive out-migration, the pervasiveness of television and media, the advertising industry, tourism and other trends that brought effect to foster new cultural needs.*

As another example, there is a threat of the permanent disappearance of a hundred verbal languages. Therefore, it is necessary to undertake some measures to make an inventory both offline and online to be accessed by the public and corporations. This is not just to provide access, but also for managing, safeguarding and protecting ICH under a national law regime.

However, all of these influencing factors might be caused by the lack of a national policy and appropriate measures for safeguarding and protecting ICH. They may consist of: a) the process of trade liberalization (globalization) that has emerged, which impacts social transformation from communalism to individualism and competition; b) technological advancement, especially in telecommunications; c) the phenomenon of intolerance or different understanding that has emerged between individual ethnic groups of people or communities; d) civil war, as occurred in Syria. All of these causes trigger damage or destruction of cultures and their values, including ICH.

Legally, the core of the problem can be seen at international and national levels. At the international level, there are at least three international legal instruments dealing with cultural heritage, namely: 1) the 1972 UNESCO Convention concerning the Protection of World Cultural and Natural Heritage; 2) UN Security Council Resolution 2347 on the Protection of Cultural Heritage; 3) the European Directive on the Protection of Cultural Heritage. However, these regulate cultural heritage in general and are not specific to ICH. UNESCO realized that it is necessary to regulate ICH to solve its problems and, as a result, it filed the 2003 UNESCO Convention on the Safeguarding of the Intangible Cultural Heritage as an international legal instrument for protecting and safeguarding ICH (UNESCO, 2003). Under this convention, every state party is mandated with an obligation to promote, safeguard and protect the ICH in their jurisdictions. For that purpose, this convention, specifically in Article 11 (a), emphasized that "Each State Party shall take the necessary measures to ensure the safeguarding of the Intangible Cultural Heritage present in its territory". Therefore, complying with this article, Indonesia, as a member state, is *ipso facto* also obliged to manage ICH in its national law.

At the national level, Indonesia has accepted but still has not yet ratified the convention. Therefore, Indonesia, although recognized as a well-known, culture-rich, multi-ethnic and cultural country, has not yet enacted a national law to safeguard and protect ICH. So, the existing intangible cultural heritage of Indonesia is not safeguarded and there are no protection measures under national laws. This situation is endangering the ICH generated by various ethnic groups and groups of individuals who are living in hundreds of different islands. Therefore, it is important to realize that Indonesia risks losing its well-known cultural richness and multicultural heritage in the rapid changes of the globalized world. This means that some of the ICH that is affected by such changes could disappear. Therefore, to prevent such negative impacts, Indonesia as a party could play an important role in taking the necessary measures to ensure the safeguarding of ICH in its territory and, among the safeguarding measures referred to in Article 2, Paragraph 3 of the 2003 UNESCO Convention, identify and define the various elements of ICH present in its territory, with the participation of communities, groups and the relevant non-governmental organizations.

Then, under Article 12(1) of the 2003 UNESCO Convention, Indonesia should have inventories of its ICH. This article provisioned that "to ensure identification with a view to safeguarding, each State Party shall draw up, in a manner geared to its own situation, one or more inventories of the intangible cultural heritage present in its territory". Then, Indonesia shall report and provide information on the legislative, regulatory and other measures in relation to inventories of ICH when submitting its report to the Intergovernmental Committee for the Safeguarding of Intangible Cultural Heritage. For that purpose, Indonesia could provide offline and online access to its ICH for protection and commercial exploitation.

The root cause of this problem can be understood from a philosophical point of view: the absence of any law regulating ICH has opened up legal uncertainty in managing and exploiting ICH. This is rooted in the absence of a national legal instrument for the management of Indonesia's ICH. To overcome this, it is necessary to initiate a new law, not just for managing such ICH, but also concerning how to create benefit by sharing the exploitation of ICH owned by ethnic groups of people in Indonesia.

For that purpose, it is important to offer some possible solutions: 1) by providing digital (online) inventory access to the public; 2) by enacting a new law on the management of ICH; 3) by registering the ICH at the Directorate General of Intellectual Property Rights of Indonesia; 4) by introducing a model of a licensing contract on the exploitation of ICH.

From these solutions, the present work seeks to elaborate on the second, a new law on ICH management. In detail, this can be analyzed in four main ways: a) reasons why there is a need to protect ICH in Indonesia; b) identification and control of ICH; c) commercial exploitation of ICH; d) introducing a model licensing contract for ICH. In more detail, these four main ideas are presented through in-depth analysis and the introduction of new ideas as solutions.

2 PROBLEMS

With reference to, and by way of clarifying, the research question described above, this part would search for answers through two detailed questions concerning the absence of a law regulating provision of public access to an inventory of ICH:

- Why has the government of Indonesia not yet enacted a new law to protect the abundance and richness of intangible cultural heritage generated by the various ethnic groups of Indonesia?
- What are the substantial matters of a new law regulating the intangible cultural heritage of Indonesia?

3 DEFINITION OF INTANGIBLE CULTURAL HERITAGE

For the purpose of analysis in this work, there are two basic concepts that should be clarified: *culture* and *intangible cultural heritage*. The first of these, culture, is the core concept in the analysis of the problems. Dealing with this concept, Kant argued that culture is, however, "not static but in a continuous process of evolution". Then, in relation to ICH, UNESCO defined culture as "the set of distinctive spiritual, material, intellectual and emotional features of society or a social group, and all it encompasses, in addition to art and literature, lifestyles, way of living together, value systems, traditions and beliefs". Article 2 of the 2003 UNESCO Convention on the Safeguarding of the Intangible Cultural Heritage (UNESCO, 2003) defined 'intangible cultural heritage' as meaning:

> *...the practices, representations, expressions, knowledge, skills – as well as the instruments, objects, artifacts, and cultural spaces associated therewith – that communities, groups and, in some cases, individuals recognize as part of their cultural heritage. This cultural heritage, transmitted from generation to generation, is recreated by communities and groups in response to their environment, their interaction with nature, and their history, and provides them with a sense of identity and continuity, thus promoting respect for cultural diversity and human creativity. For the purpose of this convention, consideration will be given solely to such intangible cultural heritage as is compatible with existing international human rights*

instruments, as well as with the requirements for mutual respect among communities, groups and individuals, and of sustainable development.

Article 2 also clarified that such ICH manifested in the following domains: a) oral traditions and expression, including language as a vehicle; b) performing rights; c) social practices, rituals and festive events; d) knowledge and practices concerning nature and the universe; e) traditional craftsmanship.

4 MANAGING INTANGIBLE CULTURAL HERITAGE IN THE NATIONAL LAW OF INDONESIA

This section discusses why it is important to safeguard and protect under a national law regulating ICH. There are many reasons that can be advanced, including: 1) Indonesia's ICH has been developed naturally or originated from different cultures, tribes and regions; 2) the Indonesian ICH has come into realization in a wide variety of ethnic groups of people; 3) most of Indonesia's ICH is still not safeguarded and legally protected. Therefore, it is important to introduce a legal draft of law to be issued for safeguarding and protecting ICH at the national level.

To clarify such a legal draft of law for safeguarding and protecting ICH, it is necessary to substantiate the main points of its articles. They may start with: 1) a definition of ICH that contains Indonesian characters in the form of values, the community norm and traditions; 2) reflection of ICH by ethnic groups; 3) ownership of ICH; 4) a national authority for safeguarding and protecting ICH; 5) cooperation with the UNESCO Intergovernmental Committee for the safeguarding of intangible cultural heritage; 6) registration of ICH; 7) digitalization of ICH; 8) online access to Indonesia's ICH inventory; 9) legal protection of ICH based on intellectual property laws, information and technology law, and the law of biological diversity; 10) safeguarding measures of ICH; 11) participation of communities, groups and non-governmental organizations in taking the safeguarding measures; 12) commercial exploitation of ICH: 12.1) by holders or owners; 12.2) by licensee; 13) infringements of ICH; 14) settlement of disputes; 15) amendments; 16) concluding clauses.

Then, to ensure the enforcement of such a proposed law on ICH, it is important to specify what kind of competent national institution is needed to manage (for safeguarding and protecting) ICH. This is a kind of governmental institution that receives its rights and obligations from the state. Then, to establish a workable and well-functioning authority for safeguarding and protecting ICH, it is necessary to specify its functions as follows: 1) to issue any guidelines, operational directives and technical regulations regarding safeguarding (preservation, protection and promotion of ICH); 2) to act as a national authority for registration; 3) to file any expression of ICH and provide its classifications; 4) to establish a national network with relevant governmental institutions; 5) to have responsibility for identifying and inventorying ICH; 6) to promote creativity of each community to make their ICH sustainable; 7) to set up a national strategy for safeguarding and protecting ICH; 8) to ensure the potential of ICH can be commercially exploited to help to heighten the welfare levels for relevant local people; 9) to function as a national dispute settlement body for ICH; 10) to enact the laws to have specific regulation at every stage of protection, and their connections to other laws, and social and economic issues. In addition, this national authority should have to establish sub-division institutions that have different and specific functions that guarantee and ensure the enforcement of all provisions of such proposed laws on ICH.

5 MULTI-DIMENSIONS OF SAFEGUARDING AND PROTECTING ICH

In terms of the safeguarding of ICH, there are at least four dimensions that require attention: the law of intellectual property rights, the law of biological and ecological resources, the law of electronic information and transactions and the law of geographical indication. All four dimensions or legal regimes are described below.

5.1 *The law of intellectual property rights*

The first dimension of inventorying ICH can be seen in the Law of Intellectual Property Rights (IPR). From this dimension, Wendland (2005) advanced a series of questions on the relationship between inventorying ICH and Intellectual Property (IP) protection. His response was that it depends on: 1) what 'inventory-making' means in practice; 2) what is inventoried; 3) how and by whom inventory-making is undertaken. These three IP questions will arise at every stage of inventory-making: research, collection, recording, cataloging, classification, publishing, disclosure, updating, and so on.

Wendland (2005) also mentioned four types of elements that can be inventoried: i) literary, musical and artistic expression for which neighboring rights copyright law could apply; ii) performances and rituals for which performer's rights could apply; iii) signs, indications, marks and symbols for which trademark law could apply; iv) know-how and knowledge relating to the patent system. The implications of documentation and registration are not the same in copyright law, trademark law (including geographical indication) and patent law.

In addition, UNESCO's Expert Meeting on Inventorying Intangible Cultural Heritage (see Wendland, 2005) advised that:

> *The Convention attaches great importance to the preparation of inventories; Article 12 states that State Parties shall draw up one or more inventories, using stronger language than other articles dealing with the role of State Parties in relation to the Convention. The Convention presents the preparation of one or more inventories as a safeguarding measure in itself and at the same time as a prerequisite for further safeguarding measures: see Article 2.3 which includes identification in the set of safeguarding measures, and Article 12 which stipulates that inventories have to be drawn up to ensure identification with a view to safeguarding.*

Furthermore, there is much ICH that has the potential to be protected under an IPR legal regime. All such ICH could be the product of human creativity. Of course, they must fulfill one of the prerequisites or elements to be protected under IPR laws. According to Article 2.1, UNESCO emphasized that there are two elements of such a product of ICH: 'human creativity' and 'distinctiveness'. These two elements can be the minimal standardized elements to be protected by IPR law. Furthermore, this is also confirmed by Article 3(b) of the 2003 UNESCO Convention provided that "affecting the rights and obligations of States Parties deriving from any international instrument relating to intellectual property rights or to the use of biological and economical resources to which they are parties".

Due to the ICH having these minimal elements, 'human creativity' and 'distinctiveness', they could be subjected to copyright, patent, trade mark, trade secret, industrial design or other forms of IPR legal regime. Therefore, it is necessary to identify which ICH can be classified for protection under a specific legal regime of IPR. For instance, ICH that is fulfilling the two elements mentioned above, such as 'performing arts', can be protected under copyright law. 'Knowledge and practices concerning nature and the universe' and 'traditional craftsmanship' can be protected under patent law. Signs, marks and symbols can be made subject to trademark law. So there are many other manifestations of ICH that could be subject to a related IPR law regime.

To resolve the problem of protection, it is necessary to identify and classify related ICH. Identified ICH could be classified and or grouped into a specific legal regime of IPR. This effort can help officers of the inventory department of ICH management identify which ICH could be commercialized or just protected. This could also help in the process of putting ICH online on the Internet as a method of publication and advertisement.

5.2 *The law of biological and ecological resources*

The second dimension of safeguarding ICH can be seen in the perspective of the 1992 UN Convention on Biological Diversity (CBD). This means that any biological and ecological resources mentioned in Article 2 of the CBD convention are also subject to the ICH convention. Article 2 of the CBD convention states that "biological resources include genetic resources, organism or parts thereof, population, or any other biotic component of ecosystem with actual or potential use for humanity". As a consequence, any digitized ICH that is related to such resources could be advertised to the public. However, those that have the potential for being commercialized should be subject to patent law, trademark law and copyright law. This means that public access to digitized ICH having CBD's defined resources should be limited for commercial reasons or benefit-taking. By contrast, the rest of them that are being defined as public domain can be opened to public access. Therefore, there is a necessity to issue a specific policy for managing, publishing and exploiting ICH resources as defined in the CBD convention.

5.3 *The law of electronic information and transactions*

The third dimension of ICH can be seen from the perspective of the law of electronic information and transactions. From this dimension, ICH information has been transformed from analog to digital product and has been placed into an online method of publication. Thus, any digital product of ICH should be subject to that law. This means that any digital and online products of ICH can also be assessed as intangible assets to be safeguarded and protected by the 2016 Act no. 19 on Electronic Information and Transactions. Therefore, any digitized ICH should be categorized as electronic information that can be provided for public access. At this level, this digitized ICH will be subject to the definition of electronic information as provisioned in Article 1(1) of the 2016 Act no. 19 on Electronic Information and Transactions:

> *Electronic information is one or a group of electronic data, including but not limited to writing, sound, pictures, map, design, photo, Electronic Data Interchanges (EDI), electronic mail, telegram, telexes, telecopy or the like, letters, sign, figures, access code, symbols, or perforation, that have been processed that having the meaning or understandable by person who are able to understand.*

For the reason of providing online access, such electronic information in the form of digitized ICH could be uploaded to the Internet as it was sorted for the need of protection and safeguarding efforts. By taking this measure, the selected digitized ICH could be accessed and exploited by third parties. Therefore, this law can be applied to protect the digitized ICH, including the cases of violation and infringement perpetrated by third parties. Of course, this digitized ICH, categorized as electronic information, could become electronic evidence to be brought before a court. Therefore, any recorded digitized ICH information can be tracked and provided as evidence in the adjudication process.

5.4 *The law of geographical indications*

The fourth dimension of ICH can be understood from the Geographical Indication (GI) point of view. Here, there are symmetries between formal recognition as GI and as ICH. For example, Gangjee (2015, p. 556) described the "protection for the clay pots of Goiabeiras, from the Brazilian state of Espirito Santo . . . Brazil provided formal recognition for these pots under their intangible cultural heritage law, but supplemented this recognition with a registration as a geographical indication". He added that the idea behind the double recognition is to provide better marketing tools for the intangible cultural heritage and if necessary, "protection in the international market".

However, there is an academic debate around this double protection, although Van Uytsel (2015) concluded that:

When applying for a geographical indication, the production process has to be described and a control mechanism checking the compliance with the production process has to be established. Combining these two elements means that know-how, skills and practices are part of the GI protection. Such know-how, skills and practices can also fulfill the criteria of the definition of ICH, due to which GI and ICH could meet in the [Japanese] GI Act.

6 DIGITIZING AND ONLINING INVENTORY ACCESS OF ICH

This section discusses two points: digitalizing and placing online inventory access to ICH. The first one, digitalizing ICH, is a process in which any data of ICH is transformed from analog to digital form using computers or digital technologies. Digitalizing ICH (digital heritage) is still problematic, because of the risk of the data being lost to posterity. In this case, there are four factors contributing to such risks: the physical environment, the policy environment, the economic environment, and the legal environment. However, the main objectives for digitalizing ICH are to improve preservation, protection and promotion of ICH. This effort is not just vital for the cultural and economic development, it is important in the construction of the future development of national identity and national self-awareness of Indonesia. This means that the existing ICH can be transferred to the next generation, living in the digital era, while respecting the values, norms and cultural expressions that were created by previous generations. The digitizing process is becoming the management both of cultural assets and a source of economic benefits to be employed by groups of individuals or communities.

This digitizing process can also be a safeguarding measure, because these measures are aimed at ensuring the viability of the ICH, including its identification, documentation, research, preservation, protection, promotion, enhancement and transmission, particularly through formal and non-formal education, as well as the revitalization of the various aspects of such heritage. Furthermore, there are at least three main objectives for digitalizing ICH: 1) reshaping the future of Indonesian society by changing the mindset or frameworks of thinking of the current generation from the old norms to move on to a more moderate and modern pattern of thinking; 2) establishing a more modern civilized nation of Indonesia; 3) maintaining or increasing the national awareness of ICH and paying respect to the creativity of ancestors and/or members of the nation's older generation.

Complying with the objective of digitizing ICH, it is necessary to make comprehensive and complete documentation of the identified ICH. For that purpose, there is much manifested ICH that could be documented. This consists of: 1) oral traditions and their expression, including language as a vehicle of the ICH; 2) performing rights; 3) social practices, rituals and festive events; 4) knowledge and practices concerning nature and the universe; 5) traditional craftsmanship. With regard to the effort of digitizing ICH, it is necessary to consider which ICH could be documented and digitized. However, it does not mean that all of these forms of ICH can be digitalized. Of course, some of them should be kept securely, due to the obligations determined by related laws of patents or trade secrets and contract law. For example, a patented ICH containing obligations for secrecy cannot be disclosed to the public, including digitizing ICH. Therefore, identification of ICH can help to categorize which ICH can be documented or not. All ICH involving secrecy or undisclosed information that is subject to patented matters could not be made available in digitalized form or online. Thus, the rest of ICH that is subject to copyright law could be digitized. To make a secure inventory of ICH, it is important to set an intellectual property protection policy. This means that any information on ICH can be accessed publicly, except for those that for potential IP protection should be secured or kept in secret for commercial purposes under patent and copyright law regimes. In other words, such IP protection shall also cover any violations, infringements or cyber-attacks to be prevented by a national or provincial authority in managing ICH.

Complying with the ideas mentioned above, Wendland (2005) emphasized that there are four types of elements that can be inventoried: i) literary, musical and artistic expression for which neighboring rights and copyrights law could apply; ii) performances and rituals for which performer's rights could apply; iii) sign, indication, and mark symbols for which trademark law could apply; iv) know-how and knowledge relating to the patent system. The IP implications of documentation and registration are not the same in copyright law, trademark law, and patent law. Wendland reminded us that there is a series of questions on the relationship between inventorying ICH and IP protection, the answers to which depend on: 1) what 'inventory-making' means in practice; 2) what is inventoried; 3) how and by whom inventory-making is undertaken. IP questions arise at every stage of inventory-making: research, collection, recording, cataloging, classification, publishing, disclosure, updating, and so on.

To digitize such copyrighted ICH, it is necessary to build up infrastructures and facilities required for the digitizing process. According to the argument of Uneson and Wittenburg, "the use of this infrastructure is to foster the transfer of ICH to the Internet, permitting free access to fully interoperable, standards-compliant corpora of primary cultural heritage documents, as well as tools to exploit these documents". In this matter, the ICH authority shall set a national policy to manage the use of the digitalized ICH inventory data, which could be filed for two kinds of inventory. The first is the filing of basic ICH information that could be updated or enriched with new information. This should be facilitated with strong protection and kept away from any Internet connection. This inventory should be immune from intervention by unauthorized third parties, whereas the second inventory shall be employed for disseminating ICH. This will publish ICH online and provide open access to the public. This is not just for publication, but will also be used for advertising or offering the ICH for potential commercialization.

Then, the second discusses provision of online inventory access to ICH. In this matter, related ICH can be made available to the public transparently. On one side, some ICH could be freely accessed, whereas the rest could be subject to limited or restricted access. Therefore, these kinds of access to copyrighted and non-copyrighted ICH can help to classify or categorize them into commercialization stages that give advantage or sharing benefit for the users. There is a necessity to place ICH into the online regime of exploitation. This step is very important to organize ICH transparently and to commercialize it in the globalized market. Furthermore, the potential commercialization of this ICH can help local people or the ICH owners, both groups of individuals and communities, to change and modernize their life through the royalties generated by licensing their ICH. However, all of these steps of ICH management shall be controlled, guided and advised by an expert ad hoc community established by the National Committee for Managing ICH.

Afterward, the second ICH inventory can be given an online method of access. An authorized officer can upload any files of ICH after determining that such files can reside online. For that purpose, it is necessary to set a management policy for ICH to make it easy and simple for the public to access it. However, a group of individuals or communities should be engaged to participate in uploading, controlling and protecting their living ICH. Besides this, it is necessary to suggest that, in relation to the commercialization of ICH, any form of cyber-attack or cybercrime and the like should be prevented by appropriate measures.

7 COMMERCIAL EXPLOITATION OF ICH IN THE FUTURE

In discussing the commercialization of ICH, there are at least two main schemes of exploitation to be considered: 1) the use of ICH by the owners; 2) the exploitation of ICH by the licensee. Both schemes are considered below.

7.1 *The exploitation of ICH by its owners*

As we know, ICH developed by local people as a result of their human creativity has great potential to be commercialized, which of course benefits their welfare. Such ICH might be created and held by a group of people or by individuals. For the purpose of commercialization, the potential of this ICH can be exploited by its owners. In particular, all such ICH generated by its holders involving copyright or patent matters can be exploited through direct purchase by the local people who developed or own them. This means that they can produce and sell any product of ICH directly to consumers by deploying their ICH for both online or offline methods of purchase.

In the case of their products containing copyrighted material, their ICH in the domain of oral tradition and expression, for example, performing arts and festive events, can be directly used for exploitation. This means that their ICH copyrighted material can be manifested for business or commercial purposes. As a result, such ICH could contribute to and benefit them in terms of shared welfare in community life. So, this is one of the efforts by which to strengthen or heighten the living standards of local people by employing their ICH.

In the case of their products containing patented material, their ICH in the domain of knowledge related to the use of natural medicine resources, including traditional treatments for health, can be directly registered to the Directorate General Intellectual Property at the Ministry of Human Rights, Republic of Indonesia, as a competent authority. However, all of these methods or processes should fulfill the requirements for such registration of patents, and pass a substantive examination. Then, the registered patent of their ICH can be used in producing any patented natural medicine or other product using their ICH.

Then, for managing their exclusive right both in copyright and patent, it is necessary to suggest that local people should establish a collective legal entity in the form of a cooperative (*koperasi*). This means that they can produce their copyrighted and patented material resulting in financial benefit that in turn could change their life from a traditional one to a modern one. The chief of the traditional *adat* law system (clan or tribe) should be automatically appointed to manage such a cooperative to ensure its functional success, so that benefit-sharing to the members of their tribe can be fairly enjoyed and their living standards raised. However, due to the lack of knowledge of managing cooperatives among such chiefs, it will be necessary to employ a newly graduated student from the Faculty of Economics to be their counterpart in advising and managing them professionally.

7.2 *Exploitation of ICH by licensees*

Due to the lack of managerial knowledge for exploiting the registered patents of ICH by the owners (local people), it is necessary to take another option for exploiting such registered patents. In this option, both local people and the investor should come into a licensing contract for commercially managing and exploiting such registered or patented ICH. This scheme of legal relationship should be drafted to realize and manage the rights and obligations of both licensor and licensee, and should ensure the balance of rights and duties (obligations) of both parties.

To realize this scheme of relationship, it is important to substantiate provisions that can be grouped into the rights and obligations of both parties for a certain period of time. These provisions shall be organized in terms of the following points: definition, describing patented ICH, steps to commercialization, infringements, maintaining confidentiality of patented ICH, royalty payments, developing the patented ICH, and conflict resolution if a dispute arises during the enforcement of such a licensing contract of the patented ICH. However, for enforcement of this kind of licensing contract to succeed, it is important to establish a joint committee to control and evaluate the rights and duties of both parties in performing such a contract. This committee may consist of two persons representing the owners, two persons representing the licensee, and one person from the government.

To have an effective and workable licensing contract, it is necessary to provide some legal advice to local people, both individual groups of people or communities who do not have knowledge of related laws and licensing matters. Certainly, lawyers should assist them in drafting and enforcing such licensing contracts of relevant ICH, and managing their rights and duties fairly. Then, it is also necessary to be reminded of several legal principles, such as good intention, fairness, and balance of rights and obligations, and ensure that legal certainty is promoted and enforced in a good manner. All of these legal principles should be defined clearly and simply enforced.

8 CONCLUSIONS

I concluded that it is necessary to issue a national policy for safeguarding and protecting ICH in a set of regulations, and to establish institutions that are required to manage its protection and exploitation. Substantially, such a proposed regulation may consist of some main points: 1) definition of ICH that has Indonesian character in the form of values, community norms, and traditions, including its expression; 2) reflection of ICH by ethnic groups; 3) registration of ICH; 4) safeguarding of ICH; 5) legal protection (especially through intellectual property regimes and other laws); 6) commercial exploitation of ICH; 7) digitalizing ICH; 8) providing online access to Indonesian's ICH inventory; 9) violation and infringements of ICH; 10) establishing a National Committee for Managing and Exploiting ICH; 11) cooperation between national and international committees; 12) settlement of disputes; 13) amendments; 14) concluding provisions.

I recommend that such legal protection under the proposed law should be issued as soon as possible to protect and safeguard ICH generated by various ethnic groups, and to reshape and help establish the national identity of Indonesia.

REFERENCES

Blake, J. (2006). *Commentary on the 2003 UNESCO Convention on the Safeguarding of the Intangible Cultural Heritage*. Leicester, UK: Institute of Art and Law.

Borrissova, V. (2010). *Digitizing cultural heritage in Bulgaria: A survey of intellectual property-related experiences and practices*. Geneva, Switzerland: World Intellectual Property Organization (WIPO). Retrieved from https://www.wipo.int/export/sites/www/tk/en/resources/pdf/borissova_report.pdf

Corbett, S. (2016). Digital vs. analogue: Reconceptualising the orphan works problem for cultural heritage institutions. In J.C. Lai & A.M. Dominicé (Eds.), *Intellectual property and access to im/material goods* (pp. 289–314). Cheltenham, UK: Edward Elgar.

Dachlan, R. (2015). Indonesia's implementation of inventory obligation under UNESCO's intangible heritage convention: Problems in the online inventories. *International Journal of Cultural Property*, *22* (1), 131–151.

Gangjee, D.S. (2015). Geographical indications and cultural rights: The intangible cultural heritage connection? In C. Geiger (Ed.), *Research handbook on human rights and intellectual property* (pp. 544–559). Cheltenham, UK: Edward Elgar.

Hastanto, S. (2005, December). *Inventory of intangible cultural heritage in Indonesia*. Presentation at the Sub-Regional Experts Meeting in Asia on Intangible Cultural Heritage: Safeguarding and Inventory-Making Methodologies, Bangkok, Thailand. Retrieved from https://www.accu.or.jp/ich/en/pdf/c2005subreg_Indo.pdf

Hastanto, S. (2008, December). *Map of Indonesian culture as Intangible Cultural Heritage Inventory (ICHI) of Indonesia*. Presentation at the 53rd Society of Ethnomusicology Conference, Connecticut, United States of America. Retrieved from http://sem2008.blogs.wesleyan.edu/files/2008/10/srihastanto paper.pdf

Kurin, R. (2004). Safeguarding intangible cultural heritage in the 2003 UNESCO convention: A critical appraisal. *Museum International*, *56*(1–2), 66–77.

Kurin, R. (2007). Safeguarding intangible cultural heritage: Key factors in implementing the 2003 convention. *International Journal of Intangible Heritage*, *2*, 10–20.

Republic of Indonesia. (2009). *Practical handbook for inventory of intangible cultural heritage of Indonesia*. Jakarta, Indonesia: Ministry of Culture and Tourism. Retrieved from https://unesdoc.unesco.org/ark:/48223/pf0000186978

Sardjono, A. (2017). Challenges for ASEAN interoperability: Lessons for research on cultural heritage protection in Indonesia. In E. Ng & G. Austin (Eds.), *International intellectual property and the ASEAN way: Pathways to interoperability* (pp. 35–46). Cambridge, UK: Cambridge University Press. doi:10.1017/9781316711606.006

UNESCO. (2003). Convention on the Safeguarding of the Intangible Cultural Heritage. *United Nations Treaty Series*, *2368*, 3–94.
UNESCO. (2012). Operational Directives for the Implementation of the Convention on the Safeguarding of the ICH, adopted by the General Assembly of the States Parties to the Convention at its Fourth Session. Paris, France, June 4–8.Paris, France: UNESCO. Retrieved from https://ich.unesco.org/en/directives
Van Uytsel, S. (2015). *The new Japanese act on geographical indications: An intangible cultural heritage perspective*. doi:10.2139/ssrn.2692449
Wendland, W. (2005, March). *Management and ownership of intangible cultural heritage*. Keynote speech at the Fourth Session of the Expert Meeting on Inventorying Intangible Cultural Heritage, Paris, France. Paris, France: UNESCO. Retrieved from https://ich.unesco.org/doc/src/00036-EN.pdf
Xiaochun, S. (2016). Growing up in the 'digital' age: Chinese traditional culture is coming back in digital era. In K.J. Borowiecki, N. Forbes & A. Fresa (Eds.), *Cultural heritage in a changing world*. Basel, Switzerland: Springer. doi:10.1007/978-3-319-29544-2_15

Culture and International Law - Juwana et al. (Eds)
© 2019 Taylor & Francis Group, London, ISBN 978-1-138-38766-9

Legal protection of culture in Indonesia through the World Heritage Center UNESCO

Dyah Permata Budi Asri
Faculty of Act, Janabadra University, Indonesia

ABSTRACT: Protection of culture in Indonesia is an exciting issue nowadays. It is often associated with cultural disputes between Indonesia and other countries such as Malaysia. The rise of Indonesian culture which claimed ownership or used by other parties without legitimacy (misappropriation) became the reason for the importance of legal protection of Indonesian culture.

Moreover, it is important to protect the Indonesian culture because Indonesia is a country that has various cultures, especially when related to much income from the culture-based tourism sector. UNESCO, through the World Heritage Center, has carried out legal protection efforts on Indonesian culture by conducting an inventory and documentation of culture.

Inventory and documentation of cultures from Indonesia into World Cultural Heritage are one of the defensive legal protection efforts for culture from Indonesia, where preventive protection aims to prevent disputes. The attempt to register Indonesian culture into a World Cultural Heritage by UNESCO is an attempt to avoid Indonesian cultures so that foreign countries will not recognize the ownership without permission.

Up to 2018, Indonesian culture which has been recognized by UNESCO as a World Cultural Heritage is 10, consisting of Wayang Kulit, Keris, Angklung, Gamelan, Batik, Noken, Subak, Sekaten, Saman Dance, and Lumpia.

Inventory and documentation efforts carried out by UNESCO through the World Heritage Center are following the principles of Indonesian cultural regulation. It is stipulated in Act Number 28 of 2014 concerning Copyright, mainly Article 38 which regulates the Expression of Traditional Culture. It is also mentioned in Act Number 15 of 2017 concerning the Advancement of Culture in which the state must undertake efforts to manage and protect Indonesian culture by conducting an inventory and documentation.

KEYWORDS: culture, inventory and documentation, preventive protection

1 INTRODUCTION

Cultural diversity is the pride of the community and is a selling point for them. Based on the 2014 data, the number of foreign tourists coming to Indonesia are more than 9.4 million or grew by 7.05% compared to the previous year.[1]

Culture is a new legal problem caused by the absence of domestic legal instruments that can provide optimal legal protection. Besides, at the international level, the regulation of culture has not become an international agreement that provides legal protection, the Act of Intellectual Property Rights contained in the Trade-Related Aspects of Intellectual Property Rights, (TRIP's), can not accommodate the wealth of traditional communities or local people optimally.

1. Data from Statistics Indonesia 2014, accessed 7th of May 2015

In the legal system of Intellectual Property Rights (IPR) in Indonesia, regulation of traditional cultures is regulated in Act Number 28 of 2014 concerning Copyright. The regulation regarding traditional culture is contained in Chapter V concerning the Expression of Traditional Culture and Protected Creation, especially in Article 38.

The definition of Traditional Culture Expression following the explanation of the Copyright Act and WIPO is the culture both tangible and intangible. The culture is an ancestral heritage that was developed and maintained for generations by certain communities. The term Traditional Cultural Expression is almost the same as folklore as regulated in the old Copyright Act of 2002.

The obligations of the state to preserve the Traditional Culture Expression is mentioned in the Article 38 paragraph 2, "The State must inventory, maintain the Traditional Cultural Expressions as referred to paragraph (1)".

The state's obligation to all forms of Traditional Cultural Expression in the Copyright Act Number 28 of 2014 has been stated explicitly. The country as the owner of traditional culture (in this case the local government) has obligations in the framework of maintaining and managing the culture, including the requirement to carry out cultural inventories, keep and preserve the culture of all forms of violations and the use of traditional culture without legal rights. It's just that the provisions affirmed in the Act up to now have not been implemented due to various constraints, including the implementation of technical regulations and also due to human resources.

At the international level, UNESCO (United Nations Educational, Scientific and Cultural Organization) a particular body under the United Nations (United Nations) which deals with the issues of Education, Science and Culture has one program that aims to secure cultural and natural heritage. UNESCO in 1972 established and made a UNESCO World Heritage site (UNESCO's World Heritage Sites) which is managed by UNESCO's World Heritage Committee, consisting of 21 groups (21 state parties) chosen by the General Assembly in a 4-year contract. A World Heritage Site is a place of culture and nature, and objects that matter to humanity and become a legacy for the next generation.

This program aims to catalog, name, dictate, document, and preserve essential places to become the world's human heritage. Registered locations can obtain funds from the World Heritage Fund by fulfilling certain conditions. This program was created on November 16, 1972, through the UNESCO general conference.

A culture originating from Indonesia that has been registered at the UNESCO World Heritage Center so far there are 6 (six) cultures including Wayang, Keris, Batik, Saman Dance, Angklung, and Noken. Until 2013, the Indonesian government through the Directorate of Internalization of Values and Cultural Diplomacy of the Ministry of Education and Culture has registered 71 cultural works from various regions in Indonesia.

For the culture of Yogyakarta, only 1 (one) is currently registered as an Indonesian Intangible Heritage, Kasongan Pottery. And in 2014 the determination increased to 89, including 1 (one) more culture from Yogyakarta namely Bedhaya Semang Dance.

Traditional Knowledge Protection, especially those that are related to Traditional Cultural Expressions must also be a concern. This thing is essential as the efforts to protect knowledge, and traditional cultural expressions can be used as one of the drivers of increased regional income.

Provision of protection for Traditional Cultural Expression becomes essential when faced with the characteristics and uniqueness of its own. There are several reasons for the need to develop protection for the Expression of Traditional Culture. The reasons are "the consideration of justice, conservation, maintenance of culture and traditional practices, prevention of seizure by unauthorized parties to the components of folklore and the development of the use of the interests of Traditional Knowledge" Protection of Traditional Cultural Expressions has a decisive role in providing support to the community to preserve the tradition.

The significance of the holding of this research is the protection of the Expression of Traditional Culture is very necessary to prevent products belonging to the Indonesian people, especially those based on Traditional Cultural Expressions, so that their ownership is not recognized without permission by other countries.

Therefore, these products need legal protection. Moreover, it is clear that all wealth based on traditional culture has very high economic value. These efforts will undoubtedly encourage the improvement of the Indonesian economy and can improve the welfare of the community.

Based on the background of the above problems, the following problem formulation can be submitted:

1. Why is protection for the expression of traditional culture in Indonesia essential to be done?
2. What is the concept of protecting traditional cultural expressions that have been carried out by UNESCO through the World Heritage Center?

The purpose of this study is:

1. Want to know the reasons for the importance of protecting traditional cultural expressions in Indonesia.
2. Want to analysed the concept of protection of traditional cultural expressions conducted by UNESCO through the World Heritage Centre.

2 RESEARCH METHODOLOGY

This research is normative juridical research. According to Soerjono Soekanto, the prescriptive juridical approach is legal research conducted by examining library material or secondary data as the primary material to be investigated by searching for the regulations and literature relating to the problem under study.[2] This normative juridical research is carried out by examining and interpreting academic matters relating to principles, conceptions, doctrines and legal norms relating to the regulation of local wisdom and traditional culture in the Act of Intellectual Property Rights.

Data sources used in this study using primary data, namely data obtained from the field through observation, interviews, and data obtained from reliable sources, which are processed by researchers. Observations, interviews and data collection in the area can be collected from the informants who have been determined in this study. Interviews are conducted in a structured and unstructured manner. Structured interviews are guided by interview guidelines that have been prepared and carried out on the speakers, namely:

1. Head of the Yogyakarta Special Province Cultural Office.
2. Head of Denpasar Bali Tourism and Culture Office.

Besides, there are secondary data sources in this study in the form of data taken from library materials consisting of 3 (three) sources of legal material, namely primary, secondary and tertiary legal materials. Furthermore, secondary detail data includes of:

1. Primary Legal Material
   a. Copyright Act No. 28 of 2014 where arrangements regarding traditional cultural expressions are regulated therein;
   b. Act Number 5 of 2017 concerning the Advancement of Culture;
   c. Minister of Education and Culture Regulation of the Republic of Indonesia Number 106 of 2013 concerning Indonesian Intangible Cultural Heritage;
   d. As well as other International Regulations and Conventions related to this research.
2. Secondary Legal Material
   Namely legal material that explains primary legal materials, consisting of Literature, Scientific Journal, Dissertation, Thesis, Research Reports and other secondary legal materials related to this study

2. Soerjono Soekanto and Sri Mamudji, *Penelitian Hukum Normatif (Suatu Tinjauan Singkat)*, (Jakarta: Rajawali Pers, 2001), 13-14.

3. Tertiary Legal Material
   Tertiary Legal Material is a supporting legal material that is legal material that provides instructions and further explanation about primary and secondary legal materials, including Large Indonesian Dictionary, English Dictionary, and Black's Act Dictionary.

Data analysis in this study uses qualitative analysis. It means that it describes the data that is processed in detail in sentences (descriptive). Qualitative analysis is carried out starting from empirical analysis, which in depth is complemented by normative analysis. Based on the results of the study concluded deductively, namely ways of thinking based on facts that are general and then drawn a specific conclusion.

3 DISCUSSION

3.1 *Regulation of intellectual property rights in the Indonesian legal system*

Intellectual Property Rights internationally are better known as Intellectual Property Right (IPR), which are related rights arising or born due to human intellectual abilities in the form of discoveries in the fields of technology, science, and art. Intellectual property rights are not a new thing in Indonesia.

Since the days of the Dutch East Indies Government, Indonesia has had Acts concerning Intellectual Property Rights which constitute the enactment of rules and regulations of the Dutch East Indies government which were in force in the Netherlands such as 1912 Autonomy, 1922 Reglement industrial Eigendom colony, and 1910 Octrooi wet.

At present, Intellectual Property Rights have become a fundamental issue and get attention, both at national and international forums. The inclusion of the Trade-Related Aspects of Intellectual Property Rights (TRIP's)[3] in the World Trade Organization (WTO) approval package in 1994 signaled the start of a new era of the development of Intellectual Property Rights around the world.

Thus, the issue of Intellectual Property Rights cannot be separated from the world of trade and investment. The importance of Intellectual Property Rights in economic and business development has spurred the start of a new era of science-based economic growth.[4]

Indonesia is one of the countries that participated in signing the agreement on the establishment of the World Trade Organization (WTO) that was also mentioned about the arrangements on aspects of trade related to Intellectual Property Rights (Agreement on Trade-Related to Aspect of Intellectual Property Rights). Indonesia ratified the international cooperation with Act No. 7 of 1994 concerning the ratification of the World Trade Organization Agreement Establishing (Agreement on the establishment of a world trade organization).[5]

The Intellectual Property Rights System is an individual right. Because of its nature which is the individual's right, a person is free to submit an application or register his intellectual work or not register.

Besides, the Intellectual Property Rights system supports the establishment of a good documentation system in the form of human creativity, thus enabling the prevention of technological results or other similar works. With the support of proper documentation, it is expected that the community can make the most of it to support its life needs or develop further so that it can provide even higher added value for the creative work or findings.

3. This discussion is an international agreement in the field of intellectual property rights related to trade. This agreement is one of the agreements under the World Trade Organization or WTO (World Trade Organization) which aims to uniform the intellectual property rights system in all WTO member countries. Intellectual Property Rights are a new trade issue discussed in the Uruguay Round trade negotiations.
4. Muhammad Firmansyah, *Tata Cara Mengurus HaKI (Hak Atas Kekayaan Intelektual) Hak Cipta, Paten, Merek, Desain Industri, Desain Tata Letak Sirkuit Terpadu, & Rahasia Dagang*, (Jakarta: Visi Media, 2008) 6.
5. Tim Lindsay et.al., *Hak Kekayaan Intelektual Suatu Pengantar*, (Bandung: PT Alumni, 2002) 25.

In understanding the importance of recognizing Intellectual Property Rights, people must understand the principles of the Rights:[6]

a. Economic Principles
In the Economic Principles, Intellectual Property Rights come from the creative results of the human thought that has economic benefits and values that will benefit the rights owner.

b. Principles of Justice
In creating an intellectual work, it requires a lot of sacrifices to develop or find intellectual work both sacrifice of energy, mind, cost and time. Therefore, it is appropriate that the creator or inventor will get protection in his ownership from the illegal use by other parties. So that it can be said that the owner has the flexibility to utilize the intellectual work.

c. Cultural Principles
The principle of culture is the development of science, literature, and art to improve the standard of living and will benefit the community, nation, and state.

d. Social Principle
The social principle regulates human importance as they are the citizens of the country. Hence, the rights that have been granted by Act on an intellectual work are a unit that is protected based on a balance between individual and community/environmental interests.

The conception of Intellectual Property Rights is divided into two categories. Those categories are Copyright and Industrial Property Rights. Specifically, industrial property rights are divided into several parts, including Patent Rights, Trademarks, Trade Secrets, Industrial Designs, Plant Varieties, and Integrated Circuit Layout Designs.

In this discussion, the concept of Intellectual Property Rights is more alluded to is Copyright. Meanwhile, the object in this dissertation is Traditional Cultural Expression, where the object in the conception of intellectual property rights falls within the scope of Copyright.

In Act Number 28 of 2014, Copyright is defined as the exclusive right of the creator that arises automatically based on the declarative principle, and due to the regulations in the Act.[7] The work must be realized in real form without reducing the restrictions following the provisions of the legislation. Furthermore, Article 1 point 2 states that an Author is a person or several persons who individually or jointly produce a work that is unique and personal. And the meaning of the creation is stated in Article 1 point 2. On those articles, the creation means every creative work in the field of science, art, and literature that is produced from the inspiration, ability, mind, imagination, dexterity, skill, or expertise expressed in real form.

Based on the description above, it can be said that concerning rights, the government provides a Copyright concept. It is an exclusive right as the right is owned and controlled by a person or group of people as the creator or holder of the Copyright monopoly. It is also used to reproduce or announce the creation by the creator or other Copyright holders.

Creations that are the object of protection of Intellectual Property Rights include the fields of science, art, and literature, consisting of:

a. Books, pamphlets, display of published papers, and all other written works:
b. The lectures, courses, speeches, and other similar creations;
c. Props made for the benefit of education and science;
d. Songs and/or music with or without text;
e. Drama, musical drama, dance, choreography, wayang, and pantomime;
f. Works of art in all forms such as paintings, drawings, carvings, calligraphy, sculpture, sculpture, or collage;
g. Applied artwork;
h. Architectural works;

6. Elsi Kartika Sari and Advendi Simangunsong, *Hukum dalam Ekonomi Edisi Kedua* (Jakarta: Grasindo, 2007) 113.
7. Article 1 Item 1 Law of Copyrights Number 28 Year 2014

i. Map;
j. Batik artwork or other motif art;
k. Photographic work;
l. Portrait;
m. Cinematograph works;
n. Translations, interpretations, adaptations, anthologies, databases, adaptations, arrangements, modifications and other works of transformation;
o. Translation, adaptation, arrangement, transformation, or modification of Traditional Cultural Expressions;
p. Compilation of Work or data, both in a format that can be read with Computer Programs and other media;
q. Collection of Traditional Cultural Expressions as long as the compilation is an original work;
r. Video games; and
s. Computer program.[8]

In the Copyright Act Number 28 of 2014, the creator is not only those who have individual rights, but also the communal communities as the holders of intellectual copyright in the form of traditional cultural expressions of specific indigenous groups.

Traditional cultural expressions are collective and are often regarded as the property of the entire community. It doesn't only belong to individuals in the community and is carried out for generations traditionally. In the traditional formula, Traditional Cultural Expression based on tradition is a system of creation, innovation, and cultural expression which is generally hereditary and usually relates to a particular community or region. It also continues to develop following environmental changes.

The exclusion of traditional cultural expressions as intellectual property in the TRIP system is not solely because there are many principles of intellectual property in TRIP's that are not in line with traditional cultural expressions. Furthermore, it is the part of the global strategies of developed countries to exploit and explore cultural expressions in various developing countries, including Indonesia, without providing reasonable compensation.

The discussion of the need for protection for Traditional Knowledge has become an essential issue in meetings of the Intellectual Property Rights Council (Council for Trade-Related Aspects of Intellectual Property Rights) at the WTO. The existence of this long debate has more to do with whether or not the protection of Traditional Knowledge is regulated separately (sui generis) or incorporated into the legislation of Intellectual Property Rights of each member country.

The injustice felt by developing countries occurs because the Expression of Traditional Culture of the nations in the third world does not receive protection as Intellectual Property in developed countries.[9] The injustice is also reflected in the Copyright Act Number 28 of 2014 where the protection concept is individual liberalism. Whereas, the Traditional Cultural Expression regulated in the Act adheres to common principles of togetherness, which do not fit in with the spirit of the Act. Therefore, it can be ascertained that the application becomes blurred, where the aspect of protection from the Expression of Traditional Culture is different from the type of Copyright.

In such a society the governing Act also reflects the transitional period. It is described as the face of the Act that rests on two legs with different steps. One foot is stepping in a modern Act style while the other foot is still following the traditional Act. Normatively the Act that regulates Copyright issues does not contain many problems to be applied in Indonesia, but culturally there will be many problems in its implementation.[10]

8. Article 40 Point (1) Law of Copyrights Number 28 Year 2014
9. Agus Sardjono, *Hak Kekayaan Intelektual dan Pengetahuan Tradisional*, (Bandung: PT. Alumni, 2010) 35.
10. Budi Agus Riswandi, *Hak Kekayaan Intelektual dan Budaya Hukum*, (Jakarta; PT. Raja Grafindo Persada, 2005) 201-202.

Indonesian people who have cultural diversity, ethnicity, customs, actually contain elements of the possible variety of large Intellectual Property Rights and also potential conflicts between nations. It might happen when the culture of the nation is ultimately claimed for ownership as foreign state property. Moreover, the cultures are the result of the creativity of indigenous peoples or certain tribes regions that are produced from generation to generation and preserved by the next generation.

Some Intellectual Property and traditional Indonesian culture have been recognized as the culture of other nations such as Pendet Dance, Wayang, and Reog Ponorogo (it were claimed to be Malaysian inheritance).[11] Likewise, the ancient manuscripts of the indigenous peoples of South SuActesi and Southeast SuActesi have been owned and digitalized by Malaysia.[12] Several cases have emerged in the last period, such as Malaysia's claim to Indonesian cultures of batik, wayang kulit, and Rasa Sayange songs.[13]

Malaysia claims that the song Rasa Sayange has been recognized by Malaysia since the colonial era. The Dutch East Indies army or the Nederlands Indische Leger (KNIL) Koninklijk introduced the song from Ambon when they came to the peninsula such as in Kuala Lumpur, Johor and Pinang Island between 1936 and 1939.[14]

Malaysia and Indonesia have taken middle courses in cases of claims of some Indonesian cultures by Malaysia. These efforts include making diplomatic[15] agreements through state representatives in each of the Foreign Ministries. But the peace agreement is not an effective way to prevent cultural heritage conflicts from being repeated. For that reason, there are still no definite answers regarding the resolution of the two countries' disputes.

The abundance of diversity of Indonesian traditional culture is one of the factors of why it is essential to preserving traditional cultural expressions for the Indonesian people. Besides that, several external factors must be considered. The first is the use of the culture by a foreign party, without considering the economic aspects and moral aspects arising from the utilization. Then, the existence of an inadequate Conventional IPR system in providing effective and efficient protection for Indonesian culture, as well as concerning efforts to support the creation of international conventions in the field of Traditional Cultural Expression.

3.2 *Legal protection of traditional cultural expression in Act Number 28 of 2014 regarding copyright*

Legal protection is a protection to human rights that are harmed by others. The protection is given to the community so that they can enjoy all the rights granted by Act. In other words, legal protection is a variety of legal remedies that must be provided by Act enforcement officers to give a sense of security, both in mind and physically from interference and various threats from any party.[16]

Indonesia's struggle as a developing country for legal protection continues to be held to formulate the right protection system for the Traditional Cultural Expression. One of them is by making a Bill on Traditional Knowledge and Traditional Cultural Expressions (RUU

11. Rights Research and Develompent, ndonesian Ministry of Law, *Perlindungan Kekayaan Intelektual Atas Pengetahuan Tradisional dan Ekpresi Budaya Tradisional Masyarakat Adat*, (Bandung, Alumni, 2013) 3.
12. Musafir Kelana and Abubakar Eby Hara. 2011. 'Quo-vadis Kekerabatan MalaysiaIndonesia' (2009) 2(2) *Jurnal Komunikasi Massa*, 97-111.
13. ibid
14. Wulan Anggiet Purnamasari, 'Penyelesaian Sengketa Perselisihan Tradisional Dan Ekspresi Budaya Antar Negara: Sengketa Lagu Rasa Sayange Antara Negara Indonesia Dan Negara Malaysia', (2015) 45(4) *Jurnal Hukum dan Pembangunan*, 8.
15. Leni Putri Lusianti and Faisyal Rani, 'Model Diplomasi Indonesia Terhadap UNESCO Dalam Mematenkan Batik Sebagai Warisan Budaya Indonesia Tahun 2009', (2012) 3(2) *Jurnal Transnasional*, Universitas Riau, 10
16. Satjipto Rahardjo, Ilmu Hukum (Bandung: PT. Citra Aditya Bakti, 6th ed, 2006) 54

PTEBT), which until now has not been enacted as a Act[17]. Arrangements regarding the Expression of Traditional Culture in Indonesia are also related to the government's efforts to provide legal protection to parties who have interests/ownership of Traditional Cultural Expressions. Protection of Expressions of Traditional Culture is regulated in Act Number 28 of 2014 concerning Copyright.

Definition of Copyright in Article 1 point 1 of Act Number 28 of 2014 concerning Copyright reads: "Copyright is the exclusive right of the creator that arises automatically based on declarative principles after work is realized in real form without reducing restrictions following the provisions of the Act invitation."

In the explanation of Article 4 of Act Number 28 the Year 2014 concerning Copyright, exclusive rights are the right that is only intended for the Creator, so that no party can use that right without the Author's permission. The word "no other party" in the explanation refers to a single right which indicates only the Creator may obtain such rights. Exclusive means particular, unique, specifications.

Act Number 28 of 2014 concerning Copyright, also regulates the Expression of Traditional Culture. Can be seen in Article 38 Paragraphs (1), (2), (3) and (4) of the Copyright Act, will be submitted as follows:

(1) The State holds copyright on Traditional Cultural Expressions
(2) The State is obliged to inventory, maintain, and maintain the Expression of Traditional Culture as referred to in paragraph (1).
(3) The use of traditional cultural expressions as referred to in paragraph (1) must pay attention to the values that live in the community of its development.
(4) Government Regulation shall regulate further provisions concerning Copyright held by the State for the Expression of Traditional Culture as referred to in paragraph (1).

Traditional Cultural Expression according to the explanation of Article 38 paragraph 1 of Act No. 28 of 2014 which includes one or a combination of forms of expression, includes:

a. Textual Verbal, both oral and written, in the kind of prose and poetry, in various themes and content of message content, in the form of literary or informative narratives;
b. Music, it includes vocal, instrumental, or a combination of them;
c. Motion, including, among others, dance;
d. Theater, including among others, folk puppet shows and plays;
e. Fine art, both two-dimensional and three-dimensional forms made of various materials such as leather, wood, bamboo, metal, stone, ceramics, paper, textiles, etc. or a combination thereof; and
f. Traditional ceremonies

The expression must show the existence of individual and collective intellectual activities to meet the requirements of traditional cultural expression. Both of them must have the characteristic of the identity and heritage of a community and has been maintained, developed or used by the community, or by individuals who have the right or responsibility to do so following the Act and standard practices/customs in the community.[18]

The concepts of protection coverage for traditional cultural expressions are closely related to the region as a "bearer" of traditional culture, so that the regional government, both provincial and district/city holds essential duties and functions in its protection and utilization.

In Act Number 5 the Year 2017 concerning the Advancement of Culture, it is also explained about the concept of protection of culture in Article 1 Point 4 of the Act. Protection is an effort to maintain the sustainability of Culture employing inventory, security, maintenance,

17. Dyah Permata Budi Asri, 'Perlindungan Hukum Preventif Terhadap Ekspresi Budaya Tradisional di Daerah Istimewa Yogyakarta Berdasarkan Undang-undang Nomor 28 Tahun 2014 Tentang Hak Cipta', (2018) 1(1) *e-journal of Intellectual Property* year 4.
18. Afrillyana Purba, Andrian Krisnawati and Gazalba Shaleh, *TRIP's-WTO dan Hukum HKI Indonesia*, (Jakarta; Rineka Cipta, 2005) 103.

rescue, and publication. In more detail on the way of inventory, protection, rescue, and publication is regulated in detail in the following articles, in the Protection Section Article 16 to Article 29 of the Act.

The state as the highest authority, and the regional government as a state representative can prevent monopoly or commercialization by foreign parties without the permission of the state as the copyright holder.

And the state also holds the role the Copyright Holder of Traditional Cultural Expressions obtains Exclusive Rights to the Copyright. The exclusive rights regulated by the Copyright Act are the right to publish, copy, translate, adapt, transform, distribute, display and announce.

A work whose period of protection is not limited is a work classified into traditional cultural expressions. This case can be seen from Article 60 paragraph (1) of Act Number 28 of 2014 which contains: Copyright on Expressions of Traditional Culture held by the state as referred to in Article 38 paragraph (1) applies indefinitely. This article is aimed at protecting traditional works. However, even though the purpose of article 60 is to protect intellectual works in the form of culture, customs and cultural values contained in indigenous communities, it will be difficult for traditional societies to use them to protect these intellectual works. On the one hand, in reality, there is no effort from the state to preserve traditional works exploited by other countries or foreign parties who do not have the right to exploit.

The legal system of Intellectual Property Rights on Traditional Cultural Expressions (which has been stipulated in Act Number 28 of 2014 concerning Copyright) has not fulfilled the needs of the community for the protection of Traditional Cultural Expressions. The rule of Act still needs improvement because the problems in the field of Copyright (especially regarding the Expression of Traditional Culture and the right of Indigenous people who owns the traditional culture) have not been fully accommodated in this Act.

The problem is that the Copyright regime that has been echoed so far is used merely in the effort of legal protection against intellectual works that are more likely to be individualistic. This thing is still a problem in efforts to protect traditional cultural expressions.[19]

Besides, indigenous and tribal peoples as the community that owns the Expression of Traditional Culture feel that exploitation of the culture has an impact on the social identity that is abused. It is even slowly distorted and loses sacred and noble cultural values and customs, turning into mere commercial commodities. This is the background of the need for a legal system that can provide comprehensive protection against Traditional Cultural Expressions (sui generis).

3.3 *The protection of traditional culture expression (EBT) from UNESCO through World Heritage Center*

Recognition of cultural aspects and traditional knowledge has now been carried out by UNESCO. UNESCO coordinates and verifies things that are considered as cultural heritage in the world. This is because UNESCO is an institution or body established by the United Nations (UN) in 1945 and is devoted to supporting peace and security by promoting cooperation between countries through education, science and culture to enhance mutual respect based on justice, the rule of Act, human rights, and essential freedom.[20]

To support these programs, the UNESCO Indonesian National Commission was formed (KNIU). KNIU is an institution tasked with launching the business and coordinating activities in the fields of education, science, culture and communication in the Government and UNESCO Program.

KNIU was established following the constitution of UNESCO 1945 on Article 7. The article reads as follows: "Each Member of State shall make such arrangements as its particular conditions to associate its principal bodies interested in educational, scientific and cultural

19. Dyah Permata Budi Asri, 'Perlindungan dan Pengelolaan Budaya Lokal di Kota Yogyakarta', (2016) 1(1) *Jurnal Kajian Hukum*, Fakultas Hukum Universitas Janabadra, 5.
20. Article 1 UNESCO constitution

matters with the work of the Organization, preferably by the formation of a broad National Commission representative of the government and such bodies".

As a form of Indonesia's participation to actualize work programs from UNESCO related to the field of culture, several International Conventions and Protocols have been ratified by Indonesia. The Convention and the Protocol are as follows:

Table 1. The list of Conventions and International Protocols that have been ratified by the Indonesian Government

No.	Convention/Protocol	Date Of Deposit	Type of Deposit
1.	Convention for the Protection of Cultural Property in the Event of Armed Conflict with Regulations for the Execution of the Convention. The Hague, 14 May 1954.	10/01/1967	Ratification
2.	Protocol to the Convention for the Protection of Cultural Property in the Event of Armed Conflict. The Hague, 14 May 1954.	26/07/1967	Ratification
3.	Convention concerning the Protection of the World Cultural and Natural Heritage. Paris, 16 November 1972.	06/07/1989	Acceptance
4.	Convention for the Safeguarding of the Intangible Cultural Heritage. Paris, 17 October 2003	15/10/2007	Acceptance
5.	Convention on the Protection and Promotion of the Diversity of Cultural Expressions. Paris, 20 October 2005.	12/01/2012	Accession

By ratifying various international conventions and protocols, Indonesia faces significant consequences and responsibilities. Multiple policies at the national level related to the field of culture, encourage the government to commit to protect and promote the diversity of cultural expressions.

In the future, Indonesia's responsibilities and roles are even more severe and prominent. Moreover, if it is associated with various developments and challenges that have the potential to destroy the existence and continuity of world cultures with all the diverse values.

Here are the culture in Indonesia which has received recognition from UNESCO as a world cultural heritage originating from Indonesia: Komodo National Park; Ujung Kulon National Park; Lorenz National Park in Papua; Tropical Rain Forest in Sumatra; Sangiran site; Borobudur temple; Prambanan temple; Shadow Puppets; Keris; Angklung; Gamelan; Batik; Noken; Subak in Bali; Sekaten; Saman dance; and spring rolls.

Whereas in 2015 Indonesia's request to submit 3 (three) Traditional Dance Groups in Bali (Three Genres of Traditional Dance in Bali), the world heritage from Indonesia was postponed from the 2016 nomination plan to 2017.[21]

UNESCO World Heritage has 981 sites, with details: 759 cultural heritage; 193 natural heritage; and 29 a mixture of cultural and natural heritage (non-material cultural works).[22] The World Heritage Center program aims to classify, name and preserve essential places to become the world's human heritage. Registered sites can obtain funds from the World Heritage Fund through certain conditions.

The cultural requirements of a country both in the form of sites and non-cultural objects have been determined in The Criteria for Selection in assessing the culture of a nation that constitutes world cultural heritage or world heritage sites/culture.

Many elements of culture in the world are threatened with extinction due to the effects of globalization policy on uniformity and lack of means, appreciation and understanding, and the lack of interest among young people to study the components of cultures (especially to maintain its sustainability.) That is the reason why in 2003, UNESCO formulated a Convention for the Safeguarding of Intangible Cultural Heritage (for further writing abbreviated ICH). Considering the importance of this, the ICH itself has been ratified by Indonesia

21. <http://whc.unesco.org/en/statesparties/id> accessed on 16th of October 2016
22. Ibid

through the Presidential Regulation of the Republic of Indonesia Number 78 of 2007 concerning the Ratification of the ICH.

ICH is an International Convention that regulates and save cultural heritage through UNESCO international institutions. ICH has the responsibility for preserving intangible cultural heritage, setting the scope for 'safeguards' under this convention. It is stated in Article 2 paragraph (1) that the scope of "intangible cultural heritage" is as follows:[23] "The intangible cultural heritage means the practices, expressions, knowledge, skills as well as the instruments, objects, artifacts, and cultural spaces, associated therewith communities, groups and, in some cases, individuals, recognize, as part of their cultural heritage.

To get world recognition for national cultural heritage, Indonesia must follow the stages and formats determined by UNESCO. In the first phase, the cultural branch must be registered as a national cultural heritage, the registration of culture as an intangible national cultural heritage, in Indonesia managed by the Directorate General of Culture, Ministry of Education and Culture. After that, it can only enter the next stage to get world recognition. After recording as a national cultural heritage, then it will propose to the world cultural heritage.

It also needs a long process to reach the world recognition. For example, the award for natural heritage in the form of a Subak landscape patterned irrigation in Bali takes 12 years to be approved at the UNESCO meeting in July 2012 finally.

It is not easy to get recognition from UNESCO. Even so, there are many advantages that we can get both regarding prestige and funding. The recognition of UNESCO means world recognition as well, which will improve the image of the Indonesian people in the eyes of the international community.[24] There is appreciation and pride of the nation when Indonesia's cultural heritage is known to the world.

In addition to obtaining funding from UNESCO related to the preservation of cultural heritage, automatically the international attention will be drawn to Indonesia. Moreover, if one day there is a problem with the inheritance. For example, the earthquake event in Yogyakarta Special Region on May 2, 2006, that caused damage to the Prambanan Temple. As one of the world-recognized sites through UNESCO, many countries offer assistance in the form of repair costs and expert support. This case is a positive impact of entering Indonesian culture into a world heritage through the UNESCO World Heritage Center.

On the contrary, Indonesian culture can be claimed by other parties, if the government does not register it with UNESCO. The reason is, there is no recognition that the culture belongs to Indonesia.

On the one hand, recognition by UNESCO has severe consequences. The first consequence is that Indonesia is obliged to maintain, preserve and pass on a relay to the next generation. Secondly, periodically, Indonesia must report to UNESCO regarding the condition of these inheritances. If Indonesia does not carry out these obligations, then UNESCO will provide sanctions namely the revocation or removal of the site or the world cultural heritage from the recognition of UNESCO.[25]

Meanwhile, Indonesia must also pay attention to the responsibility for management of cultural heritage preservation related to intangible heritage. Because, if Indonesia is negligent, then UNESCO will also provide the same sanctions, moreover, if these legacies have been established as world heritage.

The management of the Indonesian Intangible Cultural Heritage should be a shared responsibility between the Government, the Regional Government and all elements of society. All

23. *Convention For The Safeguarding Of The Intangible Cultural Heritage*, UNESCO, Paris 17 October 2003, 2.
24. When Indonesia has ratified one of the UNESCO conventions, it has the right to propose a wealth of Indonesian cultural heritage that includes three categories, site heritage, natural heritage, and intangible inheritance and if UNESCO has recognized one of these proposals, then Indonesia has the right to obtain restoration fees, or other costs related to the preservation of the world heritage.
25. UNESCO sanctions are also faced by Indonesia, which is one of the world's natural heritage in Sumatra, the Sumatra Tropical Rainforest. The natural heritage has been repeatedly recommended to be included in the "in danger" list, but the status was only set in mid-2011.

must work together concerning protection, development, marketing, investment and business, and community empowerment.

4 CONCLUSION AND SUGGESTIONS

4.1 *Conclusion*

a. We need the arrangements regarding the protection of traditional cultural expressions so that the existence of culture in Indonesia will get protection from the potential claims of ownership by other nations/external parties. The real problem that has happened is the dispute over cultural property between Indonesia and Malaysia.
b. The expression of traditional culture needs to be managed and protected to guarantee the interests of indigenous peoples as their owners. Nowadays, the existence of traditional cultural expressions can be eroded due to the globalization. There is a possibility that the culture will become extinct/disappear along with the development of globalization in the community.
c. UNESCO through the World Heritage Center recognizes a culture originating from a country as a world cultural heritage of the country. The principles carried out by UNESCO in protecting traditional cultural expressions are the principles of documentation and inventory of cultures. These cultures come from countries that are members of the intangible international cultural protection conventions. These safeguards are urgently needed to prevent Indonesian cultures from other countries' claim (preventive measures).

4.2 *Suggestions*

National and regional governments need to play a role in the identification, inventory, documentation, and registration. Another government's function is the determination of certain indigenous communities as owners of Intellectual Property Rights on Traditional Knowledge and Traditional Cultural Expressions.

This role needs to be stated in regulation on the management and protection of culture in Indonesia. The government might improve the existing Intellectual Property Rights rules and new Acts that specifically regulate the protection and utilization of traditional cultural expansions in Indonesia (*sui generis*).

REFERENCES

Purba, Afrillyana, Andrian Krisnawati and Gazalba Shaleh, *TRIP's-WTO dan Hukum HKI Indonesia*, (Jakarta; Rineka Cipta, 2005).

Sardjono, Agus, *Hak Kekayaan Intelektual dan Pengetahuan Tradisional*, (Bandung: PT. Alumni, 2010).

Badan Penelitian dan Pengembangan HAM Kementerian Hukum dan HAM RI, *Perlindungan Kekayaan Intelektual Atas Pengetahuan Tradisional dan Ekpresi Budaya Tradisional Masyarakat Adat*, (Bandung, Alumni, 2013)

Riswandi, Budi Agus, *Hak Kekayaan Intelektual dan Budaya Hukum*, (Jakarta; PT. Raja Grafindo Persada, 2005).

Asri, Dyah Permata Budi, 'Perlindungan Hukum Preventif Terhadap Ekspresi Budaya Tradisional di Daerah Istimewa Yogyakarta Berdasarkan Undang-undang Nomor 28 Tahun 2014 Tentang Hak Cipta' (2018) 1(1) *e-journal of Intellectual Property*.

———, 'Perlindungan dan Pengelolaan Budaya Lokal di Kota Yogyakarta' (2016) 1 (1) *Jurnal Kajian Hukum*, Faculty of Act, Janabadra University.

Sari, Elsi Kartika and Advendi Simangunsong, *Hukum dalam Ekonomi Edisi Kedua* (Jakarta: Grasindo, 2007).

Kelana, Musafir dan Abubakar Eby Hara, 'Quo-vadis Kekerabatan Malaysia Indonesia', (2009) 2(2) *Jurnal Komunikasi Massa*.

Lusianti, Leni Putri and Faisyal Rani, 'Model Diplomasi Indonesia Terhadap UNESCO Dalam Mematenkan Batik Sebagai Warisan Budaya Indonesia Tahun 2009' (2012) 3(2) *Jurnal Transnasional*, Universitas Riau.

Firmansyah, Muhammad, *Tata Cara Mengurus HaKI (Hak Atas Kekayaan Intelektual) Hak Cipta, Paten, Merek, Desain Industri, Desain Tata Letak Sirkuit Terpadu, & Rahasia Dagang*, (Jakarta; Visi Media, 2008).

Rahardjo, Satjipto, Ilmu Hukum, cet. VI (Bandung: PT. Citra Aditya Bakti, 6th ed, 2006).

Soekanto, Soerjono, Sri Mamudji, *Penelitian Hukum Normatif (Suatu Tinjauan Singkat)*, (Jakarta: Rajawali Pers, 2001).

Lindsay, Tim, et al., *Hak Kekayaan Intelektual Suatu Pengantar*, (Bandung; PT Alumni, 2002)

Wulan Anggiet Purnamasari, 'Penyelesaian Sengketa Perselisihan Tradisional Dan Ekspresi Budaya Antar Negara: Sengketa Lagu Rasa Sayange Antara Negara Indonesia Dan Negara Malaysia' (2015) 45 (4) *Jurnal Hukum dan Pembangunan.*

Convention For The Safeguarding Of The Intangible Cultural Heritage, UNESCO, Paris 17 October 2003, page 2

Act number 28 Year 2014 regarding Copyrights

Act Number 5 Year 2017 regarding Cultural Advancement

UNESCO Constitution

Data from Badan Pusat Statisik (BPS) Nasional (Statistics Indonesia) Year 2014, accessed on 7th May 2015

http://www.pusakaindonesia.org/kekayaan-budaya-indonesia-dan-klaim-negaralain/accessed on 28th April.

http://whc.unesco.org/en/statesparties/id, accessed on 16th October 2016

Culture and International Law - Juwana et al. (Eds)
© 2019 Taylor & Francis Group, London, ISBN 978-1-138-38766-9

The most-favored-nation principle in Indonesian investment law: Legal interpretation of Article 6 of Indonesian Investment Act No. 25 Year 2007

Emmy Latifah
International Law Department, Faculty of Law, Universitas Sebelas Maret, Indonesia

Moch Najib Imanullah
Civil Law Department, Faculty of Law, Universitas Sebelas Maret, Indonesia

Robertus Bima Wahyu Mahardika
Assistance Public Notary of Ismiyati, Indonesia

ABSTRACT: This paper has aim to provide the scientific studies on how the Indonesian Government interprets the MFN principle in its national investment law. The most-favoured-nation principle (hereinafter referred to as MFN principle) is one of the important pillars in the international trading system. The MFN principle provides an indirect standard of protection that attempts to serve an equal playing field among investors and therefore decrease economic distortions in a granting state. Indonesia, as one of the developing countries, has been recognizing the MFN principle in Article 6 (1) Indonesian Investment Act 25/2007 which states that the Indonesian government provides the same treatment to all investors originating from any States making investment in Indonesia. However, the next paragraph of Article 6 asserts that such treatment set forth in prior paragraph shall not apply to investor from certain countries having granted "privilege" under an agreement made with Indonesian Government. The exception in the form of "privilege" as stated within Article 6 (2) shows the contradiction with the previous paragraph. It is a normative legal research using secondary data. The secondary data are included primary, secondary, and tertiary legal materials. The data were collected using library research, then legal interpretation method was employed to analyze the data

KEYWORDS: MFN principle, international investment law, Indonesian investment law, article 6 of indonesian investment act 25/2007

1 INTRODUCTION

The most-favored-nation principle (hereinafter referred to as MFN principle) is one of the important pillars in the international trading system.[1] This principle has existed since the eleventh century[2] and began to spread in the fifteenth century with the inclusion of the MFN clause on the first treaty between the United States and France in 1778.[3] Further development,

1. Stanley K. Hornbeck, 'The Most-Favoured-Nation Clause' (1909) 3 *Am. J. Int'l. L* 395.
2. Endre Ustor, 'First Report on the Most-Favoured-Nation Clause' (1969) 2 *Y. B. Int'l L. Comm'n* 157, 159, U.N. Doc. A/CN.4/213.
3. Treaty of Amity and Commerce, 6 February 1778, France-United State. In Article 3 stated that:"...the subjects of the most Christian King shall pay in the Ports, Havens, Roads, Countries, Islands, Cities, or Towns, of the United States or in any part of them, no other greater Duties or Imports...than those

the MFN principle has been included in many international treaties, especially in the Friendship, Commerce, and Navigation treaties. After the failure of the Havana Charter to come into force in 1950, the inclusion of MFN principle became a general practice in international investment agreements (IIAs).[4]

Today, IIAs without MFN principle are considered as half-empty treaty.[5] The MFN principle, combined with the National Treatment provision, provides for an indirect standard of protection that attempts to provide an equal playing field between investors and therefore decrease economic distortions in a granting state.[6] In other word, MFN principle has an aim to grant equality in competitive condition and not to grant superiority or to guarantee the accumulation of advantageous rules and principles of third-party treaties.[7]

However, the implementation of MFN principle in trade and investment matter is completely different. In former case, the principle provided primarily quantitative advantages, while in the latter, the scope remains unclear. In addition, the range of measures that can be applied by a state within its borders (mainly tariff related) can not be compared to those applied with respect to an established investment, because the areas here are countless.[8]

By means of Indonesian Investment Act 25/2007 (hereinafter referred to as "Investment Act"), Indonesia regulates the implementation of investment as an effort to increase the national economic growth and realize the people welfare in the competitive economic system. One of the Indonesian basic policies within investment is to provide "an equal treatment" for all investors, originating from both Indonesian investor and foreign one with due regard to the national interest of Indonesia.[9] Furthermore, the meaning of "equal treatment" under Article 3 (1) of Investment Act is a non-discriminatory services provided to all investors, both in relation between domestic investors and foreign investors, and among the domestic investors.[10]

The Indonesian basic policy in relating to investment elaborates more detail in Article 6 (1) Investment Act which state that "...the Government (of Indonesia) shall provide the same treatment to all investors originating from any states making investment in Indonesia pursuant to the rules of law."[11] This provision clearly provide an understanding that the Indonesian Government recognizes the MFN principle in Indonesian investment law system.

However, the next paragraph of Article 6 of Investment Act makes the previous paragraph become ambiguous. Article 6 (2) state that: "...such treatment set forth in paragraph (1) shall not apply to investor from certain countries having granted privilege under an agreement made with Indonesian Government."[12] There is no sufficient explanation regarding what "privilege" means and furthermore, there is no guidance how to construe this provision. It, of course, will lead implications for the Indonesian Government as an investment destination country. On the one hand, equating treatment between domestic and foreign investors, if not done carefully and prudently, it will turn off the domestic industry. On the other hand,

which the Nations most favoured are or shall be obliged to pay; and they shall enjoy all the rights, Liberties, privileges, immunities and exemptions in trade, navigation and commerce...which the said Nations do or shall enjoy".More detail, see http://avalon.law.yale.edu/18th_century/fr1788-1.asp

4. Ibid.
5. Alejandro Faya Rodriguez, 'The Most-Favoured-Nation Clause in International Investment Agreements: A Tool for Treaty Shopping?', (2008) 25 (1) *J. Int. Arb.* 1, p. 1. Available at: <https://works.bepress.com/alejandro_faya_rodriguez/2/>
6. Ibid.
7. Scoot Vesel, 'Clearing a Path Trough a Tangled Jurisprudence: Most-Favored-Nation Clauses and Dispute Settlement Provisions in Bilateral Investment Treaties', (2007) 32 *Yale J. Int'l L.*,<http://digitalcommons.law.yale.edu/yjil/vol32/iss1/4>
8. Alejandro Faya Rodriguez, above n 5.
9. Article 4 (2) Indonesian Investment Act of 25/2007.
10. Article 3 (1) (d) Indonesian Investment Act of 25/2007.
11. Article 6 (1) Indonesian Investment Act of 25/2007.
12. Article 6 (2) Indonesian Investment Act of 25/2007.

granting discriminatory treatment to investors, both domestic and foreign, means that it could jeopardize of Indonesia's position internationally in the sense of attracting the foreign investor.[13]

This article has aim to review in depth on how Article 6 of Indonesian Investment Act should be interpreted by Indonesian Government.

2 DISSCUSSION

2.1 *The concept of most-favored-nation principle and its development*

The MFN principle has evolved in its development. Initially, the MFN principle was applied in trade relations, especially it was widely appeared in bilateral commercial treaties since at the twelfth century.[14] However, with the increasing of multilateral relations, such principle have found their way into multilateral treaties. Further its development, until the early eighteenth century, this principle was worded broadly applied to all privileges, liberties, immunities, and concessions treaties.[15]

In 1967, the International Law Commission (ILC) initiated to codify and conduct interpretation of the MFN principle. ILC then submitted Draft Article on Most-Favored-Nation Clause to the U.N. General Assembly and recommended it as a foundation for multilateral treaty in 1978 (hereinafter referred to "ILC Draft").[16] Even though such Draft did not become a treaty and is non-binding, it did codify the definition, scope, and the rules governing the operation of the MFN principle.[17]

The ILC Draft distinguishes between the definition of "MFN clause" and "MFN treatment". Article 4 of ILC Draft stated that "a most-favored-nation clause is a treaty provision whereby a State undertakes an obligation towards another State to accord most-favored-nation treatment in an agreed sphere of relation."[18] The wording "clause" in this sense covers both single provisions of treaties or other agreements and any combination of such provisions, including entire treaties, when appropriate. It also means that it does not matter whether MFN clause is short and concise or long and detailed, or whether it amounts to the whole contents of treaty or not. Article 4 indicates that the MFN clause is unilateral in which a state (as a granting state) undertakes the special obligation (MFN treatment), and the other state (as beneficiary State) accepts this obligation.

The most important example of MFN clause is embodied in Article I, paragraph 1 of the General Agreement on Tariffs and Trade (GATT). It states that:

> "With respect to customs duties and charges of any kind imposed on or in connection with importation or exportation or imposed on the international transfer of payments for imports or exports, and with respect to the method of levying such duties and charges, and with respect to all rules and formalities in connection with importation and exportation, and with respect to all matters referred to in paragraphs 2 and 4 of Article III, any advantage, favor, privilege or immunity granted by any contracting party to any product

13. According to Guiguo Wang, provide the MFN treatment is one of the mechanism to attract the foreign investment. More detail, see Guiguo Wang, "China's Practice in International Investment Law: From Participation to Leadership in the World Economy," (2009) 34 *Yale J. Int'l L.* 576. <http://digitalcommons.law.yale.edu/yjil/vol34/iss2/16>
14. Stephan W. Schill, 'Multilateralizing Investment Treaties through Most-Favoured-Nation Clauses' (2009) 27 (496) *Barkeley J. Int'l. Law* 509.
15. Endre Ustor, above n 2, 17.
16. Report of the International Law Commission on the Work of Its Thirtieth Session 8 May-28 July, [1978] 2 *Y.B. Int'l L. Comm'n* 5, 50 at. 11-12, U. N. Doc. A/CN.4/SER.A/1978/Add.1 (part 2).
17. Yannick Radi, "The Application of the Most-Favoured-Nation Clause to the Dispute Settlement Provisions of Bilateral Investment Treaties: Domesticating the 'Trojan Horse'." (2007) 18 (4) *EJIL* 4 758.
18. Stephan W. Schill, above n 14.

originating in or destined for any other country shall be accorded **immediately and unconditionally** to the like product originating in or destined for the territories of all other contracting parties" [Emphasis added].

In other words, this Article means that in respect to market access, any advantage given to any product originating in or destined for one country shall be accorded immediately and unconditionally to like products originating in or destined for all other members.

Meanwhile, the definition of "MFN treatment" as stipulated in Article 5 of ILC Draft is "treatment accorded by the granting state to the beneficiary state, or to persons or things in a determined relationship with that State, not les favorable that treatment extended by the granting state to a third state or to persons or things in the same relation with that third state."[19] This Article provides the understanding that besides the state, "persons or things" can be the object of MFN treatment. Persons or things also include persons or objects in the natural and juridical sense that can apply in all states of the world with different legal systems. The word "things" includes not only physical notions but also activities and services that are also included in MFN objects such as trade practices, port entry activities, and so forth.

Furthermore, "person or things" which subject to MFN treatment should have "determined relationship" with the beneficiary state. "Determined relationship" here means that the relation between "persons and things" with the beneficiary state should be based on clause of the treaty. In other word, the clause embodied in the treaty, which indicate the relationship between the granting and the beneficiary State, has to determine the persons or things to whom and to which the most-favored-nation treatment is applicable. Besides that, granted the MFN treatment by granting state could also be extended to "persons or things" which in the same relation with the third state. The word "same" in this context has the close meaning with "the same type of" or "the same kind of".

However, the expression "same relationship" has to be used with caution since it could lead the different implication. For example, the relationship between State A and its nationals is not necessarily the "same" as the relationship between State B and its nationals. Nationality laws of states are so diverse that the sum total of the rights and obligations arising from one State's nationality laws might be quite different from that arising from another state's nationality laws.

2.2 *The purpose and scope of most-favoured-nation principle in international investment law*

Today, there are approximately 3,000 international investment agreements (IIAs) made by investment actors,[20] and MFN principle has been markedly present in IIAs. The significance of MFN principle has not been diminished until the present day.

The purpose of MFN principle in IIAs is to provide an equality of competitive conditions between foreign investors from different nationalities seeking to set up an investment or operating that investment in a beneficiary state.[21] Foreign investors seek sufficient assurance that there will not be adverse discrimination which put them at a competitive disadvantage. In other word, MFN principle in the context of international investment means that a beneficiary state treats investor (granting state) from one foreign country no less favorably than investors from any other foreign country.[22]

It is urgent to determine the scope of MFN treatment to have a grasp over MFN treatment and its applicability in a IIAs framework. Generally, MFN treatment applies to all kinds of both "investor" and "investment activities" such as the operation, maintenance, use, sale, or liquidation of an investment. However, different treaties extend this principle in different

19. Pasal 5 ILC Draft.
20. Available at: http://investmentpolicyhub.untad.org/IIA [visited on April 15, 2018].
21. UNTAD, *Most-Favoured-Nation Treatment*, UNTAD Series on Issues in International Investment Agreements II (United Nation, New York and Geneva, 2010) 13-14.
22. Ibid 1.

terms. Although most treaties, such as NAFTA, provide limited set of activities such as the establishment, acquisition, expansion, management, conduct, operation, and sale or other disposition of investments,[23] some others such as the Energy Charter Treaty contains very general text, cover all investment-related activities, including management, maintenance, use, enjoyment, or disposal.[24] For very basic operational purposes, the treatment may go only to investor or its investment, or to both, as the common practice stands; also, the treatment may cover the pre-establishment phase or post-establishment activities.[25]

While the immense majority of investment treaties do not include binding provisions in relation to the admission of foreign investment, a number of treaties, especially those concluded in the recent past, do extend the MFN treatment even to pre-investment conditions. If the treaty concerned has not provided MFN clause for pre-investment, the obligation is limited to activities only *after* an investment has been made. However, if the treaty provides MFN clause even with regard to the pre-establishment phase, contracting parties are expected to create non-discriminatory conditions for new foreign investor and admit its investment under conditions similar to those already in place in the country concerned.

Moreover, the International Center for Settlement of Investment Disputes (ICSID) tribunal in the *Maffezini* case showed that the broad definition of MFN clause to be found in Argentina-Spain Bilateral Investment Treaty (BIT) encompassed not only substantive rights but also procedure of international dispute settlement.[26] Thus, such extension of the application of MFN principle to dispute settlement provisions had allowed foreign investors to resort dispute settlement mechanisms that were not stipulated in the BIT between the granting state and beneficiary state (basic treaty), but rather had been provided in another BIT to which the beneficiary state was a party. The tribunal in the *Maffezini* case concluded that:

> "...unless it appears clearly that the state parties to a BIT or the parties to a particular investment agreement settled on a different method for resolution of disputes that may arise, most-favoured-nation provisions in BITs should be understood to be applicable to dispute settlement."[27]

2.3 *Legal interpretation of MFN principle under indonesian investment law*

The Indonesian Investment Act Number 25 of 2007 concerning Investment was enacted as one of the steps to restructure Indonesia's investment law aiming to create a conducive investment climate. Previously, Indonesia had two Acts on investment, namely Foreign Investment Act Number 1 of 1967 concerning foreign investment and Domestic Investment Act Number 5 of 1967 concerning Domestic Investment. After around 40 years of its implementation, the Indonesian Government deemed it necessary to adjust Indonesian investment law, especially after Indonesia became a member of the WTO in 1994. Through Indonesian Investment Act 25/2007, the Government tried to adapt to the existing investment law in the world, specifically adoption of the WTO principles that have been ratified by Indonesia. The MFN principle has been becoming one of the principle has to be implemented in all trade relations created among WTO member states, including in the investment sector.

The MFN principle is outlined in Chapter V of Indonesian Investment Act Article 6 (1) and (2). Article 6 (1) states that "the Government shall provide the same treatment to any investors from any states making investment in Indonesia pursuant to the rules of law". This article

23. Article 103 NAFTA
24. Article 10 paragraph 7 the Energy Charter Treaty
25. Alejandro Faya Rodriguez, above n 5, 91.
26. *Emilio Augustin Maffezini v Kingdom of Spain*, ICSID Case No ARB/97/7 of 25 January 2000. Art IV, 2 of the Argentina–Spain BIT reads as follows:"In all matters subject to this agreement, this treatment shall not be less favourable than that extended by each Party to the investments made in its territory by investors of a third country".
27. Ibid 49.

recognizes that the MFN principle is the basis for the Indonesian government in providing equal treatments to all investors, both foreign and national investors. Further, Article 6 (2) of the Act envisages that "such treatment as referred to paragraph (1) does not apply to investor from a country obtaining the privilege from Indonesian government based on agreement."

There are three aspects of MFN provisions that have given rise to interpretative issues, which will be dealt with below in turn: the structure of MFN Treatment in International Investment Agreements; the *Ejusdem Generis* Principle; and MFN exception in regional economic integration organization

2.3.1 *The structure of MFN treatment in international investment agreements*

In order to understand the interpretation of Article 6 paragraph (2) of Investment Act 25/2007, it is important to grasp the structure of MFN in international investment agreement. The definition of MFN Treatment in Article 5 ILC Draft sets out the foundation structure of the operation of MFN treatment. This Article reads as follow:

> "Most favoured-nation treatment accorded by the granting state to the beneficiary state, or to persons or things in a determined relationship with that state, not les favoured that treatment extended by the granting state to a third state or to persons or things in the same relationship with that third state."

Article above consists of three elements of MFN treatment. *First*, MFN treatment prohibits the granting state from discriminating between "persons or things" of the beneficiary state and the third state. In IIAs context, these persons are investors, and things are investments. *Second*, MFN treatment applies where the comparators (the investors or investments) from the beneficiary and third state are in the same relationship with the granting state. In other word, they must be in like circumstances. *Third*, the investor or investment from the beneficiary state receives no less favourable treatment than the treatment which the granting state provides to the investor or investment from the third state.[28]

The ILC's definition reflects the basis structure and legal effect of MFN clause as elaborated by the ILC in *Anglo-Iranian Oil Co.*,[29] the ICJ referred to the treaty between the granting and beneficiary state containing the MFN clause as the basic treaty. The basic treaty establishes the juridical link between the beneficiary state and the third treaty and confers the rights enjoyed by the third party on the beneficiary state. Absent the MFN clause, the third-party-treaty "independent of and isolated from the basic treaty, can not produce any legal effect as between... [the beneficiary state] ...and ...[the granting state]: *it is res inter alios acta.*[30]

An MFN clause in a basic treaty does not technically incorporate by reference the provisions of the third-party treaty. As noted by the ICJ in *Anglo-Iranian Oil Co.*,[31] the MFN clause confers the rights enjoyed by the third party on the beneficiary. The MFN clause can confer no benefit if the third party's rights come to an end, for example, where the third-party treaty has been terminated.[32] In other words, an MFN clause does not, as soon as it becomes applicable, crystallize or incorporate by reference the more favourable treatment afforded by a third-party treaty. Access to more favourable treatment is available only so long as the third

28. Andrew Paul Newcombe, Lluis Paradell, *Law and Practice of Investment Treaties: Standards of Treatment* (Netherland: Wolters Kluwer, 2009) 196.
29. *Anglo-Iranian Oil Co., Case* (UK-Iran) (1952) ICJ Rep 93 (Anglo-Iranian Oil).
30. Ibid 109. In Anglo-Iranian Oil, the ICJ did not consider the meaning and scope of the MFN clause at issue because it held that it did not have jurisdiction to hear the merits of the case. On this point, see *Siemens A. G. v. Argentina* (Decision on Jurisdiction, 3 Aug. 2004) 96 [Siemens].
31. *Anglo-Iranian Oil Co.*, above n 29, 28.
32. It should be noted that under IIAs, treaty obligations continue to exist after treaty termination. For example, Art. 13(3) Czechoslovakia-Netherlands (1991) provides: "in respect of investments made before the date of the termination of the present Agreement the foregoing Articles thereof shall continue to be effective for further period of fifteen years from that date."

party is able to obtain the advantage in question.[33] As observed by the tribunal in *Siemens A.G. v. Argentina*, "the benefit available due to an MFN clause last as long as the treaty that grants them is in effect, but they do not become incorporated into the treaty containing the MFN clause."[34]

Since an MFN clause permits an investor or investment to claim the benefits that a state affords to investors or investments from third-party state, the MFN clause multilateral investment protections by creating an "integrated network"[35] of IIAs. Commentators, respondent states, and tribunals have raised concerns that a broad interpretation of MFN clauses will give rise to expansive treaty rights never intended by the state parties.[36] One concern is that MFN clauses have the potential to accord treaty rights without the corresponding limitations or exceptions that apply in the basic treaty.[37] On the one hand, IIA claimants and commentators have argued that the very purpose of MFN clauses is to ensure that the favourable treatment afforded by other IIAs is extended without discrimination.[38] The claim is made that the purpose of IIA MFN clauses is to ensure, as Georg Schwarzenberger argued over fifty years ago, "the minimum of discrimination and the maximum of favours conceded to any third state."[39] This debate has played out in several IIA awards, beginning with *Emilio Agustin Maffezini v. Spain*,[40] led to significant developments in treaty practice and IIA jurisprudence on MFN treatment.

2.3.2 *The* Ejusdem Generis *principle*

In IIAs, MFN clause provides that foreign investors and investments are entitled to the same or no less favourable treatment than the granting state provides to foreign investors and investments from third party states. Thus, in IIA claims, the issue is whether the granting state has provided less favourable treatment to investments or investors of the beneficiary state than it has accorded to investments or investors from a third state. This gives rise to two questions of application: (1) whether the investments or investors in question are comparable ("in the same relationship"); and (2) whether there has been less favourable treatment.

In order to provide respond regarding to those questions, the MFN clause is governed by the *ejusdem generis* principle. It is according to which a MFN clause only apply to issues belonging to the same subject matter or the same category of subjects to which the clause relates as stated within Article 9 and 10 of the ILC Draft. Article 9 of the ILC Draft provides that the beneficiary state of a MFN clause should acquire, for itself or for the benefit of persons or things in a determined relationship with it, only those rights which fall within the limits of the subject matter of the MFN clause, and only with respect to persons or things which are specified in the clause or implied from its subject matter to benefit from it.[41]

33. In *Case Concerning Rights of Nationals of the United States of America in Marocco*, The US claimed that MFN provisions provided it the benefits of British and Spanish treaty provisions providing for consular jurisdiction in all cases involving their nationals. However, since the UK and Spain had renounced their capitulatory rights, the US could not claim such rights. For detail, see *Case Concerning Rights of Nationals of the United States of America in Marocco* (*France v. US*) (1952) ICJ Rep 176 [Rights of US Nationals in Morocco] at 192.
34. *Siemens A.G v. Argentina* (Decision on Jurisdiction, 3 Aug. 2004) 96 [Siemens]. Available at http://ita.uvic.ca/documents/CMS_FinalAward.pdf.
35. F. Orrego Vicula, 'Bilateral Investment Treaties and the Most-Favoured-Nation-Clause: Implications for Arbitration in the Light of a Recent ICSID Case', paper delivered at *ASA Swiss Arbitration Association Conference: Investment Treaties and Arbitration*, 25 January 2002.
36. Ibid.; Jurgen Kurtz, 'The MFN Standard and Foreign Investment: An Uneasy Fit?' *6 J. World Inv. & Trade* (2004) 873.
37. Andrew Paul Newcombe, Lluis Paradell, *above n 28*, 198.
38. Ibid.
39. Georg Schwarzenberger, 'The Most-Favoured Nation Standard in British State Practice' (1945) 22 *BYIL* 99-100.
40. *Emilio Agustin Maffezini v. Spain*
41. Article 9 ILC Draft

Moreover, Article 10 goes on suggestion that the rights acquired should be those that the granting State extends to a third State within the limits of the subject matter of the MFN clause and only if the beneficiary persons or things belong to "same category" of persons or things which benefit from the treatment extended to the third party and have "the same relationship" with that State.[42] The Commentary to Draft Articles 9 and 10 underlines that the rights of the beneficiary are limited, with respect to the subject matter, in two ways, namely by the clause itself, which refers to a certain matter, and secondly by the rights conferred by the granting State on the third State.[43]

In the area of investment, the principle has been highlighted by the *Maffezini* decision[44] and not challenged by the many other cases that followed suit. A dispute arising from the treatment allegedly received by the Argentine investor Emilio Agustin Maffezini from Spanish entities, in connection with his investment in an enterprise for the production and distribution of chemical products in the Spanish region of Galicia. Spain (the Respondent) objected to the tribunal's jurisdiction since Mr. Maffezini (the Claimant) had failed to comply with an exhaustion of local remedies requirements set forth in the Argentine-Spain BIT. Mr. Maffezini admitted that the dispute had not been referred to the Spanish courts prior to its submission to ICSID, but he argued that the MFN clause in the Argentine-Spain BIT would allow him to invoke Spain's acceptance of ICSID arbitration contained in the Chile-Spain BIT and that none of the exceptions from MFN in the Argentine-Spain BIT applied to the dispute settlement provisions at issue in the case.

Based on this case, Tribunal had decision that by virtue of the MFN clause of the 1991 Argentine-Spain Bilateral Investment Treaty, the claimant had the right to import the more favourable jurisdictional provisions of the 1991 Chile-Spain Agreement and, as a result, to resort to international arbitration without being obliged to submit its dispute to Spanish courts for a period of eighteen moths beforehand.

2.3.3 *MFN exception in regional economic integration organization*

Most of the countries worldwide seek closer regional integration through the creation of free trade areas, customs unions, economic or monetary unions, or even political unions, and it implies in giving privilege to investors of other regional economic integration organization members when they make an investment in the region. Most regional organization covering investment issues limit themselves the establishment of an internal investment regime, thereby leaving it up to individual members on how they want to deal with outside investors. Basically, members of such organization have the possibility to extend the benefits of organization membership to investors of third countries making an investment in their territory, unless the regional organization itself decides otherwise.

However, given the potential benefits of regional integration, the international community has long since allowed regional organization and their members to deviate from the MFN standard if certain conditions are fulfilled. Article XXIV of the 1947 General Agreement on Tariffs and Trade (GATT) permits members of a free trade area or customs union to grant themselves preferential treatment, provided that: (a) the aim of the regional organization is to facilitate internal trade, and (b) such organization does not create new trade barriers for importers from outside its territory. The provision allowing such deviation from the MFN principle is usually referred to as a "regional organization exception". Although originally a trade issue, this exception has likewise made its way into IIAs.

There are many difficulties in this context derives from the fact that both the MFN principle and the existing regional organization exceptions typically have a very broad scope. Moreover, there is considerable vague regarding to the relationship between a regional economic integration organization exception in the context of IIAs and the actual investment policies that a regional organization and its members pursue vis-à-vis investors of non-regional

42. Article 10 ILC Draft.
43. Commentary ILC Draft
44. Maffezeni Case

organization members. Another difficulty is how to identify the investors from outside regional to which the regional organization benefits would not apply. An investing holding company, organized and located outside the regional territory, may nevertheless be owned or controlled by nationals of regional organization member states. Another question would arise if a foreign company incorporates a subsidiary in order to gain access to the benefits offered within the regional.

3 CONCLUSION

The interpretation of MFN principles in Indonesian investment law as stipulated in Article 6 Investment Act 25/2007 is carried out based on Article 24 GATT. Regional organizations are given the freedom to give privileges to their members insofar as they do not harm the non-member countries.

REFERENCES

Andrew Paul Newcombe, Lluis Paradell, *Law and Practice of Investment Treaties: Standards of Treatment*, Wolters Kluwer, Netherland, 2009.

Anglo-Iranian Oil Co., Case (UK-Iran) (1952) ICJ Rep 93 (Anglo-Iranian Oil).

Case Concerning Rights of Nationals of the United States of America in Marocco (*France v. US*) (1952) ICJ Rep 176 [Rights of US Nationals in Morocco] at 192.

Hornbeck, Stanley K., 'The Most-Favoured-Nation Clause' (1909) 3 *Am. J. Int'l. L.*

Kurtz, Jurgen, 'The MFN Standard and Foreign Investment: An Uneasy Fit?' (2004)*6 J. World Inv. & Trade*.

Radi, Yannick, 'The Application of the Most-Favoured-Nation Clause to the Dispute Settlement Provisions of Bilateral Investment Treaties: Domesticating the 'Trojan Horse'.' (2007) 18 (4) *EJIL*, 758.

Report of the International Law Commission on the Work of Its Thirtieth Session 8 May-28 July, [1978] 2 *Y.B. Int'l L. Comm'n* 5, para 50 at. 11-12, U. N. Doc. A/CN.4/SER.A/1978/Add.1 (part 2).

Rodriguez, Alejandro Faya, 'The Most-Favoured-Nation Clause in International Investment Agreements: A Tool for Treaty Shopping?' (2008) 25 *J. Int. Arb.* 1, Available at: <https://works.bepress.com/alejandro_faya_rodriguez/2/>

Schil, Stephan W., 'Multilateralizing Investment Treaties through Most-Favoured-Nation Clauses', (2009) 27 *Barkeley J. Int'l. Law*. 496.

Schwarzenberger, Georg, 'The Most-Favoured Nation Standard in British State Practice' (1945). 22 *BYIL*

Scoot, Vesel, 'Clearing a Path trough a Tangled Jurisprudence: Most-Favored-Nation Clauses and Dispute Settlement Provisions in Bilateral Investment Treaties', (2007)32 *Yale J. Int'l L.*, Available at: <http://digitalcommons.law.yale.edu/yjil/vol32/iss1/4>

Wang, Guiguo, 'China's Practice in International Investment Law: From Participation to Leadership in the World Economy,' (2009) 34 *Yale J. Int'l L.* Available at <http://digitalcommons.law.yale.edu/yjil/vol34/iss2/16>

Vicula, F. Orrego, 'Bilateral Investment Treaties and the Most-Favoured-Nation-Clause: Implications for Arbitration in the Light of a Recent ICSID Case', paper delivered at *ASA Swiss Arbitration Association Conference: Investment Treaties and Arbitration*, 25 January 2002.

Czechoslovakia-Netherlands (1991)

Emilio Agustin Maffezini v. Spain

Emilio Augustin Maffezini v Kingdom of Spain, ICSID Case No ARB/97/7 of 25 January 2000.

ILC Draft

Indonesian Investment Act of 25/2007.

Investment Agreements II, United Nation, New York and Geneva, 2010, 13-14.

Maffezeni Case

North American Free Trade Agreement

The Energy Charter Treaty

Treaty of Amity and Commerce, 6 February 1778, France-United State. <http://avalon.law.yale.edu/18th_century/fr1788-1.asp>

http://investmentpolicyhub.untad.org/IIA [visited on April 15, 2018].

UNTAD, *Most-Favoured-Nation Treatment*, UNTAD Series on Issues in International

Ustor, Endre, 'First Report on the Most-Favoured-Nation Clause' (1969) 2 *Y. B. Int'l L. Comm'n* 157, 159, U.N. Doc. A/CN.4/213.
Siemens A.G. v. Argentina (Decision on Jurisdiction, 3 Aug. 2004) 96 [Siemens].
Siemens A.G v. Argentina (Decision on Jurisdiction, 3 Aug. 2004) 96 [Siemens]. Available at http://ita.uvic.ca/documents/CMS_FinalAward.pdf.

Culture and International Law - Juwana et al. (Eds)
© 2019 Taylor & Francis Group, London, ISBN 978-1-138-38766-9

Unesco's intangible cultural heritage safeguard in Indonesia's policy of batik and printed batik 2015

Shofi Fatihatun Sholihah
Graduate Student of International Relations Department, Universitas Gadjah Mada, Yogyakarta, Indonesia

ABSTRACT: This research is aimed to discuss about whether and how UNESCO's Intangible Cultural Heritage Safeguard Convention (ICHS Convention) might be compatible to justify the import restriction policy of batik and printed batik TPT in Indonesia 2015. Republic of Indonesia's Ministry of Trade launched import bureaucratization policy to restrict 'textile and textile product' (TPT) of batik and printed batik through Permendag (Trade Minister Regulation) No. 53 Year 2015. Its economic purpose is to protect local batik and printed batik industry, due to the explossive imported batik to Indonesian textile market, especially from China. In addition, another purpose is to safeguard batik as a cultural heritage. Therefore, Indonesian government applied ICHS Convention, which legally regulated Indonesian batik as world cultural heritage, as its policy's justification means.

In my findings, imported 'batik and printed batik TPT' are not Indonesian batik's like product. It makes the justification sourced from ICHS Convention potentially weak to be applied and difficult to make sense. Moreover, the batik market is not threatened by imported batik.

The research was conducted in qualitative method, which emphasized constructivist aspect of international trade policy formulation. The researcher compared the ICHS Convention with WTO Agreement embodied in the import policy of batik and printed batik. The comparison of those regulations was supported with empirical data that has been conducted by doing documentation, literature study, and interview to related stakeholders.

From this research we know that ICHS Convention is weak to be used as its import policy's economic justification. However, normatively, ICHS Convention has strong potential to justify batik products as Indonesia's product which need to be protected in any aspect, including in the aspect of international trade for cultural products, especially in the field of creative economy and its Mark of Origin.

KEYWORDS: batik, intangible cultural heritage, safeguard convention, import restriction, international trade

1 INTRODUCTION

This research is aimed to discuss about whether and how UNESCO's Intangible Cultural Heritage Safeguard Convention (ICHS Convention) might be compatible to justify the import restriction policy of batik and printed batik TPT in Indonesia 2015. In 2015, Indonesian Ministry of Trade released a policy to restrict imported batik TPT and printed batik via Minister of Trade Regulation (Permendag) Number 53 Year 2015 about Regulation of Batik TPT and Printed Batik. It is regulated the imported batik TPT and printed batik from abroad that has been made with printing, written, and stamped techniques through bureaucratic mechanism and by sending mechanism through certain pots.[1]

According to the reigning Indonesian Minister of Trade, Rachmat Gobel, Permendag No. 53 Year 2015 was released to protect the hereditary Indonesian cultural heritage products from the batik import invasion. On the other hand, the regulation was aimed to protect the local batik businessemen, especially for the printed batik one.[2] Moreover, in Januari-Juli 2015, the imported batik increased 24,09% from the previous year in 2014.[3] This situation hurts batik reputation as the main creative economy product of Indonesia.

By seeing that issue, Indonesian government attached cultural heritage protection aspect and international trade law as a consideration of Permendag No. 53 Year 2015 about the Regulation of Imported Batik TPT and Printed Batik. The minister argued that cultural heritage protection initiative through import policy was seen to be legal since UNESCO has included Indonesian Batik as the Representative List of Intangible Cultural Heritage for Humanity. By having this recognition, Indonesian batik also have strength legal potentials through UNESCO's International Convention on Safeguarding Intangible Cultural Heritage (ICHS Convention) that has been ratified by 170 countries up to June 2016, including Indonesia, as the legal instrument.[4]

However, the spirit of ICHS Convention is completely different with WTO Agreement. Based on WTO Agreement, all countries should hold non-discrimination spirit of international trade. It means that all goods and services should not be restricted. Meanwhile according to ICHS Convention, a country whose cultural heritage is listed in UNESCO, is required to protect their listed cultural heritage. In this case, the import restriction policy through Permendag Number 53 Year 2015 is also in international trade corridor. That's why the intersection of those two regulations need to be operated and harmonized. Therefore, Indonesian government needs to seek a correlation gap between those two regulations as justification means.

Another problem was coming out that most of the printed batik is not cultural batik heritage product's like priduct. That's because according to UNESCO, batik is:

> The techniques, symbolism and culture surrounding hand-dyed cotton and silk garments known as Indonesian Batik permeate the lives of Indonesians from beginning to end. Batik is dyed by proud craftspeople who draw designs on fabric using dots and lines of hot wax, which resists vegetable and other dyes and therefore allows the artisan to colour selectively by soaking the cloth in one colour, removing the wax with boiling water and repeating if multiple colours are desired.... the craft of batik is intertwined with the cultural identity of the Indonesian people and, through the symbolic meanings of its colours and designs, expresses their creativity and spirituality.[5]

Traditional batik from the other countries sometimes may not fulfill those criterions. This situation may lead batik protection through trade restriction regulation is irrelevant.

By seeing those explanations, the researcher is interested to study whether and how ICHS Convention can be used to justify the import restriction policy of batik and printed batik in Indonesia 2015, as Indonesian government urged the protection of batik as a cultural heritage from import invasion. It is important to be researched further since the import restriction

1. AD Afriyadi, *Banyak Jadi Incaran Negara Lain, RI Perketat Impor Produk Batik* (2015) Bisnis Liputan6.com <http://bisnis.liputan6.com/read/2282998/banyak-jadi-incaran-negara-lain-ri-perketat-impor-produk-batik>.
2. F Ariyanti, *Mendag Rachmat Gobel Bakal Stop Impor Batik Dari China* (2015) Bisnis Liputan6.com <http://bisnis.liputan6.com/read/2212567/mendag-rachmat-gobel-bakal-stop-impor-batik-dari-china>.
3. S Primadhyta, *Menteri Gobel Bakal Larang Impor Batik* (2015) <http://www.cnnindonesia.com/ekonomi/20150411153228-78-45910/menteri-gobel-bakal-larang-impor-batik/>.
4. UNESCO, *The States Parties to the Convention for the Safeguarding of the Intangible Cultural Heritage (2003)* (2016) <http://www.unesco.org/culture/ich/en/RL/indonesian-batik-00170#>.
5. UNESCO, *Indonesian Batik* (2009).

policy is potentially caused disguise protectionism accusation to Indonesian government. Hopefully, this research may contribute to give pictures to those who read, especially the stakeholders and government, to arrange strategic step in intangible cultural heritage protection which intersect with international trade aspect.

1.1 *International trade as political instrument and its interstitial politic*

N. J. Wheeler and Bergink[6] (2010) said that law is not only operated for a tool to dominate others, but also to provide legitimation benefit. Furthermore, Hikmahanto Juwono (2010)[7] said that international law is involved to make a country's action is based on the law in other country's eye. Thus, conceptually, the using of ICHS Convention in import policy of batik TPT and printed batik as political instrument could not be separated from Christian Reus-Smit interstitial concept (2015), which consists of four types of reason:

- **Idiographic**, forms actor's identity and it is always related with "who am I" or "who are we" question;
- **Purposive**, forms preference of an actor with leading question "what do we want?";
- **Ethical**, Ethical deliberation happens when they address the question of 'how I should act?' or 'how we should act?', situating their purposive and instrumental decisions within the realm of socially sanctioned norms of rightful agency and conduct; dan
- **Instrumental**, – the favoured terrain of realists and rationalists – involves actors confronting two subsets of questions: one strategic-instrumental, the other resource-instrumental. The former asks 'how do I get what I want?' or 'how do we get what we want?', while the latter asks 'what do I need to get what I want?' or 'what do we need to get what we want?'.

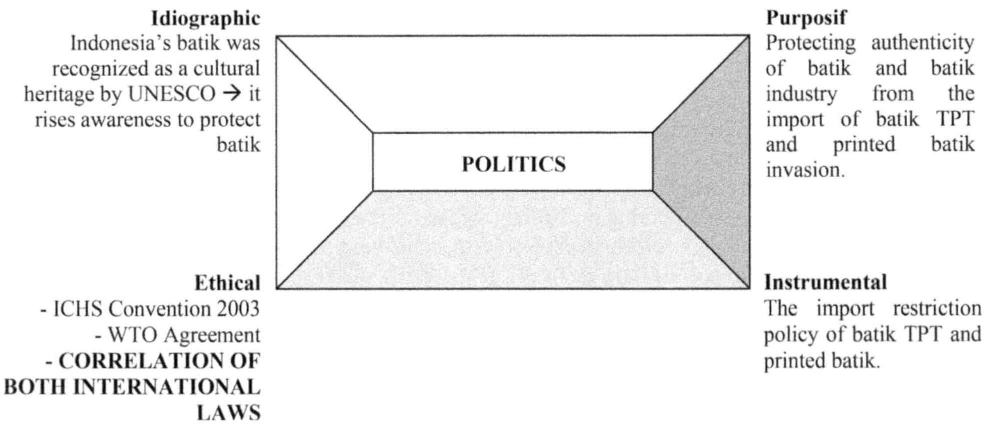

Figure 1. Conception model of interstitial politics which is applied in the politics of import restriction policy of imported batik TPT and printed batik 2015

The model above is applied to make us easier to understand the aim of policy formation of imported batik TPT and printed batik through its purposive deliberation. We may also understand the idiographic of the policy through the UNESCO's recognition for Indonesian batik. Then, ethical deliberations may be seen as a justification means of the instrumental deliberation. But, the intersection between two international laws, ICHS Convention 2003 and WTO Agreement, leads us to seek the correlation of both laws as its main menu of this research.

6. JE Bergink, *International Law as a Political Instrument* (2010).
7. H Juwono, *Understanding Int'l Law* The Jakarta Post <http://www.thejakartapost.com/news/2009/04/19/understanding-int039l-law.html>.

1.2 *Purposive and instrumental deliberation: The purpose and technical of import policy of batik TPT and printed batik*

> "There is an upward trend in imports of batik TPT and printed batik, this is a threat that we must see. Therefore, we must make an effort to preserve batik, by inhibiting the import of batik-patterned textiles, "said the Minister of Trade Rachmat Gobel." The domestic industry will not be able to compete if imports continue. Our grandchildren will not know if batik is Indonesia's cultural heritage, this is the reason for the issuance of the policy," said Rachmat.[8]

From Rachmat Gobel's statement above, there are two purpose of to restrict the imports of batik TPT and printed batik. Firstly, **normative objective** to preserve batik since it has been recognized by UNESCO, as attached in the consideration of Permendag No. 53 Year 2015. As a consequence, Indonesia has to protect their batik cultural heritage with various methods, especially through education. Later it was discovered that the Minister of Trade Regulation No. 53 of 2015 is expected to educate the public about the real batik.

Secondly, **the economic objectives** to protect the domestic batik TPT industry from the invasion of imports of printed batik. Moreover with the ACFTA mechanism, import duties charged only range from 0-5%. Plus the cost of producing batik textile, especially from China, is cheaper because the textile raw material in the form of cotton does not need to import. This makes the price of TPT of foreign printed batik is able to compete with batik and TPT of local printed batik, even the price is much lower. For example, stamped batik shirts can be priced at Rp. 100,000-Rp. 200,000 on the market. While batik TPT and imported printing batik are valued at IDR 12,000-IDR 30,000. For lower class people and/or those who do not understand batik, the choice will certainly fall to the imported printed batik. Such conditions make some batik entrepreneurs and local printed batik feel threatened.

Even so, domestic needs remain fulfilled. Indonesia has also exported a lot of batik and batik TPT abroad. Even the value is higher than the imported batik and printed batik, as listed in the following graph:

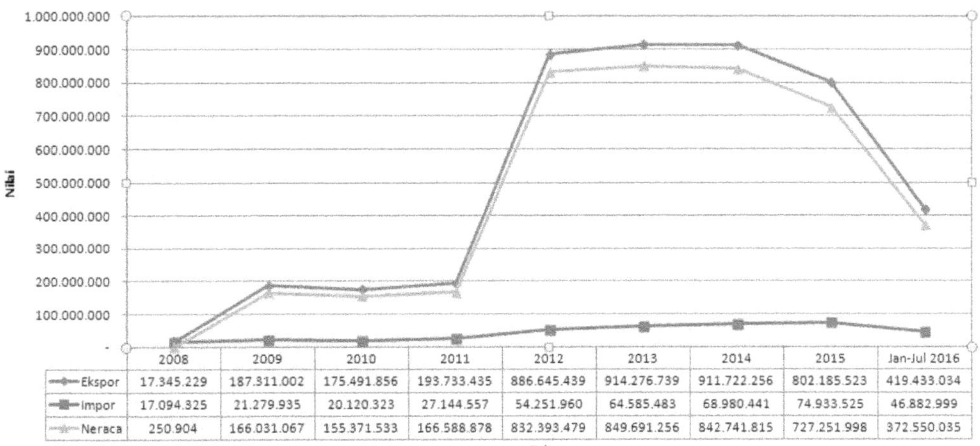

	2008	2009	2010	2011	2012	2013	2014	2015	Jan-Jul 2016
Ekspor	17.345.229	187.311.002	175.491.856	193.733.435	886.645.439	914.276.739	911.722.256	802.185.523	419.433.034
Impor	17.094.325	21.279.935	20.120.323	27.144.557	54.251.960	64.585.483	68.980.441	74.933.525	46.882.999
Neraca	250.904	166.031.067	155.371.533	166.588.878	832.393.479	849.691.256	842.741.815	727.251.998	372.550.035

Tahun

Sumber: BPS, 2016

Figure 2. Comparison of export-import value of batik TPT and Indonesian printed batik (In US dollars)

The graph above shows that the export of TPT batik and printed batik far above their imports. This situation makes BPS argue that the presence or absence of restrictions on the

8. Ariyanti, above n 2.

import of TPT batik and printed batik does not significantly influence the trade balance.[9] In addition, TPT batik and printed batik are not like products of batik. Batik TPT products from other countries, such as Malaysia, are also less qualified to be referred to as batik. Moreover, batik TPT and printed batik made with printing techniques (printing) cannot be called batik. Even so, restrictions on the import of batik TPT and printed batik have a positive correlation to strengthen the normative side of batik protection in terms of cultural heritage.

Then from the technical side, the Import Policy of Batik TPT and Printed Batik contains many points to restrict imports, including:

Table 1. Types of batik import restrictions and batik motives in the Minister of Trade Regulation No. 53 of 2015

Number	Restriction Types	Article:Paragraph
1	Import Bureaucratization	3:1; 4:1,2; 5, 7, 8:1; 9; 6
2	Verification or Search from Surveyor	14, 20
3	Restriction of Port Destination	13
4	Technical Specification Restriction: definition, domestic labeling, and marks of origin.	1:1,2; Lamp I dan II; 13; 12.

Source: (Indonesian Ministry of Trade, 2015)

According to Donald A. Ball and Wendell McCulloh, bureaucratization of trade belongs to an import license which is one of the efforts of non-tariff protectionism policies.[10] This is because the administrative conditions have the potential to disrupt the course of international trade. Likewise with the technical verification by surveyors and other types of restrictions.

1.3 *Ethical deliberation: International legal framework for batik TPT import policy and Indonesian printed batik in 2015*

The efforts to restrict the import of batik TPT and printed batik have the potential to invite accusations of disguise protectionism from other countries. Therefore, the international legal framework is used as a consideration or ethical deliberation as well as a legal basis in Minister of Trade Regulation No. 53 of 2015. The existence of approval and ratification of international law encourages countries to tend to act in accordance with their national interests and make law a means of justification.[11] The consideration is derived from the trade law and international cultural heritage protection law as follows:

1.3.1 *Instrument for the protection of cultural heritage regime*

One of the instruments of cultural heritage protection regime is Convention on Safeguarding Intangible Cultural Heritage (ICHS Convention). The aim is to provide protection against intangible cultural heritage, especially through educational channels. The ICHS Convention was accepted by Indonesia on 15 October 2007 with the status of acceptance.[12] The consequences of acceptence status are the same as ratification, namely the state has an attachment to the convention. The use of the 'acceptance' status for the ICHS Convention was chosen because at the national level, constitutional law does not require the ratification of

9. F Ariyanti, *Mendag Bakal Larang Impor Batik, Ini Kata BPS* (2015) Bisnis Liputan6.com <http://bisnis.liputan6.com/read/2213943/mendag-bakal-larang-impor-batik-ini-kata-bps>.
10. S Zulaekah, 'Penerapan Technical Barrier to Trade Melalui Pelabelan (Hang Tag) Identitas Budaya Pada Produk Batik' (2014) 9(2) *Pechtidee Jurnal Hukum* 184.
11. C Reus-Smit, 'Pendahuluan' in *Politik Hukum Internasional* (Bandung : Nusa Media, 2015).
12. UNESCO, *Decision of the Intergovernmental Committee: 4.COM 13.44.* <http://www.unesco.org/culture/ich/en/decisions/4.COM/13.44>.

international law by the head of state, but can also be by other public officials. In the case of this batik TPT import policy and printed batik, the ICHS Convention was applied by the Minister of Trade with a legal product in the form of ministerial regulations. This is in accordance with article 2 (1) (b) and 14 (2), Vienna Convention on the Law of Treaties 1969.[13]

The impact of acceptance status, Indonesia must strive to achieve the objectives of the ICHS Convention in accordance with article 1, including: to protect, ensure respect and to increase awareness about the importance of the ICH, and to provide international cooperation and assistance mechanisms.[14] Indonesia is also obliged to carry out efforts to preserve intangible cultural heritage in the form of identification, documentation, research, preservation, protection, promotion, improvement and transmission, especially through formal and non-formal education as revitalization of various aspects of cultural heritage. This is stated in article 2 paragraph 3 of the ICHS Convention. In addition, efforts that can be done by the state in protecting batik cultural heritage according to article 13 of the ICHS Convention include:

> adopting appropriate legal, technical, administrative and financial measures with the aim of: i) encouraging the establishment or strengthening of institutions for training in managing intangible cultural heritage and transmitting such inheritance through forums and places expected to perform; ii) ensuring access to intangible cultural heritage while respecting customs practices to provide access to specific aspects of the cultural heritage; iii) establishing documentation institutions for intangible cultural heritage and facilitating access to them.[15]

The use of the consideration of UNESCO's recognition of Rachmat Gobel's tenure was made to affirm to the international community that Indonesia is a party that has the rights and obligations to protect the cultural heritage of batik. Therefore, Indonesia must make every effort to avoid batik from external or internal threats in accordance with the mechanism of international cultural heritage protection regime.

1.3.2 *International trade regime instrument*

Minister of Trade Regulation No. 53 of 2015 also refers to the Marrakesh Agreement Establishing The World Trade Organization (Marrakesh Agreement Establishing a World Trade Organization, often referred to as the WTO Agreement) as one of its legal considerations. The WTO agreement is a principle source of WTO law. This agreement was formed on April 15, 1994 and entered into force on January 1, 1995. This WTO agreement contains a short basic agreement of 16 articles and various agreements and other understandings contained in the annex. As for this agreement there are four annexes, namely attachments 1, 2 and 3, called Multilateral Trade Agreements. While attachment 4, is a Plurilateral Trade Agreements.

The relationship between the WTO Agreement on the main articles and their attachments is a unity. The WTO agreement has binding power and must be applied by all WTO members. This is in accordance with articles 2 and 3 of the WTO Agreement which read:

Article 2. The agreements and associated legal instruments included in Annexes 1, 2 and 3 (hereinafter referred to as "Multilateral Trade Agreements") are integral parts of this Agreement, binding on all Members.

Artice 3. The Plurilateral Trade Agreements and associated legal instruments included in Annex 4 are binding on those Members. The Plurilateral Trade Agreements do not create either obligations or rights for Members who have not accepted them.

As a consequence that Indonesia has ratified the Marrakesh Agreement Establishing The World Trade Organization, Indonesia made Law Number 7 of 1994.[16] As for article 1 of Law No. 7 of 1994, Indonesia has agreed, acknowledged and committed itself to the rules of the

---

13. *Glossary Relating to Treaty Actions* (2016) United Nations Treaty Collection <https://treaties.un.org/Pages/Overview.aspx?path=overview/glossary/page1_en.xml#acceptance>.
14. UNESCO, 'Convention for the Safeguarding of the Intangible Cultural Heritage' October *Eva.Mpg.De.*
15. Ibid.
16. HS Kartadjoemena, *GATT Dan WTO; Sistem, Forum, Dan Lembaga Internasional Di Bidang Perdagangan* (Jakarta : Penerbit Universitas Indoenesia, 1996).

Agreement on Establishing the World Trade Organization along with Attachments (Annexes) 1, 2 and 3.[17] All international trade rules at the national level are made with due observance of the principles and provisions of the WTO, namely to eliminate discrimination in international trade. The principle was then translated into two main principles, namely the most-favored nation (MFN) and national treatment. In the MFN, the state is prohibited from discriminating trade between countries with one another. While in national treatment, the state is prohibited from discriminating to differentiate products from other countries when they reach the country.[18]

In addition, Indonesia also has the right to use the Dispute Settlement Body in resolving all problems and using WTO rules to facilitate the international trade process, whether it is for trade facilitation or as a means of the legality for international law, even as a matter of dispute resolution.

Then looking at these two principles, the Import Policy of Batik TPT and Batik Motif does not violate the MFN principle. This is because Indonesia continues to impose import rules on batik TPT and printed batik without exception, although the main problems come from the soaring import of batik TPT and Chinese printed batik in 2015. Indonesia does not only provide import restrictions for China alone. Thus, Indonesia does not reduce the same opportunity between one or several other countries to export batik TPT and printed batik to Indonesia.[19]

The inclusion of the Agreement on the Establishment of the World Trade Organization as one of the considerations at the same time can be intended as a strategic step and to convince the international community that ethically Indonesia still holds the principles of the WTO. Furthermore, for a more detailed study of articles related to the import policy of TPT batik and printed batik in 2015, this will be explained in the next section.

1.4 *Correlation of the ICHS convention law with the WTO agreement as international legal justification*

The second correlation of international law in the Minister of Trade Regulation No. 53 of 2015 is both supportive and conflictual. It is called supportive because of the relationship between the ICHS Convention and the WTO Agreement mutually supportive of restricting the import of Indonesian batik. While the conflictual relationship is shown in several articles in the Minister of Trade Regulation 53 which contradict each other with the two considerations of international law. Thus the correlation between the two laws can be a reference to see ethical deliberation of the actions of the Indonesian government in protecting batik.

1.4.1 *Supportive correlation*

Supportive correlation is indicated by the existence of articles relating to societal value in the ICHS Convention and there is a connection with the WTO Agreement. First, the WTO article which is positively correlated with other ICHS Conventions is GATT XX (f), "imposed to protect national treasures of artistic, historic, and archeological values". Broadly, national treasure of artistic, historic, and archeological values can be interpreted as cultural goods,[20] even though the actual national treasures can be interpreted freely by WTO member countries.[21] Therefore, batik can be interpreted as cultural goods of Indonesia because batik has an important artistic superiority.[22]

17. *DPR RI. UNDANG-UNDANG REPUBLIK INDONESIA NOMOR 7 TAHUN 1994 Tentang Pengesahan, Pub. L. No. UU No. 7 Tahun 1994 (1994)* (Indonesia: Kementerian Hukum dan HAM).
18. P Van Den Bossche, *The Law and Policy of the World Trade Organization; Text, Cases and Materials* (Cambridge University Press, 2nd ed, 2008).
19. Ibid.
20. Ibid.
21. JAR Nafziger and RK Peterson, *Handbook on the Law of Cultural Heritage and International Trade* (London : Edward Edgar Publishing, 2014).
22. A Biondi in Chechi, *The Settlement of International Cultural Heritage Dispute* (Oxford, London : OUP Oxford, 2014).

Then if the cultural goods are threatened, Article XX (f) in GATT can be useful to justify the protection and promotion of cultural identity. The cultural goods referred in this study are Indonesian batik which has its own identity characteristics. Although the existence of batik is not classified in cultural heritage that is threatened by its existence, efforts to preserve batik in various regions in Indonesia may provide legal force for Indonesia to protect batik in the context of trade. Moreover, until now batik is touted as a cultural heritage that must be preserved according to government policies.[23]

In Article XX (f) GATT 1994, protection and conservation of cultural heritage objects from damage caused by international trade activities are interests that are understood in international law. In addition, the article supports the principle of sovereign states freely to determine the destiny of their national cultural property within the framework of international trade.[24] Every country that is unable to maintain its cultural customs and cultural identity is considered less sovereign.[25]

Second, protection and promotion of cultural identity in Article XX (f) GATT has conformity with the ICHS Convention, especially in article 2 paragraph 3 regarding the definition of "safeguard". Also in Article 11 on the role of members to take the steps needed to maintain the cultural heritage of objects in that country. These actions would be in accordance with article 1 paragraph 1 concerning the purpose of the ICHS Convention, namely to safeguard cultural heritage, article 1 paragraph 2 to foster respect for cultural heritage, and article 1 paragraph 3 to increase awareness of the importance of maintaining cultural heritage.

Imports of batik TPT and printed batik that are booming are feared to hamper the process of transmitting knowledge of cultural heritage to the public. This makes people less able to distinguish batik from printed batik because it is tempted by cheap prices. Whereas the normative understanding of batik and its values is more important than low prices so that the transmission of knowledge and values of life in cultural heritage can be controlled properly.[26] Similarly, the essence and important elements of the national treasure are protected.[27] In addition, restrictions on the import of TPT batik and printed batik are also to emphasize the cultural sovereignty built by Indonesia as The Global Home of Batik. This means that Indonesia as the recipient of UNESCO's recognition feels that it has a big responsibility in protecting batik and is at the center of the development of world batik.[28] Although it cannot be denied that there are interests of firms and local agencies in it.

With regard to that, the third, Marks of Origin contained in article IX GATT 1994 also has a positive correlation with the ICHS Convention to protect consumers when buying batik. This is because in the Minister of Trade Regulation No. 53 of 2015, the Indonesian government requires every batik that is imported to indicate from which country the batik TPT and printed batik originated. This effort can provide education to consumers about the origin of the product. Unfortunately, the regulation on the provision of product information other than the country of origin (the words "textile printing", size, name and address of the producer/name and address of the importer) on products and/or packaging (Ministry of Trade of the Republic of Indonesia, 2015a) has the potential to have a correlation with the WTO Agreement. Because national provisions regarding marks of origin should not contain

23. ME Pangestu, 'Sambutan Menteri Perdagangan Pada Acara Hari Batik Nasional: Pidato' (Jakarta: Kementerian Perdagangan RI, 2011); TREDA, *Indonesian Batik; A Cultural Beauty* (Jakarta, 2009).
24. Matz-Luck., 'General Agreement on Tariff an Trade 1994. In A. S.-F. Rüdiger Wolfrum' in Peter-Tobias Stoll (ed), *WTO: Technical Barriers And Sps Measures* (2007) 564 <https://books.google.co.id/books?id=Wy5F2IZK-AIC&pg=PA137&lpg=PA137&dq=national+treasure+on+gatt&source=bl&ots=4O1WAb0Gcn&sig=UldtL5aogBB8PRB4B21S9MWeYG8&hl=id&sa=X&ved=0ahUKEwiHqrKi_NzNAhXEQI8KHdeCAlUQ6AEINDAD#v=onepage&q=national treasure on gatt&f=false>.
25. Ibid
26. Zulaekah, above n 10.
27. A Pescatoce in Chechi, *The Settlement of International Cultural Heritage Dispute* (Oxford, London: OUP Oxford, 2014).
28. A Pangestu, *World Batik Summit Digelar Di Jakarta* (2011) <http://nationalgeographic.co.id/berita/2011/07/world-batik-summit-2011-digelar-di-jakarta>.

obligations other than the origin of the product (GATT Working Party 1958 in Johnecheck, 2016).[29] But again, this may be normatively ignored by the ICHS Convention.

In addition, looking further at the CCD, those who agree with culture as a means to protect international trade assume that culture should not be the subject of international trade.[30] This is in accordance with the 1998 Stockholm Plan of Action Conference on Cultural Policies for Development which discusses cultural goods and services. The Plan of Action revealed that "cultural goods and services should be treated as being not like any other form of merchandise".[31] Thus, a country that is pro-culture, feels that culture must be more protected and not treated as normal trade commodities. This clause has been stated in Article XX (f) GATT 1994, so that if it could become a counter for not treating batik too much like a normal trading commodity.

Through this CCD, there are several articles which according to Graber (2006) can have a political impact to strengthen cultural policies, namely articles 10, 11, 12, 14, 15, 16, 18, and 19. If these articles also correspond to Article XX (f) General Exception of GATT 1994 and ICHS Convention, ties between the UNESCO Cultural Convention (ICHS and CCD) can complement each other. Like the article 13, with the existence of cultural integration in development policy, if it could help protect cultural heritage. In accordance with article 14 (a (ii)) the state is also given the right to facilitate access to global markets and a wider distribution network for cultural activities, goods and services.[32] Similarly, batik has made various policies, especially in limiting the import of batik TPT and this batik motif.

1.4.2 *Conflictual correlation*

Then seeing the fact that TPT batik and imported printed batik are like products from TPT batik and local printed batik, this has a correlation effect against the principle of MFN (Most Favored Nation) if it is not done properly. GATT article I paragraph 1 reveals that the MFN principle prohibits discrimination between like-products originating from or intended for different countries.[33] Meanwhile, the purpose of import restrictions is to protect the batik industry, both traditionally processed and printing. This policy will backfire for Indonesia if the ban on the import of textile printed batik is still accompanied by the production of printed batik.

In addition, TPT batik and printed batik are not like products of batik. Which is where batik is an object protected under the ICHS Convention. Some parties, such as researchers from the Yogyakarta Center for Crafts and Batik, doubt that this regulation has been properly used to protect batik. This is because commodities that are regulated focus more on printed batik (printing). More competition occurs between TPT batik and local printed batik with TPT and imported printed batik.

Furthermore, the provisions on the import of batik TPT and batik motif indicate import restrictions as clearly stated in article 2 of the Minister of Trade Regulation No. 53 of 2015, which reads: "Batik TPT and batik motif TPT which are restricted in import are listed in Appendix I which is an integral part of this Ministerial Regulation." Although there are indications of import restriction, the regulation does not require the number of TPT batik and printed batik that must be restricted in imports, but mention the HS code (harmonized system) and what types of products are restricted in imports. In addition, this type of quantitative import limitation is more in the form of licensing, where various administrative requirements are applied with the intention of limiting imports (non-automatic).[34]

---

29. W Johnecheck, 'Consumer Information, Marks of Origin and WTO Law: A Case Study of the United States – Certain Country of Origin Labeling Requirements Dispute Law: A Case Study of the United States – Certain Country Of'.
30. CB Graber, 'The New Unesco Convention on Cultural Diversity: A Counterbalance to the WTO?' (2006) 9(9) *Journal of International Economic Law* 553.
31. Ibid.
32. UNESCO, *Convention on The Protection and Promotion of the Diversity of Cultural Expression* (2005).
33. Bossche, above n 18.
34. Ibid.

Import restrictions by way of tightening these licenses are actually legitimate with justified reasons. According to Article XIII GATT 1994 concerning Quantitative Restriction Administration, quantitative restrictions must take into account non-discrimination rules, trade distribution, and import licensing procedures. This is in accordance with article 3.2 concerning the Import Licensing Agreement that non-automatic licensing must not have the effect of additional import restrictions and restrictions for those who have obtained trade restrictions. Thus, countries that implement non-automatic import licensing are expected to comply with the following conditions:

- There is no discrimination between applicants for import licenses, neutral and impartial;
- The government is obliged to provide reasons for refusing to submit a permit;
- The right to review the decision of the applicant;
- Deadline for processing applications;
- Validity of import licensing;
- The desire to issue permits for certain products in economic quantities;
- Information relevant to import licensing must be published.[35]

Meanwhile the Minister of Trade Regulation 53 of 2015 also has the potential to violate Article V paragraph 1 and 2 of GATT 1994 concerning freedom of transit, where each country has the authority to enter certain port areas with or without lowering their luggage (GATT, 1994). As mentioned in the previous section, the determination of this destination port is based on the volume of imports of batik TPT products and printed batik at the port of destination, port facilities and quarantine, the position of the production center, and port development plans (Center for Foreign Trade Policy, 2012). The verification and information-giving process is also included in one of the obstacles to international trade with a technical information mechanism, although the aim is to ensure that importers comply with domestic regulations.[36]

Unfortunately, Minister of Trade Regulation No. 53 of 2015 has not yet been implemented, so researchers cannot assess whether the regulation is implemented in accordance with WTO rules or not. Because when it was stipulated on July 14, 2015, the Minister of Trade Regulation No. 53 of 2015 will only take effect 90 days after that date. Meanwhile, two months later, there was a change in the Permandag No. discourse. 53. However, the deadline for processing import licensing applications and efforts to validate import licensing has been included in article 4 paragraph 1 and article 6 paragraph 2 of the Minister of Trade Regulation No. 53 of 2015.

1.5 *Ideographic deliberation as supporting justification*

Legal justification is less complete if there is no justification of supporters. As ideographic deliberation strengthens the identity of an item. In the policy of limiting the import of batik TPT and printed batik, the identity of Indonesian batik is important to be used as a supporting justification. As we know that Indonesians associate batik with Indonesia. Not only that, even batik is part of Indonesian society,[37] so it has important cultural, socio-economic and political significance.

In terms of culture, the development of printed batik and technology is growing rapidly in various regions through various processes of acculturation or assimilation. Batik does not only play an important role in various traditional ceremonial processions, but starts to be used in the daily life of the community. Even every region is now trying to develop motives in accordance with their respective local wisdom. The development of this batik is the fastest among countries that recognize the color barrier art with wax.

In terms of socio-economic, the presence of batik also presents various batik villages, associations, and batik organizations. Not only that, the batik industry is able to absorb a large number of workers as listed in the following graph:

35. Ibid.
36. WTO, *Technical Information on Technical Barriers to Trade.* (2016).
37. MC Howard, *Indonesian Textiles from Dress to Art* (2009) <www.iar.ubc.ca/centres/csear/.../3-howard.pdf>.

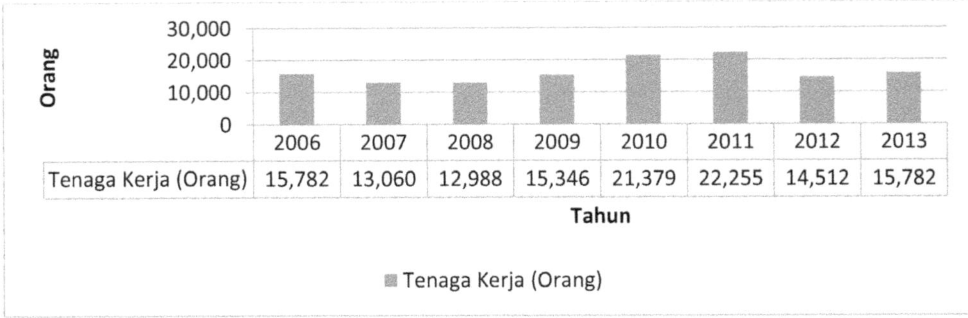

Figure 3. Data on total absorption of workers in the Indonesian batik industry in 2006-2013
Source: Indonesian Ministry of Industry, 2014

Meanwhile, in terms of politics, batik is used as a means of nation building. In 1995, President Soeharto created a trend of Papuan batik to affirm Papuans.[38] In addition, the role of batik politically is to show the national identity of the Indonesian people.

Although batik has an important meaning in society, apparently the definition of batik has not reached an agreement. The Ministry of Trade said that batik TPT is genuine batik, while the Ministry of Industry through the Center for Crafts and Batik said that batik TPT is not batik. Whereas if there is a definite agreement, Indonesia can refuse TPT batik and printed batik that are included for reasons of quality and product suitability. Products that are not in accordance with the quality and definition of the product can be returned and the import closed. Based on the interview with Heri Pramono, the researcher of the Yogyakarta Center for Crafts and Batik, Indonesia is currently developing a compulsory SNI design for batik craftsmen. This is intended to protect consumers from "imitation batik" which has the potential to cause the transmission of batik culture and knowledge to the public. Please note that some countries including Japan make imitation batik and sometimes export it.[39]

In addition, restrictions on the import of batik TPT and printed batik are also reinforced by the commitment of the Indonesian government which has always sought to protect batik as a cultural heritage.

1.6 *Use of the ICHS convention as justification for import restrictions in the framework of the 2015 batik import policy and Indonesian batik motif*

UNESCO's Convention on Safeguarding of the Intangible Cultural Heritage is important in the process of justifying the Import Policy of Batik TPT and Indonesian Printed batik in 2015, although it tends to be weak. The difference in the definition of batik, batik TPT and printed batik is one reason for the weakness of the justification of the policy of limiting the import of batik TPT and this batik motif. TPT entrepreneurs of local printed batik feel overwhelmed by the presence of imported printed batik as their product. The suitability of the commodity can be accepted, but in terms of the accuracy of the provision of cultural heritage safeguards, if the ICHS Convention becomes less relevant because the TPT batik motif has a different definition from batik according to UNESCO.

Weaknesses also exist in how the ICHS Convention is used to justify restrictions on imports of printed batik that flood if faced with reasons to protect the traditional local batik industry. This is because both are not like products, so they are less relevant to compare. In addition, imports of batik TPT and printed batik are much smaller than the export value of batik TPT

38. Ibid.
39. T Sekimoto, 'Batik as Commodity and a Cultural Object' in S Yamashita &J Seymour (ed), *Globalization in South East Asia; Local, National, and Transnational Perspective* (Barghahn Books, 2003) 262.

and local printed batik. In addition, Indonesia also still produces printed batik, which can backfire on Indonesia.

Although the factual economics of like product and export value makes justification through the ICHS Convention on restrictions on the import of TPT batik and printed batik tend to be weak, the use of justification of the ICHS Convention is juridically normative important, especially to strengthen the product and the origin (MOO) of batik. In addition, ICHS is also important to emphasize that batik is a valuable commodity and cultural heritage for Indonesia. Especially in the development of a creative economy based on culture in Indonesia, the characteristics, authenticity and ideas of batik products must be protected.

The ICHS Convention in the policy of limiting the import of batik TPT and batik motif also has the potential to strengthen the status of batik as a national treasure and Indonesian cultural heritage. This situation has a positive correlation with GATT article XX General Exception, paragraph (f) imposed to protect national treasure. Ethically, this ICHS Convention contributes to a normative justification. According to Weren A. Keegen (2000), GATT as an extension of the WTO is an agreement between countries but is functionally part of the domestic law order of each country. Thus, a positive correlation with GATT is useful as a defense reference for Indonesia to defend itself,[40] especially if there is pressure from groups who object to the restrictions on the import of batik TPT and printed batik.

The justification of import restrictions through ethical deliberation above is also supported by justification through ideographic deliberation and other two deliberative relations that cannot be separated.[41] In this case, ideographic deliberation lies behind the practices carried out by actors when trying to articulate, justify, prove, and complain about their identities through verbal processes and the process of communicative action rituals.[42] Minister of Trade Regulation No. 53 of 2015 is explicitly linked to the identity of the Indonesian people as the owner of the rights and obligations of protecting batik as a world cultural heritage.

Then the importance of batik for Indonesia would be able to answer the ideographic question of how batik became an Indonesian identity. It can also define Indonesia's identity with various roles of batik in the fields of socio-economic, cultural and political history. Moreover, Indonesia's identity as the holder of the recognition of "batik as a cultural heritage" encourages the desire to justify the restrictions on the import of batik TPT and printed batik as a means to protect batik from getting stronger. This is what Alexander Wendt said in Reus-Smit (2007) that deliberation and action around identity questions determine first the deliberative and purposive and ethical action structures, which in turn will condition instrumental reasoning and behavior.

Until now there is no country that has sued the violations of the TBT Agreement, whereby the country charged with using Article XX (f) is its legal basis[43]. So, its use is still relatively safe, because it makes Indonesia's instrumental actions based on law.[44] Nevertheless, to support the ICHS Convention as a justification of normative restrictions on the import of TPT batik and printed batik, Indonesia needs to ensure that all import restriction mechanisms are met. For example, by notifying the WTO of the protectionist actions carried out: import licensing, marks of origin, destination port restrictions, verification, and other product provisions. This is because administrative import licensing must be carried out as required in Article 12.8 of the Import Licensing Agreement: "Any Member may notify the Committee on Safeguards of all laws, regulations, administrative procedures and any measures or actions deal with this Agreement that has not been notified by other Members that are required by this Agreement to make such notifications. (GATT, 1994) "If, until now, restrictions on TPT batik and printed batik had been published and socialized both online and offline.

40. Zulaekah, above n 10.
41. Reus-Smit, above n 11.
42. Ibid.
43. Bossche, above n 18; WTO, *Dispute by Agreement of GATT 1994* (2016) <https://www.wto.org/english/tratop_e/dispu_e/dispu_agreements_index_e.htm?id=A9#>.
44. Juwono, above n 7.

Unfortunately, Minister of Trade Regulation No. 53 of 2015 did not last long. In August 2015, President Joko Widodo made a reimbursement for several ministerial posts, one of which was for the position of Minister of Trade. The position of the Indonesian Minister of Trade, which was originally held by Rachmat Gobel, was replaced by Thomas Lembong. With the change of minister, several policies began to be changed. In mid-September, there was news that the import policy of batik TPT and printed batik would be revised again.[45] After taking office, Thomas Lembong changed the Minister of Trade Regulation No. 53/M-DAG/PER/7/2015 concerning Provisions on the Import of Textiles and Textile Products (TPT) of Batik and Batik Motives with the Regulation of the Minister of Trade No. 86/M-DAG/PER/12/2015 concerning Provisions on the Import of Textiles and Textile Products (TPT) Batik and TPT Batik Motives.

In policy No. 86, administrative requirements are made simpler. Recommendations from the Ministry of Industry and the Ministry of SMEs and administrative requirements such as Registered Import Status (IT), NPWP, Customs Registration Number (NIK), Trade Permit (SIUP), and Industrial Business License (IUI) were abolished.[46] While the intent and purpose of the revised policy still remains the same as before, namely to protect batik and the batik textile industry and domestic printed batik.

This simplification of the bureaucracy is done in the context of debureaucratization, given that President Joko Widodo carried out a series of economic deregulation and debureaucratization policies contained in Jokowi's Economic Policy Packages.[47] The aim is to create ease of doing business in Indonesia. That way, Indonesia's target to reach the 40th rank in the ease of doing business can be achieved.[48] To date, the Ministry has enacted the Minister of Trade Regulation No. 86/M-DAG/PER/12/2015 concerning Provisions on the Import of Textile and Textile Products (TPT) Batik and TPT Batik Motives as the basis of national law to protect batik in Indonesia.

Idiographic deliberation supports and motivates the country's decision to impose restrictions on the import of batik TPT and printed batik to protect batik as a cultural heritage. It also supports the use of the ICHS Convention to protect batik as a cultural heritage from batik TPT and imported printed batik. Recognition is at least able to make general exceptions in GATT valid.

2 CONCLUSION

Regulation No. 53 of 2015 carries UNESCO's Intangible Cultural Heritage Safeguard (ICHS Convention) and the WTO Agreement as a means of justification. Moreover, with the widespread import of batik TPT and printed batik from China, Indonesia needs to protect it. Based on the results of the study, the ICHS Convention tends to be weak if it is used to justify the restrictions on the import of TPT batik and printed batik in terms of economy due to irrelevance and lack of like products. Moreover, UNESCO implies that the definition of batik is not found in color-barrier textile technology with other candles. Even so, the normative use of the ICHS Convention in restricting the import of batik TPT and printed batik is important to strengthen the protection of batik products. This is accommodated in GATT article XX (f) General Exception regarding the imposed to protect national treasure. Normative ethical justification is also supported by the ideographic deliberation that batik is an Indonesian national identity. Thus, purposive deliberation to protect batik can be achieved.

45. BSC, *Belum Dua Bulan Permendag Pengetatan Impor Batik Direvisi* (2015) <http://www.jurnalasia.com/2015/09/19/belum-dua-bulan-permendag-pengetatan-impor-batik-direvisi/>.
46. *Indonesian Ministry of Trade 2015*; Vicki Febrianto, *Kemendag Akan Revisi Aturan Impor Batik* (2015) ANTARA News.
47. ibid
48. A Budiman, *Kemudahan Usaha Paket Kebijakan Ekonomi Jilid XII* (2015) <https://m.tempo.co/read/news/2016/04/28/090766861/kemudahan-usaha-paket-kebijakan-ekonomi-jilid-xii>.

However, the problem again arises when the definition of batik between one institution and another in a different country. Moreover, batik is a shared culture, so identification of like products for batik and other color-barrier technologies needs to be clarified. This situation has the potential to complicate the identification process in the context of protecting batik. Therefore, further research needs to be carried out.

REFERENCES

Bergink, JE, *International Law as a Political Instrument* (2010)

Biondi in Chechi, A, *The Settlement of International Cultural Heritage Dispute* (Oxford, London : OUP Oxford, 2014)

Bossche, P Van Den, *The Law and Policy of the World Trade Organization; Text, Cases and Materials* (Cambridge University Press, 2nd ed, 2008)

Graber, CB, 'The New Unesco Convention on Cultural Diversity : A Counterbalance to the WTO ?' (2006) 9(9) *Journal of International Economic Law* 553

Johnecheck, W, 'Consumer Information, Marks of Origin and WTO Law : A Case Study of the United States – Certain Country of Origin Labeling Requirements Dispute Law : A Case Study of the United States – Certain Country Of'

Kartadjoemena, HS, *GATT Dan WTO; Sistem, Forum, Dan Lembaga Internasional Di Bidang Perdagangan* (Jakarta : Penerbit Universitas Indoenesia, 1996)

Matz-Luck., 'General Agreement on Tariff an Trade 1994. In A. S.-F. Rüdiger Wolfrum' in Peter-Tobias Stoll (ed), *WTO: Technical Barriers And Sps Measures* (2007) 564<https://books.google.co.id/books?id=Wy5F2IZK-AIC&pg=PA137&lpg=PA137&dq=national+treasure+on+gatt&source=bl&ots=4O1WAb0Gcn&sig=UldtL5aogBB8PRB4B21S9MWeYG8&hl=id&sa=X&ved=0ahUKEwiHqrKi_NzNAhXEQI8KHdeCAlUQ6AEINDAD#v=onepage&q=national treasure on gatt&f=false>

Nafziger, JAR and RK Peterson, *Handbook on the Law of Cultural Heritage and International Trade* (London : Edward Edgar Publishing, 2014)

Pangestu, ME, 'Sambutan Menteri Perdagangan Pada Acara Hari Batik Nasional : Pidato' (Jakarta : Kementerian Perdagangan RI, 2011)

Pescatoce in Chechi, A, *The Settlement of International Cultural Heritage Dispute* (Oxford, London : OUP Oxford, 2014)

Reus-Smit, C, 'Pendahuluan' in *Politik Hukum Internasional* (Bandung : Nusa Media, 2015)

Sekimoto, T, 'Batik as Commodity and a Cultural Object' in S Yamashita & J Seymour (ed), *Globalization in South East Asia; Local, National, and Transnational Perspective* (Barghahn Books, 2003) 262

TREDA, *Indonesian Batik; A Cultural Beauty* (Jakarta, 2009)

Zulaekah, S, 'Penerapan Technical Barrier to Trade Melalui Pelabelan (Hang Tag) Identitas Budaya Pada Produk Batik' (2014) 9(2) *Pechtidee Jurnal Hukum* 184

UNESCO, 'Convention for the Safeguarding of the Intangible Cultural Heritage' October *Eva.Mpg.De*

UNESCO, *Convention on The Protection and Promotion of the Diversity of Cultural Expression* (2005)

WTO, *Technical Information on Technical Barriers to Trade.* (2016)

DPR RI. UNDANG-UNDANG REPUBLIK INDONESIA NOMOR 7 TAHUN 1994 Tentang Pengesahan, Pub. L. No. UU No. 7 Tahun 1994 (1994) (Indonesia: Kementerian Hukum dan HAM.)

Indonesian Ministry of Trade 2015

Afriyadi, AD, *Banyak Jadi Incaran Negara Lain, RI Perketat Impor Produk Batik* (2015) Bisnis Liputan6.com<http://bisnis.liputan6.com/read/2282998/banyak-jadi-incaran-negara-lain-ri-perketat-impor-produk-batik>

Ariyanti, F, *Mendag Rachmat Gobel Bakal Stop Impor Batik Dari China* (2015) Bisnis Liputan6.com <http://bisnis.liputan6.com/read/2212567/mendag-rachmat-gobel-bakal-stop-impor-batik-dari-china>

Ariyanti, F, *Mendag Bakal Larang Impor Batik, Ini Kata BPS* (2015) Bisnis Liputan6.com <http://bisnis.liputan6.com/read/2213943/mendag-bakal-larang-impor-batik-ini-kata-bps>

BSC, *Belum Dua Bulan Permendag Pengetatan Impor Batik Direvisi* (2015) <http://www.jurnalasia.com/2015/09/19/belum-dua-bulan-permendag-pengetatan-impor-batik-direvisi/>

Budiman, A, *Kemudahan Usaha Paket Kebijakan Ekonomi Jilid XII* (2015) <https://m.tempo.co/read/news/2016/04/28/090766861/kemudahan-usaha-paket-kebijakan-ekonomi-jilid-xii>

Febrianto, Vicki, *Kemendag Akan Revisi Aturan Impor Batik* (2015) ANTARA News

Glossary Relating to Treaty Actions (2016) United Nations Treaty Collection <https://treaties.un.org/Pages/Overview.aspx?path=overview/glossary/page1_en.xml#acceptance>

Howard, MC, *Indonesian Textiles from Dress to Art* (2009) <www.iar.ubc.ca/centres/csear/.../3-howard.pdf>

Juwono, H, *Understanding Int'l Law* The Jakarta Post <http://www.thejakartapost.com/news/2009/04/19/understanding-int039l-law.html>

Pangestu, A, *World Batik Summit Digelar Di Jakarta* (2011) <http://nationalgeographic.co.id/berita/2011/07/world-batik-summit-2011-digelar-di-jakarta>

Primadhyta, S, *Menteri Gobel Bakal Larang Impor Batik* (2015) <http://www.cnnindonesia.com/ekonomi/20150411153228-78-45910/menteri-gobel-bakal-larang-impor-batik/>

UNESCO, *Decision of the Intergovernmental Committee: 4.COM 13.44.* <http://www.unesco.org/culture/ich/en/decisions/4.COM/13.44>

UNESCO, *Indonesian Batik* (2009)

UNESCO, *The States Parties to the Convention for the Safeguarding of the Intangible Cultural Heritage (2003)* (2016) <http://www.unesco.org/culture/ich/en/RL/indonesian-batik-00170#>

WTO, *Dispute by Agreement of GATT 1994* (2016) <https://www.wto.org/english/tratop_e/dispu_e/dispu_agreements_index_e.htm?id=A9#>

Culture and International Law - Juwana et al. (Eds)
© 2019 Taylor & Francis Group, London, ISBN 978-1-138-38766-9

The legal implication of UNESCO Convention 2001 to the law of salvage and law of find in order to protect and to preserve underwater cultural heritage

Sri Wartini
Lecturer of International Law and International Environmental Law, Faculty of Law, Universitas Islam Indonesia.

ABSTRACT: Underwater cultural heritage is regulated by Law of the Sea Convention and UNESCO Convention Year 2001. Based on the two Conventions, states have obligations to protect and to preserve the underwater cultural heritage and cooperate for that purpose. The UNESCO Convention 2001 may conflict with the Law of Salvage and the Law of Find, since according to the Law of Salvage that the Salvators may exploit the sunken vessel for commercial purposes. While based on the Law of Find recognizes the principle of "finders keepers". The research undertakes a critical examination the legal implication of the UNESCO Convention 2001 to the Law of Salvage and the Law of Find. Secondly, it analyses comprehensively the conflict between the UNESCO Convention 2001 with the Law of Salvage and the Law of Find in order to protect and to preserve underwater cultural heritage. Finally, it also analyses the possibilities to settle the conflicts. The paper is a normative research and the methodology employed in this paper is library research. While the approaches employed in the research is conceptual approach. The paper is analysed qualitatively and presented descriptively. The research finds that it is very important to harmonize and to fill the gap between the Law of Salvage and Law of Find with the UNESCO Convention Year 2001.

KEYWORDS: underwater cultural, heritage, shipwreck, salvage and finders keepers

1 INTRODUCTION

The UNESCO Convention on the Protection of the Underwater Cultural Heritage, 2001 (hereinafter UNESCO Convention 2001) is unique due to the mystery of its location under water and its historical context. The site of a wreck or a submerged worsening is the reminder of a human catastrophe, the ending of a voyage and a loss of human lives. The discovery of the site of a wreck accelerates people to step back into the past and re-experience the last moments of the ship and its crew. Once out of the water and exhibited on land, objects are deprived of their context and lose part of their importance. Therefore, several recent initiatives have commenced to offer visitors in situ experiences while at the same time safeguarding the conservation and protection of the previous site in proportion to the principles of the UNESCO Convention 2001.[1]

Before the 21st century, UCH has not received systematic protection under international law. In fact, in in recent years more and more underwater cultural heritage (hereinafter UCH) is distressed and impaired by unauthorized activities directed towards it, protecting this kind

1. UNESCO, 'The Convention on the Protection of the Underwater Cultural Heritage'. https://www.unesco.nl/sites/default/files/dossier/gb-2001convention-infokit_07-2009.pdf?download=1. < Accessed on 17 September 2018>.

of heritage has become ever more fundamental and crucial. The protection of UCH has already started based on the law of the sea and law of salvage, however, the protection has not yet carried out optimally and it caused numerous imperfections and problems. The adoption of the 2001 Convention on the Protection of Underwater Cultural Heritage indicates the establishment of a moderately inclusive legal framework in this regard. Some substantial regimes for the protection of underwater cultural heritage is shaped by this convention including preservation in situ, severe restrictions on the application of law of salvage and law of find and rules relating to the jurisdiction over underwater cultural heritage within the exclusive economic zone and on the continental shelf.[2]

UCH may help us in understanding the past, or may even turn out to be the symbol of a nation State, because they possess historical or archaeological value. For example, the RMS Titanic, a ship whose wreckage was found at sea, is a valuable historical object since it is a precise reflection of conditions at the time it sank. The General Conference acknowledged "the importance of underwater cultural heritage as an integral part of the cultural heritage of humanity" and admitted to being "deeply concerned by the increasing commercial exploitation of underwater cultural heritage, and in particular by certain activities aimed at the sale, acquisition or barter of underwater cultural heritage.

Article 303 (1) UNCLOS is silent in the protection of UCH within the EEZ or Continental Shelf or the Area. While the customary law of the sea lays out rules governing the recovery of disabled and sunken vessels, it does not recognize the need to preserve underwater cultural heritage or distinguish between shipwrecks that are culturally or historically significant and those that are not significant. Various states admit the need to protect archaeologically significant shipwrecks, but customary international law does not provide direction for achieving this goal.

Thus, there is a legal lacuna in regulation of activities directed at underwater cultural heritage situated outside the territorial sea is beyond dispute. Greatly enhanced underwater technology is directly contributing to the threat of inappropriate commercial exploitation of underwater cultural heritage located beyond the Territorial Sea, and it is this threat and regulatory lacuna that the UNSCO Convention 2001 is designed to counter the problems.[3]

Due to the monetary value of many historic shipwrecks and the accessibility of new technology has drawn a growing number of salvors into the salvage industry. Hence, there is serious debate over salvaging historic shipwrecks at the ppresent. Two such salvors are Phil Masters and Barry Clifford, both of whom left behind more traditional lifestyles to undertake salvaging historic shipwrecks.[4] Masters discovered the Feversham, a British frigate that sank in 1711; Blackbeard's flagship, the Queen Anne's Revenge; and El Salvador, a Spanish galleon that sank in 1750, carrying 240,000 gold and silver pesos. Masters stated that he wants to make El Salvador a household name like Titanic by producing documentary videos and auctioning off recovered treasure and artifacts.[5] Based on the law of salvage, there is no obligation to preserve the historic shipwrecks in-situ.

Parties to the UNESCO Convention recognise "the importance of underwater cultural heritage as an integral part of the cultural heritage of humanity and a particularly important element in the history of peoples, nations, and their relations with each other concerning their common heritage."[6] Great accentuates has been placed on the necessity of adopting an international instrument deliberated to protect underwater cultural heritage. Parties to the

2. Nie Bomin, 'On the International Legal Protection of Underwater Cultural Heritage', https://core.ac.uk/download/pdf/41460226.pdf. < Accessed on 21 September 2018>
3. UK UNESCO 2001 Convention Review Group, 2014, *The UNESCO Convention on the Protection of the Underwater Cultural Heritage 2001: An Impact Review for the United Kingdom*, http://www.jnapc.org.uk/UNESCO%20Impact%20Review%20February%202014.pdf. < Accessed on 18 September 2018)
4. Christopher R. Bryant, 'The Archaeological Duty Of Care: The Legal, Professional, And Cultural Struggle Over Salvaging Historic Shipwrecks'. (2001) 65 *Albany Law Review*, 99.
5. Ibid.
6. Article of the UNESCO Convention 2001.

Convention express concern that this heritage "is threatened by unauthorized activities directed at it" and is the subject of "increasing commercial exploitation," realizing that responsibility for its protection rests with all states.[7]

The latest discovery of the Spanish galleon, SAN JOSE, off the coast of Colombia, has created a great deal of international interest in the destiny of its valuable cargo. It was projected to have been carrying between four to seventeen billion dollars of jewels and valuable metals when it sank in a naval battle in 1708. Up to now, possible claimants include, but are not limited to: an American salvage company, the Colombian government, the Kingdom of Spain, and the Republic of Peru.[8] The famous SAN JOSE was the flag ship of one such treasure fleet. Loaded with nearly seventeen billion dollars' worth of silver, gold, emeralds, and other jewels, she was worth approximately three times Spain's annual income.[9]

The historic shipwrecks for treasure salvors of sunken ships, abandonment is the most significant issue. If a ship has been abandoned, then the law of finds applies and title passes to the finders. No insurance companies or other claimants can claim the "loot." If a court does not deem the ship abandoned or if any owner can come forward to make a claim, the law of salvage will apply. In this case, the treasure salvors only receive a portion of the proceeds of any recovered articles. Accordingly, many recent sunken ship lawsuits revolve around whether the ship has been abandoned.[10]

One such battle has emerged over the exploitation and recovery of objects from historic shipwrecks and other submerged sites which is called as the "underwater cultural heritage." The nautical archaeology community has spoken expressively of the need to protect historically essential shipwrecks from altruistic neglect by coastal States; from looting by negligent sports divers; and from, worst of all, dishonest and destructive treasure hunters. A number of coastal States have recently gone on record as declaring title to shipwrecks located within two hundred miles of their shores or, in the alternative, assertions of regulatory authority over that underwater cultural heritage. Coastal States have thus discovered that there lies within their grasp a resource that international law has yet to allocate to governmental control: the historic salvage industry.[11] In sum, historic shipwrecks are invaluable sights into the past, which can provide us with a wealth of historic knowledge, as well as a literal wealth in gold, silver, and other valuable commodities.[12]

This article consist of three parts. Part I of the article explains the crucial reason protection of the UCH and the impacts of the law of Salvage and the law of Find. Part II of this article examines the traditional admiralty laws of salvage and finds as well as UNCLOS. Part III of this article analyzes the legal implication of UNESCO Convention to the law of Salvage and the Law of Find. Part IV of this article explores and analyse the conflict between the UNESCO Convention 2001 with the Law of Salvage and the law of Find. Part V, it examines the possibilities to settle the conflict between the UNESCO Convention 2001 with the Law of Salvage and the Law of Find, and finally it is followed by conclusion.

7. Liza J. Bowman, *Oceans Apart Over Sunken Ships: Is The Underwater Cultural Heritage Convention Really Wrecking Admiralty Law?* https://digitalcommons.osgoode.yorku.ca/ohlj/vol42/iss1/1/. <Accessed on 22 September 2018>.
8. Mitchell F. Tedesco, 'Between the Devil and The Deep Blue Sea: The Shortcomings of Forcing Courts to Choose From The Law of Salvage and The Law of Finds in Treasure Salvage Cases' (2016-2017) 29 *University of San Francisco Maritime Law Journal*, 155.
9. Ibid, 157.
10. Jeffrey W. Yeates, 'Clearing Up the Confusion: A Strict Standard of Abandonment for Sunken Public VesselS', (1999-2000) 12 *University of San Francisco Maritime Law Journal*, 365.
11. David J. Bederman, 'Building New Regimes and Institutions for the Sea', (1998) 30 *University of Miami Inter-American Law Review*, 100.
12. Cathryn Henn, 'The Trouble With Treasure Historic Shipwrecks Discovered In International Waters', (2012) 19 *University of Miami International and Comparative Law Review*, Vol. 19, Spring, 143.

2 THE TRADITIONAL ADMIRALTY LAWS AND UNCLOS

The protection of UCH actually has been regulated in the Salvage Convention which gives opportunity to the state Parties to make a reservation of Article 30 of the Salvage Convention. While in the law of find there is no rule applicable to the protection of UCH. On the other hand, UNCLOS does not clearly regulate the protection of UCH. Since, the three legal regimes which each of them is not directly and explicitly regulate the protection of UCH, thus it lead to the adoption of UNESCO Convention 2001.

2.1 *The law of salvage*

The concept of saving the life and property from the perils is recognized as salvage. A party who successfully saves a person or maritime property from the sea earns the right to an award from the owner of the property. The law of salvage started since the existence of the Rhodian Code,[13] which dates from around 800 B.C. and was later adapted into various European legislation, such as England's Law of Oleron.[14] "Salvage is a reward for terrifying service" and is granted when a salvor successfully and voluntarily saved at least some parts of a maritime property that is subject to a "marine peril".[15] Salvage law gives the salvors the right to get rewards from the owner of the maritime property, such as vessel and its goods on board, but the title to the vessel remains with its owner. The claim of the salvage may not give title, because "the doctrine of salvage assumes title to the property rests in some individual," and so "even though a vessel is abandoned without the hope of recovery or return, the title of the vessel remains in her owner."[16] When the marine property has been successfully salvaged immediately returned to the owners.

In the case when a historic wreck has been abandoned, there may be no owner or successor from whom the salvor can obtain a reward. As a result, the salvor may to claim the ownership under the law of finds and claim title to the property. However, it can cause a problem in jurisdiction that operate under the law of sovereign prerogative, "where the title of all unclaimed property passes to the state".[17] Thus, there is no opportunity for the salvors to gain ownership of the historic wreck. According to Justice Russell[18] noted that "salvors who seek to preserve and enhance the historical value of ancient shipwrecks should be justly rewarded." The opinion is based on the court ruling in MDM Salvage, Inc. v. The Unidentified, Wrecked and Abandoned Sailing Vessel:[19]

The 1989 Salvage Convention replaced the 1910 Salvage Convention for states that are parties to both conventions to the extent that their provisions were incompatible. The 1989 Salvage Convention has been legally binding in several states, including the United Kingdom, Canada, and the United States.[20] The 1989 Salvage Convention recognizes that most salvage services today are performed under a contract. The 1989 Salvage Convention does not define the relationship between salvage law and protection of the underwater cultural heritage. The only reference to underwater heritage is in the form of a reservation. Parties may reserve the right not to apply the provisions of the 1989 Salvage Convention "when the property involved

13. By Mark A. Wilder, 'Application of Salvage Law and the Law of Finds to Sunken Shipwreck Discoveries Modern technology has made the location and retrieval of shipwrecks'. https://pdfs.semanticscholar.org/3bfc/4c3583c7a31cb0cc25e1ad0231f9b83219a4.pdf. <Accessed on 19 September 2018>.
14. David J. Bederman, above n 11.
15. Nathan Murphy, 'Scuttle the Abandoned Shipwreck Act: The Unnecessary Unconstitutionality of American Historic Shipwreck Preservation', (2011) 36 *Tulane Maritime Law Journal*, 164.
16. Ibid.
17. Rob Regan, 'When Lost Liners Become Found: An Examination Of The Effectiveness Of Present Maritime Legal And Statutory Regimes For Protecting Historic Wrecks In International Waters With Some Proposals For Change', (2005) 29 *Tulane Maritime Law Journal*, 316-317.
18. Ibid.
19. Ibid.
20. Liza J. Bowman, above n 7.

is maritime cultural property of prehistoric, archaeological or historic interest and is situated on the seabed,"[21] thus disregarding salvage law from national law governing underwater heritage. For instance, Canada made such a reservation in ratifying the 1989 Salvage Convention.[22]

Conventionally, the law of salvage was used to encourage people to render prompt and voluntary action to save lives and property from the perils of the sea. It is crucial to note several special circumstances surrounding the salvage of historic shipwrecks, which contrast from those of present shipwrecks. The measures that can be done by salvage has to comply with the three requirements.[23] First is the element of marine peril. The element was met when a ship was in danger of sinking because of some accident. Many in the archeological community debate that given the immaculate condition in which many ancient shipwrecks are preserved, commercial salvors are the wrongdoers who put ancient ships in peril through their rush excavating and looting, which causes the forfeiture of significant scientific and related information. Furthermore, courts are fully eager to stretch this principle to hold historic wrecks lost to the ocean floor in peril of being vanished to natural worsening, or destruction by manmade fishing and marine activities, if left in place.[24]

Consequently, when the salvors hunt for historic shipwrecks is much more expensive than the search for more modern wrecks, since it obliges more skill and knowledge and additional time to save the historic shipwrecks. Thus, it is necessary to take into account when figuring out a salvage award. Some have contended that because a salvage award is already defined by evaluating the factors, the application of the law of salvage to the new context of historic shipwreck recovery should prompt the inclusion of a new factor grounded on the need to take the preservation of historical value into consideration.

The objective of salvage is "to save and preserve property that is in marine peril from destruction, damage, or loss and to compensate the salvor with an award determined by an admiralty court".[25] It is well established that to assert a successful salvage claim, it must be shown that:

(1) the vessel or cargo was in marine peril;
(2) the salvor rendered service voluntarily;
(3) the salvor was successful either in whole or in part; and
(4) the salvor established 'possession' over the shipwreck[26]

All the requirements have to be fulfilled, however in the context of the protection of underwater cultural heritage, the court, required the archaeological value to be added as a new element in the law of salvage.[27]

A problem that often arises when courts are hearing salvage claims for historic wrecks is whether the law of salvage can be applied, since there is another doctrine, the law of finds, which has also been applicable.[28] Under the law of salvage, the salvor does not acquire ownership rights of the salvaged property after they have successfully salvaged it from the sea. Rather, the salvors merely acquire a maritime lien over the property as security for a salvage award. The law of developed to res salvage claims for historic wrecks is whether the law of salvage applies at all.

---

21. Article 30 the Salvage Convention
22. Ibid.
23. Ben Juvelier, '"Salvaging" History: Underwater Cultural Heritage and Commercial Salvage' (2017) 32 *American University International Law Review*, 1026.
24. Mitchell F. Tedesco, above n 8, 164.
25. R. Ethan Zubic, 'Pure Versus Contract Salvage – Narrowing The Scope Of An "Agreement To Volunteer" Bar To Pure Salvage', (2011) 10 *Loyola Maritime Law Journal*, 147.
26. Ibid.
27. Rob Regan, above n 17, 317.
28. David Curfman, 'Thar Be Treasure Here: Rights To Ancient Shipwrecks In International Waters–A New Policy Regime', (2008) 86 *Washington University Law Review* 183.

If a salvor does not recover or rescue any property, even though he has exerted a substantial amount of time, effort, and financial expense, he is still not entitled to a salvage reward. The law of salvage presumes that the owner desires the salvage service. For example, the salvor when providing the salvage service a salvor acts on the sake of the owner in retrieving the owner's property albeit the owner may have asked no such demand or had no understanding of the need. Under this law, the salvor is entitled to a reward from the owner in the form of a lien on the property saved.[29]

Salvage can be classified into commercial salvage and Historic salvage. Commercial salvagers make efforts to save ships and cargo from imminent danger, such as fire. This type of rescue calls for salvager action that is relatively close in time to the time of the ship's peril. While the historic salvage is "the pursuit and recovery of shipwrecks whose value is partially derived from their historic stature."[30] Historic salvagers search for ships that sunk many years ago. The value of this property comes from its historical and cultural significance. The expertise level of the historic salvager is important.

2.2 *The law of finds*

The law of finds if it is compared to the law of salvage, it is a much more recent legal development in maritime law. Its common law ancestor is the ancient property law concept of actual possession, or "finders-keepers." The policy behind the law of finds is to encourage individuals "to seek out and maximize the use of property."[31] Courts that have applied the law of finds in maritime disputes have, in essence, "rejected the salvage law theory that title to property can never be lost" and "instead applied the law of finds under the doctrine of 'animus revertendi' (the owner has no intention of returning)."[32] In contrast to the law of salvage, which does not transfer title, the law of finds gives a finder "title to the property upon a determination that property has been permanently abandoned."[33]

The law of finds, on the other hand, bestows ownership rights to the salvors when they successfully salvage the property. However, the law of finds only applies when it is determined that the salvaged property has been abandoned. The mere physical abandonment of property at sea is not sufficient to divest the owner of title. "If the vessel is a derelict, however, abandoned by her master and crew, she can be salvaged without consent." Derelict property is defined as "property on navigable waters which is abandoned and deserted by those who were in charge of it."[34] When the abandoned property has been controlled by a finder, he holds title to it. This title is reliable against the whole world, as well as the original owner.[35]

The law of finds is now commonly accepted as a maritime concept. Some courts, though, have been unwilling to apply the law of finds to shipwrecks. Previously, the law of finds was seen as more appropriate for "property such as whales and fish–that had never been owned by anyone".[36] The long-standing notion of "finders, keepers" is embodied in the maritime law of finds. This body of law was traditionally applied to maritime property, such as fish or ocean plants, which no one owns. If property is abandoned by its owner, the law of finds treats it as if it is "returned to the state of nature and thus equivalent to property" with no prior owner.

29. Omar Carmona Sánchez, 'Rights of Treasure Hunters Under Puerto Rico Law: Application of Article 285 of The Civil Code Through The Jones Act, The Puerto Rican Underwater Archaeological Protection Act and The Abandoned Shipwreck Act Of 1987' (2008) 47 *Revista de Derecho Puertorriqueno* 353.
30. Marian Leigh Miller, 'Underwater Cultural Heritage: Is The Titanic Still In Peril As Courts Battle Over The Future Of The Historical Vessel?' (2006) 20 *Emory International Law Review* 345.
31. Nathan Murphy, above n 15, 164.
32. Ibid.
33. Christian Hoefly, 'National Treasure: A Survey Of The Current International Law Regime For Underwater Cultural Heritage', (2016) 4 (August) *Penn State Journal of Law & International Affairs*, 816-817.
34. Mitchell F. Tedesco, above n 8, 164.
35. Liza J. Bowman, above n 7.
36. Christopher R. Bryant, above n 4, 02- 103.

Even if there was an owner of the property, the courts presume that the owner no longer exists. Because courts assume the owner no longer exists, a salvager is given full title to the vessel[37] rather than just possessory rights as in the law of salvage.

Courts have held that to gain title to shipwrecks under the law of finds, the "salvor must be the first finder to: (1) demonstrate an intent to acquire the property and take actual possession or control of it; and (2) demonstrate that the property was abandoned." As to the latter requirement, there is confusion in the courts. The debate centers on what constitutes abandonment and whether abandonment can be inferred "from the passage of time or from the owner's own inactivity." Courts have looked to three different types of proof to determine abandonment, including: "(1) express renunciation of ownership by the owner; (2) implication from an owner's inaction; or (3) passage of time and the lack of an identifiable owner." If salvors are unable to convince the court that the wreck is abandoned, they will usually argue that the law of salvage should apply instead.[38]

2.3 *The United Nations Convention on the Law of the Sea (UNCLOS)*

The division of ocean space into the various maritime zones provided for under the UNCLOS correspondingly necessitates that any meaningful discussion on the international legal framework on the protection of the UCH must account for this division. The UNCLOS makes reference to six maritime zones: internal waters, the territorial sea, the contiguous zone, the exclusive economic zone, the continental shelf, and the Area. The UNCLOS carefully laid out the various rights and duties of states in each of these zones. The UCH Convention (UNESCO Convention) follows this schematic dissection of the ocean into the various maritime zones of jurisdiction.[39]

UNCLOS was adopted in the 1980, it comes into force on 16 November 1994 at the time being, the development technology to make an exploitation of cultural under water has not yet regulated comprehensively. There are only two articles deal with the protection of cultural underwater. UNCLOS handles the issue of protection of underwater cultural heritage in articles 149 and 303. Article 303(1) imposes a duty to protect "objects of an archaeological and historical nature found at sea" and states that the parties "shall" cooperate for this purpose. Article 149 UNCLOS states:

> "All objects of an archaeological and historical nature found in the Area shall be preserved or disposed of for the benefit of mankind as a whole, particular regard being paid to the preferential rights of the State or country of origin, or the State of cultural origin, or the State of historical and archaeological origin".

Article 149 leaves two notable lacunas in UNCLOS. The first is the lack of a practical provision regarding underwater cultural heritage found in the waters between the outer-edge of the Contiguous Zone until the start of the Area, and the second is the vagueness of the definition of underwater cultural heritage. Article 149 raises two primary points, each fraught with ambiguity. Article 149 stipulates that objects found in "the Area" should (1) be preserved or disposed of "for the benefit of mankind," while (2) giving preferential rights to three conceivably different entities: the State of origin, the State of cultural origin, and/or the State of archaeological origin. Under the second point, the Convention similarly fails to elaborate on how to balance the three different States which could be capable of claiming preferential rights,

37. Jeffrey Cohn, 'A Legal Perspective On The Protection Of Underwater Cultural Heritage Resources In The United States: Is The Abandoned Shipwreck Act Lost At Sea, Or Is It Worthy Of Salvage?' (2016) 27 *DePaul Journal of Art, Technology & Intellectual Property Law*, 3-4,
38. Marian Leigh Miller, above n 30, 347-349
39. Lowell Bautista, 'Ensuring the Preservation of Submerged Treasures for the Next Generation: The Protection of Underwater Cultural Heritage in International Law'. Proceedings from the 2012 LOSI-KIOST Conference on Securing the Ocean for the Next Generation. https://www.law.berkeley.edu/files/Bautista-final.pdf. Accessed on 19 September 2018.

there is no elaboration about the issues. Article 149 and 303 UNCLOS provide some frameworks for the legal protection of UCH found at sea,[40] however these Articles indicate an unenforceable starting point to understanding underwater cultural heritage.

While Article 303 of UNCLOS contains much more specific language pertaining to underwater cultural heritage and introduces the primary tension between legal regimes for UCH. It mentions:

1. States have the duty to protect objects of an archaeological and historical nature found at sea and shall cooperate for this purpose.
2. In order to control traffic in such objects, the coastal State may, in applying article 33, presume that their removal from the seabed in the zone referred to in that article without its approval would result in an infringement within its territory or territorial sea of the laws and regulations referred to in that article.
3. Nothing in this article affects the rights of identifiable owners, the law of salvage or other rules of admiralty, or laws and practices with respect to cultural exchanges.
4. This article is without prejudice to other international agreements and rules of international law regarding the protection of objects of an archaeological and historical nature.

Article 303 addresses archaeological and historical objects at sea, and elaborates on three fundamental principles, namely: (i) it bestows a duty on states to cooperate to protect archaeological objects found at sea; (ii) When there is an object will be removed from the territorial sea of the coastal states should get the approval from the coastal states otherwise it infringe the laws and regulations referred to in that article; (iii) The rules in this article will not affect the rights of identifiable owners, the law of salvage or other rules of admiralty, or laws and practices with respect to cultural exchanges. It is similar to Article 149, UNCLOS only initiate to introduce protection of UCH.[41] However, the elaboration of the three fundamental aspects stipulated in Article 303 enacted through State practices, domestic laws, and subsequent conventions.

Specifically, principles two and three of Article 303 introduce the defining conflict surrounding UCH in the case to determine shipwrecks subject to salvage and finds against the in-situ preservation required by archaeological practice.[42] Article 149 and 303 of the UNCLOS will not affect the rights of the salvor to imposed the law of salvage or the law of finds. Thus, those articles are weak and ambiguous as well as unenforceable when the wreck laying in waters beyond the territorial reach of coastal states.[43] The development of advent new technologies causes the existing framework for the protection of underwater cultural heritage was inadequate, since there is possibility to make evacuation of the historical shipwreck which is formerly untouchable due the lack of technology. This led the International Law Association established the UNESCO Convention in 2001 after 4 years negotiation stated in 1998.[44]

3 THE PROTECTION OF CULTURAL UNDERWATER BASED ON UNESCO CONVENTION 2001

The understanding of the threat that unauthorized salvaging that may occur to underwater cultural heritage causes to the establishment of an international framework aimed at its protection: The UNESCO Convention 2001. The UNESCO Convention 2 primary goal is to ensure that any interference with underwater cultural heritage complies with internationally

40. Ole Varmer, 'Closing The Gaps In The Law Protecting Underwater Cultural Heritage On The Outer Continental Shelf' (2014) 33 *Stanford Environmental Law Journal*, 254.
41. Lowell Bautista, above n 39.
42. Ibid.
43. Christopher R. Bryant, above n 4, at 106
44. Markus Rau, 'The UNESCO Convention on Underwater Cultural Heritage and the International Law of the Sea', http://www.mpil.de/files/pdf1/mpunyb_rau_6.pdf. <Accessed on 20 September 2018>.

accepted archaeological standards. The negotiating parties attempted to balance between the interests of coastal states, namely the states in whose waters cultural heritage was found and those of flag states, namely the sovereigns under whose laws the submerged vessels were registered or licensed.[45]

UNCLOS maintains a slight jurisdictional balance in the Exclusive Economic Zone and Continental Shelf. It grants coastal states only jurisdiction over natural resources but not include underwater cultural heritage found in those waters. The UNESCO Convention 2001[46] was finalized on November 2, 2001. During the negotiations of the Convention, its relation to the UNCLOS was one of the most controversial issues. One of the questions was "whether a new convention could extend coastal state jurisdiction to control activities affecting "underwater cultural heritage beyond the limits"[47] established by the UNCLOS. In this context, it is relevant that Article 303(4) of the UNCLOS might be interpreted as allowing future agreements concerning underwater cultural heritage to develop the jurisdictional framework of the UNCLOS. The outcome of the negotiations is a compromise, which develops on the existing jurisdictional framework. A lots of significant states uttered opposition to this compromise.[48]

The UNESCO Convention 2001 obliges parties to regulate UCH activities within their national jurisdiction according to the Annex's standards of underwater archaeology, mandates in situ preservation, and prohibits commercial trade or speculation. It adopts the traditionalist preservation doctrine, asserting, since the archaeological resources are "finite, depletable, and non renewable" they need in situ preservation that permits sequencing and dating at stratigraphic levels. The Annex, consisting of thirty-six rules drafted by archaeologists, however it is not legally binding. Formalized industry standards such as the Annex remain dominant in developing state practice and are generally adopted by national legislatures.[49]

The UNESCO Convention 2001 creates a requirement that a vessel or national of another state notify the coastal state about discoveries of underwater cultural heritage in the coastal state's Exclusive Economic Zone or Continental Shelf. This may be understood as deliberating on the coastal state the right to demand a report from the flag state's vessel master. Moreover, the Convention grants "Coordinating State" status to coastal states, meaning that once an underwater cultural heritage artifact is discovered in its Exclusive Economic Zone or Continental Shelf (even by another state's national or commercial vessel), the coastal state becomes the administrator in charge of managing activities affecting the find.[50] Even though the Convention provides that "the Coordinating State shall act on behalf of the State Parties as a whole and not in its own interest." However, there is no authorization to conduct such action which constitute a basis for the assertion of any preferential or jurisdictional rights not provided for in international law, including the UNCLOS. Additionally, the Convention allows Coordinating States to "take all practicable measures" prior to consultations with flag states in cases of "immediate danger to the underwater cultural heritage, including looting."[51] The nature of these practicable measures is ambiguous.

The UNESCO Convention 2001 defines underwater cultural heritage as "all traces of human existence having a cultural, historical or archaeological character which have been

45. Eden Sarid, 'International Underwater Cultural Heritage Governance: Past Doubts And Current Challenges' (2017) 35 *Berkeley Journal of International Law*, 220-221.
46. The other three heritage conventions are the Convention on the Protection of Cultural Property in the Event of Armed Conflict, 95 the Convention on the Means of Prohibiting and Preventing the Illicit Import, Export and Transfer of Ownership of Cultural Property, 96 and the Convention concerning the Protection of the World Cultural and Natural Heritage. see Liza J. Bowman, above n 7
47. David Freestone, 'A Decade of The Law of the Sea Convention: Is It A Success?' (2007) *George Washington International Law Review*, 515-516.
48. Ibid.
49. Eden Sarid, above n 45, 226.
50. By Mark A. Wilder, above n 13.
51. Article 10 (5) UNESCO Convention 2001.

partially or totally underwater, periodically or continuously, for at least 100 years." The hundred-year criterion was established to avoid ownership-related problems and conflict with ordinary salvage law. The attachment of "cultural, historical, or archaeological character" as a restricting criterion was an attempted compromise between states that advocated for a wide definition and those that preferred that only "significant" underwater cultural heritage would enjoy protection. However, some believed this as unnecessary because, after all, one could argue that almost all artifacts over a hundred years old hold a cultural, historical or archaeological character.[52]

The UNESCO Convention 2001 features five fundamental principles, which are all outlined in article 2. The first is that state parties have an obligation to protect underwater cultural heritage for the benefit of humanity. In practice this means that any activity directed at or influencing underwater cultural heritage must meet international archeological standards. These standards are outlined in the Annex to the Convention. Second, priority is always given to in situ preservation of underwater cultural heritage, namely, in its original location on the ocean floor. This is in keeping with archaeological principles, which prescribe that excavation should occur only when the underwater cultural heritage is at risk or for research purposes. Third, commercial exploitation of underwater cultural heritage is prohibited. Fourth, state parties are required to cooperate with each other and promote awareness of the importance of underwater cultural heritage.[53] Fifth, the principles of international law and state sovereignty are to be secured. The premise of the Convention, it seems, is based on an assumption of wide participation and collaboration between member states. The Convention defines different cooperation mechanisms such as sharing information and collaborating in the investigation and conservation of UCH sites. It also encourages member states to enter into bilateral, regional or other multilateral agreements for the protection of UCH.

4 THE LEGAL IMPLICATION OF UNESCO CONVENTION TO THE LAW OF SALVAGE AND THE LAW OF FIND

The legal implication of the UNESCO Convention 2001 to the law of Salvage and Law of Find can be demonstrated as followed. *First*, the definition of UCH in Article 1 of the UNESCO Convention 2001 suffers from being overly broad and vague. The phrase "all traces of human existence having a cultural, historical or archaeological character". It means that everything which are found in the sea is classified as UCH if it poses archaeological character. On the other hand, why that in – situ preservation is much more preferable, and the historic shipwrecks and other underwater cultural heritage is excluded from salvage law due to the salvage law intended to save objects in danger of being lost at sea, and that historic artifacts do not fall into such a nature because they have already been lost.[54] Additionally, danger to an artifact could be augmented by endeavouring to take it to the surface instead of just leaving it where it is.

The fact is, in its proper and ordinary signification, it may rightfully be interpreted to include just about anything and everything that is found underwater. The UNESCO Convention 2001 assumes as UCH an object underwater which satisfies the above criterion and the 100-year period test and will be covered in the broad scope of the Convention's protection. These broad criteria likewise ignore the nature of UCH as a multi-use resource. This obvious archaeological bias overlooks the fact that UCH is also a fishery resource and also a sports and recreational resource. Hence, the definition affect the application of the Law of salvage

52. Eden Sarid, above n 45, 219.
53. UNESCO 'About the Convention on the Protection of the Underwater Cultural Heritage', http://www.unesco.org/new/en/culture/themes/underwater-cultural-heritage/2001-convention/. Accessed on 24 September 2018.
54. Allison Leigh Richmond, 'Scrutinizing the Shipwreck Salvage Standard: Should A Salvor Be Rewarded For Locating Historic Treasure?' (2010) 23 *New York International Law Review*, 120-121.

and the law of find. Thus, there will be no more objects of the law of Salvage and the law of find if the objects has been in the bottom of the sea for 100 years.

Second, according to Article 4 of the UNESCO Convention 2001 states "Any activity relating to underwater cultural heritage to which this Convention applies shall not be subject to the law of salvage or the law of finds, unless it:

(a) is authorized by the competent authorities, and
(b) is in full conformity with this Convention, and
(c) ensures that any recovery of the underwater cultural heritage achieves its maximum protection.[55]

Consequently, when the objects have been determine as UCH, the law of salvage and the law of find cannot be applicable unless those requirements are fulfilled. The Article put a strict requirement to the application of the law of Salvage and the Law of Find.

Third, elimination of the economic value of UCH affect a lot to the law of salvage, since the purpose of the law of salvage in some extent for commercial purposes.The UCH Convention introduces the principle that the preservation and protection of UCH is contrary with its commercial exploitation.[56] More than this, the UCH Convention pursues to eradicate UCH from commerce. On the one hand, it is extremely suspicious whether this is the most effective means to achieve the aims of the UCH Convention. The fact that UCH is consist of various resource implies that it is not only important archeologically, historically or culturally; it also has an economic value. Shipwrecks contain of numerous kinds of economic values.[57]

The most interesting and contentious aspect of the Convention is its prohibition on the commercial exploitation of UCH. One of the objectives of the Convention is mentioned in Aticle 2 (7) "that underwater cultural heritage shall not be commercially exploited." Further, the Annex of the Convention (Rule2) describing the rules to be followed, stipulates:

> "The commercial exploitation of underwater cultural heritage for trade or speculation or its irretrievable dispersal is fundamentally incompatible with the protection and proper management of underwater cultural heritage. UCH shall not be traded, sold, bought or bartered as commercial goods."

In an ostensible effort to protect the UCH, thus the prohibition of commercial exploitation is an endeavour to absolutely abolish a commercial entity's profit motive in recovering wrecks in the original place.

If the UNESCO Convention 2001 becomes customary international law, the consequence of the ban on commercial exploitation would be a near or thorough eradication of the historic wreck salvage industry. Without a profit motive, commercial salvage companies will apparently not stand survive.

5 THE CONFLICT BETWEEN THE UNESCO CONVENTION AND THE LAW OF SALVAGE AND THE LAW OF FIND

Law of Salvage and law of Find have their own objectives which are different with the UNESCO Convention 2001. The conflicting rules between law of Salvage and Law of Find with the UNESCO Convention 2001 are triggered by the different interest of the salvor, owners and states Parties of the UNESCO Convention 2001. There are two fundamental conflicting rules of the law of Salvage and the law of Find with the UNESCO Convention.

55. James A.R. Nafziger, 'The UNESCO Convention on The Protection of the Underwater Cultural Heritage: Its Growing Influence' (2018) 49 (July) *Journal of Maritime Law and Commerce* 374.
56. Patrick Coleman. 'UNESCO and the Belitung Shipwreck: The Need for A Permissive Definition of "Commercial Exploitation"' (2013) 45 *George Washington International Law Review* 851-852.
57. Yakov Malkiel, 'An Evolutionary Look at the Law, Technology, and Economics of Sunken Treasure' (2013) 44(April) *Journal of Maritime Law and Commerce* 195.

First, according to the UNESCO Convention2001, in situ preservation is always the first option.[58] This means that based on archaeological principles that excavation would not occur unless the wreck was at risk or there was a research purpose for excavating. Thus, no matter which state is sovereign, the shipwreck would ordinarily stay on the ocean floor. Thus, in situ preservation is contradict with the law of salvage and the law of find.

Second, any commercial exploitation of a sunken state vessel is fundamentally incompatible with the UNESCO Convention 2001 principles.[59] Title to a sunken state vessel should essentially be viewed as a means to ensure its preservation. This idea is reflected, for example, in the Dutch committee's statement that emphasis is now on the public interest in conserving these wrecks or their contents rather than on the economic value of salvaging them.[60] Ownership is currently therefore important not so much in order to exercise title to the [Dutch East India Company's] wrecks as to ensure their protection through international frameworks.[61]

Third, it may raise conflict of ownership. The first question that may be raised is whether UCH can be owned. If a piece of UCH belonged to a person or entity at one time, then this raises the question as to whether the piece of UCH can be regarded as an abandoned object after one hundred years? It is believed that the physical act of abandoning and the intention to abandon should be two factors that help us to decide whether sunken properties have been abandoned, however it would be very difficult to find evidence to support this. With this difficulty in mind, UCH is usually not considered to be ownerless or abandoned, however doubts exist. Therefore, it seems that UCH within the limits of national jurisdiction cannot be the subject of law of salvage or law of find. UCH may have sunken for many years, the ownership of the artifact may be determined by the law at the time when sank.. However, even if ownership of UCH can be determined, conflicts remain.[62]

6 THE POSSIBILITIES TO SETTLE THE CONFLICT BETWEEN THE UNESCO CONVENTION 2001 WITH THE LAW OF SALVAGE AND THE LAW OF FIND

The conflicting rules and interest between law of find, law of salvage and the UNSECO Convention 2001 should be solved in order to achieve the objective of the UNESCO Convention 2001. By attempting to protect historic wrecks from individuals and corporations who employ no archaeological standards, the UNESCO Convention 2001 has succeeded in creating a sort of moratorium on location and recovery efforts.[63] Hence, it is necessarily to cope up with the issue by establishing a certain kind of conditions that have to be performed by the salvors to contribute to the protection and preservation of UCH.

The Law of salvage and law of find is visible to be exercised when the requirement which are stipulated in Article 2 (1) of the UNESCO Convention 2001[64] are fulfilled. In addition, by providing the commercial incentive of salvage companies[65] and it contributes to the number of wrecks that can be found and located, many wrecks in peril of being damaged and destroyed will receive protection. Even though the drafters of the Convention seem to assume that not all wrecks are considered to be in marine peril, not all wrecks are perfectly safe in

58. Lydia Barbash-Riley, 'Using A Community-Based Strategy To Address The Impacts Of Globalization On Underwater Cultural Heritage' (2015) 22 *Indiana Journal of Global Legal Studies*, at 204-205.
59. Ben Juvelier, above n 23, 1027.
60. Eden Sarid, above n 45, 232. (219-166)
61. Ibid.
62. Ben Juvelier, above n 23, 1027.
63. Jeremy Neil, 'Sifting Through the Wreckage: An Analysis and Proposed Resolution Concerning the Disposition of Historic Shipwrecks Located in International Waters' (2010/2011) 55 *New York Law School Law Review* 902.
64. Article 2 (1) UNESCO Convention 2001, states: "This Convention aims to ensure and strengthen the protection of underwater cultural heritage".
65. Craig J. S. Forrest, 'Has The Application of Salvage Law to Underwater Cultural Heritage Become A Thing of The Past?' (2003) 34(April) *Journal of Maritime Law and Commerce* 319.

their present conditions. Thus the service which are provided by the salvors through consulting with the archaeologist the protection and preservation of UCH will be obtained and this is important to educate the people.[66]

The UNESCO Convention 2001 provides that "nothing in this Convention shall prejudice the rights, jurisdiction and duties of States under international law, including the United Nations Convention on the Law of the Sea."[67] This was meant to satisfy the maritime powers that were concerned that the Convention might adjust the balance of rights and interests established under UNCLOS. The provisions likely to receive the most criticism from treasure seekers are Article 2(7) and Rule 2 of the Annex. Article 2 (7) states that underwater cultural heritage shall not be commercially exploited. Rule 2 of the Annex elaborates this general principle, declaring that "the commercial exploitation of underwater cultural heritage for trade or speculation or its irretrievable dispersal is fundamentally incompatible with the protection and proper management of underwater cultural heritage."[68] Furthermore, underwater cultural heritage shall not be traded, sold, bought or bartered as commercial goods".

Third, the UNESCO Convention 2001 entitles coastal States, under certain circumstances, to authorize or prohibit activities conducted towards UCH located within the EEZ or on the continental shelf.[69] Meanwhile, a coastal State shall request its nationals, or the master of the vessel flying its flag, to report the discovery of or intended activities related to UCH within those areas, either to it or to all other parties. Coastal States are required to consult with other parties who have declared an interest in being consulted on how to effectively protect UCH.[70] Ultimately, protection measures consented by all consulting States shall be taken and certain urgent measures are allowable. Similar regimes exist for UCH in the Area, which could be generalized as three steps "report, consultation and protection or urgent measures." The uniqueness of this regime is that reporting must be made to all States parties.

Fourth, the 1989 International Convention on Salvage (ICS) established the prevailing international salvage regime. Compared with UNCLOS, this treaty took an advance regarding the protection of UCH even though its legal regime is not exactly related to UCH. Article 30 (1) of the ICS provides that States parties can reserve the right not to apply the provisions of the Convention "when the property involved is maritime cultural property of prehistoric, archaeological or historic interest and is situated on the sea-bed." Some scholars have pointed out that by making reservations to Article 30 (1) (d), states can exclude the "maritime cultural property" located at the seabed from the scope of salvage law.[71] In other words, the ICS or salvage law cannot be applied to UCH when reservations exist. Consequently, the ICS contributes to the protection of UCH since it allows the exclusion of salvage law at this point.

Furthermore, "salvage" is defined as "any act or activity undertaken to assist a vessel or any other property in danger in any waters."[72] Thus, marine danger is a vital precondition for applying salvage law to the marine property concerned. Some held that the ICS does not imply that the shipwreck is necessarily in peril, the "nature and degree" of which shall be properly proven.[73] In other words, even when no reservations are made, salvage law or the ICS cannot be automatically applied to UCH. So shall UCH be considered to be "in danger"? Even if some American courts have recognized the possibility that UCH is in danger, many scholars do not believe so. At any rate, this debate indicates that it is no longer likely that salvage law could be universally applied to UCH without any limitation.[74]

66. Jeremy Neil, above n 63, 899-900.
67. Article 3 of the UNESCO Convention 2001.
68. Rule 2 of the UNESCO Convention 2001 Annex
69. Article 10 (2) UNESCO Convention 2001.
70. Article 10 (3) (a) and (b) UNESCO Convention 2001.
71. Ben Juvelier, above n 23, 1026.
72. Article 1 (1) Salvage Convention 1989.
73. Bomin Nie, *On the International Legal Protection of Underwater Cultural Heritage*, https://core.ac.uk/download/pdf/41460226.pdf. <Accessed on 21 September 2018>.
74. *Ibid.*

7 CONCLUSION

Based on the analysis regarding the legal implication of the UNESCO Convention 2001 to the law of Salvage and the Law of find, it can be submitted, as followed:

First, the legal implication of the UNESCO Convention 2001 to the law of Salvage and law of Find enables the UNESCO Convention 2001 to protect and to preserve the UCH, since the UNESCO Convention 2001 can be used as a legal basic to prohibit the enforcement of the law of salvage and the law of finds toward the property in the sea when the property has been determine as the UCH, so there is no more chance to enforce the law of salvage and the law of finds. However, cooperation can be carried out when for specific purposes that the need of the salvor's service to evacuate the UCH to be performed in the museum which is much more beneficial for the educational purposes.

Second, it cannot be justified that there are serious conflicts between the law of salvage and the law of finds with the UNESCO Convention 2001. The different objectives which exist in each field of law causes the conflict, such as the principle of in-situ preservation and non commercial principle in the UNESCO Convention 2001 are contradict with the law of salvage and the law of finds. The salvors are prohibited to salvage the archeological and historical shipwrecks which are previously cause a lot of advantage for the salvors from the rewards that are granted by the owners. However, if each field of law is applied in its own scope, there will be no conflict of interest as far as each field of law respects and recognizes the jurisdiction of each field law. The UNESCO Convention 2001 still recognizes the applicability the law of salvage and the law of finds as far as in accordance with the requirements which are stipulated in Article 4.

Third, There are some possibilities to settle the conflict between UNESCO Convention 2001 and the law of salvage and the law of finds especially related to the principle of preservation in situ of underwater cultural heritage shall be considered as the first option before allowing or engaging in any activities directed at this heritage and also the principle of underwater cultural heritage shall not be commercially exploited in-situ preservation and non-commercially. Those kinds of conflict can be settled when there is cooperation and also compromise to implement the principles of the UNESCO Convention 2001 by providing certain kind of mechanism in the specific case that there is still an opportunity for the salvor to offer service in order to protect and to preserve UCH base on the archeological principle.

REFERENCES

Barbash-Riley, Lydia, 'Using A Community-Based Strategy To Address The Impacts Of Globalization On Underwater Cultural Heritage' (2015) 22 *Indiana Journal of Global Legal Studies*.

Bautista, Lowell, 'Ensuring the Preservation of Submerged Treasures for the Next Generation: The Protection of Underwater Cultural Heritage in International Law'. Proceedings from the 2012 LOSI-KIOST Conference on Securing the Ocean for the Next Generation. https://www.law.berkeley.edu/files/Bautista-final.pdf. Accessed on 19 September 2018.

Bederman, David J., 'Building New Regimes and Institutions for the Sea', (1998) 30 *University of Miami Inter-American Law Review*.

Ben, Juvelier, '"Salvaging" History: Underwater Cultural Heritage and Commercial Salvage' (2017) 32 American University International Law Review

Bomin, Nie, *On the International Legal Protection of Underwater Cultural Heritage*, https://core.ac.uk/download/pdf/41460226.pdf. <Accessed on 21 September 2018>

Bowman, Liza J., *Oceans Apart Over Sunken Ships: Is The Underwater Cultural Heritage Convention Really Wrecking Admiralty Law?* https://digitalcommons.osgoode.yorku.ca/ohlj/vol42/iss1/1/. <Accessed on 22 September 2018>.

Bryant, Christopher R., 'The Archaeological Duty Of Care: The Legal, Professional, And Cultural Struggle Over Salvaging Historic Shipwrecks'. (2001) 65 *Albany Law Review*.

Cohn, Jeffrey, 'A Legal Perspective On The Protection Of Underwater Cultural Heritage Resources In The United States: Is The Abandoned Shipwreck Act Lost At Sea, Or Is It Worthy Of Salvage?' (2016) 27 *DePaul Journal of Art, Technology & Intellectual Property Law*.

Coleman, Patrick, 'UNESCO and the Belitung Shipwreck: The Need for A Permissive Definition of "Commercial Exploitation"' (2013) 45 *George Washington International Law Review*.
Curfman, David, 'Thar Be Treasure Here: Rights To Ancient Shipwrecks In International Waters–A New Policy Regime' (2008) 86 *Washington University Law Review*.
Forrest, Craig J. S., 'Has The Application of Salvage Law to Underwater Cultural Heritage Become A Thing of The Past?' (2003) 34(April) *Journal of Maritime Law and Commerce*.
Freestone, David, 'A Decade Of The Law of the Sea Convention: Is It A Success?' *George Washington International Law Review*, (2007).
Henn, Cathryn, 'The Trouble With Treasure Historic Shipwrecks Discovered In International Waters' (2012) 19 *University of Miami International and Comparative Law Review*.
Hoefly, Christian, 'National Treasure: A Survey Of The Current International Law Regime For Underwater Cultural Heritage' (2016) 4 (August) *Penn State Journal of Law & International Affairs*.
Malkiel, Yakov, 'An Evolutionary Look at the Law, Technology, and Economics of Sunken Treasure' (2013) 44 (April) *Journal of Maritime Law and Commerce*.
Miller, Marian Leigh, 'Underwater Cultural Heritage: Is The Titanic Still In Peril As Courts Battle Over The Future Of The Historical Vessel?' (2006) 20 *Emory International Law Review*.
Murphy, Nathan, 'Scuttle the Abandoned Shipwreck Act: The Unnecessary Unconstitutionality of American Historic Shipwreck Preservation' (2011) 36 *Tulane Maritime Law Journal*.
Nafziger, James A.R., 'The UNESCO Convention on The Protection of the Underwater Cultural Heritage: Its Growing Influence' (2018) 49 (July) *Journal of Maritime Law and Commerce*.
Neil, Jeremy, 'Sifting Through the Wreckage: An Analysis and Proposed Resolution Concerning the Disposition of Historic Shipwrecks Located in International Waters', (2010/2011) 55 *New York Law School Law Review*.
Nie, Bomin, 'On the International Legal Protection of Underwater Cultural Heritage' (2015) 2 *China Ocean Law Review* https://core.ac.uk/download/pdf/41460226.pdf. <Accessed on 21 September 2018>.
Regan, Rob, 'When Lost Liners Become Found: An Examination Of The Effectiveness Of Present Maritime Legal And Statutory Regimes For Protecting Historic Wrecks In International Waters With Some Proposals For Change' (2005) 29 *Tulane Maritime Law Journal*.
Richmond, Allison Leigh, 'Scrutinizing the Shipwreck Salvage Standard: Should A Salvor Be Rewarded For Locating Historic Treasure?' (2010) 23 *New York International Law Review*.
Sánchez, Omar Carmona, 'Rights of Treasure Hunters Under Puerto Rico Law: Application of Article 285 of The Civil Code Through The Jones Act, The Puerto Rican Underwater Archaeological Protection Act and The Abandoned Shipwreck Act Of 1987' (2008) 47 *Revista de Derecho Puertorriqueno*.
Sarid, Eden, 'International Underwater Cultural Heritage Governance: Past Doubts And Current Challenges' (2017) 35 *Berkeley Journal of International Law*.
Tedesco, Mitchell F., 'Between the Devil and The Deep Blue Sea: The Shortcomings of Forcing Courts to Choose From The Law of Salvage and The Law of Finds in Treasure Salvage Cases' (2016-2017) 29 *University of San Francisco Maritime Law Journal*.
Varmer, Ole, 'Closing The Gaps In The Law Protecting Underwater Cultural Heritage On The Outer Continental Shelf' (2014) 33 *Stanford Environmental Law Journal*.
Yeates, Jeffrey W., 'Clearing Up the Confusion: A Strict Standard of Abandonment for Sunken Public Vessels' (1999-2000) 12 *University of San Francisco Maritime Law Journal*.
Zubic, R. Ethan, 'Pure Versus Contract Salvage – Narrowing The Scope Of An "Agreement To Volunteer" Bar To Pure Salvage' (2011) 10 *Loyola Maritime Law Journal*.
UNESCO Convention 2001
Rule 2 of the UNESCO Convention 2001 Annex
Salvage Convention 1989
Rau, Markus, *The UNESCO Convention on Underwater Cultural Heritage and the International Law of the Sea*, http://www.mpil.de/files/pdf1/mpunyb_rau_6.pdf. < Accessed on 20 September 2018>.
UK UNESCO 2001 Convention Review Group, 2014, The UNESCO Convention on the Protection of the Underwater Cultural Heritage 2001: An Impact Review for the United Kingdom,http://www.jnapc.org.uk/UNESCO%20Impact%20Review%20February%202014.pdf. < Accessed on 18 September 2018)
UNESCO, *The Convention on the Protection of the Underwater Cultural Heritage*. https://www.unesco.nl/sites/default/files/dossier/gb-2001convention-infokit_07-2009.pdf?download=1. < Accessed on 17 September 2018>.

UNESCO, *About the Convention on the Protection of the Underwater Cultural Heritage*, http://www.unesco.org/new/en/culture/themes/underwater-cultural-heritage/2001-convention/. Accessed on 24 September 2018.

Wilder, Mark A., *Application of Salvage Law and the Law of Finds to Sunken Shipwreck Discoveries Modern technology has made the location and retrieval of shipwrecks.* https://pdfs.semanticscholar.org/3bfc/4c3583c7a31cb0cc25e1ad0231f9b83219a4.pdf. <Accessed on 19 September 2018 >.

https://pdfs.semanticscholar.org/3bfc/4c3583c7a31cb0cc25e1ad0231f9b83219a4.pdf. <Accessed on 19 September 2018>.

Culture and International Law - Juwana et al. (Eds)
© 2019 Taylor & Francis Group, London, ISBN 978-1-138-38766-9

Regulation of fisheries resources in support of sustainable development in Indonesia

Magdariza
Lecturer of Law Faculty, Andalas University, Padang, Indonesia

ABSTRACT: As the greatest archipelagic state in the world, Indonesia has an extensive ocean territory that provides a large benefit in the sector of fisheries resources. Any regulation was established in sustain the resource management to preserve of availability and sustainability. Since the Indonesian government issuing jurisdiction of ocean territory known as Declaration of Djuanda in 1957 until established Fisheries Act with amendment and the last is Fisheries Act No. 45 of 2009. Moreover, the fisheries resources are correlated with the Naval Act, coastal management and associated legislation. In common, as the state that was ratify the United Nations Convention on the Law of the Sea (UNCLOS) 1982, the maintained regulation is intended to sustain fisheries resources as described in the Stockholm Declaration of 1972 in the development principle to attain the current demand, without reducing the ability of future generations to accomplish it.

KEYWORDS: Regulation, fisheries resource, sustainability development, archipelagic state, resource management

1 INTRODUCTION

As an archipelagic state, Indonesia has thousands of islands spread around its territory. As the largest archipelagic state in the world, Indonesia has more water than land within its territory, with two-thirds made up of water, either deep-ocean or archipelagic. At the limits of the region, there are many potential resources to develop in order to support the development of the country.

The implementation of water resource development, especially in fisheries, must be arranged according to existing regulations to preserve the sustainability of potential fisheries in the long term. The implementation of sustainable fisheries development is a realization of state sovereignty in maintaining sustainable fisheries resources for the improvement of social welfare.

Following independence, the fisheries regulations of Indonesia are statutes and regulations such as the Decree of Maritime and Fisheries Minister. In international law, there is also the legal 1982 convention of the sea (United Nations Convention on the Law of the Sea/ UNCLOS), ratified in Indonesia in 1985 under Act No. 17.

The regulations on fisheries intend to preserve the availability of fisheries resources in the long term. According to their objectives, the management of fisheries must be arranged on the principle of sustainable development of the continuity of fisheries for the future. At this point, the development is in an implementation process of preservation such that demand accomplishes principles for the present generation without reducing the capacity in the future.

The enforcement of a sustainable development principle is based on the Stockholm Declaration of 1972. Increasing international awareness encouraged the UN to organize a conference on the human environment in 1972 in Stockholm, Sweden (Putra, 2003, p. 13), resulting in the declaration. Even though the result is only in the form of a declaration, it is a step forward for states in preserving the environment from destruction and devastation by humans. An implementation of fisheries management to maintain sustainability in fulfilling current demands while supporting the fisheries demand of the next generation must also be arranged by the principle of sustainable development.

2 FISHERIES RESOURCES AND SUSTAINABLE DEVELOPMENT

2.1 *Fisheries resources*

The total water area in Indonesia as a large proportion of the territory has provided great benefits, whether in terms of recreation, sport or research, besides the utilization of resources like fisheries. Fisheries involve 'activities related to the management and utilization of resources and the environment in the fisheries business system, starting from pre-production, production, management, until marketing' (point 1 of Article 1 of Act No. 45, 2009).

Fisheries resources consist of the fish, environments, and artificial resources used in the fisheries industry (Republic of Indonesia, 2xxx, p. 34). Meanwhile, the meaning of fisheries resource is potentially all types of fish (point 2 of Article 1 of Act No. 45, 2009). With great potential in the water, fish are a recoverable resource, which means that utilization must be arranged systematically, should not be taken entirely, and should be carried out according to the applicable rules. If the resource is only taken partially, the remaining fish can still can breed. This is intended to guarantee long-term availability and preservation for future utilization. This characteristic of fisheries resource is termed a renewable resource, and seeks to preserve a balance.

Because the organisms' life cycle occurs in the water, especially at sea, catching is conducted by fisherman with simple or traditional, as well as modern, tools. Fishing activity with traditional tools is conducted by micro fisherman from the beach, sometimes using a small boat, depending on weather and capital. Meanwhile, fishing with modern tools arranged by considers any provision in correlation with the fishing activity.

Fishing is an activity carried out in an uncultivated area with or without tools, including a ship for loading, shipping, storage, refrigeration, handling, processing and/or preservation (point 5 of Article 1 of Act No. 45, 2009). Therefore, the activity can be conducted only for uncultivated fish to maintain their conservation, and fishing by ship requires a fishing permit (*Surat Ijin Penangkapan Ikan* (SIPI)). As depicted in point 6 of Article 1 (Act No. 45, 2009), it is argued that the meaning of fish cultivation is maintaining, raising and/or breeding, and harvesting the result in a controlled area, including activity with a ship for loading, storage, refrigeration, handling, management and/or preservation.

The important thing related to fisheries is resource conservation. As described in point 8 of Article 1 of the Fisheries Law, it is an attempt to protect, conserve and utilize fish, including their ecosystems, variety and genetics, to guarantee their existence, availability and continuity by preserving and increasing the quality, value and diversity of fishing resources.

2.2 *Sustainable development*

The terms of sustainable development have been known since the interest of the international community has been directed to preserving the environment, and it is beginning to be understood that when the environment is not preserved and conserved, it will bring devastation for the future. The first pillar of international community action was the Stockholm Declaration of 1972.

The declaration contained 26 principles of development, signed by 113 heads of state. It asked that the states of the world implement development to improve and increase the living conditions for the present generation without reducing those of the next one (Husin, 2009, p. 5). The Stockholm Declaration inspired the states of the world as to the importance of the future of the environment. Thereby, it was realized that environmental problems absolutely determine the life of living creatures, including humans. Between creatures and the ecology is mutual influence, and each has dependence on the other. Humans require a healthy, comfortable environment, whether in air, flora, water, or fauna, also in contrary. However, the situation has growing by human, that always emphasize on their interest and the government on each states as pursue to the economic development, along with exploitation and unobstructed environmental exploration without considering the negative impact.

The Stockholm Declaration has ratified the environmental development concept. It is not only challenging all states and populations to improve their concern about environmental devastation, but also to find alignment between development and environmental management.

Moreover, the legal development of the international environment was established in the United Nations Convention on Environment and Development (UNCED) of 1992, agreed in Rio de Janeiro, Brazil, and known as the Rio Declaration, which consisted of 27 principles. This concentrates on the importance of a conservation concept called sustainable environment, which has been ratified as a basic principle in economic development and environmental management. The emergence of the concept derives from alarming situations, such as contamination, devastation and inappropriate resource utilization.

In the Rio Declaration there is a sustainable development concept consisting of three interrelated and sustaining main pillars: economic development, social provision, and environmental conservation. According to the World Commission on Environment and Development, the sustainable development concept is 'development to accomplish the present demand, without reducing the competence of the next generation to accomplish its demand'.

3 REGULATION OF FISHERIES RESOURCES TO MAINTAIN SUSTAINABLE DEVELOPMENT IN INDONESIA

Indonesia is one of the greatest archipelagic states on earth, with water territories larger than the mainland. Thus, Indonesia has enormous potential for fisheries resources that can be utilized by its people. The use of these resources must obviously be carried out according to the associated provisions.

The sovereignty of Indonesia as an archipelagic state started from the declaration of the government on territorial waters in 1957, known as the Declaration of Djuanda. The government issued the declaration because of the open sea areas between islands. There is freedom in the high seas, such as the freedom to fish, which means foreign fishermen from other states have similar rights to catch fish in open seas. Obviously, this situation is causing suffering for the people of Indonesia, especially its fishermen, because they will lose out in fishing. Another consideration is that the area of open seas between the islands in Indonesia reduces unity between the people on different islands because they are separated by open seas. Following its declaration, the government conferred legal power upon it by establishing the regulation of Indonesian waters in Act No. 4/Government Regulation/1960.

The next was regulation was Act No. 1 of 1973 on the Continental Shelf. Article 10 describes that the implementation of exploration and exploitation of resources on the continental shelf must be heeded and must protect interests as follows: a. defense and national security; b. transportation; c. telecommunication and underwater electrical transmission; d. fisheries; e. oceanographic investigation and other scientific research; f. nature reserves. Thus, the fisheries interest has to be considered and conserved in the course of the exploration and exploitation of the continental shelf. When a dispute over interests occurs, it must be settled according to these provisions, and if a problem in protection occurs in the exploration and exploitation of the continental shelf, the government can temporarily stop or withdraw the relevant business license.

Further regulation of fisheries occurred with Act No. 5 of 1983 on the Exclusive Economic Zone (EEZ) of Indonesia. The preamble of the act stipulated that all water activities in the jurisdiction of Indonesia must preserve and reserve the biological and non-biological resources in the territorial waters deemed as the EEZ owned by Indonesia. The stipulated protection and preservation is an attempt to maintain and sustain the wholeness of the ecosystem in the Indonesian EEZ territory.

The utilization of both resources in EEZI arranged by sovereignty right as international law given to use economically the natural resources in EEZ. As described in Article 4 Paragraph 1 point (a), in its EEZ, the Republic of Indonesia had the sovereign right to execute the exploration and exploitation, management and conservation of biological and non-biological resources in the seabed, bottom ground, and the water above, as well as any activities to explore and exploit the economic zone, including development of hydro, tidal and wind power.

The EEZ regime in the international community has been developed in practice by individual states and became a provision established in UNCLOS 1982 with the intention of protecting coastal states from resource depletion and extinction through onshore and offshore fishing. The definition of an EEZ can be seen in Article 55 of UNCLOS 1982, which states that 'The exclusive economic zone is an area beyond and adjacent to the territorial sea, subject to the specific legal regime established in this Part, under which the rights and jurisdiction of the coastal state and the rights and freedom of other states are governed by the relevant provisions of this Convention'.

In order to protect and preserve sustainable natural resources in this zone, the convention also determined many regulations that must be implemented by coastal states, as described in Article 61, in that coastal states should determine the total allowable catch and guarantee it by suitable conservation and management to ensure preservation of biological resources in the EEZ without exposure to excessive exploitation. The obligation of these actions intends to maintain and improve the existing population so that it can used at a level that will bring a guaranteed maximum result, as determined by economic factors and the relevant environment. This includes the socioeconomics of coastal fishermen and the special requirements of developing states, while also paying attention to the fishing method, mutual dependence on species, and international minimum standards proposed in common, whether at the subregional, regional or global level. According to the convention, an activity that must be arranged by coastal states is consideration of the consequences for species in correlation with or depending on useful species, with the intent to maintain and improve the population of species that relate or depend on the level when their reproduction is in danger.

UNCLOS determines the activities that can be conducted in the EEZs of coastal states in relation to fisheries, including conservation as depicted in Article 61, which regulates the optimum utilization of biological resources by determination of competence in use and carrying out of agreements with other coastal states that lack such competency. Moreover, UNCLOS regulates any supply of existing fish in the EEZ of a coastal state or its territorial waters if they are in close proximity to highly migratory species, sea mammals, anadromous and catadromous species, and sedentary.

The special regulation on fisheries depicted in Act No. 9 of 1985, then amendment to Act No. 31 of 2004 and Act No. 45 of 2009 on revision of Act No. 31 of 2004, are effective regulations at present. In order to protect and preserve fish resources, management is an attempt to obtain the sustainable productivity of a biological resource, attaining conservation to guarantee an available, sustainable, increasing quality and variety of species.

In order to maintain sustainable fisheries resources, any activities conducted must be based on principles of benefit, justice, togetherness, partnership, independence, equality, cohesiveness, transparency, efficiency, sustainability and sustainable development. The principle of sustainability is that fisheries management is arranged as optimally as possible by considering the sustainable aspect of the resource, while the principle of sustainable development is fisheries management arranged intentionally and capable of improving prosperity and social welfare with emphasis on environment sustainability for the present and the future.

The management of fisheries must be supported by management planning that determines matters in coordination with fisheries, such as potential and allocation for fishing, protection, as well as cultivation in fish management areas, setting the total catch, fish size and minimum weight, species prohibited from trade, protected species, contamination prevention, and provision of conservation territory by achieving sustainable resources and environments. The provision intended to protect and preserve this sustainable supply is described in the Fisheries Act that always relies on fisheries management to attain the optimum benefit and sustainability, as well as guaranteeing resource sustainability. This is based on the sustainable development concept as depicted in the Stockholm Declaration.

Fisheries, as a water resource, are also related to maritime management, and Act No. 32 of 2014 on the ocean. This resource consists of renewable and non-renewable water resources with comparative and competitive superiority and dependable in the long term when the management related to the utilization and waters conservation; that one of implementation principle is continuity. The objective of the principle, as depicted in point (d) of Article 3, is that water regulation utilizes the water resource in sustainability as much as possible for the prosperity of the present generation without sacrificing that of the next.

The management of fisheries resources relates to the social communication who living in coastal, according to Act No. 1 of 2014 on amendment of Act No. 27 of 2007 on the management of coastal areas and small islands. Point 19 of Article 1 described this as an attempt to protect, conserve, and utilize coastal areas and small islands, including the ecosystem, to secure the existence, availability, and sustainability of coastal resources and small islands by preserving and improving their quality, value and diversity.

Another regulation important to the management of fisheries resources is Act No. 32 of 2009 on protection and environmental management. Point 3 of Article 1 of the regulation argues that sustainable development is an awareness and intentional effort combining environmental, social and economic aspects into a development strategy to secure the environment totality and safety, competence and welfare, as well as the quality of lives for the present and next generations. In the implementation of the protection and management of the environment, it is carried between sustainable and continuity with the intention to secure the accomplishment of supply for the present and the next generation. The conservation of resource is the resource management in secure the wisely utilization and sustainable for supply by preserve and improve of quality of value and diversity.

4 CONCLUSION

As a state dominated by water, Indonesia has huge potential resources in fisheries. Protection of this resource is described in established domestic regulations or ratified international rules. The problem of fisheries resource control exists not only in regulation but also in the protection and environmental management of oceans, coasts and EEZs, as well as international conventions such as the United Nations Convention on the Law of the Sea of 1982, ratified by Indonesian Act No. 17 of 1985.

Essentially, any regulation associated with fisheries resources must be based on sustainable development principles as described in the Stockholm Declaration of 1972, accomplishing current demands without reducing the competence of the next generation to do the same.

REFERENCES

Husin, S. (2009). *Hukum Lingkungan Internasional* [*International environmental law*]. Jakarta, Indonesia: Pusbangdik.

Putra, I.B.W. (2003). *Hukum Lingkungan Internasional, Perspektif Bisnis Internasional* [*International environmental law: International business perspective*]. Bandung, Indonesia: Refika Aditama.

Republic of Indonesia. (2xxx). *Identifikasi Kearifan Lokal Dalam Pengelolaan Sumber Daya Kelautan dan Perikanan Di Indonesia* [*Identification of local wisdom in the management of marine and fisheries resources in Indonesia*]. Jakarta, Indonesia: Ministry of Maritime Affairs and Fisheries.

Satria, A., Mony, A. & Muthohharoh, N.H. (Eds.). (2017). *Laut dan Masyarakat Adat, Kajian Praktik Pengelolaan Sumber Daya Laut Berbasis kearifan Lokal Oleh Masyarakat Adat di Pulau-Pulau Kecil terluar* [*Sea and indigenous peoples: Study of local wisdom-based marine resource management practices by indigenous peoples in outermost small islands*]. Jakarta, Indonesia: Kompas.

Undang No. 5 tahun 1960 tentang Peratuan Dasar Pokok-Pokok Agraria.

Undang-Undang No. 1 tahun1973 tentang Landas Kontinen.

Undang-Undang No. 5 tahun 1983 tentang Zona Ekonomi Eksklusif (ZEE) Indonesia.

Undang-Undang No. 9 tahun 1985 tentang Perikanan yang kemudian dirubah menjadi Undang-Undang No. 31 tahun 2004 dan yang berlaku sekarang adalah Undang-Undang No. 45 Tahun 2009.

Undang-Undang No. 32 tahun 2014 tentang Kelautan. Sumber Daya Kelautan.

Undang-Undang No. 45 tahun 2009 tentang Perikanan.
Undang-Undang No. 1 tahun 2014 tentang Perubahan atas Undang-Undang No. 27 tahun 2007 tentang Pengelolaan Wilayah Pesisir dan Pulau-Pulau Kecil.
United Nations Convention on the Law of the Sea (UNCLOS) 1982

Culture and International Law - Juwana et al. (Eds)
© 2019 Taylor & Francis Group, London, ISBN 978-1-138-38766-9

Legally binding instrument on business and human rights: Opportunities and challenges

Iman Prihandono
Lecturer of Public International Law, International Law Department, Faculty of Law, Universitas Airlangga, Surabaya, Indonesia

ABSTRACT: On 26 June 2014, the UN Human Rights Council approved Resolution A/HRC/26/L.22/Rev.1 on the establishment of the Open-Ended Intergovernmental Working Group (OEIWG) on transnational corporations and other business enterprises with respect to human rights. The task of this working group is to elaborate the establishment of an international instrument that binds the human rights responsibilities of multinational corporations. Up until the second session of 2016, the OEIWG has discussed the possible contents, scope, mechanism and form of this binding instrument. The supporters of this international instrument believe that this binding treaty could strengthen victims' access to remedies, as it will directly hold multinational corporations responsible for violating human rights at an international level. So far, states have failed to provide an effective remedy, therefore a joint mechanism at an international level is needed. An effective remedy could be reached by providing measures to remove the substantial procedural and financial constraints experienced by victims. These barriers have been the problem in holding the companies responsible for human rights abuses. On the other hand, experts and human rights activists reject this idea on the grounds that there will be difficulties in defining the scope of the human rights responsibilities of multinational corporations. Further, states will also use this binding treaty as a reason to transfer responsibility for the protection of human rights to companies. Thus, there is a risk that the obligation to protect human rights may be shared with corporations. This paper discusses the opportunities and challenges of the proposed international binding treaty on business and human rights. It is found that the proposed legally binding instrument is a significant step forward in the area of business and human rights. It may significantly reduce the time and resources for litigation and, in the end, provide better access to remedies for the victims of corporate wrongdoings.

KEYWORDS: legally binding instrument, business, human rights, multinational corporations, effective remedy

1 INTRODUCTION

In 2011, the UN Human Rights Council (UNHRC) approved the resolution of Principles on Business and Human Rights (UNGP).[1] For the first time, the UN has a standard which regulates the negative impact of human rights in business activities. Therefore, on its

1. United Nations Human Rights Council. (2011). Guiding principles on business and human rights: Implementing the United Nations 'Protect, Respect and Remedy' Framework'. Report of the Special Representative of the Secretary-General on the issue of human rights and transnational corporations and other business enterprises, John Ruggie, A/HRC/17/31. http://www.business-humanrights.org/media/documents/ruggie/ruggie-guiding-principles-21-mar-2011.pdf, accessed 15 January 2016.

implementation, the UNGP received several criticisms from individuals and civil society organizations. There are at least three main weaknesses in the UNGP that should be noted. First, the UNGP is not significant because it only focuses on socialization and encourages states to implement the three pillars (protect, respect, remedy) in their jurisdiction. Second, the UNGP doesn't give a mandate to follow up human rights violations by corporations at an international level. Third, the UNGP doesn't give the UNHRC the chance to strengthen standards and create a mechanism for business and human rights responsibility.[2]

Ecuador, as the proposing country for the establishment of an international legally binding instrument on human rights and transnational corporations and other business enterprise campaigns, states that the UNGP fails to solve the main issue of human rights violations by multinational corporations because there is no international responsibility mechanism and it ignores victims' rights on access to remedies.[3] In line with this argument, Joseph Stiglitz supports the formation of a binding instrument at international level that gives a legal basis for obliging the home country to challenge a corporation that violates human rights abroad.[4] On 26 June 2014, states who supported the legally binding treaty won the vote at the UNHRC and established Resolution A/HRC/26/L.222/Rev.1. Of 47 member states, 20 agreed, 14 disagreed, and 13 abstained. The resolution contains provisions on the establishment of the Open-Ended Intergovernmental Working Group (OEIWG) on transnational corporations and other business enterprises with respect to human rights.[5] The mandate of the working group is to elaborate binding international instruments, in the field of human rights, governing transnational corporations and other business entities.[6]

Nonetheless, Resolution A/HRC/26/L.22/Rev.1 has been criticized. For example, Ruggie states that the formulation of a binding treaty and how this treaty works will be very difficult, and hamper the progress made by UNGP.[7] Another argument is that the binding treaty will not solve the main problem of the enforcement of human rights related to corporate business activities which is the failure of the government in carrying out its international obligations at a national level. If the goal is to provide better access to remedies for the victims, then the national legal system needs to be improved rather than a treaty that has extraterritorial powers.[8]

From the conflict above, this article seeks to explore the opportunities and challenges of the proposed binding instrument on business and human rights. It is found that the proposed legally binding instrument is a significant step forward in the area of business and human

2. Joint Civil Society Statement on Business and Human Rights during the 17th session of the UN Human Rights Council on 15 June 2011. http://www.escr-net.org/docs/i/1605781, accessed 4 January 2017.
3. Statement on behalf of a group of countries at the 24rd Session of the Human Rights Council General Debate – Item 3 "Transnational Corporations and Human Rights" Geneva, September 2013. https://business-humanrights.org/sites/default/files/media/documents/statement-unhrc-legally-binding.pdf, accessed 5 January 2017.
4. Stiglitz, J.E. (2013). Introductory speech for the panel "Defending Human Rights".3rd UN Forum on Business and Human Rights, 3 December 2013, Geneva (pp. 4–5). http://www.ohchr.org/EN/Issues/Business/Forum/Pages/2013FBHRSubmissions.aspx, accessed 6 January 2017.
5. Human Rights Council. Twenty-sixth session agenda item 3, Elaboration of an international legally binding instrument on transnational corporations and other business enterprises with respect to human rights, A/HRC/26/L.22/Rev.1. https://documents-dds-ny.un.org/doc/UNDOC/LTD/G14/064/48/PDF/G1406448.pdf?OpenElement, accessed 7 January 2017.
6. Ibid, 9.
7. Ruggie, J.G. (2014b). A UN Business and Human Rights Treaty Update. Boston, MA: Harvard John F. Kennedy School of Government http://business-humanrights.org/sites/default/files/media/un_business_and_human_rights_treaty_update.pdf, accessed 9 January 2016.
8. International Organisation of Employers. (2014). IOE Comments on the Proposal for a Binding UN Treaty on Business and Human Rights, Geneva. http://www.ioe-emp.org/fileadmin/ioe_documents/publications/Policy%20Areas/business_and_human_rights/EN/_2014-05-12__G-523_IOE_Comments_on_a_Binding_UN_Treaty_on_Business_and_Human_Rights__final_.pdf, accessed 7 January 2017.

rights. It may significantly reduce the time and resources of litigation and, in the end, provide better access to remedies for the victims of corporate wrongdoings.

2 ISSUES ON THE FORMULATION OF A BINDING TREATY

While the general purpose of establishing a binding treaty in business and human rights is certainly desirable, serious challenges can disrupt the process. If this is ignored, then it can ruin this initiative. Here are some challenges and opportunities that should be taken seriously.[9]

First, the proposal of direct enforcement of human rights obligations on corporations, and not only on the state, is a breakthrough in traditional human rights practice. The proposed binding treaty may hold corporations directly responsible under international law for violating human rights. International law traditionally places the state to be responsible for human rights violations, and for offenses committed by individuals and/or companies within their jurisdiction's territory. Therefore, the proposed binding treaty will deviate from the first pillar of the UNGP, the state's obligation to protect. But the proposed binding treaty does not provide clear guidance on responsibilities or the standards to replace it.

The parties who oppose this binding treaty, including human rights activists, argue that the state will use the treaty as an excuse to refuse to protect human rights. This is because the obligation to protect human rights has been shared with the corporation. The facts indicate that countries that encouraged the binding treaty have not taken any significant action on UNGP implementation.

Human Rights Watch 2015 found that the states which support a binding treaty in business and human rights committed serious human rights abuses, such as: the persecution of human rights defenders, demonstrators, and journalists; restrictions on freedom of expression; legalization of child labor; arbitrary detention; and the lack of judicial independence.[10]

Second, the purpose of unclear binding treaties could be fatal. The idea of making an international standard for corporate responsibility for human rights is very interesting. In practice, however, this proposal fails to answer important questions about the content and limits of corporate responsibility that has been proposed. Can the corporation be responsible for ensuring the enforcement of human rights as regulated in all international instruments?

The parties opposed to a binding treaty argue that a balance between public interest, national politics, individual rights and the sovereignty of the state can only be administered by the state. It is the state that decides, through the process of democracy, how to protect human rights in their territory. Surely it would be difficult to imagine if the state could so easily hand over the power to regulate public policy to multinational corporations.[11]

Third, the exceptions for national corporations create a serious question about the goals or objectives of this binding treaty. The parties who reject this binding treaty object if the treaty focuses solely on the responsibilities of multinational corporations only. They assume that if the main purpose of the treaty is to get corporations to be responsible for human rights violations, there is no need to differentiate between national corporations and multinational corporations. All corporations must have the same responsibilities, no matter where the corporation is established or where they operate.

Moreover, some countries argue that national law is, in fact, sufficient to ensure the protection of human rights. National regulations should be able to regulate transnational corporations' activities within the country without requiring a new international treaty. Exceptions to national companies will only lead to different treatment. This situation will provide significant advantages to national companies and state-owned enterprises compared to foreign companies, which are required to use different and higher standards.

9. McBrearty, S. (2016). The proposed business and human rights treaty: Four challenges and an opportunity. *Harvard International Law Journal*, Online Symposium, *57*, 12.
10. Ibid.
11. Ibid, 13.

Fourth, by not involving corporations in binding treaty negotiations, it will jeopardize possible acceptance by the state. The supporters of binding treaties in business and human rights propose that companies shall be excluded from the negotiation process. Unilateral negotiations may provide a short-term victory in the form of a stronger covenant language. However, the exclusive approach will ultimately limit support for the treaty itself, which will not be effective.[12]

As Ruggie has suggested for binding treaty supporters not to go down a path that will end in a mere symbolic movement, whose practical implementation is limited to a few parties in a particular place. Moreover, there will be a high potential for serious rejection of any further form of international legalization in the field of business and human rights.[13]

John Ruggie explains why a global agreement that forces companies to follow binding rules about human rights will not be effective, so it should not be forced. Ruggie has three major objections conveyed to states that support a binding treaty for corporations. First, this arrangement will take a relatively long time to reach consent, while the current challenges in business and human rights are urgent. Second, the worse challenge is that the process of making this a binding treaty risks damaging effective short-term measures to improve the business standards of human rights that have been forced by the UNGP. Third, although this binding treaty obligation will be charged directly to the corporations, there will be serious questions that are difficult to answer on how this will be implemented.[14]

Apart from the above risks, the main concern of this binding treaty is that an unenforceable international treaty will lose its legitimacy. In other words, Ruggie argued that this binding treaty would be difficult to enforce. Ruggie sees four options for binding treaty enforcement mechanisms for business and human rights.[15]

First, enforcement through an international tribunal for the corporations. However, this is not realistic for at least some time ahead. This is because the existing international tribunal mechanism still places the state as the main actor in international law.

Second, enforcement by the host country where the company operates. Yet countries that have ratified the human rights treaties undoubtedly have an obligation to protect individuals within their territory or have jurisdiction over human rights violations by corporations. If these countries have failed to fulfill their international obligations, it will be difficult for any additional agreements to make significant changes.

Third, law enforcement by the home country where company is established or has its main office. Unfortunately, most countries tend not to use extraterritorial enforcement against offenses committed in other countries because it is an intervention in the internal affairs of another state.

Fourth, the last option, is through the establishment of a new treaty, as well as other human rights treaties. If the state agrees, the company is required to report on the implementation of their human rights responsibilities. This report is then assessed for conformity by an agency or committee established as an enforcement body by the international treaty.

Above all, if the formation of a binding treaty in business and human rights is a more desirable approach, then the following mathematical calculations need to be considered. There are about 77,000 transnational corporations, with about 800,000 subsidiaries and millions of suppliers. For example, Walmart itself has 62,000 subsidiaries and suppliers. Then, there are also millions of other national companies. In comparison, the treaty bodies committee in the United Nations mechanism is currently struggling to keep up with the developments of its 192 member states, each of which deals with only one specific right or specific group affected by human rights violations. How can a committee formed by a binding treaty for business and

12. Ibid, 14.
13. Ruggie, J.G. (2014a). A UN Business and Human Rights Treaty? http://businesshumanrights.org/sites/default/files/media/documents/ruggie-on-un-business-human-rights-treaty-jan-2014.pdf, accessed 10 January 2017.
14. Ruggie, J.G. (2008). *Treaty road not travelled* (p. 42). London: Ethical Corporation.
15. Ibid, p. 43.

human rights deal with millions of corporations, while also addressing the various rights of all people?[16]

3 THE OPPORTUNITIES OF A BINDING TREATY

Most of the supporting states of Resolution A/HRC/26/L.22/Rev.1 have agreed on certain issues. They believe that there needs to be a legally binding treaty to complement the UNGP. They also generally agree that the UN treaty that will be established will not only be limited to gross human rights violations, but on the contrary, it applies to all forms of corporate human rights violations. However, in the ensuing discussion there has been controversy over three important questions below:[17]

First, does the legally binding treaty apply only to transnational corporations, or to all forms of business actors, including state-owned enterprises? The opinion of the supporters of the binding treaty seems to be divided on the question of whether a legal instrument, which will be specifically designed to include only transnational corporations, or if it can be generally applicable to all businesses.

Establishing criteria of transnational corporations to distinguish them from other business actors is not an easy task. In Resolution A/HRC/26/L.22/Rev.1, transnational corporations are only defined as "all business enterprises that have transnational characters in their operational activities." The problem is, if the binding treaty includes only transnational corporations, there is nothing to prevent a transnational corporation or its subsidiaries restructuring or altering their legal status, and thus no longer being covered by the definition.

Second, does this binding treaty include extraterritorial obligations? A further question is whether there is an obligation for states to punish human rights abuses conducted by transnational corporations outside their sovereign territory. However, some southern countries, including China and Russia, feel that these extraterritorial obligations can jeopardize their interests. This is because foreign countries can interfere with internal matters and violate their national sovereignty.

Third, can the binding treaty regulate the direct obligation of transnational corporations? An important issue is whether this legal instrument should establish direct obligations under international law for transnational corporations. For example, the obligation that transnational corporations should recognize the jurisdiction of countries in this treaty and that the jurisdiction of an international tribunal may be applied directly to them.

In many cases, a state is only committed to carrying out its obligations arising from international treaties into its national law. A state is obliged to prevent a third party from committing human rights violations, and any offenses may then be processed through a national court. However, it will be a significant change if state obligations are reduced and shared with multinational corporations. This question is also directly related to the status of multinational corporations in international law.

Apart from a few points that need serious attention, there are several opportunities related to the shape of this binding treaty; ranging from very detailed and all-encompassing conventions, there is also a more general short-form convention, an optional protocol of an existing human rights treaty, or a stand-alone instrument that focuses on a particular theme.

Deva breaks down some of the strategic issues that should be included in this binding treaty. The proposed binding treaty should be able to provide a strong normative basis about why the company has a duty to human rights. Deva further states that the applicable human rights of the company are not limited to the rights contained in the International Bill of

---

16. Ibid.
17. Martens, J. & Seitz, K. (2016). *The Struggle for a UN Treaty: Towards global regulation on human rights and business.* Global Policy Forum (GPF) and the Rosa Luxemburg Stiftung (pp. 24–27). http://www.rosalux-nyc.org/wp-content/files_mf/un_treaty_online18.pdf, accessed 8 January 2017.

Rights, but also includes the rights set out in all human rights treaties that have been adopted by the United Nations.[18]

In addition, a binding treaty should also be able to describe the principles that govern some degree of corporate liability in relation to human rights. More importantly, it describes a number of mechanisms that focus both on state and non-state mechanisms to implement and enforce human rights obligations on companies. Finally, this treaty should be able to provide measures to remove the substantial, procedural and financial conceptual obstacles experienced by the victims in which the company is held responsible for human rights violations.[19]

Concrete proposals are not only conveyed in the form of the binding treaty, but also in the specific contents. Cassel and Ramasastry have categorized different proposals into three groups: (1) proposals that require concrete steps, especially at national level, (2) proposals that look at existing and future international mechanisms will be very supportive, and (3) proposals aimed at creating better coherence between policies at national and international levels. According to Cassel and Ramasastry, a binding treaty focused on specific branches or specific forms of human rights violations by companies may also be an option.[20]

Olivier de Schutter, formerly of the UN Special Commission on the Right to Food, described four possibilities for the content of this binding treaty. First, clarify and strengthen the duty of the state in the protection of human rights, including extraterritorial. Second, require the state, through a framework-form convention, to report on the adoption and implementation of national action planning in business and human rights. Third, impose human rights obligations directly on the company, and establish new mechanisms to monitor their compliance with these obligations. Fourth, it imposes on the state a task of mutual legal assistance to ensure effective remedies for victims who are harmed by the actions of transnational corporations.[21]

Based on the proposals that have been mentioned so far, it can be concluded that the main framework proposals of the binding treaty should be designed to address the following key points:[22]

First, a definition of responsibility and accountability in human rights violations by corporations. In principle, the binding treaty should allow transnational corporations to be responsible for human rights violations. This requires definitions of specific corporate responsibility. Therefore, this treaty should make states commit to assigning accountability to the company at a national level, whether in criminal, civil or administrative law. Then, it can also be stated in agreements, appropriate standards and lists of human rights violations that can be claimed.

Second, the binding power of due diligence, including human rights risk analysis and impact assessment. The binding treaty should encourage companies to advance guidelines and take necessary measures to prevent human rights violations in all sectors of their operations. Corporations should apply a systematic risk analysis of human rights along with their impact assessment. The guidelines and steps should be based on consistent international standards. This binding treaty is addressed directly to the corporation or business person, or to the state, which must then ensure that the businesses within its jurisdiction have carried out their due diligence duties.

Third, the mechanisms of monitoring and implementation at national and international levels. Implementation of this binding treaty requires monitoring and implementation

18. Deva, S. (2014). *The human rights obligations of business: Reimagining the treaty business* (p. 8). Hong Kong City University. http://business-humanrights.org/media/documents/reimagine_int_law_for_bhr.pdf, accessed 15 January 2017.

19. Ibid.

20. Cassel, D. & Ramasastry, A. (2015). White paper: Options for a treaty on business and human rights (p. 36). http://business-humanrights.org/sites/default/files/documents/whitepaperfinal%20ABA%20LS%206%2022%2015.pdf, accessed 15 January 2017.

21. de Schutter, O. (2016). Towards a new treaty on business and human rights. *Business and Human Rights Journal, 1*(1), 41–67. Retrieved from http://journals.cambridge.org/action/displayAbstract?fromPage=online&aid=10006521&file-Id=S205701981500005X

22. Treaty Alliance. (2015). *Enhance the International Legal Framework to Protect Human Rights from Corporate Abuse.* Joint Statement, Geneva. http://www.treatymovement.com/statement/, accessed 20 January 2017.

mechanisms at national and international levels. With respect to the monitoring of the implementation of this treaty, governments may refer to existing mechanisms, such as the Convention on the Rights of Persons with Disabilities and the Optional Protocol to the Convention against Torture and other Cruel, Inhuman or Degrading Treatment or Punishment.

Fourth, improving cooperation between countries in investigation, jurisdiction and enforcement. This binding treaty needs to encourage countries to cooperate in the field of litigation. This should be built on the principle of joint responsibility, as has been exemplified in international cooperation on the fight against corruption and transnational crime. This cooperation includes at least mutual legal assistance regarding investigation, evidence collection and prosecution, as well as the recognition and enforcement of court decisions in criminal and civil cases. This binding treaty is not to create a new mechanism at the international level, but rather to strengthen jurisdiction at a national level.

Fifth, the implementation of state extraterritorial obligations to protect human rights. Regarding the extraterritorial obligations of the state in the protection of human rights, UNGP 2011 has, in fact, been lagging behind when compared with the development of international human rights discourse at this time. Although these extraterritorial obligations are considered very conservative, the UN Committee on Economic, Social and Cultural Rights is now one step ahead and has urged countries to participate in some of their general comments. It aims to prevent violations of human rights by multinational corporations under the jurisdiction of a host country.

Sixth, the proposed treaty must define the relationship of the binding treaty with bilateral and multilateral trade agreements and investment agreements. It should assert its position in addition to other international agreements, specifically with bilateral and multilateral trade and investment agreements. The proposed binding treaty must either have a position above the other agreement, or at least contain binding decisions to effectively change or add a clause for human rights protection into existing trade or investment agreements.

4 THE PROPOSED 'ZERO DRAFT' OF THE LEGALLY BINDING INSTRUMENT

In 16 July 2018, the UN Human Rights Council's Open-Ended Intergovernmental Working Group on transnational corporations and other business enterprises with respect to human rights published the zero draft of the Legally Binding Instrument (LBI) to regulate, in international human rights law, the activities of transnational corporations and other business enterprises. This instrument aims to provide prompt, effective and adequate access to remedies and enhance accountability for victims of human rights violations resulting from transnational corporations' business activities. The existence of this LBI will be advantageous for the victims by ensuring that corporations will be held accountable and there will be proper reparation for the victims by providing clear procedures. Likewise, it determines which institutions have the duty to provide effective remedies for the victims.

Article 3 of the LBI elaborates that its scope applies to human rights violations resulting from any business activities of a transnational character. Furthermore, this instrument also covers all international human rights and those rights recognized under domestic law. The term 'transnational character' of business activities is further explained in Article 4(2) as any profit-oriented activity such as production or commercial activity conducted by a natural or legal person, including electronic activities, which take place or involve two or more national jurisdictions.

It also includes all type of business entities, regardless of size, such as firms, partnerships, corporations, companies, other associations, natural or juridical persons, or any combination thereof, irrespective of the mode of creation or control or ownership, and includes their branches, subsidiaries, affiliates, or other entities directly or indirectly controlled by them.[23] The LBI gives more importance to the linkage of corporate activities rather than to the form of the company itself.

23. United Nations Human Rights Council. (2017). Elements for a draft legally binding instrument on transnational corporations and other business enterprises with respect to human rights chairmanship of the OEIGWG established by HRC Res. A/HRC/RES/26/9. 29 September 2017 (p. 5). https://www.ohchr.org/

It appears that these articles apply a restrictive approach. The LBI covers only companies with a transnational character, thus creating uneven treatment for domestic enterprises especially in countries where the domestic law for human rights protection is weak. Based on the victim's point of view, it will prevent access to remedies for human rights violations at a domestic level.[24] As all corporations should be equally responsible for violating human rights, the exclusion of domestic corporations is contrary to the spirit of the treaty to hold corporations liable for human rights violations.[25]

Article 4(1) explains the definition of victims of corporate human rights abuses. A victim is defined as a person, whether an individual or in a group, who has claimed to have suffered harm such as: physical and mental injury, emotional suffering, economic loss and other loss through acts or negligence in the context of business activities of a transnational character. If it is needed and is in accordance with domestic law, dependents of the direct victim and persons who have suffered in assisting the victim may also be included in the term 'victim'.

Article 5 of the LBI explains two elements of the court jurisdictions arising from acts or omissions that result in violations of human rights. There two ways that a court may have jurisdiction over a case, these are: (1) the court where the acts or omissions occurred; (2) the court of the state where the natural or legal person or association of natural or legal persons alleged to have committed the acts or omissions are domiciled.

Under this article, the home states of companies have jurisdiction to adjudicate claims. This jurisdiction is to impose a duty on the state to protect human rights. This is in accordance with Principle No. 2 of the UNGP which provides extraterritorial human rights obligations to states. States should set out clearly the expectation that all business enterprises domiciled in their territory and/or jurisdiction respect human rights throughout their operations, and this includes their business operations overseas. Accordingly, home states must take steps to prevent a business entity within their jurisdiction from violating human rights when operating in foreign countries.[26] Moreover, it is also compatible with the active personality principle. This means a state must be obliged to protect human rights within corporations that are (1) registered under its laws, (2) have their principal place of business under the state's jurisdiction, or (3) have located their central place of administration on the state's territory.[27]

This article is also supported by Principle No. 25 of the UNGP, which implies that home countries should provide access to remedies in national courts for human rights violation that occurred abroad, particularly when victims have no access to effective judicial remedies in their own countries.[28] Indeed, the court jurisdiction provision under the LBI provides a significant advantage for the victim of corporate human rights abuses. Companies may be brought to their national court, and this court should not refuse adjudication which is based on reasons of court incompetence. The jurisdiction article provides a broader opportunity for victims to obtain remedies. Victims may choose which court will be the best forum to achieve the better remedy or solution. Likewise, this article shares an equal obligation for both the home and the host states to provide access to effective remedies.

Documents/HRBodies/HRCouncil/WGTransCorp/Session3/LegallyBindingInstrumentTNCs_OBEs.pdf, accessed 2 August 2018.

24. Berthet, A., Hood, P. & Hughes-Jennet, J. (2018). UN treaty on business and human rights: Working group publishes draft instrument, 26 July 2018. https://www.hlregulation.com/2018/07/26/un-treaty-on-business-and-human-rights-working-group-publishes-draft-instrument/, accessed 5 August 2018.
25. McBrearty, S. (2016). The proposed business and human rights treaty: Four challenges and an opportunity. *Harvard International Law Journal, 57*, 13.
26. de Schutter, O. (2015). Towards a new treaty on business and human rights. *Business and Human Rights Journal, 1*(1), 45. Retrieved from http://journals.cambridge.org/action/displayAbstract?fromPage=online&aid=10006521&file-Id=S205701981500005X
27. Ibid, 46.
28. Ibid, 54.

5 CONCLUSION

After a series of long discussions, the OEIWG has finally produced the zero draft on the legally binding instrument for human rights violations by companies. Many argue that this instrument will be counterproductive, because it may undermine the implementation progress of the UNGPs by states. On the other hand, many also argue that it is possible for this instrument to materialize, and it must cover at least six important issues. Perhaps, the proposed legally binding instrument has not been able to accommodate all concerns for holding companies liable for violating human rights. Nevertheless, the zero draft is a significant step forward in the area of business and human rights. The most important feature under this draft is the jurisdiction clause. Indeed, determining court jurisdiction can be burdensome for the victims of corporate abuse when seeking justice. Courts in many jurisdictions seem to be reluctant to exercise their jurisdiction. This is based on the reason that there is another court more appropriate to adjudicate the case. Therefore, the jurisdiction clause may bring a solution to the issue of which court should exercise jurisdiction in a particular case. This will significantly reduce the time and resources of litigation, which in the end will provide better access to remedies for the victims of corporate wrongdoings.

Despite its significance, the draft may face a number of challenges ahead. To be implemented, this proposal must be ratified by a significant number of states. It is very likely that the home states of many multinational corporations will be reluctant to accept this draft. One of the main reasons for this objection is the fact that this instrument may open a wave of transnational litigation against multinational companies in their home country. Further, a number of states have implemented measures to prevent human rights corporations by their companies abroad. This includes enacting legislation to oblige companies to conduct human rights due diligence. This is in accordance with the framework proposed by the UNGP. The UK Modern Slavery Act and the France Duty of Care Law are the most prominent examples of this effort. Therefore, the acceptance of this legally binding instrument proposal may not be easy. It may take a number of revisions, compromises and a series of negotiations between states before it can be implemented. Indeed, the acceptance by developed countries, the home states of multinational companies, is an important element.

REFERENCES

De Schutter, O. (2016). Towards a new treaty on business and human rights. *Business and Human Rights Journal, 1*(1), 41–67. Retrieved from http://journals.cambridge.org/action/displayAbstract?fromPage=online&aid=10006521&file-Id=S205701981500005X

McBrearty, S. (2016). The proposed business and human rights treaty: Four challenges and an opportunity. *Harvard International Law Journal, 57*, 12–14

Ruggie, J.G. (2008). *Treaty road not travelled* (p. 42–43). London: Ethical Corporation.

Berthet, A., Hood, P. & Hughes-Jennet, J. (2018). *UN treaty on business and human rights: Working group publishes draft instrument*, 26 July 2018. https://www.hlregulation.com/2018/07/26/un-treaty-on-business-and-human-rights-working-group-publishes-draft-instrument/, accessed 5 August 2018.

Cassel, D. & Ramasastry, A. (2015). *White paper: Options for a treaty on business and human rights* (p. 36). http://business-humanrights.org/sites/default/files/documents/whitepaperfinal%20ABA%20LS%206%2022%2015.pdf, accessed 15 January 2017.

Deva, S. (2014). *The human rights obligations of business: Reimagining the treaty business* (p. 8). Hongkong City University. http://business-humanrights.org/media/documents/reimagine_int_law_for_bhr.pdf, accessed 15 January 2017.

Human Rights Council. Twenty-sixth session agenda item 3, elaboration of an international legally binding instrument on transnational corporations and other business enterprises with respect to human rights, A/HRC/26/L.22/Rev.1. https://documents-dds-ny.un.org/doc/UNDOC/LTD/G14/064/48/PDF/G1406448.pdf?OpenElement, accessed 7 January 2017.

International Organisation of Employers. (2014). *IOE Comments on the Proposal for a Binding UN Treaty on Business and Human Rights, Geneva.* https://www.ioe-emp.org/fileadmin/ioe_documents/publications/Policy%20Areas/business_and_human_rights/EN/_2014-05-12__G-523_IOE_Comments_on_a_Binding_UN_Treaty_on_Business_and_Human_Rights__final_.pdf, accessed 7 January 2017.

Joint Civil Society Statement on Business and Human Rights during the 17th session of the UN Human Rights Council on 15 June 2011. http://www.escr-net.org/docs/i/1605781, accessed 4 January 2017.
Martens, J. & Seitz, K. (2016). *The struggle for a UN treaty towards global regulation on human rights and business*. Global Policy Forum (GPF) and the Rosa Luxemburg Stiftung. http://www.rosalux-nyc.org/wp-content/files_mf/un_treaty_online18.pdf, accessed 8 January 2017.
Ruggie, J.G. (2014a). A UN Business and Human Rights Treaty? http://businesshumanrights.org/sites/default/files/media/documents/ruggie-on-un-business-human-rights-treaty-jan-2014.pdf, accessed 10 January 2017.
Ruggie, J.G. (2014b). *A UN Business and Human Rights Treaty Update*. Boston, MA: Harvard John F. Kennedy School of Government. http://business-humanrights.org/sites/default/files/media/un_business_and_human_rights_treaty_update.pdf, accessed 9 January 2016.
Statement on behalf of a group of countries at the 24rd Session of the Human Rights Council General Debate – Item 3 "Transnational Corporations and Human Rights" Geneva, September 2013. https://business-humanrights.org/sites/default/files/media/documents/statement-unhrc-legally-binding.pdf, accessed 5 January 2017.
Stiglitz, J.E. (2013). Introductory speech for the panel "Defending Human Rights" during the 3rd UN Forum on Business and Human Rights, 3 December 2013, Geneva (pp. 4–5). http://www.ohchr.org/EN/Issues/Business/Forum/Pages/2013FBHRSubmissions.aspx, accessed 6 January 2017.
Treaty Alliance. (2015). *Enhance the International Legal Framework to Protect Human Rights from Corporate Abuse*. Joint Statement, Geneva. http://www.treatymovement.com/statement/, accessed 20 January 2017.
United Nations Human Rights Council. (2011). Guiding principles on business and human rights: Implementing the United Nations 'Protect, Respect and Remedy' Framework'. Report of the Special Representative of the Secretary-General on the issue of human rights and transnational corporations and other business enterprises, John Ruggie, A/HRC/17/31. http://www.business-humanrights.org/media/documents/ruggie/ruggie-guiding-principles-21-mar-2011.pdf, accessed 15 January 2016.
United Nations Human Rights Council. (2017). Elements for a draft legally binding instrument on transnational corporations and other business enterprises with respect to human rights chairmanship of the OEIGWG established by HRC Res. A/HRC/RES/26/9, 29 September 2017 (p. 5). https://www.ohchr.org/Documents/HRBodies/HRCouncil/WGTransCorp/Session3/LegallyBindingInstrumentTNCs_OBEs.pdf, accessed 2 August 2018.

Culture and International Law - Juwana et al. (Eds)
© 2019 Taylor & Francis Group, London, ISBN 978-1-138-38766-9

Humanitarianism, state sovereignty, and ASEAN mode of governance: The case for a diversified global south perspective

Nandang Sutrisno
Universitas Islam Indonesia

ABSTRACT: As the world has increasingly become more connected, it is inevitable that there is an expansion of humanitarian problems that we confront can only be solved by international co-operation. Clearly, the ongoing Rohingya crisis is the latest example that showcased the Southeast Asian region's failure in the area of humanitarian management. It suggests that ASEAN has abandoned its very purpose of its existence as it conceived in its founding document, the Bangkok Declaration. In light of this, this paper argues that this cannot be separated from the region's rigid understanding of the notion of state sovereignty. Based on this assumption, the analytical reading that this paper adopted highlights that the interpretative rigidity hurts the supposedly liberating nature of ASEAN. Thus, it is fair that this requires a healthy dose of humanitarianism to introduce a more progressive approach in intra-state dealings. In fact, the paper argues that this recommendation is highly plausible as the Bangkok Declaration itself necessitates "a primary responsibility" among its member states.

KEYWORDS: Humanitarianism, state sovereignty, ASEAN Mode of Governance, the Bangkok Declaration, Rohingya crisis

1 INTRODUCTION

In today's debate on humanitarian intervention, the leading voices are predominantly promulgated by the legal scholars in the developed world.[1] While it may be understandable from the fact that the developing world tends to prioritize the more practical dimensions that may concretely contribute to the economic and other material developments,[2] nevertheless, it is an unfortunate situation as the Western world only represents a small number of the world's population.[3] To be

1. See e.g., Mauro Barelli, 'Preventing and Responding to Atrocity Crimes: China, Sovereignty and the Responsibility to Protect' 23(2) *Journal of Conflict and Security Law* 173-201 (2018); Nicholas J. Wheeler, *Saving Strangers: Humanitarian Intervention in International Society* (Oxford: Oxford University Press, 2000); Simon Chesterman, *Just War Or Just Peace?: Humanitarian Intervention and International Law* (Oxford: Oxford University Press, 2000); Thomas G. Weiss, *Humanitarian Intervention: Ideas in Action* (Cambridge: Polity Press, 2016); Anne Orford, *Reading Humanitarian Intervention: Human Rights and the Use of Force in International Law* (Cambridge: Cambridge University Press, 2003); Thomas G. Weiss & Cindy Collins, *Humanitarian Challenges And Intervention* (New York: Routledge, 2018); Gary J. Bass, *Freedom's Battle: The Origins of Humanitarian Intervention* (New York: Alfred A. Knopf, 2008); Jennifer M. Welsh ed., *Humanitarian Intervention and International Relations* (Oxford: Oxford University Press, 2003).
2. See Kevin Gray & Bary K. Gills, 'South–South cooperation and the rise of the Global South' 37(4) *Third World Quarterly* 557-574 (2018).
3. As the American University Center for the Global South notes: 'The global South includes nearly 157 of a total of 184 recognized states in the world, and many have less developed or severely limited resources.' American University Center for the Global South, http://www1.american.edu/academic.depts/acainst/cgs/about.html.

specific, "[d]eveloping countries, currently account for 80 per cent of the world's population and 61 per cent of the global total is accounted by the population giants China and India."[4] A recent projection of the United Nations expected that "[f]rom 2017 to 2050, it is expected that half of the world's population growth will be concentrated in just nine countries: India, Nigeria, the Democratic Republic of the Congo, Pakistan, Ethiopia, the United Republic of Tanzania, the United States of America, Uganda and Indonesia (ordered by their expected contribution to total growth)."[5] The absence of voice from the non-developed world, it is not only distorting the representativeness of the state of international legal discourse; but, more importantly, it ignores the very idea of international legal system itself as a body of legal norms that serves the interest of the whole population of the world.[6] Moreover, the fact that most of global conflicts are taking place within the developing world, it is important that the theory and practice of humanitarian intervention should be engaged by more viewpoints that originated from the implicated region.[7]

Having said that, it is important to add a different take on humanitarian intervention as a matter of utmost importance in light of some recent developments in the developing world. In this vein, the recent failure of the international community to take into account the practice of humanitarian intervention by India that resulted in the independence of Bangladesh is a case in point.[8] To be precise, the debate that I will present below will be profoundly informed by the so-called Rohingya crisis in the Southeast Asian region. Specifically, this paper uses Rohingya crisis to inform the gravity of the failure of current model of interstate relationship in the region. More pointedly, it is argued that the current model is heavily centered around the principle of the inviolability of state sovereignty. This ongoing crisis has provided a window of opportunity for recasting the evolving debate, primarily, within the scholarly community of the developing countries on what it means of having a global legal system in this decentralized interstate affairs.

Hence, the primary objective of this paper is to provide a critical addition to the debate revolving around the legality of humanitarian intervention as an international legal norm. At the same time, this article is also aimed to provide a critical update on the construction of the Asian practice, in particular, in international relations that specifically touches the current humanitarian crisis. This critical point of view of the subject that represents the non-statist interest is, therefore, contains a fresh take on this increasingly important subject as the state boundaries is becoming more and more porous. In other words, this paper takes the current reality where the transnational movement of people as inevitable.[9] For that matter, it is important to make a meaningful shift in which the Third World international legal theorists adopt their own, apart from their governments. As of now, it might be argued that the existence of an independence body of scholarly community in the area of international law is clearly untenable. In light of this, it should be no surprise that the only representative of Indonesia in Asian Society of International Law, the only region's scholarly community on international is represented by a hawkish government official.[10]

---

4. Ernestina Coast, *Population trends in developing countries* (LSE Research Online, August 2005), http://eprints.lse.ac.uk/268/1/Arnold.pdf.
5. United Nations, *World population projected to reach 9.8 billion in 2050, and 11.2 billion in 2100* (June 21, 2017), https://www.un.org/development/desa/en/news/population/world-population-prospects-2017.html.
6. See Bruno Simma, 'Universality of International Law from the Perspective of a Practitioner' 20(2) *European Journal of International Law* 265-297 (2009). See also Jonathan I. Charney, 'Universal International Law' 87(4) *American Journal of International Law* 529-551 (1993); Ernst Sauer, 'Universal Principles in International Law' 42 *Transactions of Grotius Society* 181-191 (1956).
7. See Global Conflict Tracker (Council of Foreign Affairs, Nov. 26, 2018), https://www.cfr.org/interactives/global-conflict-tracker#!/global-conflict-tracker.
8. Gary J. Bass, 'The Indian Way of Humanitarian Intervention' 40 *Yale Journal of International Law* 227-294 (2015).
9. See Pranoto Iskandar & Nicola Piper, 'Why Low-skilled Migration Matters' 3 *Indonesian Journal of International & Comparative Law* 577 (2016).
10. See Asian Society of International Law, Governing Bodies, Executive Council, ASIANSIL, https://www.asiansil. org/about-us/governing-bodies/ (last visited November 28, 2018).

In consequences, as a result of being more theoretical rather than empirical in nature, the methodological aspect of the debate will be strongly influenced by recent theories in the literature of international politics. To complete the theoretical engagement, the discussion will also take advantage of many pertinent empirical investigations that are selectively choosing to enhance the theoretical claims that I advance. That said, the combination of some cutting-edge theoretical accounts with some practical developments is hopefully successfully delineating some of the most abstract ideas. Less visible, the paper will also include some of the most important ethnographic studies that aim to explain the surrounding cultural notions that shaped the current debate. Needless to say, it is fair for this paper to aspire in expanding the current scholarly position on the subject as its ultimate aim.

2 BACKGROUND

As an international issue, humanitarian intervention has existed before the existence of international law.[11] This historical fact cannot be separated from the humanitarian intervention character which is closely related to daily problems faced by the individual as moral creatures. Hence, the international law conception on humanitarian intervention covers almost all questions closely related to everyday problems of every human being in every corner of the globe. Almost every issue of humanitarian intervention more often than not correlates with the moral position of the intervening parties. Clearly, this cannot be separated from the notion of "humanitarianism" as its raison d'etre.[12] For instance, whether or not it is legally justified to intervene to other countries to stop, for example, slavery or an authoritarian regime from committing a serious human right violation. In this regard, it is clear that the major question that the humanitarian intervention as a legal norm has posed is that to what extent or what are the legal limits for intervening on behalf of the oppressed population.[13] It follows that the next important substantive requirement is that in order to be a "legitimate" humanitarian intervention it must improve the situation.[14]

Admittedly, there has been some scholarly efforts that aims to address the above question. In general, the most common positions are to be found within two extremes. At one extreme, a group of scholars adopts a position that proscribes any act of intervention in any domestic affairs of other states.[15] One of its prominent proponents, Oscar Schachter argues forcefully that any attempt to make humanitarian intervention as legitimate legal principle would provide the powerful state "an almost unlimited right to overthrow governments alleged to be unresponsive to the popular will or the goal of self-determination".[16] Clearly, this legal position cannot be separated from a literal reading of Article 2(4) of the United Nations Charter that is essentially aimed to uphold the protection of another form of human rights as one of the Charter's founding principles.[17] In other words, the illegality of humanitarian intervention is chiefly related with the supremacy of the collective human right to self-determination that manifested in the form of

11. Gary J. Bass, *Freedom's Battle: The Origin of Humanitarian Battle* (New York: Alfred A. Knopf, 2008).
12. See Michael Geyer, 'Humanitarianism and Human Rights' in Fabian Klose ed., *The Emergence of Humanitarian Intervention: Ideas and Practice from the Nineteenth Century to the Present* 31-55 (Cambridge: Cambridge University Press, 2015).
13. See Fernando R. Tesón, *Humanitarian Intervention: An Inquiry into Law and Morality* (New York: Transnational Publishers, 1988).
14. See Mary Kaldor & Christine Chinkin, *The "Doctrine of Humanitarian Intervention": And how it exposes the absence of any serious intention to help Syrians*, openDemocracy (Apr. 22, 2018), https://www.open democracy.net/ mary-kaldor-christine-chinkin/doctrine-of-humanitarian-intervention-and-how-it-exposes-absence-of-an
15. Ian Brownlie, *International Law and the Use of Force by States* (Oxford: Clarendon Press, 1991), 340-41.
16. Oscar Schachter, 'The Legality of Pro-Democratic Invasion' (1984) 78 *American Journal of International Law* 649.
17. Christopher Greenwood, 'Is There a Right of Humanitarian Intervention?' (1993) 49(2) *World Politics* 34-35.

common articles of both ICCPR and ICESCR. More pointedly, as we will see later, the revolving debate on the legality of humanitarian intervention is a conflict of human rights norms.[18]

At the other end of the spectrum, however, another group of scholars propose entirely different legal position, namely the right of humanitarian intervention is a valid, and, therefore, legitimate international legal principle. Arguably, the most distinguished proponent of this position is Christopher Greenwood who recognizes that since the end of Cold War era there have been a shifting state practice in this regard.[19] The inclusion of a cold realpolitik calculation is proven empirically that leads one author to support the counterintuitive proposal for the legalization of the unilateral humanitarian intervention as "it should ... discourage aggressive wars by states that use the pretext of humanitarianism".[20] Another supporting argument for this position comes from the outside of legal mode of reasoning, namely the ethicists who adopt the consequentialist reasoning in which "[by] allowing humanitarian intervention in some cases ... would promote overall well-being. So far from forbidding humanitarian intervention, consequentialist reasoning will support it ...."[21]

In the midst of the heated debate about the legality of humanitarian intervention, there is something missing. And that missing feature is the lack of diversity of point of view on the subject. Needless to say, it is noted that diversity of thought is the most important aspect of diversity as a mean to avoid of what John Stuart Mill describes as robing "the human race, posterity as well as the existing generation" to get to the elusive objective truth.[22] Reasonably enough, this diversity of point of views creates what one might called as a "marketplace of ideas".[23] This marketplace of ideas is relied on the assumption of infallibility, i.e. any opinion is still something up for debate and, hence, its validity is still open for further debate. In consequence, "[d]issenting speech helps maximize the benefits ... both by presenting individuals with alternatives to their beliefs and by promoting certain character traits that increase the level and independence of thought."[24] Thus, "free speech, like the free market, creates a competitive environment in which the best ideas ultimately prevail."[25]

In the same vein, the *Nature*'s editorial for its 2014 special issue on diversity unequivocally suggests that "[t]here is growing evidence that embracing diversity – in all its senses – is key to doing good science."[26] Hence, it is fair to argue, without it, international legal system will be unable to adapt effectively to changes brought about by many non-legal developments. In other words, the failure of having diversity of thought, in turn, will deteriorate the capacity of international law itself to stay relevant in an ever-changing world. As Susan Wood of Henderson Woods, LLC put it, "[d]iversity of thought introduces not only differences of perspective, but also differences in approach".[27]

For some reason or another, it is unsurprising that only a small number of the Global South based scholars who have intensively worked on international legal issues. One major consequence is that "[the] subsequent [of international and comparative law journals] geographical expansion towards Asia, Oceania and, to a lesser extent, the Middle East and Africa" is a

18. See also Geyer, above n 12.
19. Greenwod, above n 17.
20. Ryan Goodman, 'Humanitarian Intervention and Pretext for War' 100 *American Journal of International Law* 110 (2006).
21. Andrew Mason and Nick Wheeler, 'Realist Objections to Humanitarian Interventions' in Barry Holden ed., *The Ethical Dimension of Global Change* (Basingstoke: Macmillan Press, 1996), 106.
22. John Stuart Mill, On Liberty (Kitchener: Batoche Books, 2001).
23. See Irene M. Ten Cate, 'Speech, Truth, and Freedom: An Examination of John Stuart Mill's and Justice Oliver Wendell Holmes's Free Speech Defenses' (2010) 22(1) *Yale Journal of Law & the Humanities* 35-48. See also Jill Gordon, 'John Stuart Mill and the 'Marketplace of Ideas'' (1997) 23(2) *Social Theory & Practice* 235-249.
24. Cate, above n 23.
25. Joseph Blocher, 'Institutions in the Marketplace of Ideas' (2008) 57(4) *Duke Law Journal* 821-889.
26. Editors, 'Diversity Challenge' (2014) 513 *Nature* 279.
27. Susan Woods, Thinking About Diversity of Thought 3 (2008), https://digitalcommons.ilr.cornell.edu/ cgi/viewcontent.cgi?article=1106&context=workingpapers.

phenomenon that happened very recently.[28] Based on the "Source Publication List for *Web of Science*" that keeps track of the world's most cited journals, the economically developed East Asia is the only region that contributes to the list.[29] Given this fact, it is unreasonable to expect that the Global South based scholars can fully and effectively contribute to the discourse. In this light, the rest of the discussion in this paper may appropriately be seen as a modest attempt to address this literature deficiency on the question of humanitarian intervention.

3 REVISITING THE OLD DEBATE

It should be obvious from the above that there is only a handful of published scholarly works on the third world perspectives on humanitarian intervention. Arguably, the most important work of all is written by Mohammed Ayoob, a leading theorist on third world in international relations. Despite the scarcity of specific works that deal with the question of humanitarian intervention from the standpoint of the developing countries, Ayoob claims that any formulation on the third world perspectives on the international administration of war-torn territories "are linked in substantial measure to third world perspectives on humanitarian intervention."-[30] It should be clear that the conception of humanitarian intervention is central in third world conceptualization of their theories and, therefore, translated into their practices in international affairs.

Going further, Ayoob identifies that there is the so called shared substantial similarities that, chief among them, emanates from the third world's "generally suspicious orientation" toward humanitarian intervention forms their starting point.[31] Naturally, this suspicion is related with the developed countries that have consistently applied double standards in their international dealings. It is worth noting, however, the practice of double standard is unavoidable. Arguably, these Western practices of double standard has hardened the developing countries' views in supporting a more conservative global order. That said, the developing world moves to embrace the close-off model where state sovereignty as its only fundamental norm.

Strongly rooted in the Marxist tradition, B.S. Chimni, a leading figure of Third World Approach to International Law (TWAIL), constructs an imperial global state that functions solely "to realize the interests of an emerging transnational capital and powerful states in the international system to the disadvantage of third world states and peoples".[32] This imperial global state is enabled none other by international law. Suspicion runs deep, it is asserted that "the United Nations (UN) has embraced the neo-liberal agenda and is being geared towards promoting the interests of transnational capital."[33] Seen thus, any branches of international law are the enabler of this heinous system. Accordingly, the expansion of the international human rights regime should be interpreted as "the creation of a *global human rights space* that parallels the *global economic space*."[34]

In a highly decentralized legal system, such as international law, where enforcement is essentially voluntary, but, at the same time, power inequality among its participants is stark, it is uncommon to find that many global south lawyers dismissed international law as something

28. Ignacio de la Rasilla, 'A Very Short History of International Law Journals (1869-2018)' (2018) 29(1) *European Journal of International Law* 137-168.
29. See Source Publication List for Web of Science, Clarivate Analytics (May 2017), http://mjl.clarivate.com/publist_ssci.pdf.
30. Mohammed Ayoob, 'Third World Perspectives on Humanitarian Intervention and International Administration' 10 *Global Governance* 99 (2004).
31. Ibid, 99.
32. B.S. Chimni, 'International Institutions Today: An Imperial Global State in the Making'(2004) 15 *European Journal of International Law* 1-2.
33. Ibid, 2.
34. B.S. Chimni, 'A Just World Under Law: A View from the South' (2007) 22 *American University Law Review* 206.

irrelevance. At its extreme, international law is nothing but "a law of the jungle" as it serves "as an instrument to exert pressure, instrument for intervening [in] other states domestic affairs without considered as violation and it can also be used to justify states' actions."[35] In this vein, the most dramatic example that represents the rejectionists is the Asian practice that eschews the refugee laws as it considers to be representing the Eurocentric practice in refugee recognition.[36]

Supposedly, this strong suspicion toward the international legal system has hardened their interest in reviving the absolutist notion of state sovereignty in the current practice of international affairs. The developing countries embrace of the absolutist notion of sovereignty can be understood as a paradox. More importantly, the adoption of an absolutist notion of sovereignty has not only theoretically problematic but, more importantly, it has unwittingly increased the vulnerability of the population of the Global South. It is believed that a system based on a full acknowledgment of the sovereignty of each member as its basic rule will increase the independence of every sovereign in managing their own internal affairs. Interestingly enough, it raises another serious issue that is frequently serving no one but the ruling class. Moreover, it becomes the ultimate shield that cover any human rights abuses by the home-grown despots that desperate for more power. More often than not, the appropriation of the Westphalian sovereignty by the developing countries has exacerbated the domestic rule of law building process.

In particular, the ultra-nationalist rhetoric has legitimized the existence of the far-right discourse on the nation building. The post-authoritarian Indonesia is a case in point. The staggering numbers of a variety of street thug's organizations that take advantages of some of the readily available populist creeds. In addition to make a specific reference to reviving an ethnocultural pride, some are willfully appropriated religion in order to boost their sociological legitimacy. As with many other developing countries, Indonesia is a poster boy for what Robert Jackson defines as a quasi-state that lacks the capacity to function as a normal state.[37] Hence, it should be no surprise that having sociological recognition can lead to gain the coveted legal legitimacy. In fact, this extralegal player has played a decisive role in many regional elections.

In this respect, it is reasonable to expect that there has to be some limiting factors with regards to how to discipline the leviathan. One way of introducing a limiting factor is that by opening up the national legal system to the adoption of unorthodox source such as those of international law. In this transnationalized age, seizing this opportunity can be translated as embracing a pragmatic outlook in the national effort of the rule of law building. This pragmatism is to be believed as an indispensable tool in harnessing the challenges and opportunities that the democratization process presented. In an analysis of the domestic function of international law, it is noted that international law is "is a particularly useful device for certain kinds of states, namely those that are undergoing a transition to democracy. By bonding the government's behavior to international standards and raising the price of deviation, international law commitments in the constitution may help to "lock in" democracy domestically by giving important interest groups more confidence in the regime."[38]

Unfortunately, this opportunity has not been fully explored. On the contrary, the recent development seems to disregard the potentials of international law in the face of the failure of domestic legal arrangement. In the case of Indonesia, eschewing international law "has produced a distinct discourse on human rights that ... eventually hurts the very objective of the

35. Hikmahanto Juwana, 'Hukum Internasional sebagai Instrumen Politik: Beberapa Pengalaman Indonesia sebagai Studi Kasus' (2012) 5 *Arena Hukum* 106-114.
36. Sara E. Davies, "The Asia Rejection?: International Refugee Law in Asia," (2006) 52 *Australian Journal of Politics and History* 562-575.
37. Robert H. Jackson, *Quasi-States: Sovereignty, International Relations and the Third World* (Cambridge: Cambridge University Press, 1996).
38. Tom Ginsburg, 'Locking in Democracy: Constitutions, Commitment, and International Law' (2006) 38 *NYU J. Int'l L. & Pol.* 712.

human rights movement itself which promotes the rights of human beings, not only national citizens."[39] More recently, a group of civil society activists have challenged the process of the internalization of international legal norms.[40] Needless to say, at a regional level, the rejection of international law is not an isolated phenomenon. The rejection of international law has appeared to be a shared trait of many, if not all, influential countries in the Southeast Asian region.[41] Thus, it should be no surprise that one major implication is that ASEAN as the only region's project of regionalization has become the world's least developed.[42]

4 MAKING A FRESH START

What one can implied from the above discussion is that the prevailing model of interstate relationship will have difficulty in delivering its promise, i.e. to realize ASEAN as a common platform to grow the community voice of the region.[43] Moreover, as the Rohingya crisis clearly suggests, a new kind of inter-state relationship is needed. The current model that is based on the notion of the absolutism of state sovereignty has not only impeded the evolution of the interstate system but, more importantly, it has paralyzed the system to respond to any crisis that requires an immediate response. In addition to the reputational damage that it has caused, this prolonged inaction has generated many humanitarian costs that are supposedly avoidable. In fact, it may be ascribed that inaction has aggravated the humanitarian scale that propelled it as "the world's fastest growing humanitarian crisis."[44] Hence, it is fair that the Rohingya crisis should be considered as the ultimate wakeup call for the region to revisit their model of interstate engagement.

For a start, suffice it to say that it is not time for going back to the business as usual ritual. Meaning, there has to be a major breakthrough in the region's dealing with the cross-border issues. In particular, it is no longer avoidable that there are many emerging transnational issues that left individual state completely incapacitated. In many cases, it is not uncommon to find that the system generates superficial responses that satisfy nothing but diplomatic necessity. Worse, as in the case of Rohingya, the system is simply rendered non-functional.

In this light, it is important to re-examine the rigid application of state sovereignty as the underlying premise of the interstate interaction system that the region has persistently maintained. Rather than serving as an erosion of state sovereignty, ASEAN has paradoxically fomented a systematic weakening of the system. As one observer rightly put it, "[w]hen approached with multilateral institutions such as the EU in mind, ASEAN makes little sense."[45] Hence, it is reasonable to assert the claim that this system failure is resulted from the rigid application of the principle of non-interference. To be sure, this principle is a straightforward deduction of the inviolability of state sovereignty. As a result, each state member is every island to itself. In other words, any supra-national agreement, regardless its nature, is in

39. See e.g., Pranoto Iskandar, 'Constitutionalizing Human Rights Universality in Non-constitutional Legal System: Decoding Indonesian Human Rights Brouhaha' (2016) 3(1) *Indonesian Journal of International & Comparative Law*, 3.
40. See Pranoto Iskandar, 'A Democracy Needs International Law' *Indonesian Journal of International & Comparative Law Blog* (October 31, 2018), https://www.ijil.org/blog/a-democracy-needs-international-law.
41. See Davies, above n 36.
42. Pranoto Iskandar, 'Non-Citizen Rights in ASEAN: The Need to Chart a New Course' (2018) 27(2) *Social & Legal Studies* 180-199.
43. Simon Tay, 'Growing an ASEAN Voice?: A Common Platform in Global and Regional Governance' *ERIA Discussion Paper Series* (September 2013).
44. *Rohingya crisis: The world's fastest growing humanitarian crisis*, BBCNews (October 19, 2017), https://www.youtube.com/watch?v=KT7QUzJg0aM.
45. Gisle Kvanvig, ASEAN, Sovereignty and Human Rights, https://www.jus.uio.no/smr/english/about/programmes/vietnam/docs/asean-sovereignty-and-human-rights—gisle-kvanvig.pdf (last visited November 30, 2018).

practice non-enforceable. Going further, this self-imposed conception has impeded, if not thwarted, any attempt that requires domestic legal transformations.

It is clear that an immediate action that sensibly rectify the sluggishness of the region's supranational mechanism is none other than starting to accept a slightly modified conception of state sovereignty as the governing principle in the region's interstate affairs. This can be translated as a swift adoption of the implied side of being a sovereign state, i.e. a responsibility to protect the humanitarian values. This notion of sovereignty embraces a more responsibility-oriented model of domestic governance. That said, this model recognizes that there is a legitimate limit to the application of non-interference principle. For that reason, once the limit, such as the existence of a gross violation of human rights, has been crossed the applicability of the principle is qualitatively applied.

The genuine acceptance of this model is supposedly to increase the swiftness of the system, especially when it faces a plethora of debilitating humanitarian crises. To be fair, it might propel a conservative concern as it will aggravate the already fragile region. At first blush, it is a valid objection as ASEAN has been riddled with suspicion among its member states. Admittedly, this has been the very reason that behind the region's failure in conceiving its own dispute mechanism.[46] On the contrary, the injection of a healthy dose of humanitarianism will very likely be a boost for the struggling ASEAN to broach the domestic psyche of the population. As an enabler for ASEAN to engage in various issues that are close to the everyday concerns of the people will no doubt benefit the current campaign that promote the idea of "We, the ASEAN people." In the long run, needless to add, the adoption of an infused humanitarianism state sovereignty would significantly contribute to the robustness of the process of regional integration.

5 CONCLUSION

To conclude, it is important to reiterate that the historic foundational idea of ASEAN is none other than creating "One Vision, One Identity, [and] One Community" in the region.[47] Thus, it is no surprise that interfering in the internal affairs of other states is also a strong feature in the regional politics in Southeast Asia.[48] To achieve it, one should look no further than "[the] short, simply-worded document containing just five articles [that] declared the establishment of an Association for Regional Cooperation" that latter known simply as ASEAN.[49] More specifically, this founding document, better known as, the Bangkok Declaration explicitly recognized that "the countries of Southeast Asia share a *primary responsibility* for strengthening the economic and social stability of the region and ensuring their peaceful and progressive national development."[50] By recognizing that there is a "primary responsibility," it should not be controversial for the region to progressively move forward toward a more responsive system that work for the betterment of its population. In fact, the introduction of a more responsive model of interstate relations in the region is a welcome tweak toward a more humanized face of the Southeast Asia.

REFERENCES

American University Center for the Global South. (n.d.). About. Retrieved from: http://www1.american.edu/academic.depts/acainst/cgs/about.html.

46. See Edmund Sim, "The Outsourcing of Legal Norms and Institutions by the ASEAN Economic Community," (2014) 1(1) *Indonesian Journal of International & Comparative Law* 314-332.
47. See *History*, ASEAN, https://asean.org/asean/about-asean/history/.
48. Lee Jones, *ASEAN, Sovereignty and Intervention in Southeast Asia* (London: Palgrave Macmillan, 2012).
49. See *History*, ASEAN, https://asean.org/asean/about-asean/history/.
50. The Asean Declaration (Bangkok Declaration) Bangkok (August 8, 1967), https://asean.org/the-asean-declaration-bangkok-declaration-bangkok-8-august-1967/ (emphasis added).

Asian Society of International Law. (n.d.). *Governing bodies: Executive council.* Retrieved from: https://www.asiansil.org/about-us/governing-bodies/;

Ayoob, M. (2004). Third world perspectives on humanitarian intervention and international administration. *Global Governance*, 10, 99-118.

Barelli, M., 'Preventing and responding to atrocity crimes: China, sovereignty and the responsibility to protect' (2018) *23*(2) *Journal of Conflict and Security Law*, 173-201.

Bass, G.J. *Freedom's battle: The origins of humanitarian intervention* (New York,Alfred A. Knopf. 2008)

Bass, G.J., 'The Indian way of humanitarian intervention' (2015) *40*(2) *Yale Journal of International Law*, 227-294.

BBCNews. (October 19, 2017). *Rohingya crisis: The world's fastest growing humanitarian crisis.* Retrieved from: https://www.youtube.com/watch?v=KT7QUzJg0aM.

Blocher, J. 'Institutions in the marketplace of ideas' (2008) *57*(4) *Duke Law Journal*, 821-889.

Brownlie, I. (1991). *International law and the use of force by states.* Oxford: Clarendon Press, 1991).

Cate, I.M.T., 'Speech, truth, and freedom: An examination of John Stuart Mill's and Justice Oliver Wendell Holmes's free speech defenses' (2010) *22*(1) *Yale Journal of Law & the Humanities*, 35-48.

Charney, J.I. 'Universal International Law' (1993) *87*(4) *American Journal of International Law*, 529-551.

Chesterman, S., *Just war or just peace? Humanitarian intervention and international law* (Oxford: Oxford Universty Press, 2000)

Chimni, B.S. 'International institutions today: An imperial global state in the making' (2004) *15*(1) *European Journal of International Law*, 1-37.

Clarivate Analytics. (May 2017). Source Publication List for Web of Science. Retrieved from: http://mjl.clarivate.com/publist_ssci.pdf.

Coast, E. (2005, August). Population trends in developing countries. *LSE Research Online*. Retrieved from http://eprints.lse.ac.uk/268/1/Arnold.pdf.

Council of Foreign Affairs. (November 26, 2018). Global conflict tracker. Retrieved from: https://www.cfr.org/interactives/global-conflict-tracker#!/global-conflict-tracker.

Davies, S.E., 'The Asia rejection?: International refugee law in Asia' (2006) *52*(4) *Australian Journal of Politics and History*, 562-575.

Chimni, B.S., 'A just world under law: A view from the south' (2007) *22*(2) *American University Law Review*, 199-220.

Editorial: Diversity Challenge [Editorial]. (2014, Sept. 14). *Nature*, 279.

Geyer, M. 'Humanitarianism and human rights' In Fabian Klose (Ed.), *The emergence of humanitarian intervention: Ideas and practice from the nineteenth century to the present* (Cambridge: Cambridge University Press, 2015) 31-55

Ginsburg, T, 'Locking in democracy: Constitutions, commitment, and international law' (2006) *38*(4). *NYU Journal of International Law & Politics*, 707-760.

Goodman, R. 'Humanitarian intervention and pretext for war' (2006) 100 *American Journal of International Law*, 107-141.

Gordon, J., 'John Stuart Mill and the "Marketplace of Ideas."' (1997) 23(2) *Social Theory & Practice*, 235-249.

Greenwood, C. Is there a right of humanitarian intervention? (1993) 49(2) *WorldPolitics*, 34-40.

Iskandar, P. (2018, October 31). A democracy needs international law. [Web log post]. IJICL's blog. Retrieved from: https://www.ijil.org/blog/a-democracy-needs-international-law.

Iskandar, P.,'Non-citizen rights in ASEAN: The need to chart a new course' (2018) *27*(2) *Social & Legal Studies*, 180-199.

Iskandar, P., 'Constitutionalizing human rights universality in non-constitutional legal system: Decoding Indonesian human rights brouhaha' (2016) 3(1) *Indonesian Journal of International & Comparative Law*, 3-42.

Iskandar, P. & Piper N, 'Why Low-skilled Migration Matters,' (2016) *3*(3) *Indonesian Journal of International & Comparative Law*, 577-581.

Jackson, R.H., *Quasi-states: Sovereignty, international relations and the third world.* (Cambridge: Cambridge University Press, 1996)

Jones, L. (2012) *ASEAN, sovereignty and intervention in Southeast Asia* (London: Palgrave Macmillan)

Juwana, H., 'Hukum internasional sebagai instrumen politik: Beberapa pengalaman Indonesia sebagai studi kasus' (2012) 5 *Arena Hukum*, 106-114.

Kaldor, M. & Chinkin C. (April 22, 2018). *The "Doctrine of Humanitarian Intervention": And how it exposes the absence of any serious intention to help Syrians. openDemocracy.* Retrieved from: https://www.opendemocracy.net/mary-kaldor-christine-chinkin/doctrine-of-humanitarian-intervention-and-how-it-exposes-absence-of-an.

Kvanvig, G. (n.d.). ASEAN, Sovereignty and Human Rights. Retrieved from: https://www.jus.uio.no/smr/english/about/programmes/vietnam/docs/asean-sovereignty-and-human-rights—gisle-kvanvig.pdf.
Mason, A. & Wheeler N., 'Realist objections to humanitarian interventions'. In Barry Holden (Ed.), *The ethical dimension of global change* (Basingstoke: Macmillan Press, 1996), 94-110.
Mill, J.S., *On liberty*. (Kitchener, Batoche Books, 2001)
Orford, A., *Reading humanitarian intervention: Human rights and the use of force in international law*. (Cambridge: Cambridge University Press, 2003)
de la Rasilla, I., 'A very short history of international law journals (1869-2018)' (2018) 29(1) *European Journal of International Law*, 137-168.
Sauer, E., 'Universal principles in international law' (1956) 42 *Transactions of Grotius Society* 181-191.
Schachter, O. The legality of pro-democratic invasion (1984) 78(3) *American Journal of International Law*, 645-650.
Sim, E. The outsourcing of legal norms and institutions by the ASEAN Economic Community (2014) 1 (1) *Indonesian Journal of International & Comparative Law*, 314-332.
Simma, B. Universality of International Law from the Perspective of a Practitioner. (2009) 20(2) *European Journal of International Law*, 265-297.
Tay, S., *Growing an ASEAN voice?: A common platform in global and regional governance*. (ERIA Discussion Paper Series, 2013). Retrieved from Economic Research Institute for ASEAN East Asia website: http://www.eria.org/ERIA-DP-2013-16.pdf.
Tesón, F.R., *Humanitarian intervention: An inquiry into law and morality*. (New York, Transnational Publishers, 1988)
United Nations. (June 21, 2017). *World population projected to reach 9.8 billion in 2050, and 11.2 billion in 2100*. Retrieved from: https://www.un.org/development/desa/en/news/population/world-population-prospects-2017.html;
Weiss, T.G. *Humanitarian intervention: Ideas in action*. (Cambridge: Polity Press, 2016)
Weiss, T.G. & Collins C., *Humanitarian challenges and intervention* (New York, Routledge, 2018)
Welsh, J.M., (ed.). *Humanitarian intervention and international relations*. (Oxford, Oxford University Press, 2003)
Wheeler, N.J. *Saving strangers: Humanitarian intervention in international society*. (Oxford, Oxford University Press, 2000)
Woods, S. Thinking about diversity of thought (2008). Retrieved from: https://digitalcommons.ilr.cornell.edu/cgi/viewcontent.cgi?article=1106&context=workingpapers.

Culture and International Law - Juwana et al. (Eds)
© 2019 Taylor & Francis Group, London, ISBN 978-1-138-38766-9

Global governance 2.0: A cultural approach toward a global regime

Ian Montratama
Pertamina University, Jakarta, Indonesia

ABSTRACT: Global governance is facing a real challenge nowadays, especially due to incomplete participation on certain issues by great powers such as the United States. Under President Donald Trump, the US has excluded itself from the Paris Agreement for Climate Change. While in the face of potential nuclear confrontation, the US has shown its impatience toward the Kim Jong-un regime of North Korea.

The above phenomena signify the existence of a problem with the current model of global governance through the United Nations. The remodeling of global governance can be pursued by using a mature governance model from management studies. However, we argue that a more fundamental factor for creating more effective global governance is by building mutual trust and perception among the nations of the world in order to address global issues. Some states are not willing to absorb the consequence(s) of a global regime that would risk their domestic interests or conveniences. Other states appear not to care at all about the risks or threats that will be faced in the long run, because they are facing many current domestic issues that need to be addressed more urgently.

As many nations have different priorities, capacities, and perceptions toward global risks, we think the best approaches to building mutual understanding about global risks among the people of the world and addressing them by global action are (1) constructing world opinion, (2) shaping global ethics, and (3) eventually making international laws (that are in line with domestic laws). The Institute for Defense and Strategic Research (IDSR) proposes a model that can be implemented in order to achieve more effective global governance, called IDSR's Global Governance 2.0 Model.

KEYWORDS: Global risks, mutual trust and perception, Global Governance 2.0 model

1 INTRODUCTION

It is not foolish to believe that our world is in danger. Scientific research predicts that, with the current global temperature increasing by 3 °C per year, the icebergs at the poles will melt and the seawater level will rise to a level that will inundate Florida and Bangladesh. The temperature increase may also provoke the creation of storms, such as Storm Irma, which hit the Caribbean, Cuba and Florida in September 2017.

The quality of our environment has been worsened by irresponsible human acts. Firing forests to open up plantation fields has created a toxic haze across state borders. Throwing trash into the seawater has destroyed the habitat of many fish. The usage of Freon makes a hole in the ozone layer in the atmosphere that creates a greenhouse effect throughout the planet.

In addition, the possession of nuclear weapons means that the world is always in danger. The magnitude of current nuclear weapons could destroy a large area (up to 24 km^2) for tens of years due to nuclear radiation and climate change, which is called 'nuclear winter'. The high level of tension in the Korean Peninsula has put the world on the brink of nuclear war. The geopolitical structure in far eastern Asia may provoke China to get involved in a Korean war, which may spread the conflict to other regions, such as South Asia, Southeast Asia and Oceania.

Despite the fact that some sections of the world's population enjoy a better quality of life, the population in some states still suffer from extreme poverty and a lack of security. With the ethics of distributive justice, it would be socially improper if the fortunate section of the population neglected the unfortunate section. Extreme poverty needs to be addressed by global actions if it is to generate an enormous result.

The current global governance model (that we call Global Governance 1.0) seems to have failed to address the global issues. The great powers are the biggest challenge to creating and/ or running international laws or a global regime effectively. The great powers possess economic, political and military powers that make their participation in the mechanism of setting international laws vital.

In a realm of anarchy, international law should be the most effective instrument to maintain world order. However, these international laws should be in line with domestic regulations, especially with regard to the national laws of the great powers. That ideal condition would make the world order more stringent and would make international laws into an international regime that limited states' behaviors.

It would be better if as many nations as possible had domestic laws that were in line with world opinion, even before the international laws were enacted. The current situation suggests that international laws would be useless in the face of neglect from the great powers. Therefore, the move toward making international laws (as a global regime of governance) should start with influencing the making of domestic laws that reflect world opinions. If all of the great powers have made suitable domestic laws, then the United Nations can set up a relevant conference to create the appropriate new international laws.

Our proposed model (called Global Governance 2.0) is framed with the intent of establishing global public opinion and creating a global ethic in relation to certain global issues. That non-binding norm is projected to create domestic laws and eventually international laws as the ultimate outcome.

2 THE MODEL OF GLOBAL GOVERNANCE 2.0

The heading above signifies a new model that is remodeled from the current global governance model, which is predominantly governed by the United Nations. The current model has provided many treaties and written ethics that have contributed to the world peace and security that we have enjoyed so far. Learning from the League of Nations, which failed to stop World War II, the UN made its role to avoid the outbreak of World War III, through its intervention in the Korean War in 1950–1953 and the Indo-Pakistani War in 1966.

As the UN has gained more trust among nations, it has played a vital role as a unique coordination platform at a global level. Not only in international politics and security domains, but also in such areas as commercial development (such as GATT/WTO and World Bank), human rights (such as UNHCR and Amnesty International), social and economic development (such as ECOSOC, IFAD and IMF), environment protection, and humanitarian aid (such as WFP, UNICEF, FAO, and UNESCO).

The UN structure has expanded beyond anyone's expectations. Intergovernmental conferences on certain issues may lead to the creation of a new UN body. Nowadays, the UN's bodies are numerous and neat – that calls for restructuring or remodeling (or "reformation", according to President Trump's speech in the UN's General Assembly forum in September 2018).

Organizational restructuring is common practice at a corporate level. The aim is to make the organization work more effectively and efficiently. Some management tools have been invented for this, including the governance model. The cross-level projection of theory is sometimes useful. We learned in the 1980s and 1990s that many big companies try to adapt Sun Tzu's Art of War strategies into business. Meanwhile, in 1986, international relations scholars became accustomed to the term strategic partnerships (borrowed from the corporate business level) to explain co-operation between two rivals to pursue common goals, for example between the Soviet Union and China.

At the Institute for Defense and Strategic Research (IDSR), we have developed a governance model that we have called *Global Governance Model 2.0*. This model has the modest objective of bringing the best business practices to the organizational restructuring of the UN. The model needs an implementation mechanism, which we have called the *IDSR Pathway for Global Governance* (this will be discussed in Section 3). The model can be seen in Figure 1.

The model in Figure 1 signifies how the UN should be run in order to overcome global risks in the areas of security, economy, social and environment, which should be addressed in the UN General Assembly (on global risk). The UN should be oriented toward risk mitigation co-ordination among nations. Every year, the UN General Assembly (UNGA) holds a global risk conference to take UN decisions on certain global risk issues.

As global risks have expanded into environmental aspects, the UN's organs should supplement the UN's Environment Council (UNEC). UNEC will address climate change and environmental damage issues.

When organizing the UN's three main organs (UNSC, UNECOSOC and UNEC) toward risk mitigation, they should be structured into six departments, namely (a) global risk assessment, (b) ethics and legal formulation, (c) compliance assessment and tribunal, (d) finance/budget management, (e) internal audit service, and (f) human resource management. These six departments should form the structure in each of the UN's three organs.

Global Risk Assessment Department. This department has the main function of assessing global risk, as per the organ's domain. The department should be staffed with credible and appropriate experts who are equipped with adequate working equipment and infrastructure. To maintain the quality of assessments, Department A, as we will call it, should work together with relevant Non-Government Organizations (NGOs), universities, and research institutions (which we will call partners) that have been approved by the department.

Department A should be responsible for producing an *annual global risk report* – relevant to its organ. This annual report should indicate: (i) the current situations related to certain global risks; (ii) their future trends; (iii) proposed global action roadmap(s) to mitigate the

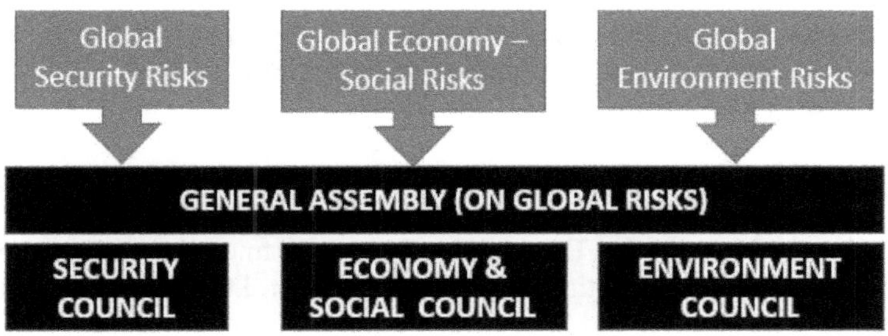

Global Risk Assessment (A)	SC's Dept. A	Ecosoc's Dept. A	EC's Dept. A
Ethics & Legal Formulation (B)	SC's Dept. B	Ecosoc's Dept. B	EC's Dept. B
Compliance Assessment and Tribunal Court (C)	SC's Dept. C	Ecosoc's Dept. C	EC's Dept. C
Finance Management (D)	SC's Dept. D	Ecosoc's Dept. D	EC's Dept. D
Internal Audit Service (E)	SC's Dept. E	Ecosoc's Dept. E	SC's Dept. E
Human Resources Management (F)	SC's Dept. F	Ecosoc's Dept. F	EC's Dept. F

Figure 1. Global Governance Model 2.0.

global risk(s). The proposed roadmap(s) should be brought to the UNGA conference to gain UNGA's approval as international law.

In order to face the possible problem of gaining a consensus for UNGA's approval for the roadmap(s), Department A should have a UN mandate to work together with its partners, in order to allow its partners to promote and educate the world's citizens to comprehend and believe in Department A's assessments. Their partners' advocacy activities should be oriented to: (a) promote world society's risk intelligent culture; (b) shape world opinion; (c) create global ethics; (d) eventually, smooth the way to generate international law (this will be discussed in Section 3).

Ethics and Legal Formulation Department. This department has the principal function of creating ethics and/or international law drafts in order to generate solid ground for global action(s). Department B, as it will be called, should be staffed with experienced and credible experts that are able to draft legal documents that are not only effective, but also conduct cultural considerations in order to avoid cultural mishaps.

Department B should responsible for: (i) deciding on the most appropriate forms of international law or ethics; (ii) formulating the best drafts of the law or written ethics. The draft should then should be brought to UNGA's annual meeting for approval.

Department B should have a mandate to work with each of the UN's member states to co-produce domestic laws, where these laws were not already compatible with the international law draft. A domestic law draft would only be needed for those nations who did not have suitable domestic laws to support the international law draft.

Compliance Assessment and Tribunal Court Department. This department has the main function of assessing whether every UN member state complies with UN international laws and/or drafts that are related to a certain organ's domain. Department C, as it will be called, makes sure that the global actions that are needed to mitigate global risks are on track. The other main function is to hold a tribunal court that relates to a certain UN organ. The International Court of Justice (ICJ) and the Permanent Court of Arbitration (PCA), which mainly handle security-related cases, may be reorganized into a Tribunal Court for Security. Meanwhile, for the other two organs, there should be a Tribunal Court for Economy and Social, and a Tribunal Court for Environment.

Department C should be responsible for: (1) monitoring every nation's policy regarding international laws and drafts; (2) providing a tribunal court for any disputes in order to mitigate global risks. The department should be staffed with credible and appropriate experts (including international level judges and attorneys) who are equipped with adequate working equipment and infrastructure.

As for Department C's Tribunal Courts, they should have a mandate to perform a legal tribunal court, as has been done in ICJ and PCA. The courts themselves can be maintained in the UN offices in The Hague, Geneva or Vienna.

Finance Management Department. This department has the principal function of managing the financial and budgeting aspect of each organ. Department D, as it will be called, should be staffed with credible and appropriate experts who are equipped with adequate working equipment and infrastructure.

Department D should responsible for: (1) producing an annual financial report – relevant to its organ – that should indicate the financial status of the organ and its affiliated agencies in an accountable and transparent manner, and (2) planning for the following fiscal budget, which should be approved by a higher authority in the UN.

The UN should give a mandate to each Department D to plan, manage, and report on the budgeting and finance aspect of its organ.

Internal Audit Department. This department has the main function of monitoring and evaluating (*monev*) to ensure that each organ and its personnel perform their duty as per their assignments. The *monev* activities are projected to operational, finance, and personnel related matters. Department E should be responsible for: (1) making sure that the organ runs as per its assignments; (2) investigating any report that relates to an organ's internal affairs.

The UN should give a mandate to each Department E to monitor, evaluate and investigate the related organ's internal activities.

Human Resources Department. This department has the main function of managing the human resources aspect of each organ. Human resources should be sourced from international recruits who are professionals and experts; representatives of the UN member states should also be included for diplomatic positions. Department F should be responsible for planning, selecting, recruiting, hiring, training, and managing the human resources of certain UN organs. The UN should give a mandate to each Department F to plan, manage, and report on the human resources aspect of its organ.

The above model may look simple. However, the objective of the model is to propose a feasible reorganization of the UN structure – with limited objections. Moreover, the route to more effective global governance lies in an agreement between domestic laws and/or policies and international laws/ethics, rather than in the UN's organizational structure. Therefore, in Section 3 we will discuss the mechanism of how global governance may effectively work as a global regime.

3 MECHANISM TOWARD GLOBAL GOVERNANCE 2.0

The essential factor for creating a global regime is not by imposing international law, but by causing the people of the world to support global actions of their own will. Therefore, we have created a pathway on how to achieve a global regime using a cultural approach as shown in Figure 2.

The model shown in Section 2 is a modest reformation. Any reform that is more substantial than that model may risk being infeasible to implement. As the ultimate goal is to have a more effective, efficient and responsive global governance, we should not frame our mindset so that UN reorganization is the only solution. It is more important to find a way to make sure that the domestic laws and policies of nations are in line with the preferred global actions in order to mitigate global risks.

The above thinking may seem to be more difficult to attain than imposing international law on certain states whose domestic laws are still not in line with international law. However, the current situation regarding the non-participation of the US in UN Climate Change and the Law of the Seas shows how hard it is to create a global regime. On the other hand, we saw how enabler technologies (i.e. social media) led to information spreading quickly and vastly across national borders. With proper social media handling, this may initiate people's understanding of the global risks and this may provoke a social movement to shape domestic regulations to comply with preferred global actions.

Understanding Global Risk. As a first step to giving people around the world an understanding of the global risks, there should be trust among people that there is: (1) a credible source of information on global risks and their mitigating ways; (2) a credible institution that may lead global actions in the right direction.

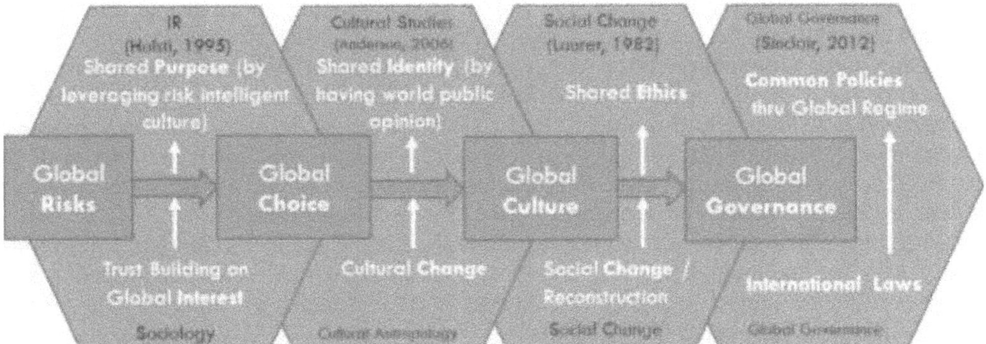

Figure 2. IDSR Pathway for Global Governance.

The creation of a credible source of information on global risks should not wait until the UN reformation is complete. Global governance signifies joint actions between state actors and non-state actors in order to govern the world. Therefore, research institutes, such as the Global Challenge Foundation, may take a key role in educating the people of the world about the global risks.

On the other hand, the UN organization should preserve their role as the spearhead of intergovernmental agencies by creating global action through a global regime in order to mitigate global risks. The UN's consistent and persistent multilateral efforts should be maintained continuously, depending on the level of global risks. The trust of both people and states should be built to its optimum level so that they believe that the UN is a credible channel for common interest that is able to act on a global level.

The global common interest should be shaped carefully along with the goal of promoting people's risk intelligent culture. People should not only be educated so that they understand about global risks, but also to enable them to integrate this knowledge into their way of life. People's culture is changing because of the shared purpose of preserving the world's quality of life. People know the risks and dangers that they are facing and that this demands changes in their very culture.

Determining Global Choice. The growing need for cultural change will be the fundamental base from which to proceed to the next level in creating the world's public opinion on global risks. Uniting the opinions of people from around the world would be very challenging without understanding that all of the people of the world actually share a common identity as global citizens.

Regardless of their nationality, ideology, race, religion, and gender, people are facing catastrophic global risks and they need to make a united effort to ensure their very existence. These global risks lead to people consenting to the few choices that they should take collectively in order to mitigate the risks.

With the help of credible research institutes, people can be exposed to these few global choices and their respective consequences. Policy recommendations at state level should also be promoted by the UN to raise people's awareness of what should be done at both the domestic and global level. The awareness of people as global citizens may raise the need for social change in order to reshape global culture.

Reshaping Global Culture. With a shared identity as global citizens, the people of the world demand a global culture that is shaped by their common interests in order to mitigate global risks. This new culture may define some dos and don'ts, musts and mustn'ts, rights and wrongs, and things that are good and bad that basically limit people's behaviors regarding something that may risk their quality of life.

The basic global culture may be tailored carefully by the UN and relevant non-state actors in order to design these world ethics. These ethics are more like non-binding and unwritten regulations and could be seen as preliminary global norms to international laws. By their character, these ethics should be easier to integrate into domestic ethics in every state of the world. The shared ethics will eventually clear the way to accommodating more formal international laws made by the UN.

Firming Global Governance. With strong global ethics and a low level of resistance from state actors, the UN may gather the political support from member states to draft relevant international laws in order to mitigate certain global risks. In Section 2, we have proposed that the three UN organs should have their own Department B that could carefully draft the written ethics and international laws. Future international laws should govern states behaviors in order to collectively conserve the world from catastrophic global risks.

In order to confirm global governance, the domestic laws of the UN's member states should comply with international laws. This compliance is necessary to make sure that a state's behavior would be subject to legal consequences in its national laws, especially for internal affairs policies that may cause global harm.

By having common policies between domestic and international laws, the global regime should prevail with the UN and its affiliated/endorsed non-state actors to govern the world for the shared interest of all people. No head of state(s) could hamper the global regime as he/

she would first need to face his/her domestic people when making any policies that opposed world public opinion.

4 CONCLUSION: SETTING WORLD PUBLIC OPINION FIRST

The proposed model of Global Governance 2.0 is rather too modest to optimize its chance of implementation. Drastic change may not be realistic and time is a critical factor in order to mitigate global risks.

Rather than debating the perfect global governance model, we need to give more attention to the cultural process of shaping world public opinion. Catastrophic global risks may, by their nature, create a common purpose that leads to global choices. We proposed global governance with a focus on empowering local indigenous communities to gain media expression in the global fora. Indigenous communities have been suffering from man-made disasters and they need to be involved as the subject (not object) of the mitigation strategy. In many cases, local communities have been blamed as the perpetrators of these disasters.

Our global governance proposal places indigenous communities at the core of global initiatives. International organizations will need to raise the issues and problems of indigenous communities. Those people who have been invisible in the media and international politics for years may have a vital role to play. Global risks, such as climate change, environmental degradation, and poverty, need to be dealt with by the participation of people as global citizens, who would embrace a risk intelligent culture.

With a developed risk intelligent culture, people may share an identity as global citizens and demand a new global culture that reflects global norms or ethics. Those global norms and ethics would bring a double-edged benefit that may shape both domestic and international laws to eventually construct a global regime.

The clear pathway above might create faster result(s) than the current global governance model, which has been shown to be flawed by being hampered by the policies of the great/major powers that intensify global risks. A solid global regime is not dictated by an intergovernmental agency like the UN, but by common policies (between domestic and international laws) and people's culture. Our proposed model signifies a top-down approach, but our proposed pathway advises a bottom-up approach.

REFERENCES

Baker, S., Kousis, M., Richardson, D. & Young, S. (1997). Introduction: The theory and practice of sustainable development in EU perspective. In S. Baker, M. Kousis, D. Richardson & S. Young (Eds.), *The politics of sustainable development: Theory, policy and practice within the European Union* (pp. 1–41). London, UK: Routledge.

Barber, C.V. (2000). *Forest, fires and confrontation in Indonesia.* Winnipeg, Canada: International Institute for Sustainable Development.

Baret, S., Hilda, E., Hatfield, S., Sanford, N. & Vazirani, J. (2013). *Developing an effective governance operating model.* New York, NY: Deloitte.

Eckersley, R. (2004). *The green state: Rethinking democracy and sovereignty.* Cambridge, MA: MIT Press.

Eckersley, R. (2005). Greening the nation-state: From exclusive to inclusive sovereignty. In R. Eckersley & J. Barry (Eds.), *The state and global ecological crisis* (pp. 159–181). Cambridge, MA: MIT Press.

Global Challenges Foundation. (2017). *Global catastrophic risks 2017.* Stockholm, Sweden: Global Challenges Foundation.

Holsti, K.J. (1995). *International politics: A framework for analysis* (7th ed.). Upper Saddle River, NJ: Prentice Hall.

Jacobs, M. (1999). Sustainable development as a contested concept. In A. Dobson (Ed.), *Fairness and futurity: Essays on environmental sustainability and social justice* (pp. 21–32). Oxford, UK: Oxford University Press.

Martínez Cantera, A.L. (2016, June 7). Indonesia's forest fires threaten Sumatra's few remaining Orang Rimba. *The Guardian*. Retrieved from https://www.theguardian.com/global-development/2016/jun/07/indonesia-forest-fires-threaten-sumatras-few-remaining-orang-rimba
Martono, N. (2012). *Sosiologi Perubahan Sosial: Perspektif Klasik, Modern, Posmodern, dan Poskolinial*. Jakarta, Indonesia: Rajawali Press.
Miranda, R.J. (2016, September 9). The indigenous Dayaks and forest-dependent communities are not to blame for the raging forest fires in Central Kalimantan, Indonesia! Retreived from https://medium.com/@randijulian/the-indigenous-dayaks-and-forest-dependent-communities-are-not-to-blame-for-the-raging-forest-fires-e96d505aeac4
Mongabay. (2016, August 23). Raging Amazon forest fires threaten uncontacted indigenous tribe. Retrieved from https://news.mongabay.com/2016/08/raging-amazon-forest-fires-threaten-uncontacted-indigenous-tribe/
O'Neill, K. (2009). *The environment and international relations*. Cambridge, UK: Cambridge University Press.
Rosenau, J. (1995). Governance in the twenty-first century. *Global Governance*, *1*(1), 13–43.
Saebani, B.A. (2016). *Perspektif Perubahan Sosial*. Bandung, Indonesia: Pustaka Setia.
Sukmana, O. (2016). *Konsep dan Teori Gerakan Sosial*. Malang, Indonesia: Intrans Publishing.
Survival International. (2016, August 18). Brazil: Amazon fires threaten to wipe out uncontacted Indians. Retrieved from http://www.survivalinternational.org/news/11391
Survival International. (2016, August 22). Top tribal conservation skills. Retrieved from http://www.survivalinternational.org/articles/3380-tribal-conservation
Tay, S. (2001). Fires, haze and acid rain: The social and political framework of air pollution in ASEAN and Asia. In W. Stefen, J. Jager & D. Carson (Eds.), *Challenges of a changing earth* (pp. 49–55). Amsterdam, The Netherlands: Springer.
United Nations. (2014, October 20). 'Largely invisible' in Millennium goals era, indigenous peoples' knowledge, traditions key to sustainable future, Third Committee told. Retreived from https://www.un.org/press/en/2014/gashc4106.doc.htm

Culture and International Law - Juwana et al. (Eds)
© 2019 Taylor & Francis Group, London, ISBN 978-1-138-38766-9

Cultural relativism approach to freedom of religion: How religious values affect business and investment in Indonesia

A.A.A. Nanda Saraswati
International Law Department, Faculty of Law, Brawijaya University, Indonesia

ABSTRACT: Indonesia has been facing renewed calls to repeal its controversial blasphemy law, particularly after Jakarta's Chinese and Christian governor, Basuki "Ahok" Tjahaja Purnama, was sentenced for 2 years in prison for blasphemy in 2017. The verdict immediately raised ethnic and religious tensions. As a normative approach, using statute and conceptual approach, this article attempts to analyze the view of judges in Indonesia towards how blasphemy law is interpreted as a permissible limitation of freedom of expression. It, thus, furthermore examines whether religion and cultural sensitivity may bring indirect effects to the business and foreign investment sector. The results show that the decision of the Indonesian Constitutional Court on judicial review of the Blasphemy Law is inclined to prioritize the concept of cultural relativism by incorporating the so-called "*Indonesian perspective*". It is based on the ideology of the State, "Pancasila". However, religious values and prohibition of "different interpretations" regarded as legitimate restrictions need to be reviewed, both in terms of substance and implementation. Revisions to certain provisions of blasphemy law are essential to determine the extent to which States can intervene in one's beliefs, speech, and expression to prevent arbitrary interpretations. It also will create legal certainty for business and foreign investment which are to respect and become adherent with the local laws, culture, and belief of the Indonesian people.

KEYWORDS: blasphemy law, religious values, cultural relativism, business, investment

1 FREEDOM OF RELIGION IN INDONESIA

Freedom of religion is a universal fundamental human right. It is a principle that supports the freedom of an individual or community, in private or public, to choose and manifest a religion or belief in teaching, practice, worship, and observance. It also includes the freedom to change one's religion or beliefs. Freedom of Religion is a broad concept which include freedom from discrimination base on religion, freedom to embrace or convert religion, and freedom to practice the religion.[1] Religion, which raises more concern in international politics, has created polarizations of perspective on several aspects of freedom of religion. This aspect oftenly revoke excessive conflicts among nations and states. This is understandable, since there are differences in social, culture, history, economy, politics, and other characterteristics that affect and provide contribution towards the formation of contradicting claimage value, including perception on what is referred as human rights.[2]

In Indonesia, normatively, freedom of religion has been protected and guaranteed as human rights, both in the constitution and a number of laws and regulations. *The*

1. Universal Declaration of Human Rights, Adopted from General Assembly Resolution 217 A on 10 December 1948
2. Darara Timotewos Gubo, *Blasphemy and Defamation of Religions In a Polarized World, How Religious Fundamentalism is Challenging Fundamental Human Rights* (London: Lexington Books, 2015)

guarantee is one indicator that Indonesia is a state of law.[3] The 1945 Constitution, article 28 E paragraph (1) states that: "*Everyone is free to embrace religion and worship according to his religion …*" Furthermore Article 29 (2) states "*The State guarantees the independence of each resident to embrace their respective religion and to worship according to his religion and belief.*" While in article 28 I stated that "*rights to religion cannot be reduced under any circumstances.*" In addition, freedom of religion is also regulated in Law No.39 Year 1999 concerning Human Rights. Article 22 states that "*Everyone is free to embrace his own religion and to worship according to his religion and belief. And the State guarantees the freedom of each person to embrace their respective religion and to worship according to their religion and belief.*"[4] Observing the condition of the above regulation, it seems that freedom is assured in Indonesia. However, such freedom is not absolute. Indonesian Constitution sets the limit in the 1945 Constitution Article 28 Paragraph J which states that: "*In exercising their rights and freedoms, each person must submit to the restrictions set by law with the sole purpose of guaranteeing the recognition and respect for the rights and freedoms of others and to fulfill just demands in accordance with moral considerations, religious values, security, and public order in a democratic society.*" Whereas Articles 70 and 73 of the Human Rights Law state that the implementation of freedom of human rights must not violate the rights of others, security, morality, public order, and the interests of the nation. The mechanism of the restriction is actually also regulated in international instruments such as the Universal Declaration of Human Rights and the ICCPR. The restrictions stipulated in the ICCPR must be carried out by legal provisions, in order to protect security and public order, health, public morals, or other people's basic rights and freedoms.[5]

Seeing both abovementioned national and international instruments, there seems to be a slight difference. In Indonesian Constitution, "religious values" is one of the reasons for limiting human rights, whereas ICCPR does not. In this regard, there was a debate about internal freedom (forum internum) and external freedom (forum externum). Indeed, the aspect of internal freedom is absolute, meaning it cannot be interfered by State under any circumstances. This component includes the right to form and hold opinions based on conscience, including those beliefs that may be deemed objectionable, or even offensive to others. It protects the right to have or hold a religion or belief, as well as the right not to have a religion or belief. On the other hand, the externum forum relates to the right to manifest a religion or belief, either alone or as a part of a community. This component includes the right practice a religion or belief through activities such as teaching, worship, or other forms of observance; the right to share a religion or belief with others; the right to publish or distribute books, literatures, and other forms of information about a religion or belief; the right to own and use buildings for worship; the right to express a religion or belief through clothing, rituals, and symbols. Due to its relation to the rights of others, forum externum can be limited by the government or state in exceptional situations with a high threshold of evidence required by those enforcing any limitations. As mentioned earlier, that The UN Human Rights Committee declares such permissible limitations if they are prescribed by law and are necessary to protect public safety, order, health or morals, or the fundamental rights and freedoms of others.

This is where such freedom is open for debate. This is because in the international level, limitations to this freedom have been carried out by a number of countries differently. On reasons for imposing limitations is due to the increase in certain situations that can lead to

3. A.V.Dicey, *An Introduction to Study of the Law of the Constitution* (London, 10th edition, Palgrave MacMillan) 223-224.
4. Law Number 39 Year 1999 on Human Rights (State Gazette Year 1999 Number 165), article 22
5. International Covenant on Civil and Political Rights, adopted by UN General Assembly, dated 19 Desember 1966, article 18

abuse towards the adherents of a religion through what we know as hate speech.[6] On form of hate speech is based on religion that has the characteristic of stating that a religion is harmful to other religions, thus promoting destruction, for example the attack or destruction of houses of worship.[7] The prohibition of hate speech has been regulated in ICCPR which states that any propaganda of war shall be prohibited by law. As well as any advocacy to national, racial or religious hatred that constitutes incitement to discrimination, hostility or violence shall be prohibited by law.[8]

Another form of limitation is often associated and even overlaps with what is referred to as "blasphemy". The idea that hate speeches, which incite discrimination and violence must be banned, seems not as controversial as blasphemy. Indonesia is one of 70 countries that have anti-blasphemy laws/policies. Blasphemy is regulated in the Criminal Code (KUHP) and Law No. 1/PNPS/1965 concerning Prevention of Abuse and/or Blasphemy of Religion (Blasphemy Law). Article 156 paragaph a of the Criminal Code reads:

> *"Sentenced to imprisonment for a maximum of five years, whoever intentionally publicly issues feelings or acts; which is basically a hostility, abuse, or desecration of a religion adopted in Indonesia; with the intention that people do not adhere to any religion which based on the One God Almighty."*

Whereas Blasphemy Law states:

> *"Everyone is forbidden to intentionally publicly tell, advocate, or seek public support, to make interpretations of a religion adopted in Indonesia or carry out religious activities that resemble the religious activities of that religion; interpretations and activities which deviate from the principles of teachings in the respective religion."*[9]

It appears that the Criminal Code does not clearly define blasphemy or its limitation. Whereas in the Blasphemy Law, there is a prohibition to interpret a religion. The words *"do interpretations that deviate from the principles of teachings in the respective religion"* are often debated, raising a request for testing the constitutionality of Blasphemy Law. The essence of the testing aims to look for the direction and interpretation of freedom of religion and see the extent to which the relevance of Blasphemy Law is related to the current social conditions in Indonesian society. The applicants consisted of lawyers and legal aid activists who were members of the Freedom of Religion Advocacy Team. Considered being unconstitutional, the applicants sued the articles in the Blasphemy Law,[10] arguing that the interpretation carried out by people should not be limited by the State. In this case, the state may not determine the interpretation of one group as an official interpretation of the State. Something that is considered true by a group/sect is not necessarily considered as truth by another group.[11] Religion is an interpretation that always develops according to the times and contexts.[12] Moreover, interpretation is a general phenomenon, both in terms of practice and the history of religion development.[13] In this context, there is no single meaning to the text/teaching, so that

6. *Legal Analysis on the Concept of Hate Crime and Hate Speech* (OSCE, Polyesterday, Skopje, 2012) 37.
7. Kathleen Mahoneey, 'Hate Speech, Equality nad the State of Canadian Law' (2009) 44 *Wake Forest Law Review*, 326
8. International Covenant od Civil and Political Rights 1966, Pasal 20 ayat 2
9. Law Number 1/PNPS/1965 on the Prevention of Abuse and Blasphemy of Religion (State Gazette Year 1965 Number 3), Article 1
10. Rita Triana Budiarti, *Kontroversi Mahfud MD: Dibalik Putusan Mahkamah Konstitusi* (Jakarta, Edition II, Konstitusi Press, 2013) 47-48.
11. Constitutional Court Decision Number 140/PUU-VII/2009 on the Prevention of Abuse and Blasphemy of Religion against the 1945 Constitution, 231
12. Akhmad, Muamar, 'Kebebasan Beragama dan Problematika HAM Universal' (2013) II(I) *Jurnal Studi Agama dan Pemikiran Islam*, 78.
13. Jefrrey Haynes, *Religion and Politics in Europe, the Middle Easr and North Africa, Routledge, New York*, 8; Also see Tijani Abd. Qadir Hamid, *Pemikiran Politik dalam Al-Quran* (Jakarta, Gema Insani Press, 2011) 9

differences in interpretation are a logical consequence of the development of religion. All interpretations are an inseparable part of human instincts, as beings who are endowed with reason to always continue to seek the truth. Thus, each interpretation has the potential for truth and also potential for errors. By limiting people from interpreting, it means tantamount to closing the possibility for the emergence of forms of interpretation that might have better truths. These restrictions betray human nature.[14] How do judges interpret this? Here's the explanation.

2 A CULTURAL RELATIVISM APPROACH

The Constitutional Court stated that it rejected all petitioners' requests in the judicial review session of Law No.1/PNPS/1965 concerning the Prevention of Abuse and/or Blasphemy of Religion.[15] Indeed, all of the 9 Constitutional Court judges did not produce a unanimous vote. Judge Harjono,[16] gave a concurring opinion while a dissenting opinion was given by Judge Maria Farida Indrati.[17] The trial of this lawsuit was the longest trial at the Court, in which 12 sessions were held in 6 months. The claim is indeed a complex involving not only groups in interest, but also perspective of normative, historical, religious, and political.[18]

In its decision, the Constitutional Court has long enough to discuss the relationship between Constitution, State, and religion. The Court began by noting that the philosophical basis of Indonesia as a state was the result of a compromise between two schools of thought, namely secular and Islamic, both of which were not adopted as the basis of the State.[19] The Court observed that the Indonesian concept of a "state of law" was not the same as the concept of "*rechstaat*" either the concept of "rule of law". This is based on the fact that the Constitution places the One and Only God as the main basis along with religious values that underlie the life of the nation and state.[20] It further stated that Pancasila is a "fundamental state foundation" where the Almighty God cannot be changed or replaced. That is the basis of Indonesia's philosophical view as a state of Pancasila, so that all activities/practices that alienate citizens from the values of Pancasila must not be allowed. Anyone is forbidden to erode the religiosity of society that has been inherited as values that inspire various legislative provisions in Indonesia, even if it is based on freedom.[21]

In its decision, the Panel of judges appeared to use a perspective of cultural relativism. Cultural relativism argues human rights are not universal. The difference is due to the condition that human beings are always a product of several social and cultural environments.[22] Each nation have different backgrounds or ideological, social, and cultural histories, hence enforcing human rights universalism to all nations or countries in the world is an impossible objective.[23] These adherents emphasize the impact of cultural differences and how they reflect the relativity of human rights principles and their applications. It is impossible to impose any

14. Court Decision Number 140/PUU-VII/2009, above n 11, 24
15. See Constitutional Court Decision Number: 140/PUU-VII/2009 dated 19 April 2010
16. Constitutional Court, Session Minutes of Case Number 140/PUU-VII/2009 Concerning Review to Law Number 1 PNPS Year 1965 on the Prevention of Abuse and Blasphemy of Religion against the 1945 Constitution, 90
17. Ibid, 95
18. Yayan Sopyan, 'Menyoal Kebebasan Beragama dan Penodaan Agama di Indonesia (Telaah atas Putusan MK No.140/PUU-VII/2009)' (2015) II(2) *Jurnal Cita Hukum*, 199
19. Stewart Fenwick, *Blasphemy, Islam and the State, Pluralism and Liberalism in Indonesia* (London and New York, Routledge, 2017) 65
20. Court Decision Number 140/PUU-VII/2009, 3.34.10, 275
21. Ibid, 3.34.5, 273
22. Satya Arianto, *Hak Asasi Manusia dalam Transisi Politik di Indonesia* (Jakarta, second edition, Pusat Studi Hukum Tata Negara FHUI, 2005) 91-92.
23. Rohidin, *Konstruksi Baru Kebebasan Beragama, Menghadirkan Nilai Kemanusiaan yang Adil dan Beradab di Negara Hukum Indonesia* (FHUII-Press, 2015) 82.

value, including the value of human rights, on a society or culture that does not accept the validity of that value. Therefore, no culture is justified in trying to force its ideas to be accepted by other cultures, or "No culture is justified in attempting to impose on others what must be understood as its own ideas.[24] The characteristics that are always present in the view of cultural relativism include:[25] each culture possess different moral code; there is no standard objection to judge that one social code is better than other social code; moral code from our society is merely one from many other codes, and has no higher status; there is no universal truth on ethics, means that there is no single moral truth that applies to everybody; moral code from a culture applies only to the respective culture's environment; and it's deemed arrogance when we try to judge other person's deed.

Such notion of cultural relativism can be seen from the opinion of the Panel which explicitly states that Indonesia has banned anti-religious campaigns and misinterpreted religion. This is a characteristic of freedom of religion according to Indonesian law, therefore it becomes one of the elements that distinguishes Indonesia from other countries, especially the West where human rights apply universally to all people everywhere, regardless of nationality, ethnicity, culture, and other distinguishing factors.[26] According to the Constitutional Court, blasphemy articles can not only be seen from the legal aspect but also philosophically which places freedom of religion in the Indonesian-ness perspective, hence the practice of diversity in other countries cannot be equated with the practices that occur in Indonesia.[27] Things such as the basis of divinity and religious values become a measure or parameter to distinguish good law from bad law, even to determine the constitutionality of a legal product.[28] Related to the issue of interpretation, although freedom to interpret is an internal dimension, but it still has to be conducted based on the principles of religious teachings. The judges' point of view is perceptible in the following reasoning:

> "*Interpretation can provide confidence in something, so that interpretation can lead to the truth and the potential for the occurrence of errors. Although the interpretation of beliefs in religious teachings is part of freedom which part in the forum internum, but the interpretation must be in accordance with the points of religious teachings through the correct methodology based on the source of the relevant religious teachings, namely the respective scriptures, hence freedom to interpret religion is not absolute. Interpretations that are not based on a common methodology recognized by adherents of the religion and not based on the source of the scriptures in question will cause a reaction that threatens security and public order when expressed or carried out in public.*"[29]

Based on the above statement, it appears that the flow of thought of the Panel of judges considers that some aspects of human rights are not absolute, therefor it can be limited based on certain considerations. Regarding restrictions, the ICCPR does not include "religious values" as a form of legal limitation. The ICCPR does not allow restrictions to be applied in the exercise of the right to freedom of expression for the purpose of guaranteeing the respect of a religion from "defamation". The ICCPR protects the rights of individuals, and in some cases, individual groups, but does not protect abstract entities such as religion, beliefs, ideas, or symbols. The UN Human Rights Committee has criticized blasphemy law and declared the

24. Henry Steiner, Philip Alston, *International Human Rights in Context: Law, Politics, Morals: Text and Materials* (New York, 3rd Edition, Oxford University Press, 2008) 518.
25. Joshua Preisa, *Pluralism, Relativism and Cultural Rights*, Paper for Workshop about Human Rights on 20 April 2004, in Pranoto Iskandar, Hukum HAM Internasional, Sebuah Pengantar Konseptual (Cianjur: IMR Press, 2010) 151.
26. Kyriaki Topidi, Lairen Fielder, *Transnational Legal Process and Human Rights, (*USA: Routledge, 2016)22; Micheline Ishay, *The History of Human Rights, From Ancient Times to the Globalization Era* (London: University of California Press Ltd, 2008) 3; Hilkka Becker, Grainne Brophy, Elaine Dewhurst, *Human Rights Law* (United Kingdom, 4th Edition, Oxford University Press) 1
27. Ibid, 274
28. Ibid, 3.34.11, 275
29. Ibid, 288-289

right to freedom of expression should not be "used to prevent or punish criticism of religious leaders or comments about religious doctrine or the subject matter of the faith."[30] Similar to this, the UN Special Rapporteur on the promotion and protection of freedom of expression stated that restrictions on the right to freedom of expression are "designed to protect individuals from direct violations of their rights" and "not designed to protect the belief system from external or internal criticism."[31] Among many things, Rabat Plan of Action states that the right to freedom of religion or belief, as stated in a number of international conventions such as the Universal Declaration of Human Rights and the ICCPR, does not include the right to adhere to a religion or belief that is free from criticism or ridicule.[32]Countries that have blasphemy laws must revoke the regulation because it has a choking effect on the enjoyment of the right to freedom of religion or belief as well as healthy dialogue or debate about religion.[33] Restrictions on freedom of religion and expression can be carried out if the expressions emit feelings/commit acts of hostility that lead to discrimination.[34] To prevent and counteract the practice of intolerance on the basis of religion, a broader set of policy actions is clearly needed.[35]

Differs to the statement from ICCPR and Rabat Plan of Action, the Panel of Judges seems to use cultural relativism view in defining "religious values" as public value. The reasoning is as follow:

> *"...the restriction on religious values as communal values of society is a legal limitation according to the constitution. Religious traditions in Indonesia do have specialties and uniqueness that the State cannot intervene in ...".*[36] *"Religion is not only free to be embraced, but religious values become a barrier to other basic freedoms solely to guarantee recognition and respect for the rights and freedoms of others."*[37] The Panel explicitly stated that the existence of "religious values" as the legal limitation to Human Rights is one charactereistics of Indonesia that differs to universal norm.[38]

3 RELIGION IN RELATION TO BUSINESS AND INVESTMENT

The previous explanation of religious values raises questions in relation to business and investment. The question that arises is whether or not religion and its values could influence business and investment activities in Indonesia. To answer these questions, we must first look at the regulation on investment in Indonesia.

In 2016, the Government Government of Indonesia enacted Presidential Regulation No. 44 of 2016,[39] which sets out the new list of negative investments which replaces the previous decree, in the 2014. Such amendments were signed by President Joko Widodo in 2016. It is one out of many efforts to increase foreign direct investment (FDI) including Indonesia's

30. Human Rights Commission, General Commentary 34, 48.
31. Human Rights Council, Report of the Special Rapporteur on the promotion and protection of the Right to Freedom of Opinion and Expression, Ambeyi Ligabo, for Human Rights Council, 28 February 2008 A/HRC/7/14 paragraph 85 in Amnesty International, 26
32. *Report of the United Nations High Commissioner for Human Rights, A/HRC/22/17/Add.4* (2013) 19, <http://www.ohchr.org/Documents/HRBodies/HRCouncil/RegularSession/Session22/A-HRC-22-17-Add4_en.pdf≥, accessed on 16 May 2017
33. Ibid, 25
34. Rumadi, 'Kebebasan dan Penodaan Agama, Menimbang Proyek Jalan Tengah Mahkamah Konstitusi RI' (2012) 1(2) *Indo-Islamika*, 269.
35. Benecdict Rogers, 'Rejecting Religious Intolerance in South East Asia' (2018) 2(1 June) Journal of Southeast Asian Human Rights, 222.
36. Court Decision Number 140/PUU-VII/2009, above n 20, 295
37. Constitutional Court, Session Minutes of Case Number 140/PUU-VII/2009, above n 20, 60
38. Ibid, 275-276
39. Presidential Regulation Number 44 Year 2016 on List of Business Fields Closed and Business Fields Open with Conditions to Investment

Table. 1. List of Closed Business Fields

No.	Areas	Business Field
1.	Agriculture	Plantation of Marijuana
2.	Forestry	Fishing of species of fish listed in Appendix I Convention On International Trade In Endangered Species Of Wild Fauna And Flora (CITES)
3.	Marine Affairs and Fisheries	Gathering (taking) of coral from nature for construction materials/lime/calcium and souvenirs/jewellery as well as living coral or dead coral (recently dead coral) from nature
4.	Industry	1. Manufacture of industrial chemicals and Manufacture of Ozone Depleting Substances 2. Manufacture of chemicals listed in Schedule 1 of the Chemical Weapons Convention as provided in Attachment I to Law Number 9 of 2008 concerning Use of Chemicals and Prohibition on Use of Chemicals as Chemical Weapons 3. Manufacture of alcoholic beverages: Wine
5.	Transportation	1. Provision and operation of terminals for passenger land transport 2. Provision and operation of weigh stations 3. Telecommunications/aids to shipping navigation and vessel traffic information system (VTIS) 4. Provision of air navigation services 5. Performance of testing of types of motor vehicles
6.	Communications and Informatics	Management and operation of radio frequency spectrum and satellite orbit monitoring stations
7.	Education and Culture	1. Governmental museums 2. Historical and archaeological remains (temples, Sultan's palaces, inscriptions, ruins, ancient buildings, etc.)
8.	Tourism and Creative Economy	Gambling/casinos

Source: The 2016 Negative Investment List

competitiveness regarding ASEAN Economic Community (AEC), where the purpose is to revise the list of business fields closed and business fields open with certain requirements when it comes to investment (Negative Investment List/DNI).

The 2016 Negative Investment List has maintained a list of business fields which are reserved for the government and in which any private investment, whether foreign or domestic, is prohibited. Based on the Law on Capital Investment,[40] Indonesian Government are authorized to prohibit investment in certain sectors due to Indonesia's national interests such as national defence, health or environmental grounds.

The business fields above shows the field where business and investment are closed from commercialization as investment activities. This settlement falls on the criteria of health, moral, culture, environment, national defense and security, as well as other national interests. Among them include casino and gambling, and also and the production of alcoholic beverages. The Presidential Regulation does not explicitly state the explanation of such list. However, the investments closed on the ground for religion and its values are explained below.

3.1 *Production of alcoholic beverages*

The legislation regarding alcoholic beverages is currently regulated in various laws and regulations. At the level of the Law or Government Regulation, legislation of alcoholic beverages is not specifically mentioned, which is only categorized as "beverage" or "processed food". For

40. Law No. 25 of 2007 on Capital Investment, Article 12 (3)

example in Law concerning Health,[41] Laws concerning Food,[42] and Government Regulation concerning Food Safety, Quality, and Nutrition.[43] For regulations under the Law, there has been the Presidential Regulation concerning Supervision and Control of Alcoholic Beverages,-[44] Regulation of the Minister of Trade Number concerning Provisions on Procurement, Circulation, Sales, Supervision, and Control of Alcoholic Beverages[45], as well as Regulation of the Minister of Industry concerning Control and Supervision of the Alcoholic Beverage Industry (which also regulates traditional alcoholic drinks).[46]

Through the 2015 Trade Regulation, Indonesia prohibits the sale of alcoholic drinks that have content ranging between 1 to 5 percent (called "type A alcoholic drinks") in the nation's minimarkets and kiosks. Previously, sales of beverages with an alcohol content higher than five percent had already been banned from minimarkets and kiosks. Since April 2015 these alcoholic beverages can only be bought in the (licensed) supermarkets and hypermarkets.[47] However, the regulation also provides exemptions for the sale of alcoholic beverages for customary uses, tourism, religious rituals, the pharmacy industry, and in places authorized by law. This means that it is still possible to enjoy an alcoholic beverage. However, as the number of larger supermarkets is limited (compared to the number of minimarkets which have mushroomed on the urban streets) it has become much more difficult to purchase alcoholic beverages or if consumed in restaurants, hotels or cafes, it has become much more expensive.[48]

The restrictions made by the government is to protect the morals and culture of Indonesian society, as it had become very easy for schoolchildren or students to buy light-alcoholic beverages (such as beer) due to the high number of minimarkets and kiosks in Indonesia. Moreover, there exists a negative attitude towards alcohol in Muslim-majority Indonesia as consumption of intoxicants (including alcohol) is generally forbidden (haram).

Recently, the above regulations have drawn controversy. This is due to the many regional regulations that are in line with Islamic law which limit or even prohibit the distribution and consumption of alcohol. A study by Buehler in The Politics of Shari'a Law: Activist Islamists and the State in Democratizing Indonesia in 2016, documented 377 regulations inspired by Islamic law were adopted throughout the period 1998-2013.[49] The basis of the Regional Government in prohibiting alcoholic beverages is in the public interest, namely the negative consequences of alcoholic beverages consumption which cause casualties and criminal behavior such as rape and other crimes that disrupt public order and violate decency. Therefore these basis are very strong in accordance with the sociological context in the region.[50] Some argue that it is very unreasonable if for the sake of investment, the interests of public in general, namely to prevent bad danger and the loss of life due to alcohol, are ignored. Alcoholic beverages violates religious teachings because it is the source of all forms of crime, such as murder, sexual crime, accidents, and drugs, therefor any government's affirmation to alcoholic

41. Law Number 36 Year 2009 concerning Health, Article 111 and 112
42. Laws Number 18 Year 2012 concerning Food, Articles 86, 89, 90, 91, 97, 99, and 104
43. Government Regulation Number 28 Year 2004 concerning Food Safety, Quality, and Nutrition
44. Presidential Decree Number 3 Year 1997 concerning Supervision and Control of Alcoholic Beverages
45. Regulation of the Minister of Trade Number 15/M-DAG/PER/3/2015 concerning Third Amendment to Regulation of the Minister of Trade Number 43/M-DAG/PER/9/2009 concerning Provisions on Procurement, Circulation, Sales, Supervision, and Control of Alcoholic Beverages
46. Regulation of the Minister of Industry Number 71/MIND/PER/7/2012 concerning Control and Supervision of the Alcoholic Beverage Industry, See also Naskah akademik Rancangan Undang-Undang tentang larangan minimal beralkohol, Badan Legislasi DPR RI, 2014
47. <https://www.bbc.com/indonesia/majalah/2015/01/150129_bisnis_bir_indonesia>
48. <https://www.indonesia-investments.com/news/todays-headlines/alcohol-free-beer-in-indonesia-strategy-to-comply-with-rules/item6342?>
49. <http://www.pikiran-rakyat.com/bandung-raya/2018/05/09/regulasi-dan-korban-minuman-beralkohol-masih-belum-sinkron-ini-penyebabnya>
50. *DPR Minta Kemendagri Tak Semena-mena Mengevaluasi Perda Miras* (2016) <https://nasional.tempo.co/read/773293/dpr-minta-kemendagri-tak-semena-mena-mengevaluasi-perda-miras>

beverages proves that the government loses sensitivity to moral, religious and social issues. Critics towards the abovementioned Regulation of the Minister of Trade is based on grounds that ignore the moral values of any religion in Indonesia. Even if it is associated with tourism, there are examples of successful governance that can develop tourism without colliding policies with religious and moral issues.[51]

3.2 *Gambling and casino*

Another field closed due to religious ground is gambling. While several South East Asian countries have been reported to increase economic growth in the gambling industry, this is not the case with Indonesia. In Indonesia, gambling is completely forbidden by the Sharia law, and so there are no legal land-based casinos or other bookmarkers or wagering services in Indonesia. Although Sharia Law are not the highest laws in the country, however in several areas it's values are taken into consideration. The majority of Muslim population in Indonesia and the recognition of other religions, makes cultural and religious values a part of the country's identity. The country does not permit the gambling officially according to religious beliefs. According to Indonesian laws, gambling is an immoral activity. It is considered wrong as it is considered as evil, addictive, and designed to rob people. This includes casino games, bingo, sports betting, lotteries, and luck-based games. People have to face penalties from the government if they are found to offer or participate in the gambling activities. It is seen as a community disease, a form of social pathology.[52] Therefore, enforcement to tackle gambling as a form of deviant behavior is continued through criminal law. This is reasonable since gambling causes real threat to social norms which can lead to either individual as well as social tensions, which could raise potential for the continuation of social order.[53] In terms of gambling as a criminal act, Law on the Control of Gambling,[54] is especially inseparable from the reason for the establishment and drafting of the law. In consideration to such Law,[55] it is explained that:

a. Gambling is in fact contrary to the ideology of Pancasila related to the values of religion, decency, and morals, which endangers lives of the people, nation, and state.
b. Therefore, efforts are required to limit such act to the smallest environment, to finally lead its elimination altogether from all regions in Indonesia.

The restrictions on gambling are considered not to be in conflict with the Constitution. Because, the limitation of the rights of every citizen, as long as it is regulated in the Law, is deemed not to contradict the 1945 Constitution. The provision states:"*in exercising rights and obligations, every citizen is obliged to obey prohibitions regulated in laws to guarantee the recognition and respect for the rights and freedoms of others to meet public's demand of justice according to moral considerations, religious values, security, and public order.*[56]Restricting the rights of every citizen to gamble through the Criminal Code and the Law on Gambling is justified by the Constitution 1945. The ban was not only applied to the applicants, but to all Indonesian citizens. The goal, for the benefit of public in general on the basis of moral, religious value, security, and public order. That in essence, gambling is in conflict with religion, decency, and Pancasila's moral value, and endangers the livelihoods and lives of the people,

51. For Example Banyuwangi, stated by Head of Surabaya City PCNU Tanfiziah Dr. Achmad Muhibbin Zuhri, M.Ag, in 2016
52. Kartini Kartono, *Patologi Sosial* (Jakarta, Raja Grafindo Persada, 2005) 57.
53. Saparinah Sadli in Muladi and Barda Nawawi Arief., *Teori-Teori dan Kebijakan Pidana*, (Bandung, Penerbit Alumni, 1998) 148.
54. Law No.7 Year 1974 concerning the Control of Gambling
55. Sugeng Tiyarto, *Kebijakan Penegakan Hukum Pidana Dalam Rangka Penanggulangan Perjudian* (Semarang; Dipanegoro University, 2006) 109
56. Article 28 Paragraph (2) of the 1945 Constitution

nation, and state.[57] Judging from the national interest, the organization of gambling has negative excesses and harms the society's moral and mental, especially towards the young generation. Even though the revenue from licenses for the operation of gambling obtained by the Government, both Central and Regional, can be used for development efforts, the negative consequences are far greater than the obtained benefits. Therefore, the Government considers it necessary to stop granting licenses for gambling, for the sake of order, peace, and welfare of the people. Thus, no gambling is permitted, so that all types of gambling are crimes. This Government Regulation is the implementation of Article 3 of Law Number 7 Year 1974 concerning the Control of Gambling, which regulates the prohibition of granting licenses for the operation of all forms and types of gambling, by the Central Government or Regional Government, both held at casinos, in crowded places, or those associated with other reasons. With the prohibition of granting licenses for the operation of gambling, it does not mean that the prohibition also applies to the organization of sporting, entertainment, and habitual games, as long as there is no gamble.[58]

4 TENSIONS FROM THE COMMUNITY

At the community level, cultural and religious values also shape the perspective of its people. Any case that relate to religion may raise sensitivity issues and conflict. One example is the reaction of the leader of Indonesia's second largest Muslim organization Muhammadiyah (an organization that has around 30 million members), Anwar Abbas, which has called for a boycott of Starbucks, saying that the international coffee chain's is support for gay marriage.[59]

This stand risks ruining the "religious and cultured" core of the Southeast Asian nation. Anwar argued that the government should revoke Starbucks' operating license as the company's support for the LGBT community is "not in line" with the nation's ideology. They argued that Starbuck should do business and business only, but don't bring ideology here.[60]

This view is related to the Indonesian population, most of whom are Muslims, others with the other 5 recognized religion. In general, the teachings of these religions are interpreted conservatively, meaning homosexuality is forbidden due to the influence the views of society as a whole in a negative way. Despite the number of individuals who share are more progressive perspective, the status quo is still strong. The ability of activists to think or act in different ways is hampered by very conservative and heteronormative discourses to maintain existing cultural and religious norms. Sometimes even religious leaders speak in public by stating that the existence of LGBT is contrary to God's nature and will,[61] stating that homosexuality is immoral and inconsistent with Islamic and other religious norms.

5 CONCLUSION

At present, Indonesia's respect for international human rights instruments such as the ICCPR is still based on Pancasila and the country's Constitution, therefor the influence and position

57. Act Number 7 Year 1974 concerning Gambling Control
58. Penjelasan atas Peraturan Pemerintah Republik Indonesia Nomor 9 Tahun 1981 tentang Penjelasan Undang-undang Nomor 7 tahun 1974 tentang Pengertian Perjudian.
59. *Muslim Leader calls for a Worldwide Boycott of Sarbucks because the coffee chain's pro-gay stance is "not in line" with Islamic Law (2017)* <https://www.dailymail.co.uk/news/article-4658116/Muslim-Anwar-Abbas-urge-Indonesians-boycott-Starbucks-LGBT.html>
60. *Muslim leader urges Indonesians to Boycott Starbucks over LGBT Stand*, (2017) <https://www.reuters.com/article/us-indonesia-starbucks-lgbt-idUSKBN19M36N>
61. *Hidup Sebagai LGBT di Asia: Laporan Nasional Indonesia; Tinjauan dan Analisa Partisipatif tentang Lingkungan Hukum dan Sosial bagi Orang dan Masyarakat Madani Lesbian, Gay, Biseksual dan Transgender*, USIAD

of religion becomes very important in the context of religious rights in Indonesia. One of them is proven by allowing restrictions on the basis of religious values. According to the author, the reasons for "religious values" and the prohibition on "deviant interpretations" which are considered as permissible restrictions in Indonesia, need to be reviewed, both concerning the substance and its implementation. Because the actual interpretation must be understood as an interpretation of the concept, and not against the concept. Even if the restrictions need to be done, it must be proportional. Revisions to several provisions governing religious freedom and blasphemy for legal certainty are very necessary to determine the extent/to which the State can intervene in one's beliefs and to avoid arbitrary interpretation. The use of universal concepts or cultural relativism together have the truth value, but do not let the State to advance human rights by discrimination, which can actually violate human rights itself.

Regarding to foreign investment, there is no direct relationship between religion and foreign investment. In general, there is no national policy on religion or religious values when deciding to cooperate with foreign investors. However, there are a number of areas that is closed for investment due to cultural and religious norms and values, such as the growing of marijuana, gambling and casino. Such areas are totally prohibited in Indonesia. If investment activities are related to values that conflict with religion and culture, it is not impossible to cause reactions and conflict among the society.

REFERENCES

A.V. Dicey, *An Introduction to Study of the Law of the Constitution* (London, 10th edition, Palgrave MacMillan)

Akhmad, Muamar, 'Kebebasan Beragama dan Problematika HAM Universal' (2013) II(I) *Jurnal Studi Agama dan Pemikiran Islam*

Arianto, Satya, *Hak Asasi Manusia dalam Transisi Politik di Indonesia*, (Jakarta, second edition, Pusat Studi Hukum Tata Negara FHUI, 2005)

Becker, Hilkka, Grainne Brophy, Elaine Dewhurst, *Human Rights Law* (United Kingdom, 4th Edition, Oxford University Press)

Budiarti, Rita Triana, *Kontroversi Mahfud MD: Dibalik Putusan Mahkamah Konstitusi* (Jakarta, Edition II, Konstitusi Press, 2013)

Church, Joan, Christian Schulze, Hennie Strydom, *Human Rights from a Comparative and International Law Perspective* (University of South Africa, Unisa Press, 2007)

Gubo, Darara Timotewos, *Blasphemy and Defamation of Religions In a Polarized* World, *How Religious Fundamentalism is Challenging Fundamental Human Rights*, (London, Lexington Books, 2015)

Hannum, Hurst, 'The Status of the Universal Declaration of Human Rights in National and International Law', 25 *Georgia Journal of International and Comparative Law*

Haynes, Jefrrey, *Religion and Politics in Europe, the Middle Easr and North Africa* (New York, Routledge)

Ishay, Micheline, *The History of Human Rights, From Ancient Times to the Globalization Era* (London, University of California Press Ltd, 2008)

Iskandar, Pranoto, *Hukum HAM Internasional, Sebuah Pengantar Konseptual* (Cianjur, IMR Press, 2010)

Kartono, Kartini, *Patologi Sosial* (Jakarta, Raja Grafindo Persada, 2005)

Preisa, Joshua, *Pluralism, Relativism and Cultural Rights*, Paper for Workshop about Human Rights on 20 April 2004

Rogers, Benecdict, 'Rejecting Religious Intolerance in South East Asia', (2018) 2(1, June) *Journal of Southeast Asian Human Rights*

Rohidin, *Konstruksi Baru Kebebasan Beragama, Menghadirkan Nilai Kemanusiaan yang Adil dan Beradab di Negara Hukum Indonesia* (FHUII-Press, 2015)

Sadli, Saparinah in Muladi and Barda Nawawi Arief., *Teori-Teori dan Kebijakan Pidana*, (Bandung, Penerbit Alumni, 1998)

Sopyan, Yayan, 'Menyoal Kebebasan Beragama dan Penodaan Agama di Indonesia (Telaah atas Putusan MK No.140/PUU-VII/2009)' (2015) II(2) *Jurnal Cita Hukum*

Steiner, Henry, Philip Alston, *International Human Rights in Context: Law*, Politics, *Morals: Text and Materials* (New York, 3rd Edition, Oxford University Press, 2008)

Tiyarto, Sugeng, *Kebijakan Penegakan Hukum Pidana Dalam Rangka Penanggulangan Perjudian* (Semarang, Dipanegoro University, 2006)
Topidi, Kyriaki, Lairen Fielder, *Transnational Legal Process and Human Rights* (USA, Routledge, 2016)
International Covenant on Civil and Political Rights
Law Number 1/PNPS/1965 on the Prevention of Abuse and Blasphemy of Religion
Law Number 39 Year 1999 on Human Rights
Universal Declaration of Human Rights, Adopted from General Assembly Resolution 217 A on 10 December 1948 Vienna Declaration and Program of Action, adopted by World Conference on Human Rights in Vienna on 25 June1993

Culture and International Law - Juwana et al. (Eds)
© 2019 Taylor & Francis Group, London, ISBN 978-1-138-38766-9

The protection of underwater cultural heritage in Indonesian law: Do sunken warships count?

Dhiana Puspitawati
Law Faculty, Brawijaya University, Indonesia

ABSTRACT: Indonesia, lie astride between two large continent, Australia and Asia; between two mass of waters, Indian and Pacific Ocean, through which crucial international navigational routes passes. Besides serving as a home for various marine biodiversity, Indonesian ocean also has a correspondingly rich underwater cultural heritage in the form of shipwrecks, sunken aircraft as well as other maritime sites. This paper focuses on the protection of underwater cultural heritage in the form of warships which were sunk during the sea battle. While a research by United Nations of Education, Science and Culture Organization (UNESCO) finds that there are approximately 3,000 shipwreck sites in Indonesian ocean, such research did not distinguish between commercial ships and warships or state vessels. Meanwhile, Convention on the Protection of the Underwater Cultural Heritage 2001 (2001 UCH Convention) clearly acknowledge warships as state vessels having their immunities according to international laws.

This paper examines the application of international laws on sunken warships whether they are considered as underwater cultural heritage and whether they still have their immunities once they became wrecks. It also discusses whether Indonesian Laws on cultural heritage include sunken warship as recognized underwater cultural heritage. It further analyses whether Indonesian laws on underwater cultural heritage confirm international laws on the same subject matter. It is argued that in order to protect underwater cultural heritage lie beneath Indonesian ocean, Indonesia needs to adopt appropriate national laws in accordance with international laws. With regard to sunken warships Indonesia also has to make specific regulations as to guarantee the immunities of such state vessels. In addition to this, further cooperation with state which own such warships is also crucial.

KEYWORDS: legal protection, underwater cultural heritage, sunken warships, immunities, Indonesian laws

1 INTRODUCTION

Since 70% of earth surface are covered by water,[1] sea transport still favorable both for international trade as well as other states' mobility including military mobilization. During the Second World War, warships have played a vital role both for a mean of transportation and for combat function. Indonesian waters at the time of Second World War has also been a vital route for the mobility of military vessels and were mainly used by warships belonging to Japan and allay forces. Indonesia is the biggest archipelagic state in the world with a sea area covering two-third of the country and its location at a crossroads of international seafaring and trading routes gives economic benefits as well as certain obligations to the country. It is argued that besides serving as the biggest home of various ocean resources, Indonesian waters also has a correspondingly rich maritime and underwater cultural heritage (UCH) in the form

1. 'National Geographic Society' in *Atlas of the World* (Washington DC, 2009) 26.

of shipwrecks, sunken aircraft as well as other maritime sites.[2] These various UCH need to be legally protected both by corresponding coastal states as well as the country of origin of the wrecks. This is because such sunken vessels, aircraft and maritime sites are often have hidden treasures and thus they often become target for illegal salvage. Previous research of the United Nations of Education, Science and Culture Organization (UNESCO) found that there were approximately 3,000 shipwreck sites in Indonesian waters. While this research focuses on the protection of underwater cultural heritage in the form of warship which were sunk during sea battle, unfortunately the research conducted by UNESCO did not distinguish between commercial shipwrecks and military shipwreck. In case of warship, it is not merely the treasures found in the wreck which is crucial to be legally protected but the historical value of such warship and its immunity need to be legally preserved as well.

Legal provisions on underwater cultural heritage, which include shipwreck can be found in several international conventions such as the United Nations Convention on the Law of the Sea 1982 (UNCLOS 1982), UNESCO Convention on the Protection of the Underwater Cultural Heritage 2001 (2001 UCH Convention) as well as various bilateral and regional treaties. Unfortunately, Indonesia is not yet a party to 2001 UCH Convention, however, this does not mean Indonesia is ignorant with regard to underwater cultural heritage. Although Indonesia does not have specific laws in underwater cultural heritage, Indonesian Act Number 5 Year 1992 which was revised by Indonesian Act number 11 Year 2010 on cultural heritage provides provisions on underwater cultural heritage. In addition to this there is Presidential Decree Number 19 Year 2007 on National Committee on the Use Valuable Goods taken from Sunken Ships, which were revised by Presidential Decree Number 12 Year 2009 on the Revision of Indonesian Presidential Decree Number 19 Year 2007. Furthermore, while under international law warships are recognized as having immunity, it is questionable whether such immunity remain once they become shipwreck? Does international law distinguish between warship wrecks sunk during sea battle and those who sunk not during sea battle? In addition to this, what if upon warships wreck illegal salvage is conducted?

This research examines the application of international laws on sunken warships whether they are considered as under water cultural heritage and whether they still have their immunities once they became wrecks. It also discusses whether Indonesian Laws include sunken warship as recognized underwater cultural heritage. It further analyses whether Indonesian laws on underwater cultural heritage confirm international laws on the same subject matter.

2 INTERNATIONAL LAWS ON THE PROTECTION OF CULTURAL HERITAGE

As stated previously that besides serving as a home of various biodiversity, ocean also serves as historical graves in relation to underwater cultural heritage, specifically with regard to shipwrecks. In such, effective protection is crucial. It follows that effective protection here refers to legal protection upon shipwrecks. Legal protection is needed to protect all hull of the ships as well as any other treasures found within the shipwrecks from irresponsible and illegal salvage for commercial purposes. Two most relevant international legal frameworks with regard to underwater cultural heritage are UNCLOS 1982 and 2001 UCH Convention as mentioned above. Following discussion examines relevant international legal frameworks on the subject matter.

2.1 *Underwater cultural heritage*

While UNCOS 1982 is considered as a comprehensive International Convention regulated the use of the ocean, this convention only marginally touches upon underwater cultural heritage. Since this Convention divides ocean space under national sovereignty, national jurisdiction

2. For various military shipwrecks and aircraft wreckages found and their location see further Jhohannes Marbun, 'An Advocacy Approach on Underwater Heritage in Indonesia, Case Study: An Auction on Underwater Heritage from Cirebon Waters in 2010' (2014).

and beyond national jurisdiction, it is argued that this condition underpinned insufficient development of national legal framework on the protection of underwater cultural heritage, especially in areas beyond national jurisdiction. UNCLOS 1982 only contains two articles on underwater cultural heritage, Article 149 and 303. Article 149 of UNCLOS 1982 on archeological and historical objects envisages as follows:

> "All objects of an archaeological and historical nature found **in the Area** shall be preserved or disposed of for the benefit of mankind as a whole, particular regard being paid to the preferential rights of the State or country of origin, or the State of cultural origin, or the State of historical and archaeological origin."[3]

From Article 149, it can be submitted that UNCLOS 1982 only provides for cultural heritage found in the area that is beyond national jurisdiction. UNCLOS 1982 is silent on objects found within national sovereignty and jurisdiction. It is imply that for such objects, national laws applies according to recognized legal regimes for each maritime zones. This Article further leave it to the country of origin to either preserved it or dispose it for the benefit of mankind. Unfortunately, this article is silent on how to preserve the objects? Is there any rights and obligations for coastal States, over which the object was found and the State of origin? If the State of origin wish to dispose the object, can it be freely salvage by any parties for individual or group's purposes? On the other hand, while UNCLOS 1982 is also silent on what it meant by archeological and historical objects, Article 303 of UNCLOS 1982 provides further provisions on salvage efforts conducted over archeological and historical objects lies within the ocean as follows:

1. "States have the duty to protect objects of an archaeological and historical nature found at sea and shall cooperate for this purpose.
2. In order to control traffic in such objects, the coastal State may, in applying article 33 [on the Contiguous Zone], presume that their removal from the seabed in the zone referred to in that article without its approval would result in an infringement within its territory or territorial sea of the laws and regulations referred to in that article.
3. Nothing in this article affects the rights of identifiable owners, the law of salvage or other rules of admiralty, or laws and practices with respect to cultural exchanges.
4. This article is without prejudice to other international agreements and rules of international law regarding the protection of objects of an archaeological and historical nature."[4]

Paragraph 1 of Article 303 UNCLOS 1982 does not specify which State, is that every State? Or associate coastal state, over which the object was found? If every State, it is unlikely that State would conduct any action in protecting such objects. Further, paragraph 2 implies that any objects removed from ocean floor under the contiguous zone should have prior approval from coastal state or otherwise it would infringe coastal state's jurisdiction. In contrary to this, paragraph 3 provides that this provisions do not affect the law of salvage, while there is no requirement of the law of salvage to get prior approval form coastal state upon salvage.[5] Paragraph 4 further implies that other existing international agreement would overweigh the provisions. In sum, UNCLOS 1982 only marginally provides provisions regarding underwater cultural heritage and in addition, it is submitted that such provisions remain unclear.

More specific international legal framework on underwater cultural heritage can be found in 2001 UCH Convention. This Convention adopted by UNESCO, a United Nation Agency specializing in the protection of cultural heritage who works for comprehensive protection of all form of heritage. Philosophical basis of the formulation of the 2001 UCH Convention was international community concern on the destruction of submerged archeological sites. The Convention was aimed to ensure the same level protection for underwater cultural heritage as that accorded to cultural heritage on land. The Convention was also aimed to guarantee

3. *Article 149 of UNCLOS 1982.*
4. *Article 303 of UNCLOS 1982.*
5. See further *Salvage Convention 1989.*

cooperation among States, especially between coastal State over which cultural heritage is found and State of origin. Unlike UNCLOS 1982, 2001 UCH Convention sets up definition of underwater cultural heritage and State cooperation mechanism. However, this Convention is silent on the ownership of heritage and national jurisdiction at sea.[6] Furthermore, although 2001 UCH Convention envisages certain provisions, which were lacking in UNCLOS 1982, Article 3 of the 2001 UCH Convention stated clearly that the Convention is in harmony with the provisions of UNCLOS 1982. Thus, it is submitted that while 2001 UCH Convention is silent on national jurisdiction at sea, the Convention refers to UNCLOS 1982 with regard to national jurisdiction at sea.

Article 1 of 2001 UCH Convention defines underwater cultural heritage as "all traces of human existence having a cultural, historical or archaeological character which have been partially or totally under water, periodically or continuously, for at least 100 years."[7] While the importance of this article is on the period of time that such objects remains under water for at least 100 years, such period of time can be lowered in national legislation to include more recent sites. Article 1 (1) (a) further envisages that such underwater cultural heritage include:

(i) sites, structures, buildings, artefacts and human remains, together with their archaeological and natural context;
(ii) vessels, aircraft, other vehicles or any part thereof, their cargo or other contents, together with their archeological natural context; and
(iii) objects of prehistoric character

Thus, the focus of this paper, warship wrecks is included within the scope of underwater cultural heritage under the 2001 UCH Convention. While Article 1 does not stated clearly that that the vessels referred by it include warships, however, Article 1 (8) includes warships as 'state vessels', as provided in Article 1 (8) the 2001 UCH Convention as follows: "State vessels and aircraft means warships, and other vessels or aircraft that were owned or operated by a State and used, at the time of sinking, only for government noon-commercial purposes, that are identified as such and that meet the definition of underwater cultural heritage."[8] Thus, it is submitted that warship wrecks which were sunk in service are included within underwater cultural heritage.

2.2 *International laws on warship wrecks*

While warship wrecks can be considered as underwater cultural heritage, the questions posed will be whether such warship wrecks still hold the sovereign immunity? Regarding this matter, there is no unanimity among States regarding the jurisdiction of the warship wrecks rather than it depends on national legislation. The 2001 UCH Convention does not provide for the jurisdiction of the States Parties over the wrecks of their state vessels, nor does it exclude it. The Convention does not regulate this issue, other than by providing protection to all kinds of wrecks. The Convention does require that the flag state be notified of activities directed at the wrecks of its state vessels in the territorial waters of other States Parties. In international waters, the flag State must agree to any activities directed at the wrecks of its state vessels.

In fact Article 2 (8) of the 2001 UCH Convention can be implicitly answer the question of whether warship wrecks still hold its sovereign immunity. Article 2 (8) of the Convention reads:

> "Consistent with State practice and international law, including the United Nations Convention on the Law of the Sea, nothing in this Convention shall be interpreted as modifying the rules of international law and State practice pertaining to sovereign immunities, nor any State's rights with respect to its State vessels and aircraft."[9]

6. UNESCO, *The Legal Protection of Underwater Cultural Heritage: The UNESCO 2001 Convention on the Protection of the Underwater Cultural Heritage (UCH)* (2014).
7. *Article 1 of 2001 UCH Convention.*
8. *Article 2 (8) 2001 UCH Convention.*
9. Ibid.

Thus, at this point, it is submitted that while the 2001 UCH Convention is silent on the issue of state jurisdiction upon warship wrecks, Article 2 (8) of the Convention implicitly recognizes sovereign immunity of warship wrecks. If this is so, further question is whether those remaining sovereign immunity applies in all warship wrecks or only to warships wreck which was sunk during sea battle? This refers to Article 1 of the 2001 UCH Convention which provides the inclusion of 'object of prehistoric character' as stated in paragraph (iii). Can it be interpreted that paragraph (ii) refers to State vessels which not necessarily sunk during the sea battle and thus does not hold the prehistoric characters? Or paragraph (iii) should be understood together with paragraph (ii)? So that only warship wrecks which sunk during sea battle can be considered as underwater cultural heritage and thus the sovereign immunity remains? UNCLOS 1982 is silent on sovereign wrecks, however, Forrest argued that warship used by a State for non-commercial purpose at the time of sinking has 'sovereign wreck' status.[10]

While warships' sovereign immunity is recognized in Article 32 of UNCLOS 1982, however UNCLSO 1982 is silent on what constitute sovereign immunity. Article 2 (1) of International Convention for the Unification of Certain Rules Concerning the Immunity of State-Owned Ships 1926 (1926 Convention), however, provides that sovereign immunity means that the warship shall not be "subject to seizure, arrest or detention by any legal process nor to any proceeding *in Rem*."[11] In such, if warship wrecks still retain its sovereign immunity, upon such warship wreck no salvage operation should be conducted. This is also stipulated clearly in Article 4 of the 2001 UCH Convention that the object of underwater cultural heritage as stipulated in Article 1 shall not be subject to law of salvage and law of find, unless (i) it is authorized by competent authorities, and (ii) is in full conformity with the Convention, and (iii) ensure that any recovery of the underwater cultural heritage achieves its maximum protection. From the provisions of Article 4 it is argued that three requirements in the application of law of salvage should be fulfilled cumulatively, not alternatively, which means that all three requirements should present. This provision overruled Article 4 (1) of the IMO Salvage Convention 1989, which still give the possibility to apply salvage laws upon warship wreck if State that owns that vessels decides so. As stated in Article 4 (1) of the IMO Salvage Convention 1989 as follows:

> "Without prejudice to article 5, this Convention shall not apply to warships or other non-commercial vessels owned or operated by a State and entitled, at the time of salvage operations, to sovereign immunity under generally recognized principles of international law **unless that State decides otherwise**."[12] (emphasize added)

Article 4 (2) of the IMO Salvage Convention 1989 further provides that if "a State Party decides to apply the Convention to its warships or other vessels described in paragraph 1, it shall notify the Secretary-General thereof specifying the terms and conditions of such application." This way it is argued that while there is possibility for a warship wreck to lose their immunity and thus can be conducted a salvage, it requires certain legal process which is uneasy. In addition to this, Meskin submitted that Article 4 (1) of the IMO Salvage Convention 1989 implies that sovereign immunity from the period at which these vessels were in service, applies to the wreck as well.[13] Thus, it can be concluded that warship wrecks still retain its sovereign immunity.

---

10. Craig JS Forrest, 'Culturally and Environmentally Sensitive Sunken Warships' *Australian and New Zeland Maritime Law Journal* <https://maritimejournal.murdoch.edu.au/index.php/maritimejournal/article/view/181>.
11. Article 3 (1), International Convention For The Unification Of Certain Rules Concerning The Immunity Of State-Owned Ships 1926
12. Article 4 (1) of the IMO Salvage Convention 1989
13. Senada Meskin, 'Legal Status of Warship Wrecks from World War II In Indonesian Territorial Waters (Incident of H.M.A.S. Perth Commercial Salvaging)' (2015) 2(2) *Brawijaya Law Journal*.

3 INDONESIAN LAW ON THE PROTECTION OF UNDERWATER CULTURAL HERITAGE

Geographical location of Indonesia between two mass oceans has made Indonesia as the most important routes in international navigation. Unsurprisingly, in term of underwater cultural heritage relics, Indonesia may be one of the richest in the world, ranging from natural archeological underwater relics to sunken aircraft and vessels along with its cargoes and other personal belonging. Unfortunately, the management of such heritage is still far from maximal[14] and thus resulted in minimum legal protection of the heritage. While Indonesian waters is a home of richest underwater cultural heritage, unfortunately, the lack of specific legal framework has made legal protection of such heritage is far from satisfactory. Indonesian legal framework on cultural heritage is emphasizes heavily on land based cultural heritage. The first cultural heritage law in Indonesia is Indonesian Law Number 5 Year 1992 on Cultural Heritage Goods, which was revised by Indonesian Law Number 11 Year 2011 on Cultural Heritage. This section examines national laws regarding cultural heritage in Indonesia. It seeks to find whether Indonesian Laws on cultural heritage include sunken warship as recognized underwater cultural heritage. It further analyses whether Indonesian laws on cultural heritage confirm international laws on the same subject matter, especially those concerning underwater cultural heritage.

4 ARE SUNKEN WARSHIPS CONSIDERED UNDERWATER CULTURAL HERITAGE?

As an important navigational routes, Indonesian waters also a home of thousand shipwrecks as well as aircraft and its valuable goods. A research conducted by UNESCO finds that there are approximately 3,000 shipwreck sites in Indonesian ocean, however, unfortunately, such research did not distinguish between commercial ships and warships or state vessels. As stated, Article 149 of UNCOS 1982 only provides the preservation of underwater cultural heritage found in the Area and leave to national laws on the preservation of underwater cultural heritage found in waters under national jurisdiction. Unfortunately, there is no national laws in Indonesia which specifically provides the protection of underwater cultural heritage. However, that does not mean that Indonesian government does not concern about cultural heritage. Indonesian law on cultural heritage can be found in Indonesian Law Number 5 Year 1992 (UU 5/1992), which was further revised by Indonesian Law Number 11 Year 2010 (UU 11/2010). While both laws is silent on the underwater cultural heritage, Article 12 (1) UU 5/1992 corresponds the word 'dive' for any action moving the cultural heritage from its place to another place. On the other hand Article 1 paragraph 1 of UU 11/2010 provides that cultural heritage includes five categories, which are cultural heritage object, cultural heritage construction, cultural heritage structure, cultural heritage site and cultural heritage region/areas. Unlike 2001 UCH Convention, nowhere in the UU 11/2010 mention about underwater cultural heritage such as sunken vessels or aircraft. Article 1 paragraph 2 envisages cultural heritage object as:

> *"...benda alam dan/atau benda buatan manusia, baik bergerak maupun tidak bergerak, berupa kesatuan atau kelompok atau bagian-bagiannya, atau sisa-sisanya yang memliki hubungan erat dengan kebudayaan dan sejarah perkembangan manusia."* (...natural objects and/or man made objects, both moving and immovable objects, which include gropus of parts ar traces having close relation with culture and human history)[15]

14. Supratikno Rahardjo, 'Underwater Cultural Heritage Management and Marine Tourism in Indonesia: Potential and Challenges' in *International Seminar on Marine Tourism Destination Management for Sustainable Development* (Bngka-Belitung, 2011). Bangka-Belitung, 21-22 September
15. Translation by Author

Where as Article 1 paragraph 5 of UU 11/2011 provides cultural heritage site as:

> "*. . . .lokasi yang berada di darat dan/atau di air yang mengandung benda cagar budaya, bangunan cagar budaya dan/atau struktur cagar budaya sebagai hasil kegiatan manusia atau bukti kejadian masa lalu.*" (. . .location in land and/or waters over which cultural heritage objects, cultural heritage construction and/or cultural heritage structure as a result of human activities of proof of past event, are located)[16]

Accordingly, Indonesian law on cultural heritage does not expressly mention any underwater cultural heritage nor sunken vessels or sunken warships, while partially recognize that certain cultural heritage might be found underwater. However, it is unlikely that shipwrecks would be considered as cultural heritage.

Furthermore the categories set up in Article 1 paragraph 1 of UU 11/2010 also very broad and open for interpretation. It is unclear whether shipwreck can be categorized as cultural heritage object. The only reference to water made by Article 1 paragraph 5 was with regard to site or location consisting cultural heritage objects, while the scope of cultural heritage objects itself still very vague. Thus, although warship wreck might be categorized as cultural heritage object located beneath the waters, the uncertainty prevails.

In addition to this, Article 26 paragraph 2 and 4 of UU 11/2010 in term of 'search' of cultural heritage reads as follows:

> "(2) Pencarian cagar budaya atau yang diduga cagar budaya dapat dilakukan oleh setiap orang dengan penggalian, penyelaman dan/atau pengangkatan di darat dan/atau di air
>
> *(4) Setiap orang dilarang melakukan pencarian cagar budaya atau yang diduga cagar budaya dengan penggalian, penyelaman dan/atau pengangkatan di darat dan/atau di air sebagaimana dimaksud pada ayat 2, kecuali dengan izin Pemerintah atau Pemerintah Daerah sesuai dengan kewenangannya.*"[17]

(2. the search of cultural heritage or suspected to be a cultural heritage can be conducted by everyone through excavation, diving and/or the salvage of cultural heritage from its location both in land and/or in water; 4. the search of cultural heritage or suspected to be a cultural heritage referred by paragraph 2 is prohibited, unless prior authorization is obtained from the government or local government according to their authority.)

Accordingly, while those two paragraphs seem contrary each other, the search and salvage (if underwater) of cultural heritage can only be done with prior authorization of relevant authority, in this case government or local government. Thus, if shipwrecks are considered as cultural heritage under Article 1 paragraph 2 and 5, unauthorized salvage of such wreck is illegal, with no consideration whether the wreck is ordinary shipwreck or warship wrecks.

In addition to this, there is also Presidential Decree Number 19 Year 2007 on National Committee on the Use Valuable Goods taken from Sunken Ships, which were revised by Presidential Decree Number 12 Year 2009 on the Revision of Indonesian Presidential Decree Number 19 Year 2007. Both Presidential Decrees, unfortunately only provides the working mechanism and procedures of national committee on the usage of sunken ships' valuable cargoes. Article 1 paragraph 1 of Presidential Decree Number 19 Year 2007 envisages the scope of sunken ships' valuable cargoes as ". . .valuable goods and cargoes onboard sunken ships which possessed historical, cultural, knowledge as well as economic values, sunk in Indonesian waters, exclusive economic zone and continental shelf of Indonesia, which has been remain on the seabed for at least 50 years." Thus, the emphasize of both Presidential Decrees is not on the shipwrecks but rather on the valuable goods and cargoes loaded on board the ships which sunk. Thus, it is submitted that shipwrecks, as well as warship wrecks are not included within Indonesian Laws on cultural heritage.

16. Translation by Author
17. Article 26 paragraph 2 and 4 of UU 11/2010

From the analyses of Indonesian laws above, it is argued that nowhere in Indonesian Laws consider shipwreck as well as warship wrecks as cultural heritage nor underwater cultural heritage, although some provision on such laws implicitly recognized cultural heritage located beneath the waters. It is unclear whether the vacuum of laws on the subject matter was due to the unratified 2001 UCH Convention by Indonesia or due to the lack of subject matter priority by the government. The non-State party of Indonesia to the 2001 UCH Convention is very unfortunate since as stated priory that Indonesian waters is a home of thousands shipwrecks along with its valuable cargoes.[18]

5 CONCLUSION AND RECOMMENDATION

Besides serving as the most favorites means of transportation with regard to international trade, the ocean also serves as a home of massive underwater cultural heritage, including ships wrecks and its valuable cargoes as well as aircraft wrecks. With massive areas of ocean, Indonesian waters is a home of thousands shipwrecks and aircraft sunk during their voyage traversing Indonesian waters. International legal frameworks protect such wrecks under the 2001 UCH Convention, which also recognized the sovereign immunity of warship wrecks, which sunk during sea battle or sunk while in service as State-vessel. Although the 2001 UCH Convention does not distinguish between ordinary shipwreck and warship wrecks, it is submitted that the interpretation of Article 1(1) (a), Article 1 (8) and Article 2 (8) of the 2001 UCH Convention refers to the recognition of warship wreck as underwater cultural heritage, which still retain its sovereign immunity if such vessel was sunk during sea-battle or during its service as a State-vessel.

Furthermore, while there are thousands of shipwrecks lie beneath Indonesian ocean, unfortunately, there is no legal protection provided by Indonesian laws to preserve such underwater cultural heritage. Indonesian laws on cultural heritage only partially mention a reference to cultural heritage located beneath the waters but does not specify what kind of objects that can be categorized as cultural heritage objects. While the laws gives scope to cultural heritage objects, yet such scope is too broad and vague. Thus, it is unclear whether shipwreck is considered as cultural heritage by Indonesian laws. Meanwhile relevant Indonesian Presidential Decree only provides working mechanism of national committee on the salvage of sunken ships' cargoes and valuable goods but silent on the issue of shipwrecks. It follows that there is also no legal protection for warship wrecks lie beneath Indonesian waters and there is no legal frameworks which provides whether such wreck still hold its sovereign immunity.

It is submitted that to protect thousands of shipwreck lie beneath Indonesian ocean, Indonesia should ratify the 2001 UCH Convention at the soonest and adopt appropriate national laws in accordance with international laws to protect underwater cultural heritage, especially warship wrecks make specific regulations as to guarantee the immunities of such state vessels. In addition to this, further cooperation with state which own such warships is also crucial.

REFERENCES

Forrest, Craig JS, 'Culturally and Environmentally Sensitive Sunken Warships' *Australian and New Zeland Maritime Law Journal* <https://maritimejournal.murdoch.edu.au/index.php/maritimejournal/article/view/181>

Marbun, Jhohannes, 'An Advocacy Approach on Underwater Heritage in Indonesia, Case Study: An Auction on Underwater Heritage from Cirebon Waters in 2010' (2014)

18. Illegal salvage has been conducted both on warship wrecks as well as other shipwrecks and their valuable goods and cargoes. Recent case on illegal salvage happen in Cirebon. For the detail of the case read further Marbun, above n 2.

Meskin, Senada, 'Legal Status of Warship Wrecks from World War II In Indonesian Territorial Waters (Incident of H.M.A.S. Perth Commercial Salvaging)' (2015) 2(2) *Brawijaya Law Journal*
'National Geographic Society' in *Atlas of the World* (Washington DC, 2009) 26
Rahardjo, Supratikno, 'Underwater Cultural Heritage Management and Marine Tourism in Indonesia: Potential and Challenges' in *International Seminar on Marine Tourism Destination Management for Sustainable Development* (Bngka-Belitung, 2011)
UNESCO, *The Legal Protection of Underwater Cultural Heritage: The UNESCO 2001 Convention on the Protection of the Underwater Cultural Heritage (UCH)* (2014)
Article 1 of 2001 UCH Convention
Article 149 of UNCLOS 1982
Article 2 (8) 2001 UCH Convention
Article 303 of UNCLOS 1982
Salvage Convention 1989

Culture and International Law - Juwana et al. (Eds)
© 2019 Taylor & Francis Group, London, ISBN 978-1-138-38766-9

The impact of information and communication technologies on the shifting of legal paradigms

Sukarmi
Law Faculty, Brawijaya University, Indonesia

ABSTRACT: The existence of these technologies in expected to remove the barriers of time or distance in communication. Now and in later times, economic, social, political, and even cultural activities will inevitably be more and more conducted by utilizing the services of computer networks and electronic telecommunication. These activities with the "paperless" approach, computers, and electronic telecommunication will take hold of a central position in everyday human activities. As such, experts in state administration law and governance law, policy makers, and observers of as well as interested parties in administrative matters related to functions of the state and the government must take into account the importance of the services of computers and electronic telecommunication in later times.

These changes and advancements in technology and communication in society will affect various social changes, in accordance with the conditions of society. The rhythms and methods of change are quite diverse. The positive and negative effects must be addressed, and it is inevitable that advances in IT demands changes and innovation; what needs to be done is efforts to minimize negative effects by preparing a variety of hardware and software. The government is demanded to be more progressive in following and anticipating the growth IT in preparing regulations. The above condition has caused many changes to occur in both society and government, in their own ways.

This condition occurs within the tradition of "common law", which prioritizes the principle of "judge-made law", as well as in the tradition of "civil law" which prioritizes the creation of written laws. This condition is what Richard Susskind terms as "hyperregulation". The law will become simply information that can be mastered by anyone, including those who possess no background in law or legal education at all. In this relationship, a paradigm shift can slowly occur, in consideration of the law as a process for seeking justice.

In such situations, legal services and working processes of the legal system will experience fundamental changes. As such, it is necessary to develop preparations for an institution that makes use of the Internet and is accessible by all people that require its use. Governmental and national apparatuses at both the central and regional levels must anticipate for this need immediately

KEYWORDS: technology information, hyperregulation, shifting of legal paradigms

1 INTRODUCTION

Information technology is technology that is used to work on data, including to process, obtain, compose, store, and manipulate data in various ways to result in high-quality information. High quality information is information that is relevant, accurate, and on time, for use in personal, business, and governmental needs. Communication technology is an expansion of communication science based on technology such as wireless, internet, facsimile, computers, and so on. The existence of these technologies in expected to remove the barriers of time or distance in communication.

Now and in later times, economic, social, political, and even cultural activities will inevitably be more and more conducted by utilizing the services of computer networks and electronic telecommunication. These activities with the "paperless" approach, computers, and electronic telecommunication will take hold of a central position in everyday human activities. As such, experts in state administration law and governance law, policy makers, and observers of as well as interested parties in administrative matters related to functions of the state and the government must take into account the importance of the services of computers and electronic telecommunication in later times.

These changes and advancements in technology and communication in society will affect various social changes, in accordance with the conditions of society. The rhythms and methods of change are quite diverse.

Even now in the context of business transactions, there has been a drastic change in communicative behaviors from paper to electronics, changing the system of life in society. Lifestyle is transforming from the realm of forms to the realm of electronics, which is called cyberspace. It has been stated that:

> *"Cyberspace is a term, popularized by Author William Gibson, for the shared imaginary reality of computer networks. Some people use cyberspace as the synonym for the Internet."*

In this virtual space, members of society perform legal activities that focus on matters that affect administration law, international law, criminal law, tax law, and so on.

An interesting phenomenon to be noticed is that Indonesia has also entered this cyber realm. This has been proven from news by the Indonesian Society of Electronic Communication and Information (MEKII: Suhono Harso Supangat) who suggested the formation of a supervisory body for the Internet and the need of "cyberlaws" to organize several crucial matters in the use of the Internet.

Such conditions on one hand are beneficial for consumers because the need of consumers for desired goods or services may be fulfilled and that there is a greater freedom to choose from a variety of types and qualities of goods and services. On the other hand, the above condition and phenomenon may result in an imbalance in the positions of businesspeople and consumers, wherein the latter is in a weaker position. The changes that occur will certainly bring about both positive and negative effects. The positive effects include making the processes of transaction and communication much more effective as well as easier. Technology makes the environment more comfortable, safer, and, more efficient to be lived in and processed. The creation of ideas that people can access is not limited by time and place. Information technology quickly changes individual ideas, values, and behaviors, not being limited by space and time.

On the other hand, there are also negative effects that follow; one of these is that the use of IT actually has serious effects, in particular considering the reach and losses caused by certain crimes. Theft of money or the purchase of goods with credit cards through the Internet can claim victims in the legal territory of another country, something that rarely occurs in conventional crimes. Second, crimes that occur in the Inter- net era include the computer system as a victim. The advancement of IT also advances the rate and type of crimes through the Internet.

The positive and negative effects must be addressed, and it is inevitable that advances in IT demands changes and innovation; what needs to be done is efforts to minimize negative effects by preparing a variety of hardware and software. The government is demanded to be more progressive in following and anticipating the growth IT in preparing regulations. The above condition has caused many changes to occur in both society and government, in their own ways. Some of these changes, at the level of both society and policy-makers and has the background of the effects of IT advancement on legal paradigms, are described below.

1.1 *Hyperregulated society*

Modern society tends to become even more complex and intricate. Because of the development of science and technology, change after change also occurs quickly, widely and deeply affecting the layers of society. To guarantee that the process of occurring changes can be organized, there is the increasing need to make one regulation after another. As a result, the norms of regulations quickly grows in all sectors and all layers of society, across nations and countries. This tendency to produce regulations that grow ever more complex is what leads to the appearance of the condition of "hyperregulation".[1]

In actuality, this condition has started to appear at the end of the 19*th* century and the beginning of the 20*th* century. As a response to the general disappointment of the phenomenon of classic capitalism and liberalism that are based on extreme individualism, humanity has enthusiastically developed the concept of "welfare state". In the understanding of a welfare state, the various social and economic problems that in earlier periods are considered free market territory in which power must not intervene, by the influence of socialism, they become an important consideration that the state must manage with full responsibility. Thus, the concept of welfare state is regarded by M. Hatta as the concept of a "Managing State" that influences the composition of the 1945 Constitution, in particular in formulating Chapter XIV of the 1945 Constitution, which contains Articles 33 and 34.

The extreme form of interventionist tendencies of the role of the government or the state in activities of society is the appearance of communist ideas and regimes in various parts of the world. As a result, the tendency of a state to regulate everything in the form of laws that bind the public starts to grow. Thus, what occurs is a condition that could be termed as "overregulation" in the progression of socio-politics, socioeconomics, and even socioculture in many places. Further consequences are that the role of the state tends to become even stronger in controlling everything, whether in politics, economy, and even culture, which is then later proved not ideal in the efforts to create peace, justice, and prosperity.

Since the middle of the 20*th* century, this weakness has been realized. In many places, movements have appeared in waves to encourage democratization, respect of human rights, and even liberalization that is linked with the efforts to privatize various state owned enterprises, which is to encourage an increased debureaucratization of government roles, and to develop deregulation policies in the sense of trimming regulations that are too complicated and inefficient. As expressed by John Naisbitt and Patricia Aburdene in their book, *Megatrends 2000*, the wave of privatization developed rapidly since the 1970s, starting from England, then to the United States and Japan, and then to almost all countries.

The growth of the tendency to privatize, deregulate, and de-bureaucratize that occurs along with waves of democratization in many places does have a positive impact on suppressing new regulations from being created and enforced. However, the productivity of regulations that were made over the course of almost a century has already grown to become very complicated. In addition, the reduction of the role of the state in producing laws and in controlling the dynamics of changes in society has been proven to not necessarily reduce the number of regulations that become reference in life; they continuously develop, though their production process is no longer merely determined by the government or even the state.

To overcome all complexities that occur in the dynamics of society, whether or not this is desirable, society is forced and even goaded by circumstances to create all kinds of regulations that are deemed necessary. As the scale and dimension of those changes become more complex, the need for regulating and controlling norms also increases and develops. As such, the development of the need to create regulations instead tends to increase from time to time, and without realization, a condition of "overregulation" tends to develop. This condition occurs within the tradition of "common law", which prioritizes the principle of "judge-made law", as well as in the tradition of "civil law" which prioritizes the creation of written laws. This condition is what Richard Susskind terms as "hyperregulation" in his book, *The Future of Law: Facing the Challenges of Information Technology.*

In the tradition of "common law", each day, court decisions are made in one region, which in time must immediately become a reference for judges in other regions in making decisions on similar cases. Even in the commonwealth system, "import" may occur from one of the

1. Armia MST, 'Perkembangan Pemikiran Dalam Ilmu Hukum' in *Perkembangan Pemikiran Dalam Ilmu Hukum* (Pradnya Paramita, 2002) 95.

United Kingdom countries to other member nations of the commonwealth, where a decision by a judge in one country can also become a reference for judges in other countries in making decisions on similar cases. The same is also true in the tradition of "civil law", where the tendency to create regulations for all changes that occur in society continues to increase as these changes quickly occur.

As quickly as the changes occur, the requirement for renewal of various existing regulations also quickly develops. The pace of changes that grows even more rapidly also leads to changes in society that are even more complex, triggering many more conflicts that need to be resolved by a judge. In addition, as change grows more complex and problems become ever more complicated, the need to create regulations in order to control the dynamics of change becomes ever greater. As a result, due to revolutions in communication and transportation technologies and the rapid dynamics of changes that occur, the tendency to produce new regulations also increases, whether in the form of decisions by judges or written regulations.

Due to the condition of "overregulation" or "hyperregulation", according to Richard Susskind, there is also the tendency for "legal alienation" to occur. The law becomes more and more alienated from society itself. The law also becomes alienated from citizens, from the environment of businesspeople, and even from legal experts themselves. As such, there needs to be a group of professionals that possess specialized expertise in the field of law, who can continuously follow developments in the field of law and work professionally in this field. Even so, legal experts themselves need to work hard and professionally. Legal experts are not only demanded to master various theories in legal science but also to understand in full the quick development of various legal regulations. The world of legal education is assured to fail in in preparing high quality human resources who work in the field of law if the curriculum orientation only contains theories that were produced in the past, without relating them to the regulations that quickly develop in actual practice.

In addition, legal experts and scholars who work in actual practice also face problems that are not simple, if they do not accustom themselves to follow the development of various legal regulations and legal dynamics. However, concerning this issue, it is not possible to follow the rapid dynamics of change without being assisted by adequate equipment with an automatized system. Within this relationship, the role of information technology in the form of computer systems and Internet communication systems, as well as other electronic legal facilities and infrastructure, becomes an absolute requirement. It is not possible for legal experts to be able to serve the quickly developing needs for legal services due to the revolution of information technology without utilizing the services of information technology itself.

The services of information technology in the field of law is not only useful for legal experts, but also important for anyone or any institution that needs legal information in a short amount of time. Both legal scholars who work in the world of education and research, and legal scholars who work in the world of business, politics and governance, as well as in society, need rapid legal services so that they themselves can provide rapid and accurate legal opinions. In all units of work of the state, governance, and business, these services of information technology are also very much needed to ensure that the dynamics of conducting everyday tasks can proceed orderly and follow principles. This is even more so in a country that follows the principle of a legal state such as Indonesia, which desires to uphold the principle of "the rule of law"; order in the legal system becomes something that is inevitable and non-negotiable.

1.2 *Shifting of legal paradigm*

In later times, the complex and intricate legal world will face a fundamental trans- formation in the form of information that the people require. As explained above, as more and more legal regulations are created and required as references, the law be- comes more and more alienated from the greater public. Even the law will become more alienated from the business world and even from legal experts themselves who are not able to keep up with legal developments from day to day. As such, the essence of law will change to become information with great economic value.

The law will become simply information that can be mastered by anyone, including those who possess no background in law or legal education at all. In this relationship, a paradigm shift can slowly occur, in consideration of the law as a process for seeking justice. As described by Richard Susskind, this paradigm shift will occur as described in the following table:

No	Today's Legal Paradigm	Tomorrow's Legal Paradigm
	Legal Services	***Legal Services***
1	Advisory service	Information service
2	One-to-one	One-to-many
3	Reactive service	Proactive service
4	Time-based billing	Commodity pricing
5	Restrictive	Empowering
6	Defensive	Pragmatic
7	Legal focus	Business focus
	Legal Process	***Legal Process***
1	Legal problem solving	Legal risk management
2	Dispute resolution	Dispute pre-emption
3	Publication of law	Promulgation of law
4	Dedicated legal profession	Legal specialists & Infoengineers
5	Print-based	IT-based legal system

(Processed from Figure8.1. "The Shift in Legal Paradigm", by Richard Susskind, 1996)

Because of the fundamental changes that occur due to the rapid growth of the utilization of electronic information technology in all fields of work, the execution of tasks related to law and legal regulations will experience fundamental changes. The concept of legal service in the future will experience a shift from the concept of *legal advising* to become merely the concept of *legal information*. Anyone can master legal information without having to become a legal scholar first. Even an engineer would be able to master legal information that rapidly develops.

In addition, legal services that are usually oriented as the "one-to-one approach" will transform to the "one-to-many approach". One person that masters legal information supported by information technology networks can provide legal information services to many people at once, and thus the nature of services change from *reactive* by answering questions that are asked to become *proactive* and no longer dependent on the questions that are asked or the problems being faced. Legal experts who master legal information in certain fields may have their services utilized by many people at once through effective utilization of technology and information networks, not only to react to a limited set of problems, but also to face any possibilities that may occur and all needs that may be required.

In this way, the payment method for legal consulting services that currently use "time-based billing" will shift to become "commodity pricing". The price for legal consultancy will no longer be calculated per hour of consultancy as is currently done, but per successfully resolved issue. Indeed, payment of legal consultancy services by the hour itself still constitutes a novelty in Indonesia. A large part of the income of attorneys in recent times is not earned as in the United States, where professional attorneys are paid by the hour or even by the minute. Yet in the future, the calculation of repayment for legal services itself will experience changes and will no longer be based on hours or minutes. One of the causes is that future legal services will no longer require person-to-person consultancy relationships. Any person who needs legal information services will no longer come to see an attorney or legal adviser; the person would only use a computer or meet a computer operator to open the web site or application for the required legal information services.

In addition, legal services that are currently "restrictive" in the sense of limiting services to limited client needs will also undergo changes. In the future, legal services will change from its tendency of having a "restrictive" nature to become services that have an "empowering" nature for the client. By using services of information technology that is properly operated, a person, a group of people, or even a multitude of people will have the chance to expand their knowledge and mastery of required legal information that enables any of them to overcome by themselves the legal issues that they face.

The current orientation of legal services can be said to be protectionist and defensive. The primary task of attorneys is to become a protector in the effort of maintaining the legal position of their respective clients. In this way, the position of legal services is very defensive in nature. In changes that will occur in the future, it will become inevitable that the work orientation of legal services in the future will become even more pragmatic. The position of clients will also no longer very much depend on the role of their attorneys, who has long acted as patrons. In addition, the problems that occur that requires legal services will also become even more focused on legalistic matters.

From a process standpoint, legal services are no longer oriented to problem solving, but rather risk management. Risks that occur due to problems are no longer to be resolved, but to be managed as well as possible. In the future, those who provide legal services will no longer resolve conflicts; instead, they will minimize the potential for conflicts. As a result, if currently large- and wide-scale publication of law is needed to communicate the law to the people, what will be more needed by people in the future is "promulgation of law", or the wide distribution of legal information.[2] What is meant by "promulgation of law" is that physically, the law constitutes information that needs to be distributed as much and as widely as possible, while the understanding of publication of law often means the emphasis of requiring to communicate the contents of law to the public. In the future, this communication objective may no longer be considered realistic because of the many laws that need to be communicated and the extent of people that need to know the existence of those laws. Thus, what is more prioritized is the distribution of legal information to as many targets as possible by opening up access for all people to find out information about the law. One way is through cyberspace, supported and facilitated by information technology.

The growth and progress of technology and information also very much affects the development of business transactions. John Nielson, one of the leaders of Microsoft, stated that within a period of 30 years, 30 percent of sales transactions with consumers will be conducted through e-commerce.[3]

This reality provides a challenge for law in facing the development and paradigm shift. Karim Benyekhlef stated an interesting view:[4]

> *"... Yet, one cannot claim to fully comprehend and understand this phenomenon if one reduces it to only its technical component. Obviously the latter might seem much more spectacular than its legal counterpart. However regardless of how impressive electronic highways may become, it remains undeniable that their integration and acceptance in the social and economic fabric will be dependent not ably on the legal guarantees they can provide. In other words, the consumer will only be inclined to use these new services if they can offer a degree of legal security comparable to that provide in the framework of traditional operations..."*

Karim Benyekhlef has the view that a person cannot be said to have truly understood the phenomenon about cyberspace if the understanding of the person is limited to only the technical elements of cyberspace, and the person has not yet realized the legal problems that come from cyberspace.

---

2. Munir AB, 'Cyber Law: Policies and Challenges (Malaysia, Singapore, Hong Kong, But- Terworth's Asia)' in *Huala Adolf, Hukum Perdagangan Internasional (International Trade Law)* (Jakarta, Rajagrafindo Persada, 2004) 161.
3. Ibid.
4. Sukarmi, *Tanggung Jawab Pelaku Usaha Atas Kerugian Konsumen Yang Disebabkan Oleh Perjanjian Baku (Standard Contract) Dalam Transaksi Elektronik* (University of Padjajaran, 2005).

Under new conditions such as these, businesspeople and various parties can no longer survive with old business strategies that force them to risk the goods or services they offer to be unmarketable; they instead must change their business strategy to the fulfillment of needs, tastes, and market purchasing power (market-oriented). In these times, the producer must become alert (*caveat venditor*) in the fulfillment of goods and/or services that consumers need.

For example, in the current development of advertising, the actors of the consumer protection movement repaid attention to *caveat emptor*, along with *caveat venditor*. The reason given for this is that presently advertising is dominated by strategies that sell image rather than quality of goods and/or services. The objective is so that consumers assume that they can have the advertised image or they can change their image if they consume the advertised goods and/or services. As a result, consumers will try hard to buy them even though the goods and/or services are not needed, do not suit their tastes, and are not appropriate to their purchasing power.

As a further consequence, in the future there will be a greater need for legal professionals to become more appreciated if they become specialists in specific fields. If the current pattern of legal professionalism continues to develop, the professionals will become very general, as if all legal scholars understand and master all fields of law. Thus, legal professionals in the future are demanded to transform into specialists that master information regarding a specific field, broadly and widely. If not, then there will be CD-ROMs and computers that can access the required sources for legal information through the Internet and other means. Each entrepreneur, project planner, designer, or legal professional that requires specific legal information can directly access the available sources of information through Internet networks, and on this basis, decisions can be quickly made and even easily accessed and distributed to various parts of the world simultaneously.

Thus, it becomes very important for legal experts and legal practitioners to form a reliable center for legal information. It has been the case for some time that legal experts and government officials have envisioned the formation of an "integrated law center". This need will become absolute in the future. However, the workings of the integrated law center itself must not be conventional. What is needed in the future is a center for legal information that is integrated into advanced information technology system networks that can be accessed any person or institution that needs to do so, whether domestic or abroad.

1.3 *The regulating role of the government in the era of information technology*

The era of technology and information has features and characteristics that are different from the era of conventional transactions and communication. Transactions conducted between businesspeople and consumers, for example, constitute the model of e-commerce transactions, wherein one of the parties acts as the end-user. In simple terms, B2C transactions are fundamentally the same as buying and selling, and the buyer is positioned as the end-user for the goods being traded. These are the characteristics of B2C transactions:[5]

- They are open to the public, wherein information is generically spread.
- The service provided is generic, with a mechanism that may be used by the multitude. As an example, because web systems are commonly used, service is provided using the web.
- The service provided is on an on-demand basis. Consumers start with an initiative and providers must be ready to respond according to needs.

By seeing the features and characteristics of the transaction models, if business people can actually optimize their abilities in transaction, they will obtain very large profits. However, a priority for this achievement is seeing the management aspect of business people. In relation

5. Sitompul A, *Hukum Internet Pengenalan Mengenai Masalah Hukum Di Cyberspace* (Bandung: Citra Aditya Bakti, 2001).

to this, Malcolm Frank in "The Realities of Web-based Electronic Commerce" suggested seven steps to achieve success in conducting transactions: [6]

- E-commerce must be seen as a business system and not a computer system. This means e-commerce must be a comprehensive solution in business, so that not only the technical side but also strategy, process, organization, and human resources are managed.
- The willingness to enter e-commerce must be fully supported by upper-level leaders. In other words, upper-level leaders are responsible for and own the-commerce business.
- Creation of the business process must be defined in exact terms to avoid the "glorification" of technology and computers as the only way to find solutions.
- There should be anticipation of possibly appearing conflicts that are caused by the transition to e-commerce. This conflict may very well come from third parties that feel disadvantaged with this new strategy.
- There should be anticipation of possible resistances to change from company internals.
- Demography and consumer needs ought to be studied to provide the best services to these groups.
- There should be preparation of staff who are skilled in the field of information technology and understand e-commerce with all its problems, including Intranet, web, database, system security, associated legal issues, and others.

The importance of the role of the government in this matter is because the required infrastructure to be developed needs investment in large amounts. To coordinate all efforts to develop Internet programs in government administration systems as above, there indeed needs to be an integrated information center, supported by investment in major amounts. As such, the role of the government becomes very important in this matter. Yet, information centers like these may also be developed by members of society themselves.

In relation to regulation, because of the quite rapid pace of change on technology and information that affects business activities, regulation on tariffs and taxes in the use of e-commerce applications as regulation that relates to electronic payment becomes very important. In addition, there are also regulation on legal stipulations that are related to privacy and security in conducting transactions, ability and support capacity of telecommunication infrastructure networks, and the technical standards applied in electronic trading as well as regulation of jurisdictional issues and applicable laws.

Indonesia has possessed Law of No. 11 of Year 2008 on Electronic Information and Transaction, which has been amended by Law No. 19 of Year 2016, but these are still generic in nature; these regulations are not sufficient to solve various legal problems that appear from developments and transactions that occur. For that, there needs to be regulations that are more specific regarding electronic transactions that deal with business (e-commerce). As an important note, the intended regulation of e-commerce is not oriented to the regulation of technological issues, but is more emphasized on the patterns of relationships among actors in e-commerce transactions. This is important, because if the regulation of e-commerce transactions is based on technological aspects, these legal regulations will inevitably become quickly out-of-date or obsolete. The reason is that changes in technology and information almost assuredly occur not in a matter of days, but seconds.

2 CONCLUSION

From what has been explained above, it is clear that in the future there will be many more demands to computerize the information and administration systems of all national and governmental organizations, including in private or business activities. These demands appear because of the changes caused by the spread of the utilization of information technology

6. Suherman AM, *Aspek Hukum Dalam Ekonomi Global* (Jakarta: Ghalia Indonesia, 2002).

services that are electronic in nature. In such situations, legal services and working processes of the legal system will experience fundamental changes. As such, it is necessary to develop preparations for an institution that makes use of the Internet and is accessible by all people that require its use.

Governmental and national apparatuses at both the central and regional levels must anticipate for this need immediately. The same is also true for private institutions and business people, who can take initiatives to develop legal information systems that are market-oriented. In this way, electronic legal information services may be developed carefully by utilizing information technologies that grow rapidly in society in the current times as well as in the future.

REFERENCES

A, Sitompul, *Hukum Internet Pengenalan Mengenai Masalah Hukum Di Cyberspace* (Bandung: Citra Aditya Bakti, 2001)

AB, Munir, 'Cyber Law: Policies and Challenges (Malaysia, Singapore, Hong Kong, But- Terworth's Asia)' in *Huala Adolf, Hukum Perdagangan Internasional (International Trade Law)* (Jakarta, Rajagrafindo Persada, 2004)

AM, Suherman, *Aspek Hukum Dalam Ekonomi Global* (Jakarta: Ghalia Indonesia, 2002)

MST, Armia, 'Perkembangan Pemikiran Dalam Ilmu Hukum' in *Perkembangan Pemikiran Dalam Ilmu Hukum* (Pradnya Paramita, 2002)

Sukarmi, *Tanggung Jawab Pelaku Usaha Atas Kerugian Konsumen Yang Disebabkan Oleh Perjanjian Baku (Standard Contract) Dalam Transaksi Elektronik* (University of Padjajaran, 2005)

Culture and International Law - Juwana et al. (Eds)
© 2019 Taylor & Francis Group, London, ISBN 978-1-138-38766-9

Ahok, blasphemy or hate speech: An international legal analysis

Hanif Nur Widhiyanti & I. Wayan Surya Hamijaya J
Law Faculty, Brawijaya University, Indonesia

ABSTRACT: Approximately one year ago, former Governor of DKI Jakarta, Basuki Tjahaja Purnama (Ahok), by a decision of the judges of the State Court of North Jakarta, Number 1537/Pid.B/2016/PN JKT.UTR, was declared to be proven to have legally and convincingly committed "religious desecration", by intentionally relating Surah Al-Maidah verse 51 in the Al-Qur'an with the word "lied" at Kepulauan Seribu. This decision of the judges raised various conflicting opinions, even among legal experts themselves. In reality, there is a significant difference between blasphemy and hate speech. Blasphemy in general is an act of insulting a religion or belief of individuals or other groups, while hate speech is the statement of opinions that reject the human rights principles of dignity and equality and attempt to humiliate individuals and groups in light of popular perceptions of them. The Ahok case has caught the attention of the international community, including legal institutions in other countries. The Dutch Parliament has stated that punishment for Ahok is an error, and freedom of opinion in Indonesia will be lost because of the case. OHCHR of Southeast Asia and Amnesty International have stated that the law of "religious desecration" in Indonesia is an injustice. Further, Amnesty International have stated that the application of "religious desecration" charges against Ahok has been misused to punish people who are simply and actually stating their opinions. The true nature of the Ahok case – whether it constitutes blasphemy or "simply" a case of hate speech – in the perspective of international law becomes something interesting to be discussed.

KEYWORDS: blasphemy, hate speech, freedom of expression, human rights

1 INTRODUCTION

Freedom of speech and freedom of expression are a part of human rights that are inseparable and legally ensured. Every person has the right to speak, state opinions, and express views so long as what the person believes is considered true. As a fundamental right, freedom of speech and freedom of expression can be used anywhere and anytime by every individual. Freedom of speech is the guarantee given to every individual to be able to speak and express opinions without restriction from the government[1]. The state as the possessor of legal sovereignty in its territory cannot reduce the freedom of speech of its citizens, because this is an act that restrains the human rights of each individual citizen. The state is required to provide the guarantee of the freedom of speech and freedom of opinion of its citizens.

Meanwhile, freedom of expression is the right that is possessed by every individual to speak whatever they wish to speak through communication and media, which can only

1. 'Meaning of "freedom of speech"', http://thelawdictionary.org/freedom-of-speech/, accessed on Friday, October 20, 2017, 10:52 PM.

be limited if this freedom of expression is used to damage the character or reputation of someone else by expressing false things[2]. Freedom of expression is a fundamental right possessed by every individual to speak and express their ideas or thoughts by not only speaking to the public, but also using existing media. In several cases, freedom of expression is also known as freedom of speech and included in it is free press. These two freedoms contain the power of someone to speak about their ideas or thoughts in front of the public. However, freedom of expression is supplemented with the expression of individual thoughts with existing media. Thus, freedom of expression includes in it freedom of speech and free press.

In relation to this freedom of expression, an interesting case occurred in Jakarta in 2016; the case of former Governor of DKI Jakarta, Basuki Tjahaya Purnama (called Ahok) was decided by the judges of the State Court of North Jakarta, Number 1537/Pid.B/2016/PN JKT. UT. This case began from a working visit by Ahok to the Fish Auction Site at Pramuka Island, Pulau Panggang Hamlet, Pulau Seribu Selatan Sub-District, Administrative Regency of Kepulauan Seribu, Province of DKI Jakarta to see the carp harvest; he was accompanied by members of the DKI Jakarta Local Parliament, Regent of Kepulauan Seribu, Head of Maritime Affairs, Fishery, and Food Stability of the Province of DKI Jakarta, and Economic Assistants, and this was attended by fishermen, religious figures, public figures, and local officials. When Ahok conducted the visit, the accused had been registered as a candidate for Governor of DKI Jakarta, for which the election was scheduled to be conducted in February 2017.

When Ahok expressed his greetings, this was what he said:

> "*...this election was moved forward, so whether or not I was reelected, I stop working in October 2017 so if we run this program well, you can still harvest even though I'm not elected as governor. So the story is that so you still have spirit, so you don't have to think, ah... if he's not elected, Ahok's programs are discontinued, no... I work until October 2017, so don't believe people, your little heart could tell you to not vote for me, as Surah Al-Maidah 51 is a lie to you – everything is your right, yah, so if you feel I can't be elected because I'm afraid to go to hell because of a lie to me, it's OK, because this is your personal calling, and the program continues. So you don't have to feel not so good, in your conscience you could not vote for Ahok, because you don't like Ahok, but if you accept the program it won't be good, it's a debt of gratitude, no – if you don't have good feelings, you'll die slowly by stroke.*"

According to the Council of Judges in Decision number 1537/Pid.B/2016/PN JKT.UTR, these words of Ahok makes it seem that Surah Al-Maidah Verse 51 has been used by other people to deceive and fool the people in regional elections. Ahok was considered to have positioned or situated Surah Al-Maidah Verse 51 as a tool or facility to deceive and fool the people in the process of electing regional leaders. The Council of Judges decided that Ahok:

1. Conducted a criminal act, whoever intentionally to the public expressed feelings or conducted actions that essentially acts to antagonize, misuse, or desecrate a religion believed in Indonesia; as mentioned in the First Alternative Charge as organized in Article 156a letter a of the Criminal Code;
2. Conducted a criminal act, whoever intentionally to the public expressed feelings of antagonism, hatred, or insult to one or more groups of the people of Indonesia; as mentioned in the Second Alternative Charge as organized in Article 156 of the Criminal Code.

2. 'Meaning of "freedom of expression"', http://thelawdictionary.org/freedom-of-expression/, accessed on Saturday, October 21, 2017, 3:14 PM.

To this decision, many people in Indonesia reacted. There were those who supported and were against; some considered the words of Ahok as "only" hate speech, but others also agreed with the Judges' Decision of the North Jakarta Court and considered it as religious desecration.[3] The case of Ahok caught the attention of the world, including legal agencies in other countries and the international community. The Dutch Parliament stated that the Ahok punishment is an error, and freedom of opinion in Indonesia will be lost because of this[4]. OHCHR of Southeast Asia and Amnesty International stated that the law of religious desecration in Indonesia is an injustice. Further, Amnesty International stated that Articles 156 and 156a are articles that can be utilized to punish people who are actually simply stating their opinions[5].

2 RESULT AND DISCUSSION

2.1 *Definition of hate speech and blasphemy*

Blasphemy and hate speech are common terms used by the international community for religious desecration and expressions of hate. National laws in each country have their own standards for regulating blasphemy and hate speech, but the terms "blasphemy" and "hate speech" are not explicitly regulated in international law. In international law, there are no legal instruments that clearly regulate blasphemy and hate speech. However, in international law, what is regulated is the guarantee of provision of human rights. Recognition of dignity and rights of people that are self-evident and cannot be revoked is the foundation of freedom, justice, and peace in the world. This recognition of dignity is what is formed into the protection of human rights by law[6].

Blasphemy and hate speech are actions that possess some similarities and several differences. Limits on the concepts of blasphemy and hate speech can be seen from what is meant by "blasphemy" and "hate speech" as well as their individual characteristics. Blasphemy is an action that is conducted by parties who intentionally speak to attack people or groups in relation to religion, whether belief in God, the holy book, or anything related to the religion in question to hurt the feelings of people or to affect hatred established by law or to affect the reduction of morals toward religion. As a common term in the public, the understanding of blasphemy can also cover words of vow related to religion in broadcast media and public rejection of the basic concepts of religion[7], wherein these two things are seen to have a "*blasphemous*" nature.

Hate speech is an action that indicates an expression of discrimination by expressing opinions to the public in written, visual, artistic, and other forms, and may be spread through the media[8]. According to UN's International Committee on the Elimination of Racial Discrimination, hate speech can be understood as the expression of opinions that ignore the essence of

3. https://nasional.tempo.co/read/news/2017/05/09/063873676/ahok-dihukum-dua-tahun-putusan-hakim-bulat, accessed on Thursday, September 21, 2017, 11:06 PM.
4. http://www.bbc.com/indonesia/dunia-39872700, accessed on Thursday, September 21, 2017, 11:20 PM.
5. https://www.cnnindonesia.com/internasional/20170510094031-106-213735/pbb-desak-ri-tinjau-ulang-hukum-yang-jerat-ahok/, accessed on Thursday, September 21, 2017, 11:25 PM.
6. *Universal Declaration of Human Rights* 1948, Preamble: Whereas recognition of the inherent dignity and of the equal and inalienable rights of all members of the human family is the foundation of freedom, justice, and peace in the world; Whereas it is essential, if man is not to be compelled to have recourse as a last resort, to rebellion against tyranny and oppression, that human rights should be protected by the rule of law.
7. Loso, 'Suatu Kajian Perbandingan Pengaturan Tindak Pidana Penghinaan Tuhan (*Blasphemy*) di Indonesia dan di Berbagai Negara Asing (A Comparative Study of the Regulation of the Crime of Blasphemy in Indonesia and Various Foreign Countries)', (2013) 25(2) *PENA: Jurnal Ilmu Pengetahuan dan Teknologi* (Universitas Pekalongan, Pekalongan) 76.
8. Article 19, *"Hate Speech" Explained (*Creative Commons Attribution-Non-Commercial-ShareLike 2.5, London, 2015) 9.

the principle of dignity and equality of human rights, and attempts to demean the position of a person or a group in the eyes of the public[9]. The action of hate speech is conducted by bringing out inner ideas to the public through media that can be accessed by many parties, or done directly through verbal expressions. The object of hate speech actions is race, skin color, gender, language, religion, opposing political ideals, citizenship, wealth, birth, the identity of a person, disability, migrant status, sexual orientation, as well as other possible matters that may become the object of hate speech actions[10].

Similarities and differences regarding blasphemy and hate speech are not significant, but this indicates that blasphemy and hate speech are actions that are similar in execution, but are different on the object of their acts. Blasphemy and hate speech are similar in that their action is to attack by showing discriminative attitudes, which is done to humiliate the object of discrimination in public eyes and to be known by the public and in media that can be accessed and understood by the people. The difference is that blasphemy is focused on discrimination toward religion and all related elements of religion, while hate speech has a wider coverage of objects, not just religion and including matters such as race, skin color, ethnicity, and others. Considering the explanations of blasphemy and hate speech, blasphemy is a part of hate speech, because one of the objects of discrimination by hate speech is religion. Thus, blasphemy is one of the forms of hate speech, wherein the act of discrimination is attacking religion and its elements.

Blasphemy and hate speech are actions categorized as criminal acts. These criminal acts are classified as verbal actions, because no physical harm is caused, but reputation and dignity are injured or harmed by these actions. The measure of blasphemy and hate speech actions is the presence of inappropriate words that are aimed to express hatred towards someone. These words that contain hatred are expressed with due intent from the party committing the acts of blasphemy and hate speech.

2.2 *Legal basis of regulation of blasphemy and hate speech*

2.2.1 *According to international law*

International law regulates human rights, but does not specifically regulate blasphemy and hate speech. Blasphemy and hate speech are not like regulations on seas, air and space, the environment, international treaties, and so on. Blasphemy and hate speech are only known as part of the problems regarding human rights, and so what regulates are the international conventions regarding human rights.

Instruments of international law that regulate human rights cover the 1948 Universal Declaration of Human Rights, the 1965 International Convention on the Elimination of All Forms of Racial Discrimination (hereinafter mentioned as ICERD), and the 1966 International Covenant on Civil and Political Rights (hereinafter mentioned as ICCPR) along with the Optional Protocol of ICCPR. These instruments of international regulate matters related to blasphemy and hate speech.

a. Blasphemy and Hate Speech According to the 1948 Universal Declaration Of Human Rights

   One of the human rights regulated by international law is freedom to speak in front of the public and freedom of expression. As one of the fundamental rights, freedom to speak in front of the public and freedom of expression are inseparable from every human. In the Universal Declaration of Human Rights, every person possesses the freedom to state opinions and express, including standing firm to opinions without interference from outside parties and seeking, receiving, and delivering information and ideas through any media without limits[11].

9. UN Committee on the Elimination of Racial Discrimination, '*General Recommendation No. 35 on Combatting Racist Hate Speech*, 26 September 2013, CERD/C/GC/35', para 7.
10. Article 19, above n 8, 14.
11. *Universal Declaration of Human Rights* 1948, Article 19.

Freedom of expression and freedom to speak in front of the public may be executed by any person, regardless of the status of the person. The words "every person" has the meaning that individuals that are born as humans, possess freedom of speech and freedom of expression, without being limited by the status of the person. Although status of work, nobility degree, minority, and others indicate a hierarchy of social status, human rights, in this case freedom of speech and freedom of expression, does not regard these. The statement of opinions in front of the public and freedom of expression also may not be limited by the media of delivery. All people have the right to use existing media to express themselves and speak in front of the public.

In relation to the freedom to speak in front of the public and freedom of expression, blasphemy and hate speech are also included in freedom to speak in front of the public and freedom of expression. The elements in blasphemy and hate speech actually fulfill the elements of freedom of speech and freedom of expression. Freedom to speak in front of the public and freedom of expression contains the rights of all people to display their ideas, information, and expressions in front of the public using existing media without any limits. The elements of blasphemy and hate speech also have the elements of displaying ideas, information, and expressions in front of the public using existing media and known to all. Thus, in relation to freedom of speech and freedom of expression, the acts of blasphemy and hate speech are part of the human rights to express themselves and speak in front of the public.

Though blasphemy and hate speech are forms of freedom of speech and freedom of expression, these two actions are actions that attack the human rights of other people. In the Universal Declaration of Human Rights, it is indeed mentioned that freedom of speech and freedom of expression cannot be limited, but this does not mean that this allows any person to ignore the human rights of other people. There are times when the human rights of someone will conflict with the human rights of another. Here, it is where the law has the role of being rules that apply in society and regulating everything regarding order in society, including regulations on societal life[12].

b. Blasphemy and Hate Speech According to the 1965 International Convention on the Elimination of All Forms of Racial Discrimination (ICERD)

The acts of blasphemy and hate speech may be categorized as acts of racial discrimination. According to the ICERD, racial discrimination is an act that differentiates, makes exceptions of, limits, or supports something based on race, skin color, lineage, citizenship, or ethnicity, which is aimed to eliminate recognition, enjoyment, or execution of equality in human rights and basic rights in politics, economy, society, culture, or other areas of public life[13]. Religion, although not mentioned in the explanation of racial discrimination according to the ICERD, can still be categorized as an object of racial discrimination, because religion as an identity is the same as ethnicity, skin color, lineage, or citizenship. What becomes the focus of racial discrimination is the differentiation, exception, limitation, or support of something based on identity to remove equality in the execution of human rights and fundamental rights. As such, when religion becomes an object of racial discrimination, the actor of racial discrimination indeed has the aim to eliminate equality of human rights, that someone has the right to freely possess religion and to practice religious teachings in education, acting, worship, and celebration of holidays[14].

12. Rizky Ariestandi Irmansyah, *Hukum, Hak Asasi Manusia, dan Demokrasi (Law, Human Rights, and Democracy)*, (Jakarta, Graha Ilmu, 2013) 16.
13. *International Convention on the Elimination of All Forms of Racial Discrimination* 1965, Article 1 Paragraph 1: "The term of "racial discrimination" shall mean any distinction, exclusion, restriction, or preference based on race, colour, descent, or national or ethnic origin which has the purpose or effect of nullifying or impairing the recognition, enjoyment, or exercise. On an equal footing of human rights and fundamental freedoms in the political, economic, social, cultural, or any other field of public life."
14. *Universal Declaration of Human Rights* 1948, Article 18: "Everyone has the right to freedom of thought, conscience, and religion; this right includes freedom of change his religion or belief, and freedom, either

Human rights in international law regulates several important matters regarding blasphemy and hate speech. Identities such as religion, race, ethnicity, skin color, citizenship, and others are not distanced from criticism. People who enjoy the rights of freedom of speech and freedom of expression can criticize things that are improper, even if those things are related to those identities. However, what is not justified is if someone criticizes by arbitrarily speaking in front of the public with the rationale that the person has the rights of freedom of speech and freedom of expression. Every person must respect the human rights of other people by obeying laws that are designated to respect human rights and freedom of other people by fulfilling requirements of morality, public order, and general welfare in a democratic society[15].

The legal sovereignty that a state possesses allows the state to rightfully limit human rights to ensure morality, public order, and general welfare. In the case of blasphemy and hate speech not to be meant as limits of freedom of speech and freedom of expression, there must be clear regulations on how freedom of speech and freedom of expression can be used to address certain identities, without attacking the human rights of others. International law possesses regulations on human rights, which may be openly adopted by states by firmly binding themselves to international law, whether adopted as national laws or by direct application in the state.

States that are members of international conventions must respect and ensure the rights of every person without regard of their identities, who are present in the territory of that state and under its jurisdiction[16]. Freedom of speech and freedom of expression are rights that are possessed by every person in a state. The state in the creation of laws may not revoke or forbid the execution of freedom of speech and freedom of expression, and so the state must ensure that these rights can be executed in the territory of the state and are ensured by law in their execution. In addition to not revoking and forbidding the execution of freedom of speech and freedom of expression, the state is not permitted to be an actor of racial discrimination in state authorities and institutions, whether national, regional, or local, and is also not permitted to sponsor, support, or defend acts of racial discrimination, whether conducted by individuals or groups[17]. In this case, the state is positioned as a protector of freedom to speak in front of the public and freedom of expression, as well as law enforcers for parties that misuse their freedom.

When there are parties that commit acts of blasphemy or hate speech, the state as a protector may execute several actions that are considered appropriate to handle these situations. The state may take effective action to review governmental, national, and regional policies, as well as to fix, eliminate, or repeal laws or policies that have the consequence of allowing or legalizing racial discrimination wherever it may occur[18], in accordance with the

---

alone or in community with others and in public or private, to manifest his religion or belief in teaching, practice, worship, and observance."

15. *Universal Declaration of Human Rights* 1948, Article 29 Paragraph 2: "In the exercise of his right and freedoms, everyone shall be subject only to such limitations as are determined by law solely for the purpose of securing due recognition and respect for the rights and freedoms of others and of meeting the just requirements of morality, public order, and the general welfare in a democratic society."
16. *International Covenant on Civil and Political Rights* 1948, Article 2 Paragraph 2: "Where no already provided for by existing legislative or other measure, each state party to the present covenant undertakes to take the necessary steps, in accordance with its constitutional processes and with the provisions of the present covenant, to adopt such laws or other measures as may be necessary to give effect to the rights recognized in the present covenant."
17. *International Convention on the Elimination of All Forms of Racial Discrimination* 1965, Article 2 Paragraph 1 Letters a and b: "States parties condemn racial discrimination and undertake to pursue by all appropriate means and without delay a policy of eliminating racial discrimination in all its forms and promoting understanding among all races, and, to this end: (a) each state party undertakes to engage in no act or practice of racial discrimination against persons, groups of persons, or institutions and to ensure that all public authorities and public institutions, national, and local, shall act in conformity with this obligation; (b) each state party undertakes not to sponsor, defend, or support racial discrimination by any persons or organizations."

legal procedures present in each state. An effective action that may be conducted by the state is prohibitions and resolution of problems in appropriate ways. When a state has reviewed policies, whether done by the state or even one of the institutions or organizations in the state, there must be a prohibition and resolution of blasphemy or hate speech; this is done so that public order is achievable in the state. It becomes important for the state to be able to review every policy or legal regulation yang that allows blasphemy or hate speech to develop, in order to be able resolve problems according to the legal regulations of the state[19].

Legal protection is an important matter for the people in order to avoid blasphemy or hate speech. The state must provide effective legal protection to be able to protect and restore human rights and fundamental rights that are violated by other people. Legal protection may be in the form of providing rights to obtain protection from a competent court or state institution related the protection of human rights, while the recovery of human rights is through obtaining compensation from the effects caused by racial discrimination[20].

Here, compensation may be in material or immaterial form, because there are no restrictions as to what form the compensation may take. When acts of discrimination are inflicted towards a person, the person must obtain equivalent compensation, seen from the material and immaterial losses suffered by that person. In addition to providing compensation and recovery, the state may be able provide the people with an education about tolerance. To prevent acts of racial discrimination, the state may take preventive measures by providing lessons, education, culture, and information regarding views to counter prejudice that leads in the direction of racial discrimination, and may introduce mutual understanding, tolerance, and friendship among other states and ethnic groups[21]. Education to the people is used to provide a good understanding regarding tolerance among groups. Thus, with the education provided by the state, this will reduce acts of blasphemy and hate speech within society, and additionally reduce conflicts in society.

c. Blasphemy and Hate Speech in the 1966 International Covenant on Civil and Political Rights (ICCPR)

---

18. *International Convention on the Elimination of All Forms of Racial Discrimination* 1965, Article 2 Paragraph 1 Letter c: "States parties condemn racial discrimination and undertake to pursue by all appropriate means and without delay a policy of eliminating racial discrimination in all its forms and promoting understanding among all races, and, to this end: (c) each state party shall take effective measures to review governmental, national, and local policies, and to amend, rescind or nullify any laws and regulations which have the effect of creating or perpetuating racial discrimination wherever it exists."
19. *International Convention on the Elimination of All Forms of Racial Discrimination* 1965, Article 2 Paragraph 1 Letter d: "*States parties condemn racial discrimination and undertake to pursue by all appropriate means and without delay a policy of eliminating racial discrimination in all its forms and promoting understanding among all races, and, to this end: (d) each state party shall prohibit and bring to an end, by all appropriate means, including legislation as required by circumstances, racial discrimination by any persons, group, or organizations.*"
20. *International Convention on the Elimination of All Forms of Racial Discrimination* 1965, Article 6: "state parties shall assure to everyone within their jurisdiction effective protection and remedies, through the competent national tribunals and other state institutions, against any acts of racial discrimination which violate his human rights and fundamental freedoms contrary to this convention, as well as the right to seek from such tribunals just and adequate reparation or satisfaction for any damage suffered as a result of such discrimination."
21. *International Convention on the Elimination of All Forms of Racial Discrimination* 1965, Article 7: "States Parties undertake to adopt immediate and effective measures, particularly in the fields of teaching, education, culture and information, with a view to combating prejudices which lead to racial discrimination and to promoting understanding, tolerance and friendship among nations and racial or ethnical groups, as well as to propagating the purposes and principles of the Charter of the United Nations, the Universal Declaration of Human Rights, the United Nations Declaration on the Elimination of All Forms of Racial Discrimination, and this Convention."

The ICCPR regulates freedom to carry out individual civil and political rights in front of the public. The ICCPR regulates several matters related to blasphemy and hate speech. What is regulated in relation to blasphemy and hate speech is freedom of speech, freedom of expression, freedom of opinion, and protection from actions that may limit those rights. Each individual has the right to have own opinions. Individuals must be free from interference from other parties in maintaining what has become their opinions. By obtaining and seeking information, ideas that are possessed by every individual has a right to be distributed to the public through various media, whether in spoken or written form[22]. In relation to blasphemy and hate speech, this constitutes the form of distributing ideas that are possessed. Someone who wishes to express opinions through various media that can be used may peruse freedom of speech and freedom of expression. Though the possessed ideas or views may be related to certain religions or groups, this still constitutes human rights in freedom of speech and expression.

Freedom of speech and freedom of expression can indeed be enjoyed by every individual, but sometimes, this may also be limited. The limiting of human rights is merely to protect other human rights. Freedom of speech and freedom of expression that may not be invoked is forming public opinion regarding religion, race, or citizenship of someone that may cause discrimination, violence, or antagonism[23]. Blasphemy and hate speech, although forms of freedom of speech and freedom of expression, must be limited to protect the freedom of others.

The state is expected to be able to provide good protection and education on the matters of freedom of speech and freedom of expression. However, in a state of emergency, the state can limit freedom of speech and freedom of expression to maintain public order. According to the ICCPR, member states of the convention can reduce their obligations to the convention if there is a state of emergency that disrupts public order and can threaten national security, as officially announced by the state. However, this must not be in conflict with the other obligations of the state in international law, and this is not merely done to conduct acts of discrimination toward certain groups [24].

When in a state of emergency, the state can limit freedom to speak in front of the public and freedom of expression merely to ensure that the public condition does not become worse. Speaking in front of the public and making expressions may worsen the current situation, making the condition of the state less conducive and causing detriment to many parties, including those who use their rights of freedom of speech and freedom of expression. With a temporary limitation, the state can focus on handling the state of emergency until it is resolved.

The ICCPR also regulates the protection of human rights for which the freedom to execute them are violated. In contrast to the ICERD, ICCPR has its own protocol in handling human rights in relation to civil and political rights, which is the Optional Protocol. The Optional Protocol handles complaints of the misuse and restriction of freedom of speech and freedom of expression. The Optional Protocol of the ICCPR is a complaint protocol that may be executed by individuals in each member state of the convention. The state, as

22. *International Covenant on Civil and Political Rights* 1966, Article 19 Paragraph 2: "Everyone shall have the right to freedom of expression; this right shall include freedom to seek, receive and impart information and ideas of all kinds, regardless of frontiers, either orally, in writing or in print, in the form of art, or through any other media of his choice."

23. *International Covenant on Civil and Political Rights* 1966, Article 20 Paragraph 2: "Any advocacy of national, racial or religious hatred that constitutes incitement to discrimination, hostility or violence shall be prohibited by law."

24. *International Covenant on Civil and Political Rights* 1966, Article 4 Paragraph 1: "In time of public emergency which threatens the life of the nation and the existence of which is officially proclaimed, the States Parties to the present Covenant may take measures derogating from their obligations under the present Covenant to the extent strictly required by the exigencies of the situation, provided that such measures are not inconsistent with their other obligations under international law and do not involve discrimination solely on the ground of race, colour, sex, language, religion or social origin."

participant to the Optional Protocol, must recognize the competence of the committee to accept and consider complaints from individuals to the jurisdiction of the committee who claims that the individual is a victim of violation by the state, in which the human right is recognized in the ICCPR convention[25].

The concepts of blasphemy and hate speech in international law are in general not regulated regarding actions and sanctions, but tends toward the regulation of human rights that may be disadvantaged due to blasphemy and hate speech. As such, the state must accommodate all forms of freedom of speech and freedom of expression of every individual under its jurisdiction, including the freedom to obtain, seek, and distribute information without limit, because this is a fundamental right that cannot be revoked from humans. However, this matter may be limited in order to create public order, maintain morals, and respect the rights and reputations of other people. Thus, public opinion that contains racist content is forbidden to be expressed because it may put others at a disadvantage and can limit the public rights of a person, whether economic, political, social, cultural, or of other public rights.

Resolution of blasphemy and hate speech according to international law is up to each individual state. International law stresses that a state may not have a supporting role toward acts of racism. The state must also review laws and regulations that can support actions of racism, and provide education to the people regarding mutual understanding, tolerance, and friendship. Conflict resolution must be conducted using the ways that are facilitated by a state. If a satisfactory resolution cannot be achieved, non-litigation procedures in international law may be invoked, if only to provide recommendation to the state and the party that is disadvantaged due to blasphemy and hate speech.

2.2.2 *Concepts of blasphemy and hate speech in the national Indonesian legal perspective*

Indonesia is a state of law[26] that recognizes applicable human rights in its jurisdiction. Recognition of human rights is a characteristic of a democratic state. Freedom of speech and freedom of expression are human rights that are recognized Indonesia. The national Constitution of Indonesia states that all citizens have the right to be of a certain religion and worship, to be free to express opinions[27], and to communicate and seek, obtain, process, and distribute information in all currently available ways[28]. The freedom to speak in front of the public and to express becomes one of the fundamental rights of Indonesian citizens. However, the state also admits that this freedom is also limited by the freedom of others, wherein this limiting is regulated by law as a binding law merely for the respect of human rights to create order in society, the nation, and the state[29].

The Indonesian law on human rights regulate freedom of speech and freedom of expression. The state recognizes the right of every individual to believe in a certain religion and to worship accordingly[30] and to express opinions in spoken and written forms in front of the public through print or electronic media, by paying attention to the values of living Indonesia[31]. The state permits every citizen to express all religious actions openly in public and opinions in front of the public, using the media available in the country. This is also what may lead those

25. *Optional Protocol to the International Covenant on Civil and Political Rights* 1966, Article 1: "A State Party to the Covenant that becomes a Party to the present Protocol recognizes the competence of the Committee to receive and consider communications from individuals subject to its jurisdiction who claim to be victims of a violation by that State Party of any of the rights set forth in the Covenant. No communication shall be received by the Committee if it concerns a State Party to the Covenant which is not a Party to the present Protocol."
26. 1945 Constitution of the Republic of Indonesia, Article 1, Paragraph 3.
27. 1945 Constitution of the Republic of Indonesia, Article 28 E.
28. 1945 Constitution of the Republic of Indonesia, Article 28 F.
29. 1945 Constitution of the Republic of Indonesia, Article 28 J.
30. Law Number 39 of Year 1999 on Human Rights, Article 22.
31. Law Number 39 of Year 1999 on Human Rights, Article 23 Paragraph (2) and Article 25.

who peruse these freedoms of expression and speaking in public to commit wrongful acts, such as blasphemy and hate speech.

Freedom is indeed absolute, but this freedom is limited to maintain order in society. The most absolute freedom is only applicable if the individual is not present in society[32]. Indonesia as a state of law limits all human rights in Indonesia, including freedom of speech and freedom of expression. The aim of this is so that every citizen and member of society in Indonesia respect the freedom and rights of other people, as well as to achieve security and public order based on democracy.

The limiting of freedom of speech and freedom of expression can be seen from the presence of laws that regulate blasphemy and hate speech di Indonesia. In positive Indonesian law, what is meant as hate speech is someone stating antagonism, hatred, or insult towards groups present in Indonesia, in front of the public[33]. Meanwhile, blasphemy can be understood as an action that deliberately expresses feelings of or constitutes antagonism, misuse, or desecration of one or more religions recognized in Indonesia and triggers someone to be of a religion not based on the Belief in a Supreme God in front of the public[34]. Seen from the explanation of blasphemy and hate speech in positive Indonesian law, the limiting of freedom of speech is the limiting of speaking in public about antagonism, hatred, insult, misuse, and desecration. Indeed, freedom of speech is fundamentally freely speaking in front of the public, which includes criticism that potentially may become acts of hate speech and blasphemy. However, these actions are considered to put the state in chaos, making it not conducive. The law requires all people in Indonesia to respect the human rights of other people as well as morals, ethics, and order in societal life[35]. Thus, acts of blasphemy and hate speech that are fundamentally forms of freedom of speech and freedom of expression must be limited to achieve public order.

2.3 *Comparison of regulations of blasphemy and hate speech according to international law and Indonesian national law*

Based on previous discussions, the following is a comparison of blasphemy and hate speech:

Sanctions enforce the people to obey the law. National law has sanctions that may be applied to the people. Sanctions are designated to be able to direct society in certain directions[36]. Thus, the application of sanctions regulated in Articles 156 and 156a of the Criminal Code (KUHP) of Indonesia directs society not to commit hate speech that causes antagonism, hatred, or actions that are classified as misuse and desecration. This is different from international law, which substantially only regulates limits without sanctions that can be applied to the people. The ICCPR and ICERD are two international legal instruments that have been ratified by Indonesia[37]. These two instruments only regulate principles of human rights in relation to blasphemy and hate speech, such as freedom of speech, freedom of expression, freedom of religion, and so on.

32. Agus Triyanta, 'Mencari Benang Merah Konstitusional Antara Kebebasan Beragama dan Penodaan Agama: Dari Konsep *Blasphemy Law* Hingga Pelarangan Ahmadiyah di Indonesia (Seeking the Constitutional Ties Between Freedom of Worship and Blasphemy: From the Blasphemy Law Concept to the Forbidding of Ahmadiyah in Indonesia)' (2013) XXXV(78) *UNISIA, Jurnal Ilmu –Ilmu Sosial* (Yogyakarta, Faculty of Law, Islam University of Indonesia) 26.
33. Criminal Code, Article 156.
34. Criminal Code, Article 156a.
35. Law Number 39 of Year 1999 on Human Rights, Article 69 Paragraph (1).
36. Yusnita Eva, 'Perspektif dan Kajian Hukum dari Beberapa Tokoh dalam Bidang Antropologi Hukum (Legal Perspective and Studies from Several Figures in the Field of Legal Anthropology)' (2010) 22(1) *Mimbar Hukum* (Gadjah Mada University, Yogyakarta) 177.
37. *Ratification Status for Indonesia* (online), http://tbinternet.ohchr.org/_layouts/TreatyBodyExternal/Treaty.aspx?CountryID=80&Lang=EN, accessed on Tuesday, February 27, 2017, 12:42 AM.

Table 1. Comparison of blasphemy regulations according to international law and Indonesian national law

	International Law		National Law		
Indicator	ICCPR	Optional Protocol ICCPR	Criminal Code (KUHP)	Presidential Decree (UU PNPS)	Law of Human Rights (UU HAM)
Definition	Forbidding of all forms of public opinion regarding religion that may cause discrimination, antagonism, or violence. This also includes citizenship and race. (Article 20 Paragraph 2)	There is no definition regarding blasphemy. What is regulated is the resolution of conflicts through non-litigation for individuals who feel they are a victim.	Forbidding of every person who intentionally commits antagonism, misuse, or desecration of religion, and inciting belief in a religion not based on the Belief in a Supreme God in front of the public. (Article 156a)	Forbidding of interpreting religion and religious practices that are not appropriate to teachings. (Article 1)	There is no definition regarding blasphemy. What is regulated is human rights that may be damaged by blasphemy or damaged by having considered to conduct blasphemy.
Elements	1. Actions constituting expression of opinions; 2. causing discrimination, antagonism, or violence; 3. conducted in front of the public; 4. with the object of action being religion in general	No elements	1. Actions constituting expression of opinions or acts that contain antagonism, misuse, or desecration of religion recognized in Indonesia, and offers to be of a religion not based on the Belief in a Supreme God; 2. conducted by one or more people; 3. conducted intentionally; 4. conducted in front of the public; 5. with the object of action being religion in general; 6. having sanctions constituting imprisonment	1. Actions constituting offers to interpret religion or religious activities deviating from the essence of the religion; 2. conducted by one or more people; 3. conducted intentionally; 4. conducted in front of the public	No elements
Sanctions	No sanctions	No sanctions	Imprisonment of at most 5 years	No sanctions	No sanctions

Table 2. Comparison of hate speech regulations according to international law and Indonesian national law

	International Law			National Law	
Indicator	ICCPR	ICERD	Optional Protocol ICCPR	Criminal Code (KUHP)	Law of Human Rights (UU HAM)
Definition	Forbidding of all forms of public opinion regarding citizenship, race, or religion that may cause discrimination, antagonism, or violence. (Article 20 Paragraph 2)	There is no explicit mention regarding the definition of hate speech. However, there is the forbidding of all forms of racist acts that differentiate, make exceptions of, limit, or support a group to eliminate equality of recognition, rights, or execution of human rights and fundamental public freedoms. Hate speech constitutes a form of a racial act. (can be seen in Article 2 Paragraph 1, Article 4, and Article 5)	Conflict resolution through non-litigation ways for individuals who feel they have become victims.	Forbidding of public statements containing antagonism, hatred, or insult toward groups of people living in Indonesia. (Article 156)	There is no definition regarding hate speech. What is regulated is human rights that may be damaged by blasphemy or damaged by having considered to conduct blasphemy.
Elements	1. Actions constituting expression of opinions; 2. may be causing discrimination, antagonism, or violence; 3. conducted in front of the public; 4. with the object of action being citizens and groups	1. Actions that have the aim to differentiate, make exceptions of, limit, or support a group to eliminate equality of recognition, rights, or execution of human rights and fundamental public freedoms; 2. with the object of action being race, skin color, lineage, citizenship, or ethnicity	No elements	1. Actions constituting expression of opinions that contain antagonism, hatred, or insult. 2. with the object of action being groups of people in Indonesia; 3. having sanctions constituting imprisonment or fines	No elements
Sanctions	No sanctions	No sanctions	No sanctions	Imprisonment of at least 4 years or fines of at most Rp. 300.	No sanctions

Table 3. Comparison of blasphemy and hate speech

Indicator	Blasphemy	Hate Speech
Definition	Similar meanings in Article 20 Paragraph 2 of ICCPR, being antagonism, misuse, or desecration of religion, or offering other people to not be of a religion (Article 156a of the Criminal Code) and interpreting religion inappropriately to its teachings (UU PNPS)	A form of public opinion regarding citizenship, race, or religion that may cause discrimination, antagonism, or violence (Article 20 Paragraph 2 ICCPR) and contain antagonism, hatred, or insult toward groups of people living in Indonesia (Article 156 of the Criminal Code)
Scope of actions	Public opinion of religion that may cause discrimination, antagonism, and violence regarding religion, offering other people to not be of a religion, and interpreting religion inappropriately to its teachings	Public opinion of religion that may cause discrimination, antagonism, and violence regarding religion, citizenship, or race
Similarities	Both are in the form of expression of opinions in front of the public that contains religion and may cause chaos in society as in the form of hatred, discrimination, or violence	
Differences	In addition to expression of opinions in front of the public, positive Indonesian law classifies other actions as blasphemy, such as people offering other people to not be of a religion and interpreting religion inappropriately to its teachings	Only in the form of expressing opinions in front of the public regarding ethnicity, religion, and race.

2.4 *Court decision of the state court of North Jakarta, number 1537/Pid.B/2016/PN JKT. UTR, on religious desecration by Basuki Tjahaja Purnama*

The State Court of North Jakarta sentenced 2 years of imprisonment to Basuki Tjahaja Purnama because he was proven to have fulfilled the elements of Article 156a of the Criminal Code. Much evidence was used as the consideration to sentence Basuki Tjahaja Purnama (Ahok) on religious desecration, including the legal facts found by the court.

However, there is still one legal fact that may be debated, which is the meaning of "desecration", which becomes one of the elements of Article 156a of the Criminal Code. The judge understands that the words of Ahok had created a negative meaning with the words "is a lie to you (*pakai dibohongi*)..." in concern of Surah Al-Maidah, Verse 51. From the full sentence of Mr. Basuki, it can also be understood that the negative meaning is not on the verse, but on people/rogues that use the verse to protect themselves. This is because, in another legal fact that was obtained by the court, Ahok has a book entitled *Merubah Indonesia* (*Changing Indonesia*), for which the essence of the legal fact is that there is a sentence that explains how people protect themselves using the verse as a "shield" to allow them to smoothly reach the peak of power.

These two legal facts explain that what was experienced by Ahok was the loss of political rights, through acts of racism that are "protected" by a verse. The ICERD, which has been ratified by Indonesia, has stated that acts of racism can eliminate the basic rights of a person, including the political rights of a person to be elected as a leader.

Thus, the words of Ahok should not be considered as blasphemy, but as hate speech, because the element of antagonizing or desecrating Islamic religious teachings is not fulfilled. The words of Ahok are directed to the people who misuse Surah Al-Maidah Verse 51, not those who concern the substance of the verse. The question is then the misuse, which according to Ahok disadvantaged his political rights as a citizen of Indonesia. The council of judges should have been able to understand the sharp contrast between blasphemy and hate speech. Regulations on blasphemy should function to protect ideas of religious nobility, benefiting and more often used by majority religious groups. Meanwhile, hate speech functions to protect minorities from campaigns of discrimination that involve violence.

3 CONCLUSION

Based on the sharp difference between regulations of blasphemy and hate speech, the words of Ahok should have been considered hate speech and not blasphemy. The words of Ahok were directed to people who misuse Surah Al-Maidah Verse 51, causing detriment to his political rights, and does not concern the substance of the verse.

4 ACKNOWLEDGMENTS

This paper is developed from the results of research by I Wayan Surya Hamijaya J, written as the Final Assignment for the Undergraduate Program, Faculty of Law, Brawijaya University, Malang, Indonesia, which is planned to become the starting point for further research.

REFERENCES

Agus Triyanta, 'Mencari Benang Merah Konstitusional Antara Kebebasan Beragama dan Penodaan Agama: Dari Konsep *Blasphemy Law* Hingga Pelarangan Ahmadiyah di Indonesia (Seeking the Constitutional Ties Between Freedom of Worship and Blasphemy: From the Blasphemy Law Concept to the Forbidding of Ahmadiyah in Indonesia)' (2013) XXXV(78) *UNISIA, Jurnal Ilmu –Ilmu Sosial* (Yogyakarta, Faculty of Law, Islam University of Indonesia).

Loso, 'Suatu Kajian Perbandingan Pengaturan Tindak Pidana Penghinaan Tuhan (*Blasphemy*) di Indonesia dan di Berbagai Negara Asing (A Comparative Study of the Regulation of the Crime of Blasphemy in Indonesia and Various Foreign Countries)', (2013) 25(2) *PENA: Jurnal Ilmu Pengetahuan dan Teknologi* (Universitas Pekalongan, Pekalongan).

Yusnita Eva, 'Perspektif dan Kajian Hukum dari Beberapa Tokoh dalam Bidang Antropologi Hukum (Legal Perspective and Studies from Several Figures in the Field of Legal Anthropology)' (2010) 22(1) *Mimbar Hukum* (Gadjah Mada University, Yogyakarta).

Article 19, *"Hate Speech" Explained* (Creative Commons Attribution-Non-Commercial-ShareLike 2.5, London, 2015)

UN Committee on the Elimination of Racial Discrimination, '*General Recommendation No. 35 on Combatting Racist Hate Speech*, 26 September 2013, CERD/C/GC/35′, para 7.

Irmansyah, Rizky Ariestandi, *Hukum, Hak Asasi Manusia, dan Demokrasi (Law, Human Rights, and Democracy)*, (Jakarta, Graha Ilmu, 2013)

Universal Declaration of Human Rights 1948

International Convention on the Elimination of All Forms of Racial Discrimination 1965

International Covenant on Civil and Political Rights 1948

International Covenant on Civil and Political Rights 1966

Optional Protocol to the International Covenant on Civil and Political Rights 1966,"1945 Constitution of the Republic of Indonesia

Law Number 39 of Year 1999 on Human Rights, Article 22.Criminal Code

Ratification Status for Indonesia (online), http://tbinternet.ohchr.org/_layouts/TreatyBodyExternal/Treaty.aspx?CountryID=80&Lang=EN. Accessed on Tuesday, February 27, 2017, 12:42 AM.

'Meaning of "freedom of speech"', http://thelawdictionary.org/freedom-of-speech/. Accessed on Friday, October 20, 2017, 10:52 PM.

'Meaning of "freedom of expression"', http://thelawdictionary.org/freedom-of-expression/. Accessed on Saturday, October 21, 2017, 3:14 PM.

https://nasional.tempo.co/read/news/2017/05/09/063873676/ahok-dihukum-dua-tahun-putusan-hakim-bulat. Accessed on Thursday, September 21, 2017, 11:06 PM.

http://www.bbc.com/indonesia/dunia-39872700. Accessed on Thursday, September 21, 2017, 11:20 PM.

https://www.cnnindonesia.com/internasional/20170510094031-106-213735/pbb-desak-ri-tinjau-ulang-hukum-yang-jerat-ahok/. Accessed on Thursday, September 21, 2017, 11:25 PM.

Culture and International Law - Juwana et al. (Eds)
© 2019 Taylor & Francis Group, London, ISBN 978-1-138-38766-9

What European human rights law can do to ensure Moslem women rights in freedom of religion in a workplace (A lesson learned from Asma Bougnaoui v Micropole SA case)

Hikmatul Ula, Ikaningtyas & Eka Rahmadini
Law Faculty, Brawijaya University, Indonesia

ABSTRACT: Some countries in Europe including Belgium, France and Britain issued a ban on the use of hijab in public and at workplace. One of the cases of concern is Asma Bougnaoui v Micropole SA in France. Micropole AS dismissed Asma Baugnaoui from her work as an IT consultant because the customer objected to the hijab worn by Bougnaoui. On the case, on March 14, 2017 the Court of Justice of the European Union (CURIA) decided that the customer's request could not be a reason for Micropole's dismissal to Bougnaoui because it was not a major of job requirement. This paper aims to analyze the use of the hijab for Muslim women in the workplace as a form of religious freedom and should be obeyed by EU countries as the consequence of the realization on the fulfillment of basic human rights in the EU. This paper also explains how the legal protections that can be granted by EU human rights law against European citizens who are subjected to discrimination in the workplace, particularly concerned with the use of hijab for Muslim women. Using statute and case approach, this paper thoroughly examines the EU's constitution, EU relationships with countries in the EU and the structure of human rights law in the EU. Basically, every country could not make discrimination policies and the law of the EU provides a mechanism for citizens to defend their right of freedom of religion and belief without discrimination in the workplace.

KEYWORDS: EU Law, Moslem Rights, Discrimination, freedom, workplace

1 INTRODUCTION

One of the basic rights of every human being is the right to be treated equally without discrimination. As stated in Article 1 of the General Declaration of Human Rights which states that: every human being is born in equality and freedom and is united in the spirit of togetherness.[1] The same thing is also regulated in the opening of the UN Charter which states that: everyone must work together to solve social, economic, political and cultural problems regardless of race, ethnicity, religion, nation, and political

1. Article 1 of the UDHR: *All human beings are born free and equal in dignity and rights. They are endowed with reason and conscience and should act towards one another in a spirit of brotherhood.*

views.[2] Thus, every country in the world must make policies or laws to uphold the value of humanity, the importance of human dignity, and must not make policies that contradict to human rights values.[3]

The equal, fair, and non-discriminatory treatment as well as freedom must be given to every line in social life, one of which is justice and freedom in worship and belief. The right to worship and belief is included in one of the fundamental rights or basic rights that cannot be reduced in any case. Also included in it is carrying out what commanded by religion, one of which is wearing hijab for Muslim women.

How unfortunate, in recent years, many countries have restricted or prohibited women from wearing clothes that relate to their religion rather than requiring women to dress in certain ways. The procedures for dress and appearance of women are even regulated in laws, policies or government regulations.

Laws or policies that limit women's opportunity to wear religious clothing are very common in Europe, where 18 of the 45 countries in the region have at least one restrictive law, policy or government regulation.[4] Even some European countries effectively prohibit certain types of religious clothing in public places.

France imposed a ban on the use of hijab which first took effect on March 15, 2004. The policy that emerged was the prohibition on the use of hijab or headscarves in public schools and educational institutions in France, which listed in the *Application de La Loi Du 15 Mars 2004; Sur Le Port Des Signes Religieux Ostensibles Dans Les Établissements D'Enseignement Publics.*[5] Later on June 22, 2009, President Sarkozy banned the use of hijabs or headscarves in public places by setting fines. This rule is listed in *LOI n ° 2010-1192: Interdisional letter la dissimulation du visage dans l'espace public* which ratified in 2010. Authorities then enacted the law by prohibiting people from covering their faces in public places, including government buildings, public transportation, and other places like restaurants and cinemas.[6] Those who do not comply with police officers' requests to reveal their faces can be subject to fines. Those who wear the headscarf will be fined 150 Euros, and those who use the veil will be fined 30,000 Euros or ordered to attend citizenship classes.

One example of a case related to discrimination of Muslim female workers in France is experienced by Asma Bougnaoui. Bougnaoui lost his job as an IT consultant at Micropole SA company, located in France in June 2009.[7] Bougnaoui had worked for Micropole SA for a year, which she later fired without any prior warning. Bougnaoui was fired after traveling to a meeting with a client at a French insurance company in Toulouse. The insurance company complained to her boss that the veil worn by Bougnaoui made him feel uncomfortable with her appearance. Then the insurance company reports to Micropole. Micropole then asks Bougnaoui to release her hijab at the next visit. Since Bougnaoui did not want to release her headscarf, Micropole finally fired Bougnaoui on the grounds that the hijab she wore would hinder the development of the company which mean the company could not interact with other clients. Bougnaoui, who did not accept the dismissal, finally submitted her case to the

---

2. Article 1 Paragraph (3) of the UN Charter: *To achieve international co-operation in solving international problems of an economic, social, cultural, or humanitarian character, and in promoting and encouraging respect for human rights and for fundamental freedoms for all without distinction as to race, sex, language, or religion;*
3. The main responsibility of a State or the government is to guarantee the fulfillment of its citizen's Human Rights. Article 30 of the UDHR: *Nothing in this Declaration may be interpreted as implying for any State, group or person any right to engage in any activity or to perform any act aimed at the destruction of any of the rights and freedoms set forth herein.*
4. *Resrtriction on Women's Religious Attire*, <http://www.pewforum.org/2016/04/05/restrictions-on-womens-religious-attire/≥, accessed on 01-12-2017 at 15.00 Western Indonesian Timezone (WIT).
5. *Application de La Loi Du 15 Mars 2004; Sur Le Port Des Signes Religieux Ostensibles Dans Les Établissements D'Enseignement Publics.*
6. *LOI n° 2010-1192: Loi interdisant la dissimulation du visage dans l'espace public.*
7. *The Guardian, Senior EU lawyer backs French woman sacked for wearing hijab*, <https://www.theguardian.com/world/2016/jul/13/european-court-backs-french-women-sacked-hijab-asma-bougnaoui≥, accessed on 02-12-2017 at 06.00 Western Indonesian Timezone (WIT).

CURIA (Court of Justice of the European Union).[8] CURIA concluded that what Micropole SA had done to Bougnaoui was a discrimination that contrary to the *Declaration des droits de l'homme et du citoyen 1789* (Declaration of Human Rights and Citizens), Labor Code, and Charter of Fundamental Rights of the European Union.[9]

In the European Union itself, there are two legal systems that run side by side, i.e. the European Union Law (EU constitution) which must be followed by EU Member States and the laws of each country in the European Union. European Union law itself is also divided into two rooms, namely the law based on the Council of Europe and the European Union itself, and CURIA which is under the European Union.

Therefore, it is necessary to look at the legality of the rules or laws made by France, because on the other hand there are European Union rules which should be a rule of law for European Union countries. This study will be more comprehensive if we look at the structure of the relationship between the laws of France and the European Union in the perspective of international law, and see the material validity of the laws prohibiting the use of headscarves for Muslim women in France in the perspective of human rights law.

2 THE LEGALITY OF PROHIBITING THE USE OF HIJAB AT WORK PLACE UNDER FRENCH LAW

France adheres to the principle of secularism.[10] The principle of secularism adopted by France is known as "*laïcité*", and the state has regarded the country as a secular Republic since the French Revolution in 1789.[11] *Laïcité* is the embodiment of the basic principles of the French Republic: *Liberté* (freedom), *Egalité* (equality), and *Fraternite* (brotherhood).[12]

The principle of secularism is stated in Article 1 and Article 2 *Loi du 9 Décembre 1905 Concernant La Séparation Des Églises Et De L'État* (Law of 9 December 1905 Regarding the Separation of Churches and Countries). Article 1 *Loi du 9 Décembre 1905 Concernant La Séparation Des Églises Et De L'État* states,

"*La République assure la liberté de conscience. Elle garantit le libre exercice des cultes sous les seules restrictions édictées ci-après dans l'intérêt de l'ordre public*".[13]

Article 2 Loi du 9 Décembre 1905 Concernant La Séparation Des Églises Et De L'État states,

"*La République ne reconnaît, ne salarie ni ne subventionne aucun culte. En conséquence, à partir du 1er janvier qui suivra la promulgation de la présente loi, seront supprimées des budgets de l'État, des départements et des communes, toutes dépenses relatives à l'exercice des cultes. Pourront toutefois être inscrites auxdits budgets les dépenses relatives à des services d'aumônerie*

8. *Curia Institution*, Source: https://curia.europa.eu/jcms/jcms/Jo2_6999/en/, accessed on 02-12-2017 at 07.50 Western Indonesian Timezone (WIT).
9. *Curia Institution – Case Law of the Court of Justce, Keyword: Judgement of the Court 14 March 2017*, Source: <http://curia.europa.eu/juris/document/document.jsf?text=&docid=188853&pageIndex=0&doclang=en&mode=req&dir=&occ=first&part=1&cid=662411≥, accessed on 02-12-2017 at 08.50 Western Indonesian Timezone (WIT).
10. The principle of secularism is an ideology that separates the rules of religion or belief and the state, but still guarantees the right to freedom of religion or belief.
11. Lina Ragep Powell, 'The Constitutionality of France's Ban on the Burqa In Light of the European Convention's Arslan V. Turkey Decision on Religious Freedom' (2013) 31(1) *Wisconsin International Law Journal*, (*Spring* 2013) p118 – 146. 29p, 122.
12. Elizabeth Adair, *Liberté, Egalité, Laïcité?: Defining French National Identity* (*Thessis*, United States of America, 2014).
13. *Article 1 LOI DU 9 DÉCEMBRE 1905 CONCERNANT LA SÉPARATION DES ÉGLISES ET DE L'ÉTAT*, Translation: The Republic guarantees freedom of conscience. This is to guarantee the implementation of religion liberately under the provisions that are subsequently imposed in the interest of public order.

et destinées à assurer le libre exercice des cultes dans les établissements publics tels que lycées, collèges, écoles, hospices, asiles et prisons. Les établissements publics du culte sont supprimés, sous réserve des dispositions énoncées à l'article 3".[14]

Under these rules, France adopted it in a constitution called *Constitution du 4 Octobre 1958* (French Constitution). This is stated in Article 1 *Constitution du 4 Octobre 1958* which states,

"*La France est une République indivisible, laïque, démocratique et sociale. Elle assure l'égalité devant la loi de tous les citoyens sans distinction d'origine, de race ou de religion. Elle respecte toutes les croyances. Son organisation est décentralisée. La loi favorise l'égal accès des femmes et des hommes aux mandats électoraux et fonctions électives, ainsi qu'aux responsabilités professionnelles et socials*".[15]

Based on the constitution, in 2004 France made a regulation regarding the prohibition on the use of religious symbols in public schools.[16] Initially, France banned headscarves in public schools on the grounds that France is a secular society, in which religious symbols in public schools and in public institutions imposed by public officials alluded to French secularism. Henceforth, the French government emphasized that this law applies to all religious symbols without exception. This law places restrictions on what a person can use in "public space", where the term public space is limited to companies regulated by the government, such as schools and institutions.[17]

Since the adoption of the law relating to the ban on headscarves in France, Muslim women in France face difficulties in several areas of life, one of which is seeking employment. As a result of this policy, several entrepreneurs in France began introducing internal regulations or implementing informal policies that prohibited the use of religious, cultural, and political symbols and ways of dressing with the aim of upholding the concept of neutrality. This foundation is the reason Micropole SA dismissed Asma Baugnaoui.

Upon this unilateral dismissal, Asma then filed an objection, and in the end, CURIA granted Asma's objection and stated that Micropole's actions could not be legally justified. If seen further, there are three legal bases used by CURIA in resolving Asma's case, i.e. the European Convention on Human Rights (ECHR), the International Covenant on Civil and Political Rights (ICCPR), and the Treaty on European Union (TEU).

Article 9 number 1 and number 2 ECHR states that every person has the right to freedom of thought, conscience and religion to change their religion or belief and perform their religion or belief in the form of worship, teaching, practices and observations made in private, in the community, or in public.[18] Whereas for freedom to manifest religion or belief, one must first submit to the law or rules that are determined in order to protect public order, the safety of

---

14. *Article 2 LOI DU 9 DÉCEMBRE 1905 CONCERNANT LA SÉPARATION DES ÉGLISES ET DE L'ÉTAT*, Translation: The Republic does not recognize, pay, or subsidize any religion. As a result, starting January 1 after the enactment of this law, the state, departments, and commune budget will suppress all costs related to cults. However, costs associated with chaplaincy services and intended to ensure free religious training in public institutions such as secondary schools, colleges, Universities, nursing homes, mental hospitals, and prisons can be included in the budget. Public religious institutions are abolished and became subject to the provisions stipulated in Article 3.
15. *Article 1 Constitution du Octobre 1958*, Translation: France will become an undivided, secular, democratic, and social Republic. It must ensure the equality of all citizens before the law, regardless of origin, race, or religion. It must respect all beliefs. This must be organized based on decentralization. The Act will promote equal access by women and men to administrative positions, elective positions, and professional and social positions.
16. *Application de La Loi du 15 Mars 2004 Sur Le Port Des Signes Religieux Ostensibles Dans Les Établissements D'Enseignement Publics.*
17. *Article 1 LOI n° 2004-228 du 15 mars 2004 encadrant, en application du principe de laïcité, le port de signes ou de tenues manifestant une appartenance religieuse dans les écoles, collèges et lycées publics.*
18. Article 9 number 1 European Convention on Human Rights states, "*Everyone has the right to freedom of thought, conscience, and religion; this right includes freedom to change his religion or belief and freedom, either alone or in community with other's and in public or private, to manifest his religion or belief, in worship, teaching, practice and observance.*"

society, and protect the rights and freedoms of others.[19] The assurance given from the enjoyment of the rights and freedoms stated in the ECHR is carried out without discrimination on any basis.[20]

The religion described in this Convention has a very broad meaning, in which the concept of religion must be interpreted as the fact that a person possesses and adheres to a belief or faith which they can manifest by wearing religious clothing in accordance with the adopted religion and imposed on public places.

Regarding religious freedom, the right to freedom of religion includes the freedom to establish a religion or belief based on its own choice and freedom, whether in a public or private place, to practice religion and belief in worship, adherence, experience and teaching. This statement is stated in Article 18 number 1 of the ICCPR. With this rule, the freedom to manifest religion or belief in worship, obedience, and practice cannot be restricted. This is in line with the one interpreted by the High Commissioner for Human Rights (hereinafter referred to as HCHR) in the General Comment number 22: The Right to freedom of thought, conscience, and religion, which states that the right to freedom to manifest religion or belief cannot be restricted to reasons other than those stated in article 18 number 3 of the ICCPR.[21]

In addition to those listed in the ECHR and ICCPR, the rules regarding the prohibition of discrimination in business are also listed in the Treaty on European Union (TEU). TEU is one of the main agreements of the European Union that forms the basis of EU law by establishing general principles of EU objectives, governance of its central institutions, as well as rules on external, foreign, and security policies.

Article 3 number 3 of TEU states that, the European Union will build an internal market that works for sustainable development in Europe, which will combat social exclusion and discrimination and promote justice, social protection, equality, and solidarity.[22] Even the European Union must also respect the diversity of culture and language, but still maintain European cultural heritage itself. Meanwhile, Article 4 number 2 of TEU explains that the European Union will respect the equality of member countries before the agreement, as well as the national identity of each member country which inherent in the structure of political and constitutional fundamentals in terms of local and regional government.[23] It is as well as respecting the important functions of member states by ensuring the territorial integrity of the country, maintaining law and order, and maintaining national security.

---

19. Article 9 number 2 of the European Convention on Human Rights states, "*Freedom to manifest one's religion or beliefs shall be subject only to such limitations as are prescribed by law and are necessary in a democratic society in the interests of public safety, for the protection of public order, health or morals, or for the protection of the rights and freedoms of others*
20. Article 14 of the European Convention on Human Rights states, "*The enjoyment off the rights and freedoms set forth in this Convention shall be secured without discrimination on any ground such as sex, race, skin color, language, religion, political or other opinion, national, or social origin, association with a national minority, property, birth or other status*".
21. General Comment No. 22: The Right to Freedom of Thought, Conscience, and Religion, <http://www.equalrightstrust.org/ertdocumentbank/general%20comment%2022.pdf≥
22. Article 3 number 3 of the Treaty on European Union states, "*The Union shall establish an internal market. It shall work for the sustainable development of Europe based on balanced economic growth and price stability, a highly competitive social market economy, aiming at full employment and social progress, and a high level of protection and improvement of the quality of the environment. It shall promote scientific and technological advance. It shall combat social exclusion and discrimination, and shall promote social justice and protection, equality between women and men, solidarity between generations and protection of the rights of the child. It shall promote economic, social, and territorial cohesion, and solidarity among Member States. It shall respect its rich cultural and linguistic diversity, and shall ensure that Europe's cultural heritage is safeguard and enhanced*".
23. Article 4 number 2 of the Treaty on European Union states, "*The Union shall respect the equality of Member States before the Treaties as well as their national identities, inherent in their fundamental structures, political and constitutional, inclusive of regional and local self-government. It shall respect their essential State function, including ensuring the territorial integrity of the State, maintaining law and order and safeguarding national security. In particular, national security remains the sole responsibility of each Member State.*"

In addition to being listed in the ECHR, ICCPR, and TEU, the rules regarding the prohibition of discrimination in business are also regulated in the Charter of the Fundamental Rights of the European Union. The rules regarding freedom of thought, conscience, and religion are listed in Article 10 number 1 of the Charter of Fundamental Rights of the European Union.[24] Whereas, the freedom to do business is stated in Article 16 where the freedom to do business in accordance with EU law and national law is recognized.[25] The Non-discrimination rules are regulated in Article 21 which states that any discrimination on the basis of nationality must be prohibited.

In Europe, there is an EU law on labor equality that requires all EU member states to prohibit employers from discrimination on the basis of religion or belief, disability, age or sexual orientation as stated in Directive 2000/78. This is in line with what is stated in article 1 of Directive 2000/78/EC which states,

"*The purpose of this Directive is to lay down a general framework for combating discrimination on the grounds of religion, or belief, disability, age or sexual orientation as regards employment and occupation, with a view to putting into effect in the Member States the principle of equal treatment*".[26]

The concept of discrimination is stated in Article 2 number 2 of Directive 2000/78/EC which states,

a. "*direct discrimination shall be taken or occur where one person is treated less favourably than another is, has been or would be treated in a comparable situation, on any of the grounds referred to in Article 1*".[27]
b. "*indirect discrimination shall be taken to occur where an apparently neutral provision, criterion or practice would put persons having a particular religion or belief, a particular disability, a particular age, or a particular sexual orientation at a particular disadvantage compared with other persons unless:*

    (i) *that provision, criterion or practice is objectively justified by a legitimate aim and the means of achieving that aim are appropriate and necessary or*
    (ii) *as regards persons with a particular disability, the employer or any person or organization to whom this Directive applies, is obliged, under national legislation, to take appropriate measures in line with the principles contained in Article 5 in order to eliminate disadvantages entailed by such provision, criterion or practice*".[28]

24. Article 10 number 1 Charter of the Fundamental Rights of The European Union states,
    1. Everyone has the right to freedom of thought, conscience and religion. This right includes freedom to change religion or belief and freedom, either alone or in community with others and in public or in private, to manifest religion or belief, in worship, teaching, practice and observance.
    The right to conscientious objection is recognized, in accordance with the national laws governing the exercise of this right.
25. Article 10 number 1 of the Charter of Fundamental Rights of The European Union states, "The freedom to conduct a business in accordance with Community law and national laws and practices is recognized."
26. Article 1 of the Directive 2000/78/EC, "The purpose of this Directive is to lay down a general framework for combating discrimination on the grounds of religion or belief, disability, age or sexual orientation as regards employment and occupation, with a view to putting into effect in the Member States the principle of equal treatment."
27. Article 2 number 2 (a) of the Directive 2000/78/EC, "direct discrimination shall be taken to occur where one person is treated less favourably than another is, has been or would be treated in a comparable situation, on any of the grounds referred to in Article 1;
28. Article 2 number 2 (b) of the Directive 2000/78/EC, "indirect discrimination shall be taken to occur where an apparently neutral provision, criterion or practice would put persons having a particular religion or belief, a particular disability, a particular age, or a particular sexual orientation at a particular disadvantage compared with other persons unless:

    (i) that provision, criterion or practice is objectively justified by a legitimate aim and the means of achieving that aim are appropriate and necessary, or as regards persons with a particular disability, the employer or any person or organisation to whom this Directive applies, is obliged, under national

Based on Article 2 number 5 Directive 2000/78/EC these instructions must be stipulated by national law, which required to protect public security, maintenance of public order, prevention of criminal violations, health protection, and for the protection of the rights and freedoms of others. The scope of Directive 2000/78/EC applies to all people, both in public and private sectors, including public agencies in relation to;

a. conditions for access to work, entrepreneurship, or employment, including selection criteria and conditions of recruitment, in any branch of activity, and at all levels of professional hierarchy, including promotion;
b. access to all types and to all levels of vocational guidance, job training, advanced vocational training, and retraining, including practical work experience
c. employment and working conditions including dismissal and payment

While the rules regarding work requirements are stated in Article 4 of Directive 2000/78/EC which states,

1. *"Notwithstanding Article 2 (1) and (2), Member States may provide that a difference of treatment which is based on a characteristic related to any of the grounds referred to in Article 1 shall not constitute discrimination where, by reason of the nature of the particular occupational activities concerned or of the context in which they are carried out, such a characteristic constitutes a genuine and determining occupational requirement, provided that the objective is legitimate and the requirement is proportionate".*[29]
2. *"Member States may maintain national legislation in force at the date of adoption of this Directive or provide for future legislation incorporating national practices existing at the date of adoption of this Directive pursuant to which, in the case of occupational activities within churches and other public or private organisations the ethos of which is based on religion or belief, a difference of treatment based on a person's religion or belief shall not constitute discrimination where, by reason of the nature of these activities or of the context in which they are carried out, a person's religion or belief constitute a genuine, legitimate and justified occupational requirement, having regard to the organisation's ethos. This difference of treatment shall be implemented taking account of Member States' constitutional provisions and principles, as well as the general principles of Community law, and should not justify discrimination on another ground".*[30]

The work requirements referred to in Article 4 of Directive 2000/78/EC which states that Member States may stipulate that differences in treatment based on the characteristics listed in Article 1 Directive 2000/78/EC do not constitute discrimination, as long as the reasons for

legislation, to take appropriate measures in line with the principles contained in Article 5 in order to eliminate disadvantages entailed by such provision, criterion or practice."

29. Article 4 number 1 of the Directive 2000/78/EC, "Notwithstanding Article 2(1) and (2), Member States may provide that a difference of treatment which is based on a characteristic related to any of the grounds referred to in Article 1 shall not constitute discrimination where, by reason of the nature of the particular occupational activities concerned or of the context in which they are carried out, such a characteristic constitutes a genuine and determining occupational requirement, provided that the objective is legitimate and the requirement is proportionate."
30. Article 4 number 2 of the Directive 2000/78/EC, "Member States may maintain national legislation in force at the date of adoption of this Directive or provide for future legislation incorporating national practices existing at the date of adoption of this Directive pursuant to which, in the case of occupational activities within churches and other public or private organisations the ethos of which is based on religion or belief, a difference of treatment based on a person's religion or belief shall not constitute discrimination where, by reason of the nature of these activities or of the context in which they are carried out, a person's religion or belief constitute a genuine, legitimate and justified occupational requirement, having regard to the organisation's ethos. This difference of treatment shall be implemented taking account of Member States' constitutional provisions and principles, as well as the general principles of Community law, and should not justify discrimination on another ground."

the nature of certain work activities are carried out by having characteristics such as determining the requirements of the original work with a legitimate and proportional purpose.

Labor law in France is listed in *Code du Travail* or the Labor Law. Legal rules on discrimination at work, in France are listed in *Article L. 1121-1, Article L. 1132-1, Article L. 1133-1, Article L. 1321-3 Code du Travail* (French Labor Law), that state,

1. "*L.1121-1: Nul ne peut apporter aux droits des personnes et aux libertés individuelles et collectives de restrictions qui ne seraient pas justifiées par la nature de la tâche à accomplir ni proportionnées au but recherché.*"[31]
2. "*L. 1132-1: Aucune personne ne peut être écartée d'une procédure de recrutement ou de l'accès à un stage ou à une période de formation en entreprise, aucun salarié ne peut être sanctionné, licencié ou faire l'objet d'une mesure discriminatoire, directe ou indirecte, telle que définie à l'article 1 de la loi n° 2008-496 du 27 mai 2008 portant diverses dispositions d'adaptation au droit communautaire dans le domaine de la lutte contre les discriminations, notamment en matière de rémunération, au sens de l'article L. 3221-3, de mesures d'intéressement ou de distribution d'actions, de formation, de reclassement, d'affectation, de qualification, de classification, de promotion professionnelle, de mutation ou de renouvellement de contrat en raison de son origine, de son sexe, de ses mœurs, de son orientation sexuelle, de son identité de genre, de son âge, de sa situation de famille ou de sa grossesse, de ses caractéristiques génétiques, de la particulière vulnérabilité résultant de sa situation économique, apparente ou connue de son auteur, de son appartenance ou de sa non- appartenance, vraie ou supposée, à une ethnie, une nation ou une prétendue race, de ses opinions politiques, de ses activités syndicales ou mutualistes, de ses convictions religieuses, de son apparence physique, de son nom de famille, de son lieu de résidence ou de sa domiciliation bancaire, ou en raison de son état de santé, de sa perte d'autonomie ou de son handicap, de sa capacité à s'exprimer dans une langue autre que le français.*"[32]
3. "*L. 1133-1: L'article L. 1132-1 ne fait pas obstacle aux différences de traitement, lorsqu'elles répondent à une exigence professionnelle essentielle et déterminante et pour autant que l'objectif soit légitime et l'exigence proportionnée.*"[33]
4. "*L. 1321-3: Le règlement intérieur ne peut contenir:1° Des dispositions contraires aux lois et règlements ainsi qu'aux stipulations des conventions et accords collectifs de travail applicables dans l'entreprise ou l'établissement; 2° Des dispositions apportant aux droits des personnes et aux libertés individuelles et collectives des restrictions qui ne seraient pas justifiées par la nature de la tâche à accomplir ni proportionnées au but recherché; 3° Des dispositions discriminant les salariés dans leur emploi ou leur travail, à capacité professionnelle égale, en raison de leur origine, de leur sexe, de leurs mœurs, de leur orientation sexuelle ou identité de genre, de leur âge, de leur situation de famille ou de leur grossesse, de leurs caractéristiques génétiques, de leur appartenance ou de leur non-appartenance, vraie ou supposée, à une ethnie, une*

31. *Article L. 1121-1 Code du Travail*, Translation: No one can limit personal or individual rights or liberties with any restrictions that are not justified by the nature of the tasks that must be carried out and are comparable to the sought objectives.
32. *Article 1132-1 Code du Travail*, Translation: No person can be excluded from recruitment procedures or from work experience or training period in a business. No employee can be penalized, dismissed, or subject to discriminatory treatment, either directly or indirectly, as defined in Article 1 of Law No. 2008-496 dated May 27, 2008 which stipulated various provisions to bring anti-discrimination laws in line with Community laws, specifically regarding remuneration, in the sense of Article L. 3221-3, incentive schemes or employees divisions, training, reclassification, assignments, qualification, classification, career promotion, initial or renewal contract transfer, sexual orientation, gender, age, family status, genetic characteristics, ethnicity groups, nationalities, races, participation in a membership, political opinion, trade union or council activities, religious beliefs, physical appearance, family name, place of residence, or because of certain health condition, dissability, and ability to speak language other than French.
33. *Article L. 1133-1 Code du Travail*, Translation: *Article L. 1132-1* will not preclude the difference in treatment arising from the original and decisive work requirements, provided that the purpose is valid and the requirements are proportional

nation ou une race, de leurs opinions politiques, de leurs activités syndicales ou mutualistes, de leurs convictions religieuses, de leur apparence physique, de leur nom de famille ou en raison de leur état de santé ou de leur handicap."[34]

This analysis on Bougnaoui case is firstly seen from the type of discrimination. As has been known, discrimination is divided into two, i.e. direct discrimination and indirect discrimination. Discrimination that occurs indirectly prohibits behavior that related to the notion of 'neutral', even though it still has a discriminatory effect on people or groups for some prohibited reasons.[35] The focus of indirect discrimination lies in the effect of behavior that will result in a person or group being treated differently.[36]

Whereas, for direct discrimination, there are many exceptions, both in general and in specific.[37] Specific exceptions in question are by showing that values or other social interests sometimes apply.[38] For example, in the teachings of Catholicism, only men can become priests, while women are not allowed. General exceptions are more flexible in their scope, but carried out at the discretion of a court or tribunal.[39] For example, employers can refuse to hire male nurses because they do not meet the requirements, or because the work is only suitable for women.

In practice, discrimination disrupts the implementation of other human rights such as the right to work, the right to freedom of expression, the right to freedom of religion, and the right to education. Considering international law and European law has prohibited the implementation of these two discrimination, States have an obligation to guarantee the right to non-discrimination by placing effective laws, policy measures, compensation, and sanctions for discrimination that occur in the private sector.[40]

In France, the legal relationship between international law and national law embraces monism. This monism understanding sees international law and national law as a system of legal unity which is binding on individuals within a country or towards countries in the international community.[41] Monism is embraced by understanding monism with the primacy of international law. This understanding of monism with the primacy of international law considers that national law comes from international law which is higher in hierarchy. Even national law is subject to international law and its binding power is based on a delegation of authority from international law.

In the French constitution, the provisions of international law are part of national law. This is because the provisions of international law are higher than national laws and directly give rise to rights and obligations for residents in the country of France. In French legal system it does not question the transformation of international treaties into national law, because

34. *Article L. 1321-3 Code du Travail*, Translation: Workplace regulations may not include: 1. Provisions that conflict with primary or secondary law or requirements set by agreement and common understanding of work practices that apply in business or establishment, 2. Provisions that impose restrictions on personal and individual and collective freedoms which is not justified by the nature of the tasks that must be done or are comparable to the objectives to be achieved, 3. Provisions that discriminate against employees in their work or their workplace, have the same professional abilities, for reasons of their origin, gender, behavior, sexual orientation, gender, age, family status, genetic characteristics, ethnicity groups, nationalities, races, participation to a membership, political opinion, trade union or work council activities, religious beliefs, physical appearance, family name, place of residence, or due to circumstances of health, or dissabilities.
35. Millie Jane Turner, *Discrimination in the workplace: Authenticity and the Genuine Occupational Qualification Exception*, (Dissertation, New Zealand, University of Otago, 2014) 5
36. Ibid, 6
37. Ibid.
38. Ibid.
39. Ibid.
40. Article 2 General Comment No. 31: The Nature of the General Legal Obligation Imposed on States Parties to the Covenant (2004)
41. Boer Mauna, *Hukum Internasional Pengertian Peranan dan Fungsi Dalam Era Dinamika Global* (Bandung, PT. Alumni, 2015) 12

according to the French legal system, the ratification of treaties and official announcements is sufficient as a condition of an international agreement being part of national law.

Thus, when viewed from the structure of law enforcement, the French prohibition on the use of headscarves in the workplace cannot be justified. This is because French law must not conflict with European Union law and international law in general. The prohibition on the use of headscarves at work is discrimination that is not permitted under European Union law. Freedom of religion without discrimination is a basic right that cannot be reduced, so that a country is not justified in making regulations that violate the principle of non-discrimination.

3 LEGAL PROTECTION OF MOSLEM WOMEN RIGHTS IN FREEDOM OF RELIGION UNDER EUROPEAN HUMAN RIGHTS LAW

The human rights mechanism in Europe was centered around two different regimes. One, supervised by the Strasbourg-based Council of Europe, dealt with democracy, human rights and the rule of law. The other, concerned with economic integration, which ultimately developed into the European Union (EU).[42] The overlapping of the two regimes in this regard is clearly manifested in two different legal institutions: the European Court of Human Rights (ECtHR), and the European Court of Justice (ECJ). The former, which belongs to the Strasbourg-based Council of Europe, has been the main safeguard for human rights protections in Europe. Its duty is to monitor the implementation of these protections under the ECHR, with a jurisdiction that primarily includes questions relating to the national laws of Council of Europe member states.

In contrast, the ECJ, which is based in Luxembourg, is not a human rights guardian *per se*. Rather, it is the highest legal institution established by the European Union, designed to uphold the process of economic integration among various member states. Its mandate is rather specific: to deal with any issues relating to the interpretation and application of the EU law, or national law that derives from the EU law, but not national law *per se*. This jurisdiction includes the fundamental freedoms and human rights within the EU law.

The overlapping functions of the two legal institutions are complicated by the fact that both involve different mechanisms and methods. There is no formal linkage between them, aside from a certain degree of overlap whereby EU members are also members of the Council of Europe. Moreover, since as mentioned earlier that the EU is not a party to the ECHR, it is not subject to scrutiny by the ECHR nor bound by its decisions. Similarly, the ECHR and its Strasbourg judicial mechanisms technically do not apply to the EU's actions, although EU members, as parties to the ECHR, have an obligation to respect the Strasbourg system in any circumstances even when applying or implementing EU law. In other words, EU member states would be subject to the EU Charter of Fundamental Rights whenever implementing EU law, and to the ECHR where they are acting on their own. However, the boundary between these two conditions is not always apparent. European law, in many cases, has been incorporated into national law, as has ECHR.[43] Thus, EU member states are subject to three distinct layers of human rights protections: the EU Charter of Fundamental Rights, the ECHR, and its own human rights law.

42. Allan Rosas, 'Fundamental Rights in the EU, with the Special Emphasis on the Case-Law of the European Court of Justice (Luxembourg)' in Gudmundur Aldredsson, Jonas Grimheden, Bertrand G. Ramcharan and Alfred Zayas (eds.), *International Human Rights Monitoring Mechanism* (Leiden, Martinus Nijhoff Publishers, 2009) 579 quoted in Patricia Waagstein, *Human Rights Protection in Europe*, FSI, Standford University

43. Jacobs Francis G, *The European Convention on Human Rights, the EU Charter of Fundamental Rights and the European Court of Justice* (European Constitution Law Network) 294 quoted in Patricia Waagstein, *Human Rights Protection in Europe*, FSI, Standford University

Table . Human rights mechanism in Europe

Council of Europe	European Union (EU)
Based on democracy, human rights and rule of law	Based on economic integration
European Convention of Human Rights and Fundamental Freedom (ECHR)	EU Charter of Fundamental Human Rights
European Court of Human Right (ECHR)	European Court of Justice (ECJ)

Based on the above provisions, matters related to fundamental rights issues can be submitted to the ECHR. The ECHR serves to ensure that countries respect the rights and guarantees set out in the European Convention on Human Rights. The ECHR is authorized to examine complaints filed by individuals or countries. An individual can submit an application to the ECHR if, according to his consideration, he personally and directly becomes a victim of violations on the rights and guarantees stipulated by the European Convention on Human Rights, by the way of using all legal solutions in the country that can provide compensation for the complained situation. If still unsatisfying, the individual has only six months after the final decision issued by the court is submitted as an application. Therefore, if there is a citizen who feels his fundamental rights are aggrieved or violated by the state (France), the person is welcome to file an objection to the ECHR as long as the national legal mechanism has been passed.

In addition, individuals can also take human rights mechanisms through the ECJ. The ECJ has the authority to interpret EU law and to ensure that it is applied in the same way in all EU countries and resolve legal disputes between the national government and EU institutions. In certain circumstances, it can be used by individuals, companies, or organizations to take action against EU institutions, if they feel their rights are violated. The ECJ is divided into two courts, i.e. the Judiciary Court and the General Court. The Judiciary Court is concerned with requests for preliminary judgments from national courts, certain actions for cancellation, and appeal. The General Courts relate to the rules of action for cancellations submitted by individuals, companies, and in some cases, the European Union government.

If an individual or company suffers a loss as a result of an action or not an act by an EU institution or its staff, the individual or company can take action against the European Union or the staff in court in one of two ways. First, indirectly through a national court that can decide to refer the case to court. Second, directly before going to the public hearing, if the decision by the European Union institution has directly or individually affected individuals or companies.

4 CONCLUSION

France as part of the European Union cannot make discriminatory rules. This is contrary to the law in the European Union which upholds the principle of equality, freedom and brotherhood. If France makes discriminatory policies or rules, the regulation is legally flawed and cannot be enforced.

The European Union has prepared a mechanism to provide legal protection for every citizen who suffer the impact of the discrimination, namely through the ECJ and ECHR. Both institutions provide guidance for individuals to submit their objections to state policies. However, local legal processes must be carried out to ensure that the state is able and willing to resolve human rights cases in its country.

REFERENCES

Adair, Elizabeth, *Liberté, Egalité, Laïcité?: Defining French National Identity (Thessis, United States of America*, 2014).

Francis G, Jacobs, G, *The European Convention on Human Rights, the EU Charter of Fundamental Rights and the European Court of Justice* (European Constitution Law Network).

Mauna, Boer, *Hukum Internasional Pengertian Peranan dan Fungsi Dalam Era Dinamika Global* (Bandung, PT. Alumni, 2015)

Powell, Lina Ragep, 'The Constitutionality of France's Ban on the Burqa In Light of the European Convention's Arslan V. Turkey Decision on Religious Freedom' (2013) 31(1) *Wisconsin International Law Journal*, (*Spring* 2013).

Rosas, Allan, 'Fundamental Rights in the EU, with the Special Emphasis on the Case-Law of the European Court of Justice (Luxembourg)' in Gudmundur Aldredsson, Jonas Grimheden, Bertrand G. Ramcharan and Alfred Zayas (eds.), *International Human Rights Monitoring Mechanism* (Leiden, Martinus Nijhoff Publishers, 2009)

Turner, Millie Jane, *Discrimination in the workplace: Authenticity and the Genuine Occupational Qualification Exception*, (Dissertation, New Zealand, University of Otago, 2014)

Waagstein, Patricia, *Human Rights Protection in Europe* (FSI, Standford University, 2009)

Universal Declaration of Human Rights

United Nation Charter

European Convention on Human Rights

Application de La Loi Du 15 Mars 2004

Sur Le Port Des Signes Religieux Ostensibles Dans Les Établissements D'Enseignement Publics

LOI DU 9 DÉCEMBRE 1905 CONCERNANT LA SÉPARATION DES ÉGLISES ET DE L'ÉTAT

Curia Institution, <https://curia.europa.eu/jcms/jcms/Jo2_6999/en/>

Curia Institution – Case Law of the Court of Justce, Keyword: Judgement of the Court 14 March 2017, <http://curia.europa.eu/juris/document/document.jsf?text=&docid=188853&pageIndex=0&doclang=en&mode=req&dir=&occ=first&part=1&cid=662411>

General Comment No. 22: The Right to Freedom of Thought, Conscience, and Religion, <http://www.equalrightstrust.org/ertdocumentbank/general%20comment%2022.pdf>

The Guardian, Senior EU lawyer backs French woman sacked for wearing hijab, <https://www.theguardian.com/world/2016/jul/13/european-court-backs-french-women-sacked-hijab-asma-bougnaoui>

Resrtriction on Women's Religious Attire, <http://www.pewforum.org/2016/04/05/restrictions-on-womens-religious-attire/>

Culture and International Law - Juwana et al. (Eds)
© 2019 Taylor & Francis Group, London, ISBN 978-1-138-38766-9

Strategy of land asset protection in small islands exchange in the concept of archipelagic state and its modeling

Imam Koeswahyono
Teaching Staff, Faculty of Law, University of Brawijaya, Malang, Indonesia
Researcher, The Centre for Agrarian Law Studies, University of Brawijaya, Malang, Indonesia

ABSTRACT: Indonesia is an archipelagic country that has more than 17,508 islands with an area of sea water of more than 75% and the length of the coastline reaching 81,000 km by taking into account the national context regarding the existing state. Thus, sustainable management of coastal and marine resources is an important part of the development strategy to improve national competitiveness. Provisions concerning the certification of small islands are also regulated in the Regulation of the Minister of Agrarian and Spatial Planning/Head of the National Land Agency Number 17 of 2016 concerning Land Management in Coastal Areas and Small Islands. Article 9 section (1) confirms that Small Islands can be granted Land Rights. Furthermore Article 11 section (1) confirms that the Granting of Land Rights in Small Islands as referred to in Article 9 is carried out in accordance with the provisions of the legislation. The issuance of Law Number 27 of 2007 concerning Management of Coastal Areas and Small Islands (Law Number 27 of 2007) as a *lex specialist* in the management system and protection of coastal and small island areas in Indonesia. The problems examined are: 1. How is the strategy to protect land assets in the outermost small islands in the concept of archipelagic state in Indonesia? 2. How is the model of land asset protection in the outermost small island in the concept of an appropriate archipelagic state in Indonesia? This paper discusses legal issues with the normative method as an effort to find models and strategies for protecting land assets in the outermost small islands in concepttualization of archipelagic state that suits the conditions of Indonesia. The answer to the first problem of the concept of archipelagic state can be made only through an integrated, sustainable whole policy of all interested parties in a coordinative institution both at the central and regional levels. The adoption of all relevant laws and regulations may include ratification of agreements between neighboring countries. Its fundamental principles are nationality, protection and recognition of local wisdom and cultural-based institutions in line with the values contained in Pantjasila. The second problem answers to the formation of cross-ministerial coordinative institutions, the involvement of all interested parties, the creation of a boundary line with one basic map and the empowerment of outermost island residents in terms of social welfare, education in archipelagic context and national resilience also as well as rights registration on the outer islands to provide legal assurance and land rights certainty.

KEYWORDS: land assets protection, archipelagic state, coastal resources, marine resources

1 INTRODUCTION

Based on the declaration in 1982 the concept of *archipelagic state*[1]was accepted and determined at the third UN marine law convention in 1982 (United Nations Convention on the Law of the Sea/UNCLOS 1982). Furthermore, this declaration was reaffirmed by Law

1. Charlotte Ku, 'The Archipelagic States Concept and Regional Stability in Southeast Asia', (1991) 23 *Case W. Res. J. Int'l L.* 463 <Available at: http://scholarlycommons.law.case.edu/jil/vol23/iss3/4> accessed on 17 August 2018.

Number 17 of 1985 concerning the ratification of the 1982 UNCLOS that Indonesia was an archipelagic state. This has brought consequences towards the integrity of Indonesia's sovereignty both at sea and on land. Indonesia is an archipelagic country that has more than 17.508[2] islands with an area of sea waters of more than 75% and the length of the coastline reaching 81,000 km when linked to the national context regarding the existing state. Thus, sustainable management of coastal and marine resources is an important part of the development strategy to improve national competitiveness.[3] In accordance with the essence of the country of Republic of Indonesia as a state of law, the development of Coastal and Small Islands Management system as part of sustainable development which has environmental insight, must be given a clear, firm and comprehensive legal basis to ensure legal assurance for the efforts to manage coastal and small islands areas. Therefore, Law Number 27 of 2007 concerning Management of Coastal Areas and Small Islands (Law Number 27 of 2007) as a *lex specialis* in management and protection of coastal areas and small islands in Indonesia was issued.

The existence of the outermost small islands of Indonesia is a property (asset) of a country/region that is prone to be recognized by other bordering countries. For this reason, a legal assurance is needed, namely by certifying the outer islands of Indonesia. The provision of Article 49 paragraph (1) of Law Number 1 of 2004 concerning National Wealth affirms that state/regional property in the form of land controlled by the Central/Regional Government must be certified on behalf of the government of the Republic of Indonesia/local government where the outermost small islands are in its administrative area. Provisions concerning the certification of small islands are also regulated in the Regulation of the Minister of Agrarian and Spatial Planning/Head of the National Land Agency Number 17 of 2016 concerning Land Management in Coastal Areas and Small Islands. Article 9 section (1) confirms that small islands can be granted Land Rights. Furthermore, Article 11 section (1) affirms that the Granting of Land Rights of Small Islands as referred to Article 9 on certification of islands is carried out in accordance with the provisions of the legislation. The purpose of island certification is to provide formal certainty or legality over those islands. Mahendra Putra's research about twelve outermost islands is prone to disputes with neighboring countries because of the absence of comprehensive regulations, the completion of several international maritime boundary agreements between Indonesia and neighboring countries, the low quality of human resources with low levels of education and the high level of poverty, deficiency of *land based spatial orientation*[4] so they are occupied and annexed by foreign countries or traded to individual citizen/corporate both openly and secretly. Ahmad Solihin's study states that there are ten disputes on border in line with Exclusive Economic Zone (EEZ) notion because it has not been resolved properly, map the sea area and immediately deposit the geographic coordinates of the baseline point to the United Nation in accordance with Article 16 (2) UNCLOS 1982.[5] By realizing the existing conditions that Indonesia is one of the big maritime countries, the state, which

2. Books that discuss marine issues such as Law of the International Sea of Mochtar Kusumaatmaja states the number of Indonesian islands is 13,000 islands, Biodiversity of Marine Sustainable Development Assets Indonesia of Rokhmin Dahuri states 17,000 and Coastal and Marine Pollution of Mukhtasor states 17,500 islands, while Melda Kamil in his book, International Law of Living Law, wrote 17,504 islands. However, based on the latest research on the latest data collection on the total number of islands and which is confirmed in the explanation of law number 6 of 1996 concerning Indonesian Waters, explains that "in the territorial waters of Indonesia there are approximately 17,508 islands which are under the sovereignty of the Republic of Indonesia", so the author uses the number of 17,508 islands as a basis for stating the total number of large and small islands in Indonesia.
3. Mukhtasor, *Pencemaran Pesisir dan Laut*, (Jakarta, Pradnya Paramita, 2007) 2.
4. Mahendra Putra Kurnia, Hukum Kewilayahan Indonesia: Dasar Lepasnya Pulau Sipadan-Ligitan dan Konsep Pengelolaan Pulau-pulau Terluar NKRI, (Malang, Bayumedia, 2008), viii and 115-12
5. Akhmad Solihin, *Politik Hukum Kelautan dan Perikanan: Isu, Permasalahan, dan Telaah Kritis Kebijakan*, (Bandung, Nuansa Aulia, 2010) 2

in this case is the government, has to make a large design of a policy on the sea (*zee beleid*) at the superstructure level of the government, National Council, High Council to the provincial level. Second, the state must form institutions and rules of the game/procedural or formal law, namely obligations and functions that are coordinative and multy-party. Third, the government, society and entrepreneurs must have the implementation.[6] In terms of land, according to Oloan Sitorus, it is necessary to raise awareness of the people residing in the outer islands and they must always be empowered in a sustainable social and economy, enhancing their intellectual capacity through education and implementing land usage policies.[7] A prominent issue is how to conduct spatial arrangement on the outer islands as can be interpreted from the provisions of Article 33 sections (1) and (2) of Law No. 26 of 2007 concerning Spatial Planning so a stewardship can be made not only land based (*grond)* but also marine-based, structurally compiled by provincial and district governments. Basically there will be problems in determining the state borders when establishing the area of a land-based area compared to the determination of the area based on waters (read: sea) because sea base by the idea of ocean policy is a huge protection policy especially for the outer islands with the same base map[8].

2 LEGAL ISUES

The problems which will be examined are:

1. How is the strategy to protect land assets in the outermost small islands in the concept of archipelagic state in Indonesia?
2. How is the model of land asset protection in the outermost small island in the concept of an appropriate archipelagic state in Indonesia?

3 THEORITICAL FRAMEWORK AND LEGAL METHOD

The theoretical framework is a rational explanation of the applied theory to solve the first and second legal problems. On the issue of authority, Ateng Syafrudin believes there is a different understanding between authority and competence.[9] Theoretically, it must be distinguished between authority (*authoriteit*) and competence (*bevoegdheid*). Authority is formal power, the power that comes from law, while competence only deals with a certain "*onderdeel*" (parts) of the authority. Competence is the scope of public legal action, the scope of government authority, not only include authority in the government's decisions making (*bestuur*), but also the authority in carrying the tasks out, and the distribution of its main authority is established in legislation. The juridical meaning of this competence is an ability provided by legislation to cause legal consequences.[10]

The definition of authority according to H.D. Stoud is:

> *"Bevoegheid wet kan worden omscrevenals het geheel van bestuurechttelijke bevoegdheden door publiekrechtelijke rechtssubjecten in het bestuursrechtelijke rechtsverkeer".*

6. Ibid, 10-11
7. Oloan Sitorus, *Konsolidasi Tanah, Tata Ruang dan Ketahanan Nasional*, (Yogyakarta, STPN Press,,2015), 55-62 and 67-75
8. Akhmad Solihin, above n 5, 10-11
9. Ateng Syafrudin, 'Menuju Penyelenggaraan Pemerintahan Negara yang Bersih dan Bertanggung Jawab' (2000) *IV Jurnal Pro Justisia*, (Bandung, Universitas Parahyangan) 22
10. Indroharto, 'Asas-Asas Umum Pemerintahan yang Baik', in Paulus Efendie Lotulung, *Himpunan Makalah Asas-Asas Umum Pemerintahan yang Baik*, (Bandung, Citra Aditya Bakti, 1994) 65

In other words it says: "competence can be explained as a whole set of rules relating to acquisition and the use of government authority by public law subjects in public law"[11]. Authorities owned by government institution in carrying out real actions *(riel)*, making/regulating or issuing decisions are always based on authority obtained from the constitution by attribution[12], delegation[13], and mandate.[14] Authority must be based on existing legal provisions, so the authority is the legal one (*legaliteit*). Thus, in issuing a decision the official (*orgaan*) is supported by the source of authority. Stroink explains the source of authority can be obtained for officials or government organs by attribution, delegation and mandate. Government (institutional) organ authority is an authority strengthened by positive law to regulate and maintain it. Without the authority, a correct and accountable juridical decision cannot be made[15].

There is a substantial difference between spatial planning that emphasizes the function (function) or designation, utilization of the area. Meanwhile, laws on land emphasize on the rights of authorization and/or ownership.[16] Registration of land rights is the main activity of land agency to run land administration known as Land Order Regulations based on Presidential Decision No.7 of 1979. Land administration activity is one of the five scopes of government activities in the land sector, namely: (a) land resources inventory, (b) land rights and legal administration, (c) land arrangement, empowerment and control, (d) land development, (e) land taxation.[17] The constitutional policy based on Article 33 section (3) of the 1945 Constitution of the Republic of Indonesia concerning the outer islands management and assets/ property of the state is the right of state's control. As a legal concept (*rechtconcepten*), the right of state's control includes the power to regulate (*regelendaad*), administer (*bestuursdaad*), manage (*beheersdaad*) and supervise (*toezichthoudensdaad*).[18]

Problems (*problemen*) often arise in policy making (*beleid*).[19] According to Mitroff and Linstone the problem is the gap between what we want and what we can fulfill in which contains ethical and aesthetic gaps. The conclusion is there will be different policy problems resulting in a policy-making process caused by differences in values, perspectives, tools to understand the facts, rationality determination and truth, as well as the discourses.[20] The second problem is regarding the method of legal protection to secure the outermost points of the state not only in terms of security and order, but also in terms of the improvement of their human resource quality and welfare.

---

11. Stout HD, de Betekenissen van de Wet, in Irfan Fachruddin, *Pengawasan Peradilan Administrasi terhadap Tindakan Pemerintah* (Bandung, Alumni, 2004) 4
12. J.G. Brouwer states that attribute is authority given to a government institution or state organization by an independent legislature. This is an original authority, which is not accepted from the former authority. Legislature creates an independent authority and it is not an expansion of former authority then given to the competence organization.
13. Delegation is an authority diverted from one government institution's to another so he (the delegator) can verify the authority in his name.
14. Mandate does not contain authority transfer but the mandate giver gives it to other (mandatary) for decision making or action taking in his name.
15. F.A.M. Stroink in Abdul Rasyid Thalib, *Wewenang Mahkamah Konstitusi dan Aplikasinya dalam Sistem Ketatanegaraan Republik Indonesia*, (Bandung, Citra Aditya Bakti, 2006) 219
16. The Establishment of National Spatial Management Coordination Team by Presidential Decree No.57 1989 and the main task is preparing the integrated National Strategy for Developing Spatial through area approach listed in 1980 Rules of Spatial Planning No.13 concerning the road before the announcement of 1992 Rules of Spatial Planning No. 24 (as changed into the 2007 Rules of Spatial Planning No. 26).
17. Sofi Puspasari dan Sutaryono, *Integrasi Agraria-Pertanahan dan Tata Ruang Menyatukan Status Tanah dan Fungsi Ruang*, (Yogyakarta, STPN Press, 2017,) 11-12
18. See Yance Arizona, *Konstitusionalisme Agraria*, (Yogyakarta, STPN Press, 1st Ed, 2015) 213-214
19. Problem is bad fact in life of individuals, organizations, institutions, or countries which is hard to be appointed and known if it does not have the whole understanding as explained by Hariadi Kartodihardjo., *Analisis Kebijakan: Pengelolaan Sumberdaya Alam: Diskursus-Politik-Aktor-Jaringan* (Sayogya Institute, RMI, P4W-IPB, PSA-IPB, Firdaus Pressindo, Bogor,2017) 156
20. Ibid, 158-159

Phillipus Mandiri Hadjon's view of legal protection for people as a preventive and repressive government action is as follows. Preventive legal protection aims to prevent the disputes, which direct government's actions so they can be more careful in decision-making based on discretion, and repressive protection aims to resolve disputes, including handling them in the judiciary.[21] Legal protection in the context of State Administrative Law is a description of legal function operation in realizing legal objectives that are justice, expediency and legal assurance. Legal protection is one that is given to legal subjects according to the rule of law, both in preventive and repressive (coercive) form, written and unwritten, in order to enforce the rule of law.

The registration of land rights issue, Article 1 section 1 of Government Regulation No.24 of 1997 states that land registration is a series of activities carried out by the government continuously, sustainably and regularly, which includes collection, processing, bookkeeping, presentation, and physical and juridical data maintenance, in the form of maps and lists about the land areas and flat units, including issuance of the proof of rights that covers the right of ownership of the land areas and flat units as well as other rights imposed upon the property. Land registration is physical data registration related to the land itself as its location, boundaries, building area or other objects on it. Juridical data rights concerns with what rights they have, who own the rights, and with the existence of other parties. Its continuous feature means that every reduction, change, or addition must be re-registered which will make certificate changing as the change of land's owner due to land rights transfer.

Object of land registration is regulated in the provisions of Article 9 section (1) of Government Regulation No. 24 of 1997 as follows:

1. Land areas owned that are entitled to rights of ownership, cultivation, and of building and using the property
2. Rights of land management
3. Waqf land
4. Ownership rights for flats
5. Mortgage rights
6. State land

The principle adopted for land registration is governed by Article 2 of Government Regulation No. 24 of 1997 as follows:

1. Simple
   The meaning is that the substance is easy to read or understand by all Indonesian citizens and the procedure does not need to pass through a convoluted bureaucracy. It only needs to go through the land registration procedure.
2. Secure
   Security means the certificate holder will feel secure if they pass through the land registration procedure carefully and accurately.
3. Achievable
   Is about people's financial ability, particularly it must ensure to not incriminate the economically weak parties. The point is to not let them be constrained by land registration because they do not have the resources to pay the cost.
4. Up-to-date
   Every data on land registration must be the latest, which shows the real situation at the present time. Any physical changes or objects on it or juridical matters on the land must have data (there is always an update).
5. Transparent
   Documents or data, both physical and juridical, are open and may be known by the public. This principle aims to know and overcome the deviated or hidden things.

21. Phillipus Mandiri Hadjon, *Perlindungan Hukum Bagi Rakyat Indonesia (*Surabaya, PT. Bina Ilmu, 1987) 29.

4 DISCUSSION

4.1 *The strategy to protect land assets in the outermost small islands in the concept of archipelagic state in Indonesia*

Considered from the philosophical point of view, there has been a debate about archipelagic concepts based on Garrett Hardin's (1968) thesis in *Tragedy of Commons* in which said that natural resources that are owned collectively will result in their destruction, because every individual accessing these resources will act rationally by maximizing his individual interests, but ignoring the impact of his greed on the community life. Elinor Ostrom (1990) criticized Hardin for underestimating human capacity to work hand-in-hand in institutions with the purpose of managing resources. Thus, there is a change of approach from rational choice to the strengthening of institutional aspects (neo-institutionalist). This idea of neo-institutionalist ignores inequality of power relations which actually results in inequality of access.[22] In his argument against Ostrom's, Arun Agrawal (2003) believed that if institution is a product of a conscious decision *(beleid)* of an individual and groups it is not unlikely that institutional choice of the ruling group is a design created to accommodate its interests.

In critical agrarian perspective, according to Benjamin White and Jun Borras of the Hague Institute of Social Studies, an approach developed by Mohamad Shohibuddin refers to the concept of Article 1 Section (2), (4) to (6) of Law No.5 of 1960 is an interdisciplinary and comparative approach in regarding agrarian sources, their technical and social relations, as well as their governance that can manifest in various policies or social dynamics, equipped with strong and continuous concern on the principles of social justice, economic equality, ecological sustainability.[23]

On the other hand, the dynamic and practical concept of archipelago as one whole unit provides broad definition on agrarian including coastal sea and outer islands, covering four processes: a. control and ownership of agrarian resources, b. usage and utilization of agrarian resources, c. division of labor and production relations in it, d. creation of surplus from all three processes along with the dynamics of their accumulation, expansion and distribution.[24] Seen from the character of the rules for managing coastal areas and smaller islands in Article 3.4 of Law No.27 of 2007, the challenges that are presented are, first, orientation based on conservation, rehabilitation and reclamation. The second deals with the promotion of people's need but but special position is placed on the business (Article 14 (Section 1), 16 (Section 2), 17, 18, 19). The third challenge is the management and implementation, harmony and synergy between the central and local governments, which leaves the choice of decentralization. The four protections of human rights and gender are not mentioned, but they recognize the Customary Law Community. Fifth, good governance is related to participation, transparency and accountability. The sixth is about relationships between people and WP3K with the concept of rights and permits that leads to fundamental mistake of equating the two. The seventh is about relations between the state and the WP3K in which wealth is controlled by the state and is preserved and utilized for the greater prosperity of all people.[25]

According to the perspective of national security [26] there are four interests in the principle of an archipelagic state. These are 1) neighboring countries, such as ASEAN and Australia, 2) countries with an interest in fisheries and the installation of communication cables, 3)

22. Agung Wardana, 'Neoliberalisasi Kawasan Perairan Teluk Benoa: Sebuah catatan Kritis Atas Praksis Perlawanan di Bali' (2017, XIX) 35 *Journal of Social Transformation Issue*, 57-62
23. Mohamad Shohibuddin, *Perspektif Agraria Kritis: Teori, Kebijakan, dan Kajian Empiris* (Yogyakarta, STPN Press, KPA, PSA-IPB, Sajogya Institute, 2018) 5-6
24. Ibid.,14
25. Maria SW Sumardjono et all., *Pengaturan Sumber Daya Alam di Indonesia, Antara yang tersurat dan Tersirat: Kajian KritisUndang-undang Terkait Penataan Ruang dan Sumber Daya Alam*, First Edition (Yogyakarta, Faculty of Law Gadjah Mada University and Gadjah Mada University Press, 2011) 183-200
26. about concept of guaranteeing the existence of the nation and the prerequisites for national development to achieve national goals, see Oloan Sitorus, above n 7, 16-17

maritime countries with an interest in sea traffic, 4) other major maritime countries such as: the USA, China, Japan, and Russia who has an interest in military strategy.[27] Based on the aforementioned study results, the strategy to protect agrarian assets in the context of archipelagic states can only be done through control or supervision by the state, through safety or security guarantees, and through law enforcement. In realizing this goal, an integrated and sustainable policy is required from all interested parties in central and local coordinative institutions. The calibration of all relevant legislation tools[28] including ratification of agreement between neighboring countries. The fundamental principle of mainstreaming the concept of archipelagic state is nationality, protection and recognition of local wisdom, institutions based on culture that is in line with the values of Pantjasila.

4.2 *The model of land asset protection in the outermost small island in the concept of an appropriate archipelagic state in Indonesia*

Model is defined as a concept that refers to a prototype or an initial idea about the procedure of protecting assets on the outer islands which is in line with the concept of archipelagic state. The model offered is referring to Aristotle's concept of *eudaimonia* as elaborated in his book *Nomoi*, through the enforcement of *nomothetic* justice. This implies that within physical materials lies a dynamic potential that is Indonesian human resources manifesting in Indonesian nation itself and agrarian resources. The form that will become the energy or *actus* (*ousia*) through a form of the Republic of Indonesia as an independent state. In other words, based on legal theory, legal facts will materialize only if the process of turning into a potential material is completed with *forma* or form. A potential material will not turn into *actus* if it does not have a form (*forma*).[29] Visual depiction of this concept is as follows:

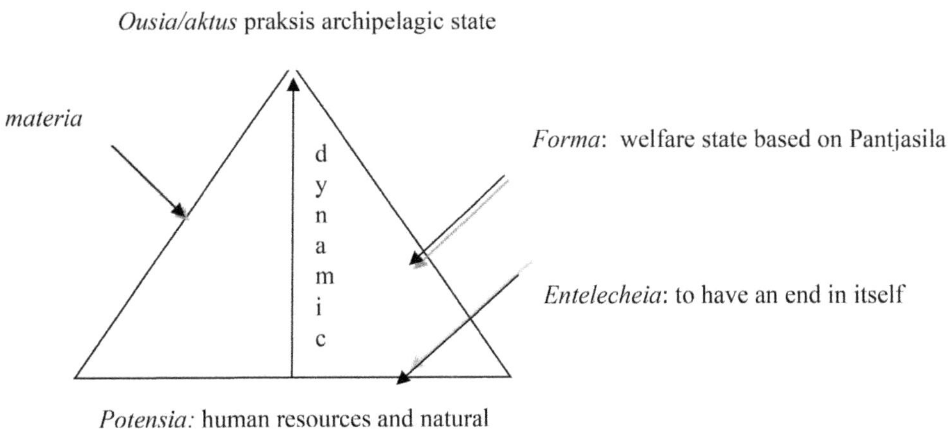

In line with Aristotle's concept, the modeling for the establishment of cross-ministerial coordinative institutions under the coordination of the Maritime Coordinating Minister, the involvement of all the interested parties, the making of a boundary with a single primary map

27. Akhmad Solihin above n 5, 100
28. Yance Arizona, *Konstitusionalisme Agraria* (Yogyakarta, 1st Ed, STPN Press, 2015) 329 compared with Ahmad Nashih Luthfi (Editor), *Asas-asas Keagrariaan Merunut Kembali Riwayat Kelembagaan Agraria, Dasar Keilmuan Agraria, Asas Hubungan Keagrariaan di Indonesia*, (STPN Press, 1st Ed, Yogyakarta, 2014) 380-387.
29. Budiono Kusumohamidjojo, *Legal Theory: The Dilemma between Law and Power* (Bandung, Yrama Widya, 2016) 9-10, materia can be in the form of tangible praxis as the state's right over the outer islands and state's authority to label lands as state's property, and the state owns the right of its management, ownership, and usage. Theoretical and practical debates over land rights are discussed by Jan Michiel Otto and Andre Hoekema (Editors), *Fair Land Governance How to Legalize Land Rights for Rural Development* (Leiden University Press, The Netherland, 2012) 7-13

created by the Geospatial Information Agency (BIG) and the empowerment of the residents of the outer islands from the social welfare aspect, education in the context of archipelagic insight and national resilience, as well as registration of land rights on the outer islands to provide legal certainty and rights of lands. In terms of the legalization of land rights, there are two paradigms that can be adopted. Referring to the notion of Jan Michiel Otto and Andre Hoekema[30], the first paradigm is that full private property installations that can be found across global and domestic policies of many nations, is not in accordance with the rights of ownership if small-scale land in rural areas. The second paradigm is that to leave customary law undisturbed which is based on the system of communal ownership (*beschikkingsrecht*) will result in the property is often taken over by the state or private sector. It is inarguable that each paradigm has advantages and disadvantages, with the latter becoming the choice of the author.[31] The rationality of choice is based on its conformity with Pantjasila, especially the second, third and fifth precepts. In addition, the second paradigm is in line with the fact that communal rights has existed first before the state was formed, and this means that the community has inherent rights with which the Indigenous people are attached to prior informed consent.[32]

5 CONCLUSION

Based on the discussion of the results of the study, the following conclusions can be formulated:

1. Strategy to protect land assets in the outermost and small islands in the concept of archipelagic state in Indonesia can be done through an integrated and sustainable policy from the interested authorities in central and regional coordinative institutions based on critical agrarian perspective. Harmonization of all relevant legislation tools includes ratification of agreement between neighboring countries. The basic principles of mainstreaming the concept of archipelagic state are nationality, protection and recognition of local wisdom, institutions based on culture that is in line with the values of Pantjasila.
2. Model of land asset protection in the outermost small island in the concept of an appropriate archipelagic state in Indonesia can be achieved through the enforcement of *nomothetic* justice with a distinction of material in which lies a dynamic potential, i.e. Indonesian human resources manifested in Indonesian people and the nation's agrarian resources. The *forma* that will become the *energeia* or *actus* (*ousia*) through a form is the Republic of Indonesia as a self-sufficing legal state. In short, based on legal theory, the legal facts will only materialize if the process of becoming a potential material finds its completion in a *forma*. The potential material will not become *actus* if it does not have a *forma*.

6 RECOMMENDATIONS

The government is expected to immediately set up a policy for the adoption of laws and regulations related to management of marine and outer islands so as to avoid overlapping authorities, policies and regulation regarding the matter. In addition, there is a need to provide adequate budget for establishing cross-department/ministry institutions to coordinate policies on defense and security of the outer islands to prevent and counteract invasion of foreign countries or corporations that violate the state's sovereignty and law.

30. Jan Michiel Otto and Andre Hoekema,
31. Ibid., 7
32. The right to be asked for approval by outside parties, including the state, if they are to use some of the natural resources in the *lebensraum* of the Indigenous people who have the *beschikkingsrecht*

REFERENCES

Arizona, Yance, *Konstitusionalisme Agraria*, (Yogyakarta, STPN Press, 1st Ed, 2015)

Fachruddin, Irfan, *Pengawasan Peradilan Administrasi terhadap Tindakan Pemerintah*, (Alumni, Bandung 2004)

Indroharto, 'Asas-Asas Umum Pemerintahan yang Baik', dalam Paulus Efendie Lotulung, *Himpunan Makalah Asas-Asas Umum Pemerintahan yang Baik*, (Citra Aditya Bakti, Bandung 1994)

Kartodihardjo, Hariadi, *Analisis Kebijakan: Pengelolaan Sumberdaya Alam: Diskursus-Politik-Aktor-Jaringan* (Bogor, Sayogya Institute, RMI, P4W-IPB, PSA-IPB, Firdaus Pressindo, 2017)

Kurnia, Mahendra Putra, *Hukum Kewilayahan Indonesia: Dasar Lepasnya Pulau Sipadan-Ligitan dan Konsep Pengelolaan Pulau-pulau Terluar NKRI* (Malang, Bayumedia, 2008)

Kusumohamidjojo, Budiono, *Teori Hukum: Dilema Antara Hukum dan Kekuasaan* (Bandung, Yrama Widya, 2016)

Luthfi, Ahmad Nashih (Ed), *Asas-asas Keagrariaan Merunut Kembali Riwayat Kelembagaan Agraria, Dasar Keilmuan Agraria, Asas Hubungan Keagrariaan di Indonesia*, (STPN Press, 1st Ed, Yogyakarta, 2014)

Otto, Jan Michiel and Andre Hoekema (Editors), *Fair Land Governance How to Legalise Land Rights for Rural Development*, (The Netherland, Leiden University Press, 2012)

Puspasari, Sofi and Sutaryono, *Integrasi Agraria-Pertanahan dan Tata Ruang Menyatukan Status Tanah dan Fungsi Ruang*, (Yogyakarta, STPN Press, 2017)

Shohibuddin, Mohamad., *Perspektif Agraria Kritis: Teori, Kebijakan, dan Kajian Empiris*, (Yogyakarta, STPN Press,KPA, PSA-IPB, Sajogya Institute, 2018)

Sitorus, Oloan, *Konsolidasi Tanah, Tata Ruang dan Ketahanan Nasional* (Yogyakarta, STPN Press, 2015).

Solihin, Akhmad, *Politik Hukum Kelautan dan Perikanan: Isu, Permasalahan, dan Telaah Kritis Kebijakan* (Bandung, Nuansa Aulia, 2010).

Sumardjono, Maria SW et. Al., *Pengaturan Sumber Daya Alam di Indonesia, Antara yang tersurat dan Tersirat: Kajian KritisUndang-undang Terkait Penataan Ruang dan Sumber Daya Alam*, (Yogyakarta, Fakultas Hukum Universitas Gadjah Mada dan Gadjah Mada University Press, 1st Ed, 2011)

Syafrudin, Ateng, 'Menuju Penyelenggaraan Pemerintahan Negara yang Bersih dan Bertanggung Jawab' (2000) IV *Jurnal Pro Justisia*, (Bandung, Universitas Parahyangan,).

Thalib, Abdul Rasyid, *Wewenang Mahkamah Konstitusi dan Aplikasinya Dalam Sistem Ketatanegaraan Republik Indonesia*, (Bandung, Citra Aditya Bakti, 2006)

Wardana, Agung, 'Neoliberalisasi Kawasan Perairan Teluk Benoa: Sebuah catatan Kritis Atas Praksis Perlawanan di Bali' (2017/XIX) 35 *Jurnal Transformasi Sosial Wacana.*

Charlotte Ku, 'The Archipelagic States Concept and Regional Stability in Southeast Asia', (1991) 23 CaseW.Res.J.Int'lL, 463 <Available at: http://scholarlycommons.law.case.edu/jil/vol23/iss3/4> accessed 17 August 2018

Constitution of the Republic of Indonesia Year on 1945

Law No. 5 of 1960 on Basic Rules of Agrarian Principles

UNCLOS 1982

Law No.22 of 2001 on Oil and Gas

Law No.1 of 2004 on National Wealth

Law No.26 of 2007 on Spatial Planning

Law No.32 of 2009 on Environmental Protection and Management

Law No.6 of 2014 on Villages

Law No.23 of 2014 on Local Government

Law No.32 of 2014 on Marine

Law No.30 of 2014 on Governmental Administration

Law No.32 of 2014 on Marine

Government Regulation No.40 of 1996 on HGU, HGB dan Hak Pakai

Government Regulation No.24 of 1997 on Land Registry

Government Regulation No.16 of 2004 on Land Management

Government Regulation No.24 of 1997 on Land Registry

Government Regulation No.11 of 2010 on Control and Utilization of Derelic/Abandoned Land

Government Regulation No.21 of 2010 on the Protection of Maritime Environment

Culture and International Law - Juwana et al. (Eds)
© 2019 Taylor & Francis Group, London, ISBN 978-1-138-38766-9

A socially just land reform model

Iwan Permadi
Associate Professor, Faculty of Law, Universitas Brawijaya. Malang, East Java, Indonesia

ABSTRACT: The enforcement of Law Number 5 of 1960 on Basic Agrarian Law (UUPA) has caused fundamental change in land-related law in Indonesia, including in land reform. The land reform program involves the land redistribution exceeding maximum boundary. Article 10 Paragraph (1) of UUPA suggests that agricultural lands must be cultivated by the owners. However, most agricultural lands are managed by giant capitalists while farmers work as their labours. This research is aimed to analyse impeding factors to put the land distribution into practice in Indonesia and to set a socially just agricultural land redistribution in the state. Four impeding factors in land redistribution are identified: (a) there is no clear implementation of regulation over excessiveness of lands; (b) there is no clear regulation over absentee land; (c) the government has difficulty formulating the form of socially just land reform and land redistribution; (d) the government has an issue over providing appropriate compensation to those whose lands are affected by land reform and redistribution; and (e) lack of land area as object of agrarian reform. Therefore, the government should formulate a proper model to realise a socially just land redistribution through government policy regarding land release to farmers who do not own any land by means of sufficient state's budget (APBN) directly paid to the farmers. The lands should not be given in freehold title status to avoid any further transfer to third parties, and the proper notarial deed given should be in the form of 'the right to use' or 'the right to cultivate'. In addition, the role of stakeholders should be taken into account and it is important to develop agriculture and food technology.

KEYWORDS: land reform, land redistribution, farmer, justice

1 INTRODUCTION

Land reform concept is closely linked to the history of the development of agrarian law of a state. In Indonesia, especially in East Java Island, in the archipelagic kingdom era, all lands sited within the area of the kingdom were owned by the King, while the people only had rights to use the lands. In other words, peasants positioned in the lowest social status were not acknowledged as legal subjects who were supposed to have rights to own and control the lands. They were acknowledged as labours of *sikep* and they were only allowed to stay on the lands owned by *sikep*.[1]

This issue surely led to ambiguity over land ownership in Indonesia, in which the majority of lands were owned by landlords, while the farmers or peasants were only entitled to cultivate the lands, for they did not have enough money to buy the lands. This situation brought to land administration-related issue, in contrary to the fact that the farmers were supposed to own the lands, not the rich.

1. Erman Rajaguguk, *Hukum Agraria: Pola PenguasaanTanah dan Kebutuhan Hidup*, (Jakarta, Chandra Pratama, 1995) 9.

After the independence of the state, social transformation regarding agrarian administration to provide justice to the society free from any intimidation serves as the main characteristic that has to be realised.[2] With the concept of justice, the government should immediately act to fairly provide welfare for the society through land reform.

Land issue in Indonesia is commonly found in villages where most ownership of lands has been transferred to the rich living far from the lands. To anticipate this issue, there has been a regulation made by the government as enacted in Act Number 5 of 1960 on Basic Agrarian Law (hereinafter UUPA). The following are Articles that serve as the basis of land reform in Indonesia:

Article 7 of UUPA:

"Excessive ownership of lands is not allowed, or it will violate common interests."

Article 10 of UUPA:

a. Every individual and legal entity that holds rights to agricultural land is principally obligated to actively cultivate the land and no extortion is allowed.
b. The implementation of the provision in Paragraph 1 will be further regulated in the Legislation.
c. Exception of the principle as enacted in Paragraph 1 will be regulated in Legislation.

Article 17 of UUPA:

As referred to the provision in Article 7, to reach the objective as intended in Article 2 Paragraph 3, there should be restriction of land ownership with the right mentioned in Article 16 by a family or a legal entity.

All the four articles serve as the basis of transformation of land structure commonly known as land reform or agrarian reform, meaning that agricultural lands must be actively cultivated by the owners.

Furthermore, the second regulation is related to the prohibition of absentee land, in which the agricultural land owned must be within the area of the district of the owner. To realise the provision, the government has issued Government Regulation Number 224 of 1961 on Land Division and Provision of Compensation, amended to Government Regulation Number 41 of 1964. Principally, the Regulation 224 of 1961 bans the absentee-based agricultural land ownership. The term 'absentee' is derived from the word 'absent' meaning 'not present'. This provision has banned the ownership of land by the person not living in the district where the land is located.

Another issue is related to measures the government should take to tackle social imbalance of land ownership. Land reform can be proposed, in which this concept deals with the structural change of agrarian control to a better one for villagers, especially for farmers. This system changes the status of land owned by landlords to the land that should be owned by the poor farmers. The term land reform in narrower scope can be defined as land redistribution.

The essence of land ownership by poor farmers requires policies from the government, one of which is known as land reform or land redistribution. Since the impeding factors seem inevitable, implementation model of just land reform is required for social justice for more even distribution of land which extends to villages.

2 RESEARCH PROBLEMS

Based on the aforementioned issues, the problems studied are presented as follows:

1. What impeding factors are encountered by the government regarding land reform in Indonesia?
2. What type of land reform model provides social justice?

2. Achmad Sodiki, Lembaga Pengkajian Pertanahan Jakarta, Pusat Studi Hukum Agraria, Universitas Brawijaya Malang. no year given.

3 RESEARCH METHODS

3.1 *Research type*

This research is categorised into normative legal research in which legal materials obtained are to be studied and will discuss the model of land reform or land redistribution that leads to social justice.

It is known that normative research in legal studies holds the characteristic seen as applied and prescriptive science. As a prescriptive science, the law studies the objective of law, values of justice, validity of rule of law, legal concept, and norms of law.[3]

3.2 *Research approach method*

This research employed statute and conceptual approaches. Peter Mahmud Marzuki argues that in academic research, the researcher is required to find the *ratio legis* and the basis of ontology of the origin of the related Act to take the philosophical content of the related Act.[4]

3.3 *Source of legal materials*

There are two sources from which the legal materials come to obtain the substance of the studied materials in this legal research:

a. Primary legal materials involve Acts, court ruling, and several official documents that contain legal provisions. What is included in the primary legal materials involves the following:

   1) Act Number 5 of 1960 on UUPA
   2) Decision of People's Consultative Assembly Number IX/MPR/2001 on Agrarian Reform and Natural Resources Management.
   3) Decision of National Land Agency Number 25 of 2002 on Guideline of Implementation of affirmation of proposal of land as a state's asset to the management of land reform.

b. Secondary legal materials involve literature, journals, papers, magazines of legal sciences, encyclopaedia, and experts' theoretical and practical thoughts related with the regulation of land reform and land redistribution, all of which were employed by considering the scientific content.

4 LAND REFORM CONCEPT IN INDONESIA

Literally, the term land reform is derived from English in which land means the ground and reform means change or transformation; land reform could be defined as the transformation of land structure. However, land reform is not only restricted to the structure of land tenure, but it also involves the reconstruction of relationship between human and land to increase the agricultural products, and this reconstruction is fundamental.[5]

The definition of land reform in Indonesia is divided as follows:

1. In a wider scope of meaning, land reform is also known as agrarian reform/five programs (*Panca Program*) that consists of:

   a. Revision of Agrarian Law

3. Philipus M Hadjon dan Tatiek Sri Djatmiati, *Argumentasi Hukum* (Yogyakarta, Gajah Mada University Press, 2005)
4. Peter Mahmud Marzuki, *Penelitian Hukum* (Jakarta, Penerbit Kencana Prenada Media Group, 2006) 93-94.
5. Hustiati, *Agraria Reform di Philipina dan Perbandingannya dengan Landreform di Indonesia* (Bandung, Mandar Maju, 1990) 31-32.

b. Abrogation of foreign rights and colonial conception on land
c. Gradually putting feudalism to an end.
d. Reconstruction regarding the ownership, land tenure, and legal relationships related with land tenure.
e. Planning, Providing, allowing the use of, and using land, water, and wealth contained within and well-planned utilisation as in accordance with the capacity and capability.

2. In narrower scope, land reform means the reconstruction regarding the ownership and land tenure and legal relationship related to land tenure.

The definition of land reform, according to UUPA, is based on the wider scope of meaning, and the formulation of definition of land reform is equal to that of Food And Agriculture Organisation (FAO), concerning related programs and acts aimed to eliminate economic and social barriers in land tenure.

The term land reform in Indonesia first introduced by President Soekarno is part of the concept in agrarian reform which is enacted in Act Number 5 of 1960 on UUPA that is the basic regulation of land reform in Indonesia. This Act holds fundamentals and basic provisions. Since this only serves as the basic principle, it only involves the highlights of the agrarian reform.

According to the provision of UUPA, the legislation regulating land reform was issued, which is aimed to manage land tenure and improve income and evenly distribute the welfare of the society especially for poor farmers. It is also aimed to give wider access to the people to develop their potential to achieve prosperity as part of national development and to bring society to welfare and justice according to *Pancasila*. In other words, land reform is a medium that helps improve the livelihood of farmers, and, therefore, the objectives achieved involve economic, socio-political, and mental-psychological objectives.[6]

There are two different views in understanding the land reform. On one hand, the UUPA is the leading part of the provision of land reform. On the other hand, some argue that the land reform provision is only in the Act Number 50 of 1960 (LN 1960-117) and in Government Regulation Number 224 of 1961 (LN 1961-280) on Establishment of Agricultural Land Area and Implementation of Land Distribution and Compensation Provision.

A.P. Parlindungan argues that UUPA is the head of land reform in Indonesia, and this view is reflected in the explanation of UUPA. Therefore, there is wider understanding than what is enacted in Act Number 56/60 and Government Regulation Number 224 of 1961. The wider understanding involves the following:

a. Abrogation of dualism of law (*adat* law and western law).
b. Legal certainty enforcement.
c. Acknowledgement of *adat* law as the basis of national agrarian law
d. Social function
e. Prohibition of latifundium and land monopoly
f. Equity between male and female societies.
g. Ceiling and minimum limit
h. Land surplus
i. Absentee land

It can be concluded that land reform should not be seen as an activity of distributing excessive land to poor farmers or labours who have no land and as a feeling of pity or active effort of the people to bring back the rights to the people more deserving.

Although it is true that the reform enacted in UUPA is based on Article 33 Paragraph (3) of the 1945 Constitution of the Republic of Indonesia, the substance is not as extensive as that of Article 33 Paragraph (3) of the 1945 Constitution that involves land, water, and all wealth contained within. UUPA is still restricted to land reform in terms of its ownership structure,

6. Sulaeman, 'Redistribusi Tanah Objek Landreform dan Permasalahannnya', (1993) *Jurnal Ilmiah Badan Pertanahan*, 1-2.

land tenure, and the utilisation and use, provision and planning. Other elements such as water, mineral, or mining are overlooked by land reform.

Another definition of land reform is a concept and strategy regarding the change in agrarian tenure structure into a better one for the village societies especially for farmers. The essence of land reform is that farmers need to have lands for their life through the efforts performed by the government and societies to reconstruct the forms of land tenure and utilisation of agrarian resources and social relationship for the sake of the welfare and prosperity of societies.

However, agrarian reform and land reform are commonly seen as equal despite the fact that it is mostly agreed that agrarian reform brings wider meaning than land reform.[7]

Prof. Boedi Harsono explains land reform with its narrower and wider definition. UUPA is not only restricted to agrarian law reform, but it also embraces the provisions regarding basic agrarian issues and their resolution. The resolution of the issues was included in the program of agrarian revolution called Agrarian Reform Indonesia[8] during the issuance of UUPA.

Agrarian Reform in Indonesia embraces 5 programs (*Panca Program*):

a. Agrarian law reform through unification of law that holds national concept and through the provision of legal certainty;
b. Abrogation of foreign rights and colonial concession on land;
c. Gradually putting feudalism to an end;
d. Reform of land ownership and land tenure and all legal relationship related to land tenure to bring the welfare and justice to societies;
e. Planning the provision and the allocation for the land, water, and natural resources contained within and well-organised utilisation as in line with the capacity and capability.

The forth program deserves more to be called land reform. All listed as parts of land reform program is commonly called land reform as well. This brings to the definition of land reform divided into two as the wider and narrower definition of the term.

Land reform and agrarian reform provide different meaning coming from several experts, but it can be concluded that land reform is a part of agrarian reform. The main aim of land reform is land redistribution to improve the structure of land tenure and ownership in societies, so that the economic development can be achieved and justice can be provided.

5 IMPEDING FACTORS ENCOUNTERED BY THE GOVERNMENT TO REALISE LAND REFORM IN INDONESIA

Since the issuance of UUPA of 1960, the land reform program, basic programs as mandated in UUPA, has not been optimally performed. In terms of the narrower understanding and definition of land reform such as re-managing and re-planning the structure of land ownership in Indonesia from landlord to poor farmers who have no lands, land reform has presented some issues for the government. Moreover, the government still fails to formulate which program is supposed to be included in agrarian reform and which one is in land reform, and which one is in land redistribution for better condition in 2000 and in the following years.

The issues encountered by the government seem to be caused by the following:

5.1 *The government has not firmly implemented regulations regarding excessive land*

The government has not firmly implemented the regulations of excessive lands as regulated in Article 7 of UUPA which regulates the prohibition of having lands that exceed the limit set.

7. I Nyoman Budi Jaya. *Tinjauan Yuridis tentang Redistribusi Tanah Pertanian dalam Rangka Pelaksanaan Landreform*, (Yogyakarta, Liberty, 1989) 9.
8. Boedi Harsono, *Hukum Agraria Indonesia (Sejarah Pembentukan UUPA, Isi dan Pelaksanaanya)*, (Jakarta, Djambatan, 2003) 23.

The maximum limit is marked by the following two elements: Right to own and Land tenure involving all types of rights of land

The regulation of the implementation is provided in Act Number 56 Prp 1960 on maximum limit of agricultural land ownership and tenure. Article 1 of Act Number 56 Prp. 1960 has determined four categories of land:

Table 1. Land categories according to maximum limit in land ownership and tenure

Category	TS	TS	KM
Non-densely populated area	15H	2OH	<50
Less densely populated area	10H	12 H	50-250
Fairly densely populated area	7,5H	9H	251-400
Very densely populated area	5H	6H	>400

Breaking the law written in the Article causes the party involved to report the excessive land owned to the government, followed by the takeover of land by the government and compensation given to the previous landowner.

According to the Provision of Government Regulation 224 of 1961, the land whose amount exceeds the maximum limit will be taken by the government. This takeover is intended for justice in which the remaining amount will be redistributed to working farmers, while this practice is only performed on agricultural lands.

The enforcement of law regarding the difficulty faced in land reform implementation for such an excessive land ownership comes from the paradigm of an individual having rights to a land. This also means there is unwillingness of the landowners whose lands are shared and redistributed and this practice may bring to more difficulty in terms of deciding the amount of fund needed to be given for compensation.

5.2 *The government has not firmly implemented regulations of absentee lands*

Absentee land is defined as prohibition of having a land outside the area of the district where a person lives. This does not apply for the members of Indonesian Armed Forces and civil servants because they sometimes need to move to different cities to work. Absentee land is caused by the following:[9]

a. The landowner has left the place in which the land is located for two consecutive years. When the person involved moves out with the permit from village head or local authority, the land left is considered as absentee land a year after two consecutive years. When the land is left without any permission, the land left is taken as absentee land after the two consecutive years.
b. Land as inheritance received by an heir living within the district outside the area where the land is located and not located in the border of the district.
c. The land is determined as absentee land after a year since the heritance is received and as long as the landowner does not do any legal act such as transferring the rights to land to another party or as long as there is no effort of changing domicile to where the agricultural land is located.
d. The purchase of agricultural land by a person not living in the district area where the land is located.
e. Based on the Guideline Number III of 1963 by the Minister of Agriculture and Agrarian, "moving to a district where the land is located" must be defined as those carrying out household and day-to-day activities.

9. Elfira Permatasari, Habib Adjie, and Hardianto Djanggih, 'Perlindungan Hukum Kepemilikan Tanah *Absentee* yang Diperoleh Akibat Pewarisan' (2018) 14(1) VARIA JUSTICIA, 7.

f. The obligation of owners of absentee land in Article 3 (1) of Government Regulation Number 224 of 1961 and the Regulation of Minister of Home Affairs Number 15 of 1974 is to propose a new right in accordance with the allocation and utilisation of land.

The issue faced by the government regarding the effort to solve absentee land, where the land will be under the control of the government when the rule of absentee land is infringed, involves the unavailability of exact data concerning the location and how large the area of land that is categorised into absentee land is.

1. The government seems to face issues to formulate the form of just land reform and land redistribution.
   In this case, there is no political will from the government to formulate specific policy regulating land reform. The policy implemented by the government is only the extension of Agrarian National Operation Project (PRONA) to provide free of charge freehold title to landowners who have not registered their lands to National Land Agency. Therefore, the government has decided to start a specific program regarding the redistribution of land and land reform that is socially just for better economic development.
2. The government faces issues regarding the provision of compensation of appropriate amount to the landowners whose lands are affected by the land reform and land redistribution program.
   The government has difficulty providing compensation of appropriate amount to landowners whose lands are affected by land reform and redistribution program. The government should do immediate action to take the rest of lands excessively owned by individuals with appropriate compensation. The lands bought by the government are to be further distributed to those who have no lands. This brings to an issue where the government will deal much with the state budget in the future.
3. Lack of land area as object of agrarian reform
   Since the 60s there has been an issue in which the land source has been limited in its availability, while this availability can serve as the object for agrarian reform and the majority came from the state's land such as conversable forest area and abandoned land. In the implementation, the functional conversion of forest area into non-forest category requires some specific requirement which can involve lengthy process. In addition, the National Land Agency also faces difficulty determining whether a land is categorised into abandoned land because the land right holder could do certain effort to avoid any potential of abandoned land status.[10]

The land of agrarian reform, as arranged in Government Regulations Draft (RPP), is derived from eight types of categories of the land status as follows:[11]

a. State's land obtained from abandoned land
b. Land of Forest Area of Conversion Production
c. State's land coming from other sources:

   1. State's land
   2. State's land formerly owned under western right;
   3. State's land obtained from no man's land and agricultural land;
   4. State's land obtained from those under self-governance
   5. State's land obtained from mineral, coal, and geothermal mining land.
   6. State's land obtained from release of forest areas;
   7. State's land obtained from exchange or any civil legal act regarding agrarian reform; and
   8. Land given by right holder to the state for agrarian reform.

10. Ministry of National Development Planning, *White Paper: Kebijakan Pengelolaan Pertanahan Nasional* (Badan Perencanaan Pembangunan Nasional (Bappenas), 2013) 20-21.
11. Article 41 Paragraph (1) and (2) of Bill of the Republic of Indonesia Number... Year... on Land

6 SOCIALLY JUST LAND REFORM MODEL

The study on the land reform must be seen from what has been done by the government. Nationally, land reform program has not been effectively implemented when it is seen from the population left with no lands. Land reform program by the government is elaborated as follows:

a. An area of 2,166 hectares held in 8 regencies in 2007.
b. An area of 3,325 hectares held in 11 regencies in 2008.
c. An area of 2,556 hectares held in 7 regencies in 2009.
d. An area of 1,983 hectares held in 9 regencies in 2010.
e. An area of 2,163 hectares held in 7 regencies in 2011.
f. An area of 712 hectares held in 4 regencies in 2012
g. An area of 1,012 hectares held in 7 regencies in 2013.
h. An area of 1,211 hectares held in 10 regencies in 2014.

From the land redistribution program having been performed by the government, it is seen that it is difficult to redistribute lands to those who have no lands or need to have lands, for the population having no lands has not been specifically figured out; the number of people who excessively have lands and the number of absentee lands are also unknown.

To figure out more the appropriate formulation of land reform, the comparison of the implementation of land reform in several countries such as China, the Philippines, Thailand, and Brazil is presented in the Table (see Table 2).

From the Table above, it can be concluded that political will from the government and its funding and all stakeholders involved play an important role in land redistribution program. Therefore, further study on those two elements is required in the Indonesian context.

Table 2. Comparison of implementation of land reform in several countries[12]

		Remarks		
No.	State	Time of Implementation	Land Reform	Impact
1.	China	First period, 5 years (1947 – 1952) Second Period, 3 years (1981 – 1983)	25% of village area in average	Growth rate in Agriculture per capita comprising 1.3% Poverty rate from 33% down to 4% of village population
2.	Philippines	14 years (1972 –1986) 8 years (1986-2004)	41 thousand hectares 5.54 million hectares of land	Housing development integrated with land redistribution Implementation of technology for farming activities developed by IRRI for paddy field agriculture
3.	Thailand	22 years (1975 – 1997)	6.22 hectares of land	Physical development such as irrigation network, water pond, farming activities, and facilities and infrastructure for irrigation, structural change of land tenure/land ownership along the period of 1987—1991, the decrease of forest damage along the period of 1961-1993 and economic indicator of success of land reform can be analysed.
4.	Brazil	8 years (2002 – 2010)	85.8 million hectares	Resolving endless conflict between giant agribusiness group and family agriculture, helping to give social compensation and wealth distribution.

12. Ibid, 19.

1. Political will from the government and its funding
   Political will from the government including its funding should be performed comprehensively. The research model offered is integrated with government's policy. The government should have prioritised land reform and redistribution for the strategic program of the government. Furthermore, the program should have been planned in state budget. The spare fund is needed recalling that in the structure of the land ownership, most lands are only owned by the rich, including the rich farmers that cannot be said as farmers as they never directly get in touch with the farming lands.
   The fund will be spent by the government on buying lands from the rich to be given to the people having no lands or peasants. This condition is in line with the substance and intention of UUPA suggesting that landowners are supposed to cultivate their own lands. The release of the land must come with requirement in which the landowners whose lands are given by the governments are not allowed to sell their land under any circumstances, but they can still inherit the lands to their heirs. Therefore, they only have rights to use, not to own the lands, for the lands given by the government are owned by the state with no notarial deed. Freehold title is not given, as there is concern that they will sell the lands when they have financial difficulties, leading them to the absence of lands to work on.
   Land reform or land redistribution program is expected to bring justice for the whole societies especially for farmers to take their lands back.
2. Maximising the role of stakeholders involved
   Increasing the role of stakeholders is essential to support land redistribution program in Indonesia. According to Howlet and Ramesh, making policy requires at least five categories of stakeholder mentioned as follows:

   a. Elected officials involving executives and legislatives;
   b. Appointed officials, as bureaucrats usually serving as the main key and central figure in the process required to make a policy or sub-system of policy;
   c. Interest group. Governments and politicians often need information given by interest group for more effective policy making or to attack their opponents;
   d. Research organisation consists of universities, groups of experts, and policy consultants; and
   e. Mass media serves as network of crucial relationship between the state and its people as a medium of socialisation and communication which reports the issues combined with the role of reporter and active analysis as advocacy of solution.[13]
      As an effort to optimise the role of stakeholders in land redistribution, agrarian reform of farming communities in Cipari is taken as an example. This case started with the conflict between PT. JA Wattie and farming community as victims of Ciseru and Cipari (Ketan Banci). In 1999, Ketan Banci called for the release of 45 ha of land of PT. Jiawati and 11.5 ha was released. This momentum has brought back the spirit of the farmers to move on to calling for the land under the control of PT. RSA.
      Table 3 below shows actors involved in the implementation of policy of land redistribution in Cipari. Each actor has his own characteristic. From actor mapping, perception and strategy played can explain standing position and its involvement in the implementation of the policy of land redistribution in Cipari.[14]
      From the case of Cipari, strategy of how to deal with the formulation of policy and how to take measures for more effective land redistribution can be learned.

3. Utilising land redistribution to accommodate the development of agriculture and food technology

13. Sutaryono, Ari Satya Dwipraja, and Dede Novi Maulana, 'Persepsi Aktor Lokal dalam Implementasi Kebijakan Redistribusi Tanah', in *Penataan dan Pengelolaan Pertanahan yang Mensejahterakan Masyarakat (Strategic research result of PPPM-STPN)* (National Library of RI: In-press catalogue (KDT), 2014) 108.
14. Ibid, 103

Table 3. Map of actors and strategy played[15]

Actor	Group	Perception	Orientation	Strategy
People who benefit	Farmer	Right (as if one is the owner)	Returning right	Struggle
	Non-farmer	Right (equal right)	As a subject of receiver	Flexible
Former right holder	Institutional	Right (equal right)	Gaining the right back	Maintaining right
Local government	Village government	Having authority	Gaining political and financial advantages	Facilitating
	Supra-village government	Part of government's program	Supporting success	struggle
Activists/ public figures	Individual	Positive condition of a struggle	Gaining right (of justice)	Struggle
	NGO	Positive condition of a struggle	Gaining right (of justice)	Struggle and organisation of farmers

Land redistribution and utilisation need to be managed. Indonesia has formulated two processes regarding the development of agriculture and food technology:[16]

a. Stage I, in 5 year period
   Identification of detailed potential, measuring the area and location of the source of TORA, and implementation of land redistribution, settling land disputes and conflicts at national-scale are the main priority at this stage. The development of agriculture and food technology has to start immediately, which could work with related government agencies and private sectors. For example, Philippines has managed to redistribute land with the area of 5.96 million Ha; Thailand managed to do so for the land with the area of 6.22 million Ha, and Brazil—after settling land disputes and conflicts at large scale—has done redistribution of 85.8 million Ha of land.
b. Stage II, in 5 year period
   The implementation of land redistribution is in line with the development of agriculture and food technology. The development of interconnection among small farmers and small-medium enterprises (SMEs) and big enterprises is performed by focusing more on exporting at international level.

7 CONCLUSION AND RECOMMENDATIONS

7.1 *Conclusion*

1. Government has encountered several issues in performing land redistribution program: such as: (a) the government has not firmly implemented the regulations regulating excessive ownership of land; (b) the government has not firmly implemented the regulation of absentee land; (c) the government has difficulty formulating the form of socially just land reform and land redistribution; (d) the government has difficulty determining the compensation of appropriate amount to landowners whose lands are affected by land redistribution and land reform; and (e) there is limited area of land as object of agrarian reform.
2. The appropriate model of land redistribution and land reform that are socially just can be performed through the government policy that holds political will to redistribute lands by the government to the farmers who have no lands under the right to use or to cultivate, in which the redistribution should be well planned in the state budget. In addition, the role of

15. Ibid, 119
16. Ministry of National Development Planning, above n 10, 31.

stakeholders should be taken into account: (a) the people who benefit; (b) former right holder: (c) local government; and (d) activists/public figures. In the utilisation of land redistribution, it is expected that farmers be well accommodated for the development of agriculture and food technology.

7.2 *Recommendations*

It is recommended that the government through National Land Agency establish a unit of officials fully in charge of realising land reform program for those who have no lands.

REFERENCES

Hadjon, Philipus M and Tatiek Sri Djatmiati. Argumentasi Hukum (Yogyakarta, Gajah Mada University Press, 2005)

Harsono, Boedi. *Hukum Agraria Indonesia (Sejarah Pembentukan UUPA, Isi dan Pelaksanaanya)* (Jakarta, Djambatan, 2003)

Hustiati. *Agraria Reform di Philipina dan Perbandingannya dengan Landreform di Indonesia* (Bandung: Mandar Maju, 1990)

Jaya, I Nyoman Budi. *Tinjauan Yuridis tentang Redistribusi Tanah Pertanian dalam Rangka Pelaksanaan Landreform* (Yogyakarta, Liberty, 1989)

Kementerian Perencanaan Pembangunan Nasional. *White Paper: Kebijakan Pengelolaan Pertanahan Nasional* (Badan Perencanaan Pembangunan Nasional (Bappenas), 2013)

Marzuki, Peter Mahmud. *Penelitian Hukum.* (Jakarta, Penerbit Kencana Prenada Media Group, 2006.

Permatasari, Elfira, Habib Adjie, and Hardianto Djanggih. 'Perlindungan Hukum Kepemilikan Tanah *Absentee* yang Diperoleh Akibat Pewarisan' (2018) 14(1) Varia Justicia.

Rajaguguk, Erman. *Hukum Agraria: Pola PenguasaanTanah dan Kebutuhan Hidup* (Jakarta, Chandra Pratama, 1995).

Rancangan Undang-Undang Republik Indonesia Nomor .... Tahun ... tentang Pertanahan

Sodiki, Achmad. Lembaga Pengkajian Pertanahan Jakarta, Pusat Studi Hukum Agraria, Universitas Brawijaya Malang.

Sulaeman. 'Redistribusi Tanah Objek Landreform dan Permasalahannnya' (1993) *Jurnal Ilmiah Badan Pertanahan*

Sutaryono, Ari Satya Dwipraja, and Dede Novi Maulana. *Persepsi Aktor Lokal dalam Implementasi Kebijakan Redistribusi Tanah. In Penataan dan Pengelolaan Pertanahan yang Mensejahterakan Masyarakat (Hasil Penelitian Strategis PPPM-STPN)* (Perpustakaan Nasional RI: Katalog Dalam terbitan (KDT), 2014)

Culture and International Law - Juwana et al. (Eds)
© 2019 Taylor & Francis Group, London, ISBN 978-1-138-38766-9

Urgency for civic education for inner Baduy tribe to raise democratic awareness in regional head elections in Lebak Banten

Jazim Hamidi
Associate Professor, Faculty of Law, University of Brawijaya, Malang, Indonesia

Airin Liemanto
Researcher, Civilization Studies Center, University of Brawijaya, Malang, Indonesia

Dwi Yono
PhD Candidate, Faculty of Law, University of Brawijaya, Malang, Indonesia

ABSTRACT: Political education is one of the democratic instruments that should receive attention to support national and regional elections. This research aims to: (1) find the legal reasoning of the instrument of political education that is often overlooked when it is linked to raising democratic awareness; (2) present models of political education to the Baduy Tangtu tribe (indigenous people) regarding the regional head election held in Lebak Banten. The theories involved are election and civic education, while the research method used is empirical-juridical with a socio-juridical approach. The research result obtained involves: (1) formulating legal argumentation over the essence of political education required in the election of a regional head; (2) developing specific models of political education for the indigenous people of Baduy Tangtu in Lebak, Banten.

KEYWORDS: Political education, indigenous people (Baduy Tangtu tribe), democratic awareness

1 INTRODUCTION

The general election is a characteristic of a democracy, either in national general elections or local general elections.[1] In Indonesia, a local general election is uncertain where it was once in the regime of a general election and once it was excluded from the regime. In the latter, the governor, vice governor, regent, vice regent, mayor and vice mayor elections, after the decision by the Indonesian Constitutional Court[2], are categorized as regional head elections (hereinafter *pilkada*).[3] The essence of the election is to give a chance for the people to take part in the election by voting for their future

1. Makinda, S. (1996). Democracy and multiparty politics in Africa. *The Journal of Modern African Studies, 34* (4), 557.
2. Constitutional Court Decision Number 97/PUU-XI/2013.
3. Law Number 10 Year 2016 on Second Amendment over the Law Number 1 Year 2015 on Establishment of Government Regulations in Lieu of Law Number 1 Year 2014 on Election of Governors, Mayors and Regents becoming Law.

leaders on their own, which is significant for their state future.[4] A general election must follow the principle of a direct, general, liberal[5], but confidential election, and an honest and fair election through the practice of democracy, and all these principles apply for isolated tribes, *adat*-law people, and indigenous people.

Lawrence M. Friedmann suggests that law and justice in the legal framework as a system is determined by three main factors: legal substance (acts), structure (law enforcers), and culture (people's awareness)[6], in addition to other supporting factors such as infrastructure, the role of experts, the role of higher education, and legal services provided by legal experts, including Soerjono Soekanto, Sunaryati Hartono, and Bagir Manan.

Jenedjri M. Gaffar argues that a general election aims to bring democracy to a state. The substance of a general election is to give room to the voice of the people in terms of establishing the House of Representatives and government as state instruments. A general election is also part of the practice of democracy, where people vote for their representatives in the parliament and in the governmental structure.[7] Some states hold the election just to elect the representatives at parliament level, while some others may hold a general election to elect state officials.

Indonesia is one of the states in the world that has practiced democracy and democratization.[8] One of the characteristics of a democratic state is that the state holds general elections. Therefore, a good general election is indicated by the political involvement of the people. This serves as the benchmark of the execution of democratic practice in a state.[9] Indonesia had held general elections from 1955 to 2014 to elect legislative members, presidents, and vice presidents.[10]

The success of a general election relies on the participation of the Indonesian people as a whole, including tribes, and traditional communities such as the Baduy. Literally, participation is defined as being an involvement of the people. In a political context, this refers to social participation in several political processes. One form of political participation is to use suffrage in a general election. The involvement of Baduy communities in a democracy (general election) rises and falls depending on the situation, the need, and the consideration of *adat* society.[11]

There was a general election in the 1980s in which the Baduy people were involved during the New Order, in which the election of the president and the vice president took place in outer Baduy. Another presidential election also took place in 2004. An election for governor and vice governor took place in 2008, an election for parliament members or legislators in 2009, an election for regent and vice regent of Lebak in 2013, an election for parliament members or legislators in 2014, and an election for regent and vice regent in 2018. The elections took place in outer Baduy, and in 2019 the Baduy community will be involved in a general election to elect the president, vice president, the House of Representatives (DPR), Regional Representatives (DPD), and Regional House of Representatives (DPRD).[12]

The term 'general election' is actually not commonly used among Baduy people. This term was brought into the Baduy community to encourage them to elect the state representatives.

---

4. Ibid, Article 59.
5. Article 2 of Law Number 1 Year 2015 on Establishment of Government Regulations in Lieu of Law Number 1 Year 2014 on Election of Governors, Mayors and Regents becoming Law.
6. Friedman, F.M. (1969). Legal culture and social development. *Law and Society Review, 4*(1), 29–44.
7. Gaffar, J.M. (2013). *Politik hukum pemilu* (2nd ed.). Jakarta, Indonesia: Konstitusi Press.
8. Nowadays, one of the political issues that has been growing is democracy and democratization. Even though many people took a skeptical point of view regarding the idea of democracy, the democratization movement grew massively in Indonesia, which was reflected in the Reformation Era of 1998. See Asshiddiqie, J. (2005). *Hukum tata negara dan pilar-pilar demokrasi* (p. 56). Jakarta, Indonesia: Konstitusi Press.
9. Rosema, M. (2007). Low turnout: Threat to democracy or blessing in disguise? Consequences of citizens' varying tendencies to vote. *Electoral Studies, 26*(3), 612–623.
10. Badan, P.P. (2014). *Laporan hasil pengawasan pemilu anggota DPR, DPD dan DPRD tahun*. Jakarta, Indonesia: Bawaslu Republik Indonesia. 7; 10.
11. Saputra, F.T. (2017). Partisipasi politik masyarakat baduy dalam pemilihan umum (studi fenomenologi partisipasi politik masyarakat Baduy pada pemilu. Proceeding of Magister of Communication Study, 1.
12. Ibid.

The people of Baduy see a general election as something of no importance, for they think it will not significantly influence their life, especially their economy; their need depends on what nature can give. However, such a condition in Baduy will not stop the general election from being held in the community. The general election should be an instrument to improve welfare because the election is not only restricted to democratic issues, but it also harnesses the power of the state for the sake of the welfare of its people.[13]

When the general election is part of the need of societies, according to the concept of Maslow, it is triggered by: (1) physiological needs such as clothing and food; (2) safety needs; (3) social needs; (4) self-esteem needs; (5) self-actualization needs.[14]

The native people of Baduy strongly cling to *adat* values handed down from their ancestors. In politics and a general election, this brings its own meaning. In the context of Maslow, Baduy people still meet their physiological needs, safety needs, and social needs in their restricted area, but they are not yet in the scope of self-actualization in the social and political frame and modernism. They (especially the people of inner Baduy) have not been able to participate in the hustle and bustle of the general election and *pilkada*. The people of inner Baduy are not directly involved, but only indirectly support what has been decided by the state in the national election or by regional governments in the regional head election.[15] Unlike what is found in inner Baduy, outer Baduy people have actively participated in the election.

Legal consequences emerge, such as whether the Baduy tribe has actively participated in the election of the regional head, whether civic education has become an urgent need for the Baduy tribe to hold a general election or *pilkada* in Lebak Banten, and what model of civic education is suitable for the Baduy tribe as an indigenous community regarding the election of the regional head in Lebak Banten.

An empirical legal research method is employed in this research with a socio-juridical approach, followed by descriptive analysis. The analytical descriptive method is not restricted to analytical elaboration, but also integrates analytical elaboration and critical analysis. Not only does it clarify but it also organizes. The descriptive analytical method is principally aimed at finding a theory, not testing a theory. This method is mainly focused on observation and natural circumstances.[16] Moh Nazir argues that the survey method involves investigation carried out to obtain facts, seen from the existing signs that lead to factual information on social, economic, or political institutions of a group or a region.[17]

Data was obtained from dialogic interviews conducted informally with three informants who knew best about the latest condition of the Baduy tribe involved. One of the informants was called Jaro Saija, the local ruler replacing Jaro Dainah. Jaro Saija, in the system of national government and administratively, is more commonly known as a Village Head of Kanekes, an extension of the government, while in the *adat* way, Jaro Saija is under *Puun*. The second source of information was Ayah Mursid, a representative of Jaro Sami (Jaro Ciebeo). Ayah Mursid acts as a spokesperson for the outer community, expected to know more about how the Baduy people develop. The third source was Asep Kurnia, an observer of the Baduy people.

However, limited time was the common issue in this research. Therefore, the observation was performed optimally by involving highly reliable, competent informants. Interestingly, modern devices were not allowed in the Baduy community during the research, according to the *adat* rule of Baduy.

13. Interview with Ayah Mursid on 9 July 2018 at 10.00 WIB in official residence of Jaro Saija (Government of Jaro/Village Head of Kanekes).
14. Maslow, A.H. (1954). *Motivation and personality*. New York, NY: Harper.
15. Interview with Ayah Mursid on 9 July 2018 at 10.00 WIB in official residence of Jaro Saija (Government of Jaro/Village Head of Kanekes).
16. Suteki & Taufani, G. (2018). *Metodologi penelitian hukum (filsafat, teori dan praktik)* (pp. 133–134). Depok, Indonesia: PT RajaGrapindo Persada.
17. Nizar, M. (1998). *Metode penelitian*. Bogor, Indonesia: Ghalia Indonesia.

The theory used in this research was the general election theory in general, and specifically civic education, as the medium of analysis. It is anticipated that there is a solution for the Baduy people, especially for the inner Baduy, because the civic education-related issues need more attention and they require socialization of the people of both inner and outer Baduy for the sake of democratization in the future.

2 DISCUSSION

2.1 *Portrayal of Baduy and its participation in Pilkada*

It is not known since when the name of Baduy was first used among the people who live in the mountainous area of Kendeng. Some argue that the name was derived from an ethnography report made by the Dutch. Hoevell (1845), Jacob and Meijer (1891), and Pleyte (1909) suggest that the people living in the area are *badoe'I, badoei*, and *badowei*. In a dichotomy, they introduced inner Baduy as Baduy Tangtu and outer Baduy as Baduy Panamping.[18]

The origin of Baduy is closely related to the Kingdom of Banten Girang, a Hindu kingdom located on the tip of Java Island. A lot of people believe that the Baduy tribe is a tribe that escaped when the Kingdom of Banten Girang was conquered by Sultan Hasanudin of Banten.[19] Geographically, according to R. Cecep Eka Permana, the Baduy people are located at 6°27′27"–6°30′ North latitude and 108°3′9"–106°4′55" East longitude. Baduy people live in the western part of Java Island in a mountainous area of Kendeng (900 mdpl)[20] with an area of 5,101.85 hectares, including 3,000 hectares of old forest (*leuwung kolot*) or sacred protected forest.[21] Administratively, the people of Baduy live in Kenakes village, in the District of Leuwidamar, the Regency of Lebak, the Province of Banten.[22]

Baduy people believe that they are the first community to exist in the world, or at least in the area of Sunda. Therefore, they cling to the belief of *Sunda Wiwitan* (the first Sundanese). This belief is based on the cosmology (perspective to nature) that their area (especially *sasaka pusaka dunia/sasaka domas* in the protected forest) is the center of the world or a sacred place (*mandala*). To keep the sacredness, *adat* law (*pikukuh*) was made.[23]

The Baduy people still exist and have managed to maintain their existence and culture for hundreds of years through the generations. St Laksono argues that a culture can be defined as being an effort by the people to conform with their surroundings. Each culture has its own color, characteristic, and structure, and so does its law.[24] Democracy, law, politics, house architecture, housing patterns, art, agricultural patterns, and mutual cooperation are some of the forms of culture maintained in the Baduy community.

In terms of democracy, the Baduy people have much in common with wider society. They have a governmental system that has existed for hundreds of years and is still well maintained. In terms of the general election, the Baduy people have their own political system, applied either in their local elections or in general elections:[25]

18. Sukirno (2018). *Politik hukum pengakuan hak ulayat* (1st ed., p. 232). Jakarta, Indonesia: Prenadamedia Group.
19. Interview with Ayah Mursid on 22 August 2013 at 11.45 and 13.45–13.55 WIB in Kampung Cijahe Desa Kebon Cau, Kecamatan Bojongmanik, *Kabupaten* Lebak.
20. Fathurokhman, F. (2016). *Hukum pidana adat baduy dan pembaharuan hukum pidana* (p. 79). Depok, Indonesia: INCA Publishing.
21. Iskandar, J. (2012). *Ekologi perladangan orang baduy pengelolaan hutan berbasis adat secara berkelanjutan* (p. 19). Bandung, Indonesia: PT. Alumni.
22. Sam, S. et al. (1986). *Tata kehidupan masyarakat baduy di Propinsi Jawa Bara*t (p. 7). Jakarta, Indonesia: Ministry of Education and Culture Project Inventory and Regional Culture Documentation.
23. Senoaji, G. (2010). Masyarakat Baduy, hutan, dan lingkungan. *Jurnal Manusia dan Lingkungan, 17*(2), 120–121.
24. Utomo, L. (2016). *Hukum adat* (p. 129). Jakarta, Indonesia: RajaGrafindo Persada.
25. Interview with Asep Kurnia, on 8 July 2018 at 19.00 WIB conducted in his home in Cisimet village, the District of Lewidamar. See also Hamidi, J., Ulum, B. & Novitasary, R. (2015). *Demokrasi lokal nurut masyarakat Baduy* (p. 103). Malang, Indonesia: Nuswantara.

a. Leader election within inner Baduy tribe
   The people of Baduy have their own rules in terms of electing a leader (*Puun*). The main principle for a person to be a leader of Baduy people is that he does not propose himself to be one, but candidates must satisfy some criteria and requirements, which are then determined based on inner feeling (*wangsit*).
b. Leader election for people outside Baduy tribe (central executives/regional, central legislators/regional)
   In general elections, to elect a president, vice president, regional head, and central legislative members of a region, the Baduy people cling to their own life philosophy closely attached to *Pikukuh karuhun* (words of ancestors), such as *Lunang* (*milu kanu menang*) or 'follow the winner', meaning that people must accept and obey the winning candidate as a leader with open arms, and *ngasuh ratu/raja, ngayak menak*, which means guiding the leader, being submissive to the state.

Mathematically, the general election in the Baduy community does not have a huge impact on voting because there is a lack of population and participation compared to that of the people of outer Baduy. This is because most of the people of inner Baduy still strongly hold to the words of ancestors, emphasizing that they are required to live together to build a state, but there are no words stating that they should stand on one side. When this is broken, there is a probability that the origin of the cosmos of Baduy people will be overturned.[26]

In reality, a general election in the Baduy community is directly performed without any intervention or force from other parties, as they have freedom to choose their leaders. The profiles of candidates are not brought to Baduy in a conventional way, which usually involves a political campaign that involves large groups of people. However, interestingly, the approach is done door to door, which allows the Baduy people to get to know the candidates personally as they meet each other face to face. They discuss with each other the programs planned, and listen and appreciate all the expectations of the Baduy people. The Baduy people should always remember the candidates' names, numbers, and the parties of the candidates the people intend to elect. Such an election is certainly different from the election of *Puun*. In the election of *Puun*, one candidate cannot be elected based on one vote for each voter, but should be represented by the trusted *adat* figure (*noken* system).[27]

A general election is not compulsory for the Baduy people, but it is held to give respect to the rule of the state. The Baduy people strongly hold to *adat* law and a simple life devoted to meeting their primary needs. However, the general election has had a special impact in which there is apprehensiveness that a conflict may be sparked among Baduy people due to different ideals regarding whom to choose. This may be contrary to the words of the ancestors, which emphasize that they should live in peace and harmony. When there is any dispute, it must be settled wisely according to *pantun*, as the fundamental perspective of life/philosophy for resolving disputes:

> "*Kutul sauruyan gagak sagalengan walik sagiringan kudu bisa sarendek saigel sabobok sapehanean kudu bisa kacai jadi salewi kadarat jadi salegok kudu bisa silih asuh silih asah, silih asih* [disputes must be resolved together with others and in line, in a well-organized way, fairly and wisely, not extending to another problem or another person and it can be resolved with love, protection, and affection]".

Moreover, the attitude of the Baduy people in a general election also has its own philosophy: *Lunang* (*milu ka nu menang*), which means 'following the winner' or whoever wins the election. The Baduy people must follow and obey the new leader, and this philosophy can be categorized as a passive participation in politics. According to Ramlan Surbakti[28], passive

26. Ibid.
27. Ibid.
28. Surbakti, R. (2007). *Memahami ilmu politik* (p. 142). Jakarta, Indonesia: PT. Gramedia Widisarana Indonesia.

participation involves activities that the government decrees, and accepting and implementing commands from the government.

When this general election in relation to the Baduy people is more profoundly observed, the Baduy people expect to have representative groups as in the general election of the New Order. With the existence of the groups, the people feel that they receive more attention from the government because they deserve to live a life with welfare, as do other citizens of Indonesia.[29]

2.2 *Urgency for civic education for the Baduy tribe*

The term 'civic education' has a similar meaning to 'civics', citizenship', and 'citizenship education'. All four terms concern the importance of education in democracy or civic education for society. The movement that reflects the importance of civic education has its own long history.[30]

Etymologically, the term 'civic education' is translated in Bahasa as *Pendidikan Kewarganegaraan/Pendidikan Politik*. This term is represented by Azyumardi Azra and the Indonesian Center for Civic Education (ICCE) team, UIN Jakarta, as a developer of the term 'civic education' in the first higher education institute[31], while *Pendidikan Kewarganegaraan* is represented by Zamroni, Muhammad Numam Soemantri, Udin S. Winataputra, and the Center for Indonesian Civic Education (CICED) team, Merphin Panjaitan, Soedijarto, and other experts.[32]

Citizenship education gained its momentum in the 1990s with varied understandings. For some experts, this type of education is identical to democracy education, human rights education, and citizenship education.

Azyumardi Azra argues that democracy education substantively involves socialization, dissemination, concept actualization, systems, values, culture, and democratic practice through education.[33] Human rights education is defined as an activity transforming the values of human rights to encourage awareness regarding respect, protection, and the guarantee of human rights as fundamentals embedded for each individual. To achieve the objective of human rights, the class must be democratic. Articles of legal acts cannot be taught verbally, but must be explained through a situation and experience familiar to the students, and the class must be taught in an interactive way.

Zamroni suggests that civic education is a democracy education aimed at preparing society to think critically and act in a democratic manner through the activities of implementing the awareness into new generations, which emphasizes that democracy guarantees human rights. Moreover, citizenship education is a process carried out by an educational institution where people study orientation, attitude, and political behavior. This leads them to political knowledge, awareness, attitude, political efficacy, and political participation, giving them the capacity to make a political decision rationally, which should be beneficial for all societies and the state.[34]

In his book *Politics* (340 BC), Aristotle stated "*If liberty and equality, as is thought by some, are chiefly to be found in democracy, they will be attained when all persons alike share in the government to the utmost".*[35]Aristotle's view was formed in the context of a city state with a very low total population. In the context of a modern state such as nowadays, despite the

29. Interview with Ayah Mursid on 9 July 2018 at 10.00 WIB in official residence of Jaro Saija (Government of Jaro/Village Head of Kanekes).
30. Branson, M.S. et al. (1999). *Belajar civic education dari Amerika*. Yogyakarta, Indonesia: LkiS.
31. Azyumardi, A. (2002). *Pendidikan demokrasi dan demokrasi di dunia Muslim*. Paper presented in National Seminar II of '*Civic Education* in College', Mataram, 22–23 April 2002.
32. ICCE Team of UIN Jakarta. (2003). *Demokrasi, HAM, dan masyarakat madani* (pp. 5–6). A research collaboration between ICCE UIN Syarif Hidayatullah Jakarta and The Asia Foundation.
33. See Azyumardi, footnote 31.
34. See ICCE Team of UIN Jakarta, footnote 32, p. 7.
35. Aristotle (1998). *Politics*. New York, NY: Oxford University Press Inc.

existence of a general election mechanism to elect state governments or village heads directly by the people, expecting full participation from all people or societies, in line with Aristotle, is not achievable.

It can be concluded that civic education, as referring to the definition given by the experts above, is an educational program that embraces nationality, citizenship regarding the relationship with a state, democracy, human rights, and civil society, all of which implement the principles of democracy and humanitarian education.

However, the term democracy, based on its etymology, consists of two words derived from the Greek *demos*, meaning people/society living in a certain region, and *cratein* or *cratos*, meaning power (sovereignty). In all, democracy is defined as a state's condition where in the governmental system, sovereignty is in the hands of society, and the highest authority is in the decisions made by society. Society holds the authority, the government is for society, and the authority itself is for the society.[36] Sovereignty is a political soul called a state, symbolized by a creator with immunity, and it is undefeatable.[37] The principle of people's sovereignty is a fundamental principle and is seen as a morality of a constitution that gives colors and characteristics to all acts concerning politics.[38]

In the author's perspective, referring to the theories discussed earlier, civic or democracy education is crucial for development in general, and especially regarding the general election and *pilkada* in Indonesia. It all makes sense because civic education is linked to socialization, dissemination, and actualization of concepts, systems, values, culture, and political or democratic practices through education. For a more developed society, it will be more effective and efficient when civic education is delivered by means of a formal educational setting (exclusive). However, it will not work for those of an isolated society, those living in coastal areas, and those living in mountainous areas, for they need education in an informal setting (inclusive), let alone for the Baduy people.

Surprisingly, according to the interview results, the people of outer Baduy see the general election and the election of regional heads (*pilkada*) in their tribe as being no different from what usually occurs in the general elections of other regions[39]; the people of the outer Baduy tribe are actively involved in the preparation of the general election, such as preparing voting booths, verifying members' cards, socialization before voting, and serving as witnesses in the voting. For the people of outer Baduy who are permanently registered as voters to vote for legislative members in Lebak, they vote following their desire and conscience.[40]

Unlike the outer Baduy people, the inner Baduy people (commonly known as the Tangtu tribe) are not informed by the culture, economy, politics, information, and technology of other regions. Ayah Mursyid from inner Baduy (a spokesperson for the existing *Puun*) opines that the people of inner Baduy are not directly involved in general elections and *pilkada* to vote for executive and legislative members in the Regency of Lebak, but they will obey whoever is elected as the new leader as long as the election is held according to a democratic political mechanism. Such a political attitude of the Baduy tribe arises because they strongly follow philosophical values from their ancestors: *Lunang* (*milu ka nu menang*) or 'following the winner', which means that the inner Baduy people will follow and obey whoever wins in the election. This is different from *Noken*, which is seen as the political attitude and political practice of the Papua people in a general election or *pilkada*.

It can be concluded that civic education related to a general election/*pilkada* among the outer Baduy people is still needed to bring them closer to politics, democracy, and their

36. Tutik, T.T. (2011). *Konstruksi hukum tata negara indonesia pasca Amandemen UUD 1945* (2nd ed., p. 67). Jakarta, Indonesia: Kencana Prenda Media Group.
37. Sarbaini, S. (2015), Demokrasi dan kebebasan memilih warga negara dalam pemilihan umum. *Jurnal Inovatif, 3*(1), 106.
38. See Gaffar, footnote 7, p. 29.
39. Interview with Jaro Saija on 10 June 2018 at 10.00–12.00 WIB in his official residence (the government of Jaro/Village Head of Kanekes).
40. Interview with the Secretary of Village (Anonymous) on 11 June 2018 in ex-secretariat room of legislative election in outer Baduy.

awareness of their political rights so that they will be able to articulate and fight for human rights in sociopolitics. Civic education is also needed inclusively and gradually for the inner Baduy tribe.

2.3 *Alternative model of inclusive civic education, especially for the Baduy people in Lebak Banten*

Several theories regarding general elections are mostly focused on civic education for political actors, political cadres, political practices, policymaking, or society (including the Baduy tribe) as active participants or pseudo-participants.[41] Continuous civic education is expected to raise wider political awareness, an understanding of human rights in sociopolitics, and tolerance. Having different opinions in relation to diversity is also expected to be common in society.

So far, the inner Baduy people follow the philosophy handed down from their ancestors: *Lunang* (*milu ka nu menang*), meaning that the people will follow whoever is elected to be a new leader in a general election or *pilkada*.[42] However, the political attitude of the outer Baduy people is different in the way that it is more adaptive to the change occurring in society in general. A general election is a manifestation of democracy, which gives people the opportunity to vote for their leader. All *adat* people have equal rights but not all of them would welcome a general election with open arms. For example, the inner Baduy people did not hold any general elections, and the outer Baduy people only started to have their general elections in the 1980s.

Therefore, the author agrees that civic education[43] needs to be continuously delivered to the people of Indonesia, not to mention to both the inner and outer Baduy people. Inclusive civic education needs to be especially given to the people of Baduy, and is more suitable to the characteristics of the inner Baduy people who strongly hold to the values given to them by their ancestors (as in *Lunang* and the message of their great-grandparents). The principle of *Lunang* in such a millennial era is quite rare, but it is still seen in the inner Baduy people. Similarly, philosophical values in the message of the great-grandparents encourage a simple life (*sak madyo*), a peaceful life, affection, and prioritizing common interests. The Baduy people are quite protective of themselves from external influences, modernization, and sociopolitical intervention from foreigners. Although they do not respond to political practices coming from the outside, they still obey whatever the result of a general election/*pilkada* held by the state may bring as long as it is done directly, publicly, free from any intervention, confidentially, honestly, and fairly (democracy).

3 CONCLUSION

The conclusions reached are based on what is discussed in this research:

1. *Lunang*-based civic education given to the inner Baduy people is a political participation practice that has been around for a long time, and remains unchanged.
2. The urgency for *Lunang*-based civic education, also called inclusive civic education, is more welcomed in the practice of democracy in Indonesia, as a result of diversity and legal pluralism in Indonesia.

---

41. Hamidi, J. (2002). *Pendidikan politik (civic education) Antara ralitas politik dan fakta hukum* (p. 67). Jakarta, Indonesia: PT. Gramedia Pustaka; Ghafar, A. (2000). *Politik Indonesia: Transisi menuju demokrasi*. Yogyakarta, Indonesia: Pustaka Pelajars.
42. Interview with Ayah Mursid on 9 July 2018 at 10.00 WIB in official residence of Jaro Saija (Government of Jaro/Village Head of Kanekes).
43. Civic education consists of paradigm, meaning, basic competence, aim, member, material scope and urgency for civic education. See Hamidi, J. (2002). *Pendidikan politik* [*Civic education*] (pp. 1–15). Bagi Kader Partai, Limited Edition.

An alternative model of inclusive political education, especially for the inner Baduy people in Lebak Banten, must be established as a pilot project in the era of democracy in this millennium.

REFERENCES

Aristotle. (1998). *Politics*. New York, NY: Oxford University Press.

Asshiddiqie, J. (2005). *Hukum tata negara dan pilar-pilar demokrasi*. Jakarta, Indonesia: Konstitusi Press.

Azyumardi, A. (2002). Pendidikan demokrasi dan demokrasi di dunia Muslim. Paper presented in National Seminar II of '*Civic Education in College*', Mataram, 22–23 April 2002.

Badan, P.P. (2014). *Laporan hasil pengawasan pemilu anggota DPR, DPD dan DPRD tahun 2014*. Jakarta, Indonesia: Bawaslu Republik Indonesia.

Branson, M.S. et al. (1999). *Belajar civic education dari Amerika*. Yogyakarta, Indonesia: LkiS.

Fathurokhman, F. (2016). *Hukum pidana adat baduy dan pembaharuan hukum pidana*. Depok, Indonesia: INCA Publishing.

Friedman, L.M. (1969). Legal culture and social development. *Law and Society Review*, *4*(1), 29–44.

Gaffar, J.M. (2013). *Politik hukum pemilu* (2nd ed.). Jakarta, Indonesia: Konstitusi Press.

Ghafar, A. (2000). *Politik Indonesia: Transisi menuju demokrasi*. Yogyakarta, Indonesia: Pustaka Pelajar.

Hamidi, J. (2002a). *Pendidikan politik (civic education) antara ralitas politik dan fakta hukum*. Jakarta, Indonesia: PT. Gramedia Pustaka.

Hamidi, J. (2002b). *Pendidikan politik* [*Civic education*] (pp. 1–15). Bagi Kader Partai, Limited Edition.

Hamidi, J., Ulum, B. & Novitasary, R. (2015). *Demokrasi lokal nurut masyarakat Baduy*. Malang, Indonesia: Nuswantara.

ICCE Team of UIN Jakarta. (2003). *Demokrasi, HAM, dan masyarakat madani*. A research collaboration between ICCE UIN Syarif Hidayatullah Jakarta and The Asia Foundation.

Iskandar, J. (2012). *Ekologi perladangan orang Baduy pengelolaan hutan berbasis adat secara berkelanjutan*. Bandung, Indonesia: PT. Alumni.

Makinda, S. (1996). Democracy and multiparty politics in Africa. *The Journal of Modern African Studies*, *34*(4), 557.

Maslow, A.H. (1954). *Motivation and personality*. New York, NY: Harper.

Nizar, M. (1988). *Metode penelitian*. Bogor, Indonesia: Ghalia Indonesia.

Rosema, M. (2007). Low turnout: Threat to democracy or blessing in disguise? Consequences of citizens' varying tendencies to vote. *Electoral Studies*, *26*(3), 612–623.

Sam, S. et al. (1986). *Tata kehidupan masyarakat Baduy di Propinsi Jawa Barat*. Jakarta, Indonesia: Ministry of Education and Culture Project Inventory and Regional Culture Documentation.

Saputra, F.T. (2017). Partisipasi politik masyarakat Baduy dalam pemilihan umum (studi fenomenologi partisipasi politik masyarakat Baduy pada pemilu 2014). Proceeding of Magister of Communication Study, 1.

Sarbaini, S. (2015). Demokrasi dan kebebasan memilih warga negara dalam pemilihan umum. *Jurnal Inovatif*, *3*(1), 106.

Senoaji, G. (2010). Masyarakat Baduy, hutan, dan lingkungan. *Jurnal Manusia dan Lingkungan*, *17*(2), 120–121.

Sukirno. (2018). *Politik hukum pengakuan hak ulayat*(1st ed.). Jakarta, Indonesia: Prenadamedia Group.

Surbakti, R. (2007). *Memahami ilmu politik*. Jakarta, Indonesia: PT. Gramedia Widisarana Indonesia.

Suteki & Taufani, G. (2018). *Metodologi penelitian hukum (filsafat, teori dan praktik)*. Depok, Indonesia: PT RajaGrapindo Persada.

Tutik, T.T. (2011). *Konstruksi hukum tata negara Indonesia pasca Amandemen UUD 1945* (2nd ed.). Jakarta, Indonesia: Kencana Prenda Media Group.

Utomo, L. (2016). *Hukum adat*. Jakarta, Indonesia: RajaGrafindo Persada.

Constitutional Court Decision Number 97/PUU-XI/2013.

Law Number 1 Year 2015 on Establishment of Government Regulations in Lieu of Law Number 1 Year 2014 on Election of Governors, Mayors and Regents becoming Law.

Law Number 10 Year 2016 on Second Amendment over the Law Number 1 Year 2015 on Establishment of Government Regulations in Lieu of Law Number 1 Year 2014 on Election of Governors, Mayors and Regents becoming Law.

Culture and International Law - Juwana et al. (Eds)
© 2019 Taylor & Francis Group, London, ISBN 978-1-138-38766-9

Renegotiation contract of mining works

Ranitya Ganindha, Rumi Suwardiyati & Setiawan Wicaksono
Law Faculty, Brawijaya University, Indonesia

ABSTRACT: Work contract renegotiations need to be carried out if there is an imbalance of rights and obligations between the parties, this is what underlies the Government to renegotiate mining work contracts. This research is a normative juridical legal research with a legislative approach and conceptual approach. The renegotiation of foreign investors can be strictly enforced by Indonesian Government without worrying about being used as the basis for suing in International Arbitration. Renegotiation the work contract should be based on the principle of proportionality that prioritizes justice for the rights and obligations of the parties, but without ignoring the sustainability of business relations between the Indonesian government and foreign investors. Through renegotiation, both parties remain accommodated in their interests. The interests of the Indonesian government to prosper the people through natural resources and the sustainability of foreign investors to invest in Indonesia, mine management in Indonesia is expected.

KEYWORDS: renegotiation, contract of work, mining

1 INTRODUCTION

The mining sector is still one of Indonesia's attractions for investors, the comparative advantage of the Earth's wealth is still a high selling point. The mining business sector is one of the business sectors that receives the highest priority from the government before and after the issuance of the Investment Law, both for foreign parties and domestic parties. For this reason, the government is trying to be able to direct and manage natural resources included in the mining business. The mining business sector includes petroleum mining, natural gas, coal, metal, tin, nickel ore, bausite, iron sand, silver and copper concentrates.[1]

In fact, Indonesia's mining wealth can be seen clearly. Indonesia has been known to be rich in mineral, coal and oil and gas goods since the beginning. Indonesian mineral reserves are ranked sixth in the world. The mining sector is still believed to be one of the most attractive investments. More broadly, mining is a complex industry in its regulation of the impact of economic development both nationally and locally, environmental aspects, socio-cultural aspects and almost certainly many large-scale mining areas are located in remote areas of a region or country.

The long history of mining contracts between Indonesia and foreign investors began when the Gesberg and Esberg Mining conducted by Freeport was the first mineral mining in Indonesia. Exploitation of minerals in the form of precious metals which include copper, gold, silver, platinum and palladium as one of the main commodities produced. Cooperation between the Government of the Republic of Indonesia and PT.

1. Amirudin Ilmar, *Hukum Penanaman Modal Di Indonesia* (Jakarta, Penerbit Prenada Media, 2004) 113.

Freeport Indonesia is carried out through an agreement outlined in a Contract of Work. The first made Contract of Work (CONTRACT OF GENERAL WORKS I)[2] in 1967 was based on Law No. 11 year 1967 concerning Basic Mining Conditions and Law No. 1 year 1967 concerning Foreign Investment. Three months after the issuance of the Foreign Investment Law, in April 1967 Freeport was the first foreign investor to enter Indonesia. After that, in the 1968 period there were 16 foreign mines, such as Inco, Bliton Mij, Alcoa, Kennecott and US Steel. At that time, the Contract of Work as a mining law product was accepted by international mining.

A work contract is an agreement between the Government of Indonesia as a Principal and a foreign company as a contractor. The company has become a single contractor with regard to the area of work contract in the mineral sector. Through the contract, the company is given various sole rights to carry out exploration, mining, processing the storage and transportation of minerals produced, as well as to market and sell or release all production from the mine and process, both at home and abroad.[3] The Government also gives sole control and management to the company for all its activities, and carries all risks arising in its operations (Article 2 paragraph (3) Generation VII Contract of Work).[4]

The Contract of Work with this provision shows how wide the authority of a mining company is. Mining companies have a lot of freedom to exploit large-scale natural resources in the mining areas under their control and then the raw mining products are sent to the investor's home country to be reprocessed. The purification of the raw mining products makes the Indonesian state as the principal does not know whether the final product of the raw mining material, whether in the form of metals such as lithium, magnesium, gold, copper, silver, titanium, etc. or in the form of radioactive materials such as radium, thorium, uranium, and so on. This makes the Indonesian Government seem to have no authority or sovereignty over its mining products and cause many losses.

The enactment of a contract of work system between the government and investors raises the legal relationship that arises between the parties, namely the government and mining investors are civil relations. Because it arises from civil relations, the relationship between the two, based on the Civil Code, has a legal status and position according to the law. The material agreed upon should also have a balanced achievement in creating rights and obligations. The rights and obligations agreed upon are of course a joint agreement between the two parties based on the principle of freedom of contract. However, the balance of rights and obligations of the parties to the mining contract often goes hand in hand, one party is more dominant than the other. Criticism and rejection of the conditions of the contract of work eventually led to strong criticism from many parties.

The criticism often raised by many parties is the imbalance related to royalties obtained by the government carried out by foreign mining companies. this is what then gets a strong reaction to the system of work contracts in mining because foreign investors can make large-scale exploitation of mining products, but the government as host country is not so significant in number, the royalties that should be used for people's welfare are not worth the amount. In the contract of work between the Indonesian government and PT Freeport, Indonesia only gets a share of 3 percent. This percentage is considered to be disproportionate if seen by the mining results that have been obtained from Indonesia

2. In the history of the Contract of Work, there were 3 periods, namely the Contract Of Works of Generation I, Generation II and Generation III. Work Contract between the Government of Indonesia and PT. Freeport Indonesia is only in Generation I and II. This is because incontract of Works Generation III, PT. Freeport did not agree to renegotiate the contract, which at that time must follow the Decree of the Minister of Energy and Mineral Resources (formerly the Minister of Mines and Energy)
3. Article 2 paragraph (1) Generation VII Contract of Work
4. Nanik Trihastuti, *Hukum Kontrak Karya: Pola Kerjasama Pengusahaan Pertambangan Indonesia*, (Malang, Setara Press, kelompok penerbit Intrans, 2013) 92.

Referring to Law No. 4 year 2009 concerning Mineral and Coal Mining which mandates the Government of Indonesia to renegotiate contracts with all foreign mining companies in the country. This law replaces Law No. 11 year 1967 which was passed in December 1967 or eight months after the signing of the Contract of Work. Based on data from the Ministry of Energy and Mineral Resources, as many as 65 percent of mining companies have principled to agree to re-discuss contracts that have been signed. However, as many as 35 percent of the total companies are still in the renegotiation stage. Among them are PT Freeport and PT Newmont. From the explanation above, it can be seen that the contract imbalance has been agreed upon, therefore the writer is interested in the research "RE-NEGOTIATION CONTRACT OF MINING WORKS"

2 DISCUSSION OF RENEGOTIATION OF WORK CONTRACTS

This study uses a normative juridical research method, with a legislative approach and a conceptual approach. The statutory approach is carried out by examining all laws and regulations relating to the legal issues being dealt with.[5] This approach is carried out by reviewing the legal basis associated with mining contracts and special mining business permits. This approach is used to analyze and review the laws and regulations related to the Mining Work Contract, especially regarding the issue of Renegotiation and special mining business licenses.

The Conceptual Approach (conceptual approach) is an approach that departs from the views and doctrines that develop in the law.[6] In this paper will examine doctrine and literature (books) relating to Mining Contracts in general and Mining Work Contracts in particular. As well as other books that are indirectly related to this paper. The author will put forward the concept that contract renegotiations may be carried out while still respecting the principles of the contract in general.

Regarding the Generation I Contract of Work renegotiated in 1991, and producing a Generation II Work Contract in which renegotiation of the Contract of Work was carried out to coincide with the extension of the Contract of Work which had been running for almost 30 (thirty) years, to be exact 24 (twenty four) years. The amendments included provisions concerning the expansion of mining areas into two blocks, namely Block A and Block B, which originally only consisted of the mining area of

Block A. And included a clause regarding the environment and work safety in accordance with the law that just came out at that time. After decades passed then there was an awareness that the Contract of Work between the Government and PT. Freeport Indonesia is considered less profitable for the Indonesian Government. The state of Indonesia which is progressing and stable both in terms of law, human resources and technological development raises a thought that the contract must be adjusted to the current condition of Indonesia. In 2009 the government established Law Number 4 year 2009 concerning Mineral and Coal (hereinafter referred to as Law Number 4 year 2009) which one of the mandates in the article is that the contract must be renegotiated and adjusted to the new mineral and coal laws as stated in article 169 of this law. Article 169 of Law Number 4 year 2009 concerning Mineral and Coal regulates at least three things, namely: (1) Respect for the Coal Mining Concession Work Contract and Work Agreement until the term of the contract/agreement expires; (2) An order to adjust the Coal Contract of Work and Work Agreement for Mining Business Exploitation which is given a grace period of one year after the promulgation of this law; and (3) Further arrangements regarding state revenues which become a reduction in contract adjustments[7].

Law Number 4 year 2009 in its transitional regulation expressly stipulates that a Contract of Work that has existed before the establishment of Law Number 4 year 2009, will remain valid until the expiry of the Contract of Work. In simple terms, this transitional rule can mean

5. Peter Mahmud Marzuki, *Penelitian Hukum* (Jakarta, Kencana Prenada Media Grup, 2005) 93.
6. Ibid, 93.
7. Article 169 b Law no 4 year 2004

that the existence of the Contract of Work status is still recognized. However, this transitional regulation also confirms that the provisions contained in the articles of the Contract of Work must be adjusted not later than 1 (one) year since Law Number 4 year 2009 is established, except for state revenues. This is an anxiety for the Contract of Work holders. Law No. 4 year 2009 raises new problems, namely points (2) related to renegotiation of Contracts of Work, which investors always consider as a deterrent to sanctity of contract. On the other hand, contract adjustment orders are a form of government sovereignty in returning the State's Right to Control over mining goods.

As for the treaty there is the principle of Contractual Freedom, contained in Article 1338 of the Civil Code which, if further analyzed, is contained in three articles, namely the principle of consensualism (the occurrence of an agreement with the consent of the parties), the basis of the binding force of the treaty/*Pacta Sunt Servanda* (the agreement applies as a Law to those who make it) and the Basic of contractual freedom (the parties are free to determine the content, extent and form of the agreement.)

Article 1338 BW states that:

"All Agreements made lawfully, apply as a law for those who make them".

The article has implications that an agreement results in a legal obligation for parties bound to execute contractual agreements and that an agreement must be fulfilled.[8] After a consensus or agreement is reached then at the same time work binding contract *(pacta sunt servanda)* as a result of the agreement. Other grounds contained in paragraph 3 of this article instruct the agreement to be executed in good faith, aimed at preventing inappropriate or arbitrary conduct in the event of the execution of the agreement.[9] That is to say, each party, though it has a higher bargaining position than any other party, should respectfully implement and implement what has been promised. The highest respect for what has been promised in this contract is often referred to as sanctity of contract.[10]

The definition of sanctity of contract in Black's Law Dicionary is "the Principle that parties to a contract, having a duty entered into it, must honor their obligations under it",[11] namely the principle that states that the parties to the contract have obligations as stated in the contract must respect/maintain their obligations under the contract.

The government is currently trying to renegotiate with various foreign companies holding contracts of work, the main reason underlying the solidity of government efforts is because these contracts are considered not in accordance with the needs of the Indonesian people in general at this time. Many contracts of work that are allegedly actually harm the state from the revenue side. Various considerations, including the issue of tax rates, concession area, as well as the interests of meeting domestic needs, are important aspects the government wants to discuss in renegotiating mining work contracts. Nevertheless, some parties are concerned that this renegotiation effort will lead to violations of the principle of freedom of contract so that Indonesia has the potential to be prosecuted in international arbitration. In addition, the imposition of renegotiation of work contracts is feared to disrupt the inflow of foreign investment into the country. Investors will think again to invest in Indonesia (related to competitive advantages that are inferior to other countries). Moving on from this, renegotiation efforts must be prepared in detail by the government. Every step and offer of negotiation must

8. Asser Hatkamp in Herlien Budiono, *Asas Keseimbangan bagi Hukum Perjanjian Indonesia* (Bandung, Citra Aditya Bhakti, 2005) 101.
9. R. Subekti, *Bunga Rampai Ilmu Hukum* (Bandung, Alumni, 1992) 18.
10. P.S. Atiyah, *An Introduction to The Law of Contract* (Oxford: Clarendon Press, 1981) 4

    It was stated that the binding power of a contract was only limited to the parties, so the contract must also be respected by the parties as well. A contract or an agreement is then said to be sacred and must be respected by the parties who are bound in it. So, then two aspects appear in the contract, namely First, as much freedom as possible to enter into a contract. Second, the contract must be treated sacred by the court, because the parties are free and there are no restrictions in entering into the contract. Thus, freedom of contract and sanctity of contract become the basis of the entire contract law.
11. Brian A. Garner, *Black's Law Dictionary* (St. Paul: West Group, 1990)

culminate in the goal of fulfilling the improvement of people's welfare but on the other hand also cling to the principle of respect for freedom of contract.

Renegotiation is one of the options for Indonesia to get something that should be entitled to royalties. The renegotiation carried out by the government is not aimed at nationalization, which is why the government still respects the rights of the mining company on the contract of work that has been made. Fear that the company will bring this case to international arbitration because Indonesia has been deemed to have violated the contract will not occur if the renegotiation is carried out in accordance with legal provisions.

The aim of the government is to renegotiate or review the Coal Mining Concession Work Contract and Work Agreement to adjust the contents of contracts and agreements with a number of mining companies holding Contract of Work and Coal Mining Concession Agreements so that the previous contract can adjust to the Minerba Law with the agreement of both parties.

From the points in the renegotiation related to the return of State Ownership Rights, there are three main considerations from the government in terms of reviewing the provisions in the Contract of Work, including:

1. The benefits for the greatest prosperity of the people are not achieved. Mining goods are included in the natural wealth contained in the earth which in Article 33 paragraph 3 of the 1945 Constitution the fourth amendment must be used for the greatest prosperity of the people. In fact, even though the mining sector provides opinions that are among the third highest deces, it still feels too small, it can be seen, the tax on gold is 3.25% of the total production as stated in Government Regulation (PP) No. 9 year 2012 concerning Non-Tax State Revenues where this regulation is applied to holders of Mining Business Permits (IUP), Business Permits
2. Special Mining (IUPK) and People's Mining Business Permit (IPR). As for the holders of Contract Works and PKP2B, they still refer to the contracts and agreements that have been agreed upon. In the Contract of Work between the Government of Indonesia and PT. Freeport Indonesia itself, the tax paid is only 3% of the total production, less than the provisions in PP. There is a willingness from Indonesia to participate in mining business. This is manifested in the provisions of the obligation to divest national shares up to 51% in the next 10 years. This is so that, when 51% of the shares are owned by Indonesia, then Indonesia can take part in making decisions in the company. For example, by making a decision to replace the majority of skilled workers with Indonesian citizens or native Indonesians, CSR policies, etc.
3. Increase the added value of mining goods by processing and refining domestically. As done so far, mining is carried out not only for minerals and/or coal, but also for the minerals that follow. This has an impact on the low value of mining goods.

When a contract has been carried out, in the process of contract, sometimes the principle of freedom of contract cannot be exercised absolutely. There are elements that allow the contract to change. One of the elements is a factor of public interest or state interests, which requires a change of contract for the benefit of the wider community.

Moving on from this, the sanctity of contract can be ruled out through the principle of permanent sovereignty over natural resources (The Principle of Permanent Sovereignty over Natural Resource). Thus, the existence of Article 169 b of Law Number 4 year 2009 can be enforced, because the government's function in implementing this provision is a regulatory function. When it is related to the public interest, the role of government functions as a contract that acts privately separately. Contract Renegotiation is a common thing that can be done. The existence of Article 169 b of Law Number 4 year 2009 concerning Mineral and Coal cannot be said to be one hundred percent injuring the sanctity of Contract due to permanent sovereignty over natural resources (The Principle of sovereignty over Natural Resources) and even so, Article 169 b as explained in the previous sub-chapter, it is generally applied and binding. So that the main function of the existence of Article 169 b is as a legal basis of the government (in the private sphere) to be able to submit a request for renegotiation of work contracts. In addition, even though Article 169 b is compelling, in reality changes to the contract of work remain based on the agreement of both parties.

Foreign investors tend to emphasize the sanctity of the contract, which is seen as the basic principle underlying their participation in this activity. Experts from the host country generally argue that these contracts should be governed by the national law of the host country based on the principles of international civil law and that the contract can be amended by the Government for the public interest. On the other hand experts from Western countries argue that these contracts are international treaties and therefore are subject to the principle of law *pacta sunt servanda.*[12]

This difference of opinion according to Zhiguo Gao will continue as long as there is a conflict of interests. However, despite these differences there is one common view that the sanctity of a contract has never been treated as an absolute principle both in theory and practice.[13] As said by R. Y. Jennings both the principle of taking rights and the principle of servant injection do not have to be viewed in an absolute or unconditional manner in their application.[14]

The principle of freedom of contract is not absolute. There are limits that fence it. These limits, among others, are not to be deviated from the rules of national law (which are public). This limit is known in Latin law which reads *pacta private juri public derogare non possunt*[15]

Limitation of public interest to this principle was also stated by Professor Yntema, as follows:[16]

> "...the principle of party autonomy in the law of contract is subject to various restriction in the different municipal laws and is not interpreted elsewhere in the same manner; these restriction are mainly imposed for reasons of public policy or in the public interest."

This principle was actually born from natural law thinking with its leader Hugo Grotius. According to Grotius, this principle is also called the theory of moral strength of a promise (the theory of the inherent moral force of a promise). Based on this theory, a promise is morally binding. This principle is also contained in Article 25 AB (Algemene Bepalingen Van Wegeving).[17] This article states that 'a person with an act or agreement must not remove the power of the legal regulations from general provisions or decency.[18]

The principle of freedom of contract is not necessarily applicable in an international contract, there is a limitation, the limitation is in the form of public interest. The theory of State interests or also called governmental interest analysis theory was pioneered by Prof. Brainerd Currie. When viewed from this angle, the Mining Contract of Work was made in 1967 where at that time the condition of Indonesia lacked capital, experts and capabilities would have been far different from now.

Based on the theory of the country's interests, what is meant by interest in this theory is actually the interest of the state (governmental interest) whose legal system is relevant to the principal case to enforce the law in the settlement of the main cases at hand which can be deduced from the policy in the relevant local law. The existence of certain policies underlying the application of a local or domestic law rule that underlies the interests of the country concerned to enforce the law in a case.[19]

12. Gao, Zhigue, *International Offshore Petroleum Contracts, Towards the Compatibility of Energy Need and Sustainable Development*, Dissertation Doctor of Science Dalhousie University, Halifax, Nova Scotia, UMIDissertation Services, Ann Rabor, Michigan, July 1993, 502
13. Ibid, 503
14. Jennings, R.Y., *State Contracts in International Lawm* (British YB International Law, 1961)156:"Neither the principle of acquired rights nor the principle of pacta sunt servanda is therefore to be regarded as being necessary absolute or unconditional in its application."
15. Ibid, 22.
16. Ibid, 23.
17. Ibid, 23.
18. Ibid, 23.
19. Bayu Seto Hardjowahono, *Dasar-Dasar Hukum Perdata Internasional: Buku Kesatu*, (Bandung, PT. Citra Aditya Bakti, 2006) 214.

Thus, an important point that needs to be considered in contract renegotiation is that the Contract of Work (KK) and Coal Mining Exploitation Work Agreement (PKP2B) are no longer lex specialis derogat legi generalis since the enactment of Law Number 4 year 2009 concerning Mineral and Coal Mining commencing from the date January 12, 2009 because it contradicts articles 128, 129, 130, 131, 132 and 133 of the Act, namely articles relating to State and Regional Revenues. In addition, the company's action to refuse to reduce the area for both KK and PKP2B is contrary to Article 53 and Article 62 of Law No. 4 year 2009.

Associated with one of the principles in contract law, namely the principle of proportionality, the contract renegotiation between the government and foreign investors is very possible. Renegotiation is carried out with the aim of rebalancing the rights and responsibilities of the parties to the place according to proportion (principle of proportionality). Six things were asked to be adapted to the new mining regulations as stipulated in Law Number 4 year 2009, namely regarding area, contract extension, obligation to divest shares, state revenue obligations (royalties), processing and refining obligations, and obligation to use goods and services domestically, being one of the efforts that can bring justice to the parties in a balanced manner, there is no one party who seems to be in a stronger position than the other party. If returned in the framework of the principle of proportionality, renegotiation of the contract of work can be done to restore the rights and obligations of the parties in a balanced manner (equilibrium) based on their respective proportions.

3 CONCLUSION

Contracts of work made between the Indonesian government and Freeport are contrary to the provisions stipulated in the 1945 Constitution of the Republic of Indonesia, especially article 33. However, the contract was made by both parties who have agreed so that it must comply with the principle of pacta sunt servanda and sanctity of contract. The Indonesian government cannot immediately change the contents of the contract without the approval of PT FPI, if this is done it can bring the Indonesian government to be sued in International Arbitration. Contract Renegotiation Efforts can be made so that each article in the Contract of Work is in accordance with the principles of social justice, the principle of natural wealth is controlled by the state, and the principle of the greatest prosperity of the people. There are international legal instruments that can be used as guidelines, including UPICCs and General Assembly resolutions 1803 (XVII), December 14, 1962.

Based on basic principles that have been recognized internationally and based on proportionality that must be done in a business contract, can be used as a basis for the Indonesian government to uphold article 169 of Law No. 4 year 2009 concerning Mineral and Coal. The renegotiation of foreign investors can be strictly enforced by the Government of Indonesia without worrying about being used as the basis for suing in International Arbitration. Renegotiation The work contract should be based on the principle of proportionality that prioritizes justice for the rights and obligations of the parties, but without ignoring the sustainability of business relations between the Indonesian government and foreign investors. Through renegotiation, both parties remain accommodated in their interests. The interests of the Indonesian government to prosper the people through natural resources and the sustainability of foreign investors to invest in Indonesia.

REFERENCES

Atiyah, P.S., *An Introduction to The Law of Contract* (Oxford: Clarendon Press, 1981).

Budiono, Herlien, *Asas Keseimbangan bagi Hukum Perjanjian Indonesia* (Bandung, Citra Aditya Bhakti, 2005).

Gao, Zhigue, *International Offshore Petroleum Contracts, Towards the Compatibility of Energy Need and Sustainable Development*, Dissertation Doctor of Science Dalhousie University, Halifax, Nova Scotia, UMIDissertation Services, Ann Rabor, Michigan, July 1993.

Garner, Brian A., *Black's Law Dictionary* (St. Paul: West Group, 1990)

Hardjowahono, Bayu Seto, *Dasar-Dasar Hukum Perdata Internasional: Buku Kesatu*, (Bandung, PT. Citra Aditya Bakti, 2006).
Ilmar, Amirudin, *Hukum Penanaman Modal Di Indonesia* (Jakarta, Penerbit Prenada Media, 2004).
Jennings, R.Y., *State Contracts in International Lawm* (British YB International Law, 1961).
Marzuki, Peter Mahmud, *Penelitian Hukum* (Jakarta, Kencana Prenada Media Grup, 2005).
Subekti, R., *Bunga Rampai Ilmu Hukum* (Bandung, Alumni, 1992).
Trihastuti, Nanik, *Hukum Kontrak Karya: Pola Kerjasama Pengusahaan Pertambangan Indonesia*, (Malang, Setara Press, kelompok penerbit Intrans, 2013).
Algemene Bepalingen Van Wegeving
Article 2 paragraph (1) Generation VII Contract of Work
Indonesia Civil Code
Indonesia Constitution 1945
Law Number 4 year 2009 concerning Mineral and Coal

Culture and International Law - Juwana et al. (Eds)
© 2019 Taylor & Francis Group, London, ISBN 978-1-138-38766-9

Legal implications of cryptocurrency: A study of disruptive financial technology in Indonesia

Reka Dewantara
Law Faculty, Brawijaya University, Malang, Indonesia

ABSTRACT: The article aims to analyze typologies of virtual currency regulations in Indonesia and how they impede or enhance disruptive financial technology. The focuses of the analysis relate to the theoretical and practical implications of *good monetary governance*. The research methods used are normative juridical with a case, conceptual and economic analysis of law approach. Systematic and hermeneutic interpretations are used to analyze the data. The development of hybrid products in new forms, such as financial technology and the emergence of business conglomerates of start-ups in Indonesia, leads to the need for an integrated regulation that supersedes the regulation in the field of supervision in monetary institutions. The financial supervisory authority and the Indonesian central bank prohibited the use of cryptocurrencies (Act Number 7 Year 2011 concerning Currency) because cryptocurrencies have no intrinsic value, so it is not really an asset one can analyze.

KEYWORDS: Cryptocurrencies, regulations, disruptive, Indonesia

1 INTRODUCTION

The use of e-commerce or transactions through Internet media continues to increase in Indonesia, as demonstrated in 2016 according to the 2016 Economic Census Data from the Central Bureau of Statistics. The e-commerce industry in Indonesia grew by 17 percent, with the total number of businesses reaching 26.2 million. Transactions in e-commerce have various payment methods, including technology-based ones, such as ATM transfers, mobile banking/Internet banking, debit cards, and credit cards, or direct payments. Based on data and statistics from the Ministry of Information and Communications of the Republic of Indonesia on e-commerce activities in 2016, technology-based payments are much more popular with 77.5 percent of total transactions, compared with direct payments of only 22.5 percent of total transactions[1].

Currently, the development of virtual currency schemes with bidirectional flow, also called bidirectional cryptocurrency (hereinafter cryptocurrency), in Indonesia is becoming popular as a phenomenon in the community. Cryptocurrency involves a programming system using cryptographic code that can be stored in a computer or smartphone device in such a way that it can be transferred and become an alternative means of making a transaction. In general, this currency is stored in the same type of file as a movie or music file on a computer or smartphone device; it can be hidden, hacked and destroyed, but can be protected by cryptographic code. Its development led to many such schemes being formed. The largest of these are Bitcoin, Dogecoin and Litecoin.[2]

1. Ministry of Information and Communications of the Republic of Indonesia (2016). *Payment method on e-commerce activity*. Retrieved from https://statistik.kominfo.go.id/site/searchKonten?iddoc=1527
2. Bovaird, C. (2017). Cryptocurrency bounces back as trader sentiment improves. *Forbes*. Retrieved from: https://www.forbes.com/sites/cbovaird/2017/09/19/cryptocurrency-bounces-back-as-trader-sentiment-improves/#1f3e897ac9a5

Act Number 7 Year 2011 concerning *Currency* (hereinafter referred to as the 'Currency Act') and Indonesia Central Bank Regulation Number 17/3/PBI/2015 concerning *Rupiah Currency Obligation that is Used in the Territory of the Unitary State of the Republic of Indonesia* (hereinafter referred to as the 'Central Bank Regulation concerning Rupiah Currency') stipulate that the rupiah is the only currency that is applicable in Indonesia, or that is valid and accepted as a legal tender in the territory of the Unitary State of the Republic of Indonesia. Therefore, any other currency (non-rupiah) used as a means of payment is not valid, and there is also a criminal provision set forth in Article 33 Paragraph 1 of the Currency Act[3].

Indonesia recognizes the existence of 'foreign exchange' or 'foreign currency' (i.e. transactions that use foreign currency as a means of payment). The intended foreign currency is a currency that is officially issued by a particular country and recognized by another country. However, the use of payments using foreign currencies in the Territory of Indonesia that results in the non-fulfillment of the legal terms of the agreement under Article 1320 of the Civil Code (BW), namely the *halal* clause, is illegal because the use of foreign currency is illegal, and there is a criminal threat in accordance with the Currency Act. There are, however, exclusions for certain matters governed in Article 4 of the Central Bank Regulation concerning Rupiah Currency:

a. specific transactions in the implementation of state budget revenue and expenditure;
b. acceptance or grant to or from abroad;
c. international trade transactions;
d. deposits in the bank in the form of foreign exchange;
e. international financing transactions.

The existence of the digital currency phenomenon, especially cryptocurrency, raises legal issues in the form of vagueness and legal consequences of cryptocurrency usage in Indonesia. The first problem lies in the status of cryptocurrency, which has no arrangements. This causes confusion to the users of this system, because cryptocurrency is not a currency that can be used in Indonesia as it is contrary to the Currency Act; in addition, it is also not a foreign currency because it is not issued or made by a recognized country. The next problem lies in the validity of the transaction agreement using the tool, due to its unclear status, so that the validity of the agreement that occurs using the transaction tool is also not known.

Based on the issues thus articulated, the author is interested in researching and analyzing the legal status and consequences of cryptocurrency usage in terms of accordance with the prevailing laws and regulations.

2 DISCUSSION

2.1 *Regulatory impact analysis concerning the typologies of virtual currency regulations in Indonesia*

In the development of the world of economics and business, information technology currently plays a very strategic role as a means of support. Non-cash payments are one of the popular transaction systems, most of which use sophisticated equipment and information technology. One form that experienced significant growth was the use of cryptocurrency as a medium of exchange. In some countries it has even been acknowledged that cryptocurrency is almost equivalent to the currency that is officially used by those countries[4]. Cryptocurrency tries to solve the

3. Any person who does not use the rupiah in: a. any transaction that has the purpose of payment; b. settlement of other obligations that must be fulfilled with money; c. other financial transactions; as referred to in Article 21 Paragraph 1 shall be subject to a maximum imprisonment of one year and a maximum fine of Rp. 200,000,000.
4. Nubika, I. (2018). *Bitcoin: Get to know the new way of investing by millennials.* Yogyakarta, Indonesia: Genesis Learning (p. 78).

problem of virtual money that did not work before, by creating a space in which the public can participate. The system can work because of the role of public participation, whereby the public provides the hardware that is a resource in each transaction of this system, so that every transaction that happens can be known by all hardware providers. Hardware providers benefit as they earn rewards in the form of one of the cryptocurrency types that the hardware is providing. Such a process is called a 'mining' process. The mining process is aimed at public participation, which can make the transaction run smoothly and safely. The existence of this mining process, in addition to providing data sources for the course of all transaction sites, also serves to maintain public participation in the running transactions. In addition, this process also gradually generates a virtual money supply, which eventually reaches a specified total. For example, the maximum supply for Bitcoin is 21 million bitcoins, which it is estimated will be reached in 2140.[5]

On the basis of this explanation, it is clear that the running cryptocurrency system is a system based on public participation without the supremacy of third parties who have authority in the configuration of the operating mechanism. In addition, the system offers a high degree of anonymity to each user. Cryptocurrency gives users and everyone else involved privacy, enabling transactions to be made by parties whose identities are unknown. The nature of this confidentiality makes cryptocurrency popular for illegal e-commerce transactions such as those involving firearms and illegal drugs.[6] With such a system, the virtue of cryptocurrency's appeal is the confidentiality and privacy provided by the cryptographic system, and the ease of making transactions with only the public key needed to transact. Further, the authenticity of each transaction will be safeguarded because each transaction must be digitally signed through a private key known only to the authorized user.

Money has the basic function of a medium of exchange, in which someone can exchange money directly for goods or services desired. Money also has a function to store value so that it can be used as a means of storage of wealth. Lastly, money functions as a unit of accounting. As the official currency of the Republic of Indonesia, the rupiah has all three functions, and by definition in *Black's Law Dictionary* is *"the medium of exchange authorized or adopted by a government as part of its currency"*, meaning that the rupiah currency is legal.[7] Indonesia has specifically regulated money using the Currency Act, where in Article 1 Point 1 it is explained that "*Currency is money issued by the Unitary State of the Republic of Indonesia, hereinafter referred to as Rupiah"*. From these two definitions it can be said that something can be described as a currency when approved or adopted by a legitimate government. In Indonesia, in accordance with the Currency Act it is stated that currency in Indonesia is the rupiah because it is issued by the legitimate government, in this case the Government of the Republic of Indonesia. Cryptocurrency is considered to be a currency used in society but is not recognized as a legitimate currency by any government. Because of the decentralized nature of this currency system, it makes governments reluctant to acknowledge it because it would compete with currencies that have been made by government. So, if cryptocurrency is said to be a currency, it is not appropriate because it does not meet the requirements of government recognition, nor the general terms of currency[8].

The conditions mentioned are cumulative or must be met fully, so that if just one of these conditions is not fulfilled then an object cannot be said to be money. Cryptocurrency does not qualify for recognition, can be distorted, is stable and the amount is compelling, so it is clear that cryptocurrency cannot be said to be money according to theory or law. This authority includes limiting the use of certain payment instruments in the framework of prudential principles. Based on this, Bank Indonesia is correct in exercising its authority in declaring that cryptocurrency in

5. Yuliana, A. & Prasetyo, H. (2014). *Tumbling bitcoin as a payment tool.* Retrieved from http://keuangan.kontan.co.id/news/gemerincing-bitcoin-as-alat-payment
6. Bort, J. (2013). *The incredible story of a security blogger, bitcoin, and 13 packets of heroin bought on the secret internet black market.* Retrieved from http://www.businessinsider.com/hackers-use-silk-road-to-frame-a-blogger-2013-7/?IR=T
7. Black, H.C. (2009). *Black's law dictionary* (5th ed.). Eagan, MN: West Publishing (p. 906).
8. Solikin, S. (2002). *Money: Understanding, creation, and its role in the economy.* Central Bank Education and Training Center (PPSK). Substitution Series (pp. 4–6).

any form is not valid as a means of payment in Indonesia, but if it is linked to the authority of Bank Indonesia to limit the use of certain payment instruments in the context of prudential principles, then Bank Indonesia may expressly prohibit the use and circulation of cryptocurrency in Indonesia. Cryptocurrency as a technology-based transaction tool is often linked or shared with electronic money, but this assumption is also not appropriate, as in addition to not having the nature of a conventional currency, cryptocurrency also cannot exactly be said to be an electronic currency. Article 1 Point 3 Bank Indonesia Regulation Number 16/8/PBI/2014 Concerning Amendment To Bank Indonesia Regulation Number 11/12/PBI/2009 Concerning Electronic Money explains the elements of electronic money, which are:

a. Issued on the basis of the value of money paid by the holder to the issuer;
b. The value of money is stored electronically in a medium such as a server or chip;
c. Used as a means of payment to a merchant who is not an electronic publisher;

The value of electronic money deposited by holders and administered by the issuer is not a deposit as to which is meant in the laws governing banking.

One element for a can be said to be electronic money that must be issued based on the conventional money legitimately deposited first, while different to cryptocurrency created by the mining process based on a computer algorithm that has nothing to do with conventional money deposited in advance by the user; therefore, cryptocurrency does not satisfy the elements of electronic money. According to Article 1 Number 5 of the Law of the Republic of Indonesia Number 19 Year 2016 About Amendment to Law Number 11 Year 2008 About Information and Electronic Transactions (UU ITE), an electronic system is "*a set of electronic devices and procedures that function to prepare, collect, process, analyze, store, display, publish, transmit, and/or disseminate Electronic Information.*"[9]

2.2 *How cryptocurrency enhances disruptive financial technology in Indonesia*

The system of cryptocurrency is peer-to-peer, meaning there is no central server in this system and it runs according to the resources of the connected users. Cryptocurrency is an electronic system that is like money. Cryptocurrency itself is an electronic agent that gives its users access to the system. Each instance of cryptocurrency data is a facilitator between users to exchange information, where in this case the information is similar to money as it is a means of payment. Information in a cryptocurrency system does not naturally become a commodity, as information is the result of a process (output) or the result of a data processing activity that is the result of one's intellectual creations. A person who possesses the information and hence the nature of the ownership of such information will be presented therein. The information is then used in economic activities, for example, as a means of payment and investment, and the person trades the information so that commercialization of the information occurs. The cryptocurrency system provides access to its users to make payments, in which case cryptocurrency is not viewed as an object or money but rather as an information system that operates in a similar nature of money, a peer-to-peer system, and each cryptocurrency unit is an electronic agent that operates on such a system to the user. The execution of such an electronic agent by sending or transferring to another party is seen as being a transaction based on the agreement of the parties receiving cryptocurrency as a means of payment. Article 22 Paragraph 2 Number 82 Year 2012 on Electronic Transaction Systems and Transmission (PP PSTE) explains: "*In the operation of Electronic Systems devoted to Electronic Information and/or Electronic Documents that may be transferable, Electronic Information and/or Electronic Documents must be unique and explain their ownership.*"[10]

Under the article, electronic information and/or electronic documents must be unique and explain the ownership of the owner must be unique and clear mastery and ownership, although cryptography of cryptocurrency ensures access to a virtual wallet address that can only be

9. Act Number 19 Year 2016 On Amendment To Act Number 11 Year 2008 concerning Information And Electronic Transactions, Article 1 Number 5.
10. Central Government Regulation Number 82 Year 2012, Article 22 Point 2.

accessed by the party who has the private key. However, the cryptocurrency system does not explain the legal identity of the owner of the virtual wallet address (name, domicile, address) so that the ownership of cryptocurrency becomes unclear. Cryptocurrency transaction verification is performed using a digital signature. A digital signature has the following conditions:[11]

a. B must be able to validate the signature of A on the message;
b. A signature must be impossible to forge by anyone;
c. In the event of a denial by A of such a signature it shall be possible for a judge or third party to resolve the matter.

The legal identity of the owner of an address in cryptocurrency is unclear, so it is not possible to verify the signature and a third party or judge cannot verify the digital signature in the cryptocurrency system. Therefore, an electronic signature is valid when it meets the objective and subjective requirements. Subjective requirements include the quality of the signer, and that the datum in the signature shall relate only to the data of the signer, as well as to the signatory's power, where those who signed the electronic document shall be those in charge of the electronic data.

The agreement is an embodiment of the will of the parties to enter into an agreement covering the execution of the agreement, how to execute, when executed, who is executing and the object of the agreement made. In connection with the cryptocurrency agreement made by the parties in pointing the object of an achievement using the cryptocurrency option. Generally the agreement is made by one party first as a form of bidding on the object in order to fulfill its performance to another party. If the contents of the offer are the will of one party then the other party shall agree to approve the offer, so if the agreement of the parties in the use of cryptocurrency as a means of transaction or fulfillment of the achievement has been agreed then the terms of the agreement (toestemming) have been fulfilled and it is executable. Generally, before the parties agree, an agreement is to be called a negotiation, that is, the adjustment of the will between the parties to find a will fulfilling the sense of justice for the parties. Negotiations made must be free of pressure or intervention from any party, so if there is a mistake in the cryptocurrency use agreement as a performance accomplishment then the agreement can be canceled.

A new electronic signature may be evidence of a legal event when it can perform two functions, namely as a signatory's identity and as a consent of the rights and obligations contained therein. In order to qualify the material, the digital signature shall be traceable. Bitcoin's inability to verify and clearly define the legal identity of the owner of a cryptocurrency address enables the user to deny ownership of a cryptocurrency, and it cannot be traced back. Cryptocurrency therefore does not comply with Article 22 of the PP PSTE, resulting in a breach of law.

The most important factor in a global economic system in each country is the banking system. The development of the modern banking system has involved various modern changes related to service mechanisms and service products. Based on the laws and regulations concerning currencies, there is no bank in Indonesia that uses or accepts cryptocurrency as one of its services. According to Altucher, in the future banks will accept cryptocurrency as part of their service system[12]. The service will use software access as an asset storage service. In addition, there will be developments where central banks in developing countries adopt blockchain technology to make their own virtual money products.

3 CONCLUSION

Cryptocurrency is also called virtual currency because it can be claimed to be used as a means of exchange/payment of a service or object. Although cited as currency, cryptocurrency does not qualify as a means of payment, either theoretically or legally. In theory, the requirements for a valid currency include: portability; durability; it can be broken down into smaller units

11. Ibid.
12. Nubika, I. (2018). *Bitcoin: Get to know the new way of investing by millennials*. Yogyakarta, Indonesia: Genesis Learning (pp. 175–176).

(divisibility); it can be standardized; it is recognized; its value is stable. Cryptocurrency does not meet these requirements. First, cryptocurrency cannot be standardized. Cryptocurrency is an open source program and cryptocurrency is run with public participation. No central authority can govern cryptocurrency so that in theory everyone who understands programming can change the cryptocurrency programming code, as long as it gets the approval of every computer running this program, because it is not possible to standardize cryptocurrency. The second requirement that is not fulfilled for cryptocurrency is recognition, in that every currency must be recognized by the competent authority. The rupiah is money and has value because Indonesia has the power to guarantee that the rupiah can be redeemed for goods and services in its territory. Therefore, the condition of recognition is the most important condition in the existence of a currency, the recognition of the difference between ordinary paper and money. Cryptocurrency is a program created by anonymous figures and has even been banned in some countries. Therefore, cryptocurrency does not meet this requirement. The last condition that cryptocurrency does not meet is that of stable value. The cryptocurrency value is constantly changing and is based on mere speculation without any definite determinant of its value. Its market value can change from very low to very high and the value continues to fall and rise according to the speculation of society. Money must have a stable value in order to be used as a means of payment. Therefore, cryptocurrency does not meet this requirement. Cryptocurrency does not qualify as being money in theory and the Currency Act recognizes only the rupiah as a legitimate means of exchange; under the Currency Act, cryptocurrency cannot be recognized as a currency in Indonesian territory.

Cryptocurrency is a phenomenon that gets great attention from the public. The use of cryptocurrency in various forms also has considerable potential, so that although this phenomenon has been running since 2009, the government or authority regulating cryptocurrency has not taken a clear position in setting cryptocurrency, see some facts that exist among others. Cryptocurrency is a system of information that is like money and is protected by cryptography. A choice of methods in setting cryptocurrency and its variants includes freeing the system to organize itself, because it is difficult for authorities to regulate certain electronic systems such as cryptocurrency. The concept of the Internet being free from government interference, being left to self-regulate and to be delivered using a reputable system, and handing cryptocurrency to the market is a risky choice because of the high potential for its use in criminal acts.

REFERENCES

Act Number 19 Year 2016 On Amendment To Act Number 11 Year 2008 concerning Information and Electronic Transactions, Article 1 Number 5.

Bort, J. (2013). The incredible story of a security blogger, bitcoin, and 13 packets of heroin bought on the secret internet black market. Retrieved from http://www.businessinsider.com/hackers-use-silk-road-to-frame-a-blogger-2013-7/?IR=T

Black, H.C. (2009). *Black's law dictionary* (5th ed.). Eagan, MN: West Publishing.

Bovaird, C. (2017). Cryptocurrency bounces back as trader sentiment improves. *Forbes*. Retrieved from: https://www.forbes.com/sites/cbovaird/2017/09/19/cryptocurrency-bounces-back-as-trader-sentiment-improves/#1f3e897ac9a5

Central Government Regulation Number 82 Year 2012, Article 22 Point 2.

Ministry of Information and Communications of the Republic of Indonesia. (2016). *Payment method on e-commerce activity*. Retrieved from https://statistik.kominfo.go.id/site/searchKonten?iddoc=1527

Suseno, S. (2002). *Money: Understanding, creation, and its role in the economy*. Central Bank Education and Training Center (PPSK), Substitution Series (pp. 4–6).

Yuliana, A. & Prasetyo, H. (2014). *Tumbling bitcoin as a payment tool*. Retrieved from http://keuangan.kontan.co.id/news/gemerincing-bitcoin-as-alat-payment

Culture and International Law - Juwana et al. (Eds)
© 2019 Taylor & Francis Group, London, ISBN 978-1-138-38766-9

Indonesia without the state policy guidelines (GBHN): Are we lost?

Riana Susmayanti
Law Faculty, Brawijaya University, Indonesia

ABSTRACT: Since the declaration of independence in August 17, 1945, Indonesia has several constitutions changes. Starting from The 1945 Constitution (UUD 1945), Constitution of The Republic of the United States of Indonesia in 1949 (KRIS 1949), Temporary Constitution in 1950 (UUDS 1950), then back to original 1945 Constitution in July 5, 1959.

Based on The 1945 Constitution, people's sovereignty was carried out entirely by the People's Consultative Assembly (MPR). As the highest state institution, the MPR sets out the Constitution and the State Policy Guidelines (GBHN). The GBHN provides the direction of national development to achieve the country's goals based on the Constitution.

On August 10, 2002, the fourth amendment to The 1945 Constitution was ratified by the MPR. These amendment changed the structure and hierarchy of the state institutions in Indonesia. The sovereignty of the people, which was originally carried out entirely by the MPR, is now implemented according to the Constitution. The MPR is no longer as the highest state institution, even losing the authority to determine the GBHN. Then, the important question is: if there is no GBHN, how to determine the direction of national development?

To answer the research question, the researcher in this normative research will use theoretical and qualitative methods. This research is aimed at political observers and constitutional law experts. This study proves the importance of the vision, mission and programs offered by the candidates of president and vice president in the presidential election. If the candidates of president and vice president are elected and win the presidential election, then their vision, mission and program will determine the direction of national development. Since there were no GBHN, then the vision, mision and of the president will determine the direction of national development. The vision, mision and program should be implemented in the period of the elected president's term of office.

KEYWORDS: GBHN, Presidential vision, mission dan program

1 INTRODUCTION

Before the amendment to the 1945 Constitution, national development in Indonesia was guided by the GBHN, namely the state direction on the implementation of the state in broad outlines as a statement of the will of the people. On the Session of the BPUPKI-PPKI[1] (May

1. BPUPKI is abbreviation for *Badan Penyelidik Usaha-usaha Persiapan Kemerdekaan Indonesia* (Committee for the Examination of efforts for the Preparation of Independence or *Dokuritsu Junbi Chōsa-kai)*, sometimes referred to as the 'Investigating Committee for Preparatory Work for Indonesian Independence'. BPUPKI was an organization set up in March 1945 by the Japanese military authority in Java during the Japanese occupation of Indonesia as the initial stage of the establishment of independence for the area under the control of the Japanese 16th Army. Read: https://en.wikipedia.org/wiki/Investigating_Committee_for_Preparatory_Work_for_Independence (accessed September 15, 2018)

Whereas, PPKI is abbreviation for *Panitia Persiapan Kemerdekaan Indonesia* (Committee for the Preparation of Indonesia's Independence or *Dokuritsu Junbi Iinkai)* sometimes referred to as 'The Preparatory

25, 1945-August 22, 1945), the Indonesian founding fathers agreed to design the GBHN as a guideline for administrators of state government to achieve the goals of the country. The GBHN was stipulated by the MPR as a representation of people's sovereignty.

People's sovereignty means the people become kings for themselves. The state is developing if the people take part in considering what is good or bad for them, the people know that they govern themselves, they have the will and do the will with responsibility[2]. Theoretically, the GBHN was the outline as a statement of the will of the people to achieve the goal of the state as a whole and integrated which comes from their will and conscience.[3]

2 GBHN AS NATIONAL DEVELOPMENT GUIDELINES

The GBHN was implemented by the Decree of the People's Consultative Assembly (Ketetapan MPR or Tap MPR) for a period of 5 years. There were 7 (seven) Tap MPR concerning GBHN, namely: i) Tap MPR No. IV/MPR/1973; ii) Tap MPR No. IV/MPR/1978; iii) Tap MPR No. II/MPR/1983; iv) Tap MPR No. II/MPR/1988; v) Tap MPR No. II/MPR/1993; vi) Tap MPR No. II/MPR/1998; and vii) Tap MPR No. IV/MPR/1999

In each session every 5 years, the MPR carried out the routine tasks of setting the GBHN which will be mandated to the President. This routine seemed not to consider the real factors of community needs and development. This can be seen from the format and formulation of the national development goals of the entire GBHN with each other in common, namely: *"National Development aims to create a material and spiritual, just and prosperous society based on Pancasila in the Unity of the Republic of Indonesia, on the free, sovereign and united in the atmosphere of a national life that is safe, peaceful, orderly and dynamic and in an independent, friendly, orderly and peaceful world."*

In fact, during the New Order era, the GBHN was not established by MPR but Wanhankamnas (*Dewan Pertahanan dan Keamanan Nasional* or National Defense and Security Council). Wanhankamnas handed it over to President Soeharto, then the President asked the MPR to make Tap MPR concerning GBHN.[4]

GBHN in 1973 was the first GBHN in the President Soeharto era, which included government efforts to organize economic life that was experiencing hyperinflation. This was reflected in the focus of the REPELITA (*Rencana Pembangunan Lima Tahun*). REPELITA was a series of five-year plans made by the government of the New Order in Indonesia:[5]

1. REPELITA I (1969–1974) focusing on basic needs and infrastructure with an emphasis on agricultural improvements (Green Revolution) to ensure food security

Committee for Indonesian Independence'. PPKI was a body established on 7 August 1945 to prepare for the transfer of authority from the occupying Japanese to Indonesia. Read: https://en.wikipedia.org/wiki/Preparatory_Committee_for_Indonesian_Independence (accessed September 15, 2018). Read also: Frans Hendra Winarta, *Suara Rakyat Hukum Tertinggi*, (Jakarta, Penerbit Buku Kompas PT. Kompas Media Nusantara, 2009) 197-198

2. Mohammad Hatta, *Demokrasi Kita, Pikiran-pikiran Tentang Demokrasi dan Kedaulatan Rakyat*, (Bandung, Sega Arsy, 2008) 46
3. Arman Anwar, *Tidak Perlu Menghadirkan Kembali GBHN*, Workshop Pancasila Konstitusi dan Ketatanegaraan "Penataan Sistem Ketatanegaraan, Tata Cara Perubahan Undang-Undang Dasar Negara Republik Indonesia Tahun 1945 dan Reformulasi Sistem Perencanaan Pembangunan Nasional Model GBHN". Kerjasama Sekretarian Jenderal MPR dengan Fakultas Hukum Universitas Pattimura, Ambon 21-22 Oktober 2016, https://fhukum.unpatti.ac.id/htn-han/566-tidak-perlu-menghadirkan-kembali-gbhn (accessed 15 September 2018)
4. Ibid
5. https://en.wikipedia.org/wiki/New_Order_(Indonesia) and https://id.wikipedia.org/wiki/Rencana_Pembangunan_Lima_Tahun (diakses 15 Juli 2018)

2. REPELITA II (1974–1979) focusing on transmigration and infrastructure on islands outside Java, Bali and Madura and growth in primary industries, including industries that process raw materials.
3. REPELITA III (1979–1984) focusing on achieving food self-sufficiency and growth in export-oriented labour-intensive industry, including industries that process raw materials into finished.
4. REPELITA IV (1984–1989) focusing on growth in capital-good manufacturing, creating new jobs and industry, including industries that can produce their own industrial machinery for development in the next Repelita..
5. REPELITA V (1989–1994) focusing on growth in telecommunications, education, and transportation infrastructure
6. REPELITA VI (1994–1998, unfinished) focusing on infrastructure to support foreign investment and free trade

After the fall of the President Suharto regime, GBHN in 1998 was the last GBHN in the New Order and Tap MPR No. II/MPR/1998 concerning the GBHN only valid for 6 (six) months. It was first revoked by Tap MPR No IX/MPR/1998[6]. Appointment of President B.J. Habibie as successor to President Soeharto on May 22, 1998, followed by the Special Session of the MPR in November 1998. Tap MPR No. II/MPR/1998 concerning GBHN was replaced by Tap MPR No.X/MPR/1998[7] concerning the Principles of Development Reform in the Framework of Rescue and Normalization of National Life as State Policy. This document became a guide for the Indonesian people to quickly get out of the economic crisis that occurred since July 1997. The latest GBHN was ratified by Tap MPR No. IV/MPR/1999 concerning GBHN 1999-2004[8], which was a legal product of the people's representatives from the General Election in 1999.

The planning of the development program in the GBHN has not been realized systemically. Before establishing the last GBHN in the transition period (from the New Order government to the Reform Era), MPR evaluated that development during the New Order was only focused on the economic sector, imbalanced with progress in other sectors. Physically, there has been progress in the economic sector but it is fundamentally fragile because it has no clear legal basis, the law is far behind, *het recht hinct achter de feiten aan.*[9]

Towards the achievement of the GBHN, there was no evaluative action from the MPR only the President's accountability report. President's accountability report presented before the MPR General Session at the end of the President's term of office. The MPR convened to hold the President accountable as a mandate. It was possible to accept, have questions, criticism even rejects the President's accountability report.

In fact, the MPR's authority to reject the President's accountability report does not have a meaningful legal meaning. If the MPR rejects the accountability report, the MPR has 2 (two) choices, namely: 1) dismissing the President from office, or 2) ordering the President to complete or correct the report. The MPR's decision to dismiss the President from office was also meaningless, because at that time the President's term of office had ended. However, if the MPR orders the President to complete or correct his accountability report, it means the MPR *de facto* prolongs the President's term of office which should end. Based on this mechanism, the system of accountability at the end of the President's term of office only gives 1 (one)

6. Ketetapan Majelis Permusyawaratan Rakyat Republik Indonesia Nomor IX/MPR/1998 Tentang Pencabutan Ketetapan Majelis Permusyawaratan Rakyat Republik Indonesia Nomor II/MPR/1998 Tentang Garis-Garis Besar Haluan Negara
7. Ketetapan Majelis Permusyawaratan Rakyat Republik Indonesia Nomor X/MPR/1998 Tentang Pokok-Pokok Reformasi Pembangunan Dalam Rangka Penyelamatan Dan Normalisasi Kehidupan Nasional Sebagai Haluan Negara
8. Ketetapan Majelis Permusyawaratan Rakyat Republik Indonesia Nomor IV/MPR/1999 Tentang Garis-Garis Besar Haluan Negara Tahun 1999 - 2004
9. http://repository.usu.ac.id/bitstream/handle/123456789/31124/Chapter%20I.pdf?sequence=4& isAllowed=y (accessed 15 September 2018)

option to the MPR, namely accepting the report and ratifying. Since it does not have a legal meaning, the accountability report at the end of the President's term is more likely to be a political than a legal event.[10]

The explanation of the 1945 Constitution (before the amendment) states that the President is subject to and is responsible to the MPR. The President's obligation to provide accountability to the MPR is stated in Article 5 par. (1) and (2) of TAP No. III/MPR/1978 concerning *Kedudukan Dan Hubungan Tata-Kerja Lembaga Tertinggi Negara Dengan/Atau Antar Lembaga-Lembaga Tinggi Negara* (Position And Relationship Of State Highest Institutions Work With/Or Country Of High State Institutions): [11]

1. The President submits and is responsible to the MPR and at the end of his term of office gives responsibility for the implementation of the GBHN stipulated by the Constitution or the MPR before the MPR Session.
2. The President is obliged to provide liability before the Special Session of the MPR which is specifically held to hold the President accountable in the implementation of the GBHN stipulated by the Constitution or MPR.

Based on historical facts, there are 2 (two) types of President's accountability report to the MPR, namely 1) Accountability report given by the President at the MPR General Session at the end of the President's term of office; and 2) Special accountability report given by the President in the MPR Special Session.

The President's accountability report at the MPR General Session at the end of the President's term of office, in practice is a report on the implementation of duties.[12] This report is assessed by the composition of the MPR members which is different from the composition who appointed the President. Accountability at the end of the term of office of the President is carried out after the formation of the MPR results of different elections, so that the composition of the MPR's membership is certainly different, even if only a few are elected to the MPR. The nature of this accountability is merely *pro forma*.[13]

While the President's special accountability report was given in the MPR Special Session[14]. President Soekarno's special accountability report was carried out before the Provisional People's Consultative Assembly (*Majelis Permusyawaratan Rakyat Sementara* or MPRS) Special Session on March 7, 1967. The President Soekarno's special accountability report, known as Nawaksara and the Nawaksara Complementary (Pelengkap Nawaksara or Pelnawaksara), was related to the G 30-PKI (September 30 Movement by Indonesian Communist Party). The G30-PKI incident caused President Soekarno to lose confidence, unable to control security and economic decline and morals. Based on TAP MPRS No. XXXIII/MPRS/1967 concerning *Pencabutan Kekuasaan Pemerintahan Negara dari Presiden Soekarno* (the Revocation of State Government Power from President Soekarno), the MPRS withdrew the mandate (dismissal) of President

10. Bagir Manan, *Lembaga Kepresidenan* (Yogyakarta: FH UII, 2006) 112-113
11. Sumali, *Reduksi Kekuasaan Eksekutif Di Bidang Peraturan Pengganti Undang-Undang (Perpu)*, (Malang, UMM Pres, 2003) 35
12. The MPR general session is a session held by the MPR based on the duties and authorities as mandated by Article 2 paragraph 2 of the 1945 Constitution, which is at least once in five years, for example inaugurating the President and/or Vice President, while the special session is carried out by the MPR based on the situation and critical state/very important condition. At the MPR Annual General Session, the President submitted a report on the progress of his administration. But if the performance is bad and there is no progress until a certain time, then the factions can ask for a Special Session. If the President's answer is no longer satisfactory, the DPR can ask the MPR to hold a Special Session. If in the Special Session the President's responsibility is not accepted by the MPR, it means the President can be dismissed.
13. Sumali, above n 11, 35 and 37
14. The MPR Special Session is a session held by the MPR at the request of the DPR or the Annual Session of the Assembly to request and assess the accountability of the President for the implementation of the Assembly's decission. This session is held if the President is considered to violate the 1945 Constitution and deviates from the GBHN. The President's accountability is carried out in a Special Session, which usually leads to dismissal efforts.

Soekarno and appointed General Soeharto as his successor under Article 8 of the 1945 Constitution (before the amendment), with the consideration that President Soekarno could not carry out his obligations and the GBHN determined by the Constitution and MPRS.[15]

Furthermore, it is necessary to explain the President's accountability report at the MPR Annual Session in 1999-2004[16]. On October 16, 1999 President Bacharuddin Jusuf Habibie (BJ Habibie) submitted an accountability report which was later rejected by the MPR at the MPR General Session on October 19, 1999[17]. An important factor in the rejection of the report was the strong suspicion that President BJ Habibie had outlined a manipulative and inaccurate indicator of economic growth.[18] On the contrary, the rejection of the report was allegedly dominated political maneuver by the Indonesian Democratic Party of Struggle (*Partai Demokrasi Indonesia Perjuangan* or PDIP), in order to increase the political image of Megawati Soekarno Putri (Chair of the PDIP). Although still likely to become a presidential candidate for the second period, BJ Habibie stated that he would not run again in the presidential election.[19]

The MPR General Assembly then elected and appointed Abdurrahman Wahid and Megawati Sukarnoputri as President and Vice-Presidents of the 1999-2004 term, and for the first time the MPR made amendments to the 1945 Constitution[20]. Since the nation's crisis and the conflict between the DPR and the presidency, the DPR asked the MPR to hold a Special Session to hear the President's accountability report. The discourse of the MPR Special Session became clearer after the President unilaterally inaugurate a temporary officials of the Indonesian National Police Chief (*Kepala Kepolisian Republik Indonesia* or Kapolri) without coordinating with the DPR. The Special Session is planned to begin on July 21, 2001 and the President will provide an accountability report on July 23, 2001. Then the President rejected the plan and declared the MPR Special Session was illegitimate and illegal, even the President issued a Presidential Decree (*Dekrit Presiden)*[21].

Based on Article 1 TAP MPR No. II/MPR/2001, The MPR Special Session revoked the mandate (dismissal) of President Abdurrahman Wahid. The President is considered violating the GBHN because he refused to report his accountability and was not present at the MPR Special Session.[22] Furthermore, based on TAP MPR No. III/MPR/2001, the MPR determined Megawati Sukarnoputri and Hamzah Haz as President and Vice President from being appointed until 2004 (continuing the the reign of President Abdurrahman Wahid). [23]

---

15. Sumali, above n 11
16. The reformation in 1998 led to the resignation of President Soeharto, who was replaced by President BJ Habibie (21 May 1998), without the President Soeharto's accountability report. Then there were four amendments in the 1945 Constitution which were successively ratified on October 19, 1999, August 18, 2000, November 10, 2001 and August 10, 2002. The amendments to the 1945 Constitution changed the constitutional structure. Then some replacement of the President, namely President Abdurrahman Wahid (October 20 1999) and President Megawati Soekarnoputri (July 23, 2001-20 October 2004). Therefore, it is necessary to explain the President's accountability report at the MPR Annual Session in 1999-2004.
17. Based on the calculation of the MPR Secretariat General's staff, the MPR finally rejected the accountability report of President BJ. Habibie after voting in a closed manner with the results of 355 members refusing, accepting accountability of 322 members, 9 abstentions and 4 invalid votes. Source: http://kepustakaan-presiden.pnri.go.id/article_index/?box=detail&id=224&from_box=list_245&hlm=1&search_ tag=&search_-keyword=&activation_status=&presiden_id=4&presiden=habibie (diakses 8 Juli 2018, pk. 16.13 WIB)
18. Tri Astuti, *Buku Pedoman Umum Pelajar: Sejarah, Rangkuman Inti Sari Sejarah Lengkap SMA Kelas 1,2,3*, (Jakarta, Lembar Langit Indonesia, 2015) 185
19. Sumali, above n 11, 36
20. Tri Astuti, above n 18, 186
21. On July 23, 2001, the President issued a Presidential Decree containing: 1) freezing the MPR and DPR; 2) return sovereignty to the hands of the people and take action and formulate the institutions needed to hold elections within one year; and 3) save the total reform movement from the obstacles of the New Order elements by freezing the Golkar Party while awaiting the Supreme Court's decision See: Tri Astuti, above n 18, 186
22. Sumali, above n 11
23. Tri Astuti, above n 18.

At the MPR Annual Session on September 27, 2004, President Megawati Sukarnoputri delivered the accountability report on the implementation of the GBHN 1999-2004 and other MPR decisions. Chair of the House of Representatives, Chair of the Supreme Audit Board, Chairperson of the Supreme Court, and Chairperson of the Constitutional Court also gave their speeches regarding the implementation of the MPR decision. The MPR Annual Session was not giving decision on acceptance or rejection of the President's accountability report and other high institutions, but only the responses or opinions of the factions to those speeches.[24]

The President's accountability should not only be interpreted as a report at the end of the term of office, but also a continuous monitoring mechanism for the President's performance, so that accountability can be requested at any time. If within 5 (five) years of the President's term of office, either the House of Representatives (Dewan Perwakilan Rakyat or DPR) or the People's Consultative Assembly (MPR) does not question, discuss or asks the President's accountability, meaning that the President has carried out his obligations properly so that there is no accountability report at the end of the term of office. The President's report on the MPR at the end of the term of office is not in the framework of accountability, but as a state massage related to the President's political obligation to convey the necessary information for the MPR to determine the level of success of the President and hopes in the future. The responsibility of the President throughout the term of office (not only at the end of the term of office) will encourage the DPR and MPR to oversee the President, not having to wait until the end of the term of office. [25]

3 THE GBHN WAS ABOLISHED BY AMENDMENT TO THE 1945 CONSTITUTION

Before the 1945 Constitution amendment, the MPR was the highest state institution because MPR held the people's sovereignty[26]. Therefore, the MPR has the authority to determine the constitution and GBHN[27], to elect and appoint and dismiss the President[28]. The President must be responsible to the MPR because national development must be carried out based on the GBHN made by the MPR, and the President is elected by the MPR.

Based on the draft amendment to the 1945 Constitution from the MPR Working Committee of 1999-2000 (Badan Pekerja MPR RI Tahun 1999-2000), it was seen the desire to amend Article 3 concerning the procedure to elect the President. As agreed, the President is directly elected by the people, then the duties and authority of the MPR must be changed.[29]

After the amendment to The 1945 Constitution, the MPR as a consultative assembly, consisting of two legislative institutions (DPR and DPD)[30], has two powers. First, authority to change and establish the Constitution. Second, authority to inaugurate and dismiss the President. While the authority of the MPR to determine the GBHN was deleted. The 1945 Constitution amendment provides new construction on hierarchy and relations of state institutions, constitutional rights, and other significant changes. The removal of the GBHN from the MPR authority has implications for national development program previously set in the GBHN.[31]

24. NU Online, *ST MPR Dimulai, Sedot Dana Rp 30 Milyar*, Kamis, 23 September 2004, Jakarta, http://www.nu.or.id/post/read/2098/st-mpr-dimulai-sedot-dana-rp-30-milyar (accessed 8 Juli 2018, Pk. 17.40 WIB)
25. Bagir Manan, above n 10, 113-114
26. Article 1 paragraph 2 The 1945 Constitution: "Sovereignty is in the hands of the people, and is carried out entirely by the MPR."
27. Article 3 The 1945 Constitution: "The MPR define the Constitution and the GBHN."
28. Article 6 paragraph 2 The 1945 Constitution: "The President and Vice President are elected by the MPR with the major votes."
29. Mahkamah Konstitusi Republik Indonesia (MKRI), *Naskah Komprehensif Perubahan UUD Negara RI Tahun 1945, Buku III Jilid 1*, 302-309.
30. Dewan Perwakilan Rakyat (DPR) is House of Representatives, similar to parliament. Dewan Perwakilan Daerah (DPD) is Regional Representative Council, which in other countries is similar to senate.
31. Mokhammad Najih, *Pengantar Hukum Indonesia* (Malang, 3rd ed Setara Press, 2013) 83-85

4 PRESIDENTIAL VISION, MISSION AND PROGRAM AS NATIONAL DEVELOPMENT GUIDELINES

As explained in the previous section, amendments to the 1945 Constitution eliminated the authority of the MPR to determine the GBHN. National development planning based on GBHN is no longer valid. Tap MPR No. IV/MPR/1999 concerning GBHN 1999-2004[32] was the latest GBHN. The GBHN 1999-2004 mandates the implementation to be outlined in the five-year National Development Program (Program Pembangunan Nasional or PROPENAS). The program then promulgated in Law No. 25 of 2000 concerning National Development Program (PROPENAS) Year 2000-2004.[33]

Furthermore, development planning was prepared based on Law No. 25 of 2004 concerning The National Development Planning System[34] was enacted to provide guidance on national development. National development plan through three stages: National Long-Term Development Plan (*Rencana Pembangunan Jangka Panjang Nasional* or RPJPN) for 20 years, National Medium-Term Development Plan (*Rencana Pembangunan Jangka Menengah Nasional* or RPJMN) per 5 years and annual Government Work Plan (*Rencana Kerja Pemerintah* or RKP).

The determination of those plans must be in the form of law to bind all parties to implement it.[35] According to Law No. 25 of 2004, the RPJP is stipulated as a Law[36], the RPJM as a Presidential Regulation[37], and the RKP also as a Presidential Regulation.[38] Therefore The RPJPN is regulated in Law No. 17 of 2007 concerning National Long Term Development Plan for 2005 - 2025[39], while the RPJMN and the RKP are regulated as follows:

1. There are four periodes of the RPJMN:[40]
   a. RPJMN I of 2005-2009 (Presidential Regulation No. 7 of 2005)
   b. RPJMN II of 2010-2014 (Presidential Regulation No. 5 of 2010)
   c. RPJMN III of 2015-2019 (Presidential Regulation No. 2 of 2015)
   d. RPJMN IV of 2020-2024
2. So far there are five RKPs:[41]
   a. RKP of 2014 (Presidential Regulation No. 39 of 2013)
   b. RKP of 2015 (Presidential Regulation No. 43 of 2014)
   c. RKP of 2016 (Presidential Regulation No. 60 of 2015)
   d. RKP of 2017 (Presidential Regulation No. 45 of 2016)
   e. RKP of 2018 (Presidential Regulation No. 79 of 2017)

32. Ketetapan Majelis Permusyawaratan Rakyat Republik Indonesia Nomor IV/MPR/1999 Tentang Garis-Garis Besar Haluan Negara Tahun 1999 - 2004
33. UU No. 25 Tahun 2000 tentang Program Pembangunan Nasional (PROPENAS) Tahun 2000-2004
34. UU No. 25 Tahun 2004 tentang Sistem Perencanaan Pembangunan Nasional
35. Point 3 in General Expalanatory of Law No. 25 of 2004 concerning The National Development Planning System
36. Article 13 paragraph (1) Law No. 25 of 2004 concerning The National Development Planning System
37. Article 19 paragraph (1) Law No. 25 of 2004 concerning The National Development Planning System
38. Article 26 paragraph (1) Law No. 25 of 2004 concerning The National Development Planning System
39. UU No. 17 Tahun 2007 Tentang Rencana Pembangunan Jangka Panjang Nasional Tahun 2005 – 2025
40. *RPJM Nasional I Tahun 2005–2009 (Peraturan Presiden No. 7 Tahun 2005), RPJM Nasional II Tahun 2010–2014 (Peraturan Presiden No. 5 Tahun 2010), RPJM Nasional III Tahun 2015–2019 (Peraturan Presiden No. 2 Tahun 2015)* and *RPJM Nasional IV Tahun 2020–2024.*
41. *RKP 2014 (Peraturan Presiden No. 39 Tahun 2013), RKP 2015 (Peraturan Presiden No. 43 Tahun 2014 jo Peraturan Presiden No. 3 Tahun 2015 tentang Perubahan Atas Peraturan Presiden Republik Indonesia Nomor 43 Tahun 2014 tentang Rencana Kerja Pemerintah Tahun 2015), RKP 2016 (Peraturan Presiden No. 60 Tahun 2015), RKP 2017 (Peraturan Presiden No. 45 Tahun 2016)*, and *RKP 2018 (Peraturan Presiden No. 79 Tahun 2017)*

Amendment to The 1945 Constitution concerning the strengthening of the presidential system also appears in Article 6A paragraph 1[42]. Initially the president was elected by the MPR, now directly elected by the people. It causes all candidates for president and vice president (presidential candidates) should compete in the presidential election to get the most people's votes.

One of the requirements to be candidates for President and Vice President is to have a vision, mission and program in organizing government.[43] The vision, mission and work program that will be implemented by the government for 5 (five) years of government if they're elected, becomes a significant important substance as a mandatory requirement for presidential candidates.[44] In registering presidential candidates to General Election Commissions (*Komisi Pemilihan Umum* or KPU), Political Parties or Joint Political Parties must submit the manuscript of the vision, mission, and program of the presidential candidates.[45] Then the KPU is obliged to facilitate the dissemination of campaign material which includes the vision, mission and program of the presidential candidates through the KPU website.[46]

The Vision, mission and program of the presidential candidates are offered during the presidential election campaign to convince voters.[47] The vision, mission and program of the presidential candidates become campaign material.[48] The vision, mission and program of the presidential candidate are made based on the principle that the President holds the power of government according to Article 4 paragraph 1 of the 1945 Constitution, and is an elaboration of the legislation.[49] The vision and mission of the presidential candidates refers to the RPJP in accordance with Law No. 17 of 2007 concerning the National Long Term Development Plan for 2005-2025, and elaborated in the elected President's annual work plan in the form of the RPJMN and RKP in accordance with Law No. 25 of 2004 concerning the National Development Planning System.[50]

Debate forums for presidential candidates as part of the presidential campaign are needed for presidential candidates to make effective dissemination of their vision, mission and program in an educational and informative manner.[51] The substance for the debate of the presidential candidates is a national vision in accordance with the state's objectives[52] in the Preamble of the 1945 Constitution.[53]

The formulation of the presidential candidates' vision, mission and program must be through academic studies so that it is realistic (can be implemented) and scientific (identified and measured). Based on the political campaign strategy, the vision, mission and programs

42. Article 6A paragraph 1: "The President and Vice President are elected in one pair directly by the people."
43. Article 5 (r) Law No. 42 of 2008 concerning Presidential Election jo Article 169 (t) Law No. 7 of 2017 concerning General Election.
44. General Explanation Paragraph 5 Law No. 42 of 2008 concerning Presidential Election
45. Article 15 (e) Law No. 42 of 2008 concerning Presidential Election jo Article 229 paragraph 1 (e) Law No. 7 of 2017 concerning General Election.
46. Article 37 paragraph 2 Law No. 42 of 2008 concerning Presidential Election jo Article 274 paragraph 2 Law No. 7 of 2017 concerning General Election.
47. Article 1 point 22 Law No. 42 of 2008 concerning Presidential Election jo Article 1 point 35 Law No. 7 of 2017 concerning General Election
48. Article 37 paragraph (1) Law No. 42 of 2008 concerning Presidential Election jo Article 274 paragraph 1 (a) Law No. 7 of 2017 concerning General Election
49. Explanation Article 15 (e) Law No. 42 of 2008 concerning Presidential Election jo Penjelasan Article 229 paragraph 1 (e) Law No. 7 of 2017 concerning General Election
50. Explanation Article 37 paragraph (1) Law No. 42 of 2008 concerning Presidential Election jo Penjelasan Article 274 paragraph 1 (c) Law No. 7 of 2017 concerning General Election
51. General Explanation Paragraph 7 Law No. 42 of 2008 concerning Presidential Election
52. There are four state's objectives in the Preamble of the 1945 Constitution: protect all the people of Indonesia and all the independence and the land that has been struggled for, and to improve public welfare, to educate the life of the people and to participate toward the establishment of a world order based on freedom, perpetual peace and social justice (*melindungi segenap bangsa dan seluruh tumpah darah Indonesia, memajukan kesejahteraan umum, mencerdaskan kehidupan bangsa, dan ikut melaksanakan ketertiban dunia yang berdasarkan kemerdekaan, perdamaian abadi, dan keadilan sosial*)
53. Article 39 paragraph (5) Law No. 42 of 2008 concerning Presidential Election jo Article 277 paragraph 5 Law No. 7 of 2017 concerning General Election

offered as campaign promises must fulfill several conditions, namely:[54] 1) focus on a clear message; 2) get the message out; 3) recruit a campaign staff, 4) build coalitions of supporters; 5) set the agenda, and 6) build momentum.

Without the GBHN, national development is more detailed and measurable because it is explained in the vision, mission and program of the elected president. It guarantees the achievement of national goals. The importance of the Presidential vision, mission and program in national development shows that the people must pay attention to the president's personal moral conduct as public officials. President as the right man in the right place must have the fiduciary capacity and character of the statesman[55]. The President must have ability and capability to continue or improve the previous president's program, but also a concept for further national development.

5 CONCLUSIONS AND RECOMMENDATIONS

Without the GBHN, the President organize national development based on his vision, mission and program. The presidential vision, mission and program is compiled based on National Long-Term Development Plan (*Rencana Pembangunan Jangka Panjang Nasional* or RPJPN) for a period of 20 years, which is then elaborated in the National Medium-Term Development Plan (*Rencana Pembangunan Jangka Menengah Nasional* or RPJMN) per 5 years dan annual Government Work Plan (*Rencana Kerja Pemerintah* or RKP). Thus the importance of the presidential vision, mission and program in national development planning, making the people must be smart and careful in electing the president in the direct presidential election.

REFERENCES

Anwar, Arman, *Tidak Perlu Menghadirkan Kembali GBHN*, Workshop Pancasila Konstitusi dan Ketatanegaraan "Penataan Sistem Ketatanegaraan, Tata Cara Perubahan Undang-Undang Dasar Negara Republik Indonesia Tahun 1945 dan Reformulasi Sistem Perencanaan Pembangunan Nasional Model GBHN". Kerjasama Sekretarian Jenderal MPR dengan Fakultas Hukum Universitas Pattimura, Ambon 21-22 Oktober 2016

Astuti, Tri, *Buku Pedoman Umum Pelajar: Sejarah, Rangkuman Inti Sari Sejarah Lengkap SMA Kelas 1,2,3*, (Jakarta, Lembar Langit Indonesia, 2015)

Dermott, Richard Mc., *A Campaign Promise You Can Trust*, (Cincinnati Ohio: Association for Quality and Participation, March/April 1999), 22.2. Proquest, The Journal for Quality and Participation

Dyzenhaus, David, *The Constitution Of Law: Legality in a Time of Emergency*, (New York, Cambridge University Press, 2006)

Hatta, Mohammad, *Demokrasi Kita, Pikiran-pikiran Tentang Demokrasi dan Kedaulatan Rakyat*, (Bandung: Sega Arsy, 2008)

Mahkamah Konstitusi Republik Indonesia (MKRI), *Naskah Komprehensif Perubahan UUD Negara RI Tahun 1945, Buku III Jilid 1*

Manan, Bagir, *Lembaga Kepresidenan*, (Yogyakarta, FH UII, 2006)

Najih, Mokhammad, *Pengantar Hukum Indonesia*, (Malang, 3rd, Setara Press, 2013)

Sumali, *Reduksi Kekuasaan Eksekutif Di Bidang Peraturan Pengganti Undang-Undang (Perpu)*, (Malang, UMM Press, 2003)

Winarta, Frans Hendra, *Suara Rakyat Hukum Tertinggi*, (Jakarta, Penerbit Buku Kompas PT. Kompas Media Nusantara, 2009)

54. Richard Mc. Dermott, *A Campaign Promise You Can Trust*, (Cincinnati Ohio: Association for Quality and Participation, March/April 1999), 22.2. Proquest, The Journal for Quality and Participation, 22-25
55. The researcher agreed to Evan Fox-Decent's dissertation work *'Sovereignty's Promise: The State as Fiduciary'*. Read: David Dyzenhaus, *The Constitution Of Law: Legality in a Time of Emergency*, (New York: Cambridge University Press, 2006) x

The 1945 Constitution
Law No. 25 of 2000 concerning National Development Program (PROPENAS) Year 2000-2004
Law No. 25 of 2004 concerning The National Development Planning System
Law No. 17 of 2007 concerning National Long Term Development Plan for 2005 - 2025
Law No. 42 of 2008 concerning Presidential Election
Law No. 7 of 2017 concerning General Election.
http://kepustakaan-presiden.pnri.go.id/article_index/?box=detail&id=224&from_box=list_245&hlm=1& search_ tag=&search_keyword=&activation_status=&presiden_id=4&presiden=habibie (accessed 8 Juli 2018, at. 16.13 WIB)
http://repository.usu.ac.id/bitstream/handle/123456789/31124/Chapter%20I.pdf?sequence=4& isAllowed=y (accessed 15 September 2018)
https://en.wikipedia.org/wiki/Preparatory_Committee_for_Indonesian_Independence (accessed September 15, 2018).
https://en.wikipedia.org/wiki/Investigating_Committee_for_Preparatory_Work_for_Independence (accessed September 15, 2018)
https://en.wikipedia.org/wiki/New_Order_(Indonesia) and https://id.wikipedia.org/wiki/Rencana_ Pembangunan_Lima_Tahun (accessed July 15, 2018)
NU Online, *ST MPR Dimulai, Sedot Dana Rp 30 Milyar*, Kamis, 23 September 2004, Jakarta, http://www.nu.or.id/post/read/2098/st-mpr-dimulai-sedot-dana-rp-30-milyar (accessed July 8, 2018)

Culture and International Law - Juwana et al. (Eds)
© 2019 Taylor & Francis Group, London, ISBN 978-1-138-38766-9

Marine resources and fisheries management based on local wisdom: The application of the customary law of Serdang Sultanate, North Sumatra

Rika Kurniaty
International Law Department, Faculty of Law, Brawijaya University, Malang, Indonesia
Coastal and Marine Research Center, Brawijaya University, Malang, Indonesia

ABSTRACT: This paper aims to examine the role of the customary marine law of the Serdang Sultanate in North Sumatra in the utilization and management of marine resources, and to explore the arrangement and recognition of national legislation on customary law in Indonesia. Excessive exploitation of marine and fishery resources is one of the biggest threats to world fisheries management nowadays. International law has provided some related rules; however, Indonesia with its character as an archipelagic country, also recognizes the management of marine resources through a framework of customary law (*hukum adat*) and local wisdom, both of which still play an essential role in the community. The government has issued various rules relating to the recognition of the existence of indigenous and tribal peoples, recognized by their customary rights and legal system (including natural resources management in the region). One of the existing customary laws in Indonesia is the marine law of Serdang Sultanate, which has had legal rules governing marine ordinances prevailing in its territory since the reign of Sultan Muhammad Shah (1424–1444 AD) This article is written normatively. The data used are secondary data collected through literature study, consisting of primary, secondary, and tertiary legal materials related to the topic.

KEYWORDS: Marine resources and fisheries management, Local wisdom, Customary law

1 INTRODUCTION

The utilization of marine and fisheries resources involves various stakeholders with different interests. It contains high conflict potential with the trigger factor being an imbalance in accessing resources in the use of technology, and an inequality in the acquisition of opportunities to extract these resources. A legal instrument is needed to regulate the use of resources that can accommodate various interests by not abandoning the principles of justice and sustainability. The government, as the holder of authority over resource management, has issued multiple laws and regulations (in such forms as laws, ministerial decrees, ministerial regulations and government regulations) which function to regulate the mechanism for the use of these resources.

Regarding the management and utilization of marine and fisheries resources by local communities or indigenous peoples, the government has issued various national legal bases in the form of recognition of the existence of indigenous peoples and recognition of their rights in managing resources: the 1945 Constitution (1945); Law Number 5 of 1960 concerning the basic rules of Agrarian Principles; Law Number 5 of 1990 concerning Conservation of Biological Natural Resources and their Ecosystems; Law Number 39 of 1999 concerning Human Rights; Act Number 23 of 2014 concerning Regional Government; Law Number 27 of 2007 in conjunction with Law Number 1 of 2014 concerning Management of Coastal Areas and Small Islands; Law

Number 6 of 2014 concerning Villages; Law Number 32 of 2014 concerning Marine Affairs; Ministerial Regulation Number 17 of 2008 concerning Conservation Areas in Coastal Areas and Small Islands; Ministerial Regulation Number 2 of 2009 concerning Procedures for Determination of Aquatic Conservation Areas; Ministerial Regulation Number 40 of 2014 concerning Participation and Empowerment of Communities in the Management of Coastal Areas and Small Islands. These rules are formally issued in the form of written rules and are binding nationally.

On the other hand, the community, especially indigenous people, has its practices for managing resources that are believed to be communal property. These rules generally exist in the form of local agreements that are not contained in written texts but are delivered in oral form from generation to generation. This instrument is often referred to as customary law, but if this regulation is born from non-indigenous people, it is referred to as a 'local agreement', although the existence of a local agreement forms it. Customary law and 'local agreements' are binding and have legal consequences in the form of sanctions for each violator.

One of the customary laws governing the sea, and still observed in the community, is the Serdang Sultanate law in North Sumatra. The Serdang Sultanate has legal rules governing maritime procedures that apply in its territory. This customary marine law of the Serdang Sultanate is a legacy of the Malacca Sultanate law, which was compiled during the reign of Sultan Muhammad Shah (1424–1444 AD). This paper aims to examine the role of the customary maritime law of the Serdang Sultanate in North Sumatra in the utilization and management of marine natural resources, and to explore the arrangement and recognition of national legislation on customary law in Indonesia.

The results of the analysis of this paper are expected to be able to examine the customary law and national law in a direction that ensures the sustainability of marine resources, while upholding respect for the rights of indigenous peoples. In other words, this paper tries to give reasons for the importance of seeing the law as a social fact. Utsman (2009)[1] explains that law as a social fact is about the legal process that is observed in society (law in action), which is related to the reciprocal relationship between law and other institutions and is non-doctrinal and empirical. Thus, it is hoped that recognition and adherence to the activities carried out by the community is a collective action with full awareness and a high sense of belonging.

2 THE ROLE OF MARINE CUSTOMARY ARRANGEMENT OF SERDANG SULTANATE, NORTH SUMATRA

The Serdang Sultanate is one of the Islamic-style kingdoms in Indonesia, which is based in the territory of North Sumatra Province. The establishment of the Serdang Sultanate was inseparable from the role of the Aceh Darussalam Sultanate during the reign of Sultan Iskandar Muda. The Serdang Sultanate was a faction of the Deli Sultanate, which was founded in 1632.

Starting from internal conflict to fight for power in the Deli Sultanate, eventually the Serdang Sultanate was formed. It was founded by the descendants of the founder of the Deli Sultanate, specifically Tuanku Umar Johan Alam Shah. He established the Middle Sultanate after being expelled from the Deli Sultanate along with his mother, Tuanku Puan Sampali.[2]

Tuanku Umar Johan Alam Shah and his mother arrived at a place that was then given the name Kampung Besar or Serdang. It was here that he founded the Serdang Sultanate and served as the first king in 1723. The sultanate reached its heyday during the reign of Sultan Thaf Sinar Basyar Shah, or Sultan Besar Serdang, in 1822–1851. In 1862, the Serdang Sultanate was attacked by the Dutch government; it suffered defeat and surrendered to the Dutch government. Subsequently, following the Act van Erkenning, dated August 16, 1862, the Serdang Sultanate was under Dutch control. At the same time, the Serdang Sultanate was still in conflict with the Deli Sultanate of the king's brother.

1. Utsman, S. (2009). *Dasar-dasar sosiologi hukum: Makna dialog antara hukum dan masyarakat.* Yogyakarta, Indonesia: Pustaka Pelajar.
2. Retrieved from http://www.kerajaannusantara.com/id/kesultanan-serdang/sejarah-umum/.

In terms of the marine resources in Serdang Sultanate, most people in the Malay Peninsula believe the sea to be a gift from God from which to make a living. In addition, regions in the Malay Peninsula are also well known as trade centers that are often visited by merchants from other countries to conduct transactional activities. The same belief applies to the people who live in the territory of the Serdang Sultanate, North Sumatra (formerly East Sumatra), where most of the Serdang people who live on the coast depend for their lives on the harvest of marine resources. Therefore, the Serdang Sultanate felt that it was necessary to formulate rules relating to maritime affairs and activities in its territory. This law was drafted as a reference to regulate procedures and all matters concerning marine activities that took place in the oceanic region of the Serdang Sultanate. As mentioned above, the Serdang Sultanate was a government of an Islamic-style kingdom established in 1723 AD with Tuanku Umar Johan as its first sultan. The history of the establishment of the Serdang Sultanate is closely related to several other kingdoms in the Malay Peninsula, including the Sultanate of Aceh Darussalam, the Sultanate of Malacca, and the Sultanate of Deli.

The customary law that regulates marine affairs in the territory of the Serdang Sultanate is adopted from similar regulations in force in the Malacca Sultanate. The customary maritime law of the Malacca Sultanate was compiled during the reign of Sultan Muhammad Shah, in 1424–1444 AD. This law must be obeyed by every ship, barge, and boat subject to the Malacca Sultanate. This customary maritime law was used until the 19th century AD, before the Dutch entered the eastern coastal region of Sumatra, including the Serdang Sultanate region.

The customary maritime law of the Serdang Sultanate contains several commonly used terms. The following are the rules contained in the marine customary law of the Serdang Sultanate, where all people on-board, including the skipper (ship captain), convert (navigator), artisan, and crew must obey the norm and customary law, applied in the port or while on-board. If a ship is going to sea, everyone on-board must obey the command of the captain of the vessel. When the boat unfurls its sail, the captain instructs his men to be on guard, including ensuring that the ship is ready to sail. People who are given the task of maintaining security must be careful in carrying out their duties. If undesirable things happen, then those responsible must be punished and fined, for example, as follows:[3]

- If the ship experiences a hazardous condition and suffers damage due to the negligence of the officers who should be on guard then, according to the law, they have to be lashed 20 times.
- If the ship is in a state of danger while the guards are unaware, then they should be sentenced to binding eight times.
- If the guards allow other ships to pass without giving a signal, then they will be subject to seven lashes of the whip.
- If the guard who is supposed to be in charge of supervising the slaves is negligent in his work and allows the slaves to flee, then the guard concerned must be flogged 60 times.
- If the officer who is supposed to keep the ship from being unstable and not let water enter the boat is negligent in carrying out their duties, then they are subject to 15 lashes.
- If the officers on guard do not pay attention to the circumstances around them so that there is a case of theft in the boat, then the officer will be punished twice by everyone in the boat.

Furthermore, regarding disposal of goods into the sea, there are rules that if a storm is expected to occur, or a tornado is happening, and it is required to jettison some of the cargo into the sea to reduce the burden on the ship, then there will be a discussion about anything that is on-board. Passengers carrying loads, both large and small, must be willing to dispose of their cargo into the sea if it has been agreed upon in the discussion forum. If the skipper is negligent in consulting people who carry the load and throws baggage into the sea indiscriminately, then the skipper will be blamed and will merit punishment.

3. Retrieved from https://www.bphn.go.id/data/documents/kontribusi_hukum_adat_dlm_pengembangan_hkm_laut_di_indonesia.pdf.

If a ship collides with a battleship, where it can cause loss of life, then this mistake must be borne by all those on-board. Everyone must pay the same amount. This rule applies without exception, both for the rich and poor, both men and women, children and adults. If a ship has an accident and a collision occurs due to hurricanes, storms, being trapped in shallow waters, or contact with other boats, causing the boat to sink, some laws regulate this. Such incidents were not considered to be caused by natural factors (wind conditions) but because of the negligence of people who should be responsible (human error).

If, for example, a hurricane occurs, endeavors must be made to save the ship to avoid more significant losses. The law states that losses incurred because of the incident must be borne and divided into three parts. As many as two-thirds must be carried by the person who is considered the most responsible for the occurrence of the accident, while the shipowner bears the other third.

Furthermore, the Serdang Sultanate established rules for entering ports and trading, and if the skipper wants to stop at a port, island or coastal port, then a consultation must be held first. If approved, the ship can go to the place where the skipper wants. If there is no consultation before anchoring, the skipper is declared to have made a mistake and deserves to be charged. If the ship arrives at a port city, then the first to be allowed to get off the boat to trade is the skipper, for a four-day period, who must be escorted by some appointed officers. After completing their business, the skipper is required to return to the ship to continue his responsibilities. Following the skipper, the next in turn is the *kiwi* (merchant), who is allowed to go ashore to trade for two days. Lastly, all the people on-board go ashore to purchase. If the time set for trading has expired and the skipper wants to buy the goods that have been taken on-board, then no one is allowed to bid a price higher than the offer submitted by the skipper. In addition, the skipper is the first person who has the right to know the cost of goods to be sold. If there are passenger ships who buy female slaves (servants) without the knowledge of the skipper, then the skipper is given the right to seize the female slaves without having to pay compensation.

Rules concerning ship detention in Serdang Sultanate: if the season is almost over, while the skipper declines to sail, then the merchants will wait at their own expense for seven days. If after seven days, the skipper does not sail then the skipper must reimburse the costs incurred by the merchants. On the other hand, if the merchants cause delays in shipping, while the season is almost over, the skipper will detain his ship for seven days at his own expense. If seven days have passed and the merchants have not arrived, the skipper has the right to set sail without having to wait. However, the skipper does not get any compensation for the costs incurred during the waiting period.

According to the law, if the season is almost over, and the captain of the boat fails to sail, the skippers will wait for their expenses for seven days. If the skipper does not navigate and the season is over, the price paid for the transportation of the cargo will be returned to the merchants. If the merchants are the reason for the delay, and the season is almost over, the skipper will stay his boat for seven days at their expense, and after that, the skipper has the right to sail without them (if they are not finished), and nothing is paid or done regarding that. If the season is not far away, and the skipper is eager to sail immediately, then he must notify the merchants and negotiate with them for yachting within 7–15 days. If the merchants are not ready at that time, the skipper has the right to leave them behind and sail immediately.

Another significant point concerns the death penalty and rules about fights on ships. There are four cases on-board that threaten the death penalty for the perpetrators.[4] Also, if someone

4. According to Serdang Sultanate common rule, the death penalty will be applied:

   a. To people who rebel against the skipper;
   b. To people who form conspiracies to kill the skipper;
   c. To someone who is carrying a sharp weapon (*keris*), while no one else has one, and uses the *keris* arbitrarily and is suspected of a dangerous action, then everyone on the ship has the right to kill that person for the sake of avoiding the threat of danger;
   d. In the event of rape or adultery.

fights on the ship, with the intention of injuring his opponent, but escapes and is precisely about the part of the vessel, then the person will be fined four Javanese *petis* trays. If someone fights on the front of the ship and attacks the place where the screen is, then the offender will be punished with the most severe death penalty. However, if this can be prevented, then the perpetrator will only be subject to a fine of one Laksa (ten thousand), or five Javanese *petis* trays. If someone fights and chases another up to the door of the skipper's room, even if he does not unsheathe a *keris*, the offender is allowed to die. However, if the perpetrator asks for forgiveness, then the punishment is for him to pay a fine of four trays of Javanese *petisis* and to cut buffalo for the skipper's party.

To prevent theft on the ship the law regulates that if a man (who is not a slave) is caught stealing either gold, silver or other valuables on a boat, then he will be punished according to the punishment imposed on land. Moreover, if the person who steals is a slave, he must first meet with his master, and if it turns out the master knows about the theft and does not inform the skipper, then the punishment for the slave is to have his hand cut off, while the master is required to pay a fine.

The adoption of customary law regarding marine affairs in the territory of the Serdang Sultanate's territory contains positive values for the sustainability of governance and the pattern of life of the Serdang people. These values include:

a. Governance order. The existence of customary marine law which is applied in Serdang Sultanate proves that governance in this kingdom has been organized and covers many areas of community life.
b. Safety. One of the objectives to be achieved by the application of the customary law on marine affairs is to provide a guarantee of protection to minimize the occurrence of things that are not desirable during a voyage.
c. Discipline. The application of the customary law regarding marine affairs in the Serdang Sultanate, directly or indirectly, will educate and control all communities or sea transportation users in the Serdang Sultanate region because there are rules and penalties to be imposed.

3 THE ARRANGEMENT AND RECOGNITION OF NATIONAL LAW ON CUSTOMARY RESOURCE MANAGEMENT IN INDONESIA

The 1945 Indonesian Constitution as the highest legislation protects the rights of customary law in communities and supports its development through three articles, namely Article 18 B, Article 28, and Article 32. Article recognition of customary community rights is stated in Article 18 B Paragraph 2, which reads that the state recognizes and respects indigenous peoples as well as their traditional rights as long as they are alive and in accordance with the development of society and the principles of the Unitary State of the Republic of Indonesia, which is regulated in law. In addition, there is also Article 28 Paragraph 3, which reads that cultural identity and traditional rights are respected following the development of times and civilizations. Whereas Article 32, besides guaranteeing the sustainability of indigenous peoples' rights, is also a mandate for the government to always provide facilities for the growth of values in the mass culture. The article declares that the state should promote Indonesia's national culture in the midst of world civilization by guaranteeing the freedom of the people in maintaining and developing their cultural values.

Things that need to be observed are the prerequisites that must be fulfilled by indigenous peoples in order to get guarantees to be able to exercise their rights in resource management, namely: the traditional rights of the community are still alive, in accordance with the development of society, in accordance with the principles of the Unitary Republic of Indonesia, and regulated in law. Despite the fact that now, most common values and rules have begun to weaken as a result of the enactment of Law Number 5 of 1979 concerning Village Government, which standardizes the form of village governance, but in its development, the government now has a strong desire to regrow the customary law. Guidance on the implementation of the guarantee and recognition of community rights must be outlined in the statute. At present, the government is working on a draft law on the Recognition and Protection of the Rights of Customary Law Communities.

From now on, the completion of Law Number 27 of 2007 in conjunction with Law Number 1 of 2014 is about the clarity of recognition of the rights of customary law communities in managing their resources. Like the 1945 Constitution, Law Number 27 of 2007 in conjunction with Law Number 1 of 2014 also provides the prerequisites for indigenous peoples to receive coastal resource management rights. These prerequisites are stated in Article 1 and Article 22, namely: settling in some geographical regions in the Republic of Indonesia because of the ties of ancestral origin, strong relations with land, territories and natural resources; having customary government institutions; having conventional law arrangements in their usual regions; the customary law community is stipulated by legislation.

In this case, Law Number 23 of 2014 concerning Regional Government relates to Chapter V of Provincial Authority in the sea and rural areas characterized by islands. This chapter regulates the authority of the province in the sea to manage marine resources, the scope of management activities and the field of management. According to this law, the area is given to the authority to regulate natural resources at sea, including: exploration, exploitation, conservation, and management of marine assets outside oil and natural gas; administrative arrangements; spatial arrangements; participation in maintaining security at sea; contributing to the preservation of state sovereignty. These activities can be carried out at most 12 nautical miles as measured from the coastline toward the open sea and islands' waters. If the distance between two rural regions involves less than 24 miles of sea, the authority to manage natural resources in the sea is divided according to distance or measured under the midline principle of the region between the two provinces.

In Indonesian regulations, the management of coastal and marine areas based on customary law is also legalized by ministerial rules and decrees. The Minister of Maritime Affairs and Fisheries Regulation is associated with the management of coastal resources according to local wisdom, where the community is the implementer of control in the Ministerial Decree of Marine and Fisheries Number 40 of 2014 concerning Participation and Community Empowerment in the Management of Coastal Areas and Small Islands. Through this ministerial decree, the public is given the opportunity to participate in all stages in the management of coastal resources and small islands, namely, at the planning, implementation, and supervision stages (Article 4).

The participation of the community in the proposed formulation of management plans must be submitted through community organizations to the provincial or district/city government (Article 6). In Article 1, it is explained that social organizations (*ormas*) are organizations that are established and formed by the community, voluntarily, based on similar aspirations, desires, needs, interests, activities, and goals to participate in development to achieve the goals of Republic of Indonesia unity based on *Pancasila*. The question is which party will determine that an organization is a mass organization that complies, or does not comply, with this regulation? How can a community assess whether these organizations can become mouthpieces for their aspirations? Therefore, a corrective measure is needed so that the public can understand the clarity of the organizations in question.

In addition to Ministerial Decree Number 40 of 2014, Government Regulation on Marine and Fisheries Number 13 of 2014 concerning the Network of Aquatic Conservation Areas is also issued. The conservation area referred to in this government regulation is a protected water area, managed with a zoning system to realize the sustainable management of fish resources and the environment. So, the network of the watershed conservation area is a collaboration between the administration of two or more watershed conservation areas in a synergistic manner that has bio-cyclic links (Article 1). However, Article 5 explains that in addition to bio-fisheries, networks can be formed based on the attachment of sociocultural, economic and governance aspects. Sociocultural aspects include community support, potential conflicts, potential threats, local wisdom, and customs.

3.1 *Analysis of the relationship between legislation and customary rules in the management of marine resources based on local wisdom*

This analysis is needed to see how far the harmonization of customary law applies in the community with legislation that legally binds the community in regulating and managing coastal resources. The analysis includes criteria for indigenous peoples and recognition of the implementation of collective management.

3.1.1 *Standards for customary law communities*

There are differences in approaches between indigenous and tribal law communities so that it is necessary to formulate criteria for indigenous and tribal peoples that can be used by all laws and regulations. Efforts to reformulate the requirements of indigenous peoples are essential to avoid multiple interpretations of the existence of indigenous peoples, which will lead to clashes between rules, but also to avoid conflicts at the community level.

The existence of indigenous and tribal peoples according to Law Number 27 of 2007 in conjunction with Law Number 1 of 2014 must have legitimacy or be recognized by the provisions of the legislation. However, until now no laws and regulations govern the recognition of a typical law community. The rule is still in the draft stage, namely the Draft Bill on Recognition and Protection of Indigenous Peoples. The thing that needs to be prepared is an institution that is tasked with verifying whether or not the existing indigenous people meet the criteria required by the legislation.

3.1.2 *Recognition of implementation of customary law*

There are some inconsistencies between the rules that have been enacted by Law Number 27 of 2007 and the management mechanisms that have existed in the community. This inconsistency can be eliminated by making improvements to both parties, both in Law Number 27 of 2007 in conjunction with Law Number 1 of 2014 and in the rules that are observed by indigenous peoples in managing coastal resources. These inconsistencies occur in several ways, namely:

a. The planning process that makes the role of the community equal to the business world. This opens the opportunity for the dominance of business interests in the mechanism of coastal resource management, in contrast to the interests of the community. This matter is considered not as per the mandate of the 1945 Constitution that requires the exploitation of natural wealth for the prosperity and welfare of the people.
b. Law Number 27 of 2007 in conjunction with Law Number 1 of 2014 grants privileges to customary law communities in the management of fisheries resources with no requirement for location permits and management permits but, on the other hand, there are requirements for considering national interests by the provisions of regulations legislation. This raises the problem of the extent of tolerance given by the state to guarantee the freedom; when the Regional Regulation becomes one of our laws and regulations, what is the position of indigenous peoples' power when the environmental regulation is more favorable to the business world?
c. Through the law, the government requires the legalization of the existence of indigenous peoples as a precondition for the granting of coastal resource management rights. However, the criteria of indigenous peoples are still different between one law and another. Also, it is not clear which institution can legalize and verify a customary law community.
d. There are always conflicts over the territory of indigenous peoples in the management of coastal resources.

4 CONCLUSION

The practice of managing marine and fisheries resources based on the customary law of the Serdang Sultanate has existed and developed for a long time in the land of North Sumatra. The customary law has quite comprehensive rules and accommodates various marine interests in the community. The existence of the customary law of the Serdang Sultanate and other customary laws has received recognition from the government through different rules and regulations ranging from the basic law to ministerial regulations. National legislation generally recognizes the existence of general law communities and the role of customary law in the management of natural resources. The rights of indigenous peoples obtain guarantees from the Indonesian Constitution. Not only that, the customary law community is a legal subject which means being a person with rights and obligations. This right is an expression of local wisdom in the management of natural resources. However, some studies state that the recognition is a conditional recognition, where these requirements are often inconsistent between one law and another. Regarding this, the solution is to determine the proportions of involvement of local government, society, and the business world. This needs to be determined by the verifier of customary law communities, as well as the need for regional regulations that regulate the boundaries of each conventional district, and the need to trace the history and structure of various customary laws in Indonesia.

REFERENCES

Camelia, A.I. (2014). Konflik wewenang pengelolaan laut daerah.

Djojodiguno, M.M. (1964). *Asas-asas hukum adat.* Yogyakarta, Indonesia: Jajayan Badan Penerbit Gadjah Mada.

Djubedi, D. (2014). *Hak ulayat laut di era otonomi daerah.* Yogyakarta, Indonesia: Genta Press.

Kamaruzzaman Bustaman-Ahmad. (2012). (PhD, Acenologi). Tahun, Indonesia: Bandar Publishing Banda Aceh.

Keputusan Menteri Kelautan dan Perikanan Nomor 40 Tahun 2014 tentang peran serta dan pemberdayaan masyarakat dalam pengelolaan wilayah pesisir dan pulau-pulau kecil. (2014).

Lynch, O.J. & Emily, H. (2002). *Whose resources? Whose common good?: Towards a new paradigm of environmental justice and the national interest in Indonesia.* ELSAM, ICEL, ICRAF.

Mochammad Nadjib, lembaga Ilmu Pengetahuan Indonesia; Memahami Budaya Ekonomi Nelayan Sebagai Dasar Meningkatkan Pilar Ekonomi Pesisir, dikutip dari Rural Talks Ikhtiar Memahami Transformasi Sosial Ekonomi Masyarakat Desa, Indonesia Human right Committee for Social Justice (IHCS).

Peraturan Menteri Kelautan dan Perikanan Nomor 13 Tahun 2014 Tentang Jejaring Kawasan Konservasi Perairan. (2014).

Peta jalan pembaharuan hukum sumber daya alam lingkungan hidup. Kementerian Hukum dan Hak Asasi Manusia.

Quina, M. & Subagiyo, H. (2015). Ulasan Undang-Undang Nomor 32 Tahgun 2014 tentang Kelautan, Penegakan Hukum di Laut: Peluang dan tantangan. *Jurnal Hukum Lingkungan Indonesia, 2*(1), 93–104.

Rahail, J.P. (1993). *Larwul Ngabal: Hukum adat Kei bertahan menghadapi arus perubahan.* Jakarta, Indonesia: Yayasan Sejati.

Rahardjo, S. (2002). *Sosiologi hukum: Perkembangan metode dan pemilihan masalah.* Yogyakarta, Indonesia: Genta Publishing.

Simarmata, R. (2006). *Socio-legal studies dan gerakan pembaharuan hukum. digest law, society and development.* Retrieved from http://huma.or.id/wp-content/uploads/2006/12/Rikardo-Simarmata.-socio-legal-studies-dan-gerakan-pembaharuan- hukum.pdf

Soekanto, S. & Mamudji, S. (2003). *Penelitian hukum normatif* (6th ed.). Jakarta, Indonesia: Raja Grafindo Persada.

Tim Badan Pembinaan Hukum Nasional, peluang dan tantangan peradilan adat dalam sistem hukum Indonesia studi kasus peradilan adat yang 'melibatkan pihak luar'. (2013).

Undang-Undang Dasar 1945 Amandemen Undang-Undang Republik Indonesia Nomor 5 Tahun 1979 tentang pemerintahan desa. (1979).

Undang-Undang Nomor 32 Tahun 2014 tentang Kelautan

Undang-undang Nomor 27 Tahun 2007 tentang Pengelolaan Wilayah Pesisir Dan Pulau-Pulau Kecil.

Undang-Undang Republik Indonesia Nomor 23 Tahun 2014 tentang pemerintahan daerah. (2014).

Undang-Undang Republik Indonesia Nomor 27 Tahun 2007 juncto undang-undang nomor 1 tahun 2104 tentang pengelolaan wilayah pesisir dan pulau-pulau kecil. (2007).

Utsman, S. (2009). *Dasar-dasar sosiologi hukum: Makna dialog antara hukum dan masyarakat.* Yogyakarta, Indonesia: Pustaka Pelajar.

Culture and International Law - Juwana et al. (Eds)
© 2019 Taylor & Francis Group, London, ISBN 978-1-138-38766-9

The protection of Preah Vihear temple in the armed conflicts situation between Cambodia and Thailand based on international law

Ikaningtyas, Herman Suryokumoro, Hikmatul Ula & Lely Manullang
Law Faculty, Brawijaya University, Indonesia

ABSTRACT: In 2011, there was an armed conflict which caused by a border dispute between Cambodia and Thailand. The armed conflict resulted in massive destruction of Preah Vihear temple that located in the border's area between Cambodia and Thailand. Preah Vihear Temple itself has been crowned as the world heritage by UNESCO in 2008. This paper aims to analyze the status of cultural heritage in armed conflict and how the legal protection for the cultural heritage in case of armed conflict. Using statute and case approaches, this paper describes the rules in international law especially international humanitarian law related to cultural preservation and takes the case of the destruction of Preah Vihear temple as the core of the study. In international humanitarian law, cultural heritage objects are protected objects, meaning they should not be targeted by the military at the time of the armed conflict. In the event of an armed conflict, parties shall also take measures to protect cultural heritage objects within their territories and cultural heritage objects in their enemy's territory.

KEYWORDS: cultural heritage, armed conflict, legal protection

1 INTRODUCTION

When an armed conflict occurs, the parties to the war must know the status of an object as a civilian object or military objectives.[1] Civilian objects are all objects that are not military objects.[2] The function or usefulness of cultural heritage objects in general is as a place of cultural objects of historical value, preserving culture, and in the purpose for developing knowledge. Essentially, the purpose of cultural heritage objects is for non-military purposes as a civilian or public object. Cultural objects are civil objects that must be protected when armed conflict occurs.

However, an armed conflict always brings the destructive effect and damage to heritage objects or cultural heritage. According to Hans van der Hoeven, in the *Memory of the World Program*, the destruction of cultural heritage objects and libraries is as old as the emergence of the concept of culture itself. The purpose of destroying cultural heritage objects is common in the history of armed conflict. The aim of which is to erase certain ethnicities, religions and memories of certain cultures, even to destroy or

1. military objectives are limited to those objects which by their nature, location, purpose or use make an effective contribution to military action and whose total or partial destruction, capture or neutralization, in the circumstances ruling at the time, offers a definite military advantage., 1977 The First Protocol to the Hague Convention 1954 for the Protection of Cultural Property in the event of Armed Conflict 1954, art 52 (2)
2. 1977 The First Protocol to the Hague Convention 1954 for the Protection of Cultural Property in the event of Armed Conflict 1954 (Protokol I), art 52 (1)

eliminate the identity and existence of certain groups. There is an assumption on parties involved in armed conflict that the destruction and devastation of cultural heritage objects play an important role in defeating their enemies.[3]

In international law, especially international humanitarian law, cultural heritage objects are protected objects, which also applies during armed conflicts. In the event of an armed conflict, the parties are required to take steps to protect cultural heritage objects within their territory and cultural heritage objects in their enemy's territory.[4] In Article 27 of The Hague Convention 1899 and 1907 Concerning the Law and Habits of War on Land, there stated provisions concerning the principle of protection of cultural heritage objects. In addition, the protection of cultural objects also received special attention in the Diplomatic Conference of International Humanitarian Law in Armed Conflict in Geneva (1974-1977), Article 53 of Additional Protocol I Geneva in 1977, Article 85 paragraph 4 (d) and 5 of the Protocol, and The Hague Convention concerning the protection of cultural heritage objects in armed conflict (Convention for the Protection of Cultural Property in the Event of Armed Conflict) which was signed in 1954 after the second world war. The purpose of the establishment of this convention is to protect cultural heritage objects from attacks and destruction in situations of armed conflict. This Convention is made based on the principles of the protection of cultural heritage objects in The Hague Regulation 1899 and 1907, and the Roerich Pact 1935. Protection of cultural heritage objects is further regulated in the implementing protocol of this convention, The First Protocol to The Hague Convention 1954 for the Protection of Cultural Property in the event of Armed Conflict 1956 (Protocol I) and The Second Protocol to the 1954 Hague Convention for the Protection of Cultural Property in the event of Armed Conflict 1999 (Protocol II).[5] In addition to these conventions there are also several international legal instruments that aim to protect cultural heritage objects, including: Constitution of UNESCO, UNESCO Convention Concerning protection of the world cultural and natural heritage 1972, UNESCO Declaration concerning the intentional Destruction of Cultural Heritage 2003, International Criminal Court (ICC) Statute 1998, and several other conventions related to the protection of cultural heritage objects.

Although the protection of cultural heritage objects has been arranged in such ways in the fore mentioned various provisions, destruction and attack on cultural heritage objects often occur in an armed conflict. Destruction, devastation, and attack on cultural heritage objects happened for not only once or twice.[6] Destruction of cultural heritage objects has begun since the 1st world war,[7] and continued to the second world war, where there were several world heritage sites that suffered severe damage, including:[8] San Agustin Church in Philippines, St. James Church in Sibenik, the City of Bath in Rome, the historical center of Florence which is the home of Renaissance arts and architectures, the Plantin-Moretus Museum in Belgium, and many more.

After the Second World War ended, the United Nations Education Scientific and Cultural Organization abbreviated as UNESCO was formed as an organization under

3. Sanja Zgonjanin, 'The Prosecution of War Crimes for the Destruction of Libraries and Archives during Times of Armed Conflict (online)' (2005) 40(2) *Libraries & Culture* (Spring 2005) 1-2, http://www.ebsco host.com/(14 November 2011, See also, François Bugnion, *The origins and development of the legal protection of cultural property in the event of armed conflict Article (online)*, 14 September 2004, by François Bugnion 50th anniversary of the 1954 Hague Convention for the protection of cultural property in the event of armed conflict. http://www.icrc.org/eng/index.jsp (5 August 2018)
4. 1954 The Hague Convention for the protection of cultural property in armed conflict, art 4(1).
5. Protocol II was signed in The Hague, Netherland on 26 March 1999.
6. The destruction of cultural heritage objects has become more severe since the introduction of aerial bombing and long-range weapons.
7. World War I resulted in the destruction of a large number of cultural objects, especially in Rheims, Leuven and Arras.
8. http://www.worldheritagesite.org/(09 August 2018)

the United Nations tasked with encouraging the identification, protection and maintenance of cultural heritage objects. UNESCO protects cultural heritage objects through international cooperation, the establishment of a world heritage list, world heritage list in danger, Cultural heritage with enhanced protection, and establishment of international legal instruments such as conventions, declarations and recommendations. The establishment of UNESCO did not automatically stop acts of destruction and attack on cultural heritage objects. Some armed conflicts cause severe damage to cultural heritage objects. Some of these devastating incidents included the destruction of the Buddha Bamiyan Monument in Taliban in 2001 armed conflict in Iraq, the attack on the Agra Fort in India, the destruction of a large number of Omeyan and Abaside Monuments destroyed by US forces during the armed conflict in Iraq, the bombing of Dubrovnik's Old City that inhabited by libraries and city archives in Croatia by Serbia because of the use of mortars and artillery in a civil war,[9] the destruction of the Mostar Bridge in Bosnia and Herzegovina, the destruction of East Asian libraries in Shanghai, the destruction of Angevine archives in Nepal,[10] attacks against Preah Vihear Temple in an armed conflict between Thailand and Cambodia in 2011, and many more.

The authors in this case focus on analyzing armed conflict between Thailand and Cambodia. The event that resulted in the destruction of Preah Vihear temple which is a world heritage site, is a special event, because the area, which became the area of armed conflict between Thailand and Cambodia, is the border area of the two countries. Right in the area there Preah Vihear temple, a cultural heritage object that has been officially registered as a world heritage object by UNESCO in 2008.[11] Armed contacts between the two countries' military forces have been going on since 2001 to mid-2011. Armed contacts around Preah Vihear temple area have caused damage to the temple. The position of the temple has a lot of adverse effects on the temple itself. Moreover, Thailand and Cambodia are both ASEAN member countries. The armed conflict between these two countries has possibilities to disrupt the stability of security in the Southeast Asian region.

2 RESULT AND DISCUSSION

2.1 *Armed conflict between Thailand and Cambodia in the area around Preah Vihear temple*

Between Thailand and Cambodia there have been regional border agreements which are a direct border between the two Countries. This border agreement was made between the French government which at that time occupied Cambodia and the kingdom of Siam (now Thailand),[12] which known as the Franco-Siamese Convention of February 13th 1904 and the Treaty Between France and Siam of March 1907. The Franco-Siamese Convention of February 13th 1904 placed Preah Vihear temple in Thailand's territory. After that on March 23, 1907, the government of the kingdom of Siam and Cambodia signed the Treaty Between France and Siam of March 1907. This agreement formed the Franco-Siamese Mixed Commission which aimed to determine the boundaries between the two countries. The joint commission mapped the location

9. Cross Curent News, *Dubrovnik Bombed Out Heritage (online)*, 1992, History Today, volume 42, number 9, http://www.ebscohost.com/(21 August 2018) 1.
10. Sanja Zgonjanin, above n 3, 2.
11. Preah Vihear Temple is listed as a cultural heritage object belonging to Cambodia, and it was Cambodia who register this temple to be included in the list of UNESCO world cultural heritage objects.
12. Monticha Pakdeekong,, 'Who Owns the Preah Vihear Temple? A Thai Position (0line)' (2018) 2(1) *Journal of East Asia & International Law*, Spring 2009, 2 <http://www.ebscohost.com> (August 21, 2018)

of the border between the two countries. This map is used by the Cambodian government to argue before the International Court of Justice (ICJ).[13]

At that time, there was a struggle between the two countries over Preah Vihear temple. Thailand's army once occupied Preah Vihear temple. So that on October 6, 1959, Cambodia unilaterally filed this case with the ICJ, which was later known as the case concerning the Temple of Preah Vihear. Then on June 15, 1962, based on a map issued by the Franco-Siam Mixed Commission, the ICJ issued a decision which essentially ruled that the Preah Vihear temple was part of the territory of Cambodia.

As determined in the ruling, the Thai side had to withdraw its troops from Preah Vihear temple, because Thai soldiers occupied the temple at that time. Thailand then withdrew its troops from the temple because Thailand respected the ICJ ruling. However, later in the decision, it was seen that the ICJ did not determine the precise or exact boundary line between the two countries. ICJ only decided that Preah Vihear temple was part of Cambodia. The decision also did not regulate the 4.6 km^2 area around the temple which part of the country. In fact, Preah Vihear temple is located on the Dangrek mountain range which is located in the territory of Thailand and Cambodia, and access to the temple is easier and more frequently accessed from Thailand. In addition, even though the two countries have formed a commission to set the boundary line between Thailand and Cambodia, or also known as the Thai-Cambodian Joint Commission on Demarcation for the Land Boundary (JBC) between Thailand and Cambodia. This commission has not conducted surveys or investigations and has not set a boundary line or demarcation in this region. ICJ has also not decided on this issue.

Preah Vihear temple at the beginning of its construction around the 17th century was a temple which built as a place of worship for Hindus which at that time was built during the reign of the Khmer king. Both the people of Cambodia and Thailand visited Preah Vihear temple for worship. Thailand and Cambodia recognize that Preah Vihear Temple is of extraordinary value to humanity and it is appropriate that Preah Vihear temple should be included in the World Heritage List.[14] In addition, both Thailand and Cambodia have agreed to register Preah Vihear Temple in the World Heritage List. Cambodia as the formally registering country, and with support from Thailand.[15]

But without approval and unbeknownst to Thailand, Cambodia submitted the registration proposal itself, even though previously Thailand had expressed its desire to join in the joint nomination of Preah Vihear temples and the surrounding area or transboundary nominations that need joint approval from Thailand and Cambodia. This has angered the Thai government because the Cambodian government unilaterally nominated the temple to enter the world heritage list at the 32nd session of the world heritage committee in Quebec City, Canada. Besides that, Cambodia's action to register the Preah Vihear temple on the World Heritage list was also criticized by the Thai government, because the Thai government considered that the issue of territorial disputes over the area around the Preah Vihear temple had not been resolved.[16]

Between one country and another, the boundaries must be clear, but the border between the two countries is unclear, so the ownership of this temple is not yet clear. Because of this uncertainty, conflicts emerged between the two countries fighting over ownership of the area around the temple. Cambodia in its demands to the ICJ, demanded that the ICJ decide five

13. Ibid., ICJ jurisdiction in upholding armed conflict between Thailand and Cambodia resulted from the fact that the Thai government has explicitly acknowledged the International Court of Justice in Geneva. Although this Court has not been in place since 1946, Thai recognition must be transferred to the successor to the Geneva International Tribunal, the International Court of Justice in The Hague, which was established in 1945 by the United Nations Charter.
14. Ibid, 6.
15. Decision of World Heritage Committee no. WHC-07/31.COM/24 concerning The Nomination of natural, mixed and cultural properties to the world heritage list - the Temple of Preah Vihear. The decision was adopted by the 31st World Heritage Committee meeting in Christchurch, (New Zealand June 23-2 July 2007) 154-156. <Accessed via http://whc.unesco.org/en/decisions/1322.> July 21, 2018
16. Monticha Pakdeekong, above n 11, 6-7.

things, namely: the legality of a French-made map in 1907 based on international law, border settlement between Thailand and Cambodia, Cambodia's sovereignty over Preah Vihear temple, withdrawal of Thailand's troops stationed in Preah Vihear temple, and the return of all objects of Cambodian statues transferred by Thailand.

Negotiations between the two countries to resolve their territorial boundaries began in 1954. In 1958 the negotiations pursued by the two parties did not meet an agreement because Thailand agreed to the agreement and protocol but would not accept the use of the word "documents annexed" because the word has a broader meaning and leads to sketches that do not have accuracy. Cambodia insists on the words "documents annexed". Therefore, there is no agreement that can be agreed upon. After that, negotiations were held again in 1997, but the negotiations stopped because there was no agreement on which map should be used by the joint commission as a basis for working to determine the boundary line (demarcation line) between the two countries. Then in 2000, both parties signed an MoU (Memorandum of Understanding).[17] This MoU was signed by the two countries on the 14th of June in 2000.[18] Following this MoU, both parties agreed to use the map in Annex I as a basis for determining the boundary line between the two countries.

Based on these facts it can also be concluded that the two countries have indeed agreed to let the joint commission work to determine the demarcation line between the two countries in the border region. Until the time of the armed conflict between the two countries on the border, there is no legal boundary line between the two countries on the border.

Regarding the ownership of Preah Vihear temple, Thailand has complied with and respected the decision of the ICJ. In carrying out all decisions of the I.C.J, Thailand withdrew all its troops from Preah Vihear temple, because of the decision of ICJ was binding, must be obeyed by the parties, and final (contentious jurisdiction). Therefore, regarding the issue of the ownership of Preah Vihear temple there are no more problems between the two countries. In the decision of the WHC (World Heritage Committe), Thailand officially stated its intention to participate in the joint nomination with Cambodia. Preah Vihear Temple as the world heritage object. In addition, in the WHC decision, the committee encouraged Cambodia and Thailand to cooperate in protecting Preah Vihear temple, due to the fact that residents living around Preah Vihear temple, both Thai and Cambodian citizens, have long appreciated the temple. Cambodia was also asked to involve Thailand in all matters relating to Preah Vihear temples, including inviting Thailand to jointly with UNESCO in testing national arrangements made by Cambodia to comply with international standards.[19]

The remaining problem between the two countries and the lack of a way to solve them until now is the problem of setting boundary lines in the two countries' border areas. The absence of a clear and legitimate boundary line has caused a conflict to arise between the two countries. The conflict can be triggered by various problems. The problem that occurs between Thailand and Cambodia is triggered by the issue of each country trying to uphold its sovereignty in their respective jurisdictions. Basically, the most important thing in solving States border problems is the agreement of the parties. This agreement must be preceded by an agreement, which includes:

---

17. Memorandum of Understanding Between the Government of Kingdom of Cambodia and the Government of Kingdom of Thailand on the Survey and Demarcation of Land Boundary. The purpose of the MoU was to conduct a survey and demarcation of land boundaries between the two countries and jointly organize it based on the Franco-Siamese Convention of 1904 and the Treaty of 1907 and additional Protocols, and to use the map issued by the Franco-Siamese Commission of Delimitation.
18. Bangkok Post, Thai-Cambodian Relations, 14 June 2000, http://m.bangkokpost.com/(31 July 2018)
19. Decision of *World Heritage Committee* No. WHC-08/32.COM/24Rev, 31 March 2009 concerning *Examination Of Nomination*, the decision was adopted at the 32nd World Heritage Committee meeting in Quebec City, Canada. 2 - 10 July 2008, pp. 226-228. See also the decision of World Heritage Committee No. WHC-10/34.COM/20, 03 September 2010 concerning Temple of Preah Vihear (Cambodia), was adopted at the 34th World Heritage Committee meeting in Brasilia, Brazil. 25 July - 3 August 2010, 116 <Accessed through http://whc.unesco.org/en/decisions/>, August 19 2018

a. Agreement on a base map that will be used as a joint work map, because both parties must use the same basic map. So there are no two or more maps, because they will cause disputes.
b. Agreement on the method of determining the limits to be used, namely the delination method (on the map) and demarcation (in the field).

Preah Vihear temples are of equal importance to Thailand and Cambodia. Residents around the temple usually use the temple as a place of worship. As ordinary people, the people around the temple are accustomed to performing worship at the temple, regardless of which the temple belongs to. Hence, socially and culturally, the temple has become part of the lives of the residents of both countries living in the border region. However, due to the border agreement, the temple was placed into Cambodian territory. All provisions agreed upon by Thailand and Cambodia in the 2000 MoU, relating to the determination of the boundaries of the two countries, should be included in an international border agreement. An international border agreement between the two countries should set clear boundaries or demarcations, also by setting clear boundary signs. If these signs have also been agreed upon by the two countries, the border agreement must be registered with the United Nations. In order for further disputes to occur between the two countries, both disputes regarding the interpretation and implementation on the contents of the agreement, the existing border agreements can be used as a legal basis for deciding which disputes might arise later. If there has been a legal boundary and has a legal force, it is hoped that there will be no more territorial conflicts in the border regions of the two countries.

However, since July 15, 2008, the Thai army re-occupied an area of 4.6 km2 around Preah Vihear temple. Thailand and Cambodia through their regional commanders met in Chong Saam Pass, Sisaket Province, Thailand, on 5 February 2011. During the meeting the two sides reached an agreement on a ceasefire agreement as soon as possible. Yet later, according to the Thai side in February 2011, the Cambodian Army violated the terms of the agreement by starting firing. This incident injured 2 Thai civilians and 8 Thai soldiers. On 7 February 2011 the Cambodian army resumed shooting at the Thai army headquarters in Phu Ma Khua and Phlan Yao districts within Thailand.[20] On October 3, 2011, a clash of weapons between the soldiers of both sides took place in three different areas around the temple, starting with firing fire to the sky into Thailand's territory by Cambodian troops.[21] The ICJ finally issued a decision ordering the two countries to withdraw their troops from the border region.

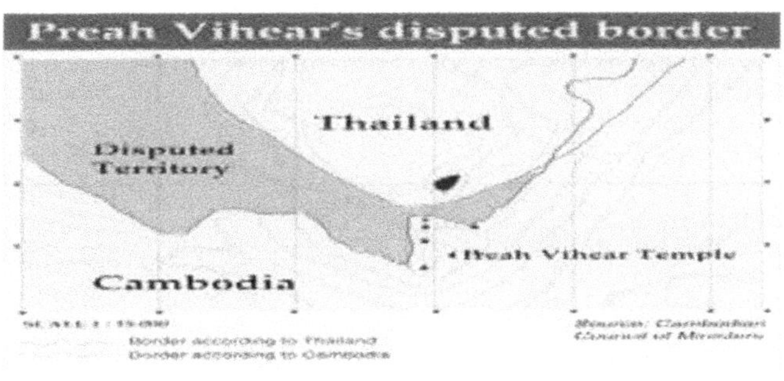

The two countries' accusations regarding who first started the armed attack were the result of resolving protracted border problems and have not met agreements for years. Border issues

20. Bangkok Post, *Feisty dispute turns into a war of words*, http://m.bangkokpost.com/. Published on 08 February 2011 at 12:00 am. (29 August 2018)
21. That is the first time to Chong Don Ao Pass and Phu Ma Khua, which was then followed by the launch of attacks on other Thai regions, namely Sattasom Hill, Phlan Yao, Chong Ta Thao Pass, areas close to Phra Viharn Temple, and Phum Srol Village.

are one of the most fundamental, crucial and sensitive issues that can trigger conflicts between countries.

2.2 *Legal protection towards Preah Vihear temple as world cultural heritage objects*

In the armed conflict that occurred between Thailand and Cambodia since 2008, it has caused damage to the Preah Vihear temple, as in the table below:

Preah Vihear Temple is a protected cultural heritage object, where Preah Vihear Temple categorization has been set in various regulations of International Law concerning legal protection of objects of cultural heritage in armed conflict. This Normative Instrument begins with the establishment of several rules of international law, including in The Hague Regulations concerning the Laws and Customs of War on Land 1899 and 1907, or the so-called The Hague Regulation, namely in article 27 which reads:

Table 1. Data of Damages in Preah Vihear Temple

Years	**Damages**	**Cause**	**Source**
October 2008	200 places around the temple, with several holes with a depth of 10 cm and two centimeters wide	Shootout between Thailand and Cambodia	Report by *The Phnom Penh Post*
April 2009	A Nine-headed dragon snake statue that considered to be the temple guardian spirit was damaged	damaged by shrapnel. The Troops also used 400 mortar and artillery shells in the temple which caused serious damage to this World Heritage site.	Report by *The Cambodia Daily*
2009	The trees around the temple were cut down. There are remnants of a small crater and blackened fire, and the temple has been damaged	Caused by grenades fired across the border	Report by *The Phnom Penh Post*
2011	In Preah Vihear temple there are traces of battle, with chips and pieces cut from columns and walls from the fourth gate, or building entrances, and along the temple's crossroads. A trace of blood was found in a carved stone door. Allegedly a trace of the last step of a Cambodian soldier who was killed.	Shootout between Thailand and Cambodia	Report by Seth Mydans, journalist of *The New York Times*
February 2011	the UNESCO flag which is a sign that the temple is protected by UNESCO is perforated	Bullet shot	Report by journalist Tom Fawthrop from English Aljazeera. (http://english.aljazeera.net/)
5 February 2011	Facade of the temple	Artillery shot	*Cambodia-Thai Shelling Damaged Preah Vihear temple.* (http://www.eturbonews.com)
6 February 2011	Wings of Preah Vihear temple collapsed	The use of mortar, Rocket, and artilleries.	

Source: Kurczy, Stephen, *Caught in the Thailand-Cambodia crossfire: Preah Vihear temple (online)*, Christian Science Monitor, 2 August 2011. http://www.ebscohost.com (20 August 2018)

"In sieges and bombardments all necessary steps should be taken to spare as far as possible edifices devoted to religion, art, science, and charity ..."[22]

In addition, in 1935 an agreement was made called the Treaty on the Protection of Artistic and Scientific Institutions and Historic Monuments or also called the Roerich Pact, which signed on April 15, 1935 in Washington DC. The first article of the Roerich Pact refers to cultural heritage objects as neutral objects.

In the additional protocols of the first to the fourth Geneva Convention, there are arrangements regarding the protection of cultural heritage objects, namely in the 1st and 2nd supplementary protocols. In article 53, it is stipulated that:

"... is prohibited from: (a) carrying out any hostile actions aimed at historical monuments, works of art, or places of worship which are cultural or spiritual heritage of a nation; (b) using such objects to support military efforts; (c) making such objects as objects of restriction."[23]

It is said that without prejudice to the 1954 Hague Convention on the Protection of cultural heritage objects in armed conflict, it means that the provisions of this Convention are additional or complementary to the conventions that existed before this Convention, which regulates the protection of cultural heritage objects. That is, parties involved in international armed conflict are prohibited from carrying out any acts of hostility directed against historical monuments, works of art, or places of worship which are cultural or spiritual heritage of the people, using these objects to support military efforts, and making objects the target of the attack.

Whereas not much different from the 1st Protocol, in the second additional Protocol to the Geneva convention on the Protection of victims in non-international armed disputes, it is also reaffirmed regarding the protection of cultural heritage objects. It is just different from the 1st protocol used in international armed disputes, the regulation in the 2nd protocol is specifically for armed disputes that are non-international, namely:

"... it is prohibited to carry out any hostile actions aimed at historical monuments, works of art or religious places which are the spiritual heritage of a nation and use it to support military efforts."[24]

In these two additional protocols, both in international armed conflicts and non-international armed conflicts, the parties are prohibited from carrying out any actions that threaten the sustainability or existence of a cultural heritage object, through the actions mandated in article 53. In armed conflicts between Thailand and Cambodia, which are international disputes, parties are required to comply with the provisions contained in the second Geneva Convention.

After World War II was completed in 1948, a new proposal was submitted to UNESCO (United Nations Educational, Scientific and Cultural Organization) by the Dutch Government. In 1951, the UNESCO General Conference finally decided to hold an Intergovernmental Conference which eventually resulted in the 1954 Hague Convention or The Hague Convention for the Protection of Cultural Property in the Event of Armed Conflict,[25] which regulates the protection of cultural objects during armed disputes.

22. 1899 dan 1907 The Hague Regulations concerning the Laws and Customs of War on Land, art. 27.
23. *Protocol Additional to the Geneva Conventions of 12 August 1949, and relating to the Protection of Victims of International Armed Conflicts 1977, art 53. Accessed from* http://www.icrc.org/eng (19 August 2018). See also Translation of Additional Protocols to the Geneva Conventions of 12 August 1949, and relating to the protection of victims of international armed conflict (Protocol I) and non-international (Protocol II), compiled by the Directorate General of General Legal Administration, Ministry of Justice and Human Rights of the Republic of Indonesia, 2003.
24. Ibid, art 16.
25. Indonesia has ratified The Hague Convention 1954 with Presidential Decree Number 234 Year 1966.

This Convention is the first convention in international law that regulates the protection of cultural heritage objects, specifically in situations of armed conflict. Article 2 on the Protection of cultural heritage objects states that, "for the purposes of this Convention, the protection of cultural objects consists of safeguards and respect for these cultural objects." Based on the provisions of this article, in this convention the protection of cultural objects consists of two forms, namely security and respect for cultural objects. Safeguards against cultural heritage objects must be carried out before the war takes place, namely in peacetime, which contained in article 3 that states, "The High Contracting Parties endeavor at a peaceful time to prepare the security of cultural objects located in their territories from the effects that can be estimated occurs during armed conflicts, by taking actions that they deem appropriate." From this article it can be seen that the parties must be able to prepare things to protect cultural heritage objects from any threats that might occur if a war broke out with other countries. In this convention, the provided protection is divided into general protection and special protection. General protection is given in general to all cultural heritage objects contained in a country. Special protection, specifically can be given to:[26]

1. A number of shelters to store moving cultural objects during armed conflicts, centers containing monuments, and other very important immovable cultural objects.[27]
2. Cultural objects located close to an important military object, including a port, train station or aerodrome.[28]
3. Transportation that is specifically used for the transmission of cultural objects, either in a territory or towards another territory.[29]

To get special protection, the objects must be registered in the International Registration of cultural objects under Special Protection (International Register of Cultural Property under Special Protection).[30] Article 23 of the Convention for the Protection of Cultural Property in the Event of Armed Conflict describes UNESCO's assistance in protecting cultural heritage objects in armed conflict, that:

1. The parties must request assistance from UNESCO for technical assistance in the implementation of the protection of their cultural objects, or in relation to other problems arising from the application of this Convention or its implementing Regulations. The organization must match the assistance within the limits set by the program and by its resources.
2. This organization[31] has the authority to issue, on its own initiative, and provide proposals to the parties to the dispute.

In UNESCO Declaration Concerning the Intentional Destruction of Cultural Heritage[32], Paragraph v:

> *"When involved in an armed conflict, be it of an international or non-international character, including the case of occupation, States should take all appropriate measures to conduct their activities in such a manner as to protect cultural heritage, in conformity with customary international law and the principles and objectives of international agreements and UNESCO recommendations concerning the protection of such heritage during hostilities."*[33]

26. The Hague Convention 1954, above n 2, art. 8.
27. Ibid, art 8 (1)
28. Ibid., art 8 (5)
29. Ibid., art 12
30. Ibid., Art 8 (6). The International Register of Cultural Property under Special Protection is under the responsibility of the Director General of the United Nations Organization for Education, Science and Culture (or in English abbreviated as UNESCO). The cultural objects included in this category include Borobudur temple and Taj Mahal.
31. UNESCO
32. UNESCO Declaration Concerning the Intentional Destruction of Cultural Heritage.
33. 2003 UNESCO Declaration concerning the Intentional Destruction of Cultural Heritage, Paragraph V.

Whereas when involved in an armed conflict, including occupation, the state must take all appropriate measures to carry out their activities in such a way as to protect cultural heritage, in accordance with international customary law and principles, the purpose of international agreements and UNESCO's recommendations regarding the protection of such heritage during hostility.

Other convention governing the protection of cultural heritage objects in armed conflict is the Additional Protocol to the Geneva Conventions of 12 August 1949, and Relating to the Protection of Victims of International Armed Conflicts (Protocol I), specifically in article 85 paragraph 5 which states the category of war crimes, which means that the crime in article 85 paragraph 4 can be tried and punished in accordance with the decision of the Court concerned in a war. The International Court of Justice can hear crimes in this article. One form of war crimes is the destruction of historical monuments, and other cultural sites.[34]

In the International Criminal Court (ICC) which is also referred to in Article 8 of the Rome Statute of War Crimes, attacks on historic buildings fall into the category of war crimes and can be tried by the ICC. In Article 2 letter d of the Statute of the International Criminal Tribunal for the Former Yugoslavia (ICTTY),[35] destruction of objects of cultural heritage can also be classified as war crimes if they occur in areas of armed conflict.

It can be concluded that the protection of cultural heritage objects in armed conflict has been comprehensively regulated in the rules of international law. Even actions in armed conflict carried out by the parties, which result in damage to a cultural heritage object can be classified as war crimes. The ICC itself is authorized to try if the concerned country is unable and unwilling to try.

In principle, world cultural heritage objects belong to all humanity, not only the state where the cultural heritage objects are located. This is why world heritage objects are said to have universal values, so that damage to cultural heritage objects belonging to anyone also means the destruction of the cultural heritage of all humanity.

3 CONCLUSION

The armed conflict that occurred between Thailand and Cambodia around the Preah Vihear temple was caused by a border dispute that has not been resolved to date. In addition, there are differences in interpretation between the two countries regarding which maps are used in determining borders. The ownership of Preah Vihear temple itself was decided by the ICJ in its decision entitled The Case Concerning the Temple of Preah Vihear in 1962. Both Thailand and Cambodia have ratified conventions on legal protection for world cultural heritage objects, as well as legal protection for world cultural heritage objects in armed conflict into their respective national laws. Among them, the Convention concerning the Protection of the World Cultural and Natural Heritage 1972, The Hague Convention for the protection of cultural property in armed conflict 1954, and the 1977 First Protocol to The Hague Convention 1954 for the Protection of Cultural Property in the event of Armed Conflict 1954 (Protocol I). It means that under any circumstances, including in situations of armed conflict both Thailand and Cambodia must protect Preah Vihear Temple which belongs to the world cultural Heritage objects.

34. This protocol, with reference to the Geneva Conventions, is a reference to the rules of international humanitarian law.
35. The decision of the ICTY (International Criminal Tribunal for the Former Yugoslavia) on the punishment to the perpetrators of destruction to Dubrovnik which has been registered in the World Heritage List has made an important case by UNESCO in formulating a more flexible international agreement in the future that can protect and provide certainty in punishing the perpetrators of destruction to world cultural heritage objects.

REFERENCES

Cross Curent News, Dubrovnik Bombed Out Heritage (online), History Today, volume 42, number 9, 1992

Decision of World Heritage Committee no. WHC-07/31. COM/24 concerning The Nomination of natural, mixed and cultural properties to the world heritage list - the Temple of Preah Vihear. The decision was adopted by the 31st World Heritage Committee meeting in Christchurch, New Zealand June 23-2 July 2007

François Bugnion, The origins and development of the legal protection of cultural property in the event of armed conflict Article (online), 14 September 2004

Memorandum of Understanding between the Government of Kingdom of Cambodia and the Government of Kingdom of Thailand on the Survey and Demarcation of Land Boundary

Pakdeekong, Monticha, 'Who Owns the Preah Vihear Temple? A Thai Position (online)' (2009) 2(1) *Journal of East Asia & International Law*

UNESCO Declaration Concerning the Intentional Destruction of Cultural Heritage.

Zgonjanin, Sanja, 'The Prosecution of War Crimes for the Destruction of Libraries and Archives during Times of Armed Conflict (online)' (2005) 40(2) *Libraries & Culture*

1954 The Hague Convention for the protection of cultural property in armed conflict

1977 The First Protocol to The Hague Convention 1954 for the Protection of Cultural Property in the event of Armed Conflict 1954

1899 dan 1907 The Hague Regulations concerning the Laws and Customs of War on Land

1907 The Hague Convention (IX) concerning Bombardment by Naval Forces in Time of War

Bangkok Post, Feisty dispute turns into a war of words, http://m.bangkokpost.com/

http://www.worldheritagesite.org/

http://www.ebscohost.com/

Culture and International Law - Juwana et al. (Eds)
© 2019 Taylor & Francis Group, London, ISBN 978-1-138-38766-9

Protection model and fulfilment of patient rights in the implementation of informed consent in Indonesia

Syafruddin & Arif Rohman
Fakultas Hukum, Universitas Borneo Tarakan, Indonesia

ABSTRACT: Law and healthcare are different sciences. But due to the frequent cases that occur related to the practice of medicine, the law contributes by providing solutions for both physicians and patients as consumers of health, although medicine has a code of professional ethics as well as standard operations as a basis for doctors in carrying out their work. Legal tools are still needed because in practice there are many medical malpractices. This study focuses on two important things: first, how judges assess express consent in the implementation of informed consent, and second, the model of protection and fulfillment of patient rights in the implementation of informed consent in Indonesia.

The research method used is normative legal research, because it is based on health law and the health minister's regulation as the main benchmark in analysis, and then integrated with court decisions relating to medical practices that have occurred in Indonesia.

The results of the discussion illustrate that the main point for doctors and health workers in carrying out their duties is the implementation of concrete agreements, both written and oral. Empirical facts show that doctors often do not carry out this procedure because the patient is unconscious during a medical action. The *judex facti* consideration is entirely based on information and documents made unilaterally by doctors without medical records; this is in violation of the provisions of Article 2 Paragraphs 3 and 4 of the Regulation of the Minister of Health Rl No. 585/Men. Kes/Per/IX/1989 concerning Medical Approval. In addition, the model for protecting patient rights in law enforcement is applying reverse evidence to doctors as defendants of malpractice in relation to the fulfillment of informed consent, because the medical profession is able to explain. From several cases, it appears that the judge's decision is not fundamental to informed consent, but tends to the negligence aspect of the doctor or medical personnel by referring to Article 359 of the Criminal Code, is negligence also called error, lack of caution.

KEYWORDS: Model, protection, patient rights, informed consent

1 INTRODUCTION

The existence of a medical code of ethics is one of the non-penal efforts of the medical profession in carrying out medical practice. The effort shows that the protection of professions that are based on science is very important. This is not sufficient for society or healthcare consumers. Thus a regulatory legal device is needed for patients to fulfill their basic needs. Eventually, the existence of the health law and several health minister regulations not only affect the community as consumers of health services, but also give a strong legal basis for the implementation of medical practice. Despite this, there are still violations committed by doctors and medical personnel, based both on mistakes and negligence, which have a negative impact on patients.

Some cases that have entered the realm of law and been handled by courts relating to medical malpractice are Judgment Nos. 46 K/Pdt/2006, 90/Pid.B/2011/PN.MDO, and 1110 K/Pid.

Sus/2012. Some of these cases are representative of the implementation of healthcare law enforcement in Indonesia. In the meantime, there are two investigations in this research, namely how the judge assesses express consent in the implementation of informed consent, and the model of protection and fulfillment of patient rights in the implementation of informed consent in Indonesia.

2 RESEARCH METHOD

The research is a study with document study categories, namely court decision analysis of medical malpractice based on judges' decision texts. To achieve our results, we reconstruct cases, identify the parties to the conflicts, the position of the cases, the parties' arguments, the judgments, and the reasons given by the judges.

3 DISCUSSION

3.1 *Judge appraisal of express consent on implementation of informed consent*

Basically, law enforcement involves: (1) legal material (regulations/legislation); (2) law enforcement officers (judges, prosecutors, police, lawyers, and correctional institutions); (3) legal facilities and infrastructure; (4) legal culture.[1] The process of law enforcement itself is closer to the general adage, which is like a currency that has two sides. Whereas between quality instruments and legal instruments must not prioritize one thing in line with the concept of the legal mind (justice).[2]

The process of law enforcement actually does not occur at the application/law enforcement stage, but can be started at the formulation stage (the lawmaking stage). Satjipto Rahardjo said that law enforcement is the effort to bring legal ideas and concepts into reality. Law enforcement is a process to realize legal desires in reality. Legal desires are the thoughts of the legislature that are formulated in legal regulations.[3]

Regarding law enforcement in the settlement of criminal cases, there is an invalidity of the principle of legality (see Nyoman Serikat Putrajaya's argument[4]).

The principle of legality is recognized as a fundamental principle by countries that use criminal law as a medium for countering crimes. However, the enactment is not absolute, in the sense that an actor can emulate an act that has occurred as a criminal offense and can be punished as long as such an act is contrary to written law, which in international criminal law is called the principle of general law that is recognized by nations.

To facilitate an understanding of judges' assessments of express consent, several cases are described below.

Judgment No. 90/PID.B/2011/PN.MDO

This case concerned a criminal act that caused the death of someone, Siska Makatey, due to negligence (Article 359 of the Criminal Code in conjunction with Article 361 of the

1. Saleh, S. (2004). Komitmen supremasi hukum di tengah kemajuan masyarakat Indonesia. Paper presented at *Dialog Nasional Profesional Aparat Penegak Hukum dalam Pelaksanaan di tengah Masyarakat yang Bersih dan Berwibawa, Jakarta, October 11, 2004* (pp. 5–6).
2. The law is justice in the context of the 21st century development has changed. Modern nationalism Century that promotes the power of reason almost never satisfies the human mind about the meaning of justice (Netherlands: *rechtsvaardigheid*) in the rhythm of the motion law in society. See Rahardjo, S. (2006). *Sisi-sisi lain dari hukum di Indonesia* (2nd ed., p. 169). Jakarta, Indonesia: Penerbit Buku Kompas.
3. Rahardjo, S. (2009). *Penegakan hukum: Suatu tinjauan sosiologis* (p. 24). Yogyakarta, Indonesia: Genta Publishing.
4. Putra, J. & Serikat, N. (2004). *Pemberlakuan hukum pidana secara retroaktif sebagai penyimbang asas legalitas dan asas keadilan. Suatu pergeseran paradigma dalam ilmu hukum pidana* (p. 37). Pidato pengukuhan guru besar, Universitas Diponegoro Semarang.

Criminal Code, Article 55 Paragraph 1 of the 1st Criminal Code). The defendants were Dr. Dewa Ayu Sasiary Prawani (Defendant I), Dr. Hendry Simanjuntak (Defendant II), and Dr. Hendy Siagian (Defendant III), and the plaintiff was the Public Prosecutor. At the Manado District Court No. 90/PID.B/2011/PN.MDO dated September 22, 2011, the amendments declared that Defendants I, II and III were not proven legally and convincingly guilty of committing a crime in the first primary and subsidiary indictment, second indictment, and third primary and subsidiary indictment. The primary indictment charged to the defendants violates Article 359 of the Criminal Code in conjunction with Article 361 of the Criminal Code in conjunction with Article 55 Paragraph 1 of the Criminal Code, which is a weighting article of the article charged in the first subsidiary charge, which violates Article 359 of the Criminal Code in conjunction with Article 55 Paragraph 1 to the 1st Penal Code of Jis; the acquittal of the defendants from the first primary indictment violates Article 359 of the Criminal Code. Given Article 361 of the Criminal Code in conjunction with Article 55 Paragraph 1 of the Criminal Code, then the defendants must also be released from the first subsidiary charge, namely violating Article 359 of the Criminal Code in conjunction with Article 55 Paragraph 1 of the Criminal Code. Release Defendants I, II and III therefore of all charges (acquittal), and recover the rights of the defendants in their abilities, position and dignity.

However, at appeal level in the Supreme Court, based on Decision No. 365 K/Pid/ 2012, it was stated that the same three defendants were proven legally and convincingly guilty of criminal acts as referred to in Article 359 of the Criminal Code in conjunction with Article 55 Paragraph 1 of the 1st Criminal Code, and all three defendants were sentenced accordingly, with imprisonment for ten months, with consideration of the judge as follows:

1. *Judex facti* (legal facts) misappropriates the law, because it does not properly consider juridically relevant matters, namely based on the results of medical record no. 041969 which has been read by expert witness Dr. Erwin Gidion Kristanto that when the victim entered the General Hospital Prof. R. D. Kandou, Manado, the general condition of the victim was weak and the victim's status was severe;
2. Before carrying out a Cesarean section operation on the victim, the defendants did not convey to the victim's family the possibility of what could occur to the victim;
3. The defendants carried out the operation on the victim, Siska Makatey. An air embolism then occurred that entered the right ventricle of the heart, which prevented blood from entering the lungs, and lung function then failed and subsequently resulted in heart failure;
4. The actions of the defendants have a causal relationship with the death of the victim, Siska Makatey, according to the certificate from the General Hospital Prof. Dr. R. D. Kandou, Manado, No. 61/VER/IKF/FK/K/VI/2010, dated April 26, 2010. Based on the review returned to the Supreme Court in Judgment Review No. 79.

In PK/PID/2013, Dr. Dewa Ayu Sasiary Prawani and colleagues were released from the indictment by the decision of a judicial review chaired by Mohammad Saleh and involving Professors Surya Jaya, Syarifuddin, Margono, and Maruap Pasaribu. However, this decision was not taken unanimously. One member of the assembly, Prof. Surya Jaya, gave a dissenting opinion. Ridwan cited the consideration of the decision that the applicant reviewed again (Dr. Dewa Ayu Sasiary Prawani et al.) did not violate the Standard Operating Procedure in dealing with Cesarean section surgery. The judicial review considered the original *judex facti* (district court) consideration to be correct, and ordered that the convicts be expelled from the correctional facility and the good name of the convicts be restored by the verdict. The decisions handed down against Dr. Dewa Ayu Sasiary Prawani and colleagues, at the first level, appeal, and cassation (judicial review) concerned negligence. The acts of the defendants as regulated and threatened with Article 76 of the Republic of Indonesia Law No. 29 of 2004 concerning Medical Practices in conjunction with Article 55 Paragraph 1 of the 1st Criminal Code, is addressing other related elements, namely:

1. The element of "person"
   The definition of 'anyone' is as a personal pronoun, which is usually used in each formulation of the articles of a criminal act from the relevant legislation, or in other words can also be interpreted as the subject of the offender. These subjects were Defendants I (Dr. Dewa Ayu Sasiary Prawani), II (Dr. Hendry Simanjuntak) and III (Dr. Hendy Siagian).
2. The element of "due to his/her error caused the death of another person"
   Before the Cesarean section operation on the victim was carried out, the defendants had not told the family about the worst possibilities, including death, that could happen to the victim if the Cesarean section surgery was carried out. In addition, the defendants who as doctors carried out the Cesarean section surgery on the victim did not conduct investigations, such as a chest Röntgen photo heart examination. Hence, this is the negligence of the defendants.

In the medical action carried out by Dr. Dewa Ayu Sasiary Prawani, there were several issues, namely:

1. Siska's case was declared an emergency at 6:30 p.m., even though it should have been declared an emergency as soon as she was hospitalized in the morning.
2. Some of the medical actions of Dr. Dewa Ayu Sasiary Prawani and her colleagues were not included in the medical record.
3. Dr. Dewa Ayu Sasiary Prawani did not know the infusion and the type of infusion drug given to the victim.
4. Although Dr. Dewa Ayu Sasiary Prawani assigned Dr. Hendy Siagian to inform the patient and her family of the action plan, Dr. Hendy Siagian did not do it. He instead handed over the approval sheet of the action that Siska had signed to Dr. Dewa Ayu Sasiary Prawani, but it turned out that the signature on it had been faked.
5. There was not good coordination in Dr. Dewa Ayu Sasiary Prawani's team when taking medical action.
6. There was no preparation for the victim suddenly experiencing an emergency.

Some of the court decisions above are related to informed consent, which has implications for medical malpractice on medical action, for patient relations, and for doctors/health personnel. The position of the patient in a very weak condition is that of being helpless and not having legal protection, specifically the Health Act, the Law on Health Workers, the Medical Practice Law, and the Law on Hospitals, which clearly places the patient as the object that needs care, so there is no legal gap in claiming their rights related to procedural errors, permanent disability, and disability or even death due to medical action. Here, the informed consent that is the basis for approval in medical action has been ignored.

Sanctions contained in the legislation in the health sector itself do not appear to be strict, because the judge refers more to the provisions in the Criminal Code article on negligence. Judges should be able to refer to the informed consent arrangement in the Minister of Health Regulation No. 290/MENKES/PER/III/2008 concerning Approval of Medical Actions, even though this regulation is the implementation of Article 45 of the Medical Practice law. All parties involved in the allegation of medical malpractice always ignore the provisions in this article.

However, in the Judicial Review of the Supreme Court of the Republic of Indonesia No. 76 PK/Pid/2013, on behalf of defendants Dewa Ayu Sasiary Prawani, Hendry Simanjuntak and Hendy Siagian, the Supreme Court declared and ruled that the convicted were not proven legally and convincingly guilty of committing the criminal act with which they were charged. Therefore the panel of judges at the judicial review level canceled the Supreme Court Decision No. 365 K/Pid/2012 dated 18 September 2012, which had in turn canceled the Manado District Court Decision No. 90/Pid.B/2011/PN.MDO.

The above case shows that aspects of informed consent are ignored by doctors. This can be proven in the form of the signature of the victim in the special action approval letter, and also in the surgical and anesthetic approval submitted by Dr. Hendy Siagian to be signed by the victim being different from the signature of the victim that is in her Identity Card (KTP) and the Askes Card. Then, after being examined by the Makassar Branch Forensic Laboratory and based on the results of the criminal laboratory's examination on June 9, 2010, Lab No. 509/DTF/2011, the criminal laboratory stated that the signature on behalf of Siska Makatey, aka Julia Fransiska Makatey, on the document was an autograph signature/'spurious signature'.

From this evidence, the aspect of informed consent and the existence of therapeutic transactions are the basis for a doctor to take medical action. With the ignored aspects of informed consent and therapeutic transactions, the criminal law teachings are included in negligence on medical action. To be able to get a doctor, a doctor who performs a medical action without it being preceded by the informed consent aspect and the related transaction, the authorized party must be able to prove it. Without there being informed consent in a medical action, there can be an element of error in accordance with Article 359 of the Criminal Code.

Juridically, the binding basis of the Regulation of the Minister of Health No. 290/MENKES/PER/III/2008 for which there are no sanctions against ignorance of informed consent is detrimental to the patient. In medical action, patients and doctors/health workers should be in a balanced position, namely the legal relationship between patients and doctors/health workers is contractual with each other in the law. This must be understood in medical action, so that actions that are suspected to be malpractice of medicine on patients can be avoided. Keep in mind that approval in medical action that contains high risk must be obtained as written approval signed by the right of consent. Whereas a medical action that does not involve risk can be given with verbal consent. There is an essence of approval from informed consent in medical action between patient and doctor/health worker.

For this reason informed consent by looking at the facts of the court decision which is allegedly malpractice conducted by medicine can be minimized, by placing an informed consent arrangement in everyone's rights. By placing informed consent as an inherent right of a person (whether patient or doctor/health worker), a balanced relationship pattern will be maintained parallel to each other. Patient rights are acknowledged by placing informed consent rights as part of patients' rights that must be respected, and strict sanctions imposed if not done. This places informed consent as a pillar of the essence of the recognition of the right to health for everyone. There has been a fundamental change in the informed consent perspective in the healthcare sector as part of the patients' rights that are protected, valued, and safeguarded for the benefit of all, as well as improving health status in Indonesia.

3.2 *Model of protection and fulfillment of informed consent in Indonesia*

Building a concept in the form of a law enforcement model related to informed consent, Decision No. 46 K/Pdt/2006 must first be elaborated: the Siloam Gleneagles Hospital malpractice case on circumcision without the consent of the patient. In this case, the plaintiff was Abraham Lodewyk Phaseary, residing in the Binong Permai Blok EE 11/13 Housing, Curug Tangerang, and the defendant was PT. Siloam Healthcare, trading as Siloam Gleneagles Karawaci Hospital, having its address at Jalan Siloam No. 6 Lippo Karawaci, Tangerang, and consisting of Dr. Rudi Hartanto, Dr. Nanda Romli, and Dr. Rizal S. Pohan. In consideration before total anesthesia was carried out, the plaintiff gave oral and written approval by signing an informed consent letter offered by the nurse only, to undergo surgical removal of the pen above the left ankle, which was to be carried out by Defendant IV as a bone surgeon.

Before the total anesthesia was carried out, the plaintiff had never discussed, never requested, and never given oral or written approval for circumcision surgery on his penis and the case against Defendants I, II, III, and IV is because, as an Ambonese Protestant Christian, the plaintiff had never had the intention and plan to be circumcised by anyone, anywhere and at any time.

After the plaintiff gave oral and written approval by signing the informed consent referred to above, Defendant III as the anesthetist then carried out a total anesthesia of the plaintiff, so that the plaintiff lost consciousness and did not remember anything else. While the plaintiff was unconscious, in addition to the operation of the pen extraction in the ankle carried out by

Defendant IV as a bone surgeon, it turned out that Defendant II had carried out invasive action (medical action which can directly affect the integrity of body tissue) illegally against the plaintiff, which was to perform circumcision surgery on the plaintiff's penis without giving an explanation to the plaintiff, and without written or oral approval from the plaintiff to the defendants. Both before and after the circumcision operation, the action of Defendant II was known and approved by Defendants I, III, and IV.

The act of the circumcision operation without the consent of the plaintiff committed by Defendant II, which was known and approved by Defendants I, III, and IV has been proven and recognized by Defendant I in Letter No. 093/RSSG/CS/XII/98, dated December 8, 1998, in which in essence Defendant I acknowledged and apologized for having carried out circumcision surgery without the consent of the plaintiff. The action of a circumcision operation without the approval of the aforementioned plaintiff has violated Article 2 Paragraphs 1, 2, and 3 of the Minister of Health Regulation Rl No. 585/Men.Kes/Per/IX/1989 concerning Approval of Medical Measures. Agreement based on Article 8 Paragraph 1 of the Regulation of the Minister of Health Rl No. 585/Men.Kes/Per/IX/1989 must be given by adult patients (such as the plaintiff) in a conscious and mentally healthy condition. The act of circumcision surgery without the approval of the plaintiff also violated the Code of Ethics of the Indonesian Hospital (KODERSI) Article 2, and Articles 9, 10 and 11 of Chapter III of the Hospital Obligations To Patients.

In addition to the action of a circumcision operation carried out illegally by the defendants without the consent of the plaintiff, it turned out that Defendant I was also not willing to provide a copy of the plaintiff's medical record requested by, and which is the right of, the plaintiff based on Article 10 Paragraph 2 and Article 14 Minister of Health Regulation Rl No. 749A/Men.Kes/Per/XII/1989, regarding Medical Records, where medical records are required by the plaintiff in the interests of basic health maintenance and treatment of the plaintiff, as well as material for verification in lawsuits.

Article 55 of Law No. 32 of 1992 concerning Health stipulates that every person has the right to compensation due to errors or negligence committed by healthcare personnel. Explanation of Article 55 of Law No. 32 of 1992 concerning Health expressly and clearly stipulates that "The granting of rights to compensation is an effort to provide protection for every person for a consequence, whether physical or non-physical, due to errors or negligence of health personnel". This protection is very important because negligence or error may cause death or permanent disability.[5]

The actions of the defendants who have carried out a circumcision operation without the plaintiff's approval and are not willing to provide a copy of the plaintiff's medical record, which is the right of the plaintiff, is an unlawful act as referred to in Article 1365 BW, which has caused a very large loss to the material good of the plaintiff, either physical or immaterial/non-physical. The plaintiff in person and through the previous attorney has repeatedly asked for accountability and demanded compensation, but there was no response and there was no good faith from the defendants to compensate the plaintiff.

The Tangerang District Court made a decision, namely No. 221/Pdt.G/2004/PN.TNG. dated March 3, 2005. The arguments are as follows: In the exception, the Defendant's Exception cannot be accepted; in the principal case (1) Refusing the plaintiff's claim for the whole; and (2) To sentence the plaintiff to pay court fees in the amount of Rp. 514,000. Then in an attempt to appeal, the plaintiff's District Court verdict was confirmed by the Banten High Court with Decision No. 54/Pdt/2005/PT. Banten, dated September 1, 2005. Subsequently, based on a special power of attorney dated March 16, 2005, an application for an appeal was filed orally on October 26, 2005 as evident from the cassation deed No. 221/Pdt.G/2004/PN.TNG, made by the Court Clerk Negeri Tangerang; an application accompanied by a memorandum of cassation containing the reasons received at the Registrar's Office of the District Court on November 9, 2005.

It was seen that throughout the evidentiary event, the plaintiff did not prove the act of general anesthesia or the failure of local anesthesia by Defendant III on the plaintiff. According

5. Physical loss is the loss or non-functioning of all or part of the body's organs, while non-physical losses are related to one's dignity.

to the panel, the assessment of this case which became the starting point of the problem, was the verification of the new anesthesia action then there would be a truth assessment whether or not the permit granted by the plaintiff to Defendant III. Based on the denial evidence from the defendant, in fact the plaintiff did not succeed in proving his claim, in which case Defendant III did not carry out general anesthesia but instead local anesthesia.

The *judex facti* does not at all consider the fact that during medical treatment the Cassation Appellant, when anesthetized by Cassation Defendant III while in the operating room, is a patient in a helpless condition who entrusts himself to the Cassation Defendants in full. All parties other than the Cassation Appellant at that time were only Cassation Respondents and nurses working for the Cassation I Respondent so that all information from the Cassation Defendants and existing documents were made unilaterally by the Cassation Defendants.

Whereas the legal fact that occurs is that the Cassation Petitioner is unconscious, even before entering the operating room, so that it is not possible for the Cassation Appellant to know whether any of the Cassation Defendants really explained that they would carry out the circumcision action, let alone to give consent to circumcision actions to be carried out by the Cassation Defendants. So it is very unfair and impossible to prove the *judex facti* legal considerations that essentially argue that the Cassation Appellant must prove that the Cassation Appellant has been totally sedated.

Instead, it was the Cassation Defendants who were supposed to prove that the Cassation Appellant was in a conscious and fully understanding condition when carrying out the circumcision action. For this reason, the Cassation Defendants should prove their argument by providing a medical record for the Cassation Applicant as requested by, and which is the right of, the Cassation Appellant, thus violating Article 10 Paragraph 2 and Article 14 of the Minister of Health Regulation No. 749A/Men.Kes/Per/XII/1989 concerning Medical Records.[6]

The decision of the Supreme Court on March 15, 1972, No. 549K/Sip/1971, stated: "Based on jurisprudence, the judge is free to give the burden of proof, more precisely if the evidence is charged to those who are better able to prove it". This is in accordance with the theory put forward by R. Subekti that, "The judge should be able to share the burden of proof, in the last level emphasizing the consideration of justice".[7] Instead it must be ensured not to let the judge order proof of something negative.

If the judge absolutely follows these rules, namely that the one who argues is burdened with proof, then the author believes that it will cause a burden of proof that is biased for him. Thus in the end it will not reach a good goal or outcome, because on one side it is told to prove something negative.[8]

The Civil Law Renewal states that the judge who is aware of the meaning of his position will not forget that in dividing the burden of proof, he must act honestly and with sportsmanship, and will not impose on a party to prove things that cannot be proven.[9] So, it is wrong and contrary to the law of *judex facti* consideration, which states that the Cassation Appellant cannot prove the existence of an act of general anesthesia against the Cassation Appellant because the Cassation Defendants should prove otherwise by submitting the medical records of the Cassation Appellant, which the Cassation Respondents did not. Likewise, regarding the granting of permits to carry out circumcision actions that have never been requested by the Cassation Appellant, so what happens after the Cassation Appellant is sedated is beyond the knowledge and awareness of the Cassation Appellant.[10]

6. A medical record is a file that contains notes and documents about patient identity, examination, treatment, actions and other services to patients at healthcare facilities.
7. Subekti, R. (2001). *Hukum pembuktian, cetakan 13* (p. 16). Jakarta, Indonesia: Pradnya Paramita.
8. Samudra, T. (1992). *Hukum pembuktian dalam acara perdata* (1st ed., p. 23). Badung, Indonesia: Penerbit Alumni,.
9. Ibid.
10. The *judex facti* consideration is based entirely on the information and documents provided unilaterally by the Cassation Appellant without being accompanied by a medical record of the Cassation Appellant, which violates the provisions of Article 2 Paragraphs 3 and 4 of the Regulation of the Minister of Health RI

Judex facti has been mistaken in applying the law and violating the applicable legal rules (*schending van het recht*) by making a consideration: "that the Defendant I is not available to provide a medical record copy to the plaintiff in the opinion that the assembly is given or not given a medical record copy also does not cause Defendant I to exist or not to commit unlawful acts in connection with the plaintiff's objection to the medical record's actions"; "Circumcision action is a medical action, while not giving a copy of a medical record is an administrative action, therefore the objection or problem is not an act that qualifies as an unlawful act in the sense of civilization". Judgment of *judex facti* has violated the law because Article 10 Paragraph 2 of the Regulation of the Minister of Health RI No. 749A/Men.Kes/Per/XII/1989, regarding medical records explicitly stipulates that: "Fill in the patient's medical record".[11]

It turned out that the Cassation Defendant I was not willing to provide a copy of the medical record of the Cassation Appellant, requested by and the right of the Cassation Appellant according to Article 14. Therefore it is not excessive if the Cassation Appellant argued that the Petitioners' Cassation failed to provide a medical record to conceal the actual facts, considering that the medical record contains all records and documents, which include, among other things, examination, treatment, actions and other services to the Cassation Appellant while receiving medical services from the Cassation Defendants, which cannot/are prohibited to be deleted, as regulated in Article 6 of the Regulation of the Minister of Health No. 749A/Men.Kes/Per/XII/1989, as follows:

1. Correction of error of note is made in the wrong writing and given initial by the officer concerned;
2. Deletion of writing in any way is not permissible. Then the *judex facti* considerations, which state that a copy of a medical record is an administrative action, are therefore erroneous because the objection or problem is not an act that qualifies as an unlawful act in the sense of civilization, because it is clearly regulated in the above provisions that medical records are documents that are very important for the basic interests of maintaining the health and treatment of the Cassation Appellant, as well as for evidence in legal proceedings.

Errors or omissions by the Cassation Defendants are strictly a violation of the law, namely:

1. The previous Cassation Appellant had never received an explanation or information from the Cassation Defendants regarding circumcision actions, violating Article 2 Paragraphs 3 and 4 of Regulation of the Minister of Health RI No. 585/Men.Kes/Per/IX/1989 concerning Medical Agreements;
2. The Cassation Appellant never gave consent or permission in any form, to anyone to carry out circumcision action against the Cassation Appellant, violating Article 2 Paragraphs 1 and 2 of the Regulation of the Minister of Health RI No. 585/Men.Kes/Per/IX/1989 concerning Medical Approval;
3. Until the Cassation Appellant was injected with drugs, the Cassation Appellant was never given an explanation nor gave approval for circumcision action, which has been

No. 585/Men.Kes/Per/IX/1989 concerning Medical Agreements, which stipulate: "(3) Approval as referred to in Paragraph 1 is given after the patient gets adequate information about the need for the relevant medical action and the risks that can be caused; (4) The method of delivery and content of information must be adjusted to the level of education and the conditions and situation of the patient". Even more explicitly, Article 8 Paragraph 1 stipulates: "Approval is given by adults who are conscious and mentally healthy". It has been proven that until the Cassation Appellant was anesthetized by Cassation Petitioner III, the Cassation Appellant never discussed, never questioned, or never asked for circumcision surgery to be performed on the penis of the Cassation Appellant.

11. Article 14 Regulation of the Minister of Health RI No. 749A/Men.Kes/Per/XII/1989, specifies: "Medical records can be used as: a. Basic healthcare and treatment of patients; b. Material of evidence in law cases; c. Material for purposes research and education; and d. the basis for payment of health service fees, materials for preparing health statistics".

acknowledged by the Cassation Defendants. If it is true that, *quod non*, the argument by the Cassation Defendants that there had been explanation and approval by the Cassation Appellant before the circumcision, the explanation and approval for circumcision actions were given under conditions of anesthesia or unconsciousness, violating Article 8 Paragraph 1 of the Regulation of the Minister of Health Rl No. 585/Men.Kes/Per/IX/1989 concerning Medical Agreements;

4. Doctors who carry out surgical/medical procedures (Cassation Respondent II) have never provided any explanation or information, while it is stipulated that information must be given by the doctor who will perform the operation, violating Article 6 Paragraph 1 of the Regulation of the Minister of Health of the Republic of Indonesia No. 585/Men.Kes/Per/IX/1989 concerning Medical Agreements;
5. Cassation Defendant III knew that there was no approval from the Cassation Appellant but still allowed Cassation Defendant II to circumcise the Cassation Appellant in violation of Article 12 Paragraph 1 of the Regulation of the Minister of Health Rl No. 585/Men.Kes/Per/IX/1989 concerning Medical Agreements;
6. Cassation Defendant I was also not willing to provide a copy of the medical record of the Cassation Appellant requested by and the right of the Cassation Appellant and can prove the unlawful conduct of the circumcision act without permission, violating Article 10 Paragraph 2 and Article 14 of the Minister of Health Regulation No. 749A/Men.Kes/Per/XII/1989, regarding Medical Records.

Thus it becomes clear that the Court of Appeal had been mistaken in overruling the consideration of the District Court, which violated the law and therefore the petition of the Cassation Appellant on this matter was considered reasonable enough to be granted, such that the decision of the Banten High Court, dated September 1, 2005, No. 54/Pdt/2005/PT. Banten and the Tangerang District Court Decision March 3, 2005, No. 221/PDT.G/2004/PN.TNG must be canceled.

Considering that for these reasons the Supreme Court is of this opinion, objections cannot be justified because the High Court ruling that upholds the District Court's ruling has been correct, that it is not wrong in applying the law, and objections regarding an award-proof evaluation of the facts cannot be considered in the examination at the cassation level, because the examination at the cassation level only relates to non-implementation or there being an error in the implementation of the law.

4 CONCLUSION

1. Informed consent is the main gateway for doctors/medical personnel in carrying out their duties, so the role of informed consent is very important. From several cases, it was found that the informed consent consideration was made the main basis by the judge in assessing the causality of an act. Approval for medical actions that involve high risks must involve written approval signed by the right of consent. Whereas, a medical action that is not risky can be given with verbal consent. The essence of approval derives from informed consent in medical actions between the patient and the doctor/health worker.
2. The model of protection and fulfillment of patient rights at the level of law enforcement (the court) is to apply the principle of inverse evidence to doctors/medical personnel, because it provides more effective and open opportunities for patients to obtain justice. Keep in mind that the application of this principle must be balanced, and not a negative thing.

REFERENCES

Putra, J. & Serikat, N. (2004). *Pemberlakuan hukum pidana secara retroaktif sebagai penyimbang asas legalitas dan asas keadilan: Suatu pergeseran paradigma dalam ilmu hukum pidana*. Pidato pengukuhan guru besar, Universitas Diponegoro, Semarang.

Rahardjo, S. (2006). *Sisi-sisi lain dari hukum di Indonesia* (2nd ed.). Jakarta, Indonesia: Penerbit Buku Kompas.

Rahardjo, S. (2009). *Penegakan hukum: Suatu tinjauan sosiologis*. Yogyakarta, Indonesia: Genta Publishing.

Saleh, S. (1992). Komitmen supremasi hukum di tengah kemajuan masyarakat Indonesia. Paper presented at *Dialog Nasional Profesional Aparat Penegak Hukum dalam Pelaksanaan di tengah Ma- syarakat yang Bersih dan Berwibawa, Jakarta, 11 October 2004.*

Samudra, T. (1992). *Hukum pembuktian dalam acara perdata* (1st ed.). Bandung, Indonesia: Penerbit Alumni.

Subekti, R. (2001). *Hukum pembuktian, cetakan 13. Kitab undang-undang hukum pidana*. Jakarta, Indonesia: Pradnya Paramita.

Keputusan Menteri Kesehatan Republik Indonesia Nomor 722/Menkes/SK/XII/2002 Tentang Pedoman Peraturan Internal Rumah Sakit.

Keputusan Menteri Kesehatan Republik Indonesia Nomor 290/Men.Kes/PER/III/2008 Tentang Persetujuan Tindakan Medik.

Keputusan Menteri Kesehatan Republik Indonesia Nomor 377/Menkes/SK/III/2007 Tentang Standar Profesi Perekam Medis dan Informasi Kesehatan.

Keputusan Menteri Kesehatan Republik Indonesia Nomor 722/Menkes/SK/XII/2002 Tentang Pedoman Peraturan Internal Rumah Sakit.

Peraturan Presiden Republik Indonesia Nomor 72 Tahun 2012 Tentang Sistem Kesehatan Nasional. Lembaran Negara Republik Indonesia Nomor 4148.

Undang-Undang Republik Indonesia Nomor 29 Tahun 2004 Tentang Praktik Kedokteran, Lembaran Negara Republik Indonesia Tahun 2004 Nomor 116, Tambahan Lembaran Negara Republik Indonesia Nomor 4431.

Undang-Undang Republik Indonesia Nomor 36 Tahun 2009 Tentang Kesehatan, Lembaran Negara Republik Indonesia Nomor 144.

Undang-Undang Republik Indonesia Nomor 44 Tahun 2009 Tentang Rumah Sakit, Lembaran Negara Republik Indonesia Nomor 5072. Tambahan Lembaran Negara Nomor 5072.

Culture and International Law - Juwana et al. (Eds)
© 2019 Taylor & Francis Group, London, ISBN 978-1-138-38766-9

Urgency of forming and managing an Adat Village (A study of Mojokerto Regency Regulation No. 47 of 2017 on the establishment of Adat Village preparations in Pacet Sub-District)

Indah Dwi Qurbani
Constitutional Law Department, Faculty of Law, Brawijaya University, Malang, Indonesia

ABSTRACT: The aim of this research is to determine the urgency regarding the formation and management of an Adat Village after Act No. 6 of 2014 on Villages came into effect. This research is categorized as normative legal research with applied and prescriptive analysis, with the purpose of normatively analyzing the urgency of formation and management of Adat Villages after Act No. 6 of 2014 on Villages took effect. The analysis was conducted through the study of the formation of regulations made by the Regent of Mojokerto, specifically No. 47 of 2017 on the Establishment of Adat Village Preparations in Pacet Sub-District, Regency of Mojokerto, East Java. The research results indicate that synchronization with the provisions of Article 97 of Act No. 6 of 2014 on Villages, and Articles 19, 20, 21 and 22 of the Minister of Home Affairs Regulation No. 1 of 2017 on Village Arrangements is required. There has not been any prior study conducted before the formation of the Regency regulation. It is advisable that study be conducted on the Adat Villages immediately. When the results of the study and verification done by the team suggest that the preparation of the Village does not merit it being a Village, the preparation needs to be discontinued, with the result that the area of the proposed Adat Village be brought back into the main Village.

KEYWORDS: Formation, Village, Adat

1 INTRODUCTION

Act No. 6 of 2014 on Villages (Act No. 6 of 2014 on Villages, 2014) is a manifestation of the recognition and respect by the State for the Village with all of its diversity. In the act, the matter of Village development consists of two aspects that are considered the main keys, namely Development and Development of Villages. (1) Development of Villages means a Village has full authority to manage its own communities. The Village's government and communities work together in order to advance and develop their own Village. This is due to the Village's authority to create programs that can improve the economy of the people. It is the Village itself that decides its needs and looks for ways to meet them. In other words, Village Development means that the Village is no longer the object of development but is itself the subject of development.

In Article 1 Paragraph 1 of Act No. 6 of 2016 on Villages, it is stated that: "A Village is a village and Adat Village or what are called by other terms, hereinafter referred to as village, is a unified legal community that has territorial limits in which it is authorized to regulate and manage government affairs, the interests of the local community based on community initiatives, origin rights, and/or Adat rights that are recognized and respected in the governmental system of the Unitary State of the Republic of Indonesia".

Villages (referred to also by other terms) have characteristics that are common to the whole of Indonesia, while the Adat Villages (referred to also by other terms) have different characteristics from Villages in general, mainly because of the strong influence of Adat (Islamic accepted practice) on the local government system, the management of local resources, and the social and cultural life of the villagers.

Villages and Adat Villages basically carry out almost the same tasks. The difference is only in the implementation of the rights of origin, especially concerning the social preservation of the Adat Village, the arrangement and management of Adat territories, the Adat peace meeting, the maintenance of peace and order for the Adat law community, and the governance arrangements based on the original arrangement. The Adat Village has government functions, village finance, village development, and has facilitation and guidance from the Regency/City government. In a position like this, the Village and Adat Village receive equal treatment from the government and the regional government. Therefore, in the future the Adat Village and Village can make changes to the face of the Village and its effective governance, implementation of effective development, community development and also community empowerment in the region.

In principle, the Adat Village is the legacy of the local community-maintained organization of local communities that continues to be recognized and championed by the leaders and communities of the Adat Village, in order to function to develop local social and cultural welfare and identity. The Adat Village has origin rights that are more dominant than the origin rights of a Village, because the Adat Village arose as an Adat community. The Adat Village is an Adat law community unit that historically has boundaries and cultural identities formed on a territorial basis, which has the authority to regulate and manage the interests of the Village community based on their rights of origin.

Associated with these explanations, Mojokerto Regency Regulation No. 47 of 2017 on the Establishment of Adat Village Preparations in Pacet Sub-District, sought to realize effective Village governance, accelerate the improvement of the welfare of the Village community, and improve the competitiveness of the Village. Furthermore, in the next point of consideration, it is stated that the purpose is to protect Adat peoples and their Adat rights, that are proven to be still alive, which are territorial, genealogical and functional, and which are deemed in accordance with the development of the people of the Republic of Indonesia. Based on the proceedings of the administrative and technical verification of the Village formation team preparing for the expansion of Pacet Village on October 24, 2017, Mojokerto Regency Regulation No. 47 of 2017 on the Establishment of Adat Village Preparations in Pacet Sub-District.[1]

Based on the provisions of the regulation of Adat Villages in Act No. 6 of 2014 on Villages as explained in the background above, and the initial reading on the considerations of Mojokerto Regency Regulation No. 47 of 2017 on the Establishment of Adat Village Preparations in Pacet Sub-District, research is needed on the urgency of formation and the arrangements of the Adat Villages after the enactment of Act No. 6 of 2014 on Villages.

Based on the research title, the type of research in this study is normative legal research[2], with the nature of prescriptive and applied research[3] (2). The aim is to conduct a normative analysis of the urgency of formation and structuring of an Adat Village after the enactment of Act No. 6 of 2014 on Villages by conducting study of Mojokerto Regency Regulation No. 47 of 2017 on the Establishment of Adat Village Preparations in Pacet Sub-District.

1. Mojokerto Regency Regulation No. 47 of 2017 concerning the Establishment of Adat Village Preparations in Pacet Sub-District.
2. Normative legal research conducted by researchers is library legal research or document study, because this research is carried out on or aimed at written regulations or other legal materials. It is library research or document study because this research is mostly carried out on legal materials in the library. The implementation of normative legal research will generally address: (1) research on legal principles; (2) research on legal systematics; (3) research on legal synchronization; (4) research on legal history; (5) research on legal comparisons. See Ibid, pp. 13–15.
3. This research is prescriptive and applied to study the purpose of law, legal concepts and legal norms so that as applied research this research has standards, procedures, provisions and signs in reviewing the legal principles of regional government. Studying legal principles means learning the basic reason for holding a statutory regulation (basic policy) and studying the objectives or reasons behind the enactment of legislation (enactment policy), so that the prescriptive nature of legal science will be apparent. See Marzuki, P.M. (2005). *Research, law* (pp. 22, 24). Jakarta, Indonesia: Kencana Prenada Media Group.

This research is normative legal research[4] (3), namely research done by examining legal materials or literature that has relevance to the subject matter under study, both primary legal material, secondary legal material and tertiary legal material. In this type of research, according to Soerjono Soekanto[5] (4), the domain of normative research includes: research on legal principles, legal systematics, the level of legal synchronization, legal history and legal comparison. In normative research this is different from social research[6] (2), and therefore the method used is also different from social research. This study examines the urgency of the formation and structuring of Adat Villages after the enactment of Act No. 6 Year 2014 on Villages (study on establishment of Mojokerto Regency Regulation No. 47 of 2017 on the Establishment of Adat Village Preparations in Pacet Sub-District).

2 RESEARCH METHODS

The approaches used in this study are a legislative approach and a conceptual approach. The legislative approach is carried out to be able to understand hierarchies and principles in legislation. The legal system recognizes the existence of hierarchies (intelligence or order), whereas a statute approach is carried out by examining all laws and regulations relating to the legal issues being addressed;[7] this approach is carried out by reviewing all forms of legislation in accordance with the hierarchy that is relevant to the legal issues being studied.

The conceptual approach is carried out by elaborating several legal concepts, legal theory and relevant legal doctrines to solve or answer existing legal issues.[8] The approach to this concept departs from the views and doctrines that develop in legal science.[9] This approach is intended to examine and analyze the study of legal concepts, in the form of principles, norms, and theories about the urgency of the formation and structuring of Adat Villages after the enactment of Act No. 6 of 2014 on Villages (Act No. 6 of 2014 on Villages, 2014) by conducting study of the formation of regulatory establishment through Mojokerto Regency Regulation No. 47 of 2017 on the Establishment of Adat Village Preparations in Pacet Sub-District.

With regard to legal material in this study, the legal literature in the light of its binding strength can be divided into three groups, namely: primary, secondary and tertiary legal materials (supporting materials).[10] Legal materials basically include, first, material that provides guidance on primary legal research material, better known as legal reference materials; in this case:

1. Constitution of the Republic of Indonesia Year 1945;
2. Law of the Republic of Indonesia No. 6 of 2014 on Villages (State Gazette of the Republic of Indonesia 2014 No. 7, Supplement to the State Gazette of the Republic of Indonesia No. 5495);
3. Law of the Republic of Indonesia No. 23 of 2014 on Local Government (State Gazette of the Republic of Indonesia 2014 No. 224, Supplement to the State Gazette of the Republic of Indonesia No. 5587) as amended by Act No. 9 of 2015 on the second amendment to Act No. 23 of 2014 about Local Government (State Gazette of the Republic of Indonesia 2015 No. 58, State Gazette of the Republic of Indonesia No. 5679);
4. Indonesian Government Regulation No. 43 of 2014 about the Implementing Regulations of Law No. 6 of 2014 on Villages (Gazette of the Republic of Indonesia 2014 No. 123,

4. Hanintijo, R. (1988). *Legal and jurimetric research methodology* (Rev. ed., p. 11). Jakarta, Indonesia: Ghalia Indonesia.
5. Soekanto, S. (1986). *Introduction to legal research* (pp. 50–51). Jakarta, Indonesia: UI-Press.
6. Marzuki, P.M. (2005). *Legal research* (p. v). Jakarta, Indonesia: Prenada Media.
7. Ibid, p. 94.
8. Ibid, p. 96.
9. Ibid, p. 95.
10. Peter Mahmud classifies sources of legal research by classifying primary legal material, secondary legal material and non-legal materials (Ibid, pp. 142–169).

Supplement to the State Gazette of the Republic of Indonesia No. 5539) as amended with Indonesian Government Regulation No. 47 of 2015 on Amendment of Government Regulation No. 43 of 2014 about the Implementing Regulations of Law No. 6 of 2014 on Villages (State Gazette of the Republic of Indonesia 2015 No. 157, Supplement to the State Gazette of the Republic of Indonesia No. 5717);
5. Regulation of the Minister of Home Affairs of the Republic of Indonesia No. 111 of 2014 on Guidelines for Technical Regulation in the Village;
6. Regulation of the Minister of Home Affairs of the Republic of Indonesia No. 113 of 2014 on Village Financial Management;
7. Ministry of Home Affairs of the Republic of Indonesia No. 114 of 2014 on Guidelines for Village Development;
8. Regulation of the Minister of Villages, Development of Disadvantaged Regions and Transmigration No. 1 of 2015 on Authority Guidelines Based on the Rights of Origin and Local Authority of Village Scale;
9. Regulation of the Minister of Villages, Development of Disadvantaged Regions and Transmigration No. 3 of 2015 on Village Assistance;
10. Mojokerto Regency Regulation No. 47 of 2017 on the Establishment of Adat Village Preparations in Pacet Sub-District.

Secondary legal material is in the form of legal encyclopedias, legal magazines, legal dictionaries, legal books, articles published in legal journals, and others related to research.

Third-level legal material is supporting material outside the legal field that is useful in this study, which will be used as a complement or support for research material with a method of reading literature related to research.

3 DISCUSSION

The principle of recognition is the recognition of the right of origin. The principle of subsidiarity is the establishment of large-scale local authority and local decision-making for the benefit of the Village community and the principle of diversity is the recognition and respect for the system of values that apply in the Village, but with fixed heed to the common value system in the life of the nation and the state.[11]

In principle, the Adat Village is a legacy of traditionally maintained local community governance organizations that continue to be recognized and championed by the leaders and communities of the Adat Village, in order to function to develop social welfare and local identity. The Adat Village has origin rights that are more dominant than the original rights of the Village since the Adat Village was born as an Adat community in the community. The Adat Village is an Adat law community unit that historically has territorial boundaries and cultural identities formed on a territorial basis, which has the authority to regulate and manage the interests of the Village community based on their rights of origin.

Basically, Adat community units are formed based on three basic principles, namely genealogical, territorial, and/or a genealogical combination with territoriality. What is regulated in this act is the Adat law community unit, which is a combination of genealogical and territorial. In this regard, the state recognizes and respects the Adat law community unit along with their traditional rights insofar as they are still alive and in accordance with the development of society and the principles of the Unitary State of the Republic of Indonesia. The implementation of the Adat law community unit exists and lives in the territory of the Republic of Indonesia, such as Huta/Nagori in North Sumatra, Gampong in Aceh, Nagari in Minangkabau, Marga in Southern Sumatra, Tiuh or Pekon in Lampung, Pakraman/Adat Village in Bali, Lembang in Toraja, Banua and Wanua in Kalimantan, and Negeri in Maluku.

11. Act No. 6 of 2014 on Villages.

The establishment of Adat Villages was for the first time guided by special provisions as stipulated in Chapter XIII of Law No. 6 of 2014 on Villages. The formation of a new Adat Village is guided by the provisions stipulated in Chapter III of Law No. 6 of 2014 on Villages.

Regarding the establishment of Adat Village as mentioned above, the main references are the Constitutional Court decisions of the Republic of Indonesia, namely:

a. Decision No. 010/PUU-l/2003 on Judicial Review of Act No. 11 of 2003 on Amendment to Act No. 53 of 1999 concerning Establishment of Pelalawan District, Rokan Hulu Regency, Rokan Hilir Regency, Siak Regency, Karimun Regency, Natuna Regency, Kuantan Singingi Regency, and Batam City;
b. Decision No. 31/PUU-V/2007 on Judicial Review of Act No. 31 of 2007 on Establishment of Tual City in Maluku Province;
c. Decision No. 6/PUU-VI/2008 regarding Judicial Review of Law No. 51 of 1999 on the Establishment of Buol, Morowali and Banggai Islands;
d. Decision No. 35/PUU-X/2012 on Judicial Review of Act No. 41 of 1999 on Forestry.

However, because the Adat law community unit which was determined to be an Adat Village carries out the function of government (local self-government) then there was an absolute requirement; namely, the existence of a clear boundary area, the existence of government, and other devices. Also added is one other institution in the life of the legal Adat community, such as shared feelings, wealth, and Adat government institutions. Table 1 lists the things set out in Act No. 6 of 2014 on Villages.

The structuring of an Adat Village is covered under Articles 96, 101, and 102 of Act No. 6 of 2014 on Villages, which state that:

- *The Government, Provincial Governments, and Regency/City Governments conduct structuring of Adat law communities and determine Adat Villages.* (Article 96 of Law No. 6 of 2014 on Villages).
- *The Government, Provincial Governments, and District/City Governments can make arrangements for Adat Villages. Arrangements for an Adat Village are stipulated in Regional Regulations. Regional Regulation as referred to is accompanied by an attachment to the regional boundary map.* (Article 101 of Act No. 6 of 2014 on Villages).
- *Regional Regulations concerning the Arrangements for an Adat Village are guided by the provisions of Articles 7, 8, 14, 15, 16 and 17 of Act No. 6 of 2014, in which Articles 7 and 8 regulate the provisions of Village Arrangement, Article 14 states the provisions for the establishment of Regional Regulations, and Articles 16 and 17 regulate the stages related to submission of Draft Regional Regulations concerning the Establishment of Adat Villages from Regency/City to Governor.* (Article 102 of Act No. 6 of 2014 on Villages).

The requirements for the establishment of an Adat Village are contained in Article 97 of Law No. 6 of 2014 on Villages, which states that the conditions for determining an Adat Village are:

a. Adat law community units and their traditional rights are actually still alive, territorially, genealogically and functionally;
b. Adat law community units and their traditional rights are deemed to be in accordance with community development;
c. Adat law community units and their traditional rights are in accordance with the principles of the Unitary State of the Republic of Indonesia.

In addition, the determination of the Adat Village is set by District Regulation in accordance with the provisions of Article 98 Paragraph 1 of Act No. 6 of 2014. The establishment of the Adat Village is performed with respect to:

a. factors in administering Village governance;
b. implementation of Village development;
c. Village community development;
d. empowerment of Village communities;
e. supporting infrastructure facilities.

Table 1. Contents of Act No. 6 of 2014 on Villages (Source: Act No. 6 of 2014 on Villages).

Chapter	About	Article
I	**GENERAL PROVISIONS**	1
II	**POSITION AND TYPE OF VILLAGE**	5–6
	Part One - Positions	5
	Part Two - Types of Village	6
III	**REFORMING OF THE VILLAGE**	7–17
IV	**AUTHORITY OF THE VILLAGE**	18–22
V	**GOVERNMENTAL ORGANIZATION OF THE VILLAGE**	23–24
	Part One - Village Government	25
	Part Two - Chief of the Village	26–30
	Part Three - The Village Head Election	31–39
	Part Four - Dismissal of the Village Head	40–47
	Part Five - Village Officials	48–53
	Part Six - Village Meeting/Assembly	54
	Part Seven -Village Consultative Body	55–65
	Part Eight - Income of the Village Government	66
VI	**RIGHTS AND OBLIGATIONS OF THE VILLAGE AND VILLAGERS**	67–68
VII	**REGULATION OF THE VILLAGE**	69–70
VIII	**FINANCE AND ASSETS OF THE VILLAGE**	
	Part One - Village Finance	71–75
	Part Two - Village Assets	76–77
IX	**VILLAGE DEVELOPMENT AND DEVELOPMENT OF VILLAGE AREAS**	
	Part One - Village Development	78
	• Paragraph 1 - Planning	79–80
	• Paragraph 2 - Implementation	81
	• Paragraph 3 - Monitoring and Control of Village Development	82
	Part Two - Development of Village Areas	83–85
	Part Three - Village Development Information Systems and Development of Village Areas	86
X	**VILLAGE - OWNED ENTERPRISES**	87–90
XI	**VILLAGE COOPERATION**	91
	Part One - Cooperation Between Village	92
	Part Two - Cooperation with Third Parties	93
XII	**VILLAGE COMMUNITY INSTITUTIONS AND ADAT VILLAGE INSTITUTIONS**	
	Part One - Village Community Institutions	94
	Part Two - Adat Village Constitutions	95
XIII	**TRIBAL VILLAGE SPECIAL PROVISIONS**	
	Part One - Structuring Adat Village	96–102
	Part Two - The Authority of the Adat Village	103–106
	Part Three - Governance of Adat Village	107–109
	Part Four - Rule Adat Village	110–111
XIV	**GUIDANCE AND SUPERVISION**	112–115
XV	**TRANSITIONAL PROVISIONS**	116–118
XVI	**CLOSING PROVISIONS**	119–122

Arranging and conducting Adat Village government is carried out in accordance with the origin of the rights and Adat law in the Adat Village that are still alive, and in accordance with the development of society and not contrary to the principles for the Government of the Adat Village in the principles of the Unitary Republic of Indonesia, as stipulated in Article 107 of Act No. 6 of 2014 on Villages. Institutional arrangements, filling the positions, and the tenure of the Chief of the Adat Village are in accordance with Adat law set out in provincial regulations pursuant to Article 109 of Law No. 6 of 2014 on Villages.

The Mojokerto District Medium-Term Development Plan (RPJMD) for 2016–2021 states that the Mojokerto Regency Development Vision is: "The realization of the Independent,

Prosperous and Dignified Community of Mojokerto Regency through Strengthening and Development of the Economic, Educational and Health Sectors."

The plan's third mission statement is: "Building economic independence with a people's dimension to improve welfare through strengthening the economic structure oriented to the development of infrastructure networks, UMKMs, agribusiness, agroindustry, and tourism."

Through this mission, the RPJMD is expected to achieve three things:

a. Increasing employment opportunities;
b. Improved community living quality;
c. Increased connectivity in support of regional growth/potential.

The plans' fourth mission statement describes: "Opening opportunities for effective communication and efficient to cultivate social trust (social trust) and stimulate creativity and innovation society based on ethical culture and local wisdom more character." Through this mission, two things are expected to be achieved:

a. Increased cultural preservation;
b. Increased utilization of culture-based tourism.

One of the active roles of the community in "innovating based on cultural ethics and local wisdom" refers to Mojokerto Regency's fourth mission statement in the RPJMD: to take the initiative to rebuild the Pacet Village indigenous community. Mojokerto and the supporting data are attached to this study. The chronology referred to ended in the establishment of Mojokerto Regency Regulation No. 47 of 2017 on the Establishment of Adat Village Preparations in Pacet Sub-District. This preparation is intended as an embryo of the Desa Adat Sendal, which will be expanded from Pacet Village, especially the Southern Pacet area. To complete Regency Regulation No. 47 of 2017 on the Establishment of Adat Village Preparations in the Pacet Sub-District, the Mojokerto Regency Bappeda made a proposal for the 'Traditional-Village Village Map', including the current Ngeprih and Gotekan areas.

'Sendi' is the name of a 'lost village', located on the slopes of Mount Welirang, in the Pacet District, Mojokerto. It is described as a 'lost village' because Sendi is the name of a village that has existed since the time of Majapahit. Sendi Village is believed by some people in Mojokerto to be the village that was used as a sanctuary for the officials and Begawan from the Majapahit Empire in its time. It is characterized by the presence of several historical sites and Majapahit relics in the area such as a 'Putuk Chair', the 'Soldier Tomb of Majapahit, Head Singo Joyo' who died in 1925, and a site by some springs. Currently, the former village of Sendi is better known to local people as the Ngeprih-Gotekan area.

In public administration, 'Sendi' as a village has existed since 1915. It was inaugurated by *Gouverment Oost-Java, Residentie Soerabaja, Regentschap Modjokerto, District Djaboeng, Desa Sendi, Oorspronkelijk Opgenomen* in 1915, as a representative of the Dutch government centered in Surabaya. The aforementioned is based on documents of the administrative divisions in East Java in 1931 (Cribb, 2010), which state that 'Residentie Soerabaja' consists of several *Regentschap* and their districts, namely:

A. Regentschap Soerabaja:	B. Regentschap Sidoarjo:
• Soerabaja • Djabakota • Goenoeng Kendeng • Bawean	• Sidoarjo • Porong • Garden • Krijan
C. Regentschap Modjokerto:	D. Regentschap Djombang:
• Modjokerto • Modjokrasi • Modjosari • Djaboeng	• Djombang • Ploso • Modjoagoeng • Ngoro

In 1931, the Dutch government carried out large-scale forest management in Java under the coordination of a Dutch government forestry company called *den dienst van het Boschwezen,* often abbreviated to *Boschwezen* (Peluso, 1991; Indonesian Ministry of Forestry, 1986). In the period 1931–1942, the Dutch government and *Boschwezen* tried to expand commercial forestry areas by including areas around the forest, which were considered to have very high potential (Peluso, 1991). One of the commercially managed forest areas was forests located in the *Regentschap Modjokerto* area.

Sendi Village, which is located on the slopes of Mount Welirang, is a village located around a forest area that is not separated from the management by *Boschwezen.* According to the author, it is possible that the Sendi Village area was incorporated by *Boschwezen* into the forest area in 1932. The event was part of the *Boschwezen* commercial forest area expansion program.

The *Boschwezen* document in 1932, owned by the Republic of Indonesia *Perum Perhutani,* documents the exchange of the land of Desa Sendi with *Boschwezen.* The document is in the form of Official Report No. 3 of 1932, dated October 10, 1932, concerning the exchange and compensation for residents of Sendi Village, Pacet Sub-District, Mojokerto Regency with *Boschwezen.* The total land area freed in this process was 762.9 Ha. In particular, for Sendi Village, the area of land exchanged was 72.55 Ha. Then, based on the Minutes of Border Arrangement dated March 27, 1935, it was determined that Sendi Village become the Anjasmoro Mountains Forest Zone and this was ratified on August 23, 1935 by the Chief Inspector of the Dutch Forestry Service in Bogor. Figure 2 shows a map of the Adat Village from the Results of Mapping in 2006.

Figure 1. Proposal for the Adat Village map that was remade by the team forming the preparation of Pacet Village expansion in Mojokerto Regency in 2017.

The total area of the Adat Village Preparation in question is 265 Ha, as stated and stipulated in Article 3 of Mojokerto Regency Regulation No. 47 of 2017 on the Establishment of Adat Village Preparations in Pacet Sub-District. However, this regulation does not mention the number of inhabitants of the Village in question, which is as follows:

1. The population of the Village of Pacet

   Number of men : 3,334
   Number of women : 3,255
   Total : 6,589
   Total families : 1,850

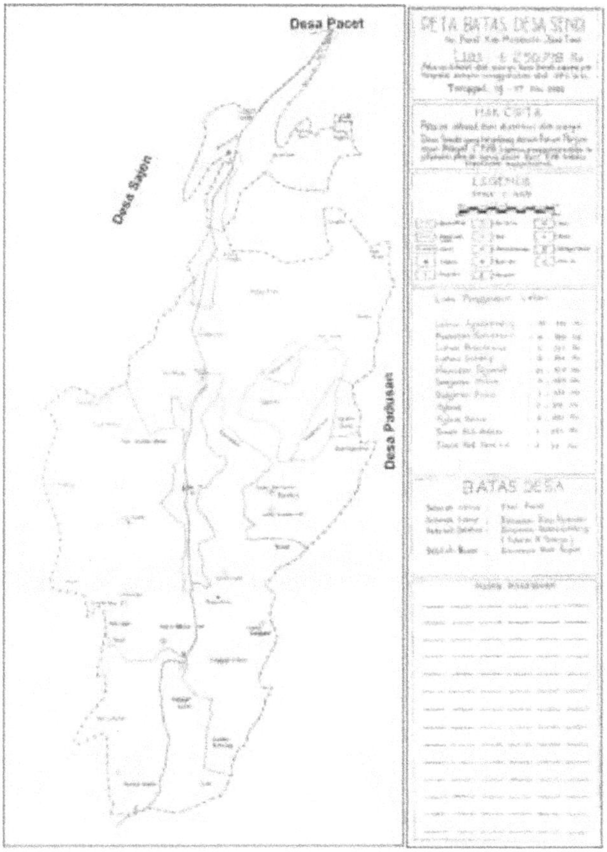

Figure 2. Adat Village, from the Results of Mapping in 2006.

2. The population of South Pacet Village

   Number of men : 302
   Number of women : 296
   Total : 598
   Total families : 227

3. The number of people living in Sendi (Village)

   Number of men : 90
   Number of women : 96
   Total : 186
   Total families : 57[12]
   (Data source: Mojokerto Pacet Village Head)

By referring to the provisions of Act No. 6 of 2014 on Villages (State Gazette of the Republic of Indonesia of 2014 No. 7, Supplement to the State Gazette of the Republic of Indonesia No. 5495) and Regulation of the Minister of Home Affairs No. 1 of 2017 concerning Village Arrangement (Official Gazette of the Republic of Indonesia 2017 No. 155), the study of the formation of Adat Villages through Mojokerto Regency Regulation No. 47 of 2017 on the Establishment of Adat Village Preparations in Pacet Sub-District are as follows:

12. Based on information from the Head of Pacet Mojokerto during the FGD dated March 16, 2018, 57 families have become one with the total population of the village of South Pacet.

1. *Has the Mojokerto District Government socialized the formation of the Adat Village with the village government and the village community concerned?* This is a provision in Article 35 of the Minister of Home Affairs Regulation No. 1 of 2017 on Village Arrangements, which states that:

   a. The District/City government, in conducting Village formation as referred to in Article 34 Paragraph 2, must socialize the Village expansion plan with the government of the Village and the Village communities concerned.
   b. The Village government to facilitate and prepare for the implementation of Village meetings referred to in Paragraph 1.
   c. Village Consultative Body holds Village meetings referred to in Paragraph 2 to obtain agreement to establish a Village through the division.
   d. The Village meeting results referred to in Paragraph 3 shall be recorded in the proceedings of meeting results to include the deliberation of the Village government with the Village community.

- Article 36 of the Minister of Home Affairs Regulation No. 1 of 2017 on Village Arrangements states that: "Provisions regarding the expansion of the Village as referred to in Article 19 to Article 26 shall apply *mutatis mutandis* to the expansion of the Village by the Regency/City Regional Government." The steps to form an Adat Village must be passed according to the provisions of Articles 19 to 26 of the Minister of Home Affairs Regulation No. 1 of 2017 on Village Arrangements, namely:
- Has the Head of the Pacet Village reported the proceedings of the results of the Village consultation to the Regent of Mojokerto?
- After receiving the report, has the Regent assigned the Village Preparation team to conduct a study and verify the requirements for forming a Village?
- Does the Village Preparation team consist of at least the elements of the local government of Mojokerto Regency in charge of Village governance, community empowerment, regional development planning and legislation, sub-district heads, and academics in the fields of government, regional development planning, development and community socialization?
- Has the verification of requirements been carried out? Which includes verification of administration by examining documents related to the minutes of the Village meeting and minutes of Village meetings, as well as the minimum age limit of the parent Village and minimum population, as well as technical verification through field observation to verify: availability of transportation and communication between region; factual verification of the condition of the closeness of the social group, the conditions of the Adat and traditions in the area of the prospective preparatory village that support the administration of candidates for the preparatory village; factual verification of economic conditions, the condition of human resources in the productive age in the area of the prospective preparatory village, which makes it possible to progress and develop properly with local potential; verification of the requirements for the number of residents of the parent Village and expansion Village; verification of the preparatory village area boundaries in the parent Village map; and verification of the availability of supporting facilities and infrastructure for the implementation of Village governance and public services has been done to check availability of (a) office facilities where the preparatory village government organizes, and (b) ease for the public to access public services.
- The results of the study and verification of the requirements of the proposed Village by the preparatory village team in the form of recommendations stating the feasibility of establishing the proposed village. Have they done the intended steps in Mojokerto Regency? Recommendations stating that it is feasible to form an Adat Village are taken into consideration by the Regent to carry out the expansion of the Village. The Regent agrees to the expansion of the Village, and stipulates Regency regulations regarding the establishment of the proposed village. In this case, in Mojokerto Regency, in the form of Mojokerto Regency Regulation No. 47 of 2017 on the Establishment of Adat Village Preparations in Pacet Sub-District.

2. In the considerations, point (b) of Mojokerto Regency Regulation No. 47 of 2017 on the Establishment of Adat Village Preparations in Pacet Sub-District mentions: "That in order

to protect all Adat law community unit along with a real Adat rights are still alive, whether they are territorial, genealogical, and that is functional deemed in accordance with the developments in the framework of the Unitary Republic of Indonesia." Based on the considerations of the contents of point (b), *whether there has been unity among Adat people of Pacet Sub-District, Mojokerto*, the criteria in Article 97 of Act No. 6 of 2014 on Villages mentions that the term Adat Village means:

a. Adat law community unit along with real Adat rights are still alive, whether territorial or genealogical, and that both are functional;
b. Adat law community unit along with Adat rights are deemed to be in accordance with the development of society;
c. Adat law community unit along with Adat rights are in accordance with the principles of the Unitary Republic of Indonesia.

In the framework of implementing government and legal certainty, it is necessary to revisit a portion of the material considering point (b), which is regulated in Mojokerto Regency Regulation No. 47 of 2017 on the Establishment of Adat Village Preparations in Pacet Sub-District.

4 RECOMMENDATION

1. It is necessary to include the provisions of territory and population in Mojokerto Regency Regulation No. 47 of 2017 on the Establishment of Adat Village Preparations in Pacet Sub-District.
2. Based on the results of the study, the establishment of an Adat Village in Mojokerto must refer to the provisions of Articles 7, 8, 14, 15, 16, 17, 97 and 98 of Act No. 6 of 2014 on Villages.
3. The results of the study on Mojokerto Regency Regulation No. 47 of 2017 on the Establishment of Adat Village Preparations in Pacet Sub-District need to be adjusted to the provisions of Article 97 of Act No. 6 of 2014 on Villages, and Articles 19, 20, 21 and 22 of Minister of Home Affairs Regulation No. 1 of 2017 on Village Arrangements.
4. In the case of the formation of an Adat Village in Mojokerto, the steps that must be taken by the Mojokerto Regency Government are as follows:
   - Conducting in accordance with the provisions of CHAPTER XIII ADAT VILLAGE SPECIAL PROVISIONS Articles 96 to 110 of Law No. 6 of 2014 on Villages. One of these stipulations (in Article 97) is that the conditions for determining an Adat Village are:
     a. Adat law community units and their traditional rights are actually still alive, in territorial, genealogical and functional terms;
     b. Adat law community units and their traditional rights are deemed to be in accordance with community development;
     c. Adat law community units and their traditional rights are in accordance with the principles of the Unitary State of the Republic of Indonesia.
   - Conducting in accordance with the provisions of Article 8 of Act No. 6 of 2014 on Villages.
   - To socialize the proposed formation of the Adat Village with the Village government and the Village community concerned.
   - The Head of the Pacet Village reports the minutes of the results of the Village Conference regarding the establishment of the Adat Village to the Regent of Mojokerto.
   - The Regent forms a Village Preparation team.
   - The Regent assigns a village preparatory team to conduct a study and verify the requirements for the establishment of an Adat Village.
   - The preparatory village formation team verifies the requirements, which include verification of administration and technical verification.

- The results of the study and verification of the requirements of the proposed Village by the village preparatory team in the form of recommendations stating the feasibility of establishing an Adat Village.
- Recommendation from the village preparatory team stating that it was feasible to form an Adat Village to be taken into consideration by the District Head to carry out the expansion of the Village. The Regent agrees to the expansion of the Village, stipulating the Regency regulations regarding the establishment of a such a village. In this case, in Mojokerto Regency, in the form of Mojokerto Regency Regulation No. 47 of 2017 on the Establishment of Adat Village Preparations in Pacet Sub-District.

REFERENCES

Act No. 6 of 2014 on Villages. (2014).

Hanintijo, R. (1988). *Legal and jurimetric research methodology* (Rev. ed.). Jakarta, Indonesia: Ghalia Indonesia.

Marzuki, P.M. (2005). *Research, law*. Jakarta, Indonesia: Kencana Prenada Media Group.

Mojokerto Regency Regulation No. 47 of 2017 on the Establishment of Adat Village Preparations in Pacet Sub-District. (2017).

Soekanto, S. (1986). *Introduction to legal research*. Jakarta, Indonesia: UI-Press.

Culture and International Law - Juwana et al. (Eds)
© 2019 Taylor & Francis Group, London, ISBN 978-1-138-38766-9

Human rights and conflict resolution: The case of Bosnia and Herzegovina

Prischa Listiningrum
Constitutional Law Department, Faculty of Law, Universitas Brawijaya, Indonesia

Rizqi Bachtiar
Governmental Science Study Program, Faculty of Social and Political Sciences, Universitas Brawijaya, Indonesia

ABSTRACT: Violence and brutality commonly occur in every conflict. However, ending the conflict can be meant bringing the order back, since there is no post-conflict law. The incorporation of human rights provisions in the peace agreement is therefore vital in preventing the future violations. By using the Bosnia and Herzegovina conflict, this paper aims to analyse the relationship between human rights and conflict resolution. The analysis is based on the review of the Dayton Peace Agreements. There are at least four key findings found by this research. First, international communities push the warring parties to sit in a negotiation of peace agreement as a result of strong political and military pressure. Second, although the agreement incorporates numerous provisions on human rights protection, it mentions nothing about accountability for the human rights abuses that happened during the conflict. Third, in implementing the agreement, international communities play an important role, particularly in ensuring the refugees and internally displaced persons are returned to their own homes, although they may well become a minority in some cases. Fourth, learning from the Bosnia and Herzegovina conflict, human rights laws can become complementary to the peace process when dealing with the protection of the rights of minorities and prevent future abuses but it is inadequate when dealing with war crimes, and the returning process of refugees and internally displaced persons.

KEYWORDS: Bosnia and Herzegovina, Conflict Resolution, Human Rights

1 INTRODUCTION

Since 1946, there have been 102 inter and intrastate conflicts, of which 91 per cent were intrastate.[1] During these conflicts, there were some atrocities resulting in the deaths of more than 20 million people.[2] The Bosnia and Herzegovina (hereinafter "BiH") conflict is one example where civil war generated devastating human rights violations, causing the deaths, disappearances, rapes, ethnic cleansing, and massive displacements.[3]

1. Christine Bell, *On the Law of Peace: Peace Agreements and Lex Pacificatoria* (Oxford University Press, 2008) 5. See also The Stockholm International Peace Research Institute, *Yearbook of World Armaments and Disarmaments* (Oxford University Press 2002); Paul Collier and Anke Hoeffler, 'Greed and Grievance in Civil War' (2004) 56(563) *Oxford Economic Papers*.
2. Gareth Evans, 'Security and Intrastate Conflict' (1994) 96(3) *Foreign Policy*.
3. Steven L Burg and Paul S Shoup, *The War in Bosnia-Herzegovina: Ethnic Conflict and International Intervention* (M. E. Sharpe, Inc 1999) 169-71.

Ending the conflict means bringing the order back. Since there is no post-conflict law, the incorporation of human rights provisions in the peace agreement is vital in preventing the future violations. However, human rights laws also demand the accountability of the past abuses. Here, the peace versus justice debate emerges since the most responsible persons are frequently the one that should be brought to the table. By using the BiH conflict, this paper aims to analyse the relationship between human rights and conflict resolution. The analysis will be based on the review of the Dayton Peace Agreements (hereinafter "the DPA"). The discussion will proceed in three sections: first, the background of the conflict and agreement; second, some key human rights elements covered and not covered by the DPA; third, the constraints of the implementation of human rights provisions. Finally, this paper examines whether human rights laws are complementary, inadequate or in contravention of the process of conflict resolution.

2 BACKGROUND TO THE CONFLICT AND AGREEMENT

There were three main causes of the conflict in the BiH: the failed transition to democracy,[4] the demand of self-determination and secession,[5] and the possibility of ethnic map drawing.[6] The conflict was also exacerbated by the interventions of the two neighbouring countries (Croatia and Serbia).

Before outbreak of the conflict in 1992, the BiH was a multi ethnic state consisting of three national groups, consisting of Muslims (43.7 per cent), Serbs (31.4 per cent), Croats (17.3 per cent), as well as the children of 'mixed marriages' that called themselves 'Yugoslavs' (5.5 per cent).[7] From 1908 to 1991, BiH was under the control of three different regimes: Austria-Hungary; then the kingdom of the Serbs, Croats and Slovenes; and finally the Socialist Federal Republic of Yugoslavia (SFRY).[8]In the era of SRFY, the BiH and the other five republics (Serbia, Croatia, Slovenia, Macedonia, and Montenegro) were granted a special right of self-determination and secession. This right was specified by the 1974 Constitution and only applied to a group of people that can be called a nation, such as Croats, Macedonians and Serbs.[9]However, the constitution did not mention what mechanism should be employed in using the right.

After the collapse of the communist regime in the late part of the 20th century, the SFRY tried to transform its political system into a democratic state. This transition can be seen from the establishment of free elections from April to December, 1990. Since the ex-communists, now calling themselves socialists, won the election, Slovenia and Croatia, as republics in which the majority of the people opposed the communists and communism, decided to exit from SFRY. They then declared independence after conducting majority-based referendums.[10] The declaration of independence conducted by the Slovenia and Croatia initiated a new trend of self-determination throughout the SFRY.

Learning from Slovenia and Croatia, the BiH also decided to hold a referendum in order to gain recognition of independence from the European Union (hereinafter "the EU"). The referendum was carried out on the 29th February to 1st March of 1992 and resulted in a

4. International Commission on the Balkans, *Unfinished Peace: Report of the International Commission on the Balkans* (Carnegie Endowment for International Peace, 1996) 26-28.
5. Christine Bell, *Peace Agreements and Human Rights* (Oxford University Press 2003) 92; International Commission on the Balkans, above n 4, 28-32.
6. Steven L Burg and Paul S Shoup, above n 3,169-71; International Commission on the Balkans, above n, 32-3; Christine Bell, above n 5, 95.
7. Ibid.
8. BBC News, 'Bosnia-Herzegovina Profile - Timeline' (2015) <http://www.bbc.co.uk/news/world-europe-17212376> accessed 9 March 2016.
9. Christine Bell, above n 5.
10. International Commission on the Balkans, above n 4, 27.

99 per cent vote in favour of independence. The referendum was participated in by almost 63 per cent of the citizens; mostly Muslim and Croats.[11] However, the Serbs did not join the referendum because the wanted to separate from the BiH.[12] Ignoring the fact, the Bosnian leader (Alija Izetbegović) announced the independence of BiH on the 2nd March 1992, and then submitted an application of recognition to the EU.[13]

After gaining recognition from the EU on 6th April 1992, a full attack in some Muslim regions was conducted by the Serbs (Arkan's forces) helped by Serbian Army.[14] As an effort to exacerbate the conflict, neighbouring countries' (Croatia and Serbia) formed a coalition to disintegrate the territory of the BiH.[15] The government of Serbia (President Milosevic) supported the Bosnian Serbs by providing financial and troops support; and Croatia (President Tudjman) persuaded the Bosnian Croats to separate from the BiH by supporting the Croatian separation movement of Herceg-Bosna.[16]

During the hostilities in the BiH, the three warring ethnic groups (Muslims, Serbs and Croats) conducted several human rights violations. The number of deaths was, and remains, debatable. The bulletin of the Bosnian Institute for Public Health, of the Republic Committee for Health and Social Welfare, reported a figure of 146,340 by October 1995; the Central Intelligence Agency of America (hereinafter "CIA") estimated a figure of 156,500 by November 1995, and Mustafa Imamovic reported a figure of 144,248. Although diverse in number, the facts seem to confirm that Muslims suffered more victims than others. Moreover, the number of troops killed was also substantial (81,500 in total, consisting of 45,000 Bosnian government troops; 6,500 Bosnian Croats; and 30,000 Bosnian Serbs).[17]

The fact shows that only 30 per cent of the BiH territory (32 out of 109) is occupied by a certain national ethnic.[18] Therefore, in order to support the claims of self-determination by the Serbs and Croats, they persuaded their members to migrate to some districts where they were in the majority. This effort was done in an offensive way, through the spread of hatred and threat. They also expelled the minorities from their homes. The number of Muslims that were forced to move away from Serb-occupied areas was 700,000 people.[19] In total, the number of refugees and internally displaced persons (hereinafter "IDPs") resulting from this conflict was more than a half of the BIH's population (roughly 2.3 million). This exodus was called the most tragic refugee crisis in Europe since the Second World War. The refugees flew away to 25 host countries, including the United States, Canada and Australia. The host country receiving the biggest number of refugees from the BiH was Germany (345,000), followed by Croatia, Serbia and Montenegro, Austria, and Sweden (288,000; 254,000; 80,000; 61,500, respectively).[20]

According to the Commission of Experts Established Pursuant to Security Council Resolution 780 (1992), the act of removing persons or certain groups from their lawful presence area, by the use of force or any kind of intimidation, can be considered as 'ethnic cleansing', which is contrary to international law.[21] In the case of the BiH, ethnic cleansing acts were carried out by the Bosnian Serbs against the Bosnian Muslims and Croats by different types of crimes against humanity; such as killing, torture, sexual assault, degrading treatment of prisoners of war, destruction of private, public and cultural property, forceful expulsion, and

11. Christine Bell, above n 5, 102; Steven L Burg and Paul S Shoup, above n 3, 117-20.
12. ibid.
13. ibid.
14. ibid.
15. International Commission on the Balkans, above n 4, 102.
16. Ibid, 89. For more information about the Croatian Community of Herceg-Bosna, see *Prosecutor v. Dario Kordi J & Mario* ^Erkez, Judgment of 22 February 2001, ICTY, para 5c.
17. Steven L Burg and Paul S Shoup, above n 3, 169.
18. Christine Bell, above n 5, 95.
19. Steven L Burg and Paul S Shoup, above n 3, 171.
20. Daniela Heimerl, 'The Return of Refugees and Internally Displaced Persons: From Coercion to Sustainability?' (2005) 12(3) *International Peacekeeping*, 377-8.
21. United Nations Security Council, 'Final Report of the Commission of Experts Established Pursuant to Security Council Resolution 780 (1992)', 27 May 1994, para 129.

attacks on medical units.[22] Simultaneously, the Bosnian Croats also committed the practice of ethnic cleansing against the Bosnian Muslims in Herzegovina.[23] Moreover, the government of Bosnian (Muslims) also did some acts against Serbs and Croats that can be considered as grave breaches of the Geneva Conventions, but could not be considered as the practice of ethnic cleansing.[24]

After a strong political and military pressure from the United States of America (hereinafter "the U.S.") since July 1995, finally the three warring parties agreed to negotiate in Dayton, Ohio in November 1995.[25] The negotiation lasted for twenty-one days and concluded with a set of agreements called "The Dayton Peace Agreement" (the DPA).[26] In December of the same year, the DPA was signed by the parties in Paris.[27]

3 KEY HUMAN RIGHTS ISSUES DEALT WITH BY THE DAYTON PEACE AGREEMENT

The DPA served as a foundation for the establishment of peace in the BiH. It consists of one general framework agreement and 11 annexes for an agreement on particular issues.[28] There are some key human rights elements dealt with by the DPA. Some of them are the formulation of power sharing, the establishment of human rights frameworks, institutional reform and the repatriation of refugees and internally displaced persons (IDPs).

A mechanism of territorial and political power sharing based on ethnic was specified in the DPA in order to accommodate the demand of self-determination, particularly in the BiH Constitution in Annex 4. First, it provides a territorial power sharing by establishing highly decentralised entities called as the Federation of Bosnia and Herzegovina and the Republika Srpska.[29] Second, it signifies a mechanism of political power within the parliamentary assembly. There are two chambers in the parliamentary assembly, which are the House of the People and the House of Representatives. Both chambers will have a composition of Muslims, Serbs, and Croats. Not only in the parliament, a form of political power sharing is also applied in the composition of the presidency.[30]

This complex composition of power sharing[31] might become an answer to accommodate the need of the warring parties, but may also become a serious impediment to the democracy. Recalling that within the BiH itself lives some minorities outside the "constituent peoples" (Muslims, Serbs and Croats), for instance the population of mixed marriage children that call themselves 'Yugoslavs'; a group which consists of 5.5 per cent of the population.[32] By 2009, there has been a claim of discrimination against the BiH before the European Court of Human Rights (hereinafter "the ECtHR") challenging these provisions of ethnic power sharing. The applicants are the citizens of the BiH that are originally of Roma and Jew ethnicity.

22. Ibid, para 134.
23. Ibid, para 147.
24. Ibid, para 150
25. Steven L Burg and Paul S Shoup, above n 3, 360.
26. Christine Bell, above n 5, 109.
27. Zoran Pajic, 'A Critical Appraisal of the Human Rights Provisions of the Dayton Constitution of Bosnia and Herzegovina' in Wolfgang Benedek (ed), *Human Rights in Bosnia and Herzegovina after Dayton, From Theory to Practice* (Martinus Nijhoff Publishers, 1999) 33.
28. The 1995 Dayton Peace Agreement <http://peacemaker.un.org/sites/peacemaker.un.org/files/BA_951121_DaytonAgreement.pdf> accessed 13 March 2016.
29. Ibid, Annex 4 art I para 3.
30. Ibid, Annex 4 art V.
31. See Christine Bell, 'Unsettling Bargains? Power-sharing and the Inclusion of Women in Peace Negotiations' (2015) <http://politicalsettlements.org/research/publications/reports/£sthash.xXlpRK49.dpuf> accessed 13 March 2016, 11-2.
32. International Commission on the Balkans, above n 4, 32. See also Christine Bell, above n 5, 95; and Steven L Burg and Paul S Shoup, above n 3, 26.

They challenged the BiH laws that impede BiH's citizens (outside the "constituent peoples") to stand for highest political office, such as the Presidency and the House of People on the ground of their ethnic background. In the judgment, the ECtHR said that the BiH laws are in violation of article 14 of the European Convention on Human Rights (hereinafter "ECHR"), in conjunction with article 3 of Protocol 1 and in violation also of article 1 of Protocol 12.[33] Therefore, in this case, the provisions of ethnic power sharing seem in contravention of the BiH's commitment as a member state of the ECHR. Recalling that the DPA also applies the ECHR as a standard of human rights protection.[34]

Despite applying the ECHR and its protocols, thirteen rights (the right to life; no to be tortured; not to be forced in slavery; liberty and security; private and family life; thought, conscience, and religion; expression, association, marry, property, education; and liberty of movement and residence) were listed[35] and non-discrimination provision was asserted[36] as a framework for human rights protection in the BiH. It is not clear why the DPA singled out thirteen rights, which mostly have been covered by the ECHR. On one hand, it can be interpreted that those rights are higher in importance than others. On the other hand, it may mean that those rights cannot be restricted for any reason.[37] It should be noted that some rights in the ECHR are limited. Moreover, the DPA also acknowledged fifteen additional human rights conventions, as listed in Annex 1 of the agreement.[38]

As a part of institutional reform, the DPA established a Constitutional Court that has a jurisdiction over any dispute arising between the entities or institutions within the BiH; as well as assessing the compatibility of the entity's constitution or law with the constitution of the BiH and the ECHR, as well as its protocols.[39] The Court shall comprise of nine judges, where four judges are selected by the the House of Representatives of the Federation of BiH; two others are selected by the Assembly of the Republika Srpska; and the other three are elected by the President of the ECtHR.[40] In my view, the inclusion of the foreign judges substantially was address to handle one of Court's functions in assessing the compatibility of the entity's constitution or law to the Constitution of the BiH and the ECHR as well as its protocols. Politically, the foreign judges presence is assumed to balancing the other judges, which nominated by the warring parties that potentially will not be neutral. However, this composition is very unique and rarely happens in any institutional reform.

Another key human rights issue covered by the DPA is the provision of refugees and IDPs. As stated before in this assignment, the war in BiH resulted in a massive number of displacements.[41] In order to return those people to their homes, there should be regulations in place to deal with this problem. Recalling the massive number of refugees and IDPs (more than a half of the BiH population), the parties realised the difficulties of the repatriation process. Subsequently, in the agreement, they called upon the United Nations High Commissioner for Refugees (hereinafter "UNHCR") to deploy a repatriation plan which may include priorities for certain areas or categories of returnees.[42] Moreover, the parties also give full access to other international humanitarian institutions, such as the International Committee of the Red Cross (hereinafter "ICRC") and the United Nations Development Programme (hereinafter "UNDP") to help and monitor the process of repatriation.[43]

33. *Sejdić and Finci v. Bosnia and Herzegovina [GC]*, no. 27996/06 and 34836/06, 22 December 2009.
34. The 1995 Dayton Peace Agreement, Annex 4 art II para 2 and Annex 6 art I.
35. Ibid, Annex 4 art II para 3 and Annex 6 art I(1)-(13).
36. Ibid, Annex 4 art II para 4 and Annex 6 art I(14).
37. James Sloan, 'The Dayton Peace Agreement: Human Rights Guarantees and their Implementation' (1996) 7 (207) *EJIL*, 209-10.
38. The 1995 Dayton Peace Agreement, Annex 1.
39. Ibid, Annex 4 art VI para 3.
40. Ibid, 1995 Dayton Peace Agreement, Annex 4 art VI para 1.
41. Daniela Heimerl, above n 20, 377.
42. The 1995 Dayton Peace Agreement, Annex 7 art I para 5.
43. Ibid Annex 7 art III para 2.

4 IMPORTANT ISSUES NOT COVERED BY THE DPA

There are some important issues that are not covered by the DPA. One of those is a social service to vulnerable group of people becoming a victim of human rights abuses, such as women and children. Although the fact shows that there were more than 12,000 cases of rape during the war. The actual number of rapes could be more because the data was gained on the basis of pregnant rape victims in the hospital. Sexual violence was not mentioned in the agreement, even though in the reality that was one of the tactics of war conducted by the Serbs; in this case having a connection with their agenda of ethnic cleansing.[44] Relating to women, it only mentions several human rights conventions that will be applied directly to the territory of the BiH, such as the 1957 Convention on the Nationality of Married Women and the 1979 Convention on the Elimination of All Forms of Discrimination Against Women (CEDAW).

I assume the lack of women representative at the negotiation table affected the perspectives and outcome of the peace agreement. In resolving this, or any conflict, women have a different way of thinking compared to men. They are often more concerned with issues relating to the socio-economic agenda, such as important gender-related issues and social services for vulnerable groups of people, such as the breadwinner women who have emerged as a result of the conflict. The experiences of Northern Ireland and Guatemala clearly show that women tend to bring something different to the negotiation, which usually results in a durable peace.[45]

The exclusion of women in the negotiation can be influenced by two factors: the patriarchal culture in the BiH[46] and the lack of international attention to the gender perspective agenda. The idea of including a gender perspective in the peace-making process was first introduced by the United Nations Security Council Resolution 1325 in 2000.[47] This 'soft' law increases the number of peace agreements mentioning women.[48] It calls for the parties to adopt a gender perspective that recognises the special needs of women and girls for rehabilitation, empowering them and respecting their human rights.[49]

Moreover, not so many provisions in the DPA are concerned with the past, such as investigating the human rights abuses during the conflict, reconciliation processes and revealing the truth, even if the latter were possible. The DPA only specified the provision of an amnesty for the returnees (except those who had conducted war crimes).[50] A question then arises, how about the accountability of people in general; not a returnee, not a war criminal? The DPA

---

44. Steven L Burg and Paul S Shoup, above n 3, 170.
45. Antonia Potter, 'We the Women, Why Conflict Mediation is not just a job for men' (2005) the Centre for Humanitarian Dialogue <http://www.hdcentre.org/uploads/tx_news/164Wethewomen.pdf> accessed 15 March 2016. See also Antonia Potter, 'Gender Sensitivity: Nicety or Necessity in peace-process management' (2004) the Centre for Humanitarian Dialogue <http://www.hdcentre.org/uploads/tx_news/27Antonia PotterGendersensitivityWEB.pdf> accessed 15 March 2016; United Nations Division for the Advancement of Women Office of the Special Adviser on Gender Issues and Advancement of Women Department of Political Affairs, 'Peace Agreements as a Means for Promoting Gender Equality and Ensuring Participation of Women – A Framework of Model Provisions' (2003) Report of the Expert Group Meeting <http://www.un.org/womenwatch/daw/egm/peace2003/reports/Finalreport.PDF> accessed 15 March 2016; Elise Feron, 'Gender and Peace Negotiations, Why Gendering Peace Negotiations Multiplies Opportunities for Reconciliation' (2015) Netherlands Institute of International Relations <http://www.clingendael.nl/sites/default/files/PB_Gender%20and%20Peace%20Negotiations_final_0.pdf> 15 March 2016.
46. Danijela Majstorovic, 'Feminity, Patriarchy and Resistance in the Postwar Bosnia and Herzegovina' (2011) 21:2 International Review of Sociology 277.
47. See also the United Nations Security Council Resolution 1820 (2008), the United Nations Security Council Resolution 1888 (2009), the United Nations Security Council Resolution 1889 (2009), the United Nations Security Council Resolution 1960 (2010), the United Nations Security Council Resolution 2106 (2013), and the United Nations Security Council Resolution 2122 (2013).
48. Christine Bell, 'Text and Context: Evaluating Peace Agreements for their 'Gender Perspective'' (2015) Political Settlements Research Programme (PSRP) <http://www.politicalsettlements.org/files/2015/10/Text-and-Context-11-October-2015.pdf> accessed 15 March 2016.
49. The United Nations Security Council Resolution 1325 (2000), para 8.
50. The 1995 Dayton Peace Agreement, Annex 7, art VI.

does not signify the status of the crime that has been done by any person in general and the due process of law for them. This practice will become a serious impediment in establishing the rule of law, increase the impunity culture, leave the victims uncompensated and have no deterrent effect on potential future abusers. However, imposing accountability will be problematic. It can destabilise the still fragile peace because the opposing ethnic groups still hate each other.[51] The case of South Africa shows that amnesty tends to bring peace if it is accompanied with a formal truth and reconciliation process, which lacks from this agreement.

In addition, the agreement does not signify the accountability of peace implementers. The DPA seems to assume that the peace implementers are neutral and innocent. However, the fact shows that some UN officials were suspected of rape.[52] Actually, it is fair-minded to know that the DPA does not mention any provision dealing with the conduct of peace implementers, except granting diplomatic immunity to them because they work under the supervision of the UN as a 'world peace-keeper'. The inclusion of peace implementers' accountability will only lead to a bias, as if the UN is one of the warring parties. However, since the experiences show that there is no guarantee that the peace implementers never commit any crimes, it becomes the responsibility of the sending institutions to ensure that their officials will act in a good manner and will be punished internally if proven to have conducted a crime.

5 DIFFICULTIES OF IMPLEMENTATION IN HOW HUMAN RIGHTS ARE ADDRESSED IN THE DPA

Generally speaking, the agreement is successfully implemented because it can anticipate the possible obstacles, such as the defaulters actions undertaken by the warring parties. This problem was addressed by accommodating all the parties (Bosniacs, Serbs and Croats) needs in the negotiation process, which was granted in the forms of power sharing agreement. In the conflict of Sri Lanka, the lack of participation in the negotiation process affected the implementation of the agreement.[53] The Sri Lanka's peace agreement was only accommodated the two biggest fractions (Tamil and Sinhalese) but leaved Muslims. Learning from that, it is important to bring all the parties representation in the table.

Another possible barrier of the implementation would be the intervention from the neighbouring countries, which has been discussed in other part of this essay as the root of the conflict. As a response to this, the DPA involved the Government of Croatia and the Federation of Yugoslavia (Serbia) in its negotiation and signature stage. This was done in order to assure that both neighbouring countries are bound by the DPA, hence they had to respect and support the implementation of the peace agreement in the BiH.

Moreover, the DPA also incorporates international actors as a neutral party in the implementation process. Ensuring the compliance of the parties is vital recalling the Darfur case. The Doha Document for Peace in Darfur failed to be implemented due to the lack of good faith from the parties.[54] Therefore, the DPA incorporates international communities in the implementation process. Although it seems like the BiH was under the protectorate of the UN.

51. See Elisabeth Rehn, 'The Human Rights Situation in Bosnia and Herzegovina: a regional Perspective' in Wolfgang Benedek (ed), above n 27, 20.
52. See Susan Bloor, 'Toll of Bosnian Rape and Death Camps Increases Steadily' (1994) Washington Report on Middle East Affairs <http://www.wrmea.org/1994-january/toll-of-bosnian-rape-and-death-camps-increases-steadily.html> accessed 15 March 2016; and Natalie Novick, 'When Those Meant to Keep the Peace Commit Sexualized Violence' (2012) <http://www.womenundersiegeproject.org/blog/entry/when-those-meant-to-keep-the-peace-commit-sexualized-violence> accessed 15 March 2016;
53. International Crisis Group, *Sri Lanka: The Failure of The Peace Process* (2006) <http://www.crisisgroup.org/~/media/Files/asia/south-asia/sri-lanka/124_sri_lanka___the_failure_of_the_peace_process> accessed 28 March 2016.
54. Omer Ismail and Annette LaRocco, 'Failing Darfur' (2012) <http://www.enoughproject.org/files/DDPDimplementation.pdf> accessed 28 March 2016.

The international community, particularly the UN, the Council of Europe and NATO have shown so much concern over the BiH conflict because this conflict has affected life in Europe as a whole. The fact that this war produced massive numbers of refugees seems to have threatened the equilibrium of European communities. The effort to bring the refugees and IDPs home generates a huge amount of work. By the end of 1997, from 1.3 million of refugees, there were only 208,000 people who had returned to the territory of the BiH, albeit mostly not to their homes. Another 504,000 were granted permanent status in the host countries. On the other hand, from the number of 1 million IDPs, only 153,000 people had returned to areas that were mostly occupied by their ethnic groups. Therefore, there were still 612,000 refugees and 816,000 IDPs that need to return or be returned.[55] If they are returned to their homes, mostly they will become a minority that is vulnerable to acts of discrimination.

In reality, the refugees and IDPs do not have a real choice to freely return to their homes of origin, as granted by the DPA.[56] This condition may indicate the failure of the improvement of the human rights situation in the BiH, because if the DPA is implemented consistently, there should be no fear of discrimination or human rights abuses. Ironically, this current condition will only consolidate the idea of ethnic divisions.[57] Seeing this situation, the Office of High Representative imposed new property laws that established the Property Law Implementation Program (PLIP). They then started to open up the housing stock and evict anybody that was occupying a property illegally. They also dismissed officials refusing to comply with new laws. This process was helped by the IPTF to ensure that local police forces were on the right track. This legal and political strategy led to the success of the mass return of non-Bosniacs (Muslims) to Sarajevo in 1998. The Sarajevo incident affected the societies' perception in general. Therefore, in September 2005, the UNHCR published that more than one million people (440,147 refugees and 560,326 IDPs) had returned to their pre-war homes.[58]

Although international communities seemed to have made only a little progress in the beginning of the implementation of the DPA, as soon as they gained trust from the relevant parties, they pushed the parties forward to comply with the agreement. By utilising legal and political pressure, international communities tried to ensure the parties' compliance. After establishing new laws as a foundation, international communities then started to push DPA enforcement through financial and military aid. This is based on the principle that a good law means nothing if it is not implemented. This hard effort is vital to any post-conflict situation, recalling that there will always be spoilers who try to ruin the peace process.[59]

6 ASSESSMENT OF THE ROLE OF HUMAN RIGHTS IN PEACE-MAKING

Accommodating human rights laws in the peace agreement is often either complementary to, or in contravention of, conflict resolution.[60] Sometimes human rights law is also inadequate in addressing certain problems.

In the DPA, human rights law complements the peace-making process when dealing with the rights of minorities. It is undeniable that the Federation of BiH is intentionally devoted as a land for the Muslims and Croats; and the Republika Srpska is devoted as a land for the Serbs. The problem arises when the fact shows that there are some Serbs living in the Federation; conversely there are some Muslims and Croats living in the Republika Srpska. Will

55. International Crisis Group, 'Minority Return of Mass Relocation?' (1998) <http://www.crisisgroup.org/en/regions/europe/balkans/bosnia-herzegovina/033-minority-return-or-mass-relocation.aspx> accessed 17 March 2016.
56. The 1995 Dayton Peace Agreement, Annex 7, art I.
57. Daniela Heimerl, above n 20, 382.
58. Ibid, 383.
59. See Stephen John Stedman, 'Spoiler Problems in Peace Processes' (1997) 22:2 International Security 5-53.
60. Christine Bell, *Negotiating Justice? Human Rights and Peace Agreements* (International Council on Human Rights Policy 2006) 9.

they be the subject of discrimination and harassment? Can their human rights be protected? In this case, the incorporation of a non-discrimination provision[61] in the agreement can be utilised as a protection for those numerical minorities.

The establishment of a human rights framework in the agreement also provides a foundation for the rule of law and, at least in theory, prevents future abuses. The fact that the Human Rights Commission is formed by the agreement[62] gives a positive sign to the enforcement of individual rights granted by the Constitution and Annex 6 of the agreement. Alternatively, if an individual has no access or has exhausted all the domestic remedies, he/she can submit a claim of human rights violations to the ECtHR.

On the other hand, human rights law demands accountability for human rights abuses. In this context, human rights law appears to hinder the peace-making process. This is due to the fact that the most responsible for human rights violations are the ones that we need to be in the negotiation table. Here, the peace versus justice debate appears; in the case of BiH, the need to end the war overrides the demand of accountability.

In addition, human rights law is sometimes inadequate to resolve the conflict, particularly when covering certain issues such as the prosecution of war crimes, or the repatriation of refugees and IDPs. Human rights law does not have a jurisdiction over individuals; therefore some human rights advocates rely heavily on international humanitarian law to address war crimes.[63] In the case of BiH, the ICTY was established by the United Nations Security Council to investigate and prosecute the individuals responsible for any acts of war crimes, genocide and crimes against humanity.[64]

Moreover, human rights law also says little about IDPs. IDPs are not the same as refugees because an IDP is a displaced person who has not crossed his or her country's boundaries;[65] whereas refugee is a displaced person that has fled to another country.[66] At present there is no international convention on IDPs. International law only has a treaty on refugees (the 1951 Convention Relating to the Status of Refugees) specifying the definition of refugees, their rights and the legal obligations of states. On the other hand, the IDPs are regulated by the 1998 Guiding Principles on Internal Displacement. It mentions that the state has a responsibility to assist and protect IDPs. However, the provisions in the refugees' convention and in the guiding principles are not sufficient to deal with a mass displacement, such as in the BiH case.

The provisions of refugees and IDPs in Annex 7 of the DPA that signifies their right to return, the assurance of their safety, the restoration of their property or compensation for unrestored property, the creation of a suitable condition for return, an access to reliable information of their destination area, and the responsible actors in facilitating their return, are all needed as a matter of some significance. Therefore, in this context the DPA seems to fill the gap.

7 CONCLUSION

Violence and brutality commonly occur in every conflict. To some extent, Luttwak believes that peace can only be brought about after letting the parties hurt each other.[67] This argument, in a practical sense, sounds right but is morally and logically wrong because there is no guarantee that peace will be achieved through a bloody war.[68] In so many cases, war will only

61. The 1995 Dayton Peace Agreement, Annex 4 art II para 4 and Annex 6 art I (14).
62. Ibid, Annex 6 art II.
63. Ellen L Lutz, Eileen F Babbitt, and Hurst Hannum, 'Human Rights and Conflict Resolution from the Practitioners' Perspectives' (2003) 27 Fletcher F. World Aff. 173, 176.
64. United Nations Security Council Resolution 827 (1993).
65. United Nations Commissions on Human Rights, Guiding Principles on Internal Displacement (1998), UN Doc. E/CN.4/1998/53/Add.2.
66. The 1951 Convention Relating to the Status of Refugees, art 1 para A(2).
67. Edward N Luttwak, 'Give War a Chance' (1999) 78(4) *Foreign Affairs* 36.
68. Anonymous, 'Human Rights in Peace Negotiations' (1996) 18 *Human Rights Quarterly* 258.

sharpen the tensions and create so many victims. Therefore, in the case of BiH, international communities pushed the warring parties to sit in a negotiation as a result of strong political and military pressure.

After difficult negotiations, finally the parties signed the DPA in Paris in December 1995. This agreement incorporates numerous provisions on human rights protection in a major effort to prevent future abuses. However, the agreement mentions nothing about accountability for the human rights abuses that happened during the conflict, except for the war crimes that fell within the jurisdiction of the ICTY; and the reconciliation programmes such as social services for the victims.

In implementing the agreement, international communities played an important role, particularly in ensuring the refugees and IDPs were returned to their own homes, although they may well become a minority in some cases. However, it is arguable that bringing them back can reintegrate both communities and society, stimulate harmony among ethnic groups and harden attitudes against the idea of ethnic division. Moreover, learning from the BiH conflict, human rights laws can become complementary to the peace process when dealing with the protection of the rights of minorities and prevent future abuses; inadequate when dealing with war crimes, and the returning process of refugees and IDPs; but in contravention when dealing with accountability relating to the issue of human rights abuses. Here, the peace versus justice debate emerges.[69]

REFERENCES

A, Potter, 'Gender Sensitivity: Nicety or Necessity in peace-process management' (2004) the Centre for Humanitarian Dialogue <http://www.hdcentre.org/uploads/tx_news/27AntoniaPotterGendersensitivityWEB.pdf> accessed 15 March 2016

———, 'We the Women, Why Conflict Mediation is not just a job for men' (2005) the Centre for Humanitarian Dialogue <http://www.hdcentre.org/uploads/tx_news/164Wethewomen.pdf> accessed 15 March 2016.

BBC News, 'Bosnia-Herzegovina Profile - Timeline' (2015) <http://www.bbc.co.uk/news/world-europe-17212376> accessed 9 March 2016.

C, Bell, 'Text and Context: Evaluating Peace Agreements for their 'Gender Perspective" (2015) Political Settlements Research Programme (PSRP) <http://www.politicalsettlements.org/files/2015/10/Text-and-Context-11-October-2015.pdf> accessed 15 March 2016.

———, 'Unsettling Bargains? Power-sharing and the Inclusion of Women in Peace Negotiations' (2015) <http://politicalsettlements.org/research/publications/reports/£sthash.xXlpRK49.dpuf> accessed 13 March 2016.

———, *Negotiating Justice? Human Rights and Peace Agreements* (International Council on Human Rights Policy 2006).

———, *On the Law of Peace: Peace Agreements and Lex Pacificatoria* (Oxford University Press, 2008).

———, *Peace Agreements and Human Rights* (Oxford University Press 2003).

D, Majstorovic, 'Feminity, Patriarchy and Resistance in the Postwar Bosnia and Herzegovina' (2011) 21:2 International Review of Sociology 277.

E, Feron, 'Gender and Peace Negotiations, Why Gendering Peace Negotiations Multiplies Opportunities for Reconciliation' (2015) Netherlands Institute of International Relations <http://www.clingendael.nl/sites/default/files/PB_Gender%20and%20Peace%20Negotiations_final_0.pdf> 15 March 2016.

G, Evans, 'Security and Intrastate Conflict' (1994) 96 Foreign Policy 3.

Heimerl, Daniela, 'The Return of Refugees and Internally Displaced Persons: From Coercion to Sustainability?' (2005) 12(3) International Peacekeeping, 377.

International Commission on the Balkans, *Unfinished Peace: Report of the International Commission on the Balkans* (Carnegie Endowment for International Peace 1996).

69. See Christine Bell (n 60) 1-19; Tom Hadden, 'Human Rights and Conflict Resolution' in John Morison, Kieran McEvoy, and Gordon Anthony (eds), *Judges, Transition, and Human Rights* (Oxford University Press 2007) 167-79; Ellen L Lutz, Eileen F Babbitt, and Hurst Hannum, above n 63, 173-92; Michelle Parvleliet, 'Bridging the Divide: Exploring the Relationship between Human Rights and Conflict Management' (2002) 11(1) *Track Two* 8-43.

International Crisis Group, 'Minority Return of Mass Relocation?' (1998) <http://www.crisisgroup.org/en/regions/europe/balkans/bosnia-herzegovina/033-minority-return-or-mass-relocation.aspx> accessed 17 March 2016.

———, 'Sri Lanka: The Failure of The Peace Process' (2006) <http://www.crisisgroup.org/~/media/Files/asia/south-asia/sri-lanka/124_sri_lanka___the_failure_of_the_peace_process> accessed 28 March 2016.

J, Morison, McEvoy K, and Anthony G (eds), *Judges, Transition, and Human Rights* (Oxford University Press 2007).

J, Stedman S, 'Spoiler Problems in Peace Processes' (1997) 22:2 International Security 5.

L, Burg S and Shoup P S, *The War in Bosnia-Herzegovina: Ethnic Conflict and International Intervention* (M. E. Sharpe, Inc 1999).

L, Lutz E, Babbitt E F, and Hannum H, 'Human Rights and Conflict Resolution from the Practitioners' Perspectives' (2003) 27 Fletcher F. World Aff. 173.

M, Parvleliet, 'Bridging the Divide: Exploring the Relationship between Human Rights and Conflict Management' (2002) 11 (1)Track Two 8.

N, Luttwak E, 'Give War a Chance' (1999) 78(4)Foreign Affairs 36.

N, Novick, 'When Those Meant to Keep the Peace Commit Sexualized Violence' (2012) <http://www.womenundersiegeproject.org/blog/entry/when-those-meant-to-keep-the-peace-commit-sexualized-violence> accessed 15 March 2016.

O, Ismail and LaRocco A, 'Failing Darfur' (2012) <http://www.enoughproject.org/files/DDPDimplementation.pdf> accessed 28 March 2016.

P, Collier and Hoeffler A, 'Greed and Grievance in Civil War' (2004) 56 Oxford Economic Papers 563.

S, Bloor, 'Toll of Bosnian Rape and Death Camps Increases Steadily' (1994) Washington Report on Middle East Affairs <http://www.wrmea.org/1994-january/toll-of-bosnian-rape-and-death-camps-increases-steadily.html> accessed 15 March 2016.

Sloan, James, 'The Dayton Peace Agreement: Human Rights Guarantees and their Implementation' (1996) 7 EJIL 207, 209.

The Stockholm International Peace Research Institute, *Yearbook of World Armaments and Disarmaments* (Oxford University Press 2002).

United Nations Division for the Advancement of Women Office of the Special Adviser on Gender Issues and Advancement of Women Department of Political Affairs, 'Peace Agreements as a Means for Promoting Gender Equality and Ensuring Participation of Women – A Framework of Model Provisions' (2003) Report of the Expert Group Meeting <http://www.un.org/womenwatch/daw/egm/peace2003/reports/Finalreport.PDF> accessed 15 March 2016.

W, Benedek (ed), *Human Rights in Bosnia and Herzegovina after Dayton, From Theory to Practice* (Martinus Nijhoff Publishers, 1999).

The 1950 European Convention on Human Rights.

The 1951 Convention Relating to the Status of Refugees.

The 1957 Convention on the Nationality of Married Women.

The 1979 Convention on the Elimination of All Forms of Discrimination Against Women

The 1995 Dayton Peace Agreement.

Prosecutor v. Dario Kordi J & Mario ^Erkez, Judgment of 22 February 2001, ICTY, para 5c.

Sejdić and Finci v. Bosnia and Herzegovina [GC], no. 27996/06 and 34836/06, 22 December 2009.

The United Nations Security Council Resolution 1325 (2000),

The United Nations Security Council Resolution 1820 (2008).

The United Nations Security Council Resolution 1888 (2009).

The United Nations Security Council Resolution 1889 (2009).

The United Nations Security Council Resolution 1960 (2010).

The United Nations Security Council Resolution 2106 (2013).

The United Nations Security Council Resolution 2122 (2013).

The United Nations Security Council Resolution 827 (1993).

United Nations Commissions on Human Rights, Guiding Principles on Internal Displacement (1998), UN Doc. E/CN.4/1998/53/Add.2.

United Nations Security Council, 'Final Report of the Commission of Experts Established Pursuant to Security Council Resolution 780 (1992)', 27 May 1994.

Culture and International Law - Juwana et al. (Eds)
 ISBN 978-1-138-38766-9

Uyghur Xinjiang problem: Cultural rights versus counterterrorism action

Fransiska Ayulistya Susanto & Setyo Widagdo
Law Faculty, Brawijaya University, Malang, Indonesia ,

ABSTRACT: This paper offers analysis of the government of the People's Republic of China's counterterrorism regulation and action in the Xinjiang Uyghur Autonomous Region in relation to the cultural rights of the Uyghur people. The Chinese government argues that its regulation and action forms part of preemptive measures against terrorism in Xinjiang. However, many believe that what is really happening is far from that; there are serious cultural rights violations. To this end, this paper will investigate whether the Chinese government's action violates the cultural rights of the Uyghur people and whether or not it can justify its actions in counterterrorism terms.

KEYWORDS: Cultural rights, Uyghur Xinjiang, derogation and limitation of human rights

1 INTRODUCTION

The Uyghur problems in Xinjiang have attracted the international community's attention. The problems became known by the international community after Human Rights Watch (HRW) released a series of articles on human rights violations in the Xinjiang Autonomous Region (XUAR). Its reports were created after the Non-Governmental Organization (NGO) found witnesses and started gathering information from them. After that, the issues were raised until the United Nations statement that the People's Republic of China (PRC) should stop its action in XUAR because it violates several human rights instruments.

However, the Chinese government stated that the reports by HRW are wrong: the government never had any intention of violating any rights of the Uyghur and Muslim minorities in Xinjiang but was forced into preemptive action against terrorist threats. What the Chinese government actually is doing is an after-effect of the high tension for a long period between Beijing and the Uyghur community.[1]

The problem in Xinjiang arose when the government launched its counterterrorism campaign in XUAR. Many residents and Uyghur people began disappearing into political re-education camps.[2] In 2017, it was estimated that more than 900,000 Uyghur people were being detained in re-education camps across the XUAR region.[3]

Moreover, the government also banned many activities related to Uyghur or Islamic culture and religion, with many people forced to abandon their tradition and ideology and follow the majority Han culture and the government's ideology. As part of the counterterrorism project,

1. Rian Tum, R. (2018). The Uyghurs in modern China. In *The Oxford Research Encyclopedia of Asia History* (p. 15). doi:10.1093/acrefore/9780190277727.013.160
2. Ibid, p. 13.
3. World Uyghur Congress. (2018). *World Uyghur Congress Submission on 3rd Universal Periodic Review (UPR) of The People's Republic of China (PRC)* (p. 4).

students also could not learn their own language and culture at school. The government banned any cultural and religion curricula in schools.

Considering the problems in the XUAR area, are the PRC and XUAR authorities violating the Uyghur people's cultural rights? And, if so, can their actions be justified under counter-terrorism action and human rights limitations and derogation?

This paper endeavors to answer both questions by analyzing the PRC's actions and the XUAR action in terms of the international instruments on cultural rights and human rights. The paper argues that the actions of the PRC and XUAR authorities violate the Uyghurs' cultural rights and are not justified under counterterrorism activity. Moreover, their counter-terrorism action is not targeting terrorists but all of the Uyghur people, from children to the elderly.

To this the end, the first part of this paper will analyze the violations of the PRC and XUAR authorities under the cultural rights' instrument. The second part of the paper will discuss the limitation or derogation of cultural rights under counterterrorism action.

2 DISCUSSION

2.1 *China's action in XUAR violates Uyghur cultural rights*

Many scholars still debate what is included under the definition of the culture of a society or group of people. Culture itself is created by human ideas, or the social behavior regarding actions which are recognized by a group. In some groups of people or ethnic communities, religious action could influence their culture deeply. In many examples we can see that lots of ethnic groups involve their religious beliefs in their way of life, such as in Islamic countries; Islam is part of their culture in the way they bury their family, the way they marry, and much more.

Culture in society is used to identify people and even their purpose of life, but it decreases each year. However, there are people who still believe that protecting some culture is associated with local wisdom and a means to a better life. Some people believe that "Culture becomes synonymous with the specific way of life of a community".[4] Under human rights, cultural rights are protected under the International Covenant on Economic, Social and Cultural Rights (ICESCR)[5], the Indigenous and Tribal Convention 1989, the Universal Declaration of Human Rights[6], the UNESCO Declaration on Cultural Diversity 2001[7] and many more.

Cultural rights are often seen as "luxury rights" when compared to other rights such as right to life, freedom from torture, and other political rights.[8] The cultural rights itself usual to get limitation or even rejection from the state law. However, for small communities or indigenous peoples, cultural rights cannot be separated from them. The state has an obligation to "protect, respect and fulfill" its citizens' cultural rights, just like the other rights.

Actually, "It is generally considered that culture rights under the ICESCR include rights of education (Articles 13–14) and the rights spelled out in Article 15".[9] In this paper the cultural rights we talk about are the right to get a cultural education and the right to take part in cultural life.

The ICESCR General Comment 21, no. 20 described the rights to take part in cultural life:

4. Ringelheim, J. (2013). Cultural rights. In *International Human Rights Law* (2nd ed., p. 286). Oxford, UK: Oxford University Press.
5. Articles 13–15, ICESCR.
6. Article 27, UDHR.
7. Article 2(b).
8. Ringelheim, no. 4, p. 286.
9. Ringelheim, no. 4, p. 286.

a. *Participation in cultural life →the rights to freely choose one's identity and engage in one's own cultural practice as well as to express oneself in the language of one's choice.*
b. *Access to cultural life → cover the rights to know one's own culture and others though education and information, the rights to follow a way of life associated with the use of goods and resources such as land, water, biodiversity, language, or specific institutions, and the rights to benefit from the cultural heritage and creation of others.*
c. *Contribution to cultural life → refers to the right to be involved in creating the spiritual, material, intellectual, and emotional expression of the community."* [10]

The state gives freedom to the citizen to choose their cultural identity as part of society. Moreover, citizens have the freedom to access and contribute to their culture. Even though cultural rights could be the object of human rights limitations, the state shall still give freedom to the citizen regarding the preservation of their culture.

The state, as the human rights protector, has an obligation to "respect, protect, and fulfill" the right to take part in cultural life. "The obligation to respect requires states to refrain from interfering with the enjoyment of life".[11] The obligation to protect also obligates the state to create regulations or actions that do not discriminate against people according to their cultural identity.[12] Moreover, the obligation to fulfill includes the obligation "*to facilitate, to promote, and provide cultural education in school curricula".*[13] In addition, minorities should have the right to take part in the cultural life of society at large as well as to conserve, promote, and develop their own culture.[14]

With regard to the PRC case in relation to the cultural rights of the Uyghur people and some Muslim minorities in XUAR, this paper will only analyze the rights to cultural education in school and the rights of the Uyghur people and some Muslim minorities to enjoy their cultural life without it being violated by the PRC government. The cultural violation in this case is justified by the Chinese government as preventative counterterrorist action in the XUAR area.

China, as the government which has been the ruling power in the Xinjiang area since 1990, closed down many mosques and Islamic schools. Moreover, the government also forbids the use of Arabic words and text in the Muslim area of XUAR.[15] After 1996, the Chinese government launched a campaign against "national separation", "religious extremists" and "illegal religious activities", as well as an "in-depth atheist education". The campaign is used to brainwash grassroots Muslim believers in the Xinjiang area.[16]

Moreover, in 2014 mass detention camps or, as many call them, "re-education camps" appeared, and they increased rapidly after the "Regulation on De-Extremification" or "transformation-through-education" (*jiaoyu zhuanhua)* was launched in March 2017.[17] "The camp goals are the replacement of religious affiliation and ethnic identity with secular, patriotic political allegiance."[18] The PRC uses the re-education camps to erase, little by little, the identity of the Uyghur culture and religion.

10. General Comment 21, no. 20, para. 15.
11. GC 21, no. 20, para. 49.
12. GC 21, no. 20, para. 50(d).
13. Ringelheim, J. See no. 4, p. 293.
14. GC 21, no. 20, para. 32.
15. Amnesty International Report 1999. People's Republic of China, *Gross Violation of Human Rights in The Xinjiang Uighur Autonomous Region*, p. 10.
16. Amnesty International, *China: "Where are They*?", p. 10. https://amnesty.dk/media/4729/china_where-are-they.pdf
17. Xinjiang Uyghur Autonomous Region Regulation on De-Extremification, *China Law Translate*, (March 30, 2017), www.chinalawtranslate.com/%e6%96%b0%e7%96%86%e7%bb%b4%e5%90%be%e5%b0%94%e8%87%aa%e6%b2%bb%e5%8c %ba%e5%8e%bb%e6%9e%81%e7%ab%af%e5%8c%96%e6%9d%a1%e4%be%8b/?lang=en, ibid. 13.
18. G. Shahih, ibid, 13.

The government also stated that the Uyghur culture and tradition are "backward compared with the modernity of Chinese culture".[19] The XUAR authorities also set a restriction on cultural activities in XUAR. Consequently, it is difficult for the XUAR people to pursue their cultural and religious activities.[20] The authorities also force the people in XUAR to be more patriotic and considerate, like "normal Chinese people".[21]

First, regarding cultural education, the PRC government insisted that students "focus only on teaching Chinese language and Han culture at the expense of their own language and tradition."[22] Students are forbidden to learn using the Uyghur language or other languages. From the interview by Amnesty International with Ilham:[23] "Ilham had been highlighting how Uyghur discontent and ethnic tensions were fueled by government policies limiting the use of the Uyghur language, severely restricting Uyghurs' ability to practice their own religion".[24]Other witnesses stated that: "At school we changed from having both Kazakh and (Mandarin) Chinese languages to having all subjects in Mandarin only, except Kazakh language classes. Even Kazakh literature is being translated into Chinese and taught."[25] The authorities in XUAR also created "The Xinjiang Regulation on Religious Affairs", passed in 2014, which required that:

> *Ban religion from education and punish teachers for failure to stop or report any activities that have "hints of religion" in schools; ban children from participating in religious activities and prohibit anyone, including parents and teachers, from introducing religion to children, including at home; ban high school students from dropping out of school for religious reasons.*[26]

From that regulation, it is clear that the PRC representatives in XUAR tried to erase the Uyghur culture from Uyghur students and the younger generation. Teachers and parents cannot teach the Uyghur culture and if they try to teach the younger generation, then punishment awaits them.

The actions of the PRC and XUAR authorities and these regulations violate the rights of the student to get cultural education under Articles 13(1) and 15(1)(a) of the ICESCR, Articles 30 and 31 of the Indigenous and Tribal People Convention 1989[27], and also, their rights under Article 27 of the Universal Declaration of Human Rights (UDHR). Moreover, the government also violates the rights of parents and teachers to teach their children or students about their culture that does not violate another's human rights and their social value under Article 15(1)(a) of the ICESCR, Articles 30 and 31 of the Indigenous and Tribal People Convention 1989[28], and also, their rights under Article 27 of the UDHR.

19. Amnesty International. *China: Submission to the United Nations Committee on the Elimination of Racial Discrimination, 96th Session, 6–30 August 2018* (Index: ASA/17/8742/2018), 10.
20. The Uyghur people's culture cannot be separated from the Muslim culture. Much in the Uyghur culture comes from Islamic culture and religion activities.
21. Richardson, S. (2017, April 24) China bans many Muslim baby names in Xinjiang. *Human Rights Watch* news release. Retrieved from https://www.hrw.org/news/2017/04/24/china-bans-many-muslim-baby-names-xinjiang
22. Amnesty International. (2018). *China: Submission to the United Nations Committee on the Elimination of Racial Discrimination, 96th Session, 6–30 August 2018* (Index: ASA/17/8742/2018), 10.
23. People who were sentenced to life in prison for separatism in PRC; he is one of the Uyghur activists.
24. Amnesty International. *China: "Where are they?"*, p. 11.
25. Human Rights Watch interview with Ainagul (pseudonym), 52, who left Xinjiang in 2017 and whose son is in a political camp and Daniar, 19, who is one of the students in the XUAR area, in Human Rights Watch Report *Eradicating ideological viruses: China's campaign of repression against Xinjiang's Muslims*, September 2018, 73 education camp, May 18, 2018. In ibid, 73.
26. Regulations of Xinjiang Uygur Autonomous Region on Religious Affairs (2014) art. 40, ibid, 19.
27. Uyghurs are an indigenous people under the Uyghur American Association, *Uyghurs as indigenous people; a new UHRP report highlights Chinese government violations of Uyghurs' indigenous rights*, December, 2018, https://uyghuramerican.org/article/uyghurs-indigenous-people-new-uhrp-report-highlights-chinese-government-violations-uyghurs, accessed on September 2018.
28. Uyghurs are an indigenous people under the Uyghur American Association, *Uyghurs as indigenous people; a new UHRP report highlights Chinese government violations of Uyghurs' indigenous rights*, December, 2018,

These articles clearly state that the citizens of the state shall enjoy their rights to learn their own culture from school, and from elders in the community such as parents. It is also the obligation of the state (PRC) to "protect, respect and fulfill" their citizens' rights even though they are minorities. However, what happened in XUAR is clearly in contradiction with this state obligation.

Second, in terms of the right to participate in a cultural life, the PRC government also violates this. Under the preventative action against terrorism, the government of PRC launched the "strike hard campaign", which was misused to punish peaceful activism and expression,[29] and blindly targeted Uyghur Muslims in the XUAR area.

There are several actions that the PRC government launched as pre-emptive action that actually violate the cultural rights of the Uyghur people. For example, the government have banned religious names or names which represent Islam for babies, because this is categorized as "excessive religious fervor".[30] Moreover, the government also forced the detainees in re-education camps to "memorize legal provisions and patriotic songs and write self-criticisms".-[31] In the XUAR, the Uyghur could also not display anything of a "religious and cultural affiliation such as wearing the hijab, growing an abnormal beard, praying regularly, fasting[32], or possessing books or articles about Islam or Uyghur culture".[33] Social customs, such as the religious aspects of burials, are being increasingly prohibited.[34] There is also some evidence that Turkic Muslims are being pressured to partake in Han Chinese holidays and traditions, such as the Chinese New Year.[35] They prohibit crying and wailing and traditional grieving songs at funerals.[36] Uyghurs could also not say Islamic greetings among each other, only Chinese greetings. It also proved that Uyghurs could not wear Kazakh clothing or Kazakh jewelry, and they cannot even serve Kazakh or Turkish dishes at home.[37] The PRC government also banned the Uyghur people in XUAR from celebrating or holding culture events, and they also banned people from following Uyghur traditions, holidays or Muslim holidays.[38]

These actions were done because the authorities insist that "such idea, dogma or belief and affinities in Islamic, Turkic, Uyghur, or Kazakh must be corrected or eradicated".[39] Moreover, the PRC government in its Xinjiang Regulation on Religious Affairs that was passed in 2014 also stated that:[40]

- *Ban any form of appearance – including facial hair and clothing – that is interpreted to "whip up religious fanaticism, [and] disseminate religious extremist ideologies";*

---

https://uyghuramerican.org/article/uyghurs-indigenous-people-new-uhrp-report-highlights-chinese-government-violations-uyghurs, accessed on September 2018.

29. Human Rights Watch Report, 'Eradicating Ideological Viruses'... ibid, 11.
30. Ibid, 12.
31. Ibid, 14.
32. IWGIA (2017). *The Indigenous World 2017*, pp. 312, www.iwgia.org/images/documents/indigenousworld/indigenous-world-2017.pdf. in Cultural Survival, *Observations on the State of Indigenous Human Rights in China*, prepared for The 31st Session of The United Nations Human Rights Council Universal Periodic Review, submitted on March 2018, 7
33. Ibid, 15.
34. Ibid, 15.
35. Darren Byler, "Images in Red: Han Culture, Uyghur Performers, Chinese New Year." In Ibid, 72.
36. Human Rights Watch. (2018). Interview with Auken (pseudonym), a middle-aged woman with two children who left Xinjiang in 2017, May 17. In ibid, 73.
37. Ibid, 73.
38. IWGIA. (2017). *The Indigenous World 2017*,, pp. 312, www.iwgia.org/images/documents/indigenousworld/indigenous-world-2017.pdf. in Cultural Survival, *Observations on the State of Indigenous Human Rights in China*, prepared for The 31st Session of The United Nations Human Rights Council Universal Periodic Review, submitted on March 2018, 7
39. Ibid, 3.
40. Regulations of Xinjiang Uygur Autonomous Region on Religious Affairs, 2014, art. 40. Ibid, 19; Ibid, 20.

- *Prohibit the circulation of many types of documents relating to religious and ethnic policies which would routinely be public information in other countries, such as drafts of religious laws and regulations.*

Through these regulations, it clear that the PRC and the XUAR authorities are trying to erase the cultural and religious distinctions of the Uyghur and Muslim minorities in XUAR. The government did not give them their cultural and religious rights as citizens or indigenous people. The government clearly violates the rights of the Uyghur and Muslim minorities in XUAR to enjoy their cultural life.

The PRC is a member of ICESCR, consequently, the PRC government shall fulfill, respect and protect their citizens' cultural rights. Article 15 of the ICESCR recognizes the right "to take a part in cultural life" is one of the rights that shall be fulfilled, respected and protected by the PRC government. However, as stated above, the government aggressively forces the Uyghurs to "change" their culture to the Han culture. That action is clearly violating the cultural rights of the Uyghur people. The authorities shall respect all of their citizens' cultures.

Under the Indigenous People and Tribal Convention 1989, Article 5(a), the government shall "recognize and protect, and due account shall be taken of the nature of the problems which face the indigenous people as a group and as individuals".[41] From that article, the action of the PRC government clearly violates the Uygur people's rights under this article. The PRC shall protect the Uyghur people's cultural rights, not try to erase their culture. The PRC government shall promote cultural understanding, not just erase the ideology or a culture that is different to the majority of state culture and state ideology.

Moreover, under Article 27 of the UDHR it also stated that "everyone has the right to freely participate in the cultural life of the community, to enjoy the arts and to share ...". Under this article, everyone shall enjoy their cultural rights and participate in the cultural life that they choose. The government, as the authorities, shall not ignore the needs of the cultural rights of their citizens. As stated above, because the PRC government banned the celebration of Uyghur or Muslim culture events or holidays, it is clear that the PRC government violated the rights of the Uyghur people to participate in their cultural events. Moreover, the government only permits XUAR people to join the celebration of Han Chinese events and holidays.-[42] Even children cannot get any knowledge or information regarding their culture because the government bans teachers and parents from teaching Uyghur or any other culture except the Han culture.

In conclusion, the PRC government and XUAR authorities violate the cultural rights of the Uyghurs and other minorities in XUAR. The government forces the people to erase their culture even until now. The PRC government shall end the violence to prevent bigger revenge by minority groups and pressure from the international society.

2.2 *China uses "counterterrorism action" as justification for its violation of cultural rights in XUAR*

In China's constitution, the protection of the freedom of religion is part of the rights of PRC citizens but it also states that the use of religion is prohibited if it "disturbs social order".[43] Moreover, it also states that "all ethnic groups in the People's Republic of China are equal". The constitution prohibits "discrimination against and oppression of any ethnic group" and especially protects these groups' use of language, "folkways, and customs".[44] It also prohibits discrimination on the basis of religion.[45] However, what actually happened is different to that.

41. Article 5 (a) of the Indigenous People and Tribal Convention 1989.
42. Byler, D. Images in Red: Han Culture, Uyghur Performers, Chinese New Year, https://livingotherwise.com/2018/02/23/images-red-han-culture-uyghur-performers-chinese-new-year/, accessed on September 2018.
43. Art. 36, Chinese Constitution.
44. Art. 4, Chinese Constitution.
45. Art. 36, Chinese Constitution.

The PRC government launched the "Strike Hard Campaign" to justify many repressive actions were necessary to eliminate and destroy what they considered to be terrorism and extremism in their territory.[46] With the global recognition of "Islamic terrorism" in China, the PRC has accelerated repression and human rights violations against the Uyghurs as a means of counterterrorism.[47] Moreover, in XUAR the authorities went further in April 2017 when they introduced the "De-Extremism Regulation".[48] The regulation is used as the counter-terrorism to the area that categorized as the highly suspected as the extremist and terrorist people are. In October, the government also released a regional regulation on cyber-security. The regulation includes banned contents from being accessed via the internet and downloading Islamic content.

On another occasion, the government stated that "Radical Muslim Uyghurs have killed hundreds in recent years, and China considers the region a threat to peace in the country where the majority are Han Chinese".[49] Because of this, the government categorized Uyghur ideas and culture as extremist and could lead to terrorism. Consequently, the government has justified taking some measured action to eliminate what it considers to be terrorism and extremism in the PRC territory and especially in XUAR.[50]

Actually, under counterterrorism action the government could violate human rights of terrorist members such as freedom of movement, the right to life, and others. Moreover, human rights themselves could be limited or derogated. Human rights can be limited if first, "some treaty provisions explicitly provide circumstances in which enjoyment of a right may be limited" and second, the "state has the possibility of derogating from their obligations in a time of emergency justifying exceptional measures".[51] Other scholars state that the limitation could be done if first, "prescribed by law"; second, to "pursue a legitimate aim"; third, if "necessary in a democratic society".[52] Consequently, if the government of a state wants to eliminate some rights from their citizens, they should have the reasons to justify their actions based on international law, or customary international law.

Regarding the cultural rights of the Uyghur people in XUAR, indeed cultural rights are not absolute rights and could be the subject of limitation or derogation and the PRC government have the right to do so. However, we shall analyses their reason for justification, and that their action is targeting the proper target.

In this case of the limitation of cultural rights, the government already creates the law for the prevention of terrorism in XUAR but the regulation violates their own constitutional law, as stated above. The regulation also violates several international instruments generally and

---

46. Measures of Xinjiang Uygur Autonomous Region for Implementing the Counterterrorism Law of the People's Republic of China adopted at the 12th Standing Committee of Xinjiang Committee of the Communist Party of China, effective since August 1, 2016. Human Rights Watch Report, "*Eradicating Ideological Viruses"...*, 23.
47. Holdstock, N., Islam and Instability in China's Xinjiang. *NOREF: Norwegian Peacebuilding Resource Centre*(n.d.):2016. http://noref.no/var/ezflow_site/storage/original/application/3ba335a7680451de2612c693a481eb96.pdf . In Clarke, M. China and the Uyghurs: The "Plasticization" of Xinjiang? Middle East Policy 22.3 (2015): 127-46. Web., in Isabella Steinhauer, Theses "International Social Support and Intervention: The Uyghur Movement-Xinjiang Province, China", 2017, University of Colorado, https://scholar.colorado.edu/honr_theses/1449, 18.
48. http://news.ts.cn/content/2017-03/29/content_12577663.htm in Network of Chinese Human Rights Defender (CHRD) Report, submitted to the committee on the Elimination of Racial Discrimination, for its Review at the 96th Session of the Combined Fourteenth to Seventeenth Periodic Report of The People's Republic of China (CERD/C/CHN/14-17) on Its Implementation of the Convention on The Elimination of All Forms of Racial Discrimination, Submitted on July 16, 2018, para 7.
49. Shih, G. (2018). *China's Mass Indoctrination Camps Evoke Cultural Revolution*, May 2018, https://apnews.com/6e151296fb194f85ba69a8babd972e4b, accessed September 2018.
50. Human Rights Watch, above no. 46, 20.
51. Mégret, F.Chapter 5 Nature of Obligations, in *International Human Rights Law* (2nd ed.), 110. Oxford: Oxford University Press, .
52. Ibid, 111.

the cultural rights under international regulation. The actions cannot be justified under a legitimate aim because the society needs to eliminate terrorism not eliminate the culture of the Uyghurs. Their culture is far from the actions and culture of terrorism. In the end, limitation of cultural rights is not necessary in a democratic society, there are other options that could be used to eliminate terrorism not just eliminate culture of the terrorism come from. That action is not proper to handle the problem.

Moreover, if the PRC government wants to derogate the cultural rights of the Uyghur people there shall be two situations happened in the country "public emergency, necessary and proportional, and the rights are derogable rights".[53] The PRC government could state that their country is under the public emergency of a terrorist attack from some people who come from Uyghur. It could be justified if it's clear that there is a public emergency in China's territory caused by terrorists. However, a public emergency can only be invoked if it strictly necessary to get the situation back to normal. In this case, even if there is a public emergency, it is not necessary to eliminate the Uyghur people's rights because their religion is not harming society. Moreover, the elimination of cultural rights is not proportional at all, such as banning them from their cultural activities, re-educating them in camps, or even forcing them to follow Chinese culture. There is another way to protect them from extremists, such as acceptance in the wider Chinese society or cultural dialog. Then, the situation of an emergency could only derogate the derogable rights and the cultural right is one of them. In the end, a cultural right is a derogable right and the PRC government could state that the situation in PRC is an emergency situation, however their action is not necessary or proportional at all.

The last part, the XUAR authorities and PRC government is not targeting the right people. The government eliminates all of the cultural rights of Uyghur people without any justification that they are terrorists or not. They just are targeting the Uyghur and Muslim minorities in XUAR. There is no court decision before citizens end up in detention or in re-education camps.

The special rapporteur on human rights and counterterrorism has recommended that "abandonment of profiling based on group characteristic and its replacement with a combination of universal controls effecting everyone equally, genuinely random searches coupled with proper monitoring to secure that they do not transform into unregulated de facto targeting specific groups, and profiling based on individual conduct instead of group membership".[54] He encourages the state to be more careful when handling the case of terrorism and not create a violation of human rights by targeting specific groups. The government shall also investigate each terrorist suspect, of terrorist not just if one member of the group or ethnic is suspected the entire member is also the same.

Consequently, what the government did in the XUAR area by eliminating the Uyghur people's cultural rights could not be justified by limiting cultural rights and the derogation of cultural rights. Moreover, the PRC is targeting the wrong person as a terrorist. The authorities shall not target all of the Uyghur people; they shall investigate the suspect properly. If they not the suspect their cultural rights shall not be limited or derogated, even if they want to prevent they shall not force their culture to change Uyghur culture.

3 CONCLUSION

The PRC government and the XUAR authorities clearly violate the cultural rights of the Uyghur people and Muslim minorities. They violate students' or children's rights to a cultural education, and the rights of Uyghur and Muslim minorities in XUAR to take part in cultural life.

Moreover, its justification for the limitation or derogation of these cultural rights cannot be justified under international law. Even if they try to prevent the spread of terrorism in PRC,

53. Mégret, F. *International Human Rights Law*, above no. 51, 113–114

54. Ibid, see Report of the special rapporteur on human rights and counter-terrorism, no. 39, para 83–89.

this does not mean they could violate innocent citizens' cultural rights and detain them in re-education camps. The PRC government should recreate a proper regulation based on necessary and proportional principles.

REFERENCES

Amnesty International. (1999). *People's Republic of China, Gross Violation of Human Rights in The Xinjiang Uighur Autonomous Region*, p. 10.

Amnesty International. *China: "Where are they?"*, p. 10–11. https://amnesty.dk/media/4729/china_where-are-they.pdf

Amnesty International. (2018). *China: Submission to the United Nations Committee on the Elimination of Racial Discrimination, 96th Session, 6–30 August 2018* (Index: ASA/17/8742/2018), p. 10.

Giglio, D. 'Separatism and The War on Terror in China's Xinjiang Uyghur Autonomous Region", Thesis presented in partial compellation of the requirements of The Certificate-of-Training in UN Peace Support Operations, Peace Operation Training Institute.

Human Rights Watch. (2018). Interview with Ainagul (pseudonym), 52, who left Xinjiang in 2017 and whose son is in a political camp and Daniar, 19, who is one of the students in the XUAR area, in Human Rights Watch Report *Eradicating Ideological Viruses: China's Campaign of Repression Against Xinjiang's Muslims*, September 2018, p. 73 education camp, May 18, 2018.

IWGIA. (2018). The Indigenous World 2017, 2017, www.iwgia.org/images/documents/indigenousworld/indigenous-world-2017.pdf in Cultural Survival, *Observations on the State of Indigenous Human Rights in China*, prepared for The 31st Session of The United Nations Human Rights Council Universal Periodic Review, submitted in March 2018.

Mégret, F. (2013). Nature of obligations. In D. Moeckli, S. Shah & S. Sivakumaran (Eds.), *International Human Rights Law* (2nd ed., pp. 96–118). Oxford: Oxford University Press.

Network of Chinese Human Rights Defender (CHRD) Report in, submitted to the committee on the Elimination of Racial Discrimination, for its Review at the 96th Session of the Combined Fourteenth to Seventeenth Periodic Report of The People's Republic of China (CERD/C/CHN/14-17) on Its Implementation of the Convention on The Elimination of All Forms of Racial Discrimination, submitted on July 16, 2018, http://news.ts.cn/content/2017-03/29/content_12577663.htm

Report of the special rapporteur on human rights and counterterrorism, no. 39.

Ringelheim, J. (2013). Cultural rights. In D. Moeckli, S. Shah & S. Sivakumaran (Eds.), *International Human Rights Law* (2nd ed., pp. 286–302). Oxford: Oxford University Press.

Tum, R. (2018). The Uyghurs in modern China. *Oxford Research Encyclopedia of Asian History*, pp. 13, 15. doi:10.1093/acrefore/9780190277727.013.160

UHRP report highlights Chinese government violations of Uyghurs' indigenous rights "Uyghur is indigenous people under the Uyghur American Association, "Uyghurs as indigenous people"; December, 2018, accessed at https://uyghuramerican.org/article/uyghurs-indigenous-people-new-uhrp-report-highlights-chinese-government-violations-uyghurs

World Uyghur Congress. (2018). World Uyghur Congress Submission on 3rd Universal Periodic Review (UPR) of The People's Republic of China (PRC), p. 4.

Chinese Constitution

General Comment 21, "Right of everyone to take part in cultural life" (art. 15, para. 1a, of the International Covenant on Economic, Social, and Cultural Rights).

International Covenant on Economic, Social and Cultural Rights.

Indigenous and Tribal Convention, 1989.

Regulations of Xinjiang Uygur Autonomous Region on Religious Affairs, 2014.

United Declaration of Human Rights.

UNESCO Declaration on Cultural Diversity, 2001.

Richardson, S. (2017). China bans many Muslim baby names in Xinjiang. *Human Rights Watch news release*, April 24, 2017. https://www.hrw.org/news/2017/04/24/china-bans-many-muslim-baby-names-xinjiang

Byler, D. 'Images in Red: Han Culture, Uyghur Performers, Chinese New Year.' https://livingotherwise.com/2018/02/23/images-red-han-culture-uyghur-performers-chinese-new-year/, accessed on September 2018.

Human Rights Watch. (2018). Interview with Auken (pseudonym), a middle-aged woman with two children who left Xinjiang in 2017, https://livingotherwise.com/2018/02/23/images-red-han-culture-uyghur-performers-chinese-new-year/

Holdstock, N. *Islam and Instability in China's Xinjiang*. NOREF: Norwegian Peacebuilding Resource Centre (n.d.):2016. http://noref.no/var/ezflow_site/storage/original/application/3ba335a7680451de2612c693a481eb96.pdf

Clarke, M. (2017). China and the Uyghurs: The "Plasticization" of Xinjiang? Middle East Policy 22.3 (2015): 127-146. Web., in Isabella Steinhauer thesis "International Social Support and Intervention: The Uyghur Movement-Xinjiang Province, China", 2017, University of Colorado, https://scholar.colorado.edu/honr_theses/1449

Shih, G. (2018). *China's Mass Indoctrination Camps Evoke Cultural Revolution*, May 2018, https://apnews.com/6e151296fb194f85ba69a8babd972e4b

Xinjiang Uyghur Autonomous Region Regulation on De-Extremification, *China Law Translate*, (March 30, 2017), www.chinalawtranslate.com/%e6%96%b0%e7%96%86%e7%bb%b4%e5%90%be%e5%b0%94%e8%87%aa%e6%b2%bb%e5%8c%ba%e5%8e%bb%e6%9e%81%e7%ab%af%e5%8c%96%e6%9d%a1%e4%be%8b/?lang=en, in ibid 13

Culture and International Law - Juwana et al. (Eds)
 ISBN 978-1-138-38766-9

Current thinking regarding the traditional sovereignty principle in international law: Reconception or reperception?

Adi Kusumaningrum
Law Faculty, Brawijaya University, Malang, Indonesia

ABSTRACT: Economic and political globalization has led to a situation where the concept of sovereignty is now regarded from a different perspective. It is widely argued that the smooth operation of new forms of international co-operation require a more flexible perception of sovereignty. Consequently, there has been an increasing trend toward proposing to abandon the normative concept of sovereignty and establish a new regime that would accommodate the realities of today's international affairs. Due to discourse and sophisticated practice, the concept of state sovereignty has been changed so that the absolute sovereignty of the state can no longer be sustained. The meaning of the word 'sovereign' has shifted from what it meant in the past. Based on the shifting meanings of state sovereignty, this study wants to analyze the current thinking regarding the traditional sovereignty principle in international law. The legal question that arises in this study is whether or not there has been a change in the nature of the traditional sovereignty principle.

KEYWORDS: Traditional sovereignty principle, international law, conception, perception

1 INTRODUCTION

Sovereignty is one of the qualifications required in order to be accepted as a state, in addition to region, people, and recognition from other states.[1] The qualifications or aspects of a state are integrated with each other. Ever since the development of early countries, sovereignty has been the foundation of the world order and international law. Sovereignty, according to the internal dimension, has provided a set of rules for the state as the sole foundation of the state's power over the citizen and the resources around the region. Meanwhile, based on the external dimension, sovereignty acts as a mechanism for avoiding foreign intervention in order to maintain the state's 'status quo', and to preserve the 'law mechanism from the social and economic disparity' among and between states.[2]

The sovereignty theory initially emerged as an attempt to analyze the internal structure of a state. This theory can be analyzed through the perspective of constitutional law and international law. With regard to the view of constitutional law, George Jellinek, in his book titled '*Allgemeine Staatslehre*', stated that a state is an organization equipped with a pure power, which is not acquired from a higher rank of power.[3]

1. Article 1 Montevideo Convention 1933 mentioned that '*the state as a person of international law should possess the following qualifications: a) a permanent population; b) a defined territory; c) government; and d) capacity to enter into relations with the other states*'. The definition of Government in the article refers to a sovereign government.
2. Amando S. Tolentino, *Sovereignty Over Natural Resources, Change of Concept or Change Perception?*, Environmental Policy and Law (44/3/2014) 300.
3. M. Solly Lubis, *Ilmu Negara* (Bandung, Alumni, 1975) 51.

In the 16th century, scientists, particularly in politics, commonly attributed the sovereignty theory to several writers, such as Machiavelli (1469–1527), Jean Bodin (1530–1596) and Thomas Hobbes (1588–1679).[4] The doctrine of sovereignty proposed by the three scientists is widely known as classical realism.[5] The classical doctrines from this century are also supported by the sovereignty theory proposed by Hugo Grotius and John Locke.

In practice, the term 'sovereignty' has several meanings. As is mentioned in the studies conducted by international law experts, the definition of 'sovereignty' is influenced by the dynamics of 'sovereignty' itself, which evolves along with the developments and changes happening among international society over a certain period of time.[6] The gradual changes in the world's social and politic situation contribute to the evolution of views upon the nature and content of sovereignty from time to time.

2 THE STATE'S SOVEREIGNTY IN INTERNATIONAL LAW AND ITS DEVELOPMENT

Sovereignty comes from the Latin word *superanus,* which means the highest.[7] According to L. Oppenheim, at the end of the Medieval Era, the term '*souverain*', which originates from the Latin word '*superanus*', was used in France to refer to the idea of authority, either in politics or in other aspects.[8] The word sovereignty is derived from the old French word '*soverainete*', which during the Middle Ages was known in Latin as '*superanitas*', '*supremitas*', or '*suprema potestas*'.[9]

Based on Black's Law Dictionary 1396, sovereignty generally means the highest, absolute, and uncontrollable authority that an independent state authorizes. This definition implies that (1) a state has the rights and power to rule their internal affairs without any foreign intervention; (2) the fact that a state has no internal limitations means that a state is controlled externally by the legal equality of other countries; (3) the nature of public international law is indicated from the existence of superior authority and it only exists due to agreement between or among independent and sovereign states.[10]

Krasner categorized sovereignty into four items, which are:

a. *Inter-dependence sovereignty*: this refers to the ability of a state to control movement across the state.
b. *Domestic sovereignty*: this emphasizes the structure of authority in a state and the ability of the structure to control behavior effectively.
c. *Westphalian* or *Vattelian sovereignty*: this provides an exception to the foreign source of authority, either in terms of *de facto* or *de jure*. In their regions, states hold sole authority for taking authoritative decisions. In the international arena, countries follow the non-intervention regulations toward other states' affairs.

4. Akehurst's, *Modern Introduction to International Law*, 7th Revised Edition, Peter Malanczuk (New York, Routledge, The Taylor & Francis Group, 2000) 17.
5. Alan Chong, 'Classical Realism and the tension between Sovereignty and Intervention: Constructions of Expediency' from Machiavelli, Hobbes, and Bosin, (2005) 8 *Journal of International Relations and Development*, 257.
6. Nico Schrijver, 'The Changing Nature of State Sovereignty', (2000) 70(1, January) British Year Book International Law, 70.
7. Astim Riyanto, *Negara Kesatuan; Konsep, Asas dan Aktualisasinya,* (Bandung, Yapemdo, 2006) 41–42.
8. L. Oppenheim in Gul Sarigul, *The Evolving Concept of Sovereignty in Air Law* (thesis Faculty of Law Institute of Air and Space Law Monreal, August 2004) 4.
9. Nico Schrijver, above no. 6, 70.
10. Lee L. F. in Amando S. Tolentino, Jr., above no. 2.

d. *International legal sovereignty*: this refers to the mutual recognition or acceptance toward a certain state as part of international society.[11]

In accordance with Krasner's four definitions of sovereignty mentioned above, there are at least two characteristics of sovereignty, which are: 1) the ability of a state to control the traffic at the state's borders and to control the activities involved within the borders of the state; 2) the regulations or principles, such as acknowledgment within the independent territorial entity juridically without any intervention, especially regarding the internal affairs of other states. In respect to this matter, Mochtar Kusumaatmadja stated that a state's sovereignty is limited to the region within which it is constituted.[12] According to Mochtar, the highest authority is controlled by two essential limitations, which are:[13]

a. The authority is limited within the border of the region in which it is authorized; and
b. The authority is terminated when another state's authority begins to take over.

Meanwhile, Shaw classified two aspects of sovereignty, which are internal sovereignty and external sovereignty in the form of a state's supremacy as the subject of international law. Shaw pointed out that a sovereign state possessed the international rights and responsibilities, as well as the international identity, indicated from the factual region with its clearly specified borders.[14]

Thus, according to the definitions and developments of a state's sovereignty in international society, as described in the previous paragraphs, the evolution of a state's sovereignty is divided into four periods, which are: 1) the initiation of an early doctrine of sovereignty in the 16th century; 2) the concept of sovereignty that was developed during the era of the Westphalia Agreement in 1648; 3) the concept of sovereignty at the beginning of the 18th and 19th centuries (transition); 4) the period of the sovereignty concept in the 20th century and the beginning of the 21st century.

2.1 *The early doctrine of sovereignty*

The concept of sovereignty primarily occurred around the 16th century and was proposed by scientists such as Machiavelli, Jean Bodin, Thomas Hobbes, Hugo Grotius and John Locke. The first three mentioned founders were called '*the former's conceptions*', who contributed to the basic construction of the sovereignty concept. During the classical era, sovereignty was known as *the Hobbesian 'mortal God', Machiavellian Price*, or *the Bodinian 'absolute and perpetual power vested in a commonwealth'*. In other words, a construction that gradually assembled a mutual law due to necessity and in order to provide intervention either in internal situations or toward others.[15]

The general conclusion of the sovereignty concept was that the sovereign had the highest authority, which belonged to the sovereign themselves by the law of God. Bodin recognized that in a society in which law exists, there must be an authority from which the law emerged.[16] Bodin added that there were certain exceptions upon the insusceptibility of a country from an integrated law such as God's law, natural law, public law for all nations,

---

11. Krasner, 'Abiding Sovereignty', (2011) 22(3, July) *International Political Science Review/Revue Internationale de science politique*, 231.
12. Mochtar Kusumaatmadja & Etty R. Agoes, *Pengantar Hukum Internasional.* (Bandung, Alumni, 2003) 17.
13. Ibid, 18.
14. Malcom N. Shaw, *International Law* (Cambridge, Sixth Edition, Grotius Publications Limited, 2009) 487.
15. Alan Chong, above no. 5, 259.
16. The form of sovereignty as conceived by Bodin was originally implemented in England during the era of Plantagenet King Henry II in 1154–1189, in France during the era of King Louis le Saint in 1226-1227, in Sicily during the era of King Fredrich II von Hohenstaufen in 1212–1250 and also in Spain in the era of Fernando the Saint in 1217–1252 and King Alfonso in 1252–1258. See Wildhaber, Luzius, 'Sovereignty and International Law', in Macdonald, R.St.J & Johnston, D.M. (Editor), *The Structure and Process of International* (The Hague, Martinus Nijhoff, 1983) 425.

or other laws that 'constrained' them from a contract. In contrast to Bodin, Hobbes viewed that sovereignty was not limited by either natural law, God's law, or customs.[17] Law was the mandate from the sovereign, the ruler, and it was absolute and people must abide by it.

A law expert from the Netherlands, Hugo Grotius (who was assumed to be the founder of international law through his work *De jure belli*), insisted that a sovereign state is free from foreign control. Furthermore, Grotius developed the classical theory by introducing the individual contributions that form the nation through the concept of representative sovereignty. Grotius said that *respublica* was founded by the voluntary unity of individuals in order to form a civil society. Grotius also believed that every country with a representative body would be acknowledged as a *respublica*.

Grotius defined sovereignty as '*the legitimate right to give itself laws, and to control its destiny*'.[18] According to him, national sovereignty was not only about facts relating to the world, but also about the norms of morality and the rights of a country to arrange their own laws in order to express '*human freedom*' eternally. In addition, Bodin and Grotuis mentioned several limitations in determining authority (*power of sovereign*) based on God's law, natural law, international law, or the contract between the ruler and the people. More importantly, Grotius added that the people were under the responsibility of the ruler (*incumbent*) in order to provide protection from any acts of injustice caused by the governance, which the people have entrusted to the ruler.[19]

John Locke, as mentioned by Hobbes, in his second book '*Treatise of Government*' issued in 1651, said that a social contract is permanent and cannot be revoked, but the legislatives only have the duty to establish constitutions for the sake of public importance. And if the trust is violated, the people will use their power to replace them with new legislatives.[20] Based on the concept raised by John Locke, it is unclear whether he laid the sovereignty on to the people or on to the legislatives. Lockes's opinion of sovereignty was less absolute compared to that of Hobbes. Locke clearly mentioned that intervention was intolerable. Apparently, Locke's vision of sovereignty was closest to the version seen in the English parliament.

2.2 *State sovereignty during the era of the Westphalia agreement*

The Westphalia Treaty in 1648, which marked the end of the Thirty Years' War against the hegemony of the Roman Empire, had brought the countries of Europe out from a long transition period in the Medieval Era to become sovereign states. After the Westphalia Treaty, the new international order was based on sovereign government, independence, and permanent territorial integrity.[21] In regards to this matter, Krasner stated that the Westphalia Treaty was generally seen as the momentum of the development of modern international law involving sovereign states, and each of them had exclusive authority within their geographic borders.[22]

The Westphalia Treaty took over the trans-national role of the Catholic Church, which had been limited due to the emphasis on the idea that international relationships should be built on the balance of power rather than by the desire of the Christian community.[23] This treaty also introduced sovereignty as the superior authority of a state, rather than individual power.

17. Gul Sarigul, above no. 8, 6.
18. Ibid.
19. Ibid.
20. Ibid, 7.
21. Ibid, 8.
22. Stephen D. Krasner, 'Rethinking the Sovereign State Model', *Review of the International Studies, British International Studies Association* (2001) 17.
23. Stephen D. Krasner, *Sovereignty, Foreign Policy*, No. 22, publish by Washingtonpost. News week. Interactive, LLC, 2001, p. 21. The most important thing is that Westphalia established requirements about

On the other hand, Westphalia also raised the issue of the monarchical state, who depended on their kings in every aspect of implementation of prerogative rights in the government. This situation encouraged the writers in that era to expose the difference between perfect full sovereignty and relative imperfect sovereignty.[24]

Westphalia was considered to be the most important and greatest document in the Middle Ages, from which emerged new regulations that impaired the authority of kings to handle religious affairs in their region, which was against the theory of national sovereignty that later became known as the Westphalian system. States who were involved in this system were considered to have a political authority system, which was based on autonomy, territory, mutual recognition, and control principles. Autonomy means that there is no external actor who has authority within the state's border. Territory refers to the fact that political authority is implemented within a certain geographical space. Meanwhile, recognition indicates the existence of acknowledgment among territorial entities that are independent juridically. This means that they have the competence to be involved in contractual agreements, commonly in the form of a treaty. Control emphasizes that a sovereign state has the authority to act and effectively regulate the traffic across its borders and within the region.[25]

2.3 *State's sovereignty in the 18th and 19th centuries*

At the beginning of the 18th century, the writers started to develop ideas and theories on states' supremacy that better complied with international law rather than with natural law. This period is the transitional development era of a modern state's sovereignty in international law.[26] The view of Jean Bodin was consistently asserted in this era and was categorized into two different concepts. One still believed that sovereignty should stay as a whole unity, while the other not only believed that sovereignty should stay as the authentic value of a state but that it should still be limited by the constituted regulations regarding the relationship between states.[27]

During the 18th and 19th centuries, the view that encouraged the implementation of relative imperfect sovereignty was greatly supported due to the foundation of the United States of America and the Swiss and German nations. Federal states began to introduce a new government structure that consisted of two-level-governance and the division of sovereignty between the federal country and the states.[28]

The principle that stated that the sovereign should not interfere in or judge other states' affairs was originally stated by two international law experts in the second part of the 18th century: Emer de Vattel and Cristian Wolff. In 1970, Wolff, in his writings, stated that intervening in other states' affairs, under any mechanism possible, was against the natural freedom of a country, and that each nation had the freedom from any will of other nations.[29]

---

religious tolerance in Germany. This treaty provided 'lip service' for cuius region, eius religio principles where a king is eligible to make religious-related regulations in his country.

24. E. B. Weins, *the New International Legal System: Perspective in International Law*, N. Jasentaliyane (Ed.) (The Hague, 1995) 65.
25. Stephen D. Krasner, above no. 22.
26. The development of the sovereignty theory in this century was mostly influenced by the sovereignty theory development during the Westphalia Treaty era. Krasner also emphasized that the basic rules related to Westphalian/Vattelian and *International Legal Sovereignty* had been acknowledged at least since the end of the 18th century. See Krasner, above no. 11, 233.
27. Ibid.
28. Ibid.
29. Ibid.

During the 19th century, the non-intervention principle was promoted by Latin American states, who were considered to be weak entities in the international system. This demand was not accepted legally by the United States until the 1930s.

2.4 *State sovereignty during the 20th century and at the beginning of the 21st century*

Ideas about the content and limitation (scope) of sovereignty kept developing during the 20th century. Even so, the core of the idea was still the same. Sovereignty was still seen as the prerequisite for acquiring the status of 'state' and was the most essential element in international law. Brownlie stated that as long as international law exists, the dynamic of sovereignty stands in the terminology of law. Ian Brownlie stated:[30]

> If international law exists, then the dynamics of state sovereignty can be expressed in terms of law, and, as states are equal and have legal personality, sovereignty is in a major aspect a relation to other states and to organizations of states defined by law.

As an equal state that has a legal personality, sovereignty is the main aspect in engaging with other states and international organizations in order to abide by the law. For Brownlie, sovereignty and equality among states are the constitutive foundation of international law. This is also supported by Bodin in the early initiation of states' sovereignty, as mentioned by Broms:[31]

> An interesting feature was that Bodin regarded the kings of small republics as sovereign as the king of the mightiest country. He wanted to show that is possible for all types of states to have international relations with one another. The princes found theory of sovereignty suitable for their own purposes to gain supremacy within their entities and at same time they considered themselves to be on the same level with other princes. This again brought up the doctrine of equality as related to the doctrine of sovereignty.

Bodin stated that every country, even a small state, is eligible to build international relationships with other states. Kings would figure out a suitable sovereignty theory that met their desires and, at the same time, considered themselves to stand equally with other kings. This what evolved the equality doctrine regarding sovereignty doctrine.[32]

The idea of sovereignty, independence, and equality that is explained by Broms above is comparable with the concept of international society regulated by international law. The idea of sovereignty that was integrated with the concepts of independence and equality played an important role in establishing international society that was regulated by international law in real life.

In the 20th century, the idea that 'sovereignty' had no clear and permanent definition began to spread out. Rather than focusing on finding the source of sovereignty, they tended to develop the elements and the implications of the sovereignty concept. In this era, the most recent literature about international law required the writer to further categorize the concept of sovereignty.

Milton Esman proposed a new concept in the literature on the subject of international law and the differences of the scope of sovereignty based on three domains of human experience: 1) politics (countries' institutions, the relationship among citizens, and the subject toward

30. Ian Brownlie, *Principles of Public International Law* (Oxford, Ninth Edition, Clarendon Press, 2008) 289.
31. Broms, Bengt, in Mohammed Bedjaoui, *International Law Achievements and Prospects* (Paris, UNESCO, 1991) 43.
32. Ibid.

government); 2) culture (the legitimate status and the language used, religious practices, and the scope of the arts); and 3) economy (production, distribution, trading, financial, social protection and other productive features of livelihood).[33] Meanwhile, the implication of sovereignty, as stated by Brownlie, is as follows:[34]

> (1) a jurisdiction, prima facie exclusive, over a territory and the permanent population living there; (2) a duty of non-intervention in the area of exclusive jurisdiction of other states; and (3) the dependence of obligations arising from customary law and treaties on the consent of the obligor.

During the 19th and 20th centuries, the industrial revolution changed the conditions of most of society. During the past two centuries, when the regulations of the sovereign state system had finally been eternalized, the world changed a lot, and it was marked in the history of human beings.[35] The model of the Westphalia sovereign country stood for quite a long time, but the principle that defined sovereignty as a non-interventional and mutually recognized authority among territorial entities juridically was often neglected.[36] During the development of international law, many violations toward the principles of sovereignty based on the Westphalia model occurred, either in terms of territory, autonomy, recognition, or control.[37]

The violations against the principle of autonomy usually involve a situation where an external actor manages to gain authoritative control of a state. The principle of autonomy is considered to be violated when the sovereign has approved a governmental structure controlled by external actors, or the external actors have acquired a level of power high enough to suppress the institutions, policies, or personnel of the weaker state. An example of the violation of autonomy is *bondholders' committees* who regulated the financial activities in several states in the Balkans and other places in the 19th century, International Monetary Fund (IMF), a protectorate whose the main authority to control the foreign policy without using the domestic policy, the requirement of 'medication' applied in the Middle and East Europe after Balkan war in 1870's and World War I, and satellite countries under the hegemony of Soviet Union Communists after the World War II.[38]

3 CURRENT THINKING REGARDING THE TRADITIONAL SOVEREIGNTY PRINCIPLE IN INTERNATIONAL LAW

The classical thinking of the '*Westphalian*' concept in the context of a state's rights to monopolize certain actions regarding its territory and its citizens has been neglected in many ways, despite attempts to maintain stability without any interventions from foreign or international authority with regard to decision-making and other activities in the national governance system.[39]

33. Milton Esman dalam Gul Sarigul, above no. 8, 11.
34. Ibid.
35. Ibid.
36. Stephen D. Krasner, *Rethinking the Sovereign State Model* above no. 22, 18.
37. The violation of territory in the Westphalian model of sovereign countries is where the structural authority is not proportional to the geographical border, such as the European Union with its supra-national bodies, and the Exclusive Economic Zone, where the coastal country has the authority to control commercial activities, such as seabed exploitation, but is not in charge of shipping.
38. Ibid. Westphalia Compromy conducted in four ways, which are: conventions, contracting, coercion, and imposition.
39. John H. Jackson, 'Sovereignty-Modern: A new Approach to an Outdated Concept', (2003) 97(782, October) *The American Journal of International Law*, 782.

Sovereignty has many dimensions;[40] for example, historically Richard N. Hass linked sovereignty with four main characteristics:[41]

1. Sovereign states are those who experience the highest authority in politics and monopolize the use of violence within their region (domestic authority);
2. States have the ability to regulate the mobility (traffic) across the region's border (border control);
3. Countries can freely determine their foreign policy (policy autonomy);
4. There is recognition from other states' governments that they are an independent entity who has the right to be free from external intervention (non-intervention).

Richard N. Hass emphasized that the components of sovereignty are never absolute, but at the same time, they offer the foundations of a world order in which each of the components will face new challenges like never before.[42]

Henry Schemers, supported by Richard N. Hass, stated that sovereignty consisted of many different aspects and none of them were permanent. The ideas of sovereignty have consistently changed, especially during recent years. Schemers concluded that a state's sovereignty was degraded under international law when international co-operation required the involved states to be bound by minimum international laws without any rights to claim that sovereignty allowed the state to resist any basic international regulation. Schemer also stated that current international society already possesses suitable facilities to handle domestic affairs with the help of other states and that they also have the responsibility to regulate territories with unsuccessful governments.[43]

Jo Anne Pamberton affirmed that at the end of the 20th century, much literature raised the topic of globalization, which portrayed the decrease or even the end of sovereign states. Globalization occurs in many aspects, either economic, cultural, environmental, etc., and this removes the territorial borders of states. Pamberton suggested that there was an urgency to reconceptualize sovereignty in order to accommodate the increasing ambiguity of states' borders and the multi-dimensions of world politics. This reconceptualization would drag sovereignty into the opposite axis from the original definition made at the end of the 16th century, when it was portrayed as the supreme, absolute, and indivisible authority.[44] Even so, the state-centric shift of perspective will not automatically neglect the sovereignty itself.

In relation to Pamberton's ideas, Nico Schrijver stated that the substances of sovereignty in international law in 2000 are different from those in 1648. Even so, the differences are not a new paradigm. Furthermore, Nico Schrijver, in his study titled '*The Changing Nature of State Sovereignty*', stated that:[45]

> It is evident that sovereignty is an enduring concept....... Sovereignty is not an absolute and static concept but more a relative and dynamic one. In these respects the substance of

40. As a note, many literatures, journal articles, and other scientific writings focused on discussing sovereignty by referring to various theories. One of them described the concept of sovereignty as '*organized hypocrazy*', the others portrayed sovereignty as an added value to a study and persuasion from science and law. Sovereignty can also be explored as a '*social contract*' that is constructed regarding the territorial rights of a sovereign country, which also consists of the stability of a country's border, the recognition of the territory as a sovereign country, and the right to negotiate of a sovereign country. The approaches used to explore these ideas of sovereignty depend on the amount of customs and practices of the country-nation, or even international society, which may change over time. See John H, Jackson, *Sovereignty- Modern: A New Approach to An Outdated Concept*, ibid, 786. See also Cynthia Weber & Thomas J. Biersteker, 'Reconstructing the Analysis of Sovereignty: Concluding Reflections and Directions for Future Research', in *State Sovereignty as Social Construct* (Cambridge University Press, 1996)
41. Ibid, 786.
42. Ibid.
43. Ibid.
44. Jo-Anne Pemberton, *Sovereignty Interpretations* (England, Palgrave Macmillan, 2009) 1.
45. Nico Schrijver, above no. 6.

sovereignty in international law in 2000 differs from that of 1648 and that sovereignty is more qualified, but this does not constitute a new paradigm. Moreover, what remains unchanged is the desire expressed in the Peace of Westphalia, for a pleasant, good and just peace, and the sweet fruits of complete and permanent peace for comfort of the ... peoples and lands owing the state allegiance.

Many law experts, in their many researches and scientific writings, analyze the new ideas of the sovereignty concept through various terms. When Jo Anne Pamberton utilized the term *reconceptualization*[46], other writers used other terms, such as *rethinking*,[47] *reimagining*,[48] *reinventing*,[49] *re-envisioning*,[50] *revisiting*,[51] *redefining*,[52] and so on.

Roland Rich stated that states depended on their sovereignty for security when facing global society who place the state in a shaky security system.[53] In regard to this matter, *Westphalian Sovereignty* adopted *humanitarian* and *development assistance* in order to protect the best interests of their citizens, surely without sacrificing all of the rights of the particular state. Therefore, C. Raj Kumar emphasized that sovereignty needed to be re-interpreted. The world development that encouraged diversity requires a rethinking in how sovereignty is defined, protected and implemented, not only among the states, but also within the states by the elite groups.[54] This rethinking should consist of reflecting on the consequences of eliminating the concept of sovereignty in international law.

During its development, a state's sovereignty has many new concepts, which Gerry Simpson called metaphysical sovereignty, extraterritorial sovereignty, deferred sovereignty, internationalized sovereignty, and de-territorialized sovereignty.[55] These new concepts caused sovereignty

46. Ibid, 3.
47. See Seng Tan, 'Whiter Sovereignty in Southeast Asia Today?', in Trudy Jacobsen, Charles Sampford, and Ramesh Thakur (Eds), *Re-envisioning Sovereignty; The End of Westphalia?* (USA, Ashgate, Burlington) 83. See Seng Tan conducted a study on sovereignty to analyze the challenges of basic status and the meaning of sovereignty in the context of South East Asia in this era. Furthermore, Tan explored the thinking and the practice of the development of the South East Asia region, which questioned the traditional understanding about sovereignty in the region.
48. Yongjin Zhang, 'Ambivalent Sovereignty; China and Re-Imagining the Westphalian Ideal, in Trudy Jacobsen, Charles Sampford, and Ramesh Thakur (Eds.), ibid, 101. The analysis of Yonjin Zhang about the debate on the country's sovereignty and the changing of the *Westphalian International System* based on historical norms and its manifestation currently involving China. Zhang identified three social and historical contexts that are suitable for China's socialization to the norms of sovereignty, which are: tradition, revolution, and globalization.
49. C. Raj Kumar, 'Corruption and Transparency in Governance and Development: Reinventing Sovereignty for Promoting Good Governance', in Trudy Jacobsen, Charles Sampford, and Ramesh Thakur (Eds.), ibid, 251. C. Raj Kumar wrote about the concept of sovereignty and its relevance in the current era. According to Kumar, the concept of sovereignty has many interpretations and should be reinterpreted, especially regarding sovereignty and the effect of corruption in government, and it has five dimensions: security, law enforcement, good governance, development, and Human Rights. Such challenges in government required the re-examining of global anti-corruption initiatives.
50. Ross P. Buckley, 'Re-Envisioning Economic Sovereignty: Developing Countries and the International Monetary Fund', in Trudy Jacobsen, Charles Sampford, and Ramesh Thakur (Eds.), ibid, 267. The writing of Ross P. Buckley analyzed the role and the impact of the IMF toward the economic sovereignty of developing countries, such as Latin America, Chile, Malaysia, and Argentina.
51. Thomas Blom Hansen and Finn Stepputat, 'Sovereignty Revisited' (2006) 35 *Annual Review of Anthropology*, 295. This article used an anthropology political sciences approach. Research tried to explore sovereignty in a de facto manner. As it is related to the discipline of science, the article analyzed sovereignty by restudying the position of the King and the everlasting customs, the modern form of authority, colonial authority, governmentality and modern sovereignty, informal rulers and other artificial authority, as well as market sovereignty.
52. John H. Jackson, above no. 39.
53. Roland Rich in Jacobsen Tayor, 232.
54. C. Raj Kumar, above no. 49, 251.
55. Gerry Simpson in Trudy Jacobsen, Charles Sampford, and Ramesh Thakur (Eds) above no. 47, 61–68.

to move further away from the Montevideo Convention. Currently, sovereignty is forced to face a buffer room, between the state and the global world, between private and public affairs, among the ideas of politics, safety, security and economy, and between bilateral agreement and economic integration. This surely degrades the value of 'sovereignty' from government. Moreover, Simpson emphasized that sovereignty has changed from its original form.[56]

Metaphysics sovereignty is an ungraspable and unknowable sovereignty, for instance the joint sovereignty over Guantanamo Bay by Cuba and the United States. In many ways, the decision regarding the *Rasul Case* in the US Supreme Court portrayed this imperialism in court, where the Federal Law of the US can even cover Cuba. *Extraterritorial* sovereignty is a phenomenon that developed within international society and shows the extension of the humanitarian mission from sovereignty (*jurisdictional*), such as the Belgian Constitution, which highlights universal jurisdiction and aims at punishing convicts accused of war crimes, humanitarian crimes, and genocide.[57] Deferred sovereignty is sovereignty that is substantially executed under the name of or by international society, such as in the case of Kosovo and Serbia.[58] Meanwhile, an example of internationalized sovereignty can be seen in a state with a protectorate, mandate, or trust system. Such sovereignty is usually applied to unsuccessful states that, according to John Rawls, are referred to as '*burdened states*'.[59] The concept of '*incipient sovereignty*' can be seen from looking at South Sudan, which is a new state that separated itself from the Republic of Sudan in 2011. Meanwhile, de-territorial sovereignty is a form of sovereignty seen during the process of decomposition or recomposition of sovereignty.

4 CONCLUSION

The writer believes that sovereignty is a fundamental concept that is the logical basis of international law, and that eliminating it would risk the stability of international law and other principles of the system of international relations. The rethinking needed to eliminate the sovereignty concept in international law is equal to the fight against the legitimacy and moral value of international law. According to the writer, the development of the system of international relations is currently urging a rethink of the concept of sovereignty, on the condition that this reconceptualization should be conducted thoroughly, since eliminating concepts without providing an adequate replacement would only provoke chaos, misunderstanding, and conflict.[60]

---

56. Gerry Simpson in Trudy Jacobsen, Charles Sampford, and Ramesh Thakur (Eds) above no. 47, 68.
57. On 11 April 2000, Belgium issued an *Arrest Warrant* to the Ministry of Foreign Affair of Congo due to them being accused as perpetrating or assisting in the violation of the Geneva Convention 1949 and the additional protocols and humanitarian crimes (*Arrest Warrant Case*). ICJ decided that Belgium should revoke the letter of arrest dated on 11 April 2000 upon Abdoulaye Yerodia Ndombasi (Ministry of Foreign Affair of Congo), and stated that Belgium had failed to respect the immunity of criminal jurisdiction upon Abdoulaye Yerodia Ndombasi, which is absolute since it is protected by International Law. Another example was Spain's enthusiasm for universal jurisdiction in the *Guatemalan Genocide Case*, and also the Higher Court of England, which figured out that the *UK Human Rights Act* 1998 was implemented in Iraq during the transition period between the war (March 2003) and sovereignty (June 2004). Based on Mousa's decision, the Court stated that the Constitution was applied for arresting Iraqis by British troops near Basra.
58. On one side, the Resolution of the Security Council of the UN clearly stated that Kosovo was still part of Serbia's sovereignty, but on the other hand, there was deferred sovereignty of Serbia on 22 September 1992 when the General Assembly refused the rights of Serbia to participate in the annual Assembly meeting, and on 1 November 2000 when Serbia was legally recognized by the UN.
59. This is a country that has no centralized government authority and cannot provide any services or provide security for its citizens. Examples of countries under the care of protectorates are: Somalia, Liberia, Timor Timur and part of Yugoslavia.
60. The concept of *state of nature* according to Hobbes is *'state of nature is a state of war all against all'*. Hobbes believed that in the *state of nature,* humans are free, rational, and knowledgeable. Hobbes said this

REFERENCES

Broms, B. (1991). In M. Bedjaoui (Ed.), *International law achievements and prospects*. Paris: UNESCO.

Brownlie, I. (2008). *Principles of public international law* (9th ed.). Oxford, UK: Clarendon Press.

Chong, A. (2005). Classical realism and the tension between sovereignty and intervention: Constructions of expediency from Machiavelli, Hobbes, and Bosin. *Journal of International Relations and Development, 8*.

Hansen, T.B. & Stepputat, F. (2006). Sovereignty revisited. *Annual Review of Anthropology, 35*.

Jackson, J.H. (2003). Sovereignty-modern: A new approach to an outdated concept. *The American Journal of International Law, 97*(782).

Jacobsen, T., Sampford, C. & Thakur, R. (Eds.). (2008). *Re-envisioning sovereignty: The end of Westphalia?* Burlington, VT: Ashgate.

Krasner, S.D. (2001). Rethinking the sovereign state model. *Review of International Studies*.

Krasner, S.D. (2001). *Sovereignty, foreign policy*, No. 22, Washington Post. News Week. Interactive.

Krasner, S.D. (2011). Abiding sovereignty. *International Political Science Review, 22*(3).

Kusumaatmadja, M. & Agoes, E.R. (2003). *Pengantar Hukum Internasional*. Bandung, Indonesia: Alumni.

Lubis, M.S. (1975). *Ilmu Negara*. Bandung, Indonesia: Alumni.

Macdonald, R.S.J. & Johnston, D.M. (Eds.). (1983). *The structure and process of international*. The Hague, The Netherlands: Martinus Nijhoff.

Malanczuk, P. (2000). *Akehurst's modern introduction to international law* (7th ed.). New York: Routledge.

Pemberton, J.-A. (2009). *Sovereignty interpretations, sovereignty interpretation*. Basingstoke, UK: Palgrave Macmillan.

Riyanto, A. (2006). *Negara Kesatuan: Konsep, Asas dan Aktualisasinya*. Bandung, Indonesia: Yapemdo.

Sarigul, G. (2004). *The evolving concept of sovereignty in air law* (Thesis, Faculty of Law, Institute of Air and Space Law, Montreal, Canada).

Schrijver, N. (2000). The changing nature of state sovereignty. *British Year Book International Law, 70*(1).

Shaw, M.N. (2009). *International law* (6th ed.). Cambridge, UK: Grotius.

Simpson, G. (2008). The guises of sovereignty. In T. Jacobsen, C. Sampford & R. Thakur (Eds.), *Re-envisioning sovereignty: The end of Westphalia?* Burlington, VT: Ashgate.

Tolentino, A.S. (2014). Sovereignty over natural resources, change of concept or change perception? *Environmental Policy and Law, 44*(3).

Weber, C. & Biersteker, T.J. (1996). Reconstructing the analysis of sovereignty: Concluding reflections and directions for future research. In *State sovereignty as social construct*. Cambridge, UK: Cambridge University Press.

Weins, E.B. (1995). *The new international legal system: Perspective in international law*. N. Jasentaliyane (Ed.). The Hague, The Netherlands.

---

after considering the condition of humans who are capable of respecting each other. Hobbes assumed that there was an equality of ability and power possessed about I bleach by humans to compete with each other. In competitions, everyone could threaten each other. The basic assumption was that every individual was encouraged by felicity that conflict became inevitable either caused by the scarcity of resources, the inexistence of sovereignty, lack of financial, etc. Hobbes mentioned in the beginning of Leviathan, that humans generally eager for a continuous authority. Therefore, since humans have the same nature, there is no equality of power in order to maintain the stability. That is why, war among humans is considered as *state of nature*.

Culture and International Law - Juwana et al. (Eds)
 ISBN 978-1-138-38766-9

Additional punishment in sexual crime cases

Faizin Sulistio
Faculty of Law, Brawijaya University, Malang, Indonesia

Nazura Abdul Manap
Universiti Kebangsaan Malaysia, Bangi Selangor, Malaysia

Nurini Aprilianda
Faculty of Law, Brawijaya University, Malang, Indonesia

ABSTRACT: This paper examines the additional penalties for sexual crimes. The purpose of this research is to find the justification of punishment in the criminal justice system that is more acceptable in accordance with the moral development of society. This normative juridical study uses conceptual and case approaches. The analysis is carried out by descriptive analysis method to establish the basic theory and practice of punishment by courts of sexual crime perpetrators. It can be concluded from this study that there are several reasons for additional punishments by the court; namely, the nature of the relationship of the perpetrator to the victim, repetition, and committing several crimes at once.

KEYWORDS: sexual crimes, penalties, perpetrator

1 INTRODUCTION

The government's response, amid a series of sexual crimes against women and children this year, has been widely welcomed by the public. However, the 'culture of rape' where many victims are ignored remains a concern. Victims are often blamed for the rape that occurred. Pressure arises in the community on the government to increase punishment for perpetrators, such as chemical castration.

Given the background described above, the authors sought to research into the adjustment of additional punishment for sexual criminal actors, especially when the victim is a child, that are more just in a judge's decision, concurrent with community development.

2 RESEARCH METHODS

This paper use a normative legal research approach that addresses normative legal problems on the basis of critical analysis and in-depth study of library materials and relevant legal documents. This legal problem is examined with an approach that is oriented to both a case approach and a statute approach, especially in determining and formulating criminal charges.

3 RESULTS AND DISCUSSION

3.1 *Court decision in sexual crime cases*

Additional punishment, in Indonesian criminal law, is imposed on the perpetrator of a crime by referring to several statutory provisions. Laws on additional punishment, in general, are regulated in the Indonesian Penal Code (KUHP) and some specific criminal laws outside the KUHP, such as aggravation with the following reasons:

1. Perpetrator position as civil servant/official.
2. Additional punishment because of the perpetrator's relationship with the victim.
3. Recidivism (offense repetition).
4. *Samenloop* or *Concursus* (the combination of two or more criminal acts).
5. Victims of criminal acts are children (Article 81 of Law on Child Protection).

3.1.1 *Criminal addition for serving in a position as a civil servant*

Addition, because of position, is determined in Article 52 of the KUHP, which indicates that when an official commits a crime against the special obligations of his position or at the time of committing a crime, used the authority, opportunity or any means given to his position, the penalty is increased by one third. The basis of the criminal additional punishment in Article 52 of the KUHP is located in the position of the perpetrator (official or civil servant); there are four aspects in committing crime:

1. Violating a special obligation of the position.
2. Using the power of the office.
3. Using the opportunity because of the position.
4. Using the facilities provided because of the position.

These four elements of civil servants, based on Article 52, can be simplified into two elements:

- Violates a specific obligation of the office.
- Abuses power, taking advantage of opportunity and misuse of facilities provided because of the position.

The reasons for the criminal additional punishment are rarely used in practice by public prosecutors and judges since this additional punishment is imposed on criminal acts related to authority abuses. The judge will not give criminal penalties to the perpetrators based on Article 52. The judge will consider whether the perpetrators have misused their authority. For example, a lecturer with civil servant status who rapes a woman he knows does not fulfill the provisions of Article 52, even though he is a civil servant. The additional punishment conditions are also not met in the case of a police officer who was supposed to be in charge of maintaining public order but committed sexual violence. Article 52 of the KUHP can only be applied to civil servants when there is a relationship between position and the criminal act committed. For example, a civil servant violating his special obligation because of the position that he was specifically assigned. For example, a police officer is assigned to protect a witness, but then he engaged in sexual violence against the witness being protected. The requirement for fulfillment of additional punishment in Article 52 can also be imposed on lecturers who are given the task of guiding students' theses, but who use the authority given to seduce and force their students to engage in sexual intercourse by threatening the grades or graduation of those students.

Additional punishment based on Article 52 of the KUHP is generally applicable to all forms of criminal acts, except crimes and violations of authority. Although the legal subject of violations of authority is the same, the civil servant, there is a difference between the criminal act and aggravation based on Article 52 of the KUHP on crimes and violations of authority. Authority phrases relate to subjects who hold positions as officials that can be interpreted as people who have a position or own a position, covertly showing that the legal subject in this offense does not apply to everyone, but applies for those who have an authority or certain position or a person who has certain personal qualities. The meaning of official is usually associated with people who have positions including civil servants and positions in general. The qualification of an official is a person who has an authority or position, and because of that authority or position, has the right to carry out certain actions as part of their work duties. Ownership of this authority is created by provisions, laws or by habit.

3.1.2 *Additional punishment of crime because of repetition (Recidivism)*

Repetition means certain criminal acts have occurred if the same person commits criminal acts who are already subject of a permanent legal decision. To put more severely, the criminal offense of recidivism could occur if a person, who has been convicted, has committed a crime again, then that person has proven his bad character. Even though he has been convicted, he recommits a criminal act and he needs to be punished more severely, even though he has been educated in a correctional institution, so that after returning to the community they can live normally.

Besides the KUHP, specifically, crimes of sexual violence are also subject to additional punishment on the repetition of criminal acts as stipulated in Article 81(4) in conjunction with Article 76D, which state that as well as the perpetrators referred to in Paragraph 3 (parents of perpetrators, guardians, people who have family relationships, child caregivers, educators, education personnel, officers who handle child protection, or crimes carried out by more than one person together), the addition of one third of the criminal threat is also imposed on the perpetrator who has been convicted of a criminal act as referred to in Article 76D.

3.1.3 *Combination of criminal acts (Concursus)*

The violation of a criminal offense is the occurrence of two or more offenses committed by one person, where the offense carried out for the first time has not been punished by the court, or between the first offense and the next one, has not been limited by a judge's decision.

In repetition, there is also more than one offense committed by one person. The main difference is that the repetition of the offense that is carried out first or earlier has been decided on by the judge in convicting the perpetrator, even if he has served it in part or in full. Whereas in terms of repetition of conditions such as repetition is not necessary.

In the context of a combination criminal acts, we can see additional punishment in the case of Korinus Neno, a farmer with ten children and a wife. His first child was Novi Neno, 19 years old. Since Novi was at senior high, Korinus has been stimulated by Novi, with the defendant often sexually harassing the victim by holding the victim's breast. One day when the victim's mother was not at home, Korinus who was drunk, planned to rape his daughter after watching pornographic videos. Finally, after threatening the victim with a knife, the defendant raped his daughter.

The defendant's actions were charged under Article 46 Paragraph 1 of Law No. 23 of 2004 on Elimination of Domestic Violence in conjunction with Article 64 Paragraph 1 of the KUHP. The panel of judges stated that the defendant, Korinus Neno, had been proven legally and convincingly guilty of committing a crime of 'Conducting Sexual Violence in the Household Scope', imposing a criminal sentence on the defendant of a prison sentence of 12 years.[1]

3.1.4 *Additional punishment in relation to a child victim*

Several cases of sexual crime committed with cruelty became a catalyst for the government to pass a law concerning chemical castration rules for perpetrators of child sexual violence. The first case occurred on February 24, 2016, involving a sexual violence recidivist with the initials RJ, aka Muksin aka Tebok, who was 44 years old. RJ sexually abused five children, including his own biological child who was only ten years old, and this was the second time RJ had done so. The first time, RJ admits that he does not know why he did it, and blamed lust because his wife worked in Malaysia since 2009, so he had to serve a sentence of four years

1. District Court No: 47/Pid.Sus/2016./PN.SOE

and nine months, and at this time the second act was carried out by RJ so that for his actions RJ was charged under Articles 76D and 76 E in conjunction with Article 82 of Law No. 35 of 2014 on Child Protection, with the threat of a minimum sentence of five years and a maximum of 15 years in prison (Kompas News, 2016).

Law No. 17 of 2016 is the second amendment of Law No. 23 of 2002 on Child Protection and regulates the additional punishment of Articles 81 and 81A concerning additional penalties, namely the additional punishment of castration, installation of chipped tracking devices (electronic tags) and also announcing the identity of perpetrators of child sexual violence to the community. Additional penalties of chemical castration and chip installation are found in Article 81 Paragraph 7. Chemical castration will be imposed on perpetrators of sexual violence against children relating to Paragraph 4 on the addition of one third of the criminal punishment if the perpetrator repeats his actions again or can be referred to as a recidivist and verse 5 concerning children, as more than one victim suffered serious injuries, mental disorders, infectious diseases, loss of reproductive function and resulting death, so that perpetrators of sexual violence against children can be sentenced to death or life imprisonment for a minimum of ten and a maximum of 20 years. The punishment for the perpetrators who commits a crime threatens to have intercourse with him or someone else.

Thus, the perpetrators of sexual violence against children can be subject to additional punishments in the form of chemical castration, the installation of electronic tags and the announcement of their identity as a perpetrator. Article 81A states that a period of no longer than two years and castration should be imposed after the convict has served a principal sentence.

The case for the perpetrators' additional punishment for criminal acts related to child victims is found in court decision No. 163/PID.SUS/2016/PN.Bla. In this case, the defendant named Rasidin was the victim's stepfather. The victim was 14 years old. In June 2014, the defendant saw the victim sleeping in front of the TV. The defendant approached the victim and groped the victim's body. The victim woke up and refused to obey the defendant's will, and then the defendant pushed the victim and took off the victim's clothes. The victim was threatened with a miserable life if they resisted. A panel of judges decided the defendant was guilty under Article 76D in conjunction with Article 81 Paragraph 3 of Law No. 35 of 2014 on amendments to Law No. 23 of 2002 on Child Protection, imposing a sentence of 15 years in prison and fines. The panel decided on additional punishment for the defendant because:

1. The defendant is a step-parent, who should protect and provide shelter for his children, but he did not do so properly.
2. The defendant's action against the victim (Dita Amelia Dwiyanti) occurred more than once.
3. The defendant's actions disturb society.

3.1.5 *Additional punishment based on the victim's relationship with the perpetrator*

The concept of punishment in line with the nature of the perpetrators in KUHP is actually not explicitly a criminal additional punishment, but the legislators have considered criminal threats arising from the nature of the perpetrator's relationship to the victim. In the KUHP, for example, Article 52 does not apply for crimes or criminal acts on authority abuses because the KUHP has taken into account criminal threats against officials who abuse their positions as stipulated in Article 421. This concept is also stated in Article 46 in conjunction with Article 8(a) of Law No. 23 of 2004 on Elimination of Domestic Violence, which stipulates that a 12-year prison sentence is imposed for sexual violence committed against a person who remains within the household. This concept, in the authors' view, is an implicit additional punishment which is directly given to the perpetrator for the nature of his relationship with the victim of a crime.

Criminalization of the nature of the perpetrators' relationship to these victims can be seen in case no. 416/Pid/Sus/2015/PN Sgl. The defendant, Herman, was a fisherman with seven children, three girls and four boys. He had a wife of 21 years, but had suffered one year of illness and had not had a husband-and-wife relationship for six months. Since moving from

Lampung to Bangka, Herman frequently drank alcohol. One day Herman had sexual intercourse with his third daughter, Rodian Als Yana, who was three months pregnant, at Rambak Beach, Bangka Regency. The pregnancy turned out to be the result of her father's assault. Rodian Als Yana had been raped by her biological father ten times between the ages of 14 and 20. She was under threat of being killed if she told anyone. The defendant was charged by the Public Prosecutor with a single charge using Article 46 of Law No. 23 of 2004 on Elimination of Domestic Violence. The panel of judges sentenced him to ten years in prison. The judge argued that the circumstances which incriminated the defendant's actions damaged the future of the victim. In addition, the actions of the defendant disturbed the community and damaged the order of values, morals, norms and laws in religious, family and community life.

The concept of additional punishment related to the nature of the perpetrator is explicitly applied specifically to sexual violence crimes against children in the Government Regulation in Lieu of Law (*Perppu*) No. 1 of 2016 on the Second Amendment to Law No. 23 of 2002 on Child Protection. Article 81(3) in the case of a criminal act of violence or threat by forcing a child to have intercourse with him or with another person carried out by parents, guardians, people who have family relations, child caregiver, educators, education staff, apparatus who handles child protection, or is carried out by more than one person or together, the criminal plus one third of the maximum criminal sanction.

In Article 81(3), this category of perpetrators has a close relationship with victims, both because of blood relations, guardianship and parental custody. The case of additional punishment is related to the perpetrator who has a close relationship with the victim and who is convicted under the Child Protection Law, also in the case of 163/PID.SUS/2016/PN.Bla with the defendant Rasidin.

In the practice of criminal judicature, some of the above provisions are rarely used as the basis for explicit punishment addition that contains the judge's argument. However, the additional punishment provisions related to the nature of the perpetrator, the child as a victim and some of the provisions that are the basis of the additional punishment above can be analyzed through a full court decision, whereas the ruling of additional punishment is usually related to the actions of perpetrators such as disturbing the public or the perpetrator's actions to bring trauma to the victim.

3.2 *Court decision with addition of punishment*

On an ideal level, to realize a judge's decision that reflects the legal values and sense of community justice, there are several elements that must be fulfilled properly. Gustav Radbruch suggested that ideally in a decision must contain the *idea des recht*, which includes three elements: justice (*Gerechtigkeit*), legal certainty (*Rechtsicherheit*) and expediency (*Zwechtmassigkeit*).

The legal rules established in procedural law are to prove that the perpetrator is guilty if the evidence is more tend to show the perpetrator's mistake. This court procedure is expected to reveal the truth, it is just too difficult to design procedural law rules that can provide the right results and satisfy the parties involved. The theory of the criminal justice system only examines the procedures and evidence that are well calculated in order to be consistent with legal objectives. One of the objectives of law is to achieve justice and the balance between rights and obligations.

Judges' decisions, if examined theoretically, and judicial practices sometimes lead to disparities in terms of prosecution. According to Packer the use of criminal sanctions randomly/indiscriminately/generously and used coercively will cause the criminal facilities to be a prime threat.[2] Likewise, Jeremy Bentham said that criminal law should not be used if it only causes groundless, needless, unprofitable or inefficacious.

2. Herbert L Packer, *The Limits of the Criminals Sanctions* (California, Stanford University Press, 1968) 87.

Criminal law and prosecution could be seen as ocean between land, where the prosecution function will bridge between error and justice.[3] This prosecution is intended to uphold the peace, safety and happiness of all humans. The context in criminal law is that a person will not endure and suffer from the mistakes of others. It is just that in its development, it is felt that criminal law cannot fulfill the sense of justice and achieve the objectives of preventing and overcoming crime.[4] The aim of prosecution in practice is always unsatisfactory because there is always a turbulence of thought between justice and certainty and the benefits of law, which have never met at an ideal level. Therefore, the prosecution is only a reflection of values and fulfills the desire for revenge solely. The most important issue in criminal law is the best form of criminal law is along with the conditions in society, criminal law reform is a necessity that brings civilization reform.[5] Therefore, criminal law should consider the opinion of Roeslan Saleh specifically related to criminal prosecutions, that criminal law as the most sensitive juridical glass, toward changes in culture, changes of social conditions in general. In criminal law, humans are bound in a way that is not only profound but also multi-aspect. Criminal law touches not only humans who commit crimes, but also offends victims.[6]

A description of the justice concept from the judge's decision above is giving bold attention to the state of the victim. Therefore, the judge, imposing an additional punishment, must pay attention to the following matters:

1. A court decision must provide a space of justice for victims of criminal acts.
2. Carried prosecution must provide a balance between the mistakes of perpetrators of crimes and the recovery of victims.
3. Use of means of restitution or compensation from the perpetrator/state against the victim.

4 CONCLUSION

Starting from the formulation of the problem and the analysis presented in the discussion, several conclusions can be drawn, as follows:

1. Additional punishment is regulated by legislation. This arrangement is contained in the KUHP and special laws, such as the Child Protection Law. This additional punishment is related to criminal acts committed by officials, recidivists, criminal acts involving relations between perpetrators and victims, as well as child victims. In the judgment of the court, additional punishment based on the provisions of the legislation is rarely used in the argument by the judge in the decision. The additional punishment can be analyzed implicitly through an analysis of the court's decision in its entirety. Whereas the additional punishment decision in custom is only related to the impact of the perpetrator's actions on the victim or related to the purpose of the sentence given.
2. Justice, in a court decision, can be reflected if the judge's decision considers the error aspect and accountability of the perpetrator, provides a balance between the mistakes of the perpetrator of the crime and the recovery of the victim and there is restitution or compensation from the perpetrator/state against the victim (harm principle).

3. Robin West, *Normative Jurisprudence* (London, Cambridge, 2015) 199.
4. Eva Achjani Zulfa, *Pergeseran Paradigma Pemidanaan* (Bandung, Indonesia: Lubuk Agung, 2010) 1.
5. Rosylin Muraskin and Albert R Roberts, *Vision For Change. Crime and Justice In The Twenty-First Century* (Upple Saddle River, NJ: Prentice Hall, 1996) 1.
6. Roeslan Saleh, *Hukum Pidana Sebagai Konprontasi Manusia Dan Manusia* (Jakarta, Indonesia: Ghalia Indonesia, 1983) 29.

REFERENCES

Muraskin, R. & Roberts, A.R. (1996). *Vision for change. Crime and justice in the twenty-first century.* Upper Saddle River, NJ: Prentice Hall.

Packer, H.L. (1968). *The limits of the criminals sanctions.* Stanford, CA: Stanford University Press.

Saleh, R. (1983). *Hukum Pidana Sebagai Konprontasi Manusia Dan Manusia.* Jakarta, Indonesia: Ghalia Indonesia.

West, R. (2015). *Normative jurisprudence.* London, UK: Cambridge University Press.

Zulfa, E.A. (2010). *Pergeseran Paradigma Pemidanaan.* Bandung, Indonesia: Lubuk Agung.

Culture and International Law - Juwana et al. (Eds)
© 2019 Taylor & Francis Group, London, ISBN 978-1-138-38766-9

Customer religiosity as the supporting factor for the success of sharia financing in micro business empowerment

Siti Hamidah
Law Faculty, Brawijaya University, Indonesia

ABSTRACT: The term religiosity is associated with diversity, solidity of belief, and appreciation of the religion one is adhering to. It shows the aspects of religion that are lived by individuals within their heart. In Islam, religiosity is reflected in the practice of faith, sharia and morals. It means that religiosity can be measured by the presence of religious institutions in all aspects of life. Islamic Financial Institutions, one of which, is a business entity based on Islamic principles and teachings. In carrying out its activities in Indonesia, this institution is based on Fatwa of the National Sharia Council of the Indonesian Ulema Council.

In practice, adherence to the provisions of sharia is deviated a lot. One of the causes is the factor of legal awareness. Based on the above background, this paper reveals customer understanding and awareness based on religiosity as the supporting factor for the success of financing for micro business actors. Low customer understanding and experience build understanding of contracts that are not in accordance with sharia provisions. Sharia contracts are often interpreted as debt agreements with the obligation to pay for the interest. However, the customer's understanding of the values of the contract, including trust, fairness, honesty, and mutual benefit, is very good in which it is inseparable from the socio-cultural influence of the local community.

KEYWORDS: religiosity, sharia financing, micro business empowerment

1 INTRODUCTION

Ibrahim Hosen mentioned that one of the functions of Islamic law is *tanzim wa islah al-ummah*; i.e. managing as well as possible and facilitating the process of social interaction so that a harmonious, safe and prosperous society can be realized (*baldatun tayyibatun wa rabbun ghafur*).[1] Therefore, in the economic field, it is appropriate for Islamic economic law to realize a prosperous society including in economic life; among others through Islamic financial institutions.

Islamic economics in Indonesia is developed based on the values of justice, togetherness, equity, and benefits in accordance with sharia principles. The principle of sharia, in this case, is based on the fatwa issued by an institution that has authority in establishing a fatwa in the field of sharia, namely the Fatwa of the National Sharia Council of the Indonesian Ulema Council (DSN-MUI). The Fatwa of the National Sharia Council is a reference for Islamic financial institutions including *Baitul Maal wat Tamwil* (BMT).

Referring to its objectives, Islamic financial institutions direct the economic activities of the people to *muamalah* in order to create economic justice, improve the quality of life of the people through opportunities for productive business activities, tackle the poverty problem, maintain

1. Amrullah Ahmad, et al, *Dimensi Hukum Islam dalam Sistem Hukum Nasional* (Jakarta, Gema Insani Press, 1966) 89-90.

economic and monetary stability, and save the dependence of Muslims from the non-Islamic economy (conventional).[2] Regarding to the compliance of sharia in *muamalah*, several studies have found interesting phenomena. For example, during the implementation of the solemnization of a marriage, some customers request to make a handshake that is believed to affect the validity of the agreement.[3] Other research also found the same thing, besides shaking hands, the Holy Qur'an is also placed on the table where the two parties make a transaction.[4]

The above two examples illustrate people's behavior in realizing trust; in addition to manifesting one of the principles of the Islamic engagement law of Illahiyah[5] in the business transaction process. The society does not only want a concept that is realized in various products and types of agreements, but also demands to display them in behavior; among others at the time the contract is pronounced.

It is different from the paradigm that has been familiar in the business world, which is only considered as profit making. This phenomenon shows the tendency of religiosity values to return to business activities. This is what causes the naming of financial institution customers who are bound for emotional religious reasons with the term emotional customer. These customers choose more financial institutions because of their inner and emotional bonds in carrying out religious duties and orders.[6] From the perspective of the implementation of a statutory law, handshake and presenting the Holy Book during the contract execution, are not strictly regulated. Even, the teachings of Islam do not require them to be in the requirements and terms of agreement.

Islamic financial institutions have several concepts as a basis for channeling funds to the public. Among the various contracts, profit sharing or *mudaraba*[7] is a contract that has more advantages than others,[8] because the concept strongly supports the realization of justice among the parties through equal opportunities in sharing profits and taking risks. The concept of profit sharing, known as *mudaraba*, is very appropriate in reviving the productive sector, especially micro-entrepreneurs who have capital constraints. Although in practice the *mudaraba* contract no longer uses profit sharing in accordance with the fatwa, but it is carried out almost the same as the interest system; i.e. determining fixed installments.

---

2. Warkum Sumitro, *Asas-Asas Perbankan Islam dan lembaga-Lembaga terkait BAMUI, Takaful, dan Pasar Modal Syariah di Indonesia* (Jakarta, PT Raja Grafindo Persada, 2004) 17-18.
3. Jazim Hamidi, et al, *Persepsi dan Sikap Masyarakat Santri Jawa Timur terhadap Bank Syariah*, (Malang, Banking Research Institute of East Java Region in collaboration with Bank Indonesia, 2006) 154.
4. Prayudo Eri Yandono, *Implementasi Etika Bisnis dalam Perspektif Hubungan Principal-Agent pada Kontrak Pembiayaan Mudharabah di Baitul Maal wat Tamwil (*Dissertation of Doctoral Degree in Economics, Not published, Faculty of Economics and Business, Brawijaya University, Malang, 2013) 243.
5. Illahiyah principle is a principle stating that every human behavior and deeds will not escape the provisions of Allah. That is mentioned in Surah Al-Hadid verse 4, that "...and He is with you wherever you are. And Allah, of what you do, is Seeing". (*the Holy Qur'an and translation.* Revised Edition. Ministry of Religion, Grafindo, 1994). It is similar to the *muamalah* activities, the act of agreement will never be separated from the values of tawhid. Thus, humans have responsibility for this. Responsibility to the community, responsibility to the second party, responsibility to oneself and responsibility to Allah. As a result, humans will not do what they want carelessly because all their actions will get a reward from Allah. See Muhammad Suakir Sula, *Asuransi Syariah (Life and General): Konsep dan Sistem Operasional* (Jakarta, Gema Insani Perss, 2004) 723-727; AM. Hasan Ali, *Asuransi dalam Perspektif Hukum Islam: Suatu Tinjauan Analisis Historis, Teoritis dan Praktis,* print 1, (Jakarta, Prenada Media, 2004) 125-126.
6. Emotional customers initially were the main market share of Islamic Financial Institutions when they first established and operated in Indonesia. However, when the emotional customer number has reached the saturation point and the competition in the market share of Islamic Financial Institutions for emotional customers is getting tighter, then the actors of Islamic Financial Institutions begin to switch to the rational customer. This change in market share should be followed by higher levels of professionalism.
7. The type of sharia bank fund disbursement to customers is based on the concept of profit sharing in which the bank acts as the funder and the customer as the *mudarib*, by agreeing on the profit ratio on the results of the business.
8. Atin Meriati Isnaini, 'Reconstruction Principles of Justice Funding Aqad Banking System in Partnership with Shari'ah' (2013) 4(6, November) *Academic Research International* www.journals.savap.org.pk (ISSN-L: 2223-9553, ISSN: 2223-9944) 71-77.

The above deviations are agreed by the parties, especially customers. It might be caused by several possibilities. First, the customer does not understand the Sharia contract. Second, halal term is not considered essential. Third, the inability of the customer to refuse because he/she is in a weak position compared to other parties (Islamic Financial Institutions are more dominant from the financial side), so customers are forced to accept the contract even though they actually do not understand the contract. Fourth, the Sharia Financial Institution has provided a contract in the form of a standard contract or a non-negotiable standard.

The main character of the Sharia contract is based on Islamic law. In Indonesia, Islamic financial institutions are also subject to Indonesian agreement law; the Civil Code. There are some fundamental differences between the two because Islamic law is based on the divine principle that governs all human actions while the Civil Code is a Dutch inheritance. In western law, it holds a separation between God's relationship with humans and humans with humans[9]. In the Civil Code, the value of *illahiyah* is not recognized since the agreement has been free from the sacred element. This is different from the *santri* (moslem students) community in Indonesia who commonly hold religious values. So, it is natural that the people who still adhere to these religious values demand to do things that are in accordance with their religious rituals in making transactions. However, the second phenomenon above raises the assumption that the *illahiyah* value which was originally upheld in the *santri* community in understanding the sharia contract has shifted in accordance with the Civil Code. In the other word, long as it is in accordance with the Civil Code, the sharia contract has been considered to fulfill the legal requirements of the agreement.

Reviewing further from the perspective of law enforcement, the above two phenomena are in the opposite position. The first phenomenon shows the desire to fulfill the provisions of sharia, even asking to do things that are not regulated in legal norms. On the contrary, there are things that are contrary to what should be done.

In the context of law enforcement, the aspects of society and culture play an important role. This research examines and explains the phenomenon of the meaning of sharia contract, especially the Sharia contract conducted by the community in making transactions with Islamic Financial Institutions. It has been well-known that legal theory has a role in the re-establishment of society. Many legal philosophers, such as Hegel's philosophy, admit to having given a comprehensive solution to all problems[10].

This paper goes from the legal issue of the gap between das sein and das sollen. Islamic Financial Institutions of Indonesia are obliged to implement sharia principles. There are several contract practices that are not in accordance with sharia, even "excessive" in interpreting sharia. This is something interesting. Exploring the customer's understanding of the concept of the Shariah contract is very important to be carried out in order to know their perception of the important principles that exist in the Sharia contract.

2 DISCUSSION

In *mudaraba* financing, Islamic Financial Institutions are the fund owners. This first party gives confidence to micro business actors in developing their business while the second party is called a customer (*mudarib*). Trust in managing funds is used to carry out productive and

9. Basically, the principle of *Pacta Sunt Servanda* has similarities with the *illahiyah* principle. According to its history, the principle of *Pacta Sunt Servanda* is familiar in the church law; it mentions that an agreement occurs when the two parties are strengthened by an oath. This implies that every agreement made by both parties is a sacred act that is associated with religious elements. However, in its development, the principle of *Pacta Sunt Servanda* is meant by "pactum" which means agreeing not to be strengthened by oaths and other formalities while the *nudus pactum* is enough to agree. See Salim, *Hukum Kontrak Teori dan Teknik Penyusunan Kontrak* (Jakarta: Sinar Grafika, 2004), 10.
10. W. Friedmann, *Teori & Filsafat Hukum, Telaah Kritis atas Teori-Teori Hukum (Susunan I),* (Jakarta, Rajawali Pers, 1990) 19.

profitable businesses, by mutually sharing profits in accordance with the profit-sharing ratio agreed upon and set forth in the *mudaraba* financing agreement. The rights and obligations of the parties are regulated in the agreement or contract of *mudaraba* financing.

Mudaraba financing agreement is a contract that has a risk of the occurrence of asymmetric information from customers. So, the first party must be really careful before giving a decision. All information about prospective customers must be obtained completely in order not to pose a risk in the future. Some aspects that are taken into consideration by the first party are a good level of profitability, elements that contain low uncertainty, low business monitoring costs, a good rate of return, a short period of time for refunds, and a supporting financial cash flow report. The analysis phase is carried out to further explore the proposed application which is carried out by the marketing department; it is by focusing on the juridical aspects of prospective customers, technical production, marketing, and collateral assessments to determine the value of collateral. This stage certainly does not allow an analysis based on the religiosity of the second party as a matter of first party consideration because this will be debated as a sensitive matter.

Similarly, in the next stage, the decision by the breaker committee is to complete the required documents, especially the original collateral document (Motor Vehicle Ownership or land/building certificate), signing of the *mudaraba* financing agreement and disbursement of financing. However, in terms of the customer's perspective, it is the willingness to keep the contents of the agreement and apply the mandate.

In exploring customer's understanding of religious values and their realization in the contract, there are several elements that become benchmarks. First is the understanding of the process, the second is collateral, the third is the profit determination ratio, and the fourth is the values contained in the *mudaraba* contract.

2.1 *Customer understanding of* Mudaraba *contract*

The process of obtaining *mudaraba* financing commonly takes a long time, because of the precautionary principle. *Mudaraba*, as a type of partnership contract, requires parties to share benefits and risks. The first party, in deciding to accept or reject an application, requires a relatively long time with the aim of obtaining complete information of the prospective customer, as well as a careful calculation of the business to be financed with the aim of avoiding the risk at the future.

The length of this process often leads to customer dissatisfaction. From the results of interviews with customers, it turns out that the customers did not question the suitability of the *mudaraba* contract signed with the one they should. The focus and attention of the customer is more on the amount of funding needed to develop its business, not in the process and calculation of the *mudaraba* contract based on the concept of profit sharing. Both parties in realizing the mudaraba financing agreement are not in accordance with the provisions of the Fatwa of DSN-MUI. The Fatwa of DSN-MUI No. 07/DSN-MUI/IV/2000 concerning *mudaraba* financing (*qiradh*) is a special fatwa concerning *mudaraba* financing which serves as a guideline for the implementation of financing for the Sharia Financial Institution in Indonesia.

The disagreements include, among other, the first party does not finance all business needs but only part of the need. The second party also does not explain the ratio or profit-sharing ratio but only determines exactly the obligations that must be paid by the customer, without considering whether the business being financed is in profit or loss. This is contrary to the first provision of the Fatwa of DSN-MUI which states that, "Sharia Financial Institutions, as providers of funds, bear all losses due to *mudaraba* unless *mudarib* (customers) make deliberate, negligent, or violate the agreements."

Determining fixed unilateral profits also indicates a discrepancy with the provisions of the two Fatwas of DSN-MUI relating to benefits that require:

a. It must be reserved for both parties and should not be required only for one party.
b. Part of the proportional profit for each party must be known and stated at the time the contract is agreed upon and must be in the form of a percentage (ratio) of profits according to the agreement. Change in the ratio must be based on the agreement.

c. The fund provider bears all losses due to *mudaraba* and the manager may not bear any loss except as a result of intentional error, negligence, or breach of the agreement.[11]

Reviewing from the agreement of this contract, then it would be more appropriate to use the debt contracts. Meanwhile, based on the Fatwa of DSN-MUI concerning capital provisions (a sum of money and/or assets provided by the fund provider to *mudarib* for business purposes) it is expressly required that "capital cannot be in the form of receivables and must be paid to *mudarib*, either gradually or not which is in accordance with the agreement in the contract.[12]" The last part of the process of creating the *mudaraba* financing agreement between the first party and the customer is in the form of reading and signing of the contract of *mudaraba* financing in the form of a written agreement namely "*mudaraba* profit sharing contract". This contract has been standardized and has been prepared in advance by the finance bookkeeping administration department to be read and signed by each party. As a standard contract in general, parties who have a stronger position usually use the opportunity to determine certain clauses in the contents of the contract. Therefore, the contract, that is supposed to be designed by the parties, is not found in the contract format of standard agreement. As a result, it raises an unbalanced position, because it is more beneficial for one party.

It can be concluded that the actual *mudaraba* financing contract that is not a *mudaraba* agreement that is in accordance with the character of the *mudaraba* contract. Even though in reality the parties can still receive and carry out the profit-sharing cooperation as stated in the contract. The factor that encourages the continuation of the contract is the willingness and trust between the parties. Because the parties believe that financing will be able to improve economic prosperity through a growing business.

Basically, the *mudaraba* contract is based on trust. This principle of trust (*amanah*) implies that each party is sincere (voluntary) and has good faith in *mudaraba* transaction, and believes that each party will not exploit its partners. With this volunteerism, each party will depend on the honesty of its partners.

In analyzing phenomena that rely solely on volunteerism and honesty, it should be studied based on the pillars and the terms of the contract, as well as the contracts which are forbidden in Islam. Islam prohibits a contract that is carried out without volunteerism, besides that there is also a prohibition on the contract which is carried out in an innocent manner (*al-akl bil bathil*), and must still comply with the prohibition in the transaction; for example, when it contains *usury, maysir* and *gharar*. Indeed, voluntary (*ridha al-taradhi*) is an abstract mental attitude. Therefore, in realizing this inner attitude, the implementation of the courtesy is required. The term of the *mudaraba* agreement is realized by shaking hands with each other in addition to the presence of the Holy Qur'an placed near the parties who are making agreement.

Based on the above description, it appears that the customers actually do not understand the essence of the character of the *mudaraba* contract. However, the contract is still carried out due to the needs, trust, and sincerity. Reviewing from the law regarding the contract, it has not fulfilled the pillars and the terms of the contract according to sharia, even though based on Article 1320 the Civil Code it has fulfilled the requirements.

Customer compliance is also related to security or collateral. This collateral is intended to guarantee the orderly repayment so that it is paid on the accurate time and amount based on the agreement that they have agreed upon previously.

Provisions on collateral are actually not an obligation, but it changes into a policy that requires someone to secure funds that have been distributed. Thus, the customer promises to bind themselves to submit collateral and make binding in accordance with the applicable laws and regulations in which it is an integral part of this agreement.

---

11. The second provision of the Fatwa of DSN-MUI No. 07/DSN-MUI/IV/2000 Concerning Financing of *Mudaraba* (*Qiradh*)
12. Ibid.

Actually, *mudaraba* financing with the concept of partnership cooperation does not require the delivery of collateral. Some Imam of Islamic law schools even state that the *mudaraba* contract is null and void if it requires collateral. The other Imam stated that it is only the collateral contract but the *mudaraba* contract is still valid. However, Imam Maliki and Imam Shafi'i argued that in the *mudaraba* agreement, the action is totally illegitimate because *mudaraba* is a cooperative agreement regarding joint efforts with the parties to agree on the profit sharing of business profits.[13]

Based on the Fatwa of DSN-MUI, *mudaraba* provisions on collateral are more flexible in their practices. DSN-MUI stipulates that "basically, *mudaraba* financing has no collateral; however, to anticipate that the *mudarib* does not commit irregularities, Islamic Financial Institutions may request collateral from *mudarib* or the third parties. This guarantee can only be disbursed if the *mudarib* is proven to have violated the matters agreed upon in the contract".

The customer's opinion about the guarantee obligation in the financing agreement is considered not burdensome. Collateral is a natural thing as is the custom in other financial institutions. It shows a lack of understanding of the *mudaraba* concept so that they equate it with a debt agreement which encourages reasonable thinking of collateral in contracts that should only be about sharing benefits and risks.

2.2 *BMT customer's understanding on values in the* Mudaraba *contract*

The presence of Islamic Financial Institutions, although it has not fully carried out the concept in accordance with Sharia duties, is recognized to reduce the practice of loan sharks; in addition to developing a productive business and micro business investment.

In exploring the customer's understanding of sharia values in the *mudaraba* contract, the researcher determines in advance some important values in the sharia contract, especially the *mudaraba* contract. This contract gives the parties the position as partners who work on the basis of trust or belief. On this basis, every profit or income earned must be divided according to the agreement. The same thing applies if a loss occurs in which it must be shared equally. This fair share will not be achieved if there is no openness and honesty among the parties. Thus, it is expected that this collaboration will benefit both parties. Based on the above description, it can be concluded that there are 4 main values inherent in this contract, namely (1) trust, (2) fair, (3) honesty and (4) mutually beneficial relationships.

The trust value firstly arises from the Sharia Financial Institution, because they will not channel the financing to the customers they do not trust. The customers also believe that they feel chosen because the Islamic Financial Institution trusts their reputation. This trust will lead to the continuation of the next collaboration.

Trust or belief is a major factor in this contract relationship. In a variety of business relationships, trust is very important in *mudaraba* contract because trust is the foundation for Islamic Financial Institutions as legitimate in deciding and providing business financing to customers as the *mudarib*. Trust is a form of decision taken by Islamic Financial Institutions to take risks in a relationship that is based on a feeling of confidence that each party will do something as expected and will always act in a pattern of mutual support and will not take actions that harm the institution and others.

Respondents believe that the principle of trust and trustworthiness is a condition for achieving halal and blessed property. Halal and blessed property will be used to obtain happiness in the world and the hereafter. To obtain halal and blessed property, one must adhere to ethical values; those derived from religious values and culture that are upheld by the community, with the main aim of building trust so that the business can last long.

The second value is justice. One customer interpreted the value of justice as a fair treatment because he/she was helped, so they had to pay; especially because of the verses of the Holy

13. Sutan Remy Sjahdeini, *Perbankan Islam dan Kedudukannya Dalam Tata Hukum Perbankan Indonesia* (Jakarta, Pustaka Utama Grafiti, 1999) 168.

Qur'an in the contract. Based on the *mudaraba* financing agreement signed by the parties, the *mudaraba* financing agreement includes the verses of the Holy Qur'an. One of the verses included in the contract is Surah Al-Ma'idah verse 8 which means, "...Be just; that is nearer to righteousness. And fear Allah; indeed, Allah is Acquainted with what you do". This verse implies that the substance of a value of justice is to protect the rights and obligations of every human being and lead to the right path and accepted by Allah, as the word of God in the Holy Qur'an Surah Asy-Shuraa verse 17, which means, "It is Allah who has sent down the Book in truth and [also] the balance".

Third is the value of honesty. The meaning of honesty is reflected in the use of *mudaraba* funds honestly and in accordance with a mutually agreed contract. The value of honesty is indeed believed by business people as a collateral and a basis for good and long-term business activities. In business, honesty finds its form in the fulfillment of the terms of the agreement, and guarantees the quality of goods and services, as well as fair employment relationships.

The last value in the *mudaraba* agreement is to provide mutual benefits to the parties. The phrase "mutual benefits" implies that the income earned in a certain period a small portion is used to share profits with Islamic Financial Institutions without any element of lies, fraud or manipulation of revenue engineering. *Mudharib* attitude or behavior leads to the behavior of an economic agent in accordance with the moral demands that are commendable and not merely selfish.

This *mudaraba* agreement will run well if it contains trust, honesty, justice and mutual transaction between the parties. Firmly holding trust/trustworthiness, honesty, openness and fairness are the solid foundation in the behavior of a businessman.

3 CONCLUSIONS

The level of understanding of BMT customers on the concept of *mudaraba* contract is still low. However, honesty and obedience based on religious reasons have encouraged the customers to keep the contents of the agreement, even though the agreement actually does not meet the requirements of sharia. Understanding that is not yet intact on the contract is generally only based on information from the Sharia Financial Institution; in addition to personal experience of being a customer of a conventional financial institution and experience owing to loan sharks or family. The above description forms an understanding of the *mudaraba* contract that is not in accordance with the provisions of sharia.

However, the understanding of BMT customers on contract values; i.e. trust, fairness, honesty and mutual benefit, is generally very good. This should be the main thing for Sharia Financial Institutions to foster successful financing.

REFERENCES

Ahmad, Amrullah, et al, *Dimensi Hukum Islam dalam Sistem Hukum Nasional.* (Jakarta: Gema Insani Press, 1966)

Ali, AM. Hasan, *Asuransi dalam Perspektif Hukum Islam: Suatu Tinjauan Analisis Historis, Teoritis dan Praktis*, print. 1, (Jakarta, Prenada Media, 2004)

Al-Quran dan terjemahannya.

Friedmann, W., *Teori & Filsafat Hukum, Telaah Kritis atas Teori-Teori Hukum (Susunan I)*, (Jakarta, Rajawali Pers, 1990)

Isnaini, Atin Meriati, 'Reconstruction Principles Of Justice Funding Aqad Banking System In Partnership With Shari'ah' (2013) 4(6)*Academic Research International* <www.journals.savap.org.pk≥< ISSN-L: 2223-9553, ISSN: 2223-9944, 71-77.

Salim, *Hukum Kontrak Teori dan Teknik Penyusunan Kontrak* (Jakarta: Sinar Grafika, 2004)

Sjahdeini, Sutan Remy, *Perbankan Islam dan Kedudukannya Dalam Tata Hukum Perbankan Indonesia* (Jakarta, Pustaka Utama Grafiti, 1999)

Sula, Muhammad Suakir, *Asuransi Syariah (Life and General): Konsep dan Sistem Operasional, cet.1* (Jakarta, Gema Insani Perss, 2004)

Sumitro, Warkum, *Asas-Asas Perbankan Islam dan lembaga-Lembaga terkait BAMUI, Takaful, dan Pasar Modal Syariah di Indonesia* (Jakarta, PT RajaGrafindo Persada, 2004)

Hamidi, Jazim, et. al, *Persepsi dan Sikap Masyarakat Santri Jawa Timur terhadap Bank Syariah* (Malang: Lembaga Riset Perbankan Daerah Jawa Timur bekerja sama dengan Bank Indonesia, 2006).

Yandono, Prayudo Eri, 2013, *Implementasi Etika Bisnis dalam Perspektif Hubungan Principal-Agent pada Kontrak Pembiayaan Mudharabah di Baitul Maal wat Tamwil*, (Disertasi, Program Doktor Ilmu Ekonomi, Tidak dipublikasikan, Fakultas Ekonomi & Bisnis, Universitas Brawijaya, Malang)

Hamidah, Siti, Kajian Yuridis terhadap Penggabungan 2 (dua) Akad pada Perjanjian Mudharabah wal Murabahah, (DPP-SPP, Fakultas Hukum Universitas Brawijaya, Malang, 2013)

Culture and International Law - Juwana et al. (Eds)
© 2019 Taylor & Francis Group, London, ISBN 978-1-138-38766-9

Yama and *niyama*: Ethical points in a sixteenth-century Javanese *tutur* text

Abimardha Kurniawan & Titik Pudjiastuti
Literature Studies, Faculty of Humanities, Universitas Indonesia, Indonesia

ABSTRACT: This paper discusses the concepts of ethics in the *Uttaraśabda* – a Javanese *tutur* text from circa the sixteenth century. In the *tutur* textual corpus, the descriptions of ethical issues focusing on good or bad conduct becomes a special term called *yama*, 'reining, control'. The concept of *yama* cannot be separated from its opposite called *niyama*, 'positive duties, observances'. In the old Javanese literary tradition, there is a genre named *śāsana* (for example, *Wratiśāsana, Ṛṣīśasana* and *Ślokāntara*), which specifically contains a list of ethical issues. Although most of the *Uttaraśabda* text comprises the dialogs on philosophical basics of the *maweda* ritual, in certain passages there are some explanations of ethics that should be obeyed by every religious practitioner. They integrate, as inseparable parts, in the whole textual unity, as they also determine whether a religious practice is successful or not.

Through hermeneutics and intertextual approaches, it can be seen that although the ethical concepts in *Uttaraśabda* are oriented to an individual person who makes an effort to achieve liberation (*kalĕpasan*) by practicing yoga, they are essentially integrated into a universal concept of social relations, especially interhuman relationships. When they are traced back, the ethical guidelines in *Uttaraśabda* are based on the elementary stages of *Patañjali's* (circa fourth CE) *aṣṭangga* yoga. They are also generally imbued by the points of *dharmaśāstra*. The textual sources used in this study are the manuscripts from *Merapi-Merbabu*. The manuscript collection from this scriptoria still needs more reviews to unearth their significance in the humanities.

KEYWORDS: *tutur, yama niyama,* ethics, hermeneutics, intertextual

1 INTRODUCTION

The Javanese *tutur* text, *Uttaraśabda*, is relatively unknown. Although there is no internal information that gives a clue about when and where it was composed and who was the composer, it can be approximated that *Uttaraśabda* is a textual product from the post-*Majapahit* era (*terminus a quo*), and it grew in the religious circle. Its language characteristics bear a resemblance to the early Javanese Islamic texts.[1] Therefore, we surmise that *Uttaraśabda* was composed around the sixteenth century.

The speculation about the ritual named *maweda* – the recitation of sacred formulas or mantras to make the divine power attend into the practitioner's body – dominates *Uttaraśabda* textual substance. The practice of the *maweda* ritual is generally similar to yoga. Its main goal is mystical union to the Supreme Reality. If we understood that *Uttaraśabda* contains a theoretical description of yoga – even with a specific perspective – then we can assume that the text

1. GWJ Drewes, *Een Javaanse Primbon Uit de Zestiende Eeuw: Opniew Uitgegeven En Vertald* (Leiden : E.J. Brill, 1945); GWJ Drewes, 'The Admonitions of She Bari' (1969) 9 *Bibliotheca Indonesica*; GWJ Drewes, 'An Early Javanese Code of Muslim Ethics' (1978) 18 *Bibliotheca Indonesica*.

of *Uttaraśabda* is a later development of the earlier theoretical traditions, especially those that had developed in the corpus of old Javanese religious texts.

One of the significant parts within the structure of an old Javanese religious text related to the yoga tradition is the issue on religious ethics, morals or the instruction about good and evil that every practitioner must obey.[2] The religious ethics formulation is presented through a technical term named *yama* (root √*yam*) 'restraint'.[3] *Yama* cannot be separated from *niyama* 'observance'. Both of them support each other to constitute an ethical structure that has universal and particular values simultaneously.

Yama is often considered to have universal value, but it is also often articulated in various ways. *Uttaraśabda* has a different articulation of *yama* (and *niyama*) to other religious texts. So, how does *Uttaraśabda* articulate the concept of *yama*? Is there a relationship between *yama* (and *niyama*) in *Uttaraśabda* with the ethical concepts in other texts? This paper will discuss these two issues by comparing *Uttaraśabda* to other texts which also have discussions on *yama* and *niyama*.

2 METHODOLOGY

The *Uttaraśabda* text is documented in about 26 manuscripts: eight manuscripts originating from Java,[4] while the eighteen other manuscripts are from Bali.[5] The manuscripts from each region have editorial differences, although substantially they do not contradict each other. Because the textual edition of *Uttaraśabda* has never been published, this study will based on the raw textual material. However, to reduce the problems that arise due to textual variation in every manuscript, this study will create a limitation by choosing two selected textual sources: one manuscript from Java and one from Bali. The Javanese manuscript taken as the textual source is manuscript PNRI 1 L 170. It originated from Mt. Merbabu in Central Java (dated from 1585 Śaka Merapi-Merbabu, circa 1668 AD). While the Balinese version used is Kirtya's manuscript, in other words, K 247. This is a copy of a manuscript owned by *Gria Pemaron, Munggu, Badung*. The other manuscripts will also be used as comparison if there are incorrect or elusive readings in the textual sources.

Understanding the concept of *yama* and *niyama* in *Uttaraśabda*, means that we should place this text in a tradition web of ethical thought in general. However, by considering the cultural relativism, we should also consider the that ethical concept in *Uttaraśabda* needs to be comprehended from a certain perspective. Therefore, an intertextual approach will be relevant to apply in this study. *Yama* in *Uttaraśabda* is conceptually inseparable from the earlier textual traditions – as the text is essentially a mosaic of citations from previous texts[6] – especially the texts with ethical concepts of *brāhmana* life, both from old Java and India. Interpreting the differences and distinctiveness of the *yama* concept in *Uttaraśabda* means making a comparison with other texts. Thus, the scope of comparative data used in this study must at least have an explicit description of *yama* in its formal structure.

2. K Bertens, *Etika* (Jakarta : Gramedia Pustaka Utama, 1993).
3. M Monier-Williams, *A Sanskrit-English Dictionary* (Oxford: Clarendon Press, 1899).
4. TE Behrend, *Katalog Induk Naskah-Naskah Nusantara Jilid 4 Perpustakaan Nasional Republik Indonesia* (Jakarta: Yayasan Obor Indonesia., 1998); Kartika Setyawati, I Kuntara Wiryamartana and Willem Van der Molen, *Katalog Naskah Merapi-Merbabu Perpustakaan Nasional Republik Indonesia* (Yogyakarta and Leiden: Penerbitan Universitas Sanata Dharma and Opleiding Talen en Culturen van Zuidoost-Azië en Oceanië Universitiet Leiden, 2002).
5. Th Pigeaud, *Literature of Java: Catalogue Raisonné of Javanese Manuscripts in the Library of the University of Leiden and Other Public Collections in the Netherlands* (The Hague: Martinus Nijhoff., 3 Volumes); Jan Just Witkam, *Inventory of the Oriental Manuscripts of the Library of University Leiden* (Leiden: Ter Lugt Press, 19 Volumes).
6. Judith Still and Michael Worton, *Intertextuality: Theories and Practices* (Manchester: Manchester University Press, 1990).

2.1 *Yama and niyama in old Javanese texts*

In their development along history, the concepts of *yama* and *niyama* have experienced many changes in number and arrangement. Although the technical term *yama* has been known since the Vedic era, there are no details about the list of mental qualities included in it. These details just appear in the later texts, such as *upaniṣad, puraṇa, dharmaśāstra*, as well as *tantra* and *āgama*. There are variations between five and ten ethical points that are included in *yama* or *niyama*.[7] Not only in the texts from India, the same conditions also occurred in the old Javanese texts.

An old Javanese text, *Sarasamusccaya* (265—266) describes ten categories of properties which include *yama* and ten which include *niyama*. The ten traits included in *yama* according to *Sarasamusccaya* are: (1) *ānṛśaṅsya*, (2) *kṣamā*, (3) *satya*, (4) *ahiṅsā*, (5) *dama*, (6) *ārjjawa*, (7) *prīti*, (8) *prasābha*, (9) *mādhuryya*, (10) *māddawa*. An explanation for each point mentioned is:

> *ānṛśaṅsya, si harimbawa, tan swārtha kewala, kṣamā, si kělan ring panas tis, satya, si tan mṛṣowāda, ahiṅsā, manukhe sarwwa bhāwa, dama, si upaśama wruh mituturi manahnya, arjawwa, si duga-dugāběněr, prīti, si gěng karuna, prasābha, hěning ning manah, mādhurya, manis ning wulat lawan wuwus, māddawa, pěs ning manah.*

Thus, (1) *ānṛśaṅsya* means a sympathetic person who is not selfish; (2) *kṣamā* means someone who ...; (3) *satya* means someone who does not like to lie; (4) *ahiṅsā* means to make all beings happy; (5) *dama* is someone who is calm and knows how to speak his mind; (6) *arjawwa* is someone who is always open; (7) *prīti* is someone who has great compassion; (8) *prasābha* is someone who is clear in his mind; (9) mādhurya means sweet in appearance and speech; (10) *māddawa* means soft inside.

Meanwhile, according to *Sarasamuccaya*, ten points concerning *niyama* are: (1) *dāna*, (2) *ijwā*, (3) *tapa*, (4) *dwāna*, (5) *swādhwāya*, (6) *upasthanigraha*, (7) *brata*, (8) *upawāsa*, (9) *mauda* and (10) *snāna*. The explanations of these are:

> *dāna, weweh, annadānādi, ijwā, dewa pūjā, pitṛpūjādi, tapa, kāyasangśoṣaṇa, kasatan ikang śarīra, bhūśayyā, jalatyāgādi, dwāna, ikang śiwasmaraṇa, swādhwāya, wedābhyāṣa, upasthanigraha, kahṛtaning upastha, brata, annawarjjādi, upawāsa, mauda, wācangyama, kahṛtaning ujar, haywa kěcěk kuněng, snāna, trisangdhyā sewana, madyusa ring kāla ning sandhya.*

Thus, (1) *dāna* means always to give; (2) *ijwā* means to give *pujas* to the deity and ancestors; (3) *tapa* or *kāyasangśoṣaṇa* means that his body dries up, sleeps on the ground without layer and abstains from water; (4) *dwāna* means meditation to the soul; (5) *swādhwāya* means to always study *weda*; (6) *upasthanigraha* means to control the genitals; (7) *brata* means ...; (8) *upawāsa* means to fast; (9) *mauda* or *wācangmaya* means to hold speech and not always talk; (10) *snāna* means doing trident *puja*, bathing/purifying oneself when the time changes.

As far as we know, there is no old Javanese text which gives ten categories of *yama* and *niyama* besides *Sarasamuccaya*. On average, the old Javanese texts give five points of *yama* and *niyama*.

An old Javanese text that comes from around the fourteenth century, named *Dharma Patañjala*, gives details of five *yama* and five *niyama* that parallel *Patañjali's Yogaśūtra* (2.30–2.45). The *Dharma Patañjala* (32) explanations about each point that are included in the groups of *yama* and *niyama* are as follows:

> ***yama*** *ngaranya*, ***ahingsā, satya, astainya, brahmacāri, aparigraha,***
>
> ***ahingsā*** *ngaranya, tan pamati-mati, sahana ni prāṇi tan pātyana ikā kabeh, lāwan patyanta takut ni māwak pati, matangnyan māhābrata ngaran sang wiku tan pamāti māti, hana ta wuwusning waneh, tan aparak wang-wang māti-māti sattwa, yan carwa ri sang hyang, athawā bhojana kunang, mangkana pakěnanya, tātan mangkana sang yogi, nihan*

7. Sudarshana Devi, *Wṛhaspati-Tattwa: An Old Javanese Philosophical Text* (New Delhi: International Academy of Indian Culture, 1957); Sharada Rani, *Ślokāntara, an Old Javanese Didactic Text. Critically Edited and Anotated* (Nagpur: International Academy of Indian Culture, 1957).

waneh tanpa matyana sattwa yan parwaṇikāla, tatān mangkana sang yogi, pisan ingusirān pamaty ana sarwa sattwa, ya ta sinangguh ahingsā ngaranya, ***satya*** *ngaranya, tan madwa ri bratanya, tan madwa mowus, tan pangahala nguniweh malinga mas, ya sinangguh* ***astainya*** *ngaranya,* ***brahmacāri*** *ngaranya, yatanyan tan kalalaran asamādhi, ya doning tan parabi, yekā brahmacāri ngaranya,* ***aparigraha*** *ngaranya, tar pangaku sarwa drawya, nāhan lakṣaṇaning* ***yama*** *brata.* (*Dharma Patañjala* 32; Acri, 2011, pp. 309–311)[8]

[*Yama* means *ahingsā, satya, astainya, brahmacarī, aparigraha. Ahingsā* means not to kill any living things that are not allowed to be killed or to kill beings who fear death. Therefore, it is special that a priest does not kill. Some are taught that is, not associating with people who often kill animals, if it is not intended as an offering to the gods, or just to be eaten, so it should be. A yogin should not be like that. In addition, do not kill animals during the turn of the month. Then, he will be expelled if he kills all animals. That is what is called *ahingsā. Satya* means, not being ambivalent in action, not ambivalent in speech, not speaking ill of [others]. Not stealing gold, that is what he calls *astainya. Brahmacāri* is the name, it does not pollute its silly efforts by not marrying a woman. That is what is called *brahmacāri.* Called *aparigraha*, it does not claim *egala* who belongs to him. That is what is included in *yama*.]

Furthermore, the text of *Dharma Patañjala* also outlines the five points of *niyama*, namely:

niyama *ngaranya,>* ***śauca, santoṣa, tapa, swādhyāya, īśwarapraṇidhāna***,

śauca *ngaranya, maradināwak, lāwan ambĕk haywa ta kawaśa dening rāga dweṣa moha, maradina mowus, haywa muwusakĕn manglareri waneh, maradina molah, haywa makolah durbhyāsana, maradin amangan, haywa pinangan ikang senuhutakĕn panganĕn sang wiku, lāwan inumĕnirājñāna, yekā sinangguh śauca ngaranya, <**santoṣa** ngaranya,> solihanira nasi atah santoṣaknanira, athawā solihnira tinanĕm i patapanira, ya santoṣaknanira, <**tapa** ngaranya,> ikang indriya kabeh prihĕn sakitana, ri brata lāwan samādhi, yatanyan tan padadyakĕna rāga yan panon wiṣaya kalinganya, tan garjita yan pangrĕngö kidung menak, athawā panggĕla kunang, ilatnya muhārāmet pinangan, yan pamangan rasa menak, nahan laca-laca ning tapa ngaranya, **swādhyāya** ngaranya agĕlĕm angunyakĕn mantra, astāwa ri bhaṭāra, **īśvarapraṇidhāna** ngaranya, umangĕn-angĕn kasūkṣman bhaṭāra ri rat kabeh, nguniveh ry awaknira asthityana bhaṭāra, yatanyan siddhi samādhi, yekā īśvarapraṇidhāna ngaranya.* (*Dharma Patañjala* 32; Acri, 2011, pp. 310–312)

[*Niyama* includes among others, *auca, santoṣa, tapa, swādhyāya* and *īśwarapraṇidhāna. Śauca*, means cleansing the body and mind so as not to be overcome by anger, jealousy and delusion. Cleansing speech so as not to harm others. Cleanse the deed, so as not to run bad habits. . . .]

Other old Javanese texts which also mention the five points of *yama* and *niyama* are *Wṛhaspatitattwa* (60—61) and *Wratiśāsana* (4). Each point mentioned in both texts is identical and parallel. It is just that *Wṛhaspatitattwa* used the term *daśaśīla* 'ten conducts' to refer to a combination of five *yama* and five *niyama*. The description of *yama* and *niyama* in the Wratiśāsana (4–5) are as follows:

Ahingsā*, nga, tan pamati-mati,* ***brahmacarya****, nga, tan kĕneng stri,* ***satya****, nga, tuhu mojar,* ***awyaharikam****, nga, tan pawyawahara,* ***asteya****, nga, tan cidra ring drĕwyaning len. Ika ta kalima* ***yama*** *brata ling bhaṭāra Rudra.*

[*Ahingsā* means not to kill. *Brahmacarya* means untouched by women. *Satya* means correct in saying. *Awyaharikam* means not having disagreements with others. *Asteya* means not violating the property of others. That is five *yama* as said by Lord Rudra.]

Akrodha, nga, tan kataman krodha, guru śuśrūṣa, nga, lot karakĕt ing guru, makanimitta hyunira angrĕngwa warah sang guru, śoca, nga, nitya soccarccananing bhaṭāra, aralagawa,

8. Andrea Acri, *Dharma Patañjala: A Saiva Scripture from Ancient Java, Studied in the Light of Related Old Javanese and Sanskrit Texts* (Leiden: Leiden University, 2011).

nga, tan barang-barang ring pinangan, apramadha, nga, tan palĕh-palĕh, mangabyasa sang hyang kabujanggan. Ika ta kalima, niyama brata ling bhaṭāra Śiwa.

[*Akrodha* means not being struck by anger. *Guruśuśrūṣā* means always approaching the teacher, because of his desire to hear the teachings from the teacher. *Śoca* means always worshiping *bhaṭāra. Aralagawa* means not eating carelessly. *Apramadha* means not neglecting to study the *kabujanggan*. These are the five *niyama* as said by *Bhaṭāra Śiwa*.]

2.2 *Yama in Uttaraśabda*

In *Uttaraśabda*, a description of *yama* is conveyed after the *Uttaraśabda* asks about everything that follows good and evil conditions (*ala ayu*). *Ajñanaśura* then answers it with a description of *yama*. According to these initial conversations, it is known that *yama* is not something strange. It exists in the same sphere (and perhaps it is very close) to human life, which contains both good and evil simultaneously. *Yama* refers to human behavior that must be avoided.

Uttaraśabda follows the textual tradition which states that *yama* consists of five points, such as the P*atañjali' Yogaśūtra, Wratiśāsana* and *Wṛhaspatitattwa*. However, *Uttaraśabda* uses technical terms that are very different, such as *surat, maka, jogor, manik* and *purbalodra*. Maybe they are very strange. The first four terms among the five were adopted from the names of Lord Yama's troops (*yamabala*) in the old Javanese and Balinese eschatological narratives. Their names are *Suratma* and *Jogormanik* (Hinzler, 1981). In this case, it seems clear that *Uttaraśabda* identifies *yama* as the ethical concept through *yama* as the name of the god.

2.3 *Surat*

***surat** ngaranya, sukambĕknya lamun katuwukan kaarĕpnya, priyatin lamun anganggo ala. ya ta **surat** ngaranya.*

[*Surat* means if he is satisfied with all his desires, is concerned when wearing something bad. That is *surat*.]

The literal meaning of *surat*, 'lines, writing, pictures',[9] is not related to the concepts presented in the text. Perhaps, the term letter is an adaptation of the Sanskrit word *surata*; 'great pleasure or joy'.[10] Unfortunately, the relationship between letters and *surata* cannot be ascertained yet. The term letter is conceptualized as a feeling of pleasure when someone satisfies himself with clothes, jewelry or any material that can be used as a physical decorator (in contrast to the Balinese version of the text which places the word *bhūṣana*, 'jewelry, party dress', as the object, K 247). Instead, he will be sad if he only wears bad clothes.

The concept of *yama* and *niyama* in other texts never mentions good and luxurious clothing or jewelry. Even so, excessive desire for material things is still not a good thing. That can trigger greed (*lobha*). It is possible that the nature of the letter relates to *śauca* 'maintaining purity' in *Patañjali's* concept. According to him, the purity of the mind can only be achieved if one detaches himself from all worldly desires (*Yogasūtra*, 2.40–2.41). Indeed, in its tradition, someone who takes the path of asceticism will leave all luxury, including luxury in clothing and jewelry. He will replace everything with clothes from bark (*daluwang*), resulting in a very poor appearance in the eyes of most people.

2.4 *Maka*

***maka** ngaranya, ĕnting sukanya lamun ingucap ing abĕcik, agung yan ingalĕm, arohara yan ingucap tan yogya, brangta yan winada, kroḍa yan cinalan, ya ta **maka** ngaranya.*

9. PJ Zoetmulder, *Old Javanese-English Dictionary* (The Hague: Martinus Nijhoff, 2 volumes, 1982).
10. Ibid; Monier-Williams, above no. 3.

[*Maka* means lost his happiness when said to him of a good, feels high when praised, is always tempted to say something inappropriate, confusion when blamed, and angry when reproached. That is *maka*.]

In this context, it is very difficult to find the literal meaning of *maka*. For a while, this word must be accepted as a technical term that is applied specifically, with the terminological meaning given by the text. The term is conceptualized as an attitude of refusing kindness, arrogance and anti-criticism. The Balinese version has a simpler formulation, for example, feeling happy when getting praise and concerned when getting criticism (K 247). So, essentially, the Balinese text conceptualizes it as the attitude of someone who has a desire for praise from others but he does not understand his shortcomings.

Praise is like a fire that stores danger. It is something to watch out for. The *Mānawa Dharmaśāstra* text (2.162–22.163) states that 'a *brāhmana* must always be aware of praise as he is aware of poisons. A *brahmin* must always be willing to suffer ridicule, as he is willing to experience eternal happiness. Someone who is ridiculed, can sleep calmly, walk among the crowd calmly. However, the mocking person must be prepared to meet destruction'.

2.5 *Jogor*

jogor *ngaranya, sukatinya yan andělěng anak rabinya, sanak wwang atuwa, kadang wraga mitra karahnya, ya ta mogha trěsna manahnya, suka yan tumon sarwa ana, priyatin lamun tumon ing ora, ya ta* ***jogor*** *ngaranya*

[*Jogor* means that someone is happy to see his wife's children, siblings, parents, relatives and partners. That is, his mind is suddenly filled with desire – happy when he sees all who are (material) and concerned about meeting the immaterial. That is *jogor*.]

Similarly, the literal meaning of the word *jogor* is not clear. This impasse will be resolved by reference to the terminological meaning given by the text. The term *jogor* is conceived as the nature of someone who is always happy about material things that can be reached by the senses. Unfortunately, he does not like essential things that are abstract/immaterial and not accessible to the senses. This is contrary to the *Uttaraśabda* text view which always emphasizes the essential, especially the Supreme Reality.

Therefore, the boundaries of association need to be given to practitioners of world *asketisme*. A practitioner must limit his association, including with his own family and relatives. Everything can break down concentration and make it difficult for an *asketis* to find the path of yoga, because everything is like a property that has the potential to generate craving (*tṛṣṇa*). Maybe, in the term we see there is a nuance of *aparigraha*, 'not bound by property', although the text of *Uttaraśabda* emphasizes family and friends as the most beloved property.

2.6 *Manik*

manik *ngaranya, sukamběknya lamun katuwukan pangan inum, ika sukawaknya makula makule lawan anakrabi, anuwuki karěping raga mwang arsa, arungsing lamun amangan kurang, alara si kang aměgatana, sěḍěngane warěg apan dene brangta, ya ta* ***manik*** *ngaranya*

[*Manik* means that someone is happy to be satisfied with eating, he also enjoys gathering and having sexual relations with women, satisfying all his physical and pleasure desires, restlessness when eating less, and will hurt anyone who prevents them.]

If translated literally, the meaning of the word *manik* (Skt. Maṇi) is 'jewel, pearl, crystal'.[11] However, it is difficult to determine the relationship between literal understanding and the terminological information given by the text.

11. Zoetmulder, above n 9.

The term *manik* represents the concept of not overeating (*aralagawa*), which is one item of *niyama* in the old Javanese text *Wṛhaspatitattwa* and *Wratiśāsana*. In addition, the pleasure to gather (*macula*) and sexual intercourse (*makule*) with women, is a form of negation of the *brahmacarī* attitude. Indeed, bead requires a practitioner to stay away from women as a source of sexual desire. However, if it is associated with the previous *jogor* points, the nature of the bead does seem conditional. Because, *Wratiśāsana* divides the *brahmacarī* category into three types: (1) *śukla brahmacarī* who has never experienced contact with a woman from birth (not married); (2) *suwala brahmacarī* who chooses to marry only once; (3) *kṛṣṇa brahmacarī* which allows himself to have a wife (maximum) four people. Possible bead points for the three types of *brahmacarī*. It is just that, when he is bound to carry out a spiritual process, he is not allowed at all to come into contact with women.

However, the concept of *manik* in this case is a combination of *aralagawa* and *brahmacarī* – avoiding pleasure in eating and preventing self in sexual pleasure.

2.7 *Purbalodra*

> ***purbalodra*** *ngaranya, lĕgātinya lamun angucapi wong, amukul anuduk, angaranana wong asaḍu, amala wong tan padosa, amrih amet sarya, dahat amet alaning wong, kĕḍĕh adĕngkya ring kya, gĕgĕlātinya yan tan katuwukan ambĕknya maring ala, ya ta* ***purbalodra*** *ngaranya.*
>
> [*Purbalodra* is his name, he will be relieved when he absorbs people, punches, stabs, accuses saints (doing evil), harms innocent people so that their desires are achieved. He really wants to look for the ugliness of others, as if he must envy them. His heart will regret if all his desires are not satisfied with badness. That is *purbalodra* his name.]

The term *purbalodra* is a combination of two ancient words (Skt. Pūrva), 'ruling' and *lodra* (Skt. Rudra), 'anger'. So, literally this term can be interpreted as 'controlled by anger' (Poerwadarminta, 1938 s.v. *purba* and *lodra*).

The term *purbalodra* has a complex meaning. This term describes the attitude of someone who always desires evil things to harm others, both by deed, speech and mind. Crime in deeds is shown through a hitting attitude (*amukul* < *pukul*) and piercing (*anuduk* < *suduk*) a saint (*wong asadu*). Crime in speech is done by absorbing other people (*angucapi wong*), while the form of evil of the mind is shown through jealousy (*dĕngkya* < *dĕngki*).

The *Uttaraśabda* text itself describes three forms of crime through the terms *wacika, manasika* and *kayika*. Each term is interpreted as follows: *wacika* – the word is the style of 'fruitful speech'; *manasika* – angĕn-angĕna ala 'minded or bad intentions', and if: if the initiative is 'to produce all desires to kill'. When looking at the description given by the text, *purbalodra* has a conceptual relationship with an anti-violence attitude (*ahingsā*), whether it is violence caused by physical actions, speech or thought. All the violence will make others wretched. Thus, there is an extension of meaning for the term *purbalodra*. Violence is not only limited to physical violence.

3 SOME MATTERS RELATED TO ETHICAL PROBLEMS

Ethical concepts in *Uttaraśabda* are not only detailed in five points. Indeed, the *Uttaraśabda* text does not describe what attitudes are included in *niyama*. However, it can be considered in parts of the text that teach the behavior of a spiritual practitioner. In this section, two characteristics will be discussed, namely: (a) maintaining physical and spiritual purity; (b) ethics that apply in the relationship between teacher and student. Both are included in the *niyama* group.

3.1 Śauca *(holiness)*

Śauca, purifying oneself from all objects that give rise to physical or spiritual blemishes. *Patañjali* explains *śauca* as an aversion to all things physical and avoids contact with them.

The essence of self-purification is the attempt to control the senses tightly to achieve the highest knowledge (*Yogaśūtra*, II.40–41). Meanwhile, as a commentator for *Patañjali*, the old Javanese text *Dharma Patañjala* gives a more detailed explanation. *Śauca* is the purification of three main parts in the structure of human personality: physical body (*crew*), speech (*wuwus*) and mind (*ambĕk*), in addition to preventing forbidden food and drinks from entering the body (*Dharma Patañjala* 32; Acri, 2011, p. 310).

Unlike the *Dharma Patañjala*, the text *Wṛhaspatitattwa* and *Wratiśāsana* means *śauca* in a ritualistic framework by worshiping the Supreme Reality (*arcana*). The *Wratiśāsana* text gives a more detailed explanation:

> *kunang ikang śauca, nitya śaucārcana, yan mapa ta lwir ning śaucārcana, parahupananta ri bhaṭāra śiwāditya, manggĕlara śūrya śewana, manggĕlara swānuṣṭhāna, mabhasma, majapa, sabhātya yan wruha ring snānawidhi.* (*Wratiśāsana*, fol. 13r–v).
>
> [Next is *śauca*, consistently carrying out the purification prayer. Then, what is called the purifying *puja*? Your cleansing source is *Bhaṭāra Śiwāditya*, carrying out the *sewana* solar system, concentrating, *bhasma*, reciting *japa*, gathering [with the teacher] to understand the procedure of purification.]

Quite clearly, *Wratiśāsana* chooses the daily ritual *śūrya śewana* carried out by the *Brahmins* of the *Soulis* every few moments after the sun rises in the morning as (one of the) purges. The purpose of sanctification refers to *Śiwāditya*, one of the manifestations of *Śiwa* as the sun. In practice, at the beginning of the ritual, *śūrya śewana* did involve cleansing the body with water, but the general purpose of the ritual was thorough cleansing. Each part of the ritual involves worshiping spells. From here, both in the *Wratiśāsana* and *Wṛhaspatitattwa* texts, ethical phenomena do not appear explicitly, which are the path of purification both physically and mentally. The orientation emphasizes the ritual.

Meanwhile, in the text of *Uttaraśabda*, it is clearly stated that there are two ways of cleansing, namely, purification both physically and mentally. The division of these two individual structures involves two different facilities, which are actually inseparable from one another because essentially the *Manon*, as the provider of sanctification, is present in all things (omnipresent). Like the purification ritual in general, the *Uttaraśabda* text shows that the means of cleansing the external body is water (*bañu* or *toya*), but with the status of purifying water (*toya suci sinucen*) because there are conditions that must be fulfilled. Whereas the inner aspect, the means of purification is something esoteric (I want to be holy). Furthermore, *Uttaraśabda* describes the ritual cleansing of the body (*anuceni śarīra*), complete with the *pūja* mantra for each part. At this level, the *Uttaraśabda* text is in line with *Wratiśāsana* and *Wṛhaspatitattwa*.

In addition, after all the rites of purification with water were carried out, *Uttaraśabda* also used the term *īśwara pāwitra*, which literally means 'supreme cleansing'. The terminological concept is explained through the following dialog:

> punapa ta kang sinangguh īśwara pāwitra pwakulun?
> sira sang angucap rahayu sadina.
> punapa ta kang sinangguh rahayu satata pwakulun?
> punapa si sira sang apakṣa anagih pakrĕti saking pangeran yayi?
> [What is called *īśwara pāwitra Tuanku*?
> He is the one who expresses goodness throughout the day.
> What is called good at all times, my Lord?
> Who is he who always wants to ask for deeds from God, brother.]

With *īśwara pāwitra*, the *Uttaraśabda* text seems to specify a hierarchy in the process of purification. The main form of sanctification is more ethically oriented, that is, always having good speech (utter utterance or *rahayu satata*). Perhaps what is highlighted by the *Uttaraśabda* text in that section is only goodness in speech, but in the whole text, goodness also includes deeds of the mind. Indeed, in the perspective of *dharmaśāstra*, the mouth as a tool of speech is the most powerful and holiest organ. The mouth is like a *brahmin* who acts as a buffer for the

Vedas. The *Vedas* themselves are always delivered orally (see *Mānawa Dhārmaśāstra* I.92–94). Therefore, a practitioner must realize that the source of goodness remains the Lord (Prince), so to God, one must ask for all deeds (*apakiha*, the piety of the Lord). Then, the *Uttaraśabda* text provides a form of puppet play: man as a puppet and God is the mastermind.[12] So, from here, the ethical consequences of one's actions are still determined by the attitude of devotion to the Supreme Reality.

3.2 *The relationship between guru and disciple*

Among the ethical issues discussed earlier, *Uttaraśabda* also touched on ethical issues in seeking knowledge. The term *svādhyāya* – which is classified by *Patañjali* as one of the items of *niyama* – is understood as an independent learning effort (self-study), specifically to achieve union with the intended deity (*iṣṭādevata*) (*Yogaśūtra*, II.44). Besides 'learning', the term *adhyāya* can also mean 'reading' (Monier-Williams, 1899). Perhaps because of that, the *Patañjala Dharma* interpreted it as a willingness to cast spells and *stava* (Acri, 2011, p. 310). So, it is not illustrated by the pedagogical situation between the teacher and the student of the *svādhyāya Patañjali* concept. In contrast to the *Wratiśāsana* (...) and *Wṛhaspatitattwa* (60–61), which are closer to the *āgama* tradition such as *Pauskarāgama*, both include the term *guruśuśrūsa* 'obedient to the teacher'. *Wratiśāsana* explains that *guruśuśrūsa* is:

> *sari-sari tan adoh ri pāda sang guru, makanimitta hyunirān warahĕn ri śāsana sang wiku, yathānyan tan umangguhakna ng pāpa marga, apan yan kurang warah-warah sang wiku sangkeng guru, tan enak wruh nira ri eyopadeya, ring pāñcāśikṣa, nguniweh ri tĕlas sang hyang kriyopadeśa, mārganing humung sira ng kabhyudaya muwang kaniraśrayan.*
>
> [at any time not moving away from the feet of the teacher, because of his desire to be taught a lesson about discipline of a *wiku*, so as not to meet the path of misery. Of course after it is finished all of learning.]

The *Uttaraśabda* text not only provides an ethical limit for a student, but also for a teacher. For a student, there are not many ethical limitations given by the text compared to the teacher, and even impressing that the rule was addressed to the teacher or the person who delivered the teachings (*upadesa*). The failure of a student to accept teachings, and he will become unaware (*tan wikan*), is once again determined by the attitude of a teacher. So, the concept of *guruśuśrūsa* is not highlighted in the text, although the obedient attitude of a student automatically remains in the pedagogical relation embraced by the text:

> *Sang rĕsi manih yayi tan pamalaku paguruyuga, tan pangiṣṭi pawesastra, tan parĕp pinuṣpantara, anatur boga, upaboga, ananggapi sakeng pakenak. Tan wikan sang winarah upadesa ri sang rĕsi, tan pamalaku sang rĕsi-upadesa. Ya ta sinangguh wiku rinahasya yan mangkanaa. Alpameka* [baca: *ala papeka*] *sang rĕsi, amalaku pangupadesa amrih ayasa. Tan yogya yan mangkanaa. Ana sukanira sang winarah lawan sang awarah, asung uparĕngga ri guru-upadesa. Suka kang aweh lan kang winehan. Kabudayan araning sang rĕsi yan mangkanaa.* (*Uttaraśabda*, PNRI 1 L 140)
>
> [The *rsi* also does not ask for *paguruyuga* offerings, does not expect to give clothes, does not expect offerings of various flowers, gives all pleasures, receives all pleasures. Someone who is given teachings by the *rsisi* will not understand without undergoing the teachings of the *rsisi*. If so, that is what is called I woe to it, really woe to the *rsi* when delivering teachings with the aim of getting rewarded, it is not appropriate to be like that, it is happiness for those who are taught and teach, give decoration to the teachings of the teacher, even those who give and who are given.]

---

12. For a similar case in *suluk* texts, see PJ Zoetmulder, *Manunggaling Kawula Gusti: Pantheisme Dan Monisme Dalam Sastra Suluk Jawa* (Jakarta, Indonesia: Gramedia Pustaka Utama, translated, 1991).

Based on the text quoted above, it can be seen that there is a moral rule for a teacher (*rsi*) as a patron of knowledge, for example, not demanding respect (*yaśa*) or not asking for compensation from what has been done to his client (*winarah*). He must carry out his social function sincerely on the basis of the *dharma* which has been immanent in him. Such an ethos seems to be based on the character of *aparigraha* – non-avarice, non-possessiveness – one of the points of *yama*. However, as a supporter of the tradition of knowledge or *Vedas*, a teacher has a very special position in the structure of society. Therefore, it is really outside the ethical boundary to expect rewards from groups that are stratified under it.

4 CONSEQUENCES

Any act that violates the standard will have negative consequences. The *Uttaraśabda* text explains that the consequences that a person will face if they satisfy themselves (*anuwuki* <*tuwuk* 'satisfied') in actions that should be restrained (*yama*) are sin and hell (*papa naraka*). In addition, he will have the next punishment, which is to fall into the cycle of birth and suffering (*karma*) to cleanse the soul (*ātma*) of all inherent sins. At this point, there is an allusion between the *Uttaraśabda* text and the concept of *pañcagati saṃsara* 'five conditions of misery' in Buddhist texts such as, for example, *Kuñjarakarṇa* (see Van der Molen, 2011). However, once again, *Uttaraśabda* gives a different explanation. Classification (or stratification) of punishment is distinguished on the basis of the area within the human being which is the source of sin: whether physical, verbal or mental. From *Uttaraśabda*'s perspective, evil originating from the mind has the worst consequences.

Although the *Uttaraśabda* text provides guidance for liberating humans from the cycle of birth, namely through *maweda* or reading of sacred formulas, the rituals of soteriology must begin by obeying the prescribed ethical protocols. That is why *Patañjali* places *yama* as the most basic part in the eight parts of yoga (*aṣṭāṅgayoga*). Sanctification – including union with the Highest Reality in *samadi* – self must begin from ethical awareness in the realm of social life.

The *Uttaraśabda* text does not give a picture of legal sanctions (both criminal and civil) and social sanctions for those who violate restrictions. The ethical points in *Uttaraśabda* are more oriented to individuals as religious practitioners than as members of society who must submit to the prevailing legal system. Perhaps, the *Uttaraśabda* text has surpassed all these legal rules and moved to a more advanced level. Although *Uttaraśabda* uses the term *yama*, what seems dominant is actually *niyama*. The points in *Uttaraśabda* that really show the good character in other texts are: (a) bead (specifically for interdiction with women/*brahmacarī*); (b) *purbalodra* (aspects of verbal and physical violence in it/*ahiṃsā*). The nature of crime in these two points, at least, can be found in old Javanese legal texts such as *igdigama* and *Kuṭara Manawa*, complete with penalties. Apparently, the *Uttaraśabda* text prioritizes morality over legal law, even though both can be connected to one another.

5 CONCLUSIONS

In ethical concepts, basically, the text of *Uttaraśabda* does not detach itself from tradition and the development of ethical concepts in religious texts, both in the old Javanese and Indian literary domains. There are five points in *Uttaraśabda*, where it shows clear continuity with the tradition of yoga texts after *Patañjali*. Uniquely, the *Uttaraśabda* text builds alternative ways that distinguish it from other old Javanese texts such as the *Patañjala Dharma, Wratiśāsana* and *Wṛhaspatitattwa*. The technical terms used are also very different (perhaps because the *Uttaraśabda* text developed when Indian influence had long faded), although if we look closely there is still conceptual continuity between these technical terms and the previous tradition. From this, an intertextual approach is very relevant to be used to understand ethical concepts in this *Uttaraśabda* text.

In addition, if various theories state that the points are more universal because they involve social relations between the individual and his community, but the meaning in *Uttaraśabda* transcends all of them. He is not only in the legal domain, but has penetrated the moral sphere that applies specifically to certain groups, namely clergy or *brahmins*. It cannot be denied, considering the text of *Uttaraśabda* lives and develops in a religious environment, such as the *Merapi-Merbabu* scriptoria, and in the neighborhood of Gĕria – the residence of the *Pandanda* in Bali. So, what is actually highlighted and dominant in the version of the *Uttaraśabda* version is *niyama* in the perspective of other yoga texts

REFERENCES

Acri, A. (2011). *Dharma Patañjala: A Saiva scripture from ancient Java, studied in the light of related old Javanese and Sanskrit texts*. Leiden, The Netherlands: Leiden University.

Behrend, T.E. (1998). *Katalog Induk Naskah-Naskah Nusantara Jilid 4 Perpustakaan Nasional Republik Indonesia*. Jakarta, Indonesia: Yayasan Obor Indonesia.

Bertens, K. (1993). *Etika*. Jakarta, Indonesia: Gramedia Pustaka Utama.

Devi, Sudarshana, (1957). *Wṛhaspati-Tattwa: An old Javanese philosophical text*. New Delhi, India: International Academy of Indian Culture.

Drewes, G.W.J. (1945). *Een Javaanse Primbon Uit de Zestiende Eeuw: Opniew Uitgegeven En Vertald*. Leiden, The Netherlands: E.J. Brill.

Drewes, G.W.J. The admonitions of she bari. 9 *Bibliotheca Indonesica*

Drewes, G.W.J. (1978). An early Javanese code of Muslim ethics. *Bibliotheca Indonesica, 18*.

Monier-Williams, M. (1899). *A Sanskrit–English dictionary*. Oxford, UK: Clarendon Press.

Pigeaud, T. *Literature of Java: Catalog raisonné of Javanese manuscripts in the library of the University of Leiden and other public collections in the Netherlands*. The Hague, The Netherlands: Martinus Nijhoff.

Rani, Sharada, (1957). *Ślokāntara, an old Javanese didactic text. Critically edited and annotated*. Nagpur, India: International Academy of Indian Culture.

Setyawati, K., Wiryamartana, I.K. & Van der Molen, W. (2002). *Katalog Naskah Merapi-Merbabu Perpustakaan Nasional Republik Indonesia*. Yogyakarta and Leiden: Penerbitan Universitas Sanata Dharma and Opleiding Talen en Culturen van Zuidoost-Azië en Oceanië Universitiet Leiden.

Still, J. & Worton, M. (1990). *Intertextuality: Theories and practices*. Manchester, UK: Manchester University Press.

Witkam, J.J. *Inventory of the oriental manuscripts of the library of the University of Leiden*. Leiden, The Netherlands: Ter Lugt Press.

Zoetmulder, P.J. (1982). *Old Javanese–English dictionary*. The Hague, The Netherlands: Martinus Nijhoff.

Zoetmulder, P.J. (1991). *Manunggaling Kawula Gusti: Pantheisme Dan Monisme Dalam Sastra Suluk Jawa*. Jakarta, Indonesia: Gramedia Pustaka Utama.

Partha Ajñāṇaśūra. K 247/IIIb/9. Palm-leaves, Balinese script. Singaraja, Indonesia: Gedong Kirtya.

Sĕrat Oettara-sabda. 1 L 170. Palm-leaves, Buda script. Jakarta, Indonesia: Perpustakaan Nasional RI.

Wratiśāsana. S/IV/11/DOKBUD. Palm-leaves, Balinese script. Denpasar, Indonesia: Pusat Dokumentasi Budaya Bali.

Culture and International Law - Juwana et al. (Eds)
© 2019 Taylor & Francis Group, London, ISBN 978-1-138-38766-9

Museum management: A critical point in making museums relevant

Ahmad Zuhdi Allam
Architect, Indonesia

Kresno Yulianto
Lecturer of Museum Studies, Faculty of Humanities, Universitas Indonesia

ABSTRACT: As a public space, museum is always influenced by its context, either political and social. Therefore, today's fast changing society and political transformation has pushed museum to be an adaptive and inclusive institution. However, not many museums in Indonesia are able to transform themselves to be more relevant in current age. This condition will make public getting further from their heritage that preserved in the museum. Unfortunately, academic efforts to disentangle this problem is relatively little since many scholars have already skeptical about museum management in the country. Thus, museum and heritage regulation is still considered incomprehensive to respond today's challenge.

In order to find the origin of this problem, research on museum activities was conducted in five museums of Jakarta, national capital and barometer of museum development in Indonesia. The five museums chosen have different types of collection and owner. In this research, data was collected through observation and interviews with museum workers. Unsurprisingly, the results presented in this paper shows that museum management is the most critical aspect in transforming museum to be more adaptive and inclusive. This paper also offers new approach for regulator to overcome problems regarding museum management issue.

KEYWORDS: curator, curatorial works, DKI Jakarta, Indonesia

1 INTRODUCTION

1.1 *Museum, society, and curatorial activity*

As a form of cultural authority,[1] museum has knowledge as its fundamental component.[2] Thus, as a site where 'proofs' of science and human history is stored, a museum cannot be seen as a neutral space; it is a contested site (Marstine, 2006).[3] There is an underlying paradigm that 'control' museum.

This paradigm evolves as time goes by. In the 19th century, where museum started to be opened for public, a museum is a vital part of European industrialization and colonialism. Paradigm underlying in most museums at the time is promoting colonial state's domination of its imperial area (through ethnography collection) and human domination on natural

1. Julia D Harrison, 'Ideas of Museums in the 1990s' (1994) 13(2) *Museum Management and Curatorship* 160.
2. TAM Ewin and JA V. Ewin., 'In Defernce of the Curator: Maximising Museum Impact' (2016) 31(4) *Museum Management and Curatorship* 322.
3. Janet Marstine, 'Introduction' in Janet Marstine (ed), *New Museum Theory and Practice: An Introduction* (Oxford: Blackwell Publishing, 2006).

(through biology and geology collection). The aim of collection arrangement in the museum is to make people – mostly working class – to be more awed and respect for their nation's achievement.[4]

At the end of 19th century, the museum has been an established institution. It created a new type of job: curator, which is responsible for the understanding of museum collection and its arrangement. Van Mensch (1992 & 2004) marked the birth of curator as a profession as 'first museum revolution'. For decades, the museum is controlled solely by the curator.[5] In the middle of 20th century, museum's growing role in society has pushed the birth of 'second museum revolution', which acknowledge the educational role in the museum and institutionalized its role. The traditional museum function has shifted towards its social function that universal and dynamic.[6]

The acknowledged educational function of museum led the museum to be more exposed to its social context: dynamic global politic, the rise of capitalism, fading colonialism, and postmodern philosophy. These external factors drove museum to be transformed continually.[7] As a result, many scholars suggest the change of museum relationship with its audiences. Monologue conversation from curator to society should be shifted to be more reciprocal. This approach is later known with "New Museology" paradigm. It pushes museum to be more society-oriented, speak through action, and giving devotion to social change and progress. The development of "New Museology" affects the change of "values, meaning, control, interpretation, authority, and authenticity in a museum".[8] "New Museology" paradigm led to "curatorial redistribution" [9] and push more active role for society, either as the visitor or curatorial function controller.[10] The participation of community caused by "New Museology" has replaced traditional curatorial process in the.[11] The community was not only museum's audience, it became a museum collaborator [12] that need to be involved in museum planning.[13] The complexity in curatorial activities in the museum, especially that related to society, pushed the 'third museum revolution' in 1990's. This revolution stressed the growing role of management in the museum, as well as, marketing and public relation to responding to the challenge of sustainability institution.[14]

4. Jennifer Barrett, *Museums and the Public Sphere* (West Sussex: Wiley-Blackwell, 2011).
5. Elaine Heumann-Gurian, 'Curator: From Soloist to Impresario' in Fiona Cameron and Linda Kelly (eds), *Hot topics, public culture, museums* (London: Cambridge Scholars, 2010).
6. Peter van Mensch, 'Towards a Methodology of Museology' (1992); Peter van Mensch, 'Museology and Management: Enemies or Friends? Current Tendencies in Theoretical Museology and Museum Management in Europe' in E Mizushima (ed), *Museum management in the 21st century* (Tokyo: Museum Management Academy, 2004) 3.
7. Nick Merriman, 'Museum Visiting as Cultural Phenomenon' in *The New Museology* (London: Reaktion Books., 1989); Michael Shanks, 'Public Archaeology/Museology/Conservation/Heritage' in Colin Renfrew and Paul Bahn (eds), *Archaeology: Key Concepts* (New York: Routledge, 2005) 164; Barrett, above n 4; Noerhadi Magetsari, *Perspektif Arkeologi Masa Kini Dalam Konteks Indonesia* (Jakarta: Penerbit Buku Kompas, 2016).
8. Vikki dan Clive Gray McCall, 'Museums and the "New Museology": Theory, Practice, and Organisational Change' (2014) 29(1) *Museum Management and Curatorship* 19.
9. Deirdre C Stam, 'The Informed Muse: The Implication of "The New Museology" for Museum Practice' (1993) 12(3) *Museum Management and Curatorship* 267.
10. McCall, above n 8; Christina Kreps, 'Appropiate Museology in Theory and Practice' (2008) 23(1) *Museum Management and Curatorship* 23.
11. Mathieu Viau-Courville, 'Museums Without (Scholar-)Curators: Exhibition-Making in Times of Managerial Curatorship' (2017) 68(271–272) *Museum International* 11.
12. Maria Wronska-Friend, 'Why Haven't We Been Taught All That At School? Crosscultural Community Projects in North Queensland, Australia' (2012) 55(1) *Curator* 3.
13. Nina Simon, *The Participatory Museum* (Santa Cruz: Museum 2.0., 2010).
14. van Mensch, 'Museology and Management: Enemies or Friends? Current Tendencies in Theoretical Museology and Museum Management in Europe', above n 6.

The above description shows that curatorial activity in the museum is closely related to the museum's view of society because the curator and its activities are the heart of the museum. The curator is the official voice of the museum authority.[15] The expertise of a curator (curatorship) is the most fundamental form of knowledge authority in the museum.[16] The decision about what paradigm is applied in the museum is in the hands of the curator.[17] The definition of the curator's work, not just an administrative matter; this is a philosophical issue as to how the museum's authority can be trusted and how it interacts with the audience.[18] Regarding the development of the role of the curator,[19] makes an easy-to-understand description of the evolutionary stages of the curatorial function that in line with van Mensch idea of museum revolution:

1. Curator = keeper + researcher + conservator
2. Curator = keeper + researcher + conservator + exhibitor
3. Curator = keeper + researcher + conservator + exhibitor + educator
4. Curator = keeper + researcher + conservator + exhibitor + educator + manager
5. Curator = keeper + researcher + conservator + exhibitor + educator + manager + marketing officer+ public relations officer.

However, the implementation of a certain paradigm is influenced by the context of the museum, either political or economic. Longair[20] advises that in understanding a more holistic curatorial practice, a more diverse perspective is needed, both geographically and historically because the curator works and is influenced by the social and political context. Thus, the role of museum curators and curatorial works in Indonesia and in other countries may be different despite having the same paradigm of museology. However, In Indonesia, most voices in museology academic are focusing what should curators do, while giving a little attention to the reality of curatorship in the museum.

In Indonesia, there are not many studies on curatorial activities and/or curator roles in museums. Most of the studies are discussing about what curatorial/curatorial activities should take place in the museum;[21] not about the empirical study on museum. It is noted that only one academic thesis that observe curatorial activities, specifically curatorial management[22], in National Museum of Indonesia and a paper on curatorial management at the art museum in Jogjakarta.[23] On the other hand, the efforts to unveil the underlying paradigm under curatorial activities in Indonesia are less desirable by researchers. The conducted academic study to relate theory and practice of museology in Indonesia is relatively small if called none; it is usually a management review or study of theoretical models only. It could be because researchers, and the general public, are already skeptical of museums and human resources working

15. Heumann-Gurian, above n 5.
16. Sarah Longair, 'Culture of Curating: The Limits of Authority' (2015) 8(1) *Museum History Journal* 1.
17. Marstine, above n 3.
18. Heumann-Gurian, above n 5.
19. Irena Veselko, 'What Are the Core Competencies Needed in a Museum? A View from Slovenia' in Jane A Legget (ed), *Staff and Training in Regional Museum* (Paris: ICOM-ICR, ICOM-ICTOP, and Regional Museum Murska Sobota., 2011).
20. Longair, above n 16.
21. Luthfi Asiarto, 'Human Resource Management: Training in Indonesia' in *Comparative Museology & Museography in ASEAN* (Manila: Association of Southeast Asian Nations, Committee on Culture and Information, 1997); James Bennett, 'The Changing Meaning of Research in Professional Development Training for the Museum Worker' (2011) 5(7) *Museografia* 33; Junus Satrio Atmodjo, 'Peta Permasalahan Museum: Faktor Peran' (2011) 5(7) *Museografia* 41; Oki Laksito, 'Kompetensi Profesi Museum Indonesia' (2012) 6 (10) *Museografia* 19.
22. Mawaddatul Husna Rizqika, 'Model Manajemen Kuratorial Dalam Paradigma Museologi Baru: Studi Kasus Museum Nasional' (2017).
23. Mikke Susanto, 'Manajemen Kuratorial Pameran Seni Rupa Di JOGJA GALLERY Antara 2006-2008' (2012) 6(10) *Museografia* 83.

there.[24] The lack of research in this field makes a gap between the knowledge and practice of museology, which in the end adds to the gloomy world of Indonesian museums and results in the increasingly abandoned museums of society. It is true that the Government of the Republic of Indonesia has been standardizing museums and certification curators for the past few years to implement Government Regulation No. 66 of 2015, bu the study of curators and curatorial activities in accordance with the Indonesian context still needs a lot to be done to support the museum policy.

Although Jakarta is the capital, the largest city of Indonesia, has a lot of museums, and has better human resources working in museum than other regions,[25] study of curatorial activities in museums in this region has never been done before. There are two considerations that make DKI Jakarta become the focus in research, among others.

1. The development of museum practices in terms of quality of management and quality of human resources in Indonesia, according to Kreps (2008), concentrated in metropolitan cities. Thus, museums in Jakarta area can be used as a barometer of museum development in Indonesia.
2. There are 71 museums in DKI Jakarta that have been registered by the Ministry of Education and Culture (Depdikbud). However, not all museums confirmed its existence. The author's search results show that there are 59 museums in DKI Jakarta with various types of collections and owners. This number (59 museums) constitutes 14% of the number of museums in Indonesia, 428 museums (Association of Indonesian Museum, 2016). Thus, there are many museums that can be selected as research objects.

Therefore, the purpose of this study is to get an overview of curatorial activities undertaken in museums in DKI Jakarta and observe how these curatorial activities have reflected museum attitude towards society in today's uncertain era.

1.2 *Studies and regulations of museum in Indonesia*

According to Tjahjopurnomo, et al. in "History of Museums in Indonesia" (2011), museum was as old as colonialism in Nusantara. Since 17th century, European had established museum-like institution to keep their discoveries in Nusantara. One of them, who often written in the textbook of Indonesian museum history, is Georg Eberhard Rumpf (1628-1702) who collected variety of flora and shells in his house in Amboina (now Ambon). In 1778, Bataviaasch Genootschap van Kunsten en Wetenschappen was established in Batavia (now Old Jakarta) as a safekeeper of archaeological and ethnological finding in Nusantara. Later, this institution transformed into National Museum of Indonesia. In the next decades, nobels of Nusantara also following this trend: KRA Sosrodiningrat IV established Museum Radya Pusaka in Solo at 1890 and Sri Sultan Hamengkubuwono VIII established Museum Sonobudoyo in Yogyakarta at 1935. Like museums in Europe, the museums in Nusantara at that time was managed by collection-related experts.

After the Independence, museums are managed by Indonesian. However, not much attention given in Soekarno Era (1945-1965) since the nation was busy in Physical Revolution and constructing nation political identity. In 1956, John Irwin, UNESCO consultant for Indonesian government, observed that curator in Indonesia was not more that "clerk and caregiver".[26] While Amin Sutarga, museum professional, in 1962 pointed that one of Indonesian museum problems was "lack of specialization-educated museum professional" (Tjahjopurnomo, et al, 2011). In the New Order (1965-1998) Indonesian government routinely held various training

24. Edy Sedyawati, *In Celebrating Indonesia: Fifty Years with the Ford Foundation 1953-2003* (New York: Ford Foundation, 2003); Ali Akbar, *Museum Di Indonesia: Kendala Dan Harapan* (Jakarta: Penerbit Papas Sinar Sinanti, 2010); Atmodjo, above n 21; Kresno Yulianto, *Di Balik Pilar-Pilar Museum* (Jakarta Selatan: Wedatama Widya Sastra, 2016).
25. Kreps, above n 10.
26. Asiarto, above n 21.

activities in order to increase museum professional capacity, including curator training. Within the framework of training, curator was defined as "subject specialist, have knowledge of the collection; able to develop their knowledge through study, maintain relationships with other workers, understand other collections, and conduct research; able to prepare exhibitions, either temporary, permanent, or running; has an effective collection acquisition policy; and understand the audience that the museum serves".[27] Unfortunately, in 1997 Tedjo Susilo considered the effort given by government cannot impact more positively: human resource of museum remained as an unresolved problem. Susilo suspected that the root of the problem was the absence of formal education in the field of museums, both at the secondary school and university level. Actually, there has been an effort from the government to open a museology department in universities but it did not materialize because of the lack of educators in this field (Susilo, 1997).

The same sentiment was stated by Christina Kreps who spent years as a consultant for museum development in the Nias Heritage Museum. Kreps (2008) argues that museum development and staff training in Indonesia are very ineffective because they do not pay attention to the condition of each museum and do not provide enough space to explore curatorial activities of local people. On the other hand, Indonesian society in general has not fully appreciated the value of the museum.[28] In the language of the Founder of the Nias Heritage Museum, Pater Hammerle, "they did not understand . . .".[29]

After the Reformation, there are some new laws that giving more freedom to express for people (Law No. 40 on Press of 1999) and distribution of power between central and regional governments (Law No. 32 on Regional Autonomy of 2004). However, this legal base did not have a significant impact on museum management. In fact, according to Junus Satrio Atmodjo, Chair of the Indonesian Archeology Experts Association 2007-2017, Regional Autonomy worsens the situation: the museum experiences "involution". The change in the ownership status of some museums from the central government to the local government was suspected to be the root of the problem of museum quality deterioration in which "the museum began to lose its image as a public space".[30] Akbar (2010) summarizes people's views on museums in Indonesia into 7K & 7S: kuno (old-fashioned), kusam (dull), klenik (heresy), ketinggalan (lagging), kurang (lacking), kritis (critical), kasihan (pitiful), seram (spooky), suram (gloomy), serius (serious), statis (static), sekali (once), sia-sia (useless), and sepi (deserted). Akbar's summary was not much different from the results of the study conducted by Ministry of Culture and Tourism in 2004 which found some mistaken public views about the museum:

- The museum is an institution that deals with only with pasts.
- The museum has no dynamics.
- The museum is a place to store ancient objects.
- The community still does not feel the benefits of attendance (Yulianto, 2016).

To prevent more degradation, latest regulations in the preservation of cultural heritage, Law No. 11 on Cultural Heritage of 2010, which supersedes Law No. 5 on Cultural Heritage of 1992 encourages wider community participation, division of cultural affairs between local and central government, and encourages the use of cultural heritage for the welfare of the community. The implication of the implementation of the law is the creation of good governance and transparency where the public can know and be involved more in museum matters.[31] Law No. 11 on Cultural Heritage of 2010 has been the base of Government Regulation No. 66 on Museums of 2015. In this regulation, the museum has an understanding as "an institution that functions to protect, develop, use collections, and communicate them to the

27. Ibid.
28. Sedyawati, above n 24.
29. Kreps, above n 10.
30. Atmodjo, above n 21.
31. Yulianto, above n 24.

public" (Chapter I, Article 1, No. 1). From this understanding it can be seen that in general the museum has activities: i) protecting collections, ii) developing collections, iii) utilizing collections, and iv) communicating collections to the public.

This regulation requires several things related to the establishment of museums, including: (i) having a vision and mission; (ii) having a collection; (iii) having a location and/or building; (iv) having human resources; (v) has a fixed funding source; and (vi) having a name "Museum" (Chapter II, Article 3, No. 2). From this requirement, it is implied that important activities are not only related to collections but are vital for the sustainability of the museum, which is to have human resources and a fixed source of funding. The activities mandated by the museum owners include:

- Collection Management (Chapter IV, Articles 13-31)
- Administration Management of Collection (Article 14-Article 22)
  - Accession and Registration of Collection (Article 15-Article 17)
  - Deaccession and Transfer of Collection (Article 18 and Article 19)
  - Loan of Collection (Article 20-Article 22)
- Technical Aspect of Collection (Article 23-Article 31)
  - Storage (Article 24-Article 28)
  - Conservation (Article 29-Article 31)
- Museum Security (Chapter V, Article 32-33)
- Development (Chapter VI, Article 34-Article 43)
  - Assessment (Article 34-Article 38)
  - Cooperation (Article 39-Article 40)
- Use of Museum (Chapter VIII, Article 41-Article 43)
- Funding (Chapter IX, Article 48-Article 51)

In addition to the above activities, there are also regulations related to human resources in the museum (Chapter III). First, it is the duty of the museum owner to provide human resources to manage the museum (Article 11), consists of at least head of museum, technical staff, and administrative staff. Head of Museum has the duty and responsibility for the entire museum management process in accordance with the museum's vision and mission. What is meant by "administrative staff" is the personnel who carry out administrative work; employment; finance; security; and/or domestic affair, while the workers included as "technical staff" are:

a. Registrar: technical officer who carry out activities in recording and documenting collections;
b. The curator: technical officer who, because of his/her expertise in competence, is responsible for managing the collection;
c. Conservator: technical officer who carries out preservation and conservation activities on the collection;
d. Exhibition officer: technical officer who carry out design and spatial layout activities in the museum;
e. Educator: technical officer who carry out educational activities and deliver information on collections; and
f. Public relations and marketing: technical officer carrying out communication and marketing activities of Museum programs.

2 METHODOLOGY

This research conducted with qualitative approach and designed as grounded theory research. Qualitative approach is used because important variables to be tested in this research are not clearly defined. The grounded theory research design is used so that researchers obtain general abstractions regarding the process, action, or interaction based on the views of the research participants. This process uses several stages of data collection and refinement and searches for relationships between various categories of information.[32] Qualitative approaches and grounded theory research designs are assessed precisely by studies conducted for several reasons:

1. Research seeks to explore and understand the views and activities of curators and professionals in museums (human) and museum organizations (social groups).
2. As described in the Introduction, the study of curatorial activities and the role of curators in museums has not been widely carried out.
3. The so-called "curators" differ in every social and political context, while the study of the role of curators based on empirical data in DKI Jakarta has never been done. Therefore, it is necessary to collect data from participants in order to get an abstraction about the 'curator' in this region.

According to Budiasih (2014), in the grounded theory research design, data collection is directed by theoretical sampling, which means that sample selection is based on the relevant theoretical constructions. Therefore, the selected museum in this research represents different collections and owners. Differences in museum collections are used because it can show the correlation between collections with a variety of curatorial activities in the museum (Peters, 2016). Differences between museum owners useful to know the purpose and mission of the museum and its curatorial activities. According to Government Regulation No. 66 of 2015, Government, Local Government, Citizen, and Adat Community can establish a museum. As for Citizen and Adat Community who desire to establish a museum needs to form "foundation" as a legal entity Foundation. Based on the reasons above, there are five museums selected as research objects, namely Museum Bank Indonesia, Museum Satriamandala, Museum Listrik & Energi Baru, Museum MACAN, and Museum Sejarah Jakarta (See Table 1)

The main data in this study are curatorial activities in the museum and supporting data are the activities of the Directorate of Preservation of Heritage and Museum (Dit. PCBM), Directorate General of Culture, Ministry of Education and Culture, as an extension of the government tasked with fostering and regulating museum activities in Indonesia, especially in the five museums studied.

As with qualitative research in general,[33] the data in this study were obtained through observation, interviews, and document collection. Observations were made by visiting the museum to observe directly the curatorial activities carried out. Interviews were conducted with curatorial officials in the museum to obtain data on curatorial activities that could not be observed through observation. If there are no curatorial officials, interviews are conducted with the Head of the Museum or the person responsible for curatorial activities in the museum. Documents collected are documents that represent curatorial activities in the museum. Three ways of collecting data above are done to ensure data validity

Table 1. Collection and Owner of Observed Museums.

Museum	Collection	Owner
Museum Bank Indonesia	Banking history and numismatic	Government
Museum Satriamandala	Military history	Military
Museum Listrik & Energi Baru	Science and technology	State owned corporation
Museum MACAN	Arts	Private
Museum Sejarah Jakarta	Regional history	Local Government

32. John Creswell, *Research Design: Qualitative, Quantitative, and Mixed Methods Approaches, 4th Edition* (Los Angeles: Sage Publication, Inc., 2014).
33. Ibid.

3 CURATORIAL ACTIVITY IN FIVE MUSEUMS IN JAKARTA

Curatorial activities observed in these five museums are adapted from Veselko evolution of curator's function (2011). They are collection management, research, conservation, exhibition, education, management, marketing, and public relations. Like other qualitative researchs,[34] the data in this study were obtained through observation, interviews, and document collection. Observations in this study were conducted by visiting the museum to observe directly the curatorial activities. Interviews were conducted with museum officials to obtain curatorial activity data that could not be witnessed through observation. If there is no curator in the musuem, the interview is conducted with the head of the museum or workers responsible for the curatorial activities. The documents collected in this study are documents that represent curatorial activities in museums.

3.1 *Collection management*

Collection management activities refer to museum activities that are fundamental to the collection, such as acquisition, documentation and inventory, storage, borrowing, securing, and asseccioning of collections.[35] Good collection management is also marked by the presence of collection management policy.[36] It is found that five museums do collection management activities, although only Museum MACAN has collection management policy.

3.2 *Research*

Research in museums generally conducted on collection;[37] exhibition;[38] visitors;[39] museum management or organization.[40] In conducting research, museums can work with other museums, universities, or other institution.[41] Every museum officer claimed that research (about physical condition, data validity, and significance) on collection is regularly conducted when the collection registered. Although not every museum has a special taskforce for handling research activity – only found in Museum Listrik & Energi Baru, Museum MACAN, and Museum Sejarah Jakarta, they are open for other parties to conduct research in their museums.

3.3 *Conservation*

All the studied museums undertake conservation activities, although not all have conservators. Only Museum Bank Indonesia, Museum MACAN, and Museum Sejarah Jakarta have employees serving as conservators. The observed five museum managers also claimed that their preventive conservation activities were in accordance with the characteristics of each

34. Ibid.
35. Gatot Ghautama and Prioyulianto (eds), *Pedoman Museum Indonesia* (Jakarta: Direktorat Pelestarian Cagar Budaya dan Permuseuman, Direktorat Jenderal Kebudayaan, Kementerian Pendidikan dan Kebudayaan, 2012).
36. Nicola Ladkin, 'Collection Management' in *Running A Museum: A Practical Handbook* (Paris: ICOM, 2004).
37. Ibid; Ghautama and Prioyulianto, above n 35.
38. Yani Herreman, 'Display, Exhibits and Exhibitions' in *Running A Museum: A Practical Handbook* (Paris: ICOM, 2004).
39. Vicky Woollard, 'Caring for the Visitor' in *Running A Museum: A Practical Handbook* (Paris: ICOM, 2004); Paal Mork, 'Marketing' in *Running A Museum: A Practical Handbook* (Paris: ICOM, 2004); Ghautama and Prioyulianto, above n 35.
40. Gary Edson, 'Museum Management' in *Running A Museum: A Practical Handbook* (Paris: ICOM, 2004); Ghautama and Prioyulianto, above n 35.
41. Ghautama and Prioyulianto, above n 35.

collection, although only the Museum Bank Indonesia and the Museum Sejarah Jakarta stated that they use the conservation standards of ICOM.

3.4 *Exhibition*

Noted that of the five museums studied, four museums have permanent exhibitions. Only the Museum MACAN does not have a permanent exhibition because, according to its officials, visitors will not be bored to come to the museum and for the collection to have enough time to 'rest'. The exhibition at Museum MACAN is changed every four months. Thus, the exhibition at this museum is only temporary. On the other hand, Museum Satriamandala has never changed its permanent exhibits since the museum was established, although minor improvements have been made several times. In addition to Museum MACAN, temporary exhibitions are also held at Museum Bank Indonesia, Museum Listrik & Energi Baru, and Museum Sejarah Jakarta. Other than permanent and temporary exhibition, there is also travelling exhibition that conducted by all museum, except Museum MACAN.

3.5 *Education*

Today, there are many methods and medias museum can provide as a form of educational tool. All museums have collection labels, guides, and publications in the form of brochures/print guides. However, only the Museum MACAN whose entire collection is on display has a label. Four other museums only attach labels to certain collections. Except for the Satriamandala Museum, all museums studied have specialized employees, either permanent employees or apprentices, as guides.

- Museum Bank Indonesia has a selective collection labels; guides; brochures; guidebook; child-specific audio guide; interactive media; a theater room that plays videos for children; 'museum-goes-to-school' program; and special activities, such as training, public discussion, talkshow, and competitions for students.
- Museum Satriamandala has selective collection labels, guides, guide book, and incidental 'museum-goes-to-school'.
- Museum Listrik & Energi Baru has selective collection labels; guides; brochures; educational space; interactive media; a theater room that plays videos for children; workshop space; 'museum-goes-to-school' program; and special activities, such as training and competitions for students.
- Museum MACAN has collection labels, guides, brochures; print guides; a free museum visitation program for schools, educational space (children's art room); interactive media; education kit for students; guidebook for children; and special activities, such as school visits, specialist arts training, and educator forums.
- Musuem Sejarah Jakarta has collection labels; guides, and publications in the form of brochures/print guides; theater; 'museum-goes-to-school' program; and such as seminar and discussion.

3.6 *Management*

According to Edson (2004), the nature of museum management is an attempt to help the organization, regardless its size and complexity, achieving consistent results in the realization of the museum's vision and mission. The research found that museum management activities that run optimally only found in Museum Listrik & Energi Baru, and Museum MACAN. Museum Satriamandala has a conventional museum organizational structure, but half the positions are not filled. Although management activities at Museum Bank Indonesia and Museum Sejarah Jakarta run every day, the organizational structure of the two museums is not conventional because it based on the structure of its parent organization that is irrelevant to the operational activities of the museum in general.

3.7 *Marketing*

Museum marketing activities are not only interpreted as 'selling' educational services offered by the museum, but also as an effort to encourage as many people to come to the museum. In addition, the marketing of today's museums is 'relational' that encourages people to have reciprocal relationships with museums and reflected by the high intensity of visiting. It aims to create loyal museum visitor.[42] Of the five museums studied, the existence of a museum workforce specifically assigned to perform marketing activities was found at Museum Listrik & Energi Baru and Museum MACAN. Related to the strategic museum marketing strategic plan, only the Museum MACAN has it.

3.8 *Public relation*

This museum-oriented shift becomes more visitor-oriented, demanding the existence of public relations or at least public relations management activities in the museum. In general, public relations is defined as "something that summarizes all planned communications, inward and outward, between all organizations and their audiences in order to achieve specific objectives based on mutual understanding".[43] Of the five museums studied, not all have a special unit for public relations activities. It is noted that only the Museum Bank Indonesia, Museum Listrik & Energi Baru, and Museum MACAN that owns the unit.

In practice, public relations within the museum can be seen from museum journals, publications (brochures, leaflets, research reports, or museum profiles), websites, social media, reading series, and more. Museum journals are only offered by Museum MACAN in the form of email subscription. All the museums observed have museum profiles as a medium of communication. Other types of publications is only found in Museum Bank Indonesia and Museum MACAN. Research report is only published by Museum MACAN. Until 2014 the Museum Sejarah Jakarta routinely publishes research reports, but stopped because of the efficiency done by the Government of DKI Jakarta. Of the five museums, all museums, except Museum Listrik & Energi Baru have working websites. Social media is only used in Museum Bank Indonesia, Museum MACAN, and Museum Sejarah Jakarta.

There are several things that can be discussed. First, "collection management", "research" and "exhibition" activities are found in every museum. It is noted that all museums do "collection management", although not all museums have complete instru-

Table 2. Comparison of curatorial activities in five observed museums.

Curatorial Activity	Museum Bank Indonesia	Museum Satriamandala	Museum Listrik & Energi Baru	Museum MACAN	Museum Sejarah Jakarta
Collection Management	yes	yes	yes	yes	yes
Research	yes	yes	yes	yes	yes
Conservation	yes	yes	yes	yes	yes
Exhibition	yes	yes	yes	yes	yes
Education	yes	partial	yes	yes	yes
Management	partial	partial	yes	yes	partial
Marketing	partial	partial	partial	yes	partial
Public Relations	yes	partial	partial	yes	partial

42. NG Kotler, P Kotler and W Kotler, *Museum Marketing and Strategy* (San Francisco: Jossey-Bass, 2008).
43. Yulianto, above n 24.

ments for managing collections, such as curators (Museum Satriamandala, Museum Listrik & Energi Baru, and Museum Sejarah Jakarta) or integrated collection management policies (all museums, except Museum MACAN). The "research" activity is found in all the studied museums, although with different types of research. The "exhibition" activities are found in every museum, despite having different exhibition collection and presentation approaches. Second, the "marketing" activity is still done partially by four museums because they do not have strategic museum marketing plan that vital in positioning museums in the community. Third, "public relations" activities have not been fully implemented by the three museums because no special unit is responsible for this activity (Museum Satriamandala and Museum Sejarah Jakarta) or inconsistently conducted (Museum Listrik & Energi Baru). Fourth, "management" activities are not running optimally in three museums, because of lacking human resources (Museum Satriamandala) and organizational structure that is not relevant in managing museums (Museum Bank Indonesia and Museum Sejarah Jakarta). Fifth, "education" activities in a museum (Museum Satriamandala) are still conducted partially where educational methods/media founded are collection labels (not in every collection), guides (not conducted by specialized guiding staff), paid guidebooks, and travelling museum (not routinely conducted).

Sixth, Museum MACAN, which carries out eight curatorial activities fully has many differences with other museums: art museum, newly founded (it was established in 2017 while other museums was founded on, at least 10 years ago), owned by the community (other museums owned by the government/local government), regular ticket price is Rp 100,000, and relatively much higher than other museums (average regular ticket price of four other museums Rp 6,000). It should be noted that this particularity does not necessarily indicate the reason why the Museum MACAN carries out full curatorial activities. These peculiarities are only things not found in or different from other museums. Seventh, Museum Satriamandala which carries out only four curatorial activities has differences: owned by military and unable to recruit its own contract labor, and has a severe lack of manpower resources (half of museum officer position is unfilled).

4 MANAGEMENT AS CRITICAL POINT IN MAKING MUSEUM RELEVANT

According to Edson (2004), the essence of museum management is an effort to help organizations, regardless of the size and complexity of their organization, achieve results consistent with the realization of the museum's vision and mission. Thus, the vision and mission of the five museums need to be analyzed specifically to determine the background of the presence or absence of a curatorial activity. The analysis strategy used is the strategy of "finding a theme" (Saldaña, 2014) with eight types of curatorial Veselko (2011) as the "theme". Table 3 to 7 shows the analysis, while Table 8 shows a comparison of the results of the analysis of vision and mission among the five museums.

It should be noted that despite **Government Regulation no. 66 of 2015** requires the vision and mission of the museum, the Museum Satriamandala does not have a vision, mission, and only has a duty, while the Museum MACAN only has a mission. This condition, according to Dit. PCBM, is still permissible due to the diverse museum conditions. So that in this study the task of the Museum Satriamandala was considered as a substitute for its vision and mission.

Based on the table above, it can be seen that the vision and mission of Museum Bank Indonesia mandates activities of "collection management", "exhibition", "education," management", "marketing", and "public relations". While "research" and "conservation" activities are not textually mandated.

Based on the table above, it can be seen that the task of the Museum Satriamandala mandates activities of "collection management", "conservation", "exhibition", "education," marketing ", and" public relations ". While "research" and "management" activities are not textually mandated.

Table 3. Vision and Mission analysis of Museum Bank Indonesia.

Vision
Being source of knowledge about the history of the Central Bank of Indonesia, and reliable, informative, modern and interesting policy communication (***exhibitions and education***) that are managed professionally (***management***).
Mission
Providing educational facilities to the public (***education and public relations***) in an attractive manner by utilizing appropriate information technology (***exhibitions***) regarding:
• the function and role of Bank Indonesia from time to time;
• a cultural heritage building owned by Bank Indonesia and collections related to the history of Bank Indonesia, including its preservation; and
• economic, monetary and banking knowledge needed by the local community (***marketing, public relations and collection management***).

Table 4. Analysis of Museum Satriamandala's task.

The task of the Satriamandala Museum
• Formulate, manage, maintain and present objects of historical collections of the struggle of the nation and tradition of the TNI (***collection, conservation and exhibition management***).
• Carry out arrangements and guidance in the framework of public services to members of the TNI and the community (***education, marketing, and public relations***).

Table 5. Vision and Mission analysis of Museum Listrik & Energi Baru.

Vision
Recognized as a world-class new electricity and energy museum (***marketing and public relations***) that develops, excels and trusted; becomes a modern, innovative (***exhibition***) museum and is loved by the community (***marketing and public relations***) as an educational recreation venue (***educational***) that future-oriented and relying on human potential (***management***).
Mission
• Making MLEB a fun place to play and learn through display collections, innovative activities and facilities (***collection, exhibition and education management***).
• Realizing MLEB as an ambassador for knowledge in the field of electricity and renewable energy in an effort to build the nation's character that is energy efficient (***education***).
• Participate in educating the community through educational activities (***education***) by conducting synergies with relevant institutions/companies/institutions (***public relations***) and positioning MLEB as a means of information on historical development and electricity technology and new environmentally friendly renewable energy (***collection and education management***).

Based on the table above, it can be seen that the vision and mission of the Electricity & New Energy Museum mandates activities of "collection management", "exhibition", "education," management "," marketing", and" public relations ". While "research" and "conservation" activities are not textually mandated.

Based on the table above, it can be seen that the Museum MACAN mission mandates activities of "collection management", "research", "exhibition", "education," marketing ", and" public relations ". While "conservation" and "management" activities are not textually mandated.

Based on the table above, it can be seen that the vision and mission of the Museum Sejarah Jakarta mandates activities of "collection management", "research", "conservation", "exhibition", "education," marketing ", and" public relations ". While "management" activities are not textually mandated.

Table 6. Mission analysis of Museum MACAN.

Mission

- Dedicated to supporting interdisciplinary education (education) and cultural exchange (education and public relations),
- Offers a wide variety of public programs, and a dynamic exhibition program (exhibitions, education and public relations),
- Become an important platform for local and international artists to present their work to a global audience (marketing and public relations),
- Commission new works by artists that broaden perspectives on contemporary art in and beyond Indonesia (collection, research, exhibition and education management),
- Offer professional development opportunities for artists, curators, and other arts-focused young professionals to help build upon the energy of Indonesia's vibrant arts ecology (research, education and public relations).

Table 7. Analisis visi dan misi Museum Sejarah Jakarta.

Vision

Being a representative museum for Jakarta History that explores the history of urban development, culture, society and politics (***research***) and becomes the pride of the citizens of Jakarta and Indonesia (***marketing and public relations***).

Mission

- Increase public awareness about the history of the development of the city of Jakarta (***education***).
- To make exhibitions related to the history of Jakarta (***exhibition***).
- To preserve and maintain all artifacts, historical items and museum collections (***collection management*** and ***conservation***).
- Provides the right historical storyline through IT (***exhibition***).

Based on the comparison of the results of the analysis of the vision and mission of the five museums above, it was found that the five museums had a vision and mission that mandated activities of "collection management", "exhibition", "education", "marketing", and "public relations". It was noted that there were only two museums whose vision and mission mandated "research" activities, namely the Museum MACAN and. While "conservation" activities are only mandated by the vision and mission of the Museum Satriamandala and the Museum Sejarah Jakarta. The "management" activities are only mandated by the vision and mission of the Museum Bank Indonesia and the Museum Listrik & Energi Baru.

In addition to the vision and mission, other aspects discussed in this section are management organizations. The many organizations that exist above the museum organization have

Table 8. Comparison of curatorial activities mandated in vision and mission of five observed museums.

Kegiatan Kuratorial yang diamanatkan visi dan misi	Museum Bank Indonesia	Museum Satriamandala	Museum Listrik & Energi Baru	Museum MACAN	Museum Sejarah Jakarta
Pengelolaan Koleksi	√	√	√	√	√
Penelitian	X	X	X	√	√
Konservasi	X	√	X	X	√
Pameran	√	√	√	√	√
Edukasi	√	√	√	√	√
Pengelolaan	√	X	√	X	X
Pemasaran	√	√	√	√	√
Hubungan Masyarakat	√	√	√	√	√

implications for many regulations and the decision making process in a museum. The museum's organizational structure can reflect how the museum works in realizing its vision and mission as well as being an indicator of what museological perspective is applied in the museum. Table 9 shows the location of museum organizations in their respective parent organizations. Table 10 shows the organization of five observed museums according to their levels (low, middle, and top).

The table above shows that museum organizations are at different levels within the parent organization. The similarities between the four museums whose organizations are at level 3 and 4 (Museum Bank Indonesia, Satriamandala Museum, New Energy & Energy Museum, and Museum Sejarah Jakarta) are state property. The peculiarities of the Museum Sejarah Jakarta (location of the organization at level 4) are the property of the regional government.

The table above shows that the organizational structure in each museum is different. The museum's organizational structure is similar to the latest museum organizational structure, namely the third museum revolution period, only the Museum MACAN's organizational structure. While the organizational structure of the Museum Listrik & Energi Baru has shown the existence of an aspect of the third museum revolution, namely marketing, although not as collaborative as the Museum MACAN organizational structure. The Museum Satriamandala still uses the functional museum organization model used in the second museum revolution. Two other museums, the Museum Bank Indonesia and the Museum Sejarah Jakarta, have a unique organizational structure.

In the case of the Museum Bank Indonesia, the first uniqueness is the existence of two top management in the museum. This dualism of leadership, according to one interviewee interviewee, is "dynamic" where the pattern of relations between these two positions depends on the holder. The second uniqueness in the museum organization is the name of the office that is more similar to the position in the bank than the museum. This happened because the Museum Bank Indonesia was not a work unit separate from Bank Indonesia. In operational activities as a museum, the technical and administrative functions of the museum are carried out by the Supporting Team, while top management and middle management are supervisors and decision makers.

The organizational structure owned by the Museum Sejarah Jakarta was only applied by the Provincial Government of DKI Jakarta in 2015 with the spirit of efficiency/streamlining of government organizations. This can be seen from an organization headed by one person for four museums. This unusual organizational structure, according to the museum manager, is quite confusing for parties outside the museum to date and parties in the museum at first (in the language of one of the speakers, "rather rude"). Until now the manager of the museum is

Tabel 9. Organization of five observed museums on its parent organization.

Organization Level	**Museum Bank Indonesia**	**Museum Satriamandala**	**Museum Listrik & Energi Baru**	**Museum MACAN**	**Museum Sejarah Jakarta**
Level 1	Bank Indonesia	Tentara Nasional Indonesia	Perusahaan Listrik Negara	Yayasan Museum MACAN	Pemerintah Provinsi DKI Jakarta
Level 2	Dept. Komunikasi	Pusat Sejarah	Pusdiklat	**Museum MACAN**	Dinas Pariwisata dan Kebudayaan
Level 3	**Museum Bank Indonesia**	**Museum Satriamandala**	**Museum Listrik & Energi Baru**		Museum Kesejarahan Jakarta
Level 4					**Museum Sejarah Jakarta**

Table 10. Museum Organizations

Level Manajemen	Museum Bank Indonesia	Museum Satriamandala	Museum Listrik & Energi Baru	Museum MACAN	Museum Sejarah Jakarta
Top Management	• Kepala Museum • Kepala Tim Museum	Kepala Museum	Manajer Museum	Direktur Museum	Kepala Museum Kesejarahan Jakarta *(bertanggung jawab atas empat museum)*
Middle Management	Masing-masing *top management* memiliki: Analis Senior/ Asisten Direktur	• Ka. Seksi Umum • Ka. Seksi Koleksi • Ka. Seksi Bimbingan dan Informasi	• Koor. Bidang Umum • Koor. Bidang Pengembangan • Koor. Bidang Program Publik • Koor. Bidang Marketing	• Ka. Bidang Program Edukasi & Publik • Ka. Bidang Layanan & Fasilitas Pengunjung • Ka. Bidang Pameran • Ka. Bidang Desainer • Ka. Bidang Komunikasi • Konsultan Pengembangan • PT. GMM • Manajer Teknologi Informasi • Manajer Keuangan & Akunting • Manajer SDM • Manajer Pengadaan • Asisten Kurator • Konservator • *Image Service*	• Kepala Tata Usaha • Tim Ahli • Ka. Satuan Pelaksana Koleksi dan Perawatan • Ka. Satuan Pelaksana Sarana dan Prasarana • Ka. Satuan Pelaksana Informasi dan Edukasi • Ka. Satuan Pelayanan Museum Sejarah Jakarta

(Continued)

Table 10. (*Continued*)

Lower Management	Masing-masing *middle management* memiliki tim *supporting* yang terdiri atas: • Analis/Manajer • Official Assistant/ Asistant Manajer • Pelaksana Junior/ Staf	Staf untuk masing-masing bidang.	• Staf Bidang Umum • Staf Subbidang Pengembangan & Penelitian • Staf Subbidang Perawatan dan Pengamanan Koleksi • Staf Program Publik • Staf Subbidang Kegiatan dan Kerjasama • Staf Subbidang Pemasaran dan Humas	• *Registrar* • *Education Officer* • *Public Program Coordinator* • *Education & Public Program Support* • *Desainer Grafis* • Staf Merchandiser • Staf Administrasi & Asisten Direktur	• Staf Tata Usaha • Staf Satuan Pelaksana Sarana dan Prasarana • Staf Satuan Pelaksana Informasi dan Edukasi • Staf Satuan Pelayanan Museum Sejarah Jakarta

still doing trial and error in adjusting the operational activities of the museum in this organizational structure.

Based on communication with DPCBM, one of the phenomena that hampers museum management in Indonesia, especially museums owned by the government/local government, is the fast rotation of employees. This phenomenon is found in all museums owned by the government/regional government studied, especially for top management. At the Museum Bank Indonesia, position holders of Team Leaders and Senior Analysts/Assistant Directors are always rotated for a certain period. The rotation that only happens to the holders of these positions is also due to only those who are registered as employees of Bank Indonesia. Other employees (Supporting Team) are employees who are specifically recruited by the Museum Bank Indonesia only and many of them are contract employees. At the Satriamandala Museum, the Head of the Museum and Pasi were TNI officers who could be rotated from the Satriamandala Museum, even from Pusjarah TNI. The sexy team members are employees recruited by Pusjarah TNI with employment status as civil servants (PNS) or contract employees. At the Museum Listrik & Energi Baru, the rotation of employees outside the museum by the PLN Training Center was only carried out by the Museum Manager. Other employees are permanent museum employees, many of whom have worked for more than ten years. In contrast to other museums, rotation in the Museum Sejarah Jakarta may occur every employee with the status of a civil servant who works in this museum, without knowing the position, because they are counted as local government employees, not museum employees. The status of civil servants as museum employees, according to the manager of the Museum Sejarah Jakarta, is considered problematic for the employee recruitment process. They stated that many young people wanted to work in this museum, but it was difficult to accept because of the status of the PNS where the recruitment process considered "other aspects".

In general, museums owned by the government/regional government must get approval from the above organizations to recruit permanent workers. The contract workers can be recruited directly by museums owned by the government/local government, except the Satriamandala Museum. According to the museum manager, there are 30 positions in the Satriamandala Museum's organizational structure, but currently it is only filled by 15 employees. These fifteen employees carried out all operational activities at the Satrimandala Museum, regardless of their work specialization.

At the Museum MACAN, the only museum owned by the community under study, additional employees still need approval from the Museum MACAN Foundation, even though the selection is done by the museum manager only. Currently, the museum's employees number 35 people with an average age of under 40 years and all are able to speak English. This amount, according to the Museum MACAN Director, needs to be added so that this can develop more aggressively. He also said that he had not found a significant problem in the recruitment process.

Another thing that needs to be considered related to management activities is that of the five museums studied, only the Museum Bank Indonesia and the Museum MACAN have curators/assistant curators when data collection is carried out. The managers of three other museums claim that their museum has a curatorial position which is currently not filled.

Based on the explanation above, it can be concluded that the management of the museum that runs normally is only in the Electricity & New Energy Museum and the Museum MACAN. The Museum Satriamandala has a museum organizational structure in general, but half of the positions in this museum are not filled. Management activities at the Museum Bank Indonesia and the Museum Sejarah Jakarta run every day. However, the organizational structure of these two museums is unusual because it still follows the nomenclature of the parent organization which is relatively irrelevant to museum operations in general.

5 CONCLUSION

The result from the study shows that 'marketing' and 'public relation', which is critical in making museum more ready in responding society's progress, is still conducted with half effort in most museums. The fact that these two activities done partially shows that they do know about the importance of these activities. However, there are some conditions that make them cannot fully do it. In the case of Museum Bank Indonesia and Museum Sejarah Jakarta, the organization of museums is still made like its parent organization, Bank Indonesia and Government of DKI Jakarta respectively. Meanwhile, Museum Satriamandala has a severe lack of manpower which handicapped the museum activities. From this research can also be drawn some suggestions, whether for further research, practice, or stakeholders:

1. There should be more researchs in collecting empirical evidence of curatorial activity in museums and researchs on museum management in Indonesia.
2. In an effort to encourage the museum to be more serious in doing 'marketing' and 'public relation', museum management should be the focus of museum development program in Indonesia where the training or orientation program of the museum head is necessary.

REFERENCES

Akbar, Ali, *Museum Di Indonesia: Kendala Dan Harapan* (Jakarta: Penerbit Papas Sinar Sinanti, 2010)

Asiarto, Luthfi, 'Human Resource Management: Training in Indonesia' in *Comparative Museology & Museography in ASEAN* (Manila: Association of Southeast Asian Nations, Committee on Culture and Information, 1997)

Atmodjo, Junus Satrio, 'Peta Permasalahan Museum: Faktor Peran' (2011) 5(7)*Museografia* 41

Barrett, Jennifer, *Museums and the Public Sphere* (West Sussex: Wiley-Blackwell, 2011)

Bennett, James, 'The Changing Meaning of Research in Professional Development Training for the Museum Worker' (2011) 5(7) *Museografia*

Creswell, John, *Research Design: Qualitative, Quantitative, and Mixed Methods Approaches, 4th Edition* (Los Angeles: Sage Publication, Inc., 2014)

Edson, Gary, 'Museum Management' in *Running A Museum: A Practical Handbook* (Paris: ICOM, 2004)

Ewin, TAM and JAV. Ewin., 'In Defernce of the Curator: Maximising Museum Impact' (2016) 31 (4) *Museum Management and Curatorship*

Ghautama, Gatot and Prioyulianto (eds), *Pedoman Museum Indonesia* (Jakarta: Direktorat Pelestarian Cagar Budaya dan Permuseuman, Direktorat Jenderal Kebudayaan, Kementerian Pendidikan dan Kebudayaan, 2012)

Harrison, Julia D, 'Ideas of Museums in the 1990s' (1994) 13(2) *Museum Management and Curatorship*

Herreman, Yani, 'Display, Exhibits and Exhibitions' in *Running A Museum: A Practical Handbook* (Paris: ICOM, 2004)

Heumann-Gurian, Elaine, 'Curator: From Soloist to Impresario' in Fiona Cameron and Linda Kelly (eds), *Hot topics, public culture, museums* (London: Cambridge Scholars, 2010)

Kotler, NG, P Kotler and W Kotler, *Museum Marketing and Strategy* (San Francisco: Jossey-Bass, 2008)

Kreps, Christina, 'Appropiate Museology in Theory and Practice' (2008) 23(1) *Museum Management and Curatorship*

Ladkin, Nicola, 'Collection Management' in *Running A Museum: A Practical Handbook* (Paris: ICOM, 2004)

Laksito, Oki, 'Kompetensi Profesi Museum Indonesia' (2012) 6(10) *Museografia* 19

Longair, Sarah, 'Culture of Curating: The Limits of Authority' (2015) 8(1) *Museum History Journal* 1

Magetsari, Noerhadi, *Perspektif Arkeologi Masa Kini Dalam Konteks Indonesia* (Jakarta: Penerbit Buku Kompas, 2016)

Marstine, Janet, 'Introduction' in Janet Marstine (ed), *New Museum Theory and Practice: An Introduction* (Oxford: Blackwell Publishing, 2006)

McCall, Vikki dan Clive Gray, 'Museums and the "New Museology": Theory, Practice, and Organisational Change' (2014) 29 (1)*Museum Management and Curatorship*

van Mensch, Peter, 'Towards a Methodology of Museology' (1992)

van Mensch, Peter, 'Museology and Management: Enemies or Friends? Current Tendencies in Theoretical Museology and Museum Management in Europe' in E Mizushima (ed), *Museum management in the 21st century* (Tokyo: Museum Management Academy, 2004)

Merriman, Nick, 'Museum Visiting as Cultural Phenomenon' in *The New Museology* (London: Reaktion Books., 1989)

Mork, Paal, 'Marketing' in *Running A Museum: A Practical Handbook* (Paris: ICOM, 2004)

Rizqika, Mawaddatul Husna, 'Model Manajemen Kuratorial Dalam Paradigma Museologi Baru: Studi Kasus Museum Nasional' (2017)

Sedyawati, Edy, *In Celebrating Indonesia: Fifty Years with the Ford Foundation 1953-2003* (New York: Ford Foundation, 2003)

Shanks, Michael, 'Public Archaeology/Museology/Conservation/Heritage' in Colin Renfrew and Paul Bahn (eds), *Archaeology: Key Concepts* (New York: Routledge, 2005) 164

Simon, Nina, *The Participatory Museum* (Santa Cruz: Museum 2.0., 2010)

Stam, Deirdre C, 'The Informed Muse: The Implication of "The New Museology" for Museum Practice' (1993) 12 (3)*Museum Management and Curatorship*

Susanto, Mikke, 'Manajemen Kuratorial Pameran Seni Rupa Di JOGJA GALLERY Antara 2006-2008' (2012) 6(10) *Museografia*

Veselko, Irena, 'What Are the Core Competencies Needed in a Museum? A View from Slovenia' in Jane A Legget (ed), *Staff and Training in Regional Museum* (Paris: ICOM-ICR, ICOM-ICTOP, and Regional Museum Murska Sobota., 2011)

Viau-Courville, Mathieu, 'Museums Without (Scholar-)Curators: Exhibition-Making in Times of Managerial Curatorship' (2017) 68 (271–272)*Museum International*

Woollard, Vicky, 'Caring for the Visitor' in *Running A Museum: A Practical Handbook* (Paris: ICOM, 2004)

Wronska-Friend, Maria, 'Why Haven't We Been Taught All That At School? Crosscultural Community Projects in North Queensland, Australia' (2012) 55(1)*Curator*

Yulianto, Kresno, *Di Balik Pilar-Pilar Museum* (Jakarta Selatan: Wedatama Widya Sastra, 2016)

Culture and International Law - Juwana et al. (Eds)
© 2019 Taylor & Francis Group, London, ISBN 978-1-138-38766-9

Sinking of a fishing vessel as the sovereignty of coastal state for environment

Amelia Rahmi Syaiful
Centre for International Law Studies, Research Cluster for Sustainable Ocean Policy, Faculty of Law, University of Indonesia

Melda Kamil Ariadno
International Law, Faculty of Law, University of Indonesia

ABSTRACT: Foreign-flagged ships scuttling undertaken by coastal States such as Australia, Indonesia and Malaysia are special measures in order to reduce the foreign fish ships coming into their territorial waters, in addition to special measures aimed to prevent and provide protection against the environment at sea. Countries have the right to make related policies as scuttling efforts to prevent, reduce and control pollution of the marine environment which is caused due to an infringement by foreign ships in territorial waters. Article 194 of measures to prevent, reduce and control pollution of the marine environment related to UNCLOS 1982 in coastal States, this rule provides States must take all the necessary action in accordance with the Convention, both individually as well as collectively according to the need to prevent, reduce and control pollution of the marine environment caused by any source by using this way for the most practical ways on them and in accordance with their abilities, as long as these countries must seek to comply with their policies. This action was carried out by coastal States such as Australia, Indonesia and Malaysia in the course of law enforcement not only for third countries avoiding the decline of the quality of resources both from the population, the number of catches as well as the condition of the ecosystem that is the habitat of fish. This provision in accordance with the principle of sustainable development that the country responsible for the guarantee activity in their jurisdiction and control do not damage the environment of other States.

KEYWORDS: sinking of fishing vessel, sovereignty, economic exclusive zone, coastal state, enforcement at sea, environmental studies

1 INTRODUCTION

The ocean, with its enormity and mystery, has ever been part of human consciousness, and thus it is the very foundation of human life. History has recorded that oceans have two certain functions as communication media and as resources of large capacity warehouses. Along with the development in the era of globalization, these cited functions is then developed to create legal rules related to the sea. As stated in the principle of *res communis* where areas beyond, and not subject to incorporation into, state territory; thus available for unilateral use and exploitation by all states.

Freedom at sea means being free from threats or dangers of pirates in using or utilizing the sea; and thus it does not conflict with absolute sea control.[1] This is particularly supported by

1. Mochtar Kusumaatmadja, *Pengantar Hukum Internasional: Buku 1 – Bagian Umum* (Bandung : Bina Cipta, 8th ed, 2001).

a perspective disclosing that the maritime areas are under national sovereignty or jurisdiction as referred to the territorial seas. This premise is the basic principle of international law of the sea, where coastal maritime states are allowed to make restrictions on the sea which can mean that these states can form maritime boundaries around its coastlines, as marine territories, and claim to be the territory of the coastal state included in making the rule of law.

Every country has the right to regulate its own country. However, in taking this view, it is clear if viewed from international perspectives, the concept of sovereignty is relative. In other words, when a country has a dispute with another country, the court in deciding something shall be regarded to highlight which country has the relevant argument and shall give the land to a country that nominally submits a good legal case. In this regard, if viewed in terms of the sea, the sovereignty applies if foreign vessels or foreign-flagged vessels enter the sovereignty of other states. It indicates that these ships shall comply with the regulations in the marine territory of the States sovereignty they are visiting. Sea control, seen in terms of defense, shall guarantee the use of the seas for national interests and prevent other states from using the marine potential in excess.

The United Nations Convention on the Law of the Sea (UNCLOS 1982), also called the Law of the Sea regulates the maritime zones, rules governing the Protection and Conservation of Marine Environment. It has served as the basis for the regulation and general obligations of member states.[2] Prevention of marine pollution is regulated in Part XII of UNCLOS 1982 from article 192 to article 237. UNCLOS 1982 has adopted an environmental protection system proposed by the Stockholm 1972 Declaration in which UNCLOS recognized the country's sovereignty over natural resources in its territory.

UNCLOS 1982 obliges states to protect (protect and conserve) the environment and natural resources from exploitation that are not environmentally friendly and hence this provision is part of UNCLOS 1982, as well as the coastal state like Indonesia, Malaysia and Australia have ratified UNCLOS 1982, thus the coastal states shall implement these provisions into national legislation specifically related to the act of sinking foreign vessels.

The state as the main subject of international law has rights and obligations. These are implicated in the regulation of each country that is related to state sovereignty. The sovereignty of such country then cannot be separated from the power of a country to regulate the territory, whether on land, sea, or air. State sovereignty in the sea is obtained by the coastal state to facilitate regulation of waters. Through the ratification of the state against UNCLOS 1982, coastal states such as Indonesia, Australia and Malaysia referred to the rules of international law of the sea.

The act of sinking of foreign-flagged vessels seeks to avoid a decline in the quality of resources both from the population, number of catching, and the condition of its ecosystem such as fish habitat. The sinking of foreign ships is kind of special action conducted by the coastal state in an effort to safeguard the country's sovereignty. This is based on the mandate of UNCLOS 1982 as references for the coastal state to enforce the law and this action is part of the country's efforts to avoid overfishing in the future because if it happens this may threaten the sustainability of fisheries and marine resources, special measures by the coastal states in the hope of bringing deterrent effect on offenders (at least those who commit serious crime essentially.

2 STATES AS THE SUBJECTS OF INTERNATIONAL LAW

State has sovereignty in taking care of its domestic affairs, as well as carrying out internal sovereignty. Internal sovereignty of particular states is manifested in the state's authority to determine the political system, domestic policies, as well as matters relating to the formation of a

2. R. Churchill and AV Lowe, *The Law of the Sea* (Manchester University Press, 1988).

national legal system, in which the determination of all these things cannot be interfered by other states.[3]

The state can act as a legal person (juristic person) in the rules of international law only by human mediation as a subject of international law, which results in a right and obligation for each country that participates in the rule. The legal subject then develops into a sovereignty if in contact with national law, in line with this, the state does not depend on other countries to make domestic policies. The act of sinking foreign-flagged vessels, however, is based on violations committed by foreign nationals in maritime zones. The sinking of foreign-flagged vessels is a special action that has been implemented by several countries as an implication of the existence of the Fisheries Law and specifically regulated in the legislation. This action was caused by illegal, unregulated and unreported fishing (IUUFishing) fishing activities as well as the existence of indicators that the vessel was allegedly dangerous for marine life.

The concept of the state territory provides the principle of non-intervention in matters that cover domestic jurisdiction and principles to respect the territorial integrity of other countries.[4] As already suggested, the coastal state has sovereign rights related to the enforcement of laws and regulations, this enforcement is then implied by the coastal state in special actions in the form of sinking foreign vessels. Sovereignty bestows full rights, or supreme authority, on a country within its territorial waters, familiarly called Sovereign rights in an EEZ are offset by the obligations of the coastal states to make conservation efforts.[5] With regard to this issue, the policy is concerned with maintaining fish resources as part of suistanable development.

3 METHOD

This research study is conducted in regard to normative juridical research focused on understanding the application of norms in positive law.[6] Returning briefly to the above explanation, this research is carried out to analyze and to reflect the variety of activities conducted by the coastal states in view of sources in the form of international law, national law and legal theories. Legal research analyzes the relationship between the sovereignty of a coastal state with specific actions in the form of sinking foreign-flagged vessels.

Moreover, the scientific method used to conduct the current research is the legislation approach, by conducting studies related to the laws, and thus, the regulations in relation to the sovereignty of states at maritime zones are associated with the sinking of ships.

4 RESULT AND DISCUSSION

4.1 *United Nations on the Law of the Sea*

The implication of Article 62 point 2 of the 1982 Convention on the Law of the Sea, on the Burning and/or sinking of foreign-flagged vessels is part of the coastal state's obligation to conserve natural resources in the territorial waters both in sovereignty zones and rights to sovereign and thus in the future it shall not experience over exploitation in order to maintain the stability of the sea.

Basically, the territorial waters both outside and within the sovereign territory are a means for other countries to utilize fish resources in a coastal state, however it will not be in line if it

3. Suryo Sakti Hadiwijoyo, *Perbatasan Negara Dalam Dimensi Hukum Internasional* (Yogyakarta : Graha Ilmu, 2011).
4. Malcolm Shaw, *International Law* (Cambridge : Cambridge University Press, 1997).
5. Chairul Anwar, *Zona Ekonomi Eksklusif Di Dalam Hukum Internasional Dilengkapi Dengan Analisis Zona Ekonomi Eksklusif Indonesia Dan ZEE Di Asia-Pasifik* (Jakarta : Sinar Grafika, 1995).
6. Valerine J.L.K, *Modul Metode Penelitian Hukum Edisi Revisi* (Jakarta : Fakultas Hukum UI, 2015).

is not accompanied by the wise protection and management of fish resources based on sustainable principles. The coastal state has the power to make laws and regulations by respecting sovereign rights.

There is now considerable evidence that ratification at UNCLOS 1982 has provided the right to regulate law enforcement at sea to several states such as Indonesia, Australia and Malaysia. States have governments responsible for regulating the entire territories. Such as Indonesia, as the largest archipelagic country in the world, it shall be as much as possible to maintain marine sovereignty based on the 1982 Convention on the Law of the Sea, Indonesia's framework for using exclusive rights to sea areas also makes it easy to carry out jurisdictions in its territory.

The rules regarding the obligation for the coastal state to make policies related to prevention and protection of marine environment are regulated by 1982 UNCLOS Article 192, this rule is an implication of the existence of state sovereignty in the sea in terms of making rules. Countries have sovereign rights to exploit their natural wealth in accordance with environmental policies and obligations to protect and conserve the marine environment, afterwards, the state will take it either individually or together as it should, all actions are needed to prevent, reduce and control pollution of the marine environment from any source. Specific action in the form of sinking of foreign vessels is part of state control under the country's jurisdiction in order to avoid environmental pollution in coastal countries and neighboring countries.

The purpose of establishing special actions is to make coral reefs for fish dwellings, this is in line with the principle of sustainable development giving the concept that future generations will feel the same as the current generation. In principle 21 the Stockholm Declaration affirms that states have a United Nations Charter and the principles of international law sovereign rights to exploit their own resources in accordance with their own environmental politics and the responsibility to guarantee activity in their jurisdiction or supervision that does not damage the environment of other countries or areas outside national jurisdictional boundaries.

Assessed in international law, this action includes efforts to protect the territory of sovereignty and seen from the internal aspects of sovereignty that the action taken is the exclusive right or authority of the state to form its institutions, the right to make the desired law and actions to comply how these institutions work.[7] The implementation of this action is an application part of territorial jurisdiction where a country implements and enforces the country's national law on everything that happens in the region concerned. Special actions are part of the judicial process that is carried out before the decision has been approved such as the ship shall be stranded, sunk or burnt.

Some law enforcers in coastal countries are instructed to maximize this rule such as the navy, as well as the coast state coast guard in the process of climbing, arresting, carry out investigations up to the process of sinking and/or burning the ship. However, countries have their own basic rules in their fisheries law, there is sufficient preliminary evidence when no special measures are applied and then all foreign-flagged fishing vessels that violate the EEZ are drowned, there is a judicial process carried out by the authorities of each country. The implementation of the existence of sovereignty is by implementing the sources of international law and respecting the sovereignty of other countries by not intervening or interfering with the internal problems of other countries if not requested, one source of international law which later became a guide for the coastal state was the 1982 United Nations on the Law of the Sea reinterpreted by parties that had ratified the fisheries law.

On conditions set forth in article 73 paragraph (3) of UNCLOS 1982, it clarifies the sinking of foreign-flagged vessels by other countries as a way to respect the sovereignty of other countries by not interfering with policies. Regarding this sovereignty when the state deals with other countries there is certainly a guarantee of the existence of sovereignty from the country,

7. Boer Mauna, *Hukum Internasional: Pengertian, Peranan Dan Fungsi Dalam Era Dinamika Global* (Bandung: Alumni, 2nd ed, 2000).

meaning a jurisdiction over the territory in which this action is the authority to impose the law in the coastal state.

The sinking of foreign-flagged ships is due to sea problems in the territorial waters that cannot be resolved through a moratorium. In each coastal country there are differences in practices and rules related to special actions because these countries are limited by the existence of state sovereignty. The sovereignty of the coastal state in upholding and implementing regulations and the judiciary is a manifestation of article 56 paragraph (1) letter (a) in UNCLOS. Efforts made by the coastal state through the implementation of this action as a form of protection and preservation of the marine environment, in this case keep the fish resources that are inside can still be enjoyed in the future.

4.2 *Indonesia*

Law number 45 of 2009 concerning amendments to Law No. 31 of 200 concerning Fisheries Article 69 paragraph (1) and paragraph (4) is the legal basis of the drowning of illegal fishing vessels which do not have official documents or violate legal provisions of Indonesia.

In the explanation in article 69 paragraph (4) what is meant by "sufficient preliminary evidence" is preliminary evidence to suspect that there is a criminal offense in the field of fisheries by foreign-flag fishing vessels, for example foreign-flagged fishing vessels do not have SIPI (fishing licenses) and SIKPI (Permit for Fishing Vessel), as well as clearly catching and/or transporting fish when entering the territory of the Republic of Indonesia fisheries management. Fisheries investigators or supervisors jointly carry out this special action with sufficient preliminary evidence. Fisheries supervisory ships have the duty to carry out the supervisory and law enforcement functions in the field of fisheries in the Indonesian fisheries management area. This special action is considered as a deterrence effect or a deterrent to territorial violations that can harm and threaten the state's sovereignty.

The sinking of foreign fishing vessels entering Indonesian sea areas and stealing fish is demonstrated as an attempt to create a deterrent effect on the perpetrators. This action resulted in an increase in national fish stocks, which experienced an increase of 6.5 million tons to reach 9.9 million tons. This figure is assessed from 2016 stock assessment activities with 11 Fisheries Management Areas (WPP).

4.3 *Australia*

The seas around Australia's coastline are increasingly threatened with the presence of waste and pollution made in the sea. Australia regulates the loading and disposal of waste at sea based on the Environment Protection (Sea Dumping) Act 1981. Under these rules, the Commonwealth has the aim of minimizing the threat of pollution by prohibiting the disposal of marine waste which is considered too dangerous for marine environments, as well as regulating the disposal of waste that is permitted to reduce environmental impacts.

Foreign fishing vessels trigger the risk of increasing environmental and biosecurity of marine and land resources and human health in our remote coastal communities through the presence of marine pests on the bilge, rodents, live insects (such as mosquitoes, termites, borer and ants), domestic animals as well as birds on board as well as diseases among crew members. Such only action is regarded as the last action chosen by the Australian government, because there is a risk of sea pest infestation, in sinking foreign fishing vessels in the Marine Park. Australia implements actions in the country's environmental laws as a special environmental measure of the state's obligation to protect and conserve the marine environment.

4.4 *Malaysia*

The Malaysian government has made this action as part of an effort to eradicate the IUUF. In other words, this action has not been stated to be perfect by the government of Malaysia because it is highly necessary to learn the procedures carried out by MMEA as law enforcement agencies that carry out this action. Therefore, this action is a last resort in the hope of giving psychological effect such as to not commit crimes for the further perpetrators.

The Malaysian government has implemented the action as part of the process of investigating fisheries crime because it can be conducted when there is local court decisions. There are no standard rules related to procedures for sinking foreign-flagged vessels in Malaysia. The purpose of the sinking of foreign-flagged vessels in Malaysia is to form artificial coral reefs for fish habitat to improve the economy of local fishermen.

Malaysia's actions in combating illegal fishing are carried out such as arrests, high fines, seizures and sinking of ships. The results obtained by Malaysia in the act of sinking foreign-flagged ships were the wrecks of ships that had been sunk into homes for large lion and grouper.

5 CONCLUSION

By way of conclusion, the researchers would simply like to draw the attention once more to the fact that Australia, Indonesia and Malaysia are implementing measures to sink foreign-flagged vessels for law enforcement for perpetrators who have committed to violate their territories. As well, the coastal states have ratified UNCLOS 1982 as the main reference in making policies at the sea because it is an obligation for these states to contribute to decision-making, planning and implementation that enhance to sustainable development policies.

REFERENCES

Anwar, Chairul, Zona Ekonomi Eksklusif Di Dalam Hukum Internasional Dilengkapi Dengan Analisis Zona Ekonomi Eksklusif Indonesia Dan ZEE Di Asia-Pasifik (Jakarta: Sinar Grafika, 1995)

Churchill, R. and AV Lowe, *The Law of the Sea* (Manchester University Press, 1988)

Hadiwijoyo, Suryo Sakti, *Perbatasan Negara Dalam Dimensi Hukum Internasional* (Yogyakarta: Graha Ilmu, 2011)

J.L.K., Valerine, *Modul Metode Penelitian Hukum Edisi Revisi* (Jakarta: Fakultas Hukum UI, 2015)

Kusumaatmadja, Mochtar, *Pengantar Hukum Internasional: Buku 1 – Bagian Umum* (Bandung: Bina Cipta, 8th ed, 2001)

Mauna, Boer, Hukum Internasional : Pengertian, Peranan Dan Fungsi Dalam Era Dinamika Global (Bandung: Alumni, 2nd ed, 2000)

Shaw, Malcolm, *International Law* (Cambridge : Cambridge University Press, 1997)

United Nations Convention On The Law Of The Sea (UNCLOS) 1982.Indonesia, Undang-Undang nomor 45 tahun 2009 tentang Perubahan atas Undang-Undang nomor 31 tahun 2004 tentang Perikanan.______, Kitab Undang-Undang Hukum Acara Pidana.Australia, *Sea Dumping Act* 1981______, *Fisheries Management Act* 1991______, *Maritime Power Act* 2013Malaysia, *Fisheries Act* 1982

Culture and International Law - Juwana et al. (Eds)
© 2019 Taylor & Francis Group, London, ISBN 978-1-138-38766-9

Local community perceptions toward world heritage inscription of Kota Tua Jakarta

Burhanuddin Aziz & Agi Ginanjar
Universitas Indonesia, Indonesia

ABSTRACT: Local communities play an essential role in reviving and sustaining Kota Tua Jakarta. Community is also one of the most important stakeholder in managing the World Heritage. The community's participation can be varied from involvement in the decision-making processes at the highest level down to economic involvement and the promotion of the destination at the lowest level. What shape community perceptions ultimately takes depends on the circumstance of destinations. This study attempts to analyze the current community perceptions toward the inscription of Kota Tua Jakarta as World Heritage by UNESCO. Using partial least squares-structural equation modeling (PLS-SEM), this research investigates questionnaires completed by a sample of residents of Kota Tua Jakarta Area. Social exchange theory (SET) was developed as a framework based in order to elaborate the relationships. The findings of this study show that local community strongly support the inscriptions of The World Heritage status. This research expands upon the community perceptions literature in the context of Kota Tua Jakarta. In addition, the results have practical implications for local authorities responsible for the sustainable conservation management of Kota Tua Jakarta.

KEYWORDS: local community, kota tua jakarta, perceptions, world heritage inscriptions

1 INTRODUCTION

In preserving archaeological remains, the government cannot do this individually but requires an extension to facilitate the implementation of policies and public support, for example by embracing the local community. In the Archaeological Messages and Messengers article[1] it is explained that why reaching the public is important, namely: misunderstanding and misinterpretation of heritage; support from the public and government; and as an effort to maintain the existence of archaeological sites. The above facts explain why the local community is important to be involved in the preservation of cultural heritage, especially those who care and focus on this problem.

According to Carman (in Cooper et.al, 1995) in archeology studies, a branch of science that addresses cultural preservation issues is known as cultural resource management (CRM) or known by other names as archaeological heritage management (AHM) and archaeological resource management (ARM) depending on where this terminology is used. Archaeologists in America use the term CRM more often while in the UK more AHM terms are developed. In Indonesia, the term often used is cultural resource management (MDSB). But it is common if experts in Indonesia also use the term CRM which is also widely used, as Edi Sedyawati also uses this terminology to explain that cultural resource management (CRM) is a cultural result

1. Francis P McManamon, 'Archaeological Messages and Messengers' in G Fairclough et al (eds), *The Heritage Reader* (New York, Routledge, 2000) 2.

that will be valued and utilized requires proper handling and management, which efficient and effective in addition to being able to answer the need for knowledge (Sedyawati, 2003).

Looking at the description from the above description, it can be concluded that in managing cultural resources many parties are needed to get involved because it involves the interests of many stakeholders in it. One of the important stakeholders in the preservation of cultural heritage is the local community, because in addition to their direct use of cultural resources they will also have an impact on policies related to cultural heritage.

Several studies related to the influence of the community on cultural heritage have been carried out. One of them is done by Rasoolimanesh, et al (2017), with George Town's cultural heritage objects. Located in the northeast of Penang Island in northern Malaysia, George Town was declared a World Heritage Site in July 2008 by UNESCO. Since it was developed centuries ago, George Town has been used as a place of trade and cultural exchange between east and west. George Town develops from a trading port to a historic multicultural city (Think City, 2014). George Town is home to various cultures (especially Chinese, Indian and Malay) and religion, all living together peacefully. Therefore, George Town has tangible and intangible cultural heritage properties (for example, historical buildings that represent various cultures and religions within the George Town core zone, festivals, costumes, languages, art, music, and lifestyles) that show values extraordinary universal (UNESCO, 2008).

The most recent research related to the community in the Kota Tua Jakarta is from Susiana Dewi Ratih (2016) who wrote a dissertation on "Organizing Stakeholders in the Empowerment of Tourism Communities Case Study: Old Town DMO Jakarta, 2011-2015". Adrianus Waranei Muntu (2017) wrote a thesis with the title "Analysis of the Participation of Local Communities in the Development of Travel Attractions in the Kota Tua Jakarta". This thesis focuses on the participation of local communities in developing the tourist attraction of the Kota Tua Jakarta to find out the forms of participation, factors that influence their participation and the impact of their participation.

From previous research collected, it turns out that there has been no specific research that addresses or analyzes the influence of local communities that utilize Kota Tua Jakarta area as a whole. Therefore, this research becomes important to be carried out in the framework of the development of archeology in general and CRM specialization in particular.

1.1 *Local community perceptions of world heritage site inscription*

The local community is an important and effective stakeholder, where they can have a very valuable impact on various developments in the future. Stakeholder theory explains that the interests and perceptions of various stakeholders must be considered important if they expect the development of a site to be successful and sustainable. To understand the importance of perceptions among various communities that are important stakeholders in the preservation of cultural heritage and what they expect.

Utilization of a historical area as a place of activity proves that the area still exists with historic ancient buildings in the present but still requires special attention and requires a large role from stakeholders so that the historical area can be useful also for the next generation. Although the budget for preservation of the region is still very limited, the role of stakeholders that will continuously support sustainable conservation efforts.

1.2 *Community factors and residents' perceptions*

1.2.1 *Theoretical framework*

SET is a theory that bridges various disciplines in the social field. SET theory has taken over the concept of costs, rewards and benefits derived from economics and applied them to the disciplines of anthropology, sociology and social psychology. Social exchange occurs between two or more individuals, whether in a group or not, with the existence of profitable transactions and relationships. According to Murdvee (2009), basically, SET theory focuses on the social relations and personality of individuals who form resources and profits.

In general, if conclusions are drawn from the opinions of the social science expert, it is found that SET leads to the benefits or benefits of an endeavor. The context of SET here is right with this research because this theory is applied to construct hypotheses related to the effects of community cultural attitudes, community gain, community members 'gain, and status consistency on residents' perceptions, with the aim of making interesting findings for research further research. SET theoretically explains the positive and negative perceptions of the community regarding their support for conservation efforts.[2] According to SET's theory, the community will increase their support for preservation of cultural heritage if it feels beneficial their motives include support for tourism development.

1.2.2 *Influencing community factors based on SET*

There are several factors that influence the role of the local community in preserving cultural heritage in the Kota Tua Jakarta. In this study, the factors used to determine the influence of the community on conservation in the Kota Tua Jakarta include community attachment (CA), community cultural attitude (CAT), community involvement (CINV), community gain (CG), community members gain (CMG), and consistency status (SC). To find out the role of the community based on SET, 12 hypotheses were made.

H1 - Effect of Community Attachment on Positive Perceptions

Community attachments pay attention to feelings, emotions, and a sense of belonging from the community. This section will look at the relationship between the love and belonging to the community and the preservation of Kota Tua Jakarta. There have been several previous studies discussing the relationship between community attachment to community perception.[3] Some found a significant relationship between community attachment to positive perceptions[4], but there were also those who found a relationship between community attachment and positive perceptions were non-significant. However, when using SET theory to find out the relationship between community attachment to positive perceptions, there is a significant relationship between community attachment to positive perceptions. This is because the community that has an inherent sense of love and belonging will pay attention to the benefits that will be gained from the preservation of cultural heritage in the Kota Tua Jakarta. Local communities that have strong ties will feel happy with the development of Kota Tua Jakarta. Thus the first hypothesis in this study is

Hypothesis 1: Community attachments have a positive effect on positive perceptions of the community.

H2 - Effect of Community Attachment on Negative Perceptions

The influence of community attachments on negative perceptions has also been done in previous studies.[5] Some found a significant relationship between community attachments to positive perceptions[6], but there were also those who found a relationship between community attachment and positive perceptions were non-significant.[7] However, when using SET theory to determine the relationship between community attachments to negative perceptions, there is a significant relationship between community attachments and negative perceptions. This is because the community that has an inherent sense of love and belonging will pay attention to the costs that will be incurred from the preservation of cultural heritage in the Kota Tua Jakarta. Communities that

2. Ibid.
3. P Latkova and C Vogt, 'Residents Attitudes Toward Existing and Future Tourism Development in Rural Communities' (2012) 51(1) *Journal of Travel Research* 50; C Tosun, 'Host Perceptions of Impacts: A Comparative Tourism Study' [2002] *Annals of Tourism Research* 231.
4. Latkova and Vogt, above n 4; S Rasoolimanesh et al, 'The Effects of Community Factors on Residents Perceptions Toward World Heritage Site Inscription and Sustainable Tourism Development' (2017) 25(2) *Journal of Sustainable Tourism* 198.
5. Latkova and Vogt, above n 4; Rasoolimanesh et al, above n 5.
6. Rasoolimanesh et al, above n 5.
7. Latkova and Vogt, above n 4.

have strong ties will be worried about the development of Kota Tua Jakarta. Thus the second hypothesis in this study is

Hypothesis 2: Community attachments have a positive effect on negative community perceptions.

H3 - Effect of Cultural Attitudes on Positive Perceptions

Kota Tua Jakarta according to SET theory, cultural values and beliefs held by the community will influence the perception given. If there are policies or developments carried out on Kota Tua Jakarta area that are in accordance with the culture and trust of the community, then the community will agree and support. Because with the development that is in accordance with the culture and beliefs of the community, the community will be able to easily introduce and promote their culture to people who visit the Kota Tua Jakarta. In addition, the community will also feel proud of the development of Kota Tua Jakarta. There are several researchers who have conducted research on the relationship between the development of a region to contribute to the preservation of local culture, a sense of community pride in its culture, and also the preservation of cultural identity possessed.[8] So, to describe the relationship between cultural attitudes and positive perceptions the third hypothesis is made, namely

Hypothesis 3: Cultural attitudes have a positive effect on positive perceptions of the community.

H4 - Effect of Cultural Attitudes on Negative Perceptions

If there are policies or developments carried out on the Kota Tua Jakarta that are not in accordance with the culture and beliefs of the community, the community will not agree and support. Although the community has positive perceptions of the development of an area because it is in accordance with their culture and beliefs, but usually they also feel worried about negative things that can happen due to the development of an area. Thus the relationship between cultural attitudes towards negative perceptions has a positive relationship. That way, the hypothesis that corresponds to the relationship between cultural attitudes to negative perceptions is

Hypothesis 4: Cultural attitudes have a positive effect on negative community perceptions.

H5 - Effect of Community Involvement on Positive Perceptions

There are several previous studies that use SET theory to determine the relationship between community perceptions and community involvement.[9] Using the SET theory can be explained the relationship between the willingness and readiness of the community towards community participation in the preservation of an area. The existence of community involvement can provide opportunities for the community to participate in the preservation of Kota Tua Jakarta. The relationship between community involvement in positive perceptions in the conservation of the area in Kota Tua Jakarta can be written in the fifth hypothesis, namely

Hypothesis 5: Community involvement has a positive effect on positive perceptions of the community.

H6 - Effect of Community Involvement on Negative Perceptions

Community involvement can make the community participate in the process of reciprocal relations with stakeholders of a cultural heritage area. For example, to the government or the private sector. The relationship between community involvement in negative community perceptions of conservation in the Kota Tua Jakarta as in hypothesis 6, namely

Hypothesis 6: Community involvement has a negative effect on negative community perceptions.

H7 - Effect of Community Gain on Positive Perceptions

The development of cultural heritage areas can provide positive things for the communities that act in the region. For example, the number of visitors to cultural heritage areas can increase income for the community. There are several studies that examine the increase of

8. Andereck et al, above n 2; Rasoolimanesh et al, above n 5.
9. Latkova and Vogt, above n 4; Tosun, above n 4.

income to the community towards the community's perception of the preservation of cultural heritage areas (Andereck & Nyaupane, 2011; Andereck etc., 2005; Jurowski etc., 1997; Latkova & Vogt, 2012; McGehee & Andereck, 2004). In accordance with the SET theory, that the community will feel more interested in doing something if they get a reward or profit, for example an increase in income. Thus the relationship between community gain and positive perceptions of the community can be illustrated by the following hypothesis:

Hypothesis 7: Community gain has a positive effect on the positive perception of the community.

H8 - Influence of Community Gain Against Negative Perceptions

Economic effects that can increase income for the community make the community more supportive if there is a preservation of cultural heritage areas rather than the absence of the development and preservation of cultural heritage areas. The relationship between community gain and negative community perceptions to preserve cultural heritage in the Kota Tua area can be illustrated by the following hypothesis:

Hypothesis 8: Community gain has a negative effect on the negative perception of the community.

H9 - Effect of Community Members Gain Against Positive Perceptions

In addition to providing economic improvement for the community, the development of cultural heritage areas can also improve the economy for community members. Community members who receive many benefits from the use of cultural heritage areas will be more supportive of the preservation of cultural heritage areas. That way the relationship between community members gain on positive perceptions of preservation of cultural heritage in the Kota Tua Jakarta can be described by the ninth hypothesis, namely,

Hypothesis 9: Community members gain have a positive effect on positive perceptions of the community.

H10 - Effect of Community Members Gain Against Negative Perceptions

The benefits gained by community members from preserving cultural heritage areas naturally make community members support the existence of conservation. This is because with the preservation of cultural heritage areas, community members can use the area to do business. So that the relationship between community members gain and the negative perceptions of the community to preserve cultural heritage in the Kota Tua Jakarta can be hypothesized with the following 10 hypotheses:

Hypothesis 10: Community members gain has a negative effect on negative community perceptions.

H11 - Effect of Status Consistency on Positive Perceptions

Based on SET theory, the consistency status of a tribe, gender, certain cultures in a particular community can provide benefits for an individual and can also influence their perception. In addition, the desire to show what is owned, for example in the form of cultural festivals, religious activities, food, art, and lifestyle can increasingly make the community support the preservation of cultural heritage areas. Art exhibitions and other activities attract visitors to a particular area. And for communities that show off their culture, they will feel more proud and their status is considered. Thus the status of consistency has a positive influence on the preservation of cultural heritage areas, as well as what happens in the cultural heritage area of the Kota Tua Jakarta. The following hypotheses illustrate the relationship between status consistency and positive perceptions of the community for the preservation of cultural heritage in the Kota Tua Jakarta:

Hypothesis 11: Status consistency has a positive effect on positive perceptions of the community.

H12 - Effect of Status Consistency Against Negative Perceptions

The community's great support for the preservation of cultural heritage in the Kota Tua Jakarta because of the influence of consistency status makes the community do not have negative perceptions of the preservation of cultural heritage. Effect of consistency status on community negative perceptions to preservation of cultural heritage in the Kota Tua area as in the following hypothesis 12:

Hypothesis 12: Status consistency has a negative effect on negative community perceptions.

Support for WHS Inscription

Community perceptions of the preservation of cultural heritage in the Kota Tua Jakarta give effect to the support provided by the conservation community in the Kota Tua Jakarta. There are two hypotheses related to conservation support in the Kota Tua Jakarta provided by the community.

H13 - Effect of Positive Perceptions on Community Support to WHS Inscription in the Kota Tua Jakarta

For communities that receive many benefits from the preservation of cultural heritage in an area will provide support for conservation. Especially with the existence of economic effects obtained from the preservation of cultural heritage areas makes local support even greater. The relationship between positive perceptions of the community and their support for the preservation of cultural heritage in the Kota Tua Jakarta can be illustrated by the following hypothesis:

Hypothesis 13: Positive perceptions from the community have a positive influence on their support for the preservation of cultural heritage in the Kota Tua Jakarta

H14 - Effect of Negative Perceptions on Community Support to WHS Inscription in the Kota Tua Jakarta

Communities that receive negative impacts from the preservation of cultural heritage will not provide support for preservation of cultural heritage in an area. Because the negative impact that is received by the community will make the community negative perceptions bigger. Thus the relationship between the negative perception community towards community support for the preservation of cultural heritage in the Kota Tua Jakarta can be illustrated by the following hypothesis:

Hypothesis 14: Negative perceptions of the community have a negative influence on their support for the preservation of cultural heritage in the Kota Tua Jakarta.

2 RESEARCH METHOD

2.1 *Instrument development*

In the questionnaire used in this study using a questionnaire format for ordinal scale that is by using the sequence response scale. In making the questionnaire with the questionnaire format adjusted in ordinal format, that is in the preparation of the questionnaire set a number of appropriate response options.

In this study, the choice of responses provided there are five alternatives, namely strongly disagree, disagree, neutral, agree, and strongly agree. The selection of five alternatives for the response statement in this questionnaire because this amount is enough, not too much or not too little.

2.2 *Data collection procedure*

The source of the data used in this study came from a sample of local community of the Kota Tua Jakarta. To obtain the sample, the researcher used part of the non-probability sampling method, namely convenience sampling. This method is a sampling method by selecting respondents from local community members who at the time the researcher collected data was the right time and place in accordance with the research area determined by the researcher.

Data collection techniques conducted by researchers are interviews and questionnaires. Both of these techniques were chosen because in this study researchers used a quantitative approach. Interviews are conducted before giving questionnaires to prospective respondents. This interview is useful to ensure that prospective respondents are local community members of Kota Tua Jakarta. After the interview is completed and the prospective respondent is pleased to fill out the research questionnaire, the questionnaire is given to the respondent.

2.3 *Data analysis approach*

PLS-SEM is an analytical method used for research that has the purpose of predicting and developing theory. In addition, PLS-SEM can also be used to predict endogenous latent variables or identify key variables if research is exploratory research or expansion of an existing structural theory. Data used in PLS SEM does not have to meet the requirements for assuming data normality, so PLS-SEM can also be used for data that is not normally distributed. The data should be data with an interval measurement scale. However, PLS-SEM can also be used on other measurement scales.

2.4 *Kota Tua tentative list world heritage site*

Geographically, Kota Tua Jakarta borders the Fish Market, Sunda Kelapa Harbor and the Java Sea to the north. Then, south of the Kota Tua Jakarta borders the Batu Bridge road and Asemka road. In the west, the Kota Tua Jakarta is bordered by the Krukut River and on the east is the Ciliwung River. The Kota Tua Jakarta has important buildings located in different areas. In the core zone area there are several important buildings such as Taman Fatahillah, Fatahillah Museum (Jakarta History Museum), Puppet Museum and Ceramic Museum.

3 ANALYSIS AND RESULTS

3.1 *Profile of respondents*

Table 1 shows profile of the respondent of this research, there were 27 male respondents (54%) and 23 female respondents (46%). The age range of respondents is divided into 4 groups: 10-25 years (30%), 26-40 years (26%), 41-55 years (28%) and 55 years and above (16%). Residents members in Kota Tua Jakarta came from various ethnics in Indonesia. i.e. as many as 7 people (14%); followed by Betawi as many as 7 people (14%), Javanese as many as 16 people (32%), Chinese as many as 6 people (12%) and others ethnic as many as 2 people (4%).

Table 1. Profile of the respondents

Characteristics	Frequency	Percentage	%
Gender	Male	27	54
	Female	23	46
Age (Years)	10 to 25	15	30
	26 to 40	13	26
	41 to 55	14	28
	55 and above	8	16
Ethnics	Arab	7	14
	Betawi	7	14
	Javanese	16	32
	Sundanese	12	24
	Chinese	6	12
	Others	2	4
Education	Elementary School	6	12
	Junior High School	17	34
	Senior High School	17	34
	Degree/Postgraduate	6	12
	Others	4	8
Employment Sector	Student	10	20
	Artist	13	26
	Own Business	5	10
	Private Sector	3	6
	Others	19	38

The majority of respondents had a junior high school (34%) and senior high school (34%). Most of respondents were employed as artist (26%), while the least number of respondents work in the private sector (6%).

3.2 *Model assessment using PLS-SEM*

Model suitability assessment used in PLS-SEM there are 2 types, namely assessment on measurement models and structural models. The assessment of the measurement model is an assessment of the external model which is done by looking at the relationship between indicators and their latent variables. While the structural model assessment is an assessment of the inner model that is done by looking at the relationship between latent variables.

3.3 *Assessment of the measurement model*

Assessment of measurement models is done using validity and reliability. There are 2 types of validity, namely convergent validity and discriminant validity. Convergent validity can be seen from the AVE value. Convergent validity can validate that each latent variable can represent the indicators. In convergent validity, the AVE value is at least 0.5, so that each latent variable is at least half the indicators. In contrast to discriminant validity, the validity used to determine the differences between latent variables. So that each variable, if combined, does not become the same dimension. Discriminant validity can be calculated by comparing the results of AVE with cross loading. Reliability of a PLS-SEM model can be assessed using Cronbach's Alpha and composite reliability.

The AVE value for each latent variable has more than equal to 0.5, so each latent variable that is used reliably becomes a representative of the indicators. Good composite reliability if the value is more than 0.6. In this study all the values of composite reliability for each latent variable have a value of more than 0.6, so that all latent variables have ideal reliability. Then when viewed from the value of Cronbach's Alpha shows that the value of each latent variable is more than 0.7, so it can be interpreted that the latent variable in this study has good reliability.

Discriminant validity can be assessed by comparing the correlation between latent variables and the root value of AVE (which is bold in Table 3). The root value of AVE which is higher than the correlation value between latent variables can mean that the indicator variables used in each latent variable are valid.

3.4 *Assessment of the structural model*

In Table 4 *T-Value* Result on *Inner Model. T-Value* of the relationship among variables. By using this value, the researcher could test the hypotheses that had been made earlier. The results demonstrated that there were significant effects, namely (1) community involvement (CINV) gave positive effect to local community's positive perceptions (PP), in this case Hypothesis 3a, (2) community gain (CG) gave positive effect to resident's positive perceptions (PP), in this case Hypothesis 4a, (3) community gain (CG) gave positive effect to local community's negative perceptions (NP), in this case Hypothesis 4b, and (4) local community's positive perceptions (PP) gave positive effect to the support to the preservation of cultural heritages in the area of Kota Tua Jakarta (SUP). Apart from the four effects, other community effects were not significant. With this significance test, it was known that community involvement and community gain, were the ones that mostly gave positive effect to positive perception, where the local community's support for Kota Tua Jakarta WHS inscription was very much effected by the presence of local community's positive perception.

In this study it was found that the value of the R-Square positive perception has a value of 0.69022 so that it can be categorized that the relationship between positive perception to the support for WHS inscriptions is very substantial. Whereas negative perception only has a

Table 2. Assessment results of the measurement model

Construct/Item	Loading	Composite Reliability	Cronbach's Alpha	AVE
Community Attachment (X1)		0.846287	0.766114	0.587038
Inscription of Kota Tua Jakarta as a WHS is important to me	0.844335			
I have positive feelings for Kota Tua Jakarta	0.821605			
I feel a sense of belonging to this place	0.83187			
I have emotional attachment to this place	0.517888			
Cultural Attitude (X2)		0.855712	0.746482	0.667742
The local and traditional culture should be preserved	0.865547			
The lifestyle of local residents should be protected	0.901621			
My traditions and culture is very important for me	0.664181			
Community Involvement (X3)		0.887095	0.845601	0.613643
The local communities of Kota Tua Jakarta Area have been involved in the management of the Kota Tua Jakarta	0.822042			
The local communities of Kota Tua Jakarta	0.825628			
The local communities of Kota Tua Jakarta Area participates in the development of Kota Tua Jakarta	0.77167			
The local communities of Kota Tua Jakarta Area participates in the utilization of Kota Tua Jakarta	0.850558			
The local communities of Kota Tua Jakarta has been consulted for the preservation of Kota Tua Jakarta	0.626003			
Community Gain (X4)		0.890781	0.816386	0.731094
Kota Tua Jakarta is getting better with the presence of preservation	0.862995			
The facilities in Kota Tua Jakart are getting better with the preservation of Kota Tua Jakarta	0.850733			
I feel safer and more comfortable with the presence of preservation of Kota Tua Jakarta	0.851337			
Community Members' Gain (X5)		0.902444	0.855489	0.698589
I observe there is an increase of visitor numbers in Kota Tua Jakarta	0.816149			
I observe increasing number of people concerned about Kota Tua Jakarta	0.870234			
I recognize an increasing number of people visiting Kota Tua Jakarta after the preservation process	0.873631			
I see the benefits of Kota Tua Jakarta's utilization	0.779563			
Status Consistency (X6)		0.918928	0.868039	0.790862
I am proud to be part of the local communities that concerned about the preservation of Kota Tua	0.902058			
The preservation of Kota Tua Jakarta provides opportunity for community to show their hobby, expertise, identity or culture	0.85221			
The preservation of Kota Tua contributes in revitalizing and showing religious and traditional events	0.912477			
Positive Perception (Y1)	0.791389	0.898253	0.849099	0.688467
The preservation of Kota Tua Jakarta opens more job opportunities for the communities	0.839717			
The preservation of Kota Tua Jakarta will make investment increase to my community	0.814178			
The preservation of Kota Tua Jakarta increases local cultural image and I am proud of it	0.871529			
Negative Perception (Y2)		0.847088	0.772824	0.529955

(*Continued*)

Table 2. (*Continued*)

The preservation of Kota Tua Jakarta does not make my community grow	0.851046			
The preservation of Kota Tua Jakarta makes my community cannot do any activities	0.820141			
The preservation of Kota Tua Jakarta damages the environment	0.628008			
The utilization of Kota Tua Jakarta caused traffic congestion, noises, and pollution	0.683252			
Support for WHS Inscription (Z1)		0.762779	0.70428	0.458635
Local communities should participate in the preservation of Kota Tua Jakarta	0.519757			
Local communities should make use of Kota Tua Jakarta	0.905999			
Local communities should develop Kota Tua Jakarta	0.543731			
Local communities should protect Kota Tua Jakarta	0.669264			

Table 3. Discriminant validity.

Constructs	CA	CAT	CINV	CG	CMG	SC	PP	NP	SUP
CA	**0.766184**								
CAT	0.480048	**0.817154**							
CINV	0.458226	0.347062	**0.783353**						
CG	0.376199	0.54453	0.415251	**0.85504**					
CMG	0.433534	0.373566	0.373362	0.544536	**0.835816**				
SC	0.470439	0.28493	0.327064	0.467002	0.655062	**0.889304**			
PP	0.411809	0.446444	0.595984	0.729239	0.62041	0.55564	**0.829739**		
NP	-0.12303	-0.36426	-0.27706	-0.58678	-0.48822	-0.37659	-0.63632	**0.72798**	
SUP	0.359206	0.370847	0.216329	0.257982	0.389972	0.509341	0.365908	-0.10038	**0.677226**

Table 4. Results of hypothesis testing

Variabel	T-Value	Conclusion
CA -> PP	0.556488	Not Significant
CA -> NP	1.493621	Not Significant
CAT -> PP	0.130134	Not Significant
CAT -> NP	0.901301	Not Significant
CINV -> PP	3.735522	Significant
CINV -> NP	0.657489	Not Significant
CG -> PP	3.152889	Significant
CG -> NP	2.964236	Significant
CMG -> PP	1.666437	Not Significant
CMG -> NP	1.609465	Not Significant
SC -> PP	1.744301	Not Significant
SC -> NP	0.730096	Not Significant
PP -> SUP	3.667727	Significant
NP -> SUP	1.432589	Not Significant

value of 0.430598 so the relationship between negative perception and WHS support for writing is categorized as moderate.

The amount of a variant of a variable that can be measured directly can be seen from the value of communality. Communal values are closest to 1, the indicators can explain the latent variables more. In this study, the closest value is communality from consistency status that is

Table 5. Results of R-Square and Communality

Constructs	R-Square	Communality
Community Attachment		0.587038
Cultural Attitude		0.667742
Community Involvement		0.613643
Community Gain		0.731094
Community Members' Gain		0.698589
Status Consistency		0.790862
Positive Perception	0.69022	0.688467
Negative Perception	0.430598	0.529955
Support for WHS inscription	0.163369	0.458633

equal to 0.790862, with these results it can be seen that consistency status is a latent variable that can be explained by the biggest indicators.

4 DISCUSSION

The results of the structural model assessment indicate that community attachments not significantly affect the positive perceptions and negative perceptions of the community towards the preservation of cultural heritage in the Kota Tua Jakarta. This is consistent with previous studies, that community attachments do not have a significant effect on positive perceptions and negative perceptions of the community. In contrast, from other studies, they found that there were positive effects of community attachments on positive perceptions and negative community perceptions. Although the results of this study are in accordance with previous studies, however, when viewed with SET theory, the perception of the community in the Kota Tua Jakarta turns out to be quite significant. According to SET theory, community attachments can have a significant impact on positive perception and negative perception. For communities that have community attachments to the Kota Tua Jakarta, the local community will support the preservation of cultural heritage in the Kota Tua Jakarta. On the other hand, local communities that do not have attachments (community attachments) to the Kota Tua Jakarta tend not to support the preservation of cultural heritage in the Kota Tua Jakarta.

This study assesses the cultural attitudes of the community in positive perceptions and negative perceptions regarding the support of cultural preservation in the Kota Tua Jakarta. As a result, cultural attitudes have no effect on positive perceptions and negative perceptions. These results show that local community in the Kota Tua Jakarta who want to preserve their local culture do not necessarily have positive perceptions of the development of cultural heritage in the Kota Tua Jakarta. This can be caused by the perception of the local community who feel that there are policies or developments carried out on the Kota Tua Jakarta that are not in accordance with the culture and beliefs of the local community. Concerns about negative things that can happen to cultural attitudes because the development of an area can also be a cause of local community in the Kota Tua Jakarta does not support the preservation and development in the Kota Tua Jakarta. This result is in accordance with the definition of cultural attitudes by Yarygin (2017), that cultural attitudes are a way of thinking about something related to their way of life and customs. Thus, communities in the Kota Tua Jakarta can be less likely to support the preservation of Kota Tua Jakarta area if there are things that are not in accordance with their customs.

Community involvement has a significant influence on positive perceptions. The results of this study show that community involvement improves positive perceptions of WHS inscription in the Kota Tua Jakarta. This is because the existence of community involvement can provide an opportunity for the local community to participate in the preservation of Kota Tua Jakarta. The results of this study are in accordance with the definition of community involvement by Tikare Youssef, etc. (2001) which states that community involvement is a process in which stakeholders influence and share control over setting priorities and policy making. With the involvement of community in the Kota Tua Jakarta to policy making in preservation of cultural heritage in the Kota Tua Jakarta, they will be more supportive of preservation of cultural heritage in the Kota Tua Jakarta because they are included in every policy making process and priority arrangements, so that the final result of the preservation of cultural heritage policies in the Kota Tua Jakarta also includes local community thinking in the Kota Tua Jakarta. Other results from this study show that community involvement has no significant effect on negative perceptions. This result is consistent with Rasoolimanesh's (2017) study, that the effect of community involvement that is not significant to negative perceptions indicates that the communities involved in the World Heritage Site conservation program and tourism development are comparable to those who are not involved. This is seen in terms of their perception of the negative impact of tourism development.

The findings of this study indicate that community gain has a positive effect on positive perceptions and negative effects on negative perceptions. In this study, assessed community gains were income, facilities, and security and comfort in the Kota Tua Jakarta. The development of cultural heritage areas can provide positive things for the local communities that act in the region. For example, the number of visitors to cultural heritage areas in the Kota Tua Jakarta can increase income for the local community in the Kota Tua Jakarta. Although the number of visitors to the Kota Tua Jakarta can cause more rapid damage to cultural heritage in the Kota Tua Jakarta, with the large profits obtained by the local community in the Kota Tua Jakarta, the community will be more likely to have positive perceptions than negative perceptions of preservation of reserves culture in the Kota Tua Jakarta. The results of this study are in accordance with SET's theory, that communities in the Kota Tua Jakarta will feel more interested in doing something, in this case support for the preservation of cultural heritage in the Kota Tua Jakarta, if they get rewards or benefits, for example an increase in income.

The results of this study indicate that community members gain a negative effect on positive perceptions and negative perceptions. This can mean that community members gain affects positive and negative perceptions for the local community in the Kota Tua Jakarta. Local community members who receive many benefits from the use of cultural heritage areas will be more supportive of the preservation of cultural heritage areas. However, if local community members do not receive much benefit, they may become more negative perceptions of the preservation of cultural heritage in the Kota Tua Jakarta. These results are consistent with SET's theory, that members of the community in the Kota Tua Jakarta who do not get a benefit tend not to support the improvement and development in the Kota Tua Jakarta.

In this study, the status of consistency had a non-significant effect on positive perceptions and negative effect on the negative perceptions of the community in Kota Tua Jakarta towards the preservation of cultural heritage in the Kota Tua Jakarta. This result is consistent with previous studies,[10] namely the status of consistency influences the positive perceptions of the people in George Town on the George Town site as a World Heritage Site and tourism development. According to Cropanza and Mitchell (2005) the consistency status of a tribe, gender, certain culture in a particular community can provide benefits for an individual and can also influence his perception. The desire to show what is owned by the community in the Kota Tua Jakarta, for example in the form of cultural festivals, religious activities, food, art, and lifestyle can make the community in the Kota Tua Jakarta support the preservation of cultural heritage in the Kota Tua Jakarta.

Other findings in this study are the R-square value of positive perceptions has a higher value than negative perceptions, which are sequential values of 0.69 and 0.43. According to Rasoolimanesh (2017), R-square values are variance indicators which are explained by a set of predictors for each criterion. In this study, the researchers wanted to find out the positive perceptions and negative perceptions of the community towards the preservation of the old city of Jakarta from the effects of each variable used in the study. R-square values on positive perceptions that are much higher when compared to negative perceptions in this study indicate

10. Rasoolimanesh et al, above n 5.

that the variables used in this study have a lot of strong influence on positive perceptions rather than negative perceptions. Or it could be said that the community-related variables used in this study were good predictors of the positive perceptions of the community towards the preservation of the Kota Tua Jakarta, rather than the negative perceptions of the community towards the preservation of Kota Tua Jakarta. So if you want to know more about negative community perceptions of the preservation of Kota Tua Jakarta, you need to use other better predictors.

The results of this study also found positive perceptions of communities in the Kota Tua Jakarta had a positive influence on their support for WHS inscription in the Kota Tua Jakarta. This is in accordance with previous research[11], that the population with a more positive perception will be more willing to participate in the preservation and development of the World Heritage Site George Town. The resident also believes that the local government and state government must support tourism promotion and develop long-term plans to manage conservation and tourism development efforts at the World Heritage Site George Town. The results of this study indicate that local communities in Kota Tua Jakarta that receive many benefits will provide conservation support in the Kota Tua Jakarta. Especially with the economic effects obtained by local communities in the Kota Tua Jakarta from WHS inscription makes local communities support even greater. The results of this study also show that negative perceptions of the local community still provide support for the preservation of cultural heritage in the Kota Tua Jakarta, although the results are not as significant as the positive perceptions of community support for preservation of cultural heritage in the Kota Tua Jakarta. The local community still supports the WHS inscription in Kota Tua Jakarta with the aim of increasing their positive impact and reducing negative perception. This result is consistent with previous research[12], namely the population of George Town suggests that the George Town site as a World Heritage Site and developed as tourism has a detrimental effect on members of the community and on the community as a whole. Nevertheless, residents in George Town still support and participate in efforts to preserve and develop tourism at the George Town World Heritage Site to increase the positive impact and reduce negative impacts.

5 CONCLUSION

From the entire results of this research it was known that the entire variables used to recognize the local community's supports on the preservation of cultural heritage in the area of Kota Tua Jakarta were valid and had good reliability. The findings in this research indicated that positive perceptions were excellent predictors to know the local community's supports on WHS inscription in the Kota Tua Jakarta. Asides of significance of the relation between positive perceptions' variables and community's supports on preservation that significantly provided positive effect, community's supports on cultural heritage preservation could be viewed from R^2 values that shown high positive perceptions' values. Nevertheless, in the research it was found that even local communities with negative perceptions still supported the WHS inscription in the Kota Tua Jakarta. This was shown by the results of the test on the hypothesis of relation between negative perceptions and the supports that displayed results which were local community with negative perceptions did not have negative effect on the preservation of cultural heritage in the area of Kota Tua Jakarta. Although they had negative perceptions, the local communities still supported the cultural heritage preservation in the area of Kota Tua Jakarta with the intention of increasing their positive impact and lessened the negative perceptions. UNESCO's recognition of ethnic wealth and cultural heritage in the Kota Tua Jakarta should be maintained. Preservation of Kota Tua Jakarta is the responsibility of stakeholders, one of which is the local community. The local community is considered

11. Ibid.
12. Ibid.

important in the WHS inscription in Kota Tua Jakarta because the local community is life in the Kota Tua Jakarta. Because of the importance of the local community in WHS inscription in Kota Tua Jakarta, it is necessary to know how the community's perception of the preservation of the Kota Tua Jakarta. From the results of this study, it can be seen that the local community has a positive perception of the WHS inscription in Kota Tua Jakarta. This can mean that the local community agrees with the WHS inscription in Kota Tua Jakarta and wants to be included in every preservation process of the Kota Tua Jakarta cultural heritage. So that local authorities should include the local community in the preservation and monitoring process of the Kota Tua Jakarta. In addition, it can also provide training to the local community so that the local community develops and is able to participate in the WHS inscription process.

6 RECOMMENDATIONS FOR FUTURE STUDIES

From the findings of this research it is suggested to be one of the inputs in cultural resource management research or CRM in applying aspects of the local community to cultural heritage areas. The high positive perception of the local community towards the Kota Tua Jakarta makes them important to be involved directly and more deeply in the preservation of cultural heritage, especially cultural heritage that is in the category of World Heritage and still tentative List. This is because it can accelerate the preservation process itself.

ACKNOWLEDGMENTS

The authors would like to thank Konsortium Kota Tua Jakarta Inc. and UPK Kota Tua Jakarta for collaboration in data collection stage.

Funding

This work was supported by Universitas Indonesia (UI) under the research grant entitled PITTA 2018.

Notes on Contributors

Burhanuddin Aziz is a graduate at Universitas Indonesia. He got his bachelor degree in Tourism Studies from Universitas Gadjah Mada in 2014 and started the M.Hum programme in Archaeology since August 2016. Aziz is among the awardee of the Indonesia Endowment Fund for Education. His research focus on cultural resource management, urban heritage, and tourism policy and management.

Agi Ginanjar is lecturer in Archaeology Departement at Universitas Indonesia. He is also as supervisor of S1 and S2 research in Faculty of Humanities. His research focus on cultural resource management, communication, and management.

REFERENCES

Andereck, K et al, 'Residents Perceptions of Community Tourism Impact' (2005) 32(4) *Annals of Tourism Research* 1056

Latkova, P and C Vogt, 'Residents Attitudes Toward Existing and Future Tourism Development in Rural Communities' (2012) 51(1) *Journal of Travel Research* 50

McManamon, Francis P, 'Archaeological Messages and Messengers' in G Fairclough et al (eds), *The Heritage Reader* (New York, Routledge, 2000) 2

Rasoolimanesh, S et al, 'The Effects of Community Factors on Residents Perceptions Toward World Heritage Site Inscription and Sustainable Tourism Development' (2017) 25(2) *Journal of Sustainable Tourism* 198

Tosun, C, 'Host Perceptions of Impacts: A Comparative Tourism Study' [2002] *Annals of Tourism Research* 231

Culture and International Law - Juwana et al. (Eds)
© 2019 Taylor & Francis Group, London, ISBN 978-1-138-38766-9

Community involvement in the establishment of marine conservation zones (The Indonesia Law Review)

Maria Maya Lestari
Doctoral Program, Faculty of Law, Indonesia University, Indonesia

Melda Kamil Ariadno
Dean, Faculty of Law, Indonesia University, Indonesia

ABSTRACT: The government of Indonesia has committed to the international world and shall establish 20 million hectares of Marine Protected Areas for Indonesia by 2020. The ocean, due to its vastness and the diverse resources available in, requires the cooperation among a variety of parties ranging from planning to the establishment of conservation areas, such as the role of traditional fishing communities and eligibly existing local wisdom. With regard to this issue, the ideally crucial problem is that Indonesia adheres to the flow of positive law, thus to involve the community as a part that encourages the planning and establishment of marine conservation areas shall be supported by the rule of law. For such obvious reason, conducted with qualitative analysis techniques, the current study is carried out using library research method through inventory of various laws and regulations and will be analyzed descriptively in regard to how Indonesian legislation accommodates the role of communities from planning to the establishment of marine protected areas. Based on results obtained in this line of research, the government of Indonesia, either in general or in particular, has regulated and accommodated the role of communities and local culture in part in various laws and regulations.

KEYWORDS: community involvement, marine conservation zones, Indonesia, traditional fishing communities, local wisdom

1 INTRODUCTION

One tool or way to protect the marine environment can be demonstrated by establishing marine conservation areas. The entire surface of the earth of oceans and seas covers 70% of the earth's surface area which is one global biosphere[1] unit hence it needs to be protected through conservation approach. From such observations, each country shall protect the marine environment, although there is no scientific uncertainty in regard to how, what and how much loss can be caused through the precautionary principle of allegation towards possible impacts on such pollution and destruction shall be prevented at the beginning, if it is not conducted then it also belongs to unlawful deeds.[2]

The marine protected areas are compulsory for every country without exclusion.[3] In this regard, Indonesia is very concerned about the formation of the MPA's, considering

1. Warwick Gulle, 'Environmental Protection and The Precautionary Principle: A Response to Scienti:C Uncertainty in Environmental Management', (1997) 14(1) *Environmental and Planning Law Journal,* 52., according to international law, an act of doing nothing is also an illegal act.
2. UNCLOS, art. 192

Indonesia's marine areas are one of the richest areas in variety of marine biodiversity.[4] This special mandatory is also strengthened after six countries working on CTI-FF have signed the agreement initiated by Indonesia to safeguard the seas in regard to the state's compulsory to provide 20% of its seas as conservation areas.[5] Indonesia has been bound by this International agreement, both regionally with the CTI-FF agreement and globally with the 2030 agenda for Sustainable Development (known as SDG's)[6] and therefore Indonesia is also mainly responsible for carrying out its obligations, especially in the establishment of marine conservation zones in its marine areas. Hence, in accordance with the statement of the President of Indonesia at the CTI Summit in Manado, Indonesia plans to establish 20 million hectares of marine conservation areas by 2020.[7]

The government, on the other hand, cannot carry out conservation areas on only single party. There are other elements that are also directly connected to the ocean space such as fishermen communities along with local cultures existed for thousands of years. The establishment of the marine conservation areas shall have consequences starting from the prohibition, limitation to the statutory duty to preserve the conservation areas. And in turn, in order to prevent conflicts of interest with the fishing community, the government also involves the community from the planning stage to the establishment and protection of conservation areas.

As a country that adheres to positive law, the participation of fishing communities has been regulated and recognized by various laws and regulations. And therefore it is argued that the traditional fishing communities and their local cultures have received legal recognition to participate from planning to the establishment of marine conservation areas.

2 METHODOLOGY

The current formulated research employs doctrinal research method, familiarly defined as "essentially library based study, which means that the materials needed by a researcher may be available in librarias, archives and other data bases."[8] In order to solve the legal problems that exist in this study, the researchers plan to use a statute approach carried out by comprehending all laws and regulations relating to legal issues[9] how the relationship between the role of the community and the establishment of conservation areas in Indonesian national law.

3 DISCUSSION

3.1 *Marine Protected Areas (MPAs)*

Basically, MPAs are forms of conservation carried out at seas. Conservation according to the Webster's Third New International Dictionary is well-defined as:

> "*deliberate, planned, or thoughtful preserving, guarding, or protecting. . .planned management of natural resource to prevent exploitation, destruction, or neglect. . ..wise utilization of*

3. Lauretta Burke et.al., *Reef at Risk Revisited in the Coral Triangle*, (Washington: World Resources Institute, 2012) 6-8.
4. CTI-FF Regional Plan of Action (RPOA) Goals, Goal 3 Marine Protected Areas (MPAs) Established and Effectively Managed, Target 1.
5. CTI-FF Regional Plan of Action (RPOA) Goals, Goal 3 Marine Protected Areas (MPAs) Established and Effectively Managed, Target 1.
6. SDGs number 14 tentang sea life
7. S.B. Yudhoyono, Speech by Dr. Susilo Bambang Yudhoyono, President of the Republic of Indonesia, at the Coral Triangle Initiative Summit, Manado, 15 May 2009.
8. Anwarul Yakin, *Legal Research and Writing* (Selangor, Malaysia: lexis nexis, 2007) 10.
9. Peter Mahmud Marzuki, *Penelitian Hukum* (Jakarta: Prenadamedia, 2014) 93.

a natural product. . ..a field of knowledge concerned with coordination and plans for the practical application of data from ecology, limnology, pedology, or other sciences that are significant to preservation of natural resources."[10]

The term Marine Protected Area (MPA) actually includes a variety of arrangements regarding the conservation of biodiversity and ecosystem services related to their achievement.[11] Marine Protected Areas (MPAs)/Marine Conservation Areas according to The International Union for Conservation of Nature (IUCN) are defined as follows:

> "A clearly defined geographical space, recognised, dedicated and managed, through legal or other ef- fective means, to achieve the long-term conservation of nature with associated ecosystem services and cultural values"

Commonly, MPAs always implement two protection measures which include the conservation of biodiversity and sustainable fisheries management. By protecting geographical areas, including both resident species and their biophysical environments, MPAs offer an ecosystem-based approach to conservation and fisheries management.[12]

Based on the Regulation of the Minister of Maritime Affairs and Fisheries of the Republic of Indonesia number PER.2/MEN/2009 concerning Procedures for Establishing Marine Conservation Areas Article 1 point 1, stated that Marine Conservation Areas are Marine protected areas, managed through zoning system, to achieve sustainable management of fishery resources and its environment.

The purpose of establishing marine conservation areas is to protect and preserve fishery resources and important ecosystem types on watershed to ensure the sustainability functions of their ecological; to achieve sustainable use of fishery resources and their ecosystems and environmental services; to preserve local wisdom in the management of fishery resources in and/or around marine conservation areas; and to improve the social welfare around the marine conservation areas.[13]

3.2 *Regulations concerning society involvement (fishermen) in the establishment of MPAs*

3.2.1 *Law Number 32/2009 concerning Environmental Protection and Management*

Recognition of community involvement and local wisdom in protecting the environment in general has been accommodated in Law No. 32/2009 concerning Environmental Protection and Management (UUPPLH) under the umbrella of the "environmental rule of law" in Indonesia. Where due to such recognition and the existing local wisdom, the concept of environmental protection in Indonesia is also characterized by long-standing local cultural values. The community role is regulated in article 70 of UUPPLH as follows:

1. The community has the similar rights and opportunities and highly deserve to play an active role in the environmental protection and management.

10. G. Carleton Ray dan Jerry Mc. Cormick-Ray, *Marine Conservation Science, Policy, and Management,* (Hoboken, New Jersey: Wiley Blackwell, 2014) 4.
11. The International Union for Conservation of Nature (IUCN), *Guidelines for Applying the IUCN Protected Area management Categories to Marine Protected Areas*, (Gland: IUCN, 2012), https://www.iucn.org/sites/dev/files/import/downloads/uicn_categoriesamp_eng.pdf; see also Laffoley, D. d'A, et.al, Aquaculure and Marine Protected Areas: Exploring Potential Opportunities and Synergies, (Gland: IUCN, 2017), Hal. 6, downloaded from the official website: IUCN Library System https://portals.iucn.org/library/node/46692
12. Wilson, J., Darmawan, A., Subijanto. J., Green, A., and S. Sheppard, *Scientific design of a resilient network of marine protected areas. Lesser Sunda Ecoregion, Coral Triangle. Asia Pacific Marine Program.* (The Nature Conservancy: Report 2/11, 2011), 3
13. Regulation of the Minister of Maritime Affairs and Fisheries of the Republic of Indonesia number PER.2/MEN/2009, Article 2 (1)

2. The role of community can be in the form of: social supervision; giving suggestions, opinions, proposals, objections, complaints; and/or submission of information and/or reports.
3. The role of community is carried out to enhance awareness in environmental protection and management; to improve independence, community empowerment, and partnership; to develop community capabilities and pioneering; to develop community responsiveness to conduct social supervision; and to develop and maintain local culture and wisdom in the context of preserving environmental functions.

3.2.2 *Law Number 1/2014 concerning management of coastal areas and small islands (UUWP-3-K)*

Although this law does not discuss the direct role of community in the establishment of conservation areas, it is stated in Article 60 that society plays a role in proposing traditional fishing areas into Coastal and Small Islands Zoning Plans especially (RZWP-3-K); propose the area of Customary Law Community into RZWP-3-K; conduct management activities of Coastal and Small Islands Resources based on customary law in force and do not conflict with the provisions of the legislation; report to law enforcers due to allegations of pollution, pollution and/or destruction of Coastal and Small Islands Areas which are detrimental to their lives; up to providing information, filing a lawsuit and other important rights.[14]

3.2.3 *Law of the sea (Law No. 32 of 2014)*

This law specifically regulates the community participation in relation to seas and marine protection. Under this law within article 70 regulates the role of community in the form of community involvement in matter of the implementation of maritime development both organized by the central government and regional governments.[15] This community participation, can be conducted individually, groups, professional organizations, business entities, or other social organizations in accordance with the principles of openness and partnership.[16] For marine development program, community participation can be carried out in form stated as follows:[17]

1. preparation of the Marine Development policy;
2. Marine Management;
3. Marine development; and

Provide feedback in evaluation and supervision activities.

In addition, the community also plays a role in preserving cultural values and nautical insight and even revitalizing the laws and local wisdom in the marine sectors; and play a role in the protection and dissemination of underwater cultural heritage through the efforts of preservation, restoration and conservation.[18]

3.2.4 *Regulation of the Minister of Marine and Fisheries number PER.02/MEN/2009 concerning Procedures for the establishment of Marine Conservation Areas*

This regulation is a rule that specifically regulates the stipulation and procedure for establishing marine conservation areas especially in Indonesia. Such establishment is designed to achieve the goals of sustainable use of fishery resources and their ecosystems, as well as the environmental services contained therein, through keep maintaining the existed local wisdom, thus it can guarantee the availability, sustainability and improvement of the quality of its values and diversity, to improve the social welfare, especially around the marine conservation area. [19] According to

14. Read further in article 60 UUPPLH
15. Law of the Sea Number 34 of 2014, article 70 (1)
16. Law of the Sea Number 34 of 2014, article 70 (2)
17. Law of the Sea Number 34 of 2014, article 70 (3)
18. Law of the Sea Number 34 of 2014, article 70 (4)
19. Regulation of the Minister of Maritime Affairs and Fisheries number PER.02/MEN/2009 concerning Procedures for the establishment of Marine Conservation Areas, article 2 (2)

this provision, in regard to the establishment of marine conservation areas, the community has played a role even from the proposal of prospective marine conservation areas.

The society can submit proposals regarding which areas are eligible to be nominated as marine conservation areas.[20] The community also plays a role in providing information about data on how far along their support towards establishment of conservation areas, potential conflicts that may arise due to such establishment, potential threats to existing local wisdom, local customs and the value of fisheries and aesthetics. It aims not to make mistakes either in the establishment of the area or its function that is not in accordance with the geographical and ecological conditions of the sea.

In addition, the role of the community in the socialization will subsequently be able to prevent conflict between the government as the establishing party and the community as proposers or users.[21] The important role of the community when establishing conservation areas also refers to significant input from the community at times of socialization. This is important because fishing communities as users and who are always in the sea need to know which points are the reserve area or which have been designated as conservation areas. Considering that later, after being designated as a conservation area, there will be certain coordinates that will be the core zone that cannot be used because it is the main area of conservation within the territorial waters.

3.3 *Local wisdom at sea under the context of marine conservation*

Various local knowledge and culture that may have existed for a long time in some areas of the archipelago such as the Panglima Laot in Aceh which is a customary law of the sea that applies for generations to the people of Aceh. The concept of the Panglima Laot currently[22] is regarded as a complete legal concept along with fisheries management procedures and legal sanctions. In addition, when referring to the modern legal concept of marine conservation areas, the concept of Panglima Laot also regulates how the sea area and its fishery products can be sustainable.[23] This is absolutely in accordance with the ecological criteria where marine conservation areas shall pay attention to biodiversity, naturalness, ecological linkages, representativeness, uniqueness, productivity, natural areas, rare fish habitats, fish spawning areas, and care areas.[24]

The concept of conservation of other fisheries that also existed for long periods of time before national law existed was the Mane'e concept of the Talaud people. Mane'e is a uniquely cultural heritage of traditional fishing, which is performed by indigenous parents on the beach to fish with spells and coconut leaves and forest ropes.

This ritual is conducted to invite fish in thousands of tails, which then allows all residents to catch them only with their bare hands. It is a local wisdom which contains a prohibition for local people and from outside to take fish or other seafood in the area which will be a Mane'e event.[25] Another concept of local wisdom governing conservation of fisheries is called Sasi in Maluku. Sasi refers to traditional systems of natural resource management and includes

20. Regulation of the Minister of Maritime Affairs and Fisheries number PER.02/MEN/2009 concerning Procedures for the establishment of Marine Conservation Areas, article 9 (1)
21. Regulation of the Minister of Maritime Affairs and Fisheries number PER.02/MEN/2009 concerning Procedures for the establishment of Marine Conservation Areas, article 15
22. Under the concept of Iskandar Muda government, the commander of the sea emphasizes more in the context of war and tax (excise) for ship stops; See in the Study Team on Legal Culture of the National Law Development Agency (BPHN), Customary Law Contribution in the Development of Law of the sea in Indonesia, (Jakarta, BPHN: 2015) 24.
23. Sulaiman, 'Hukum Adat Laut dalam Pengelolaan perikanan di Kabupaten Pidie Jaya Provinsi Aceh', (2013) 2(3 September-December) *Yustisia,* 17-18.
24. Presidential Regulation of the Republic of Indonesia Number 51 of 2016 concerning Beach Boundary Limits, article 4 number 2.
25. Study Team on Legal Culture in the National Law Supervisory Agency (BPHN), Customary Law Contribution in the Development of Law of the Sea in Indonesia, (Jakarta, BPHN: 2015) 40.

proportions on harvesting resources on land and at sea. Marine Sasi describes specific rules and regulations governing access to fishing areas, fishing gear, target species, and harvest time and location. Marine Sasi also combines a set of institutional roles with various levels of influence that are owned by religious authorities and government.[26]

Around the world, another concept of fisheries conservation, the village of Lamalera on the island of Lembata on Flores is known as the home of traditional whale hunting. The local wisdom they uphold is that the people of Lamalera have their own rules for catching whales. There are taboos for the Lamaleras when it comes to whale hunting. For example, it is forbidden to hunt pregnant whales, young whales, and mating whales. This capacity to recognize these specific taboos can only be learnt through extensive periods of experience.[27]

4 CONCLUSION

Based on results obtained in this line of research, the establishment of conservation areas in Indonesia has accommodated the communities' interests accorded to the rights of fishing and local wisdom. Even from the process of proposing which areas are eligible to become conservation areas, the community has been involved to be able to submit proposals. Currently, the legal rights of the community and local wisdom have been recognized and regulated in the legislation. With regard to this issue, there is now considerably a matter of attention that it is necessary to clarify the geographical boundaries and coordinates of any areas recognized as conservation areas based on local wisdom/customary provisions. Further improvements are also necessary under the legal system and maritime zones regarding the boundaries of areas included in customary law. By way of conclusion, through the role of customary law and traditional fishing communities, the obvious effort shall assist the government in preserving conservation areas.

ACKNOWLEDGEMENT

This paper is development of sub-chapter 4 the research dissertation. The researchers would like to express the deepest appreciation to UI DRPM, which has kindly provided PITTA grant assistance for the project research and scientific publications.

REFERENCES

Burke, Lauretta et.al., *Reef at Risk Revisited in the Coral Triangle, (Washington: World Resources Institute*, 2012)

CTI-FF Regional Plan of Action (RPOA) Goals, Goal 3 Marine Protected Areas (MPAs) Established and Effectively Managed, Target 1.

Gulle, Warwick, 'Environmental protection and the precautionary principle: a response to scienti: cuncertainty in environmental management', (1997) 14(1)*Environmental and Planning Law Journal.*

Kurniasari, Nendah, Elly Reswati, 'Local Wisdom of the Lamalera Community: An Expression of Human Relations with the Sea', (2011) 6(3)*Buletin Riset Sosek Kelautan dan Perikanan.*

Laffoley, D. d'A, et.al, Aquaculure and Marine Protected Areas: Exploring Potential Opportunities and Synergies, (Gland: IUCN, 2017), downloaded from the official website IUCN Library System https://portals.iucn.org/library/node/46692

Mc.Leod, Elizabeth, at.al., 'Sasi and Marine Conservation in Raja Ampat Indonesia' (2009) 37 *Coastal management*

Marzuki, Peter Mahmud, *Penelitian Hukum*, Prenadamedia, Jakarta, 2014

26. Elizabeth Mc.Leod, at.al., 'Sasi and Marine Conservation in Raja Ampat Indonesia' (2009) 37 *Coastal management*, 657.
27. Nendah Kurniasari and Elly Reswati, 'Kearifan Lokal Masyarakat Lamalera: Sebuah Ekspresi Hubungan Manusia dengan Laut', (2011) 6(2) *Buletin Riset Sosek Kelautan dan Perikanan,* 31.

Sulaiman, 'Hukum Adat Laut dalam Pengelolaan perikanan di Kabupaten Pidie Jaya Provinsi Aceh', (2013) 2(3 September-December) *Yustisia*
Ray, G. Carleton dan Jerry Mc. Cormick-Ray, *Marine Conservation Science, Policy, and Management*, (Hoboken, New Jersey: Wiley Blackwell, 2014)
Toba, M.K., et.al, Coastal and Marine Degradation, in book *The World Environment 1972-1992 two Decades of Challenge*, (Oxport: UNEP dan Springer Science Business Media, 1992)
Study Team on Legal Culture in the National Law Supervisory Agency (BPHN), Customary Law Contribution in the Development of Law of the Sea in Indonesia, (Jakarta, BPHN: 2015)
Wilson, J., Darmawan, A., Subijanto. J., Green, A., and S. Sheppard, Scientific design of a resilient network of marine protected areas. Lesser Sunda Ecoregion, Coral Triangle. Asia Pacific Marine Program. (The Nature Conservancy: Report 2/11, 2011)
Yakin, Anwarul, *Legal Research and Writing* (Selangor, Malaysia: lexis nexis, 2007)
Yudhoyono, S.B. 2009 Speech by Dr. Susilo Bambang Yudhoyono, President of the Republic of Indonesia, at the Coral Triangle Initiative Summit, Manado, 15 May 2009
The International Union for Conservation of Nature (IUCN), Guidelines for Applying the IUCN Protected Area management Categories to Marine Protected Areas, (Gland: IUCN, 2012), https://www.iucn.org/sites/dev/files/import/downloads/uicn_categoriesamp_eng.pdf
Law No. 34 of 2014 concerning Seas
Law number 32 of 2009 concerning Environmental Protection and Management
Presidential Regulation of the Republic of Indonesia Number 51 of 2016 concerning Beach Boundary Limits
Regulation of the Minister of Marine and Fisheries number PER.02/MEN/2009 concerning Procedures for establishment of Marine Conservation Areas
Regulation of the Minister of Maritime Affairs and Fisheries of the Republic of Indonesia number PER.2/MEN/2009, Article 2 (1)
Sustainable Development Goals
UNCLOS

Culture and International Law - Juwana et al. (Eds)
© 2019 Taylor & Francis Group, London, ISBN 978-1-138-38766-9

Hikayat Sultan Taburat and its views concerning diversity

Rias A. Suharjo & Titik Pudjiastuti
Universitas Indonesia, Indonesia

ABSTRACT: *Hikayat Sultan Taburat* is a manuscripts from Pecenongan which scribes in the late of 19 century in jawi script. This text tells about the story of Sultan Taburat and his offspring's adventure in Thar Al Arqan. Muhammad Bakir and Safirin are the scriber of this text. They are intellectual people from Betawi and the head of Langgar Tinggi mosque caretaker in Pecenongan. Their jobs are scribes the manuscripts for rent and religious leader in Pecenongan. In the HST manuscript which they scribes, tolerance values in the diversity are reflected in the text as a norm that subtly taught toward HST reader. In this paper, how the HST text's view point related to the toleration in the diversity will be disclosed. To reach out those research aims, the theory of philology used to identify and explain HST from the text and the context, and then reviewed. HST is a text that born in context of Pecenongan society which are diverse in the late of nineteenth century. The result of this study indicate that some tolerance attitude of HST in addressing diversity are relevant to be applied in the present. The finding of this study expected can be used for consideration to addressing diversity in the present.

KEYWORDS: Manuscript, Pecenongan, diversity, Hikayat Sultan Tabura

1 INTRODUCTION

Batavia, now Jakarta, has been a popular major town from traders around the world since the 17th century. The Dutch established a trading partnership called VOC in this town- which was previously located in Ternate. Before being named Batavia, this town was named Jayakarta and under the authority of the Banten kingdom.

The population of Batavia town varied. Niemeijer states that in the 17th century, Indians, Chinese, Malays and Europeans had lived in Batavia. In addition, Batavia was also inhabited by Javanese, Ambonese, Bandanese, Butonese, Makassarese, Bugis, Sumbawa, Balinese and others.[1]

Based on the population census of 1673 and 1788 conducted by the Dutch government, the composition of dominant Batavians was Chinese, Betawi ethnic group, Dutch, and Javanese.[2] Based on the census of 1673, the composition of Batavians was Mardijkers (5,362 inhabitants), Chinese (2,747 inhabitants), Dutch (2,024 inhabitants), Moorish and Javanese (1,339 inhabitants), Balinese (981 inhabitants), Straits-born Dutch (726 inhabitants) and Malay (611 inhabitants). In addition to those previously mentioned, there were groups of people who were recorded in the census as slaves totaling 13,278 people. Aziz states that the census of 1788 shows the composition of the Batavian people who were inside the fortress included slaves (4,221 inhabitants), China (1,320 inhabitants), Muslims (551 inhabitants), Europe (475 inhabitants), Indigenous Christians (376 inhabitants) and Mestizo (249 inhabitants).[3] The

1. HE Niemeijer, *Batavia: Masyarakat Kolonial Abad XVII* (Jakarta: Masup Jakarta, 2012) 31–32.
2. Abdul Aziz, *Islam Dan Masyarakat Betawi* (Jakarta: PT. Logos Wacana Ilmu, 2002) 18.
3. Ibid 15.

composition of the Batavian people who were outside the fortress in 1788 mentioned by Aziz consisted of Dutch (430 inhabitants), Mestizo (150 inhabitants), Mardijkers or freed slaves (2,803 inhabitants), China (32,508 inhabitants), Ambon (391 inhabitants), Banda (528 inhabitants), Moor (1491 inhabitants), Malay (9,851 inhabitants), Buton (890 inhabitants), Makassar (3,692 inhabitants), Bugis (5,707 inhabitants), Timor (208 inhabitants), Mandar (1,310 inhabitants), Sumbawa (1,425 inhabitants), Bali (13,700 inhabitants), Java (28,724 inhabitants), and Slaves (30,520 inhabitants) with a total population of 138,622 people.[4]

Diverse societies led to social friction which leads to discriminatory actions. It is also stated by Niemeijer that in the 17th century, communities in Batavia were discriminatory and racist, especially regarding skin color and religious life.[5] These two things were important parts of life in Batavia which influenced political policies of the colonial government at that time.

At the end of 19th century, Pecenongan wasone of the bustling trading areas in Batavia. There was a large printing press named G. Kolff & Co. The printing press was owned by a European who lived in Pecenongan. Chinese citizens also lived there. It is proven from the existence of several manuscripts originating from Pecenongan stating that the target readers of the newspapers were *Baba*, the term for men of Chinese ethnic group.

> *Saya memberi tau kepada sekalian pembaca/2/dan sekalian Tuan-Tuan dan Baba-Baba dan Nona-Nona sekalian, harap/3/yang empunya ini hikayat kepada Tuan-Tuan sekalian, janganlah/4/dibikin kotor, dan dibikin pecah, dan yang menjadikan/5/syak di hati yang empunya.*[6]
>
> *Harap kepada Tuan, Baba, dan Nyonya. Habis dibaca harap dikirim sewanya.*[7]
>
> (To all readers/2/and Gentlemen and Baba and Ladies, the owner of this *hikayat* call for/3/all of you, please don't make this *hikayat* dirty, break and disappoint the *hikayat* owner).[8]
>
> (Please, Sir, Baba and Madame. After reading this *hikayat*, please send the payment).[9]

In addition to the printing press established by the European, *bumi putera* (native Indonesians) also owned a manuscript rental business. Those manuscripts were rented out for reading entertainment and knowledge text. On average, each manuscript was rented for 10 cents a day. One of the large manuscript rental places in Pecenongan was owned by Fadhli's family, a family of Muslim religious leaders who also established Langgar Tinggi Mosque at that time.

Langgar Tinggi Mosque was managed by the heirs of Fadli family for generations. Some of the mosque chiefs and caretakers were also copying texts, such as Syafian, Syafirin, Muhammad Bakir and Ahmad Beramka.

The three writers who were quite productive in Pecenongan scriptorium were Syafian, Syafirin, Muhammad Bakir and Ahmad Beramka. Syafirin had an older brother named Syafian. Muhammad Bakir was Syafian's son, while Ahmad Beramka was Syafirin's son. Muhammad Bakir was known to be the most active writer in the late 19th century.

Stories written by Muhammad Bakir varied. His manuscripts are stored in the National Library of the Republic of Indonesia. Chambert-Loir and Kramadibrata state that among the manuscripts are puppet (*wayang*) story, *panji* story, Islamic story, symbolic poetry and adventure story.[10]

---

4. Ibid 16.
5. Niemeijer, above n 1, 32.
6. *Hikayat Sultan Taburat* (Manuscript collection of the National Library of the Republic of Indonesia, Ml. 183 B).
7. Ibid.
8. Ibid.
9. Ibid.
10. Henry Chambert-Loir and Dewaki Kramadibrata, *Katalog Naskah Pecenongan Koleksi Perpustakaan Nasional* (Jakarta: Perpustakaan Nasional Republik Indonesia, 2013).

One of the manuscripts written by Fadhli's family is *Hikayat Sultan Taburat*. The effort to inventory the text of HST was done by tracing catalogs of Malay and regional texts, both inside and outside the country. Unfortunately, no text of HST was found other than those contained in the nine manuscripts stored in the National Library of the Republic of Indonesia. The nine HST manuscripts stored in the National Library of the Republic of Indonesia are Ml.183 A, Ml.183 B, Ml.183 C, Ml.183 D, Ml.183 E, Ml.257 A, Ml.257 B, Ml.258 and Ml.259. Texts on the manuscripts were written in jawi scripts. The languages used were mostly Malay, Betawi, Javanese, and Arabic.

As far as the investigation was carried out, two names werereferred to as the copyists of HST, Safirin and Muhammad Bakir. This investigation was carried out by searching for information in the manuscript which included copyist's note on the exordium, the body of the text, and closing section. Besides, the searches were carried out by paying attention to the ownership signs and the authorship signs such as script characters and signatures.

In this *hikayat*, there are lessons about benefaction and tolerance through adventurous stories of the characters. The story is not just an entertainment, as the *hikayat* is also full of symbolic meanings aimed by the copyist so that the readers get the lessons. The following are the author's statements in the script of HST which has code of Ml. 183 D, Ml. 183 E, Ml. 258 and Ml. 259 intended for tenants or readers.

> *"...buat jadi pengajaran kepada orang yang membaca hikayat ini dengan mengetahui dan mengerti tamsil/9/ibaratnya. Barang siapa yang mengetahui maksudnya hikayat yang suda lalu itu, maka hendaklah/10/diambil buat ingatan akan menjadi pelajaran kehidupan dalam dunia ini*"[11]
>
> "so that it will be a lesson for the *hikayat* readers to understand the imagery/9/the analogy. Anyone who knows the meaning of the last *hikayat*, hopefully they/10/remember it as the lesson of life"[12]

[275] Ini hikayat Sultan Taburat
Diambil tamsil dengan ibarat/1/

[275] This is *Hikayat Sultan Taburat*
Taken from the imagery from the analogy/1/.[13]

Ambil tamsil dan ibaratnya
Supaya jadi dapat faedahnya/3/.[14]

Take the imagery and its analogySo that it will be useful/3/.[15]

Maka bole dijadikan tamsil dan ibarat dan penawar adanya.[16]

So it may be used as the imagery and analogy and the antidote of heartache.[17]

---

11. *Hikayat Sultan Taburat* (Manuscript collection of the National Library of the Republic of Indonesia, Ml. 183 D) 2.
12. Ibid.
13. *Hikayat Sultan Taburat* (Manuscript collection of the National Library of the Republic of Indonesia, Ml. 183 E) 275.
14. *Hikayat Sultan Taburat* (Manuscript collection of the National Library of the Republic of Indonesia, Ml. 258) 120.
15. Ibid.
16. *Hikayat Sultan Taburat* (Manuscript collection of the National Library of the Republic of Indonesia, Ml. 259) 193.
17. *Hikayat Sultan Taburat*, above n 14, 193.

Safirin and Muhammad Bakir were known to have the position as the chairmen and caretakers of Langgar Tinggi Mosque. In addition, Kramadibrata and Suharjo mention that Muhammad Bakir was a teacher for children in learning religion.[18] Their position as religious leaders in Pecenongan would have contributed to their work. This position created a sense of responsibility for Muhammad Bakir to give advice and lesson to his readers. *Hikayat Sultan Taburat* was created to convey lessons in the society life and religious life. Since the family of religious leaders in Pecenongan also dealt with manuscript copying or leasing, HST was then created as the medium of teaching.

HST is a teaching text using adventurous stories of the characters. The story begins when Sultan Taburat marries his son, Indra Buganda Syafandarsyah with Princess Mahrum Sari. After getting married, Indra Buganda Syafandarsyah decides to leave his country and his wife to wander. He is the crown prince in the Country of Thar Al Arqan. As the crown prince, he needs to get knowledge and experience to rule his country in the future.

In his adventure, he disguises himself as Captain Manshur Takbir. He faces various obstacles such as fighting against enemies and drifting in the sea. However, he can overcome those obstacles. He also has a wife named Mahrun Siti. After completing his journey, he lives with his two wives.

Both of his wives are pregnant for a long time and have not given birth. The palace astrologist tells him to look for medicines throughout the country. In the middle of his journey, he has a memory loss because his mind istricked by aGenie. Afterwards, he marries Rinumsari, the daughter of the hermit who has healed him. Then the story continues with the adventures of his children and his grandchildren.

The next story is about Indra Maulana Syafandarsyah from Raman Giri Hill. He is the son of Indra Buganda Syafandarsyah and Rinum Sari, the daughter of the Ascetic RamanRaman. Once upon a time, he loses his way to the country of Takzir. He meets Princess Mangal Jamjam and Gumanda Sula, the daughters of Maharaja Muhammad Syahrab. Indra Maulana hasbeen tortured several times by Gumanda Sula and Putri Mangal Jamjam. However, he gains much knowledge and magical objects from the persecution. With his struggle, Indra Maulana can meet his brothers in the country of Thar Al Arqan. They finally become kings in their respective countries.

Princess Mangal Jamjam has a child named Darmasatiya Syamsunari who has bad personality. Indra Maulana has two twin children named Antamanikam Rawan Galaran and Darmasatiya Qamrul Alam. They have good personality. One day, Indra Maulana's children are deceived by Darmasatiya Syamsunari. However, Darmasatiya Syamsunari is exposed to bad things. He is separated from his mother because he is kidnapped by a heartbroken thief.

This research wants to reveal the perspective about tolerance contained in manuscripts copied at the end of the 19th century in Pecenongan. *Hikayat Sultan Taburat*'s manuscript was selected as the main corpus for this research because the manuscript was written by the family of religious leaders in Pecenongan— an area which had diverse ethnic communities at the end of the 19th century. The perspective about tolerance can be analyzed from the text in this manuscript.

Philology and Codicology were used as the tool to answer the research problems. The research main corpus was a manuscript from the end of the 19th century. Therefore, codicology is necessary to analyze physical aspects of the manuscript, which has the potential to influence the identification of the text. Philology is applied to deal with problems related to the text, for example the problem of literacy and textual criticism. Furthermore, philology is used to "read" the text. Philology is used to make texts legible. What is meant by "legible" in this case is not only that the text is clear enough to be read, but it means that the text can be understood from its context.

18. Dewaki Kramadibrata, *Lakon Jaka Sukara* (Depok: Yayasan Naskah Nusantara, 2010) 1; Rias Antho Rahmi Suharjo, *Analisis Paratekstual Terhadap Hikayat Wayang Arjuna Karya Muhammad Bakir* (UGM, 2012) 73–74.

2 HST TEXT VIEWING THE DIVERSITY

In the text of the HST there are various views on how views and how to respond to diversity in terms of studying, in religious life, and in everyday relationships.

2.1 *Acquiring knowledge*

In a part of the Ml. 258 manuscript content, it is mentioned that Indra Maulana learned from all the teachers that he encountered. He learned *mengaji* ('reading the Qur'an, the Islamic holy book') from the lemma (i.e., Islamic scholars of religion and law). Besides learning from the ulema, he also learned from Christian priests. Because he learned from diverse teachersand learned diverse lessons, he became a learned person (i.e., someone with much knowledge). It is mentioned that before doing all the learning, he was an ignorant person. Moreover, he called Si Bodo (a fool people) because of his stupidity.

In an excerpt from the aforesaid story, Muhammad Bakir illustrates how the character named Indra Maulana learned from Christian priests and teachers of Christianity. It is told that one night he arrived at a village. It was populated by many people who were Christians, Jews, and the Majusi (i.e., fire worshippers, followers of an ancient religion), among others. To him, the village was not just a place to stop a while on his way somewhere else. Instead, he came there for something, namely, learning under the guidance of Christian priests. It is as stated in the excerpt in the original written language of Old Malay as follows:

> *Maka pada malam itu (8) ia turun pada suatu kampung. Maka di sana banyak daripada kaum Nasrani dan Majusi dan Yahudi. (9) Maka disanala(h) ia be[r]lajar (10) daripada pe[r]lajaran itu.Maka beberapa lamanya* ***tahulah ia daripada membaca suratan cara Nasrani*** *(11) itu serta ia tahula(h) membaca segala kitab-kitab Injil.*

which more or less means as follows:

'Then that night he came to a village. There were many Christian, Majusi, and Jewish people there. Then he studied the lessons there. Then after a while he knew how to read the writing in the Christian way and he knew how to read all Bibles'

It is mentioned that after studying and learning for some while in the village, he came to know how to read the script or writing in the Christian way. As for the sense of the word script, in this case it could mean the special set of letters used in writing. What is meant by the Christian way of writing here is the script commonly used by Christians. In view of the context of the era when the manuscript was transcribed, apparently what is meant by the Christian way of writing is the Latinscript of the era.

The excerpt as follows:

> *Maka dengan kuasa Tuhannya, maka Indra Mulana (12) pun tahulah dalam agama Nasrani dan Majusi dan Yahudi itu habisla(h) dipelajari(nya) daripada segala (13) warna kepandaian itu.*

which approximately means as follows:

> 'Then, by the grace of God, Indra Maulana knew how to learn from the Christian and Majusi and Jewish religions and learned all the colors of cleverness'

Indra Maulana came to know not only Christian religious lessons but also lessons about the Jewish and Majusi religions. All were already studied by Indra Maulana. He had studied all the colors of cleverness. The term *all the colors of cleverness* has the sense of all that was beneficial for improving Indra Maulana's insight.None of the three kinds of lessons was unbeneficial to Indra Maulana. All the colors of cleverness could be learned by Indra Maulana because of God's will. All was done and obtained due to the grace of God. Indra Maulana felt awed by all the knowledge that he had obtained. He was awed by the power of God, in this case, in relation with what the colors of know ledge were like.

Dan telah diketahuinya terang dengan kuasanya Tuhan itu. Maka heranlah Indra/14/ Mulana melihat segala budi pekertinya segala bangsa itu yang beragama itu sekalian dengan budi/15/bahasa yang baik dan perkataan yang halus-halus dan kelakuan yang baik seperti pengasihan samanya/16/manusia.

which more or less means as follows:

'And he had known the light by the grace of God. Then Indra Maulana marveled at seeing all the characters of all the religious races with their good language, gentle words, and good behavior like to love fellow human beings'

It is implied that Indra Maulana felt awed by the characters of all of the different religious races. The expression *character* appears to contain a sense which is broad in scope. It covers not only goodness but also what the attitudes and views of these religious peoples were like.

As for what is meant by character, it is mentioned by the one transcribing the manuscript that what are included in it are good language, gentle words, and good behavior, namely, to love fellow human beings.

What is meant by good language is courteous speech. Being courteous in speaking implies an understanding of customs and manners of making good communication. Certain people who would possess courtesy in language use would be those who have gentle or soft words, namely, words which are no trough ones and not those that are abusive ones like curses, swearwords, and invectives. The intended words are not those of the average common people.

The good behavior meant by Indra Maulana was associated with any attitude expressing love for fellow human beings. The attitude of loving fellow members of the human race is taught in every religion. Such attitudes were the ones learned by Indra Maulana from the people embracing religions respectively in the text.

2.2 *In religious life*

In the HST text, narrator declare his views about religious life. He said that all people in those country have good and bad attitude. People who obedient in his religion has good attitude. The narrator says that among the people belonging to those races, there were those who had bad character and there were also those who had good character. Indra Maulana had the view that people who held fast to their religion or practice the teachings of their religion would be good in behavior regardless of what race they belonged to. However, if any of them went against the teachings of his or her religion, he or she would become bad or evil. Not all the people in the village were good. There were also some who were bad, namely, those who did not put to practice the teachings of their religion.

Maka setengahnya adalah yang jahat perangainya dan adalah yang baik perangainya, ya'ni/ 17/segala bangsa itu jikalau yang memegang agamanya maka semuanya baik barang laku-nya. Dan yang tiada/18/[59] menurut agama maka jadila(h) jahat pekertinya. Maka heran-lah Indra Mulana itu sebab melihat keadilan Tuhan/1/melakukan masing-masing hambanya dengan masing-masing agamanya dan (ke)percayaannya itu.

meaning approximately as follows:

'Then a part of them were bad in character and the other part were good in character, namely that people of all those races who held to their religion would all be good in any of their deeds. And those who did not obey their religion would become bad in characterr. Then Indra Maulana was filled with wonder because he saw God's fairness in treating God's subjects with their own religions and faiths'

Each of God's subjects has his or her religion and faith. God is the All Just because God gives each subject a religion and a faith. That was something that made Indra Maulana feel awed. He was in awe upon seeing how just God was in managing God's subjects.

It mentions that a part of the people were a group who believed in wood and stone as source of power. The group worshipped wood and stone. It indicates that there were also some people who believed in the power of the moon and the sun. They worshipped the moon and the sun. There were also a group of people who believed in the power of fire and water. Fire and water were the elements that they worshipped. Another part of the people believed in the power of birds and various other animals. Power which they could obtain in a cemetery.

The following excerpt:

> *Maka setengahnya bangsa itu adala(h) yang (2) percaya kayu dan batu. Dan setengahnya percaya bulan dan matahari. Dan setengahnya percaya api dan/3/air. Dan setengahnya yang percaya burung dan segala binatang. Dan setengahnya percaya Kuburan. Maka sekaliannya/4/itu di dalam agamanya tiada lain hanya yang dibicarakan pekerjaan baik dan jahat juga.*

means more or less the following:

> 'Then a part of the race were people who believed in wood and stone and a part believed in the moon and the sun. And a part believed in fire and water. And a part were those who believed in birds and various animals. And a part believed in graves, believed in ancestors. Then all that in their religions still discussed no other than good and bad doings'

The implication is that though these people differed in what they believed, in their respective faiths the essence of the teachings was still also a discussion concerning good deeds and bad deeds.

It is to mention that the religions taught that badness was to be given in return for badnessand goodness was to be given in return for goodness. All the religions taught their followers to believe in the one and true God. None of the religions did not return in the end to belief in God. The religions are still the same though the teachings for *thaharah, fiqih*, and purifying oneself with water are found in only one or some but not in all of them.

The excerpt as follows:

> Maka semuanya itu dalam agamanya pulang percayaanla(h) kepada Tuhan yang sebenar-benarnya juga. Dan tiadalah (7) padanya hukum thaharah dan fiqih dan bersuci.

means more or less as follows:

> 'Then all that in each of the religions went back to the belief in the one and true God. And there was no law concerning thaharah and fiqih and self-purifying with water'

It is mentioned that from the holy-book studies Indra Maulana could now have though and not only nature or instinct anymore. He, who formerly only knew hunting by shooting an arrow at a bird, was now no longer satisfied with that. It was also the knowledge obtained from reading parts of the holy books related to the dynamics of human kind and the world that made his mind almost perfect.

The excerpt as follows:

> *Maka itulah ia jadi beruba(h) kelakukannya dan/15/bukan seperti adat yang se(h)ari-(h) ari tatkala ia keluar dari lubang bukit. Maka baharula(h) hampir/16/sempurna akalnya Indra Mulana itu.*

meaning more or less as follows:

> 'Therefore, he became changed in behavior and was not like what he was in his daily custom when he went out of the hole in the hill. Only then was Indra Maulana's mind almost perfect'

Is to mention that only then Indra Maulana's mind was almost perfect. It was even actually not yet perfect because it is still said to be almost so. However, it was still better than it was when he went out of the hole in the hill, in which he was still without the necessary knowledge at all.

What he liked most to do then was even only to kill a bird with an arrow. And it was even also in order to have it as only something to eat. He had changed into a human being who could think.

Thus, besides being awed concerning God's power and justness over God's subjects who differed in knowledge and belief, he also acquired knowledge of worldly matters all the time he was in the village.

2.3 *Memories of companionship*

In the manuscript here identified as Ml. 258 it is mentioned that Indra Maulana longed for the good times that he had when he played with Christian people. He did not make any difference among his friends and did not pay attention to what religion any of his friends embraced.

One excerpt as follows:

> *Maka Si Pandai Memanah Mata teringatlah/5/pada masa kecilnya teruniaya orang. Dan teringatlah pada masa bermain-main petak/6/dan bermain-main gala(h) dengan segala Nasrani itu pada waktu terangnya bulan./7/.*[19]

means more or less as follows:

> 'Then *Si Pandai Memanah Mata* remembered that in his childhood he was mistreated by people. and he remembered the times he played hide-and-seek and played with a pole together with all those Christians at the time of the bright moon'

Si Pandai Memanah Mata, literally meaning Clever In Shooting Eye With Arrow, is Indra Maulana's other name, referring to him as the one who hit the bull's eye with an arrow. At one time, he remembered the times in his childhood when he was still a small boy with someone mistreating him; Princes Mangal Jamjam and King Gumanda Sula. However, besides being mistreated, he also remembered the good times when he played hide-and-seek and played with a pole with his Christian playmate sat the times the moon was bright. Though in his childhood Indra Maulana experienced mistreatment when still small, what made him happy at heart was the times when he played with playmates at the time the light of the moon was shining brightly.

3 CONCLUSION

At the end of the 19th century, Muhammad Bakir mentioned that there were some people who were reluctant to read the *hikayat*. For them, *hikayat* is a story that "is not accepted by reason". In response to this, Muhammad Bakir and Syafirin offered a middle ground. They mentioned that in reading *hikayat*, it should not only be a pleasure, because in the *hikayat* there was a lesson. Therefore, in order to obtain benefits, the reader should take a picture and be like that contained in it. One of the *hikayat* that was written was *Hikayat Sultan Taburat*.

Hikayat Sultan Taburat was mentioned by the schriber, made to be used as one of the learning resources for his readers. *Hikayat Sultan Taburat* is not a story that can only be enjoyed as an entertainment material, but also a variety of knowledge can be obtained in it.

HST is a text created at the end of the 19th century in a regional environment that has a diverse population, in terms of ethnicity, religion, and social class. In the text of HST there are several views in addressing this diversity. In this paper, we have discussed how the text views about studying, religious life, and everyday relationships.

In the text view of Sultan Taburat's saga, to gain knowledge, one can learn from anyone with the aim of gaining knowledge. Narrated, Indra Maulana studied with scholars and priests

19. *Hikayat Sultan Taburat*, above n 14, 119.

so he became smarter than before. Learners are no longer limited by ethnicity, race or religion in studying. He may study anyone who can enlighten him.

In religious life, the text of the HST has several views. The first view regarding the attitude of religious people. People who obey their religion would all be good in their deeds. People who are religious will be polite in acting. People who are obedient in religion are said to be doing all their good deeds to others. And those who do not obey their religion would be a bad character. It is said that the evil person (surely) does not practice the teachings of his religion properly.

Religious people tend to be good language, gentle words, and good behavior like to love fellow human beings. People who are rude to fellow humans, according to the text of the HST, are not people who "hold" their religion. People who "hold their religion" are soft-hearted with good attitudes.

In the text of the HST it is stated that all that in each of the religions went back to the belief in the one and true God. Script writers did not mention or justify which God should be chosen. The author only gives the keyword to the reader: So all of that in his religion returns to the true belief to God ('Then all that in each of the religions went back to the belief in theone and true God '). Presumably the choice of words is wise to advise various readers. The author would preserve himself from the attitude of justification in religion.

The narrator also gives readers the knowledge that friendship does not distinguish between ethnicity, race, or religion. Indra Maulana is said to be playing with people who have different religions. He does not feel disturbed and feels happy playing together. The difference does not deter him in a friendship.

Some things that can be concluded from the perspective of the HST text on diversity is that diversity is beautiful, diversity provides knowledge, and diversity is also the power of God. All that goes back to how we thank it.

REFERENCES

Aziz, Abdul, *Islam Dan Masyarakat Betawi* (Jakarta: PT. Logos Wacana Ilmu, 2002)

Chambert-Loir, Henry and Dewaki Kramadibrata, *Katalog Naskah Pecenongan Koleksi Perpustakaan Nasional* (Jakarta: Perpustakaan Nasional Republik Indonesia, 2013)

Hikayat Sultan Taburat (Manuscript collection of the National Library of the Republic of Indonesia, Ml. 183 B)

Hikayat Sultan Taburat (Manuscript collection of the National Library of the Republic of Indonesia, Ml. 183 D)

Hikayat Sultan Taburat (Manuscript collection of the National Library of the Republic of Indonesia, Ml. 183 E)

Hikayat Sultan Taburat (Manuscript collection of the National Library of the Republic of Indonesia, Ml. 258)

Hikayat Sultan Taburat (Manuscript collection of the National Library of the Republic of Indonesia, Ml. 259)

Kramadibrata, Dewaki, *Lakon Jaka Sukara* (Depok: Yayasan Naskah Nusantara, 2010)

Niemeijer, HE, *Batavia: Masyarakat Kolonial Abad XVII* (Jakarta: Masup Jakarta, 2012)

Suharjo, Rias Antho Rahmi, *Analisis Paratekstual Terhadap Hikayat Wayang Arjuna Karya Muhammad Bakir* (UGM, 2012)

Culture and International Law - Juwana et al. (Eds)
© 2019 Taylor & Francis Group, London, ISBN 978-1-138-38766-9

Local wisdom on sustainable food crop protection: Subak agricultural land protection in Bali among local, national and international law

Sugama Putra, R. Ismala Dewi & Heru Susetyo
University of Indonesia, Indonesia

ABSTRACT: This paper discusses the problems of *subak*, especially the problem of changing the function of *subak* agricultural land and the factors that influence it. In essence *subak* can not withstand external party intervention. *Subak* can not afford to resist any intervention, because they have no political power, and their organizations are weak. The lack of *subak* protection policy in Bali is inseparable from the intervention of local government that has not been in favor of *subak* or side with other sectors. Therefore, a responsive law which is compatible to international human rights law is needed to accommodate the aspirations of the *subak* community in order to create an effective law against the *subak* community. One way of protecting *subak* communities and *subak* farmlands in Bali is to implement a law on sustainable food crop protection.

KEYWORDS: Land Conversion, Agricultural Land Protection, Subak, Bali

1 INTRODUCTION

In Indonesia, farmers should be given incentives and get empowerment programs, other than that if there are parties who convert agricultural land into non-agricultural land then it can be sanctioned, this is due to the guarantee of farmland protection and incentives and empowerment by law. However, the facts show that the conversion of agricultural land to non-agricultural land is still occurring, as it is not yet in line with the implementation of sustainable agriculture sustainable food protection law at the lower regulatory level.

In line with the foregoing, some argue that one of the most serious problems is the conversion of agricultural land to non-agricultural land in rural to suburban areas, leading to dramatic reductions in technically irrigated agricultural land into residential and industrial areas.[1] The impact then national rice production is reduced and forced to import rice from neighboring countries such as Thailand and Vietnam. Against this problem, there is a view that the concept of agrarian policy in Indonesia is often very interesting at the level of abstract but rather at the level of implementation to be the opposite.[2]

The protection of agricultural land against its function is regulated in The Indonesian State Regulation No. 41 of 2009 on Sustainable Land Farming Protection. Article 3, it is stated that the protection of sustainable agricultural land is organized with the aim of: a. protecting the area and agricultural land on a sustainable basis; b. ensure the availability of sustainable agricultural land; c. realizing food self-sufficiency, resilience, and food; d. protecting the ownership of agricultural land belonging to farmers; e. increase the prosperity and welfare of

1. Suparjo Sujadi, 'Analisis Dan Prediksi Permasalahan Pertanahan Di Masa Mendatang' (2004) 4 *Jurnal Hukum dan Pembangunan* 364.
2. Achmad Sodiki, *Politik Hukum Agraria* (Jakarta, Konstitusi Press, 2013).

farmers and communities; f. improve farmer protection and empowerment; g. improve the provision of employment for decent living; h. maintain an ecological balance; and i. realizing the revitalization of agriculture.

Nevertheless, the objectives as stated by article 3 can not be realized if the scope of protection of sustainable food crops has not been fulfilled. Article 4 of The Indonesian State Regulation No. 41 of 2009 concerning Sustainable Land Protection of Food Agriculture, that the scope of the intended includes: a. planning and determination; b. development; c. research; d. utilization; e. coaching; f. control; g. supervision; h. information Systems; i. protection and empowerment of farmers; j. financing; and k. community participation.

The guarantees of the protection of agricultural land against its transfer of functions are affirmed in Article 44. It is stipulated by the article that the land which had already designated as Sustainable Food Farm is protected and prohibited for conversion. This law shall provide strict sanctions to any person who transfers agricultural land to non-agricultural land as set forth in Article 70 governing administrative sanctions, as well as Articles 72, 73 and 74 which govern the criminal provisions

Lawmakers recognize that land is the most important factor for farmers to carry out their activities so that it is expected that farmers and the community will become more prosperous. This is in line with the opinion of Egbert de Vries who views that the problem of farmers, especially in Java is the lack of land. The impact of this shortage of land area had forced farmers to seek land to the tops of the mountains, raising concerns about the consequences of deforestation by farmers. Egbert de Vries came to the conclusion that Javanese farmers, however, wanted to remain farmers.[3] Opinion of Egbert de Vries is still relevant when it is associated with the case of Salim Kancil in Lumajang Regency who died for defending his farm against the illegal sand miners.

Despite legislation that guarantees the protection of agricultural land over its transfer through sustainable agricultural land protection policies, the government's efforts to protect the farms have not shown positive results. This is because there is still a change in the function of agricultural land as revealed in the working meeting of Commission IV of the House of Representatives of the Republic of Indonesia with the Minister of Agriculture which was held on September 11, 2017.

Ironically, the problem of the transfer of agricultural land function has been in contact with a cultural heritage in Bali, namely *Subak*. This has been much expressed through researches, writings, even media coverage both print and electronic. Like the following example, it is mentioned that in Bali rife development of golf courses, luxury hotels, and other tourism facilities. Thus, farmland and farmers' fortunes are sacrificed. The development of tourism in the Island of the Gods destroyed many *subak* that have existed since the ancient times.[4] On the other hand, it is clear that the 25 hectares of *Subak* Muwa on the edge of the Monkey Forest road are only 2 hectares, the rest is changed into restaurant, hotel and gallery services. The disappearance of some *subak* is not only observed from the decrease of planting area, but more importantly is the loss of a cultural equivalent.[5]

If so, the above problem does not reflect the peace for the *subak* farmers in carrying out their daily activities because at any time the land will be the target of other parties for non-agricultural purposes. Is not the law indeed held to overcome the conflicting interests[6], so that all interests need to be protected equally[7] and finally the goal of the law can be realized, that is peace.[8]

3. Egbert De Vries, *Pertanian Dan Kemiskinan Di Jawa* (Jakarta, Yayasan Obor Indonesia, 1985).
4. Koerniatmanto Soetoprawiro, *Pengantar Hukum Pertanian* (Jakarta, Gapperindo, 2013).
5. Hery Listyawati, 'Kegagalan Pengendalian Alih Fungsi Tanah Dalam Perspektif Penatagunaan Tanah Di Indonesia' (2010) 22(1) *Mimbar Hukum* 37.
6. J Van Kan and JH Beekhuis, *Pengantar Ilmu Hukum* (Jakarta, Ghalia Indonesia, 1990).
7. LJ Van Apeldoorn, *Pengantar Ilmu Hukum* (Jakarta, Pradya Paramita, 2011).
8. Peter Mahmud Marzuki, *Pengantar Ilmu Hukum* (Jakarta, Kencana, 2014).

Based on the case mentioned above, this paper is intended to discuss the protection of *subak* in terms of law, especially related to *subak* farming so that the law can really be felt for the *subak* community. Another reason why this article is raised is that *subak* has its own characteristics compared to agriculture in other areas, because *subak* is a cultural model, and has even been recognized by UNESCO as one of the world cultural heritage. However, it does not mean agricultural land in other areas is not important to protect, agricultural land must be protected from its function. This policy of protection of sustainable agricultural land should be implemented all over Indonesia because Indonesia is an agrarian country.

Therefore, subak farming land needs to be protected from overturning its function into non-agricultural land, so that subak as an irrigation system in agriculture can be sustainable as a characteristic of Balinese culture and the pride of the Indonesian nation, which the world has recognized as one of the world cultural heritage.

2 THE DYNAMIC TREND OF CHANGE OF *SUBAK* FUNCTION OF *SUBAK* AGRICULTURAL LAND IN BALI

2.1 *Concept of* subak

The views of experts in understanding *subak* are greatly varied. Sutawan said that the *subak* that is very popular in Bali is basically a container or organization where the gathering of farmers with determination and high spirits to cooperate together in an effort to get water with the aim of producing food crops, especially rice and palawija. As an irrigation institution of traditional farmers, *subak* is estimated to have existed in Bali since almost a millennium. *Subak* is also a unique irrigation system, especially in terms of religious rituals are very dense and often done by farmers *subak* members.[9] Windia views *subak* as an irrigation system from a technological side that is appropriate for the *subak* members concerned. The correspondence of *subak* system technology is shown by members of *subak* through understanding of the way of utilization of irrigation water based on Tri Hita Karana which integrates with the making of building and physical network of irrigation, how to operate, coordination of operation and maintenance performed by pekaseh (chairman) *subak* institutional and information for its management (Windia, 2006).[10]

Sirtha said the main of *subak* function is to regulate irrigation for agriculture. In carrying out such a task, several *subak* community activities, among others, arranging irrigation networks, arranging the distribution of water, arranging the rotation of cropping patterns, and carry out ceremonial activities. Implementation of *subak* organization based on customary law, that is law which grow and develop from habits living in Balinese society (Hinduism society). *Subak* as a cultural phenomenon has three characteristics: first, as a system of cultural values, such as values, norms, laws, and special rules, for example, awig-awig *subak* are provisions made by *subak* society, which is used as a code of conduct to achieve order; secondly, as a form of social system which is a pattern of *subak* community activities, for example, *subak* community activities in arranging irrigation, cultivating land, planting seeds, harvesting, or doing ceremonial activities in temple *subak*, is a pattern of behavior and interaction conducted continuous; and third, as a physical being, is the most concrete form, such as irrigation networks, rice fields, and building equipment. The three *subak* forms are strung together within the framework of culture, which undergoes changes due to the influence of development and the dynamics of society. Concrete components of culture change faster than abstract components. Therefore, the physical component undergoes the most rapid change, followed by changes in the components of social systems, and components of cultural values or norms.[11]

---

9. Nyoman Sutawan, *Organisasi Dan Manajemen Subak Di Bali* (Denpasar, Pustaka Bali Post, 2008).
10. Wayan Windia, *Transformasi Sistem Irigasi Subak Yang Berlandaskan Konsep Tri Hita Karana* (Denpasar, Pustaka Bali Post, 1990).
11. Nyoman Sirtha, *Subak: Konsep Pertanian Religius Perspektif Hukum, Budaya Dan Agama Hindu* (Surabaya, Paramita, 2008).

Graders define *subak* as "a collection of fields from the same channel or the same branch of a channel, receiving water and irrigating". Korn defines *subak* as "a legal entity visible from the wealth possessed in the form of money, some plots of dry and wet soil, temples and small buildings to meet." These two *subak* boundaries indicate a different point of view. Grader reviewed the *subak* from its physical aspect, while Korn reviewed the *subak* of three aspects, namely the religious aspect of the temple as a place of praying of *subak* people; social aspects such as activities in meeting in *subak* hall; as well as physical aspects in the form of buildings, material wealth in the form of dry soil and wet soil owned by *subak*.[12]

Traditional institutions grow and flourish in society. Naturally, institutions in the sense of early institutions arise as quirks in the pattern of human behavior, to become habitual. If the habit is then attached hope and sanctions, then the institution is born. If the institution is organized and well established or institutionalized, then the organization is established. In accordance with that view, it can be said that *subak* is a social order that grows from habit. Once established, the *subak* requires a container or organization that serves as its implementation.

According to Ter Haar, a civic organization that functions as a legal alliance, is an organization based on customary law. The fellowship as a social life in groups, which behaves as one unity to the external and inner world, has its own order, has its own management, its own property, both tangible and intangible. In accordance with Ter Haar's view, *subak* in the sense of being a social organization is a regular social unity, whose members feel attached to each other because of mutual interests, have leaders who can act in and out, and have material and immaterial treasures. The characteristics, among others, (1) have shared water resources; (2) has one or several beduguls/temples (shrine) as a place of worship to God Almighty in its manifestation as Dewi Sri; and (3) have full autonomy, both inward and outward. The characteristics of *subak* are manifested in traditional social organizations that have the following characteristics. First, there are groups of people who share common interests; second, which arranges its group in a particular arrangement; third, own property; and fourth, to have administrators who can act as one unity.[13]

In the legislation, among others, contained in Regional Regulation No. 9 of 2012 Bali Province on *Subak*, in Article 1 number 4 mentioned *subak* meaning that "*Subak* is a traditional organization in the field of water use and or plant governance at the level of farming on indigenous peoples in Bali which are socio-cultural, religious, economic nature that has historically continued to grow and develop ".

Subak has three components, namely physical components, components of social systems, and components of cultural values. Physical component of *subak* infrastructure and facilities. The components of the social system are the management of the physical component. Components of cultural values in the form of values, norms, laws, and special rules.

The organizational structure of *subak* varies according to the width of the rice field area and the number of its members. Generally, the composition of *subak* administrators consists of a pekaseh (head of *subak*), withdrawal (scribe) or secretary, and kesinoman (interpreter) or person who submits pekaseh information to *subak* residents. The long historical developments experienced by *subak* from generation to generation look at the development or changes in its organizational structure. Since 1343 AD, when Bali was under the auspices of the Majapahit Kingdom, a sedahan who was appointed to coordinate several *subak* areas in order to wage tax collection imposed on *subak* residents.

In the reign of colonial rule, the Dutch East Indies saw subak as a very effective institution functioned for agricultural taxation (landrente). Therefore, in 1925 repetition of soil measurements was done more perfectly and definitely known as a classifier. It caused the subak organizational structure to change again, namely in the kingdom was appointed a great sedahan in charge of coordinating the sedahan.

12. Ibid.
13. Ibid.

After Indonesia gained independence, subak organizational structure did not undergo substantial changes, but with the government's intention to improve water utilization efficiency, not infrequently separate irrigation networks were then merged into one. These irrigation networks could cover more than one village, so subak organizational structures undergo changes in accordance with the development and needs of the organization.

Subak also has a philosophical foundation, namely Tri Hita Karana (three causes of happiness), which embodies into three elements, namely (1) elements of parhyangan (private) that is a subak temple building as a manifestation of devotion to God Almighty; (2) element of pawongan (semi public) that is manifestation of harmonious relationship among subak people; and (3) elements of palemahan (public), which is the form of wetland and all the irrigation infrastructure and facilities.

Various traditional values of subak can be seen in the application of the philosophy of Tri Hita Karana (THK) as the main philosophy of subak. Therefore, in an effort to understand the various traditional values held by subak, will be examined based on the application of the philosophy within subak. THK comes from the words: tri means three, hita means prosperity or happiness, and karana means cause. Thus THK means the three components/elements that cause prosperity or happiness, which is closely related to one another, including: the relationship between man and God Almighty (*parhyangan*), the relationship between man and man (*pawongan or bhuana alit*), and the relationship between man and nature (*palemahan or bhuana agung*). This means to gain material and spiritual well-being or happiness, human beings need to create and nurture the harmony of mutual relationships between humans and God Almighty, the relationship between man and man, and the relationship between man and the natural environment. THK philosophy is not only applied in *subak*, but has popularized, entrenched and animated almost all the living and livelihood of the Hindu community in Bali.

Implicitly Tri Hita Karana contains a message that man manages natural resources and environment wisely and wisely to maintain its sustainability. Does not God have created the universe and everything it is because of His love for mankind? Nature is a gift of God that can provide a source of life and livelihood for humanity. Therefore, nature must be preserved and preserved so that it can be utilized not only by the present generation, but also by successive generations. The concept of Tri Hita Karana is presumably acceptable to every nation in the world and may even have applied it in their daily life even though they do not recognize the term or concept of Tri Hita Karana. The way undoubtedly differs from country to country according to tradition, culture, and religion respectively. The concept of Tri Hita Karana is very relevant to the concept of sustainable development (sustainable development) which is now so popular and often used as a reference by every development planner in various sectors.

As an irrigation system managed by farmers independently for seasonal crops, especially paddy, *subak* has several interrelated elements: (1) irrigation water management farmer organization; (2) irrigation networks/irrigation facilities and infrastructure; (3) food production; (4) irrigated rice field ecosystem; and (5) religious rituals associated with rice cultivation. In order to realize the preservation of *subak*, then all these elements must be preserved.

Thus, it can be said that if one of the elements is not working then all elements will be disturbed or even all elements become no longer functioning. For example, if the ecosystem element of irrigated rice field is converted to non-agricultural land then the impact of *subak* will not become a system anymore. In other words that *subak* farmland which is converted into non-agricultural land will certainly eliminate *subak* culture. Moreover, if an agricultural land in the over-function has been attached to the right to land, it is difficult or even impossible to be returned to agricultural land.[14]

14. Soedjarwo Soeromihardjo, *Mengkritisi Undang-Undang Pokok Agraria* (Jakarta, Cerdas Pustaka Publisher, 2009).

2.2 *Issues and problems related to subak*

Some of *subak* problems, either directly or indirectly that can trigger the conversion of *subak* farming land, will be described by borrowing the study of Gede Sedana through his book entitled "Halting *Subak* Extinction in Bali"[15], as follows:

2.3 *Quantity and quality of irrigation water*

The limited availability of available water at the source level is one of the serious problems for farmers and *subak* including farmers' organizations in developing countries. In the dry season for example, farmers are feeling the lack of water that has an impact on land utilization and plant growth that even lead to crop failure. Evidently, it can be seen from the decreasing quantity of Lake Buyan water in certain period where this lake is the source of water for the rivers in Central Buleleng Regency.

Limited quantity of irrigation water will affect farming activities in *subak*, as in the implementation of cropping pattern and planting schedule. There is often a shift in planting schedules and also changes in cropping patterns as a result of reduced irrigation water. Moreover with the influence of global warming and climate change. The impact caused by climate change is the uncertainty of the availability of irrigation water, which further decreases the productivity of the plant. In fact, not infrequently in the harvest failure.

The increasing availability of irrigation water is increasingly a problem due to the increasing use of water at the level of surface water supply and underground water by various sectors (not exclusively used for agriculture). Consequently, there is a conflict of interest in the use of water. Conflicts of interest in the utilization of water resources also occur between *subaks* with the tourism sector, household and industrial sector because the utilization is "not well organized". Excessive use of underground water, siphoning of water sources for the benefit of drinking water and the tourism industry causes disruption of irrigation water discharge for agricultural purposes.

Conversely, during the rainy season, excessive amount of water can damage the irrigation networks and result in higher financing costs for *subaks*. Almost every year *subaks* must pay for the rehabilitation/repair of irrigation networks especially at the farm level. At the primary network level (primary and secondary networks) is currently still the responsibility of the government that is the Public Works Department. However, if under certain conditions where the *subak* farmers are in need of irrigation water while the irrigation network is damaged, the government officials together with the farmers will rehabilitate immediately without having to wait for the improvement from the government. *Subak* has realized that waiting for the repair from the government takes a relatively long time because it must go through the administrative bureaucratic process of budgeting the cost of repair or rehabilitation.

The quality of irrigation water greatly affects the growth of crops to be cultivated by farmers in an effort to increase productivity. In irrigated areas located in urban areas (although currently often encountered in rural areas) it is often seen that the quality of irrigation water is very bad due to the disposal of household waste, industry directly to irrigation channels and to rivers. The problem of poor quality of irrigation water is due to *subak* irrigation channel which sometimes becomes one with drainage.

Handling the quality of irrigation water is actually already a concern from the government through the Village Rules (Awig Awig) that prohibit its citizens to throw garbage carelessly let alone in the channel. However, this regulation can not be implemented maximally by the people because of the weak law enforcement. Meanwhile, household and industrial waste disposal, such as the textile industry, is still widely found in *subak* channels that receive direct water flow from the industrial sewer. Under these conditions, *subaks* has no significant strength to warn or forbid it. Moreover, the *subak* channel is very long from upstream to the paddy fields.

15. Gede Sedana, *Menghentikan Kepunahan Subak Di Bali* (Denpasar, Pustaka Larasan, 2017).

2.4 *Weak capital structure*

Generally, farmers in Bali as well as in Indonesia have problems related to the capital domination either used for their direct farming needs on farms in the fields as well as indirectly. In some observations or direct observations made by Gede Sedana (as in the area of Orange Irrigation Area, Mambal Irrigation Area, Tegal Irrigation Area and so on) it is seen that most of the farmers' farming capital ownership is relatively low.

This condition is indicated by the limited use of fertilizer production facilities (especially fertilizer KC1 and SP36) for the crops. One of the impacts of this problem is that farmers use production facilities such as KCI fertilizer that is inconsistent with the recommendation of the Agricultural Service because the price of fertilizer is considered expensive and considered not to have a significant effect. Furthermore, the weakness of the capital of farmers is worsened again with the condition of farmers who have status as *penyakap*.

2.5 *Weak organizational capability and farming technology*

Associated with activities that have economic nuances, not many *subaks* able to become an institution that has the role to provide income for the group itself. Currently, most of *subak* have not done the selling activities of their products (grain) together, but the direct party of transactions with farmers. In addition, there is also a bookkeeping system or administration in *subak* that has not been good, so it is a problem that needs to be addressed, including the stewardship, which the board has served more than 10 years.

The *subak* farmers use their organization to focus more on irrigation, social and ritual activities at the *subak* level. Whereas in the future these activities will greatly require greater funding so that economic activities are institutionalized is needed to alleviate the burden of individual members for the dues. The limited ability of farmers including *subak* managers in the aspects of management, organization and administration become part of the weakness in the activity in the institutional. Through *subak* organizations, farmers have the opportunity to increase their bargaining power in economic activities, especially when dealing with transactions with others.

Technically, most of the farmers in some areas both in Indonesia and in Bali are still seen using experience or tradition in doing farming activities both crops and livestock. In fact many new technologies in agriculture have been introduced to *subak* farmers, but not many have adopted/applied them because only a small percentage of farmers apply them. Thus, land and crop productivity as well as livestock are relatively low. Some of the factors that are suspected to affect this condition are the financial limitations of farmers to buy production facilities, limited knowledge levels, land tenure status, limited land area of controlled rice fields, and so forth.

2.6 *Limitations of accessing information and technology*

Up to present, subak ability to access information through information technolog is still very limited. Most of the farmers (*subak*) obtain information from Agricultural Field Instructor (PPL – Penyuluh Pertanian Lapangan), friends and mass media. Limited ability to access market information poses a problem to anticipate the provision of products needed by consumers. The existence of PPL as an important source of information for *subak* farmers is needed especially in providing information about agricultural technology. But on the other hand, the limited number of PPL in *subak* area can be a barrier to obtain information quickly and completely.

The limited access to information and technology is also caused by the lack of mass media use by farmers especially on agricultural information. The ability to access information and technology is still dominated by farmers who are classified as innovators and not many in *subak*.

2.7 *Price fluctuations*

Price is one of the most decisive factors for success of farmers to gain profit. Farmers are always faced with erratic product price levels and often differ from one place to another due to various factors that are so unpredictable that they often get prices that are not feasible, especially the price of grain.

At each harvest, the price of unhulled rice produced by farmers often decreases so that farmers' income becomes low while production costs for rice farming remain high. The result is that the income received by farmers will be low as well. As is known that the management of farming is always very determined and depends on the natural situation, such as the season. At the time of the rainy season, the farmers plant rice and then when harvest will coincide and over supply occurs. Farmers can not "resist" nature to avoid simultaneous planting and harvesting times. This condition is difficult for farmers.

In addition, price fluctuations are also influenced by the presence of buyers, especially *pengijon* who have bargaining power is high enough when compared with the farmers. In fact, if farmers can store their grain for a certain period of time, this price fluctuation will help them to get a better price level. But farmers are often pressed for immediate cash to meet the needs of their families.

In the face of the challenge of price fluctuations, especially the price of grain is needed of the "hands" from outside such as the government is obliged to regulate the price of grain, especially during the harvest season. The government needs to regulate through regulation so that the farmers are not harmed because the price plummeted, and vice versa during the famine season does not lead to "panic" of consumers. The government also needs to make regulations so that the price of rice is not high. This regulation shall be carried out in full supervision so as to proceed in accordance with the regulation itself at the market level.

2.8 *Reluctance of younger generation*

The interest of the younger generation to engage in the agricultural sector is low. Farming in paddy fields is considered less supportive of improving the welfare of farmers than working in the industrial and service sectors and going hunting for jobs in cities rather than replacing their parents as farmers. Therefore, the farmers who manage the rice fields are those who have a relatively old age, which is above 45 years. This age-old age condition has a less favorable tendency toward adoption of agricultural innovation, especially farm management in paddy field.

The aversion of the younger generation to farming will also be a challenge for the future if agricultural policies have not provided direct improvements to agricultural activities, especially in paddy fields. As long as the farming activities in paddy fields for rice crops have not been felt beneficial and have not become a proud job, the younger generation will decrease to continue the work of their parents. It is no exaggeration to say that "no farmer wants his son to become a farmer in the future".

In the future development of agriculture, the role of the young generation is crucial because they have a higher tendency to adopt innovations more quickly, especially with regard to crop farming such as rice and palawija cultivated in paddy fields. Strong motivation is needed for the younger generation to work in the paddy field, and this condition can not be released with the available incentives and expectations to be achieved in conducting farming activities.

2.9 *Higher land tax*

Farmers managing paddy fields suffer strong economic pressures from non-technical factors unrelated to crop and irrigation technology. The factor is the increasing value of land tax, especially in locations that have experienced rapid development of non-agricultural development. Determination of land tax by the government is conducted on the basis of location known as the Land & Building Tax Imposition Base (NJOP). Determination of the value of this tax is felt very detrimental to farmers in the paddy fields because the value becomes very high because the price of the land around it is very high, when compared with the value of production (on and crops or other crops), then the tax value is a factor reducing the income of farmers from the farm in his paddy field. In fact, in some locations farmers are not getting proper income so they are forced to sell their rice fields, therefore the land is relatively narrow. While other farmers do over the profession by leasing or contracting the land of rice fields and then leave work in the agricultural sector. This condition if left then slowly and massively farmers will switch professions and the land also turned to non-agricultural sector. Therefore, the fear of extinction of subak is not to be a figment.

3 IMPLEMENTATION OF REGULATION OF SUBAK AGRICULTURAL LAND PROTECTION IN BALI

3.1 *Central and regulatory regulations*

Some problems that have been put forward by Sedana above should be able to tap the hearts of policy makers, because *subak* organizations should not be allowed to fight alone against the flow of modernization, let alone there is a view that *subak* can not stand the intervention of external parties. *Subak* can not afford to resist any intervention, because they have no political power, and its organizational weakness.[16] Even as it is known in 2020, Indonesia will enter the WTO free trade so that with the condition of the peasants (including *subak* farmers) today is like showing the fight between the frail against the mighty or the fight of a featherweight against a heavyweight opponent (Pitana & Setiawan (eds.), 2005). The question is whether the match is balanced? Of course wise intellectuals of the law know the answer and know how to make the match a balanced one. Therefore the State should be present so that the fragile can compete during the era of free trade in the future, by placing the law as an instrument capable of overcoming the problem.

In the effort to protect the weak farmers and protect the farmland from transferring its function to non-agricultural land, in 2009 The Indonesian State Regulation No. 41 of 2009 on Sustainable Agricultural Land Protection has been enforced so that it is expected that the right to food can be guaranteed and the community (especially farmers) can prosper prosperous. Related to the right to this food should not be underestimated because Indonesia has experienced a sad experience with the case of famine that caused the death of 250 inhabitants in Yakuhimo, in Papua.[17]

The following will describe the regulations concerning the protection of sustainable agricultural land that has been applied:

a. The Indonesian State Regulation Number 41 of 2009 on Sustainable Land Farming Protection
b. Government Regulation Number 1 of 2011 on Stipulation and Transfer of Sustainable Land Farm Food Function
c. Government Regulation No. 12 of 2012 on the Incentive for Sustainable Land Farming Protection
d. Government Regulation Number 25 of 2012 on Sustainable Land Farming Information System
e. Government Regulation No. 30 of 2012 on Sustainable Land Agriculture Farm Financing
f. Regulation of the Minister of Agriculture Number: 41/Permentan/OT.140/9/2009 on Technical Criteria of Agricultural Allotment Area

16. Wayan Windia, Wayan Sudarta and Wayan Sri Astiti, *Sistem Subak Di Bali: Kajian Sosiologis* (Denpasar, Udayana University Press, 2015).
17. Suparjo Sujadi, 'Masalah-Masalah Hukum Aktual Dalam Wacana Reformasi Agraria Di Indonesia' (2007) 1 *Jurnal Hukum dan Pembangunan* 90.

g. Regulation of the Minister of Agriculture Number 07/Permentan/OT.140/2/2012 on Technical Guidelines on Criteria and Requirements for Sustainable Land, Farming and Land Reserves Reserves
h. Regulation of the Minister of Agriculture Number: 79/Permentan/OT.140/8/2013 on Guidance of Land Suitability on Commodities of Food Crops;
i. Regulation of the Minister of Agriculture Number: 80/Permentan/OT.140/8/2013 on Criteria and Procedure of Assessing High Achievers of Farming on Sustainable Agriculture Land
j. Regulation of the Minister of Agriculture Number: 81/Permentan/OT.140/8/2013 on Technical Guidelines for the Procedure of Land Transfer Function of Sustainable Food Agriculture

The observers of *subak* in Bali there are those who assume that Law No. 41 of 2009 on Sustainable Agricultural Land Farm Protection will not be done in Bali. This is fair because they are not legal scholar who deeply understand the legal system, so they are pessimistic with the enforcement of the law for the weak *subak* community.[18]

The complete regulation of the above central government product can not be implemented if it has not been implemented into local regulations. One of the principles of Indonesian law in Indonesia embraces the theory introduced by Hans Kelsen.[19] However, not all legislation should be supplemented to a lower regulatory level for implementation. Law No. 41 of 2009 is not so, because it must be equipped to the lower regulatory level in the form of regional regulations, so that if there is an area that has not issued a regional regulation on the law then of course the protection of sustainable agricultural land can not be implemented in the area.

Several regions in Indonesia have implemented Law No. 41 of 2009 into local regulations to protect farmers and agricultural lands in their areas. Following are the areas that have issued regulation on sustainable areas for sustainable agriculture: North Sumatera, South Sumatera, Lampung, West Java, Central Java, Banten, Yogyakarta, West Nusa Tenggara, South Kalimantan, East Kalimantan, Central Sulawesi, South Sulawesi, Gorontalo, and Papua.

The above regional regulation is a level at the provincial level, so it needs to be followed up again to local regulations at the district/city level. Several districts/cities have already issued regulations on the protection of sustainable agricultural land.

In fact there are districts/municipalities, local regulations issued earlier than provincial regulations at the provincial level. This is certainly not uncommon because there may be different interests so that if there is a conflict of law, the district/municipality level regulations can be defeated by provincial level regulations. However, it becomes a dilemma when districts are keen to protect farmers and agricultural lands through their local regulations, but on the other hand the province has not yet looked at its position. Such a thing seems to happen in Bali, the provincial level has not yet determined the attitude but there are districts that have determined their policy stance to protect farmers and agricultural lands such as in Jembrana through Jembrana District Regulation No. 5 of 2015 on Sustainable Land Farming Protection.

Why Bali Provincial Government has not yet determined the attitude, it may be appropriate to put forward the following view which states that the finger of a regent or governor or other ruler is more efficient to determine the policy[20], so it is possible that agricultural land will be the target of his ambition for Revenue as much as possible, with the consequences of weak peasants suppressed. In that case, it is true what Charles Sampford said with his Chaos Theory which states that behind the positive law there is always a more decisive interaction between human beings than the statutory formulation.[21]

18. Windia, Sudarta and Sri Astiti, above n 16.
19. Hans Kelsen, *Pure Theory of Law* (Berkely, University of California Press, 1978).
20. Listyawati, above n 5.
21. Charles Sampford, *The Disorder of Law: A Critique of Legal* (Basil Blackwell Inc., 1989).

3.2 *State law and customary law*

Legal research on *subak* among others have been studied by Nyoman Sirtha. In essence this legal research discusses the government's policy in carrying out development in the field of irrigation which led to the occurrence of two irrigation systems, namely *subak* irrigation system based on customary law and technical irrigation system based on state law. One conclusion states that state law and adat law in the case of irrigation arrangements are motivated by complementary cooperation, although sometimes contradictory, but after the laws of the country are modified in accordance with the cultural patterns of society, the two legal norms are adjusted to each other.[22]

Holding on to the above research, it can be said that state law (statutory law) and customary law can also be applied to other types of development such as in agriculture to protect farmers and farmland. Besides, there are already districts in Bali that have issued local regulations on the protection of sustainable agricultural land. There are even some *subak* that accommodate the provision of agricultural land protection through awig-awig *subak* such as *Subak* Demung and *Subak* Abianuwung Village.[23] Thus, it would be wise for policy makers in Bali to strengthen the efforts that have been done by issuing regional regulations at the province.

However, considering that there has been significant social change in Bali, sustainable food crop protection policy should be applied with caution. This is due to the shift of *subak* own community in looking at the land (though not all), for example the *subak* officials who even participate into a broker so that the change of agricultural land function increasingly apprehensive. Therefore, in order to effectively enforce the laws of *subak* society, it is relevant to propose the ideas of Philipe Nonet and Philip Selznick.

Philipe Nonet and Philip Selznick in his book "Law and Society in Transition: Toward Responsive Law", 1978, have formulated a legal concept that can meet the demands that law be made more responsive to urgent social needs and to justice issues social, while maintaining the institutional results that have been achieved by the rule of law.

The concept of "Responsive Law" is the answer to criticism that the law is often detached from social reality and the ideals of justice. This concept is also an attempt to reintegrate legal theory, political philosophy, and social studies. The proposed thesis is not a theory capable of solving all practical problems, but the thesis provides a perspective and criteria for diagnosing and analyzing legal and community problems with special emphasis on institutional dilemmas and critical policy choices.

According to Nonet and Selznick, there is a need for a Theory of Law and Social Theory capable of (1) strengthening the value of the law and (2) demonstrating alternatives to coercion and legal emphasis, so that a responsive legal thesis is intended for it.

Nonet and Selznick developed the concept of responsive law by comparing three legal typologies in accordance with the social stages:

a. Repressive legal type, ie law as a repressive servant of power;
b. The type of Autonomous law, namely the law as a distinguished institution capable of taming repression and protecting its own integrity; and
c. Responsive legal type, the law as a facilitator of response to social needs and social aspirations.

These three legal typologies should be viewed as related to each other in a stage of social development. These three legal typologies are not only different legal typologies but also evolutionary stages in the relationship between law and the political order and the social order.

22. Sirtha, above n 11.
23. I Nyoman Wardi et al, *Pertumbuhan Penduduk Dan Dampaknya Terhadap Budaya Subak Dan Lingkungannya: Studi Kasus Di Kabupaten Tabanan Provinsi Bali* (Denpasar, Pusat Penelitian Lingkungan Hidup Universitas Udayana, 2015).

Each type of law deals with another problem in the social order, for example the type of repressive law of its own order which attracts all attention, in the type of autonomous law in question is a matter of legitimacy of social order that is legitimacy based on the idea that social order is lawful if the use of power is based on constitutional principles, formal procedures, in free judicial institutions (which are the ideals of the classical liberal 'rule of law'). While the type of responsive law in question is the purpose and social order derived from the desire to make the law more aimed at serving people and institutions to achieve the intended objectives, so that to be achieved not only formal justice but also substantial justice.

Philip Nonet's and Philip Selznick's responsive legal ideas should be considered for policy makers in Bali to be present for their people in agriculture, as the government's role is highly anticipated by the *subak* community.[24] Bali provincial government can invite *subak* community through its representatives that is pekaseh to convey the desire of *subak* community in the future, so it can be followed up with a responsive policy. *Subak* people's willingness to maintain the preservation of *subak* should be supported, while the *subak* community who do not want the *subak* must be explained first that sustainable agriculture sustainable agriculture policy is not just talk of farm protection or sanction, but also the main incentive given to the *subak* community as well as empowerment program in favor of *subak* farmers

Thus, *subak* issues that have been expressed by the *subak* observers can be solved immediately through the policy of sustainable agriculture so that the prosperous *subak* farmers and *subak* can be sustainable as Ajeg Bali. Without *Subak* Bali will not be interesting anymore.

3.3 *International law on sustainable agriculture*

As international agricultural trade increases, international law becomes more important to agriculture and food production. While world trade is one of the most important spheres of international law related to agriculture, agricultural and food issues can be raised in many other spheres of international law. For example, global environmental law can relate to agriculture in the use and maintenance of international waters, forest resources, and the atmosphere.[25]

International human rights affect agriculture in many areas, including agricultural labor, the right to food, ecological rights, and property rights. Another emerging area of the law that affects agriculture is the establishment and use of international dispute settlement mechanisms. On a micro-level, international law is affected by states whenever they establish mechanisms to obtain compensation or reparation for international agricultural violations. And finally, universal and extraterritorial state jurisdiction is important in the cases of human rights and environmental violations on the territories of other countries.[26]

In agricultural system, farmer is among the most important factor in securing sustainable agriculture. However, in Indonesia, farmers' rights are not really fulfilled by other stakeholders. Whereas, farmers' Rights are critical to ensuring the conservation and sustainable food and agriculture and consequently for food security. Article 9 of *the International Treaty on Plant Genetic Resources for Food* (2004) recognizes the enormous contribution that the local and indigenous communities and farmers of all regions of the world, particularly those in the centers of origin and crop diversity, have made and will continue to make for the conservation and development of plant genetic resources which constitute the basis of food and agriculture production throughout the world. It gives governments the responsibility for implementing Farmers' Rights, and lists measures that could be taken to protect, promote and realize these rights: *The protection of traditional knowledge relevant to plant genetic resources for food and agriculture; The right to equitably participate in sharing benefits arising from the utilization of plant genetic resources for food and agriculture; The right to participate in making decisions, at the national level, on matters related to the conservation and sustainable use*

24. Windia, Sudarta and Sri Astiti, above n 16.
25. See http://nationalaglawcenter.org/overview/international-law-organizations/
26. Ibid.

of plant genetic resources for food and agriculture; and The right that farmers have to save, use, exchange and sell farm-saved seed/propagating material, subject to national law and as appropriate.

Among the objectives if the *International Treaty of Plant Genetic Resources for Food* are the conservation and sustainable use of plant genetic resources for food and agriculture and the fair and equitable sharing of the benefits arising out of their use, in harmony with the Convention on Biological Diversity, for sustainable agriculture and food security.[27]

Another important legal basis for protecting sustainable agriculture is the Committee on World Food Security (CFS), 43nd Session, 2016, which endorsed the recommendations on "Sustainable agricultural development for food security and nutrition: what roles for livestock?" as follows: Support the protection and strengthening of traditional knowledge systems which promote sustainability and the use of experiential knowledge in research and development;[28]

Last but not least, article 11 of International Covenant on Economic Social and Cultural Rights clearly mentioned that: *The States Parties to the present Covenant recognize the right of everyone to an adequate standard of living for [herself or himself] and [her or his] family, including adequate food, clothing and housing... The States Parties to the present Covenant, recognizing the fundamental right of everyone to be free from hunger, shall take, individually and through international co-operation, the measures, including specific programmes, which are needed...*

Everyone has the right to food. The right to food is essential for a dignified life and is vital for the realisation of many other rights, such as the rights to health and life. Food is important not just for survival, but also for the full development of one's physical and mental capabilities. States are obliged to develop, individually and through international cooperation, a range of measures of production, conservation and distribution of food to ensure that everyone is able to access enough food to be free from hunger and malnutrition.[29]

4 CONCLUSION

Firstly, *subak* is a container or organization where the gathering of farmers with determination and high spirits to cooperate together in an effort to get water with the aim of producing food crops, especially rice and palawija has been seriously threatened because it continues to experience degradation of land transfer function for other sectors, plus the threat triggered by factors such as the quantity and quality of irrigation water, the weakness of the capital structure, the lack of organizational capability and farming technology, the limited access to information and technology, price fluctuations, the aversion of the younger generation to farming, and the higher land tax .

Secondly, from the legal perspective, either local, national or international legal grounds, have actually provided legal basis for sustainable agriculture. Yet, the policy makers in Bali have not implemented the law on protection of sustainable agriculture land, except only one district that has issued the local regulation, namely is Jembrana District. This situation should provide a reflection for policy makers in Bali as well as in other regions in Indonesia. Some regions have stepped forward but Bali is lagging behind in terms of agricultural land protection policy. Therefore, if policy makers in Bali are serious enough to protect *subak* farmers and their farmings, they shoud regulate and implement sustainable and responsive agriculture through a a sustainable agriculture safeguard policies. The policies must be made at provincial levels (as a Perda or Governor Regulation) and then at districts/regencies levels.

27. See http://www.fao.org/3/a-i0510e.pdf
28. See Committee on World Food Security recommendation http://www.fao.org/3/a-bq854e.pdf
29. See https://www.escr-net.org/rights/food

REFERENCES

De Vries, Egbert, *Pertanian Dan Kemiskinan Di Jawa* (Jakarta, Yayasan Obor Indonesia, 1985)

Kelsen, Hans, *Pure Theory of Law* (Berkely, University of California Press, 1978)

Listyawati, Hery, 'Kegagalan Pengendalian Alih Fungsi Tanah Dalam Perspektif Penatagunaan Tanah Di Indonesia' (2010) 22(1) *Mimbar Hukum* 37

Marzuki, Peter Mahmud, *Pengantar Ilmu Hukum* (Jakarta, Kencana, 2014)

Sampford, Charles, *The Disorder of Law: A Critique of Legal* (Basil Blackwell Inc., 1989)

Sedana, Gede, *Menghentikan Kepunahan Subak Di Bali* (Denpasar, Pustaka Larasan, 2017)

Sirtha, Nyoman, *Subak: Konsep Pertanian Religius Perspektif Hukum, Budaya Dan Agama Hindu* (Surabaya, Paramita, 2008)

Sodiki, Achmad, *Politik Hukum Agraria* (Jakarta, Konstitusi Press, 2013)

Soeromihardjo, Soedjarwo, *Mengkritisi Undang-Undang Pokok Agraria* (Jakarta, Cerdas Pustaka Publisher, 2009)

Soetoprawiro, Koerniatmanto, *Pengantar Hukum Pertanian* (Jakarta, Gapperindo, 2013)

Sujadi, Suparjo, 'Analisis Dan Prediksi Permasalahan Pertanahan Di Masa Mendatang' (2004) 4 *Jurnal Hukum dan Pembangunan* 364

Sujadi, Suparjo, 'Masalah-Masalah Hukum Aktual Dalam Wacana Reformasi Agraria Di Indonesia' (2007) 1 *Jurnal Hukum dan Pembangunan* 90

Sutawan, Nyoman, *Organisasi Dan Manajemen Subak Di Bali* (Denpasar, Pustaka Bali Post, 2008)

Van Apeldoorn, LJ, *Pengantar Ilmu Hukum* (Jakarta, Pradya Paramita, 2011)

Van Kan, J and JH Beekhuis, *Pengantar Ilmu Hukum* (Jakarta, Ghalia Indonesia, 1990)

Wardi, I Nyoman et al, *Pertumbuhan Penduduk Dan Dampaknya Terhadap Budaya Subak Dan Lingkungannya: Studi Kasus Di Kabupaten Tabanan Provinsi Bali* (Denpasar, Pusat Penelitian Lingkungan Hidup Universitas Udayana, 2015)

Windia, Wayan, *Transformasi Sistem Irigasi Subak Yang Berlandaskan Konsep Tri Hita Karana* (Denpasar, Pustaka Bali Post, 1990)

Windia, Wayan, Wayan Sudarta and Wayan Sri Astiti, *Sistem Subak Di Bali: Kajian Sosiologis* (Denpasar, Udayana University Press, 2015)

Culture and International Law - Juwana et al. (Eds)
© 2019 Taylor & Francis Group, London, ISBN 978-1-138-38766-9

Interpretation and conflict in the conservation of private property cultural heritage in Indonesia

Yuni Rahmawati
Universitas Indonesia, Indonesia
Balai Pelestarian Cagar Budaya and Museum Serang, Indonesia

Agi Ginanjar
Universitas Indonesia, Indonesia

ABSTRACT: This paper discusses the problems that often arise in the determination of cultural heritage, especially the establishment of buildings either owned partly or wholly by the public as stakeholders. Generally, the problem is the difference in interpretation between the public as stakeholders and the government that has the authority to define the building as cultural heritage, and ultimately the difference leads to conflict. The purpose of this research is to develop the concept of preservation of cultural heritage in the form of public and private property, with an emphasis on the interpretation of the owners as important stakeholders and the government in terms of authority, point of view, and rights and obligations; in addition, finding a reliable policy to reduce conflicts of interest in the determination of state-owned cultural heritage. This study uses qualitative methods with in-depth interviews of the public, landowners and the owners of buildings designated as buildings and cultural heritage areas, and policy makers. The results indicate that generally the public does not object to the preservation of property they have, but most do not agree with the status of cultural heritage. The conflicts that arise in the preservation of cultural heritage include an imbalance of rights and obligations of the owner, and the absence of the owner's authority in the process of preservation of the cultural heritage.

KEYWORDS: culture heritage, private property, conflict, authority, rights and obligations

1 INTRODUCTION

Generally, in Indonesia, ownership of cultural heritage, whether it is a building or an area, does not always belong to the government, unlike in European countries, such as Austria, Germany and Italy.[1] The ownership of cultural heritage can also involve a private property. This is regulated in Article 12 items 1 and 2 of Law No. 11 of 2010 on Cultural Heritage (UU No. 11/2010/CB), which claims that each individual can own and/or take control of cultural heritage when the number and its kinds have met the state's needs. In Article 1 item 7, it is stated that ownership is the most powerful and comprehensive right on cultural heritage by paying attention to the social and obligation functions in its conservation. This means that in the process of preserving cultural heritage, one should prioritize the rights of ownership, particularly for private property cultural heritage. Actually, the law to protect these ownership rights by managing several ownership rights related to ownership such as compensation in a

1. D Abfalter and H Echlaner, 'Strategic Management and Cultural HeritageSites: New Entrepreneurial Challenges for Private Owners of Castle and Stately Homes' (2002) *International Journal of Arts Management, 4* (3), 8.

form of money and/or non-monetary as well as incentives in a form of advocates, aids, or other forms which are non-financials to support the preservation of cultural heritage. In addition, these ownership rights are also protected by the obligation of the owners to ask permission when they develop and document the cultural heritage. However, the application of these rights is also questionable.

In Indonesia, private property cultural heritage preservation, both buildings and areas, causes several problems related to the preservation process. It starts from the process of registry, stipulation and maintenance up to its utilization. Owners, as important stakeholders in the process of private property cultural heritage house preservation, are less involved in: (1) the process of registry and stipulation; (2) maintenance process relying indecisively on the owners or the government; (3) the application of owners' rights and obligations in the conservation of private property cultural heritage houses is based on Law No. 11 of 2010 which is still questionable; (4) and other problems related to the conservation of private property cultural heritage. Moreover, these cultural heritage private properties are cultural heritage buildings and areas that are still occupied by the owners as residential buildings or other functions that are closely related to today's life and are included in the cultural process of the owners. Undoubtedly, a lot of problems will surely arise when the interpretation of their conservation process does not accommodate the owners' cultural process.

One of the arising problems in the conservation of cultural heritage in the form of private property are the tendencies of the owners to eliminate the status of cultural heritage from the residence that they own. The results of early 2018 interviews with four owners of cultural heritage private properties indicated that they did not want the cultural heritage status attached to their houses for various reasons. With the stipulation of their house as cultural heritage, they interpreted it that their house would be subject to various regulations that would limit their movement in optimizing the use of their houses. Additionally, they were concerned that the government would take over their houses. This shows real problems related to cultural heritage conservation in the form of private properties, particularly problems related to the owners as important stakeholders that actually have the authority to determine the value of their inheritance.

In archaeological source management, the owners are important stakeholders in private property cultural heritage conservation.[2] The law also acknowledges that ownership is the most powerful and comprehensive right on cultural heritage. However, such acknowledgment has not really realized. For example, an authority to determine the value of an inheritance can only be done by the government. The owners of a cultural heritage house are not given the space to determine which inheritance should be appropriately preserved. It can be seen that the status stipulation flow of cultural heritage in Law No. 11/2010/CB only considers the recommendation of a Team of Experts of Cultural Heritage (TECH). Even when the community has the right to register an inheritance to become a cultural heritage, a feasibility study to determine whether the inheritance is appropriate to be stipulated as cultural heritage can only be conducted by TECH without the representatives from the community (owners) within the study.

On the other hand, European countries have started to provide authorities to determine the values of a certain inheritance to the community. In Britain, for example, at the moment, English Heritage acts as non-government body that is responsible for managing the cultural resources in Britain, which involves the community, including the owner of the inheritance in the selection process of historical monuments that are appropriate for preservation. This fundamental transformation that was conducted by the British government through English Heritage and other subsidiary institutions also changed the direction of management systems of the cultural resources in Britain. Other European countries eventually adopted this concept in their effort to plan a management system of cultural resources for the public interest.[3]

2. A Wright, 'Private Property, Public Archaeology: Resident Communities as Stakeholders in American Archaeology' in *World Archaeology* (North Carolina: Appalachian State University, 2015) 212.
3. RM Thomas, 'Archaeology and Authority in the Twenty-First Century' in Fairclough, Graham et al. (Eds.), *The heritage reader* (New York : Routledge, 2008) 139.

The problems in private property cultural heritage preservation are actually problems that mostly occur in Indonesia. For example, in Surabaya, the house where Bung Tomo delivered his speech to encourage the spirit of Indonesian people through the radio was demolished after the owner sold it to another party. Another case was the removal of cultural heritage signs on the former house of Mr. Soetadisastra in Rangkas Bitung, Lebak by the owner. Additionally, there are many other cases in Indonesia related to private property cultural heritage conservation.

Judging from the real problems in house preservation as private property cultural heritage, research concerning house preservation as private property cultural heritage especially in Serang needs to be undertaken, focusing on the owners as important stakeholders in private property cultural heritage preservation. The problems related to private property cultural heritage are quite complicated problems due to the possibility of similar or different wants from both parties, namely the government as the executors of the laws of cultural heritage and the owners of cultural heritage houses. Thus, it is important to conduct research related to this private property cultural heritage by focusing on the owners as important stakeholders in compiling the concept of private property cultural heritage preservation.[4]

Based on the description concerning the problems as stated above, this research focuses on three problems, namely: (1) what is the owners' authority in the process of assessing private property cultural heritage in Serang; (2) what is the point of view of house owners on cultural heritage conservation; (3) what are the rights and obligations of the owners of cultural heritage houses in cultural heritage preservation.

The purpose of the research is to produce a concept of cultural heritage conservation in the form of private property, by focusing on the owners as important stakeholders in terms of authority, point of view, as well as rights and obligations based on academic considerations.

2 RESEARCH METHOD

This research applied a qualitative approach. This was used because it contains the element of in-depth interviews, and has the characteristic of triangulation which is highly necessary to discover wants, necessities, owners' point of view and problems related to private property cultural heritage preservation in Serang.

In the data collection, the informants should meet the following criteria:

1. They should master or comprehend something through an enculturation so that the something is not only comprehended but also applied.
2. They should be considered as dealing with or be involved with the activities that are being studied.
3. They have sufficient time to be asked for information.
4. They do not have a tendency to deliver information as a result of their own 'packaging'.
5. They are initially 'quite unfamiliar' to the researchers so that they are more desirable to be some kind of teachers or informants.[5]

By paying attention to the above requirements, the informants of this research will be as follows:

1. The owners of cultural heritage houses.
   The data taken from these informants cover the wants, necessities and points of view. These three points when they are related to the concept of values, values authority, cultural process, and public outreach that have been done.

4. P Howard, *Heritage management, interpretation, identity* (London: Continuum, 2003).
5. Sugiyono, *Metode Penelitian. Kuantitatif, Kualitatif, Dan R&D* (Bandung, Indonesia: Penerbit Alfabeta, 2016) 293.

2. Head of Cultural Division of the Office of Education and Culture of the Regional Government of Serang/Banten Province.
   The data collected cover the preservation that has been done, problems that were encountered in the private property cultural heritage house preservation, regional regulations related to private property cultural heritage houses, compensation toward the owners, stipulation process and so on.
3. Head of Office of Cultural Heritage Preservation of Serang.
   The data gathered cover the process of registry and stipulation of private property cultural heritage houses.

The instruments in the interview consist of notebooks, a tape recorder and a camera. In addition, the data collection technique involved triangulation. Triangulation, in this credibility test, means data checking from various sources in various ways and at various times. In this research, the data source for triangulation was by way of interview with the same question to more than one person. It was done whether or not compensation, incentives and socialization of cultural heritage to several informants exists. The time and technique of the triangulation cannot be done due to the time limitation of the research.

The questions that were asked of the owners were given to find out five important points in the following codes:

1. Value (Code: 01)
   Sample question: How do you feel about owning this house?
2. Cultural Process (Code: 02)
   Sample question: Apparently, you have been staying a long time in this house; what causes you to keep preserving this house?
3. Public Authority (Code: 03)
   Sample question: Has the government ever asked your opinion about this house's preservation?
4. Interpretation (Code: 04)
   Sample question: Have you received any aid from the government? What are the forms of the aid (compensation, incentive, socialization)?

In the data analysis, Miles and Hubermas model, namely reduction data, display data and conclusion drawing/verification so that getting findings in a form of a description about any problems that arise, any problems that are dominant, any factors that may affect the cause of the problems and other things that may arise in the process of the research. Conclusion drawing in qualitative research is in the form of interpreting the obtained data during the process of the research. From the conclusion, the recommendation can be given based on academic considerations.

3 DISCUSSION/ANALYSIS

3.1 *The authority of owners of cultural heritage houses in the assessment process*

A cultural inheritance will be a cultural resource when it has a certain value.[6] The process of determining the meaning and value of a cultural inheritance, according to Blunstone (2000), was not merely done by the professionals but also by the people who use and visit that inheritance.[7] In terms of people involved in the stipulation process, Bond and Worthing (2015) claimed that an identification process is necessary in determining who are the

6. WD Lipe, 'Value and Meaning in Cultural Resources' in Henry Cleere (ed.), *Approaches to the archaelogical heritage* (New York: Cambridge University Press, 1984) 1.
7. S Bond and D Worthing, *Managing built heritage. The role of cultural values and significance* (UK: Wiley Blackwell, 2001) 157.

stakeholders involved in the conservation process, and those who were identified as the stakeholders should be involved in determining the important value of an inheritance.[8]

The stakeholders include the owners and residents of the inheritance in the past and present, the community that uses the inheritance in the past and present, and those who have a relation to the cultural inheritance. This relation can be related to someone's memory and attachment to the form of a cultural inheritance or symbol that arises from the cultural resource. In several cases, this memory and symbol are not only from tangible objects but also from intangible objects.[9]

The owners and the surrounding community also have authority in determining the value of an archaeological inheritance. The value is not something that is attached to past material inheritance. The value depends on the individual background of culture, intellect, history and psychology that have seen it.[10] It is possibly based on the perception of the owners, that the historical house they own does not meet the value and benefit of a cultural resource. At the moment, the community prefer to develop their own minds/interpretations about the past and which value is most important for them, than merely accept the interpretation/thoughts and knowledge of the government.[11] Perception/interpretation differences of each stakeholder regarding the value of a cultural resource can produce conflicts in preserving private property; moreover, when one of the stakeholder's points of view, which are actually very important, are neglected. The Project Management Institute (PMI) (2006) claimed that management that neglects one of the stakeholders could cause harmful effects in achieving its objectives.[12]

The authority of the community in cultural heritage preservation has actually been discussed in the law. In the preamble part, item (c) of the Law of Cultural Heritage, it was stated that cultural heritage, in the form of objects, buildings, structures, sites and territories, needs to be managed by the government and the regional government by improving the community participation to protect, develop and use the cultural heritage. The word 'community participation' here means that actually the authority of the community in preservation exists and the law has accommodated it. However, the application is far from that expected.

The results of observations and interviews in the field showed that the owners do not have the authority to determine the value of cultural inheritance in the process of private property cultural heritage conservation in Serang. The process of registration of a residence into the national registry system does not involve the owners as the party that will have influence on the preservation process when the residence is eventually stipulated as cultural heritage. The registration process into the list of cultural heritage in the national registry system is only based on the point of view of the team of experts that have conducted several inventory activities, without paying attention to the owners' point of view as important stakeholders in the preservation. Moreover, the owners are important stakeholders in private property cultural heritage house preservation. As stated by the informant, Meru: 'There was not any data collection information from me, though. There was not any. I do not know whether the data collection occurred, even if it did, I do not know'. The information concerning his house, included in the list of cultural heritage, was obtained from his friends.

This incident provides a general picture that stipulating the values is still dominated by a certain party that is considered expert, when in fact, as mentioned by Bond and Worthing (2015), each stakeholder should be involved in determining the important value of an inheritance. Moreover, the owners act as the important stakeholder in private property cultural heritage preservation.

Based on Law No. 11 of 2010 concerning cultural heritage, the party that is entitled to determine the value of a cultural inheritance in Indonesia is the TECH. This is a group of

8. Ibid.
9. Ibid, 104-105.
10. Lipe, above n 6, 2.
11. Thomas, above n 3.
12. M Hajialikhani, 'A Systematic Stakeholders Management Approach for Protecting the Spirit of Cultural Heritage Sites' in *ICOMOS 16th General Assembly and Scientific Symposium* (Quebec: ICOMOS, 2008) 2.

preservation experts from various backgrounds who have certified competence to provide recommendations on the stipulations, ranking and removal of cultural heritage. TECH have conducted studies on cultural inheritance properties that have been registered. The studies were conducted to determine whether the values stated in the laws on a cultural inheritance exist or not. These studies will eventually produce recommendations for the stipulation of cultural heritage by the regional/municipal government.

Authority granting in determining the value to the people has actually been accommodate by Law No. 11/2010/CB in Article 11, which states that:

Objects, buildings, structures, locations, or geographical space units that, based on the research, have a special meaning for the community or Indonesian nation but they do not meet the criteria for cultural heritage as stated in Article 5 up to Article 10 can be proposed as cultural heritage.

This means that cultural inheritance that does not meet the criteria of cultural heritage in Articles 5–10 in the Law of Cultural Heritage can still be proposed as cultural heritage when they have certain values (special meanings) from the community point of view. This shows that the community is authorized to provide their views in assessing a certain value in cultural inheritance.

Unfortunately, the Law of Cultural Heritage included in Article 11 has not accommodated the community perception, in this case, the owner, concerning whether important value is the basis in determining his property as cultural heritage. Moreover, based on the Law of Cultural Heritage, it is very possible that each individual (other person) to register a cultural inheritance that is not his without considering the perception of the owner. It is stipulated in Article 29 item 2 of Law No. 11 of 2010 concerning cultural heritage that: 'Each person can participate in registering objects, buildings, structures, and locations that are assumed as cultural heritage even though he does not own or have control over it'. If we only count on Article 29 item 2, then each individual is entitled to register a cultural inheritance without considering the perception of the owner; when in fact, the ownership rights are the basic rights that should be paid attention to and the most powerful and comprehensive rights on cultural heritage.

Thus, a special rule is required in the law or its derivatives that arranges the authority in determining the value for the owners of private cultural inheritance property. Authority is not the only thing that the owner views regarding the value on the inheritance he owns, but there should be an authority to provide an approval when another party registers his house as cultural heritage. The approval for 'yes or no' should definitely be started with good communication with the owner about the cultural heritage. This is compatible with one of the principles of stakeholder management; namely, the manager should consider the importance of each stakeholder appropriately in making decisions and their implementations.

3.2 *The point of view of owners of cultural heritage houses on preservation*

In determining whether a private property should be designated a cultural heritage house, generally there are differences in the point of view of the government and the owners in terms of the value contained in the cultural inheritance in the form of private property. The government's point of view sees certain values such as values of history, knowledge, education, religion and/or culture, so that they need to be preserved. In the meantime, from the point of view of the house owner, he only sees its functions as a private property without certain important values so that preservation is not necessary.

The results of the interviews with homeowners show that the majority of the owners of cultural heritage houses approve of conservation. The results differed from the researchers' preliminary assumption that the homeowners disagreed with cultural heritage conservation. They also view that the houses they own are houses with certain important values that need to be preserved as stated by the owners below:

> *This house should stay this way, because compared to current houses, it is more comfortable this way, and the height of the ceiling should also stay the same. We can say that there are not many houses in this model at the most offices are like this, old offices. It is unfortunate,*

it was going to be changed at one time but we feel better to yield than to change it. When we feel unfortunate then it is unfortunate. (Mas Meru, the owner of the House at Jl. Ahmad Yani No. 41)

The same thing happened to the perception of the owner of a house who had previously removed the cultural heritage sign, namely the owner of the Benjol House and the house at Jl. R.M.H.S. Djajadiningrat No. 43:

Yes it should be preserved, if this is the culture of the Chinese people then so be it, one of the remains of the Chinese people is like this... the model was like this a long time ago... these types of models should have... this came from a long time ago until the fifth generation up to me that I know of, there is a further generation or something like that. (Mr. Yandi, the owner of Benjol House)

These interview excerpts from the owners of the houses above show that they actually agree with preservation even though the point of view of the owners are more subjective compared to those of the government based on the law. Nonetheless, such agreement is a positive thing in the process of cultural heritage preservation.

An interesting aspect was that when they were asked questions related to the status of cultural heritage, the majority of the owners disagreed that their houses have the status of cultural heritage, as stated below:

Yes, what is it for ? Private property is not everybody's house, so be it whether it is a cultural heritage or not, and in addition, whether there is a sign with writings or not, there are not any benefits. Unless there are benefits for us in any form, but since there are not any benefits, so what is it for ? (Mr. Meru, house owner at Jalan Ahmad Yani No. 41)

Cultural heritage is just lip service... there is not any evidence, that's my opinion. That's why I disagree... it is only lip service, no action taken. (Ms. Aliyyah, house owner of Kaujon)

The results of the interviews show that they agree with preservation but not with the status of cultural heritage. In fact, the stipulation of cultural heritage itself is a legal legitimation of a cultural resource to be preserved as stated in the Law of Cultural Heritage No. 11 of 2010. With the existence of the status of cultural heritage, the process of preservation will be easier and more legal. Then questions arise, if the owners agree with preservation, why do they disagree with the status of cultural heritage? Further discussions will explain why this occurs.

3.3 *Rights and obligations of the owners of cultural heritage*

One of the factors that becomes a red line is if the owner of the house felt that they did not get any benefit by having the status of cultural heritage. On the contrary, they feel that they will have more losses because of the abundant rules and also feel concern that their house will be taken over by the government, as stated by a house owner below:

However. on one side, we will experience losses... so it is like this when we want to change something, we need to get a permission, because it is in the law right, but if we do not have any status, we can do anything we want... we are free to change or build or do whatever, it is as simple as that actually. There are not any complicated reasons. (Mr. Meru, house owner at Jl Ahmad Yani No. 41)

I do not want to since this house will be taken from the government... overtaken by the government, no way. (Ms. Aliyyah, house owner in Kaujon)

The statements above show that there are concerns when their houses are stipulated as cultural heritage, the difficulties of renovating, even having concerns over losing their house to the government. The Clarkson Center for Business Ethics (1999) noted the principles of stakeholder management, among which are: (1) consider the importance of the stakeholder appropriately in making decisions and their implementation; (2) managers should listen and communicate openly with the stakeholders about their worries, contributions and risks that are assumed due to their involvement with the related party. This means that in conducting preservation with the concept of stakeholder management, a manager should consider the importance of the owners as important stakeholders to minimize any worries and risks that are not acceptable to the owners.

Aside from being worried about difficulties in renovating (developing) houses and the possibilities of being taken over by the government, they also worried about the difficulties in selling their private property with a status of cultural heritage, as stated by the owner of the 1928 architectural house at Jalan Ahmad Yani:

> *...Say this is a cultural heritage, I do not know who I am supposed to sell it to. Say I sell some time in the future, if I cannot change it, who will buy the house? In the meantime, this land will be used for offices say, or a mall say, then who will buy this house? No one right? Then I am at a loss, right?*

Concerns regarding difficulties in developing, selling and taking over have their basis after all, as everything is written within the rules. In the Law of Cultural Heritage Article 1 item 29, it is stated that a development should involve research, revitalization and adaptation. The development of cultural heritage should be conducted by paying attention to the principle of usage, security, maintenance, originality and values that are attached to it. Thus, if a private property cultural heritage house will be adapted into a more suitable form with the necessities, the owners should ask for permission of the government, even though the ownership is entirely in the hands of the owners.

The owners of cultural heritage are also given an obligation to secure and maintain the cultural heritage as stated in Articles 61 and 75 of Law No. 11 of 2010 concerning cultural heritage. Aside from that, in Article 75 item 2 it is confirmed that if the owners do not conduct good maintenance (abandoned) then the cultural heritage will be taken over by the state. Based on those articles, the obligations of preserving private property cultural heritage lies on the owner's shoulders. On the other hand, the Regional Government of Serang have not prioritized the program of private property cultural heritage house preservation, as expressed by the Division Head (HD) of the Education and Cultural Office of Serang:

> So now we are not focusing on private properties, but more into ancient tombs as well as buildings that have been categorized as cultural heritage and used as public facilities such as Ancient Mosque. It is not about financial issues, we have different orientation, and Jogja is special because it focuses on cultural city... There will be a progress in the future (private property cultural heritage preservation).

Aside from arranging the obligations of the owners, regulations to arrange the rights of cultural heritage owners, namely compensation and incentives for the owners who have conducted protection on the cultural heritage that they own are required. According to the law, compensation is a reward in the form of money and/or non-monetary from the government or regional government. Incentives are supports in the form of advocates, aids or other non-monetary forms to encourage cultural heritage preservation, from the government or the regional government.

The results of the research related to compensation show that all house owners involved in this research claimed that they have not ever received any compensation in a form of maintenance fund aids:

> *There has not been any government aid as long as I have lived here, at least.* (Owner of an ancient house at Jl. M.H. Suprijamhari No. 127)
>
> *I maintain this house by myself.* (Owner of an ancient house at Jl. M.H. Suprijamhari No. 69).
>
> *There was not any. I did it all by myself.* (House owner at Jl. Ahmad Yani No. 41).

There was not any, not even a single dime, if so, I feel grateful already. Actually I did not ask for help, but the prohibitions are the problems. (Owner of Benjol House)

So far, there is not any budget from the government, either from the regional or central governments for a compensation fund for the owners of cultural heritage houses in Serang. In fact, the law has arranged that there is an obligation for the government to create a compensation budget for the owners of cultural heritage. In Article 98 item 3, it is stated that: 'The government and regional government allocate budgets for the protection, development, usage, and compensation of cultural heritage, while paying attention to proportional principle'.

Providing compensation from the government has started to be applied by several regions in Indonesia such as the Special Region of Yogyakarta (SRY) and Central Java Province. The activity in providing compensation for cultural heritage protection by the Office of Cultural Heritage Preservation of SRY has started in 2008 and is ongoing. This activity is intended to provide rewards to the community of owners or managers of cultural heritage or institutions that have high commitment in preserving and protecting buildings and structures that they own/control. With the existence of rewards given to owners/managers of cultural heritage, it is expected that it can improve the community appreciation to actively participate in order to protect and preserve the past cultural inheritance.

An interesting factor that also needs to be paid attention to in providing this compensation is that the amount of compensation funds should be proportional, as stated in the Law of Cultural Heritage Article 98 item 3: 'The government and regional government allocate a budget for the protection, development, usage, and compensation of cultural heritage by paying attention to proportional principles'. The meaning of proportional here means that the amount of compensation should be adjusted to the condition of the house. This proportional principle eventually reminds the importance of valuation of economy value of a cultural heritage. Even though there are still many pros and cons among the conservationists about the valuation of economic value of this cultural heritage, it is necessary for the importance of preservation.

Aside from compensation, the law also states that there is an incentive for the owners of cultural heritage. Incentives can be in the form of advocates, aids or other non-monetary forms to encourage preservation of cultural heritage, from the government or regional government. Incentives can also be in a form of reductions in tax on land and the buildings erected on it and/or income tax can be given by the government or regional government to the owners of cultural heritage that have conducted cultural heritage protection based on the terms of the rules and regulations. However, the owners of cultural heritage houses in Serang have not experienced these tax reductions, as stated by Mr. Yandi, the owner of Benjol House:

There are not any [tax reductions]. As a matter of fact, I asked for a tax reduction several times but it was not granted. I even wrote a letter to the head division of the tax on land and the buildings erected on it, I pleaded for assistance since this is a cultural heritage... [His response] is still in process. I did that when I was in Ciceri, when I was in Ciwaru I also did it. I also did so to the office; I also wrote letters to the head division to get a response but it turns out there are not any tax reductions ...

Aside from tax reductions, incentives can also be in the form of advocacy assistance when certain cases occur that require aid. Unfortunately this advocacy assistance has not been applied, especially in the case of the owner of Benjol House, who encountered difficulties in obtaining a certificate for his house:

...Making certificate is very difficult. With the red tape at the National Land Board (NLB), the forces reasons that the rules are not applied and saying that old time forces are in the past since my parents do not know about it... I knew it when it comes to my turn. When my parents processed the making of the certificate, they did not get anything; our money had been taken by irresponsible individuals.

The rights of the owners of cultural heritage that have not been applied eventually triggered the reluctance of owners to have a status of cultural heritage on their houses. There are not any inapplicability between the rights and obligations. There are also not any inapplicability between rights and rules. It makes sense that eventually there is a tendency for rejection by house owners of cultural heritage status on the houses they own.

4 CONCLUSION AND RECOMMENDATIONS

Based on the conflicts which occur due to the differences in interpretation, private property cultural heritage house preservation has a number of special problems that obviously require the concept of special preservation. The buildings are not well maintained because the obligation of maintenance lies at the hand of the owners, and not all owners are able and willing to maintain. From the owners point of view, wishes and needs are often neglected in the preservation process and other problems lead to the reluctance of owners to have a cultural heritage status on their house.

In the preservation of private property cultural heritage houses, the owner is an important stakeholder. Written and unwritten regulations have declared the owner as the party mostly affected during the preservation process. Hence, it is a must to involve the owner in each stage of preservation, from the stage of registry, stipulation and maintenance up to utilization. The key to owner's involvement is communication. The communication should not merely be a formality, but an open communication that can really create mutual understanding. The government can understand the wishes, needs and points of view of the owner. Likewise, the owner can understand the right concepts of conservation. From such communication, it is easy to achieve a win-win solution of conservation concepts. Conservation can still be achieved, yet the rights of the owner as the strongest right holder can still be fulfilled.

In Indonesia, the budget for the cultural sector is frequently of a low priority. Therefore, it is not surprising that we are left behind in the cultural sector. Nonetheless, gradually the cultural budget needs to be increased. In the future, the compensation and incentives for cultural heritage owners who have applied protection need to be routinely allocated to motivate the owners in applying maintenance for the sake of conservation. The budgetary allocation is also needed to assist the maintenance of cultural heritage whose owners have financial shortcomings. Additionally, reserve budgets should also be available in case the owner of a cultural heritage private property wishes to sell the house. The budgetary issue should be enforced through regional or governmental regulations.

Presently, cultural heritage inclusion in the community's cultural process has frequently proven to make the conservation process easier. Therefore, it is expected that the government is able to support programs that are beginning to be carried out by Rumah Kaujon's owner and encourage other house owners to join the cultural class of house owners and the surrounding community.

The paradigm of private property cultural heritage conservation needs to be changed. *First*, the authority in policy making in conservation should not only be in the hands of the government but should also be in the hands of the owner as an important stakeholder. *Second*, there should be a balance between rights and obligations of private property cultural heritage owners. *Third*, the principles of authenticity that should actually be applied are the principles of authenticity with new paradigms that balance tangible and intangible authenticities. *Last*, there should be regular open communication among stakeholders.

Concerning the specificity of the nature of private property, a regulation that is derived from the law needs to be discussed in detail. It is expected that there will be a specific regulation regarding private property conservation in the central and regional regulations that has not been made by the Regional Government of Serang. This regulation should cover the processes of regulation up to the utilization by granting the authority to the owner as well as detailed regulations on the rights and obligations of the owner, particularly regarding the owner's rights which have been neglected all these times. Unless it is immediately realized, it may trigger conflicts in the conservation process of private property cultural heritage.

Concerning the interpretation and conflict issue, the recommended preservation concept in private property cultural heritage preservation is the stakeholder's management concept that underlines open communication, applicability of owners' rights and obligations, and granting authority to owners as important stakeholders in conservation.

REFERENCES

Abfalter, D. & Echlaner, H. (2002). Strategic management and cultural heritage sites: New entrepreneurial challenges for private owners of castle and stately homes. *International Journal of Arts Management*, *4*(3), 8–18.

Bond, S. & Worthing, D. (2016). *Managing built heritage. The role of cultural values and significance* (2nd ed.). Chichester, UK: Wiley Blackwell.

Hajialikhani, M. (2008). A systematic stakeholders management approach for protecting the spirit of cultural heritage sites. In *ICOMOS 16th General Assembly and Scientific Symposium, Quebec, Canada*. Paris, France: International Council on Monuments and Sites.

Howard, P. (2003). *Heritage management, interpretation, identity*. London: Continuum.

Lipe, W.D. (1984). Value and meaning in cultural resources. In H. Cleere (Ed.), *Approaches to the archaeological heritage*. New York: Cambridge University Press.

Sugiyono. (2016). *Metode Penelitian. Kuantitatif, Kualitatif, Dan R&D*. Bandung, Indonesia: Penerbit Alfabeta.

Thomas, R.M. (2008). Archaeology and authority in the twenty-first century. In G. Fairclough, R. Harrison, J.H. Jameson Jr. & J. Schofield (Eds.), *The heritage reader* (pp. 139–148). New York: Routledge.

Wright, A. (2015). Private property, public archaeology: Resident communities as stakeholders in American archaeology. In *World Archaeology*. Boone, NC: Appalachian State University.

Culture and International Law - Juwana et al. (Eds)
© 2019 Taylor & Francis Group, London, ISBN 978-1-138-38766-9

Why Indonesia should respect the rights of asylum seekers and refugees

Arie Afriansyah
Fakultas Hukum, Universitas Indonesia, Depok, Indonesia

ABSTRACT: Since the 1970s, Indonesia has experience as a transit country for asylum seekers and refugees. Despite non-membership of the Refugee Convention, it appears that Indonesia has served more than any other member state. Despite all of its efforts, Indonesia still needs to share its burden with the international community in general, especially within the region. Indonesia's dependence on the the International Organization for Migration (IOM) will not be a sustainable option as it also depends on other countries. This paper analyzes the legal aspects of refugee management within the context of Indonesia and its legal system. First, it discusses the laws that relate to the interaction between refugees and the Indonesian people. Second, this research will discuss how Indonesia applies Indonesian national law when it comes to the treatment of refugees during their period of resettlement. Third, this research will offer a proposal regarding the appeal to the international community in sharing the burden of managing refugees as they await the process of resettlement.

KEYWORDS: asylum seekers, Indonesia, immigration, refugees, resettlement

1 INTRODUCTION

The legal protection for cross-border refugees has been conceived as a 'global public good', where the states concerned share the burden of such protection.[1] As discussed in detail later, the principle of burden sharing or responsibility sharing underlies the 1951 Refugee Convention,[2] as embodied in its preamble and Article 35, and assumes 'an expectation of reciprocity' between states.[3] Unfortunately, in the current reality, such burden in handling the issues of asylum seekers and refugees has been very uneven in parts of the world. This situation has been heavily influenced by the notoriously trending policies of the destination countries on 'cooperative deterrence'[4] and 'diverse non-entrée measures'.[5] Such impact is no exception to Indonesia, a state that is struggling to manage asylum seekers and refugees together with its neighboring southeast countries.

1. Alexander Betts, *Protection by Persuasion: International Cooperation in the Refugee Regime* (Ithaca, NY: Cornell University Press, 2009), 25–27.
2. Convention relating to the Status of Refugees (adopted 28 July 1951, entered into force 22 April 1954) 189 UNTS 137 (Refugee Convention)
3. Amy Nethery and Carly Gordyn, 'Australia-Indonesia Cooperation on Asylum Seekers: A Case of 'Incentivised Policy Transfer'' (2014) *Australian Journal of International Affairs, 68*(2), 177–193, 181.
4. Thomas Gammeltoft-Hansen and James C. Hathaway, 'Non-Refoulement in a World of Cooperative Deterrence', (2015) *Columbia Journal of Transnational Law, 53*(2), 235–284.
5. Susan Kneebone, 'Australia as a Powerbroker on Refugee Protection in Southeast Asia: The Relationship with Indonesia', (2017) *33*(1) *Refuge: Canada's Journal on Refugees* 29–41, 30.

Indonesia has always served as a transit state for asylum seekers and refugees.[6] This can be first traced back to the refugees of Indochina, specifically the asylum seekers and refugees of Vietnam from the 1970s to the 1990s.[7] Recent cases have supported Indonesia's role as a transit state for the asylum seekers and refugees of the Rohingya. Other than that, Indonesia also serves as a transit state for the refugees of Afghanistan and other countries.[8] In the case of Vietnam and the Rohingya, Indonesia has shown good faith in the handling of asylum seekers and refugees, separate from the reality that Indonesia is just a transit state. The good faith that Indonesia has shown is rooted in its international obligations not to reject or return any asylum seekers that go into Indonesia on their way to Australia or New Zealand. As of January 2018, there are 13,895 individuals who seek protection remaining in Indonesia.[9]

The issue of asylum seekers does not end in granting access. Furthermore, Indonesia has additional responsibilities in handling asylum seekers[10] that have received refugee status until that refugee can receive certainty from other third safe countries of their acceptance. Not being a member party of the Refugee Convention,[11] Indonesia does not have a policy to integrate refugees into its population but at the same time Indonesia could not return them to their original countries, as it will violate the international norms of non-refoulement.[12] These conditions lead to the current situation where Indonesia becomes the transiting, processing and waiting country for those who seek asylum. These refugees are living in limbo, as the waiting period for resettlement is uncertain (longer period is common)[13] and they are not eligible to work but are self-reliant[14] and some of them are living autonomously among local people.[15]

The process of placement of refugees to third party states needs specific attention. This is due to Indonesia's role as a member of the international community, where on one side it is seen as reluctant to violate the rights of refugees and on the other side, acknowledges the fact that Indonesia has limits in the handling and protection of refugees within their sovereign borders. Various results can emerge from the interaction between the refugees and Indonesian

6. See Robyn Sampson, Sandra Gifford, Savitri Taylor, (2016). The Myth of Transit: The Making of a Life by Asylum Seekers and Refugees in Indonesia. *Journal of Ethnic & Migration Studies, 42*(1), 1132–1152.
7. Antje Missbach, *Troubled Transit: Asylum Seekers Stuck in Indonesia* (Singapore: ISEAS-Yusof Ishak Institute, 2015), 30–42; Tom Brown and Antje Missbach, 'The Boats May Have 'Stopped', but More Refugees are Stuck in Limbo in Indonesia', The Conversation <http://theconversation.com/the-boats-may-have-stopped-but-more-refugees-are-stuck-in-limbo-in-indonesia-56152>, accessed on 15 April 2016.
8. Missbach, ibid, 42–44.
9. According to the UNHCR, this number includes 10,168 refugees and 3,727 asylum seekers, of whom 9,742 were male and 4,153 were female. Monthly report (January 2018) issued by UNHCR Jakarta Office (file on author).
10. It is interesting to note that Indonesia does not differentiate terms 'asylum seekers' and 'refugees' as in the legal meaning. It refers to 'refugees' (*pengungsi*) as all people who seek further protection with differentiation where they are coming from, internally (similar to Internally Displaced Persons/IDP – *Pengungsi Dalam Negeri*) or outside Indonesia (foreign refugees – *Pengungsi Luar Negeri*).
11. Convention relating to the Status of Refugees (adopted 28 July 1951, entered into force 22 April 1954) 189 UNTS 137 (Refugee Convention).
12. See Nils Coleman, '*Non-Refoulement* Revised Renewed Review of the Status of the Principle of *Non-Refoulement* as Customary International Law', (2003) 5(1) *European Journal of Migration and Law*, 23–68; Jean Allain, 'The Jus Cogens Nature of Non-Refoulement', (2001) *International Journal of Refugee Law, 13*(4), 533–558, p. 538; Phil C.W. Chan, (2006) 'The Protection of Refugees and Internally Displaced Persons: Non-Refoulement Under Customary International Law?' (2006) *International Journal of Human Rights, 10* (3), 231–239.
13. Joe Cochrane, 'Refugees in Indonesia: Hoped for Brief Stay, Many May Be Stuck for Life', 26 January 2018, The New York Times <https://www.nytimes.com/2018/01/26/world/asia/indonesia-refugees-united-nations.html>, accessed on 11 June 2018.
14. Yunizar Adiputera & Atin Prabandari, *Addressing Challenges and Identifying Opportunities for Refugee Access to Employment in Indonesia.* (Yogyakarta, Indonesia: Institute of International Studies, 2018), 3.
15. Thomas Brown & Antje Missbach, 'Refugee detention in Indonesia', 12 May 2017, Lowy Institute <https://www.lowyinstitute.org/the-interpreter/refugee-detention-indonesia>, accessed on 11 June 2018.

society. Legal and social problems that occur within Indonesian society usually involve asylum seekers and those who have obtained refugee status living independently outside the immigration detention centers and community houses.[16] The current situation is creating a 'ticking bomb' where both refugees (including asylum seekers) and the Indonesian community have experienced negative impacts in the waiting period due to lack of support from the international community.

Most of the available literature focuses on the protection of asylum seekers and refugees by highlighting Indonesia's non-comprehensive policies and its lacks of infrastructure concerning the issues, without acknowledging Indonesia's right to seek assistance from the international community in handling these 'transiting protected migrants'.[17] This article seeks to fill that gap, by providing an analysis of the opportunities for Indonesia to seek further assistance from the international community in handling asylum seekers and refugees in Indonesia.[18] As an alternative solution, this paper argues that Indonesia needs to share its burden with the international community in general, especially within the region, specifically in the treatment of refugees that still reside in Indonesia during the process of resettlement to a third party.

Based on the background above, this research will discuss three main points. First, it discusses the international law that obliges Indonesia to protect asylum seekers and refugees. Second, it will discuss how Indonesia applies its national law when it comes to the management and treatment of asylum seekers and refugees especially during their waiting period of resettlement.[19] Third, this research will offer a proposal regarding the appeal to the international community on sharing the burden of managing refugees as they await the process of resettlement. It will conclude with highlights of some policy recommendations for the government of Indonesia in improving its diplomacy for asylum seekers and refugees management.

2 INTERNATIONAL OBLIGATIONS OF INDONESIA AND THE RELATIONSHIP WITH REFUGEE HANDLING

Even though Indonesia is not a state party to the Refugee Convention or the 1967 Protocol,[20] it is still bound to protect asylum seekers and refugees as a consequence of other sources of international legal duties, both treaty-based and custom-based. It is important to note that

16. Asylum seekers who live and stay independently are those who are coming to Indonesia legally (usually benefiting from Indonesia's free-visa countries or visa-on-arrival policies) but then declare themselves to the UNHCR and IOM in Indonesia as asylum seekers (*Pengungsi Mandiri*).
17. See, for example, Missbach, *Troubled Transit: Asylum Seekers Stuck in Indonesia*, above no. 2; Savitri Taylor & Brynna Rafferty-Brownt, 'Waiting for Life to Begin: the Plight of Asylum Seekers Caught by Australia's Indonesian Solution', (2010) *22*(4) *International Journal of Refugee Law*, pp. 558–592; Adiputera & Prabandari, *Addressing Challenges and Identifying Opportunities for Refugee Access to Employment in Indonesia,* above no. 9; Sampson, Gifford, & Taylor, 'The Myth of Transit: The Making of a Life by Asylum Seekers and Refugees in Indonesia', above no. 1; Nikolas Feith Tan, 'The Status of Asylum Seekers and Refugees in Indonesia', (2016) *International Journal of Refugee Law* 28(3), 365–383; and Antje Missbach, 'Doors and Fences: Controlling Indonesia's Porous Borders and Policing Asylum Seekers' (2014) *35 Singapore Journal of Tropical Geography* 228–244.
18. Example of regional burden sharing previously was discussed in Richard Towle, 'Processes and Critiques of the Indo-Chinese Comprehensive Plan of Action: An Instrument of International Burden-Sharing?' (2006) 18(3–4) *International Journal of Refugee Law* 537-570.
19. This research observed three immigration detention centers that house some asylum seekers and refugees who have obtained their status from the UNHCR in Jakarta, Medan and Kupang in the year 2016.
20. The debate on whether Indonesia should ratify the Convention of 1951 is not included in the scope of this paper. See further in Dita Liliansa dan Anbar Jayadi, 'Should Indonesia Accede to The 1951 Refugee Convention and Its 1967 Protocol?', (2015) *5*(3) *Indonesian Law Review* 324–346; Sara Ellen Davies, *Legitimizing Rejection: International Refugee Law in Southeast Asia* (Leiden, The Netherlands: Brill, 2008), 129–130. There was a plan to accede these instruments but it seems did not get the approval from the parliament of Indonesia. See Enny Soeprapto, 'Promotion of Refugee Law in Indonesia' (2004) *2*(1) *Indonesian Journal of International Law*, 57–66, 65.

Indonesia has acceded to most human rights treaties.[21] Indonesia's international obligations regarding the protection of refugees and/or asylum seekers are mainly based on the obligation of the principle of non-refoulment. Meanwhile, Indonesia's international obligations are related to the protection of human rights,[22] as Indonesia has admitted or ratified various international human rights instruments, which include the Universal Declaration of Human Rights (UDHR), the International Covenant on Civil and Political Rights (ICCPR), the Convention on the Rights of the Child (CRC) and the Convention Against Torture and Degrading Treatment or Punishment Other Cruel, Inhuman or Degrading Human Dignity (CAT).

Thus, under international human rights and customary law, it is safe to claim that asylum seekers and refugees in Indonesia are at least protected from *refoulement*, torture or other cruel, inhuman or degrading treatment or punishment, the right to liberty and security, and the right to education.[23]

2.1 *Non-refoulement principle*

This principle has been argued to have attained the status of customary international law and thus bound Indonesia[24] as part of the international community.[25] In addition, support for the treaty-based provisions is widely found in major human rights treaties such as the Convention Against Torture (CAT)[26] explicitly and the ICCPR,[27] together with the CRC[28] implicitly. Article 3 of CAT unambiguously prohibits *refoulement* in clear terms where there are considerable grounds that a person would be in danger of being persecuted upon return to his/her original country.[29] Despite no specific provision on prohibition of refoulement, such protection may be inferred from the readings of Article 6 for the right to life and Article 7 for the prohibition of ill treatment.[30] Similar to the ICCPR, the CRC does not have an explicit provision on the prohibition of refoulement. However, the Committee on the Rights of the Child interpreted Article 22 as prohibiting refoulement where there is a 'real risk of irreparable harm to the child', especially to unaccompanied and separated children outside their country of origin.[31]

---

21. Indonesia signed but did not ratify the Convention for the Protection of All Persons from Enforced Disappearance. Office of the High Commissioners of Human Rights, 'Ratification Status for Indonesia', <http://tbinternet.ohchr.org/_layouts/TreatyBodyExternal/Treaty.aspx?CountryID=80&Lang=EN>, accessed on 12 June 2018.
22. Given the history of the Convention of 1951 on the Status of Refugees and the limitations of the convention itself, it is important to also refer to other human rights instruments. See David Weissbrodt, (2008). *The human rights of non-citizens.* Oxford, UK: Oxford University Press.
23. Nikolas Feith Tan, above no. 17, 376.
24. Indonesia has never adopted a manner to become a persistent objector to the principle.
25. See Nils Coleman, above no. 12, 23–68; Jean Allain, 'The Jus Cogens Nature of Non-Refoulement', (2001) *International Journal of Refugee Law* (13(4), 533–558, p. 538; Phil C.W. Chan, (2006) 'The Protection of Refugees and Internally Displaced Persons: Non-Refoulement Under Customary International Law? (2006) *International Journal of Human Rights, 10*(3), 231–239; Elihu Lauterpacht and Daniel Bethlehem, 'The Scope and Content of the Principle of Non-refoulement: Opinion' in Erika Feller, Volker Türk, and Frances Nicholson (Eds.), *Refugee Protection in International Law: UNHCR's Global Consultations on International Protection* (Cambridge, UK: Cambridge University Press, 2003), 87–177.
26. Convention against Torture, UNTS
27. International Covenant on Civil and Political Rights (ICCPR), UNTS
28. Convention on the Rights of Child (CRC), UNTS
29. Article 3 CAT states that: 'No State Party shall expel, return ("refouler") or extradite a person to another State where there are substantial grounds for believing that he would be in danger of being subjected to torture'.
30. Human Rights Committee, 'General Comment 20, Article 7' in 'Compilation of General Comments and General Recommendations Adopted by Human Rights Treaty Bodies', UN doc HRI/GEN/1/Rev.1, 1992, 30, para. 9; Manfred Nowak, *Covenant on Civil and Political Rights, CCPR Commentary* (2nd ed., NP Engel 2005) 185.
31. Committee on the Rights of the Child, 'General Comment No 6: Treatment of Unaccompanied and Separated Children Outside their Country of Origin', UN doc CRC/GC/2005/6, 1 Sept 2005, para. 27.

An important principle that needs to be analyzed in relation to asylum seekers and refugees is the principle of non-refoulment. Article 33 Paragraph 1 on the Convention on Refugees 1951 states that:

> No Contracting State shall expel or return ("refouler") a refugee in any manner whatsoever to the frontiers of territories where his [or her] life of freedom would be threatened on account of his [or her] race, religion, nationality, membership of a particular social group or political opinion.

The provisions of Article 33 Paragraph 1 should be seen in conjunction with Article 1A (2) of the 1951 Convention on the Status of Refugees.

Based on the two rules mentioned above, the principle of non-refoulment applies to refugees as defined in Article 1A(2) of the Convention on the Status of Refugees of 1951 and applies to those who are not excluded by the 1951 Convention on the Status of Refugees. The principle of non-refoulement is also relevant to asylum seekers, which are those for whom the refugee status has not been formally defined. According to the principle of non-refoulement, actions that should not be taken include deportation, extradition, and the refusal of entry by state authorities at the border.

In essence, the principle of non-refoulement is a principle that cannot be reduced in any form that emphasizes the responsibility of the state to not allow refugees and/or asylum seekers to be placed in danger as defined in the 1951 Convention on the Status of Refugees.

2.2 *Freedom from torture or other cruel, inhuman or degrading treatment or punishment*

Protection of asylum seekers and refugees under this principle is very related to the conditions experienced during their stay in Indonesia. All irregular migrants coming to Indonesia are subject to immigration detention. Then, after registration as asylum seekers, they still need to stay in immigration detention centers throughout Indonesia. Exacerbated by the tougher policy of refugee-receiving countries,[32] asylum seekers and refugees could spend a longer time in Indonesia with limited capacity. This leads to over-crowding in most of the immigration detention centers throughout Indonesia.[33]

It is safe to argue that asylum seekers and refugees are protected from torture in absolute and non-derogable terms under Article 1 of the CAT.[34] In addition, prohibition of torture has been argued to have attained the status of customary international law and generally accepted to be *jus cogens*.[35] Indonesia is also obliged to ensure no cruel, inhuman or degrading treatment or punishment and ill treatment in general including its

32. Colum Lynch, 'Trump to Cut Number of Refugees in U.S. by More Than Half', 26 September 2017, Foreign Policy, <http://foreignpolicy.com/2017/09/26/trump-to-cut-number-of-refugees-in-u-s-by-more-than-half/>, accessed on 11 June 2018; Tess McClure, 'New Zealand's Refugee Policy is Closer to Trump's 'Muslim Ban' Than You Might Think', 1 February 2017, VICE, <https://www.vice.com/en_nz/article/aej3aj/is-new-zealands-refugee-policy-closer-to-trumps-muslim-ban-than-you-think>, accessed on 11 June 2018; Daisuke Kikuchi, 'New Justice Minister Has No Plans to Boost Japan's Refugee Intake', 10 August 2017, Japan Times, <https://www.japantimes.co.jp/news/2017/08/10/national/politics-diplomacy/new-justice-minister-no-plans-boost-japans-refugee-intake/#.Wx_KpC97H_Q>, accessed on 11 June 2018; Lizzie Dearden, 'Refugee Crisis: Number of Asylum Seekers Arriving in Norway Drops by 95%', 1 July 2016, Independent, <https://www.independent.co.uk/news/world/europe/refugee-crisis-number-of-asylum-seekers-arriving-in-norway-drops-by-95-a7114191.html>, accessed on 11 June 2018.
33. As of January 2018, eight out of 13 Indonesian immigration detention centers have over-capacity. Report of the Directorate General of Immigration, Ministry of Law and Human Rights, Republic of Indonesia. (File on author).
34. Non-derogable nature is coming from Article 2(2) CAT.
35. Erika de Wet, 'The Prohibition of Torture as an International Norm of jus cogens and Its Implications for National and Customary Law' (2004) *15 European Journal of International Law* 97; Joshua A. Decker, 'Is the United States Bound by the Customary International Law of Torture - A Proposal for ATS Litigation in the War on Terror' (2006) 6 Chicago Journal of International Law 803; Aoife Duffy, 'Expulsion to Face

immigration detention centers.[36] Such obligations are supported in a general obligation that Indonesia should ensure that: 'All persons deprived of their liberty shall be treated with humanity and with respect for the inherent dignity of the human person'.[37]

In relation to child protection, the CRC also obliges member states to refrain from any torture or other cruel, inhuman or degrading treatment or punishment of children.[38] It is also highly encouraged not to use the term 'detention' anymore and change to 'care' instead.[39] In addition, it is important to refer to the principle of the best interests of the child.[40] If it is associated with the practice of handling refugee children, then there are some things to note: (1) the availability of a supportive environment for children to learn and retain their native language; (2) availability of an environment for children to perform religious practices or beliefs; (3) availability of an environment for children's play and recreation.[41] In essence, the environment for refugee children should be conducive to the growth and development of the child, both physically and psychologically.

Indirectly, the provisions contained in the UDHR relating to how the state should treat and deal with refugees should be noted. In this case, Article 5 of the UDHR states that: 'No one shall be subjected to torture or to cruel, inhuman or degrading treatment or punishment'.[42]If it is associated with the principle of non-refoulment, then if a country, for example, deported refugees and/or asylum seekers, the country indirectly allows the refugees and/or asylum seekers to be subject to torture or cruel, inhuman and other treatment degrading human dignity. The action of returning refugees and/or asylum seekers is, indirectly, a violation of Article 5 of the Universal Declaration of Human Rights.

Another legal protection is coming from Article 2(1) of the ICCPR that requires states to respect all individuals within its territory 'without distinction of any kind, such as race, color, sex, language, religion, political or other opinion, national or social origin, property, birth or other status'. If related to the handling of refugees in the country's territory, the article puts a burden on the state parties to ensure the handling of refugees is done with the best abilities, regardless of their 'status' as refugees, the origin of the refugees and the other factors mentioned in Article 2(1).

2.3 *The right to liberty and security*

Not being criminals under Indonesian law, asylum seekers and refugees also have the right to liberty and security. The ICCPR prohibits arbitrary detention under Article 9(1) and the UN Human Rights Committee underlined that any detention of asylum seekers and refugees must be 'reasonable, necessary and proportionate'.[43] However, it is important to note that any person who comes to Indonesia without proper identification documents is categorized as an 'illegal immigrant' and subject to immigration detention.[44] The detention period will last until the person is deported or a maximum of ten years[45] and if the case goes to court, the person

---

Torture? *Non-refoulement* in International Law' (2008) *20*(3) *International Journal of Refugee Law*, 373–390, 384.

36. Articles 6–7 CAT.
37. Article 10 CAT.
38. Article 37(a) CRC.
39. Nikolas Feith Tan, above no. 17, 374.
40. See UNICEF, 'Refugee Children: Guideline on Protection and Care', https://www.unicef.org/violencestudy/pdf/refugee_children_guidelines_on_protection_and_care.pdf.
41. Ibid.
42. Universal Declaration of Human Rights, downloaded from http://www.un.org/en/universal-declaration-human-rights/.
43. UN Human Rights Committee (HRC), *Communication No. 2094/2011: Views adopted by the Committee at its 108th session (8–26 July 2013)*, 20 August 2013, CCPR/C/108/D/2094/2011, para. 9.3, <http://www.refworld.org/docid/52270fe44.html>, accessed 13 June 2018.
44. Indonesia, Law No. 6 Year 2011 on Immigration, Article 83(1)(b).
45. Article 83(1–2), ibid.

can end up with a maximum of five years imprisonment.[46] Despite this regulation, the ICCPR provides protection to asylum seekers by obliging Indonesia to have reasons for detention and allow a right of review.[47]

In terms of detention for children, the CRC provides protection by prohibiting arbitrary and unlawful deprivation and further requires that detention may only be used 'as a measure of last resort'.[48] States have been strongly encouraged to find other options to avoid putting children into detention unless there are reasonable grounds to justify such detention. This is even mandated for unaccompanied or separated children.[49] As of April 2018, there were 3,776 asylum seeker and refugee children in Indonesia, this number included 3,477 children with families, 225 unaccompanied and 74 separated minors.[50] Given these figures, Indonesia has a tough duty to ensure that these children are not deprived of their liberty and security.

2.4 *The right to education*

Some have argued that this right is the one frequently violated by states in handling children of asylum seekers and refugees.[51] The CRC mandates free primary education without any derogation on any basis including immigration status and nationality.[52] The Committee on the Rights of the Child underlined that 'States should ensure that access to education is maintained during all phases of the displacement cycle' and thus, children who are in detention also have the right to education.[53]

Previously, there have been reports that Indonesia did not allow and provide basic education for children who are asylum seekers and refugees.[54] This does not mean that Indonesia prevents non-Indonesians having access to education. The government heavily subsidizes public elementary and high schools and this is managed by the local authorities. It is common for public schools to prioritize Indonesian children as the vacancies in public schools may be limited. Again, the admittance of children to the schools is the policy of the local authorities and the schools themselves. However, given the awareness of the importance for children to attend school, a steady increase of children of asylum seekers and refugees are now admitted to public schools.[55] Apart from formal education, the government of Indonesia also provides on-site informal education within the immigration detention centers.[56]

---

46. Article 119(1), ibid.
47. Article 9(2) (4), ICCPR.
48. Article 37(b), CRC.
49. The Committee on the Rights of the Child in states that "unaccompanied or separated children should not, as a general rule, be detained," and "detention cannot be justified solely on… their migratory or residence status, or lack thereof". UN Committee on the Rights of the Child (CRC), *General comment No. 6 (2005): Treatment of Unaccompanied and Separated Children Outside their Country of Origin*, 1 September 2005, CRC/GC/2005/6, <http://www.refworld.org/docid/42dd174b4.html>, accessed 13 June 2018.
50. Monthly report (April 2018) issued by UNHCR Jakarta Office (file on author).
51. Alice Farmer, 'The Impact of Immigration Detention on Children', (2013) *44 Forced Migration Review*, 14–16, 15.
52. Articles 2(1) and 28(1), CRC.
53. Committee on the Rights of the Child, 'General Comment No 6: Treatment of Unaccompanied and Separated Children Outside their Country of Origin', UN doc CRC/GC/2005/6, 1 Sept 2005, paras 41 and 63.
54. Amy Nethery, Brynna Rafferty-Brown, and Savitri Taylor, 'Exporting Detention: Australia-Funded Immigration Detention in Indonesia' (2012) *26*(1) *Journal of Refugee Studies*, 88–109, 93; Human Rights Watch, *Barely Surviving: Detention, Abuse, and Neglect of Migrant Children in Indonesia* (USA: Human Rights Watch, 2013) 73.
55. UNHCR, 'Indonesia Facts Sheet, December 2016', <http://www.unhcr.org/id/wp-content/uploads/sites/42/2017/05/Indonesia-Fact-Sheet-December-2016.pdf>, accessed 13 June 2018; Oktina Hafanti, '*Sebuah Sekolah Negeri di Makassar Menyambut Anak-Anak Pengungsi*' (A Public School in Makassar Welcomes Children of Refugees), 19 March 2018, UNHCR Indonesia <http://www.unhcr.org/id/11439-sebuah-sekolah-negeri-di-makassar-menyambut-anak-anak-pengungsi.html>, accessed on 13 June 2018.
56. Field observation of immigration detention centers in Jakarta, Kupang and Medan in 2016.

3 INDONESIAN NATIONAL LAW AND THE RELATION WITH THE REFUGEE ISSUE

Until the end of 2016, Indonesia did not have a comprehensive national regulation on managing asylum seekers and refugees who need protection under international law. This can be seen as being due to the position of Indonesia as a non-member party of both the Refugee Convention 1951 and the Optional Protocol 1967. In addition, Indonesia has always realized that it is not a destination country for these asylum seekers and refugees. Starting in 2017, Indonesia enacted national regulations at the level of presidential regulations to manage foreign refugees while they are residing in Indonesia temporarily. Unfortunately, this article highlights that such regulations are not solving the problem regarding how Indonesia shares its burden in managing the costs and efforts in handling asylum seekers and refugees.

3.1 *National law and policy prior to 2016*

3.1.1 *General protection under human rights*

The importance of the protection and fulfillment of human rights in Indonesia can be traced from the Constitution of the Republic of Indonesia of 1945 (the Constitution NRI 1945). The section on human rights in the Constitution NRI 1945 uses the phrase 'any person', which means it does not discriminate who is entitled to protection. Not discriminating does not mean blind protection, but there are restrictions set forth in the 1945 Constitution.[57]

Related to the presence of refugees in Indonesia, new provisions in the 1945 Constitution that protects their existence, includes Article 28A of the 1945 Constitution that guarantees that every person has the right to life. [58] Furthermore, Article 28G(1) also guarantees the protection of privacy and family life. Then, Article 28D states that every person has the right to security, protection and legal certainty. Furthermore, Article 28 Paragraph 1 states that the rights mentioned above, the right to life and, indirectly, the right to guaranteed personal dignity and family life with recognized standing before the law are rights which cannot be restricted under any circumstances.

Another human rights provision is Law No. 39 Year 1999 on Human Rights (Law 39/1999). Article 2 of the law states that the state of Indonesia recognizes and upholds human rights and human freedoms. However, in view of this article, reference should also be made to the provisions of Article 67 of the law which states that anyone who is in the territory of the Republic of Indonesia must comply with the legislation, the unwritten laws and international law on human rights that have been accepted by the Republic of Indonesia.

Aside from the aforementioned regulations, there is also the Decision of Indonesian People's Consultative Assembly (*Ketetapan MPR*) No. XVIII/MPR/1998 on Human Rights (TAP MPR No. XVIII/MPR/1998). Article 2 of the TAP MPR No. XVIII/MPR contains provisions that emphasize the importance of ratifying various instruments of the United Nations on Human Rights, as long as such instruments are not contrary to Pancasila and the 1945 Constitution. Further, Article 5 of TAP MPR No. XVIII/MPR declares the Human Rights Charter as a reference in drafting the human rights bill. Thus, it can be seen that Indonesia has always paid attention to international legal instruments on human rights, not merely referring to the national desire.

Regarding the presence of refugees in Indonesia, they have rights as guaranteed not only in the international legal instruments, but also national laws ranging from the 1945 Constitution and other legislation. Against these rights, refugees residing in the Republic of Indonesia have a fundamental obligation which otherwise implement these basic obligations, it will affect the implementation of the rights concerned.

57. See Art. 28I Indonesia 1945 Constitution.

58. Indonesia (1), *Undang-Undang Dasar Negara Republik Indonesia Tahun 1945* [1945 Constitution of the Republic of Indonesia], Art. 28A.

3.1.2 *Specific policies on asylum seekers and refugees*

Initially, Indonesia regulated the management of asylum seekers and refugees as embodied in the circular letter of the Prime Minister (Ali Sostroamidjojo) No. 11/R.I/1956 of September 7, 1956 on the Protection of Political Fugitives (*Perlindungan Pelarian Politik*).[59] At that time, there was no mass influx of people escaping from persecution. Rather, in that period, newly emerging states were not politically stable and there were some occasions of persons escaping from their own countries due to political views.[60] Being an administrative instrument, this circular letter has a number of important protection principles. First, 'political refugees' (*pengungsi politik*) are protected on grounds of 'human rights and fundamental freedom in accordance with international customary law'.[61] Second, it defines a political refugee as a non-Indonesian citizen who commits a political crime in his/her original country or which may be committed outside or within Indonesian territory.[62] Third, the letter excludes acts that do not have political motives.[63] Such a clause implies that ordinary criminals shall not be eligible for protection and may be categorized as an 'exclusion clause' under the Statute of the Office of the United Nations High Commissioner for Refugees[64] and the Refugee Convention.[65] Finally, the letter eventually excludes political fugitives from protection if their actions are contrary to Indonesia's national interests such as crimes against humanity, crimes against the state's order and crimes directed against a religion which exists and is legally recognized in Indonesia.[66]

Indonesia, in 1975, faced the mass influx of asylum seekers from Indochina.[67] In responding to this situation, Indonesia issued Presidential Decision No. 38 of 1979 on Coordination of the Solution of the Problems on Vietnamese Refugees. This instrument was created to coordinate tasks among the relevant ministries in managing the arrival of 'boat people' in Indonesia, including the Ministry of State Defense, the Ministry of Foreign Affairs and the Ministry of Internal Affairs. Under this policy, Indonesia would not grant the refugees settlement, as it is not party to the Refugee Convention. However, Indonesia allowed entry for these asylum seekers for a temporary period until the international community, through the UNHCR, made final repatriation or resettlement.[68] Therefore, Indonesia also allowed UNHCR access, signing an agreement pursuant to which the agency could conduct registration and refugee status determination.[69] The Indonesian government provided an island (Galang Island) as a temporary place for around 10,000 Indochina asylum seekers. Located in the Riau Archipelago, its purpose was to allow easy access for the local government, while preventing interaction between the local population and the asylum seekers.[70]

59. Enny Soeprapto, 'Promotion of Refugee Law in Indonesia' (2004) *2*(1) *Indonesian Journal of International Law* 57–66, 58.
60. Bhatara Ibnu Reza, 'Challenges and Opportunities in Respecting International Refugee Law in Indonesia' in Angus Francis and Rowena Maguire (Eds.), *Protection of Refugees and Displaced Persons in the Asia Pacific Region* (Ashgate, 2013) 117–134, 123; Antje Missbach, *Troubled Transit: Asylum Seekers Stuck in Indonesia* (ISEAS – Yusof Ishak Institute, 2015) 157.
61. Article 1, Circular Letter 1956.
62. Article 2, Circular Letter 1956.
63. Article 3, Circular Letter 1956.
64. UN General Assembly, Statute of the Office of the United Nations High Commission for Refugees, 14 December 1950, A/RES/428(V), para. 7(d).
65. Article 1(F)(b), Refugee Convention.
66. Article 4, Circular Letter 1956.
67. Soeprapto (IJIL), 61.
68. Bhatara Ibnu Reza, 125.
69. Agreement between the government of the Republic of Indonesia and the United Nations High Commissioner for Refugees regarding the Establishment of the Office of the UNHCR Representative for Indonesia (15 June 1979).
70. Antje Missbach, 'Waiting on the Islands of'Stuckedness'. Managing Asylum Seekers in Island Detention Camps in Indonesia: From the Late 1970s to the Early 2000s', (2013) *6*(2) *Austrian Journal of South-East Asian Studies*, 281–306, 288.

As asylum seekers are coming from outside Indonesia and they are not Indonesian citizens originally, Indonesia considers the issues as falling under its immigration law. Indonesia firstly enacted its immigration law in 1992 but then replaced it with Law No. 6 of 2011 on Immigration (Law 6/2011). Those who were coming to Indonesia without proper or valid travel documents would have immigration sanctions imposed and be subject to immigration detention.[71] Article 1 Paragraph (1) of this law defines immigration as things or happenings in respect of traffic of people entering or leaving Indonesian territory and its oversight in order to safeguard the enforcement of state sovereignty of Indonesia. Referring to this definition, the influx of asylum seekers to Indonesia or discharge of refugees to be placed in a third country can be constructed as matters of immigration. It also includes supervision of both asylum seekers and refugees who are awaiting placement in a third country.

Under Law 6/2011, refugees[72] can be classified as alien. According to Article 1 point 9 of Law No. 6 of 2011, an alien is a person who is not a citizen of Indonesia. Since as alien is not a citizen of Indonesia, when he/she gets into the territory of Indonesia, they are required to have a valid visa and other valid travel documents.[73] If violating this requirement, they will be placed in a detention center. [74] However, regarding refugees, the law does not mention specific responses to them. It only regulates the handling of victims of human trafficking and human smuggling, which to them are exempt from immigration administrative action. [75]

As the institution responsible for immigration affairs under the Ministry of Legal Affairs and Human Rights, the Director General of Immigration from the Ministry of Legal Affairs and Human Rights in 2010 issued an internal regulation (Peraturan Direktur Jenderal Imigrasi No. IMI-1489.UM.08.05/*Perdirjen Imigrasi* 2010) that applied nationally on the Management of Illegal Immigrants (*Penanganan Ilegal Imigran*). Under this regulation, asylum seekers who are coming to Indonesia are categorized as 'illegal immigrants' but once they get an 'attestation letter' and are granted the status of refugee from the office of the UNHCR, they then are allowed to stay temporarily in Indonesia.[76] This instrument also ensures that the government of Indonesia will not be responsible for supporting the logistical needs of asylum seekers and refugees who are under the UNHCR's protection.[77]

In April 2016, the Director General of Immigration replaced the 2010 regulation with a more specific policy on managing asylum seekers and refugees under Indonesian Immigration Law. In Regulation No. 0352.GR.02.07/2016 on the Handling of Illegal Immigrants Declaring to be Asylum Seekers or Refugees, Indonesia tried to manage the presence of asylum seekers in Indonesia in a more detailed arrangement including the division of responsibilities between the Directorate General of Immigration, the UNHCR and The International Organization for Migration (IOM). With this regulation, the cooperation, which was conducted between the three institutions, was formalized in a legal instrument. Again, it is important to note that such an instrument would only apply within the Ministry of Legal Affairs and Human Rights. Since the management of asylum seekers and refugees is crosscutting areas of responsibilities, then this regulation only works in very segmented institutions.

In 1999, Indonesia had a national law that mentions specifically the handling of asylum seekers and refugees in Indonesia, Law No. 37 of 1999 on Foreign Relations (Law 37/1999). Article 25 states that 'The authority to grant asylum to foreigners vested in the President by taking into consideration the Minister'. Then, Article 26 regulates the 'granting asylum to foreigners carried out in accordance with national legislation and with due regard to the laws,

71. Indonesia, Law No. 6 Year 2011 on Immigration, Article 83(1)(b).
72. Refugees do not include internally displaced persons.
73. Indonesia (3), *Undang-Undang tentang Keimigrasian [Law on the Immigration],* UU. No. 6 Tahun 2011, LN No. 52 tahun 2011, TLN. No. 5216, Art. 8 para. 2.
74. See Article 81, Law No. 6 of 2011.
75. The administrative measures on immigration may be the inclusion in the list of prevention or deterrence to deportation from the territory of Indonesia. See Art. 75 Law No. 6 of 2011.
76. Articles 1–5, Perdirjen Imigrasi 2010.
77. Article 6, Perdirjen Imigrasi 2010.

customs and international practice'. Then, in relation to refugees, Article 27 states that 'the President sets policy for refugee management from abroad by taking into consideration the Minister's opinion'. The minister referred to here is the Indonesian Minister of Foreign Affairs. From the last provision, it can be seen that Indonesia had a plan to make a national policy on managing asylum seekers and refugees in Indonesia. Unfortunately, it was not until 16 years later that a such policy was enacted. This legal policy will be discussed in the following section.

3.2 *Presidential Regulation No. 125 Year 2016*

Recently, in December 2016, the government of Indonesia finally enacted a national regulation specifically on the management of asylum seekers and refugees.[78] Under Presidential Regulation No. 125 of 2016,[79] the Coordinating Minister nationally coordinates the handling management for political, legal and security aspects. Such management will be implemented across government institutions and divided into some stages or events: the rescue/discovery; the placement/sheltering; the security; and the immigration monitoring/control.

In the event of discovery or rescue of asylum seekers at sea, the Indonesian Search and Rescue Agency (*Basarnas*) becomes the coordinating actor.[80] When the rescue is on land, the Indonesian Police (POLRI) will be the ones that have the main responsibility. Soon after the rescue, those asylum seekers should be placed in the closest immigration detention center for further processing.[81] In terms of finding shelter for these asylum seekers, in the case of a mass influx and limited space in immigration detention centers, the local government is mandated to provide such temporary shelter(s).[82] This is because the local government has the authority to assign public space(s) for a certain purposes. For those whose application is rejected by the UNHCR, they will be placed in an immigration detention center and be deported in accordance with the current regulations.[83] The Indonesian Police is mandated to ensure the security of asylum seekers and refugees during their stay in Indonesia. Such security is not only for asylum seekers and refugees but also for the people of Indonesia.[84] In order to monitor all of the asylum seekers and refugees, the Directorate General of Immigration has the main responsibility and coordinates all relevant institutions.[85] Finally, the government of Indonesia, in this regulation, is committed to providing a national budget for managing asylum seekers and refugees through those relevant institutions.[86]

This Presidential Regulation is a major breakthrough in the handling of asylum seekers and refugees in Indonesia. The important point of this regulation is the state's recognition of asylum seeker and refugee status, which has only been done through circulars imposed by the Directorate General of Immigration previously. With this recognition, the status of asylum seekers and refugees is applicable across institutions under the government of Indonesia. In other words, this policy is a more comprehensive handling of asylum seekers and refugees. In contrast to refugee handling in earlier eras, this policy not only focuses on the smuggling aspect of human displacement, but also covers aspects of discovery, shelter, security and immigration control.

78. The enactment of this regulation is argued to become the implementation of Indonesia's commitment of the Bali Declaration on People Smuggling, Trafficking in Persons and Related Transnational Crime, The Sixth Ministerial Conference of the Bali Process on People Smuggling, Trafficking in Persons and Related Transnational Crime, Bali, 23 March 2016.
79. The unofficial translation of the law can be found on http://www.refworld.org/pdfid/58aeee374.pdf.
80. Articles 5–7.
81. Articles 10–20.
82. Articles 24–28.
83. Articles 29–30.
84. Articles 31–32.
85. Articles 33–39.
86. Article 40.

It is critical to note that, despite the positive development in formalizing the government's recognition of asylum seekers and refugees in Indonesia, the real impacts of the regulation may not be seen until at least two years of implementation.[87] During 2017 and 2018, the government was still occupied with dissemination of the regulation to relevant ministries, agencies and local governments. In addition, relevant ministries seem to be having difficulties in designing a proposal of national budget since some of them are new in the involvement of the issues of asylum seekers and refugees.

Based on the description of the Indonesian national law pertaining to the refugee issue, Indonesia has had national laws relating to the handling of asylum seekers and refugees and even set up rules that adjust to the social situation in Indonesia related to refugees. However, despite the legal efforts made by the government of Indonesia in protecting asylum seekers and refugees, it seems that such avenues will not be effectively achieved unless Indonesia appeals to the international community for a shared-burden in managing the issues.

4 CONCLUSION

For the purpose of illustrating Indonesia's burden in handling asylum seekers and refugees, this article has highlighted some legal concerns regarding how Indonesia perceives its legal commitment under refugees' global protection. Indonesia is not a party to the Refugee Convention but has articulated its behavior toward positive management of asylum seekers and refugees. Realizing that it is not the destination country, Indonesia also feels that care management for those who are still remaining in Indonesia, both for Refugee Status Determination (RSD) or resettlement, becomes a burden that should be dispersed under the concept of burden sharing. This concept has become a legal principle where it emanates from various treaty obligations and general principles of law, which have been recognized by states.

Unfortunately, global burden sharing is now very different because it is influenced by the trends in protectionism and inward looking of destination countries' policies in restricting or even reducing the admittance of asylum seekers and refugees. With this condition, Indonesia should be more aggressive in persuading destination countries to contribute to the management of asylum seekers and refugees. Without underestimating the roles of the UNHCR and IOM, state to state cooperation is more preferable as they have complete authority in managing the pending asylum seekers and refugees in Indonesia.

Much state-led formal cooperation has been conducted especially involving Australia. However, as shown previously, these arrangements are focused more on 'shifting-burden' as opposed to 'sharing-burden'. Therefore, even though Indonesia has its new specific regulation for refugees (Presidential Regulation 125/2016), it will experience paying the costs (directly or indirectly) in managing the indeterminate stay of asylum seekers and refugees in Indonesian territory.

REFERENCES

Adiputera, Y. & Prabandari, A. (2018). *Addressing challenges and identifying opportunities for refugee access to employment in Indonesia*. Yogyakarta, Indonesia: Institute of International Studies.

Allain, J. (2001). The *jus cogens* nature of non-refoulement. *International Journal of Refugee* Law, *13*(4).

Betts, A. (2009). *Protection by persuasion: International cooperation in the refugee regime*. Ithaca, NY: Cornell University Press.

Chan, P.C.W. (2006). The protection of refugees and internally displaced persons: Non-refoulement under customary international law? *International Journal of Human Rights*, *10*(3).

Cochrane, J. (2018, January 26). Refugees in Indonesia: Hoped for brief stay, many may be stuck for life. *The New York Times*. Retrieved from https://www.nytimes.com/2018/01/26/world/asia/indonesia-refugees-united-nations.html

87. Yunizar Adiputera & Atin Prabandari, above no. 14, 4.

Coleman, N. (2003). Non-refoulement revised renewed review of the status of the principle of non-refoulement as customary international law. *European Journal of Migration and Law*, *5*(1).
Davies, S.E. (2008). *Legitimizing rejection: International refugee law in Southeast Asia*. Leiden, The Netherlands: Brill.
de Wet, E. (2004). The prohibition of torture as an international norm of *jus cogens* and its implications for national and customary law. *European Journal of International Law*, *15*.
Decker, J.A. (2006). Is the United States bound by the customary international law of torture - A proposal for ATS litigation in the War on Terror. *Chicago Journal of International Law*, *6*.
Duffy, A. (2008). Expulsion to face torture? Non-refoulement in international law. *International Journal of Refugee* Law, *20*(3).
Farmer, A. (2013). The impact of immigration detention on children. *Forced Migration Review*, *44*.
Gammeltoft-Hansen, T. & Hathaway, J.C. (2015). Non-refoulement in a world of cooperative deterrence. *Columbia Journal of Transnational Law*, *53*(2).
Kneebone, S. (2017). Australia as a powerbroker on refugee protection in Southeast Asia: The relationship with Indonesia. *Refuge: Canada's Journal on Refugees*, *33*(1).
Lauterpacht, E. & Bethlehem, D. (2013). The scope and content of the principle of non-refoulement: Opinion. In E. Feller, V. Türk & F. Nicholson (Eds.), *Refugee protection in international law: UNHCR's global consultations on international protection*. Cambridge, UK: Cambridge University Press.
Liliansa, Dita dan Anbar Jayadi. (2015). Should Indonesia accede to the 1951 Refugee Convention and its 1967 protocol? *Indonesian Law Review*, *5* (3).
Missbach, A. (2013). Waiting on the islands of 'Stuckedness'. Managing asylum seekers in island detention camps in Indonesia: From the late 1970s to the early 2000s. *Austrian Journal of South-East Asian Studies*, *6*(2).
Missbach, A. (2014). Doors and fences: Controlling Indonesia's porous borders and policing asylum seekers. *Singapore Journal of Tropical Geography*, *35*.
Missbach, A. (2015). *Troubled transit: Asylum seekers stuck in Indonesia*. Singapore: ISEAS-Yusof Ishak Institute.
Nethery, A. & Gordyn, C. (2014). Australia–Indonesia cooperation on asylum seekers: A case of 'incentivised policy transfer'. *Australian Journal of International Affairs*, *68*(2).
Nethery, A., Rafferty-Brown, B. & Savitri Taylor, S. (2012). Exporting detention: Australia-funded immigration detention in Indonesia. *Journal of Refugee Studies*, *26*(1).
Nowak, M. (2005). *Covenant on civil and political rights, CCPR Commentary* (2nd ed.). NP Engel.
Reza, Bhatara Ibnu. (2013). Challenges and opportunities in respecting international refugee law in Indonesia. In F. Angus & R. Maguire (Eds.), *Protection of refugees and displaced persons in the Asia Pacific region*. Ashgate.
Sampson, R., Gifford, S. & Taylor, S. (2016). The myth of transit: The making of a life by asylum seekers and refugees in Indonesia. *Journal of Ethnic & Migration Studies*, *42*(1).
Soeprapto, E. (2004). Promotion of refugee law in Indonesia. *Indonesian Journal of International Law*, *2*(1).
Tan, N.F. (2016). The status of asylum seekers and refugees in Indonesia. *International Journal of Refugee Law*, *28*(3).
Taylor, S. & Rafferty-Brown, B. (2010). Waiting for life to begin: The plight of asylum seekers caught by Australia's Indonesian solution. *International Journal of Refugee Law*, *22*(4).
Towle, R. (2006). Processes and critiques of the Indo-Chinese comprehensive plan of action: An instrument of international burden-sharing? *International Journal of Refugee Law*, *18*(3–4).
Weissbrodt, D. (2008). *The human rights of non-citizens*. Oxford, UK: Oxford University Press.
Brown, T. & Missbach, A. (2017). *Refugee detention in Indonesia*. Retrieved from https://www.lowyinstitute.org/the-interpreter/refugee-detention-indonesia
Brown, T. & Missbach, A. (2016). *The boats may have 'stopped', but more refugees are stuck in limbo in Indonesia*. Retrieved from http://theconversation.com/the-boats-may-have-stopped-but-more-refugees-are-stuck-in-limbo-in-indonesia-56152
Dearden, L. (2016). *Refugee crisis: Number of asylum seekers arriving in Norway drops by 95%*. Retrieved from https://www.independent.co.uk/news/world/europe/refugee-crisis-number-of-asylum-seekers-arriving-in-norway-drops-by-95-a7114191.html
Hafanti, Oktina, (2018). *Sebuah Sekolah Negeri di Makassar Menyambut Anak-Anak Pengungsi* [A public school in Makassar welcomes children of refugees]. Retrieved from http://www.unhcr.org/id/11439-sebuah-sekolah-negeri-di-makassar-menyambut-anak-anak-pengungsi.html
Indonesia signed but did not ratify the Convention for the Protection of All Persons from Enforced Disappearance. Office of the High Commissioners of Human Rights, 'Ratification Status for

Indonesia', Retrieved from http://tbinternet.ohchr.org/_layouts/TreatyBodyExternal/Treaty.aspx?CountryID=80&Lang=EN

Kikuchi, Daisuke, (2017). *New justice minister has no plans to boost Japan's refugee intake*. Retrieved from https://www.japantimes.co.jp/news/2017/08/10/national/politics-diplomacy/new-justice-minister-no-plans-boost-japans-refugee-intake/#.Wx_KpC97H_Q

Lynch, C. (2017). *Trump to cut number of refugees in U.S. by more than half*. Retrieved from http://foreignpolicy.com/2017/09/26/trump-to-cut-number-of-refugees-in-u-s-by-more-than-half/

McClure, T. (2017). *New Zealand's refugee policy is closer to Trump's 'Muslim Ban' than you might think*. Retrieved from https://www.vice.com/en_nz/article/aej3aj/is-new-zealands-refugee-policy-closer-to-trumps-muslim-ban-than-you-think

The unofficial translation of the law can be found on http://www.refworld.org/pdfid/58aeee374.pdf

UN Committee on the Rights of the Child (CRC). (2005). *General comment No. 6 (2005): Treatment of unaccompanied and separated children outside their country of origin*. Retrieved from http://www.refworld.org/docid/42dd174b4.html

UN Human Rights Committee (HRC). (2011). *Communication No. 2094/2011: Views adopted by the committee at its 108th session (8 – 26 July 2013)*. Retrieved from http://www.refworld.org/docid/52270fe44.html

UNHCR. (2016). *Indonesia facts sheet, December 2016*. Retrieved from http://www.unhcr.org/id/wp-content/uploads/sites/42/2017/05/Indonesia-Fact-Sheet-December-2016.pdf

UNICEF. *Refugee children: Guideline on protection and care*. Retrieved from https://www.unicef.org/violencestudy/pdf/refugee_children_guidelines_on_protection_and_care.pd

Universal Declaration of Human Rights, Retreived from http://www.un.org/en/universal-declaration-human-rights/

Convention against Torture

Circular Letter 1956.

Committee on the Rights of the Child, 'General Comment No 6: Treatment of Unaccompanied and Separated Children Outside their Country of Origin', UN doc CRC/GC/2005/6, 1 Sept 2005, para. 27.

Convention relating to the Status of Refugees (adopted 28 July 1951, entered into force 22 April 1954) 189 UNTS 137 (Refugee Convention).

Human Rights Committee, 'General Comment 20, Article 7' in 'Compilation of General Comments and General Recommendations Adopted by Human Rights Treaty Bodies', UN doc HRI/GEN/1/Rev.1, 1992, 30, para. 9.

Human Rights Watch (2013). *Barely surviving: Detention, abuse, and neglect of migrant children in Indonesia*. USA: Human Rights Watch.

ICCPR.

Indonesia 1945 Constitution.

Indonesia, Law No. 6 Year 2011 on Immigration.

International Covenant on Civil and Political Rights (ICCPR)

Refugee Convention.

UN General Assembly, Statute of the Office of the United Nations High Commission for Refugees, 14 December 1950, A/RES/428(V), para. 7(d).

UNHCR

UNTS

Culture and International Law - Juwana et al. (Eds)
© 2019 Taylor & Francis Group, London, ISBN 978-1-138-38766-9

Revisiting heritage regulations and their impact in Indonesia (Case Study: Onrust Archaeological Park)

R. Ahmad Ginanjar Purnawibawa & Supratikno Rahardjo
Department of Archaeology, Faculty of Humanity, Universitas Indonesia

ABSTRACT: With Law No. 11 on Cagar Budaya (Heritage Protection) officially signed, heritage management in Indonesia starts a new chapter. The Indonesian government not only regulates protection to sustain heritage but also expects heritage to be beneficial for national economic activity as well as national character building. However, the lack of definitive rules and multiple or different interpretations has led many regions to issue local regulations according to their interpretation. This encourages the emergence of conflicts that adversely affect the management of cultural heritage in Indonesia. One such case occurred in Onrust Archaeological Park, Jakarta. As one of the important sites of historical events in Jakarta, even Indonesia, the conflict that arose resulted in the park being unable to develop further and losing its value. Through a literature review and in-depth interviews with stakeholders, this research aims to revisit the heritage regulation on Onrust Island and try to comprehend its impacts on the management of the park.

KEYWORDS: heritage, impacts, law, Onrust Archaeological Park, regulations

1 INTRODUCTION

In recent decades, international law has seen a remarkable intensification of interest in cultural heritage and a significant expansion of the legal tools for its protection. Several conventions have been negotiated to address the issues that occur in heritage protection, such as the 2001 Underwater Cultural Heritage Convention and the 2003 Declaration on the International Destruction of Cultural Heritage.[1] In Indonesia, aspects of cultural heritage protection legislation were marked by the issuance of Monumenten Ordonnantie Staatsblad 238 No. 19 in 1931, four months earlier than the publication of the Charter of Athens as a milestone in the history of global collaboration in heritage conservation efforts. Monumenten Ordonnantie consists of 14 articles that regulate terminology, categories, registration and violation. Overall, it illustrated that the protection of cultural heritage was the government's responsibility, the community involvement was intended to devotion to the state right of society less accommodated.[2]

After the independence of Indonesia, the Monumenten Ordonnantie (MO) was still used as the main legal standing in the New Order Government Period. In this period, the People's Consultative Assembly (MPR) repeatedly issued a resolution called TAP MPR concerning the outline of state policy as the basis for development planning. These regulations indicated that the MO was unable to provide solutions for the problems that occurred in that period. Finally, after the Indonesian government accepted the UNESCO Convention 1972 in the

1. Francioni, F. & Gordley, J. (2013). *Enforcing international cultural heritage law*. Oxford, UK: Oxford University Press.
2. Fitri, I., Ahmad, Y. & Ratna. (2016). Cultural heritage and its legal protection in Indonesia since the Dutch East Indies government period. *Advances in Social Science, Education and Humanities Research, 127*, 81.

1980s, the Indonesian government issued a new regulation on cultural heritage called Law No. 5 on *Benda Cagar Budaya* (BCB; Items of Cultural Heritage) in 1992. This law regulated terminology, specification and protection. However, Law No. 5 on BCB still maintained the concept of centrality in terms of registration, planning and management of heritage. The government also ignored the importance of a multidisciplinary approach as an administration structure in heritage protection, as the office was still dominated by archaeologists.[3]

Subsequently, the Indonesian government published the newest law concerning heritage protection in October 2010. Law No. 11 on *Cagar Budaya* (Heritage Protection). This law was expected to be a fundamental base as well as the new perspective to protect and manage cultural heritage in Indonesia.[4] The new aspects regulated for in this law are a more comprehensive heritage category, decentralization and a multidisciplinary approach in heritage conservation. Another major difference is the inclusion of utilization of heritage to provide a better living for the people. The new law explicitly encourages the participation of communities in safeguarding and managing cultural heritage by maintaining its sustainability, as mentioned in Article 1 Paragraph (33), which described utilization of cultural heritage for the benefit of the maximum people's welfare by maintaining its sustainability.

However, Law No. 11 on Cagar Budaya is not a perfect product, and experts have raised a number of criticisms. Tanudirjo (2010) mentioned that the definition of each category is still not correct and tight, which is not only inappropriate from an academic perspective, but can also lead to misunderstandings, as well as emphasizing the confusion in the terminology of 'situs' or site, and 'area' or region mentioned in Law No. 11 on Cagar Budaya, which were never mentioned in previous laws.[5] Tanudirjo also alludes to the inclusion of an underwater heritage category in Law No. 11 on Cagar Budaya, as the Indonesian government has still not accepted and adopted the UNESCO Convention on Protection of the Underwater Cultural Heritage (2001).[6] Another criticism is the open interpretation of the law and that the elucidation, supposed to be mentioned in the government regulation, has not yet been published. This year (2018) marked seven years' delay of the publishing of the government regulation; consequently, at provincial and municipal level the law is open to interpretation and interpreted differently by practitioners.

The problem mentioned previously has led to disharmony in heritage management in many places because Law No. 11 on Cagar Budaya is of legal standing and provides guidance for heritage workers and practitioners to perform their work properly. One such problem appears in Onrust Archaeological Park, Jakarta, which is a group of islands located in Jakarta Bay that are designated as an archaeological park, serving educational and preservation purposes. Due to differing understandings by stakeholders and interpretation of the laws, the park is managed by different agencies with different agendas. Without an integrated approach and cooperation, the park experiences exploitation without a comprehensive measure to protect its value and integrity. The problem that emerged in the park is the main focus of this research, which relies on a literature review of the applied laws and in-depth interviews with stakeholders. This research aims to analyze the conflict that emerged in the Onrust Archaeological Park.

2 ONRUST ARCHAEOLOGICAL PARK AND ITS LEGAL ASPECTS

Onrust Island, Cipir Island, Kelor Island and Bidadari Island have enlivened the cultural landscape in Jakarta Bay since 1619 when the Verenigde Oostindische (Dutch East India) Company (VOC) made Onrust a base and shipyard, and used other islands for support. Strategic location and favorable sea topography in Onrust supported the VOC's vision of monopolizing the spice

3. Ibid.
4. Ibid.
5. Tanudirjo, D.A. (2010). Undang-Undang Cagar Budaya 2010 Dalam Perspektif Arkeologi. In *Diskusi Pembahasan Undang-Undang tentang Cagar Budaya.*
6. Ibid.

trade in the archipelago. To support their cause, the VOC built barracks, forts, port, windmills and storage. Before the collapse of the VOC in 1799, the islands withstood attacks from VOC rivals in the archipelago. After that, the Kingdom of the Netherlands took over all VOC assets, including the four islands. They were used as a military defense, prison, weather station and eventually as a quarantine for hajj pilgrims before being allowed to return to Indonesia. Currently, most of the archaeological remains in Onrust Archaeological Park are ruined due to the looting of building materials carried out by local residents in 1968.

As an archaeological site, the value of the islands is immeasurable. These islands are witnesses to the Indonesian nation's journey over hundreds of years. These values and identities are currently attached to the ruins of existing buildings. Although most are in ruins, some remaining ruins are significantly iconic, such as the Martello Fort in Cipir Island. The character of the site itself is also very rare because its heritage represents conflicting identities. Evidence of the nation's past wounds exist, side by side with evidence of the Indonesian struggle for independence. This unique character is one of the important values of the Onrust Archaeological Park. Another important legacy is the Hajj Barracks on the island of Onrust, which began to be used in 1911; in addition to being evidence of historical developments in health science and health management, they also share heritage with multivocal narratives.

Since being designated in 1972 as a protected island because of its historical significance by Governor Ali Sadikin through *Daerah Khusus Ibukota* (DKI; Special Capital Region) Jakarta Governor Decree No. CB/11/2/16/1972, Onrust Archaeological Park has continued to grow and become one of the leading tourism destinations in Jakarta. Data gathered from 2011 also shows the rise in visitors to the island and, in 2017, as many as 51,000 visitors were recorded (Thousand Islands in Figures, 2015; Department of Tourism and Culture, DKI Jakarta, 2016; data.jakarta.go.id, accessed April 24, 2018). The risks that occur as a consequence of the rise of visitors, the development of tourism, and the fragile nature of the archaeological heritage made regulation to protect the park more important than ever.

Currently, Onrust Archaeological Park is protected by Governor Decree No. 2209, year 2015, concerning designation of Onrust Island, Cipir Island, Kelor Island and Bidadari Island as cultural heritage areas. Cultural heritage areas are defined in Law No. 11 on Cagar Budaya, Article 1 Paragraph 6, as geographic space units that have two or more cultural heritage sites, located close to each other and/or showing typical spatial characteristics. As a consequence of the cultural heritage area category pinned on the park, the government was obliged to facilitate its management by forming a management agency or body. Examples of such cases were implemented in the Sangiran Early Men Site and Borobudur, which have their own management agencies. In 2002, through Governor Decree No. 134, the Jakarta provincial government formed a technical unit to manage the park, called *Unit Pengelola Teknis Taman Arkeologi Onrust*. This unit then merged with another agency, in 2016, as decided in

Figure 1. Cipir Island of Onrust Archaeological Park.

Governor Decree No. 323 concerning organization and working procedures of *Unit Pengelola Museum Bahari* (Maritime Museum) management. Hence, the Onrust Archaeological Park was then managed under the Maritime Museum management. Onrust Archaeological Park also became the subject of a few other regulations, such as Local Regulation No. 1 of 2012 concerning 2030 spatial plans, and Governor Decree No. 36 of 2014 concerning the Jakarta Old Town master plan. Both regulations controlled the principal of development in Onrust Archaeological Park and emphasized the importance of balancing economic interest through tourism and ideological interest through heritage preservation.

3 REGULATIONS' IMPACTS ON ONRUST ARCHAEOLOGICAL PARK MANAGEMENT

The impact of regulations or laws on heritage management is inevitable. The term *cagar budaya* (equal to heritage) itself is a term defined by law. On one hand, archaeologists are more familiar with terms such as archaeological remains or archaeological ruins. As the subjects of law, the heritage and heritage workers are bound to follow the law itself. On the other hand is the legal status and protection provided by the nation to the associated heritage. The Onrust Archaeological Park is the same after designation; as a cultural heritage area by law, the park is bound by the same terms. In this research, we found that there are two issues that strongly affect heritage management in Onrust Archaeological Park. The first issue is the regulation related to the management agency, while the second issue is the regulation that relates to the development of the area, which directly and indirectly might affect the park.

3.1 *Management context*

The management context of Onrust Archaeological Park is undoubtedly complicated. As mentioned previously, the provincial government delegates the task of managing the park to the Maritime Museum as site manager. In this case, the provincial government has fulfilled its obligations in accordance with the mandate in the law, wherein the government must facilitate the management of cultural heritage through the establishment of a management body. However, as stipulated in Law No. 11 of 2010 concerning cultural heritage, the management body can be formed from elements of government, business and society. Maritime museums are institutions that only represent elements of the government, while the two elements of other stakeholders tend to be ignored in the decision-making process.

As a management body established by the government to manage the park, the Maritime Museum is supposed to uphold its own authority. As site manager, the Maritime Museum is obliged to arrange development planning, implementation and evaluation of the park management. However, on the other hand, the Maritime Museum, as site manager, is also restrained by the system. As stated by the Head of the Maritime Museum (in an interview on February 20, 2018), the Maritime Museum, as an agency, is under the authority of the Jakarta Tourism and Culture Office. The impact is that the site manager's authority is very limited, and the manager's vision must be in accordance with the tourism service, namely the development of the Onrust Archaeological Park as a tourism destination. Subsequently, this will lead to greater conflicts as tourism development tends to ignore the principles of preservation.

Aside from the DKI Jakarta Department of Tourism and site manager, in Jakarta, there is a Cultural Heritage Expert Team, which was formed according to Law No. 11 of 2010 concerning cultural heritage. This team serves the purpose of providing recommendations, ranking and removal of the legal status of cultural heritage. However, as granted by the provincial government, this team also holds the authority to make decisions about proposed projects related to cultural heritage, especially projects related to revitalization, adaptation, and utilization where the possibility of altering the cultural heritage from its original state occurs. This team consists of experts in the fields of archaeology, architecture, and history that hold their value in strict heritage preservation. Sometimes, this can be seen as an obstacle from a developer's perspective. As an example, in 2017, the site manager proposed a new master plan to revitalize the park, including new zoning and reconstruction of the old buildings for tourism attraction. While the new zoning concept was acceptable, the reconstruction plan for the fort on Onrust Island was postponed by the Cultural Heritage Expert Team, as the plan was seen as a threat to the authenticity and integrity of the island as a whole.

Governor Decree No. 323 of 2016 clearly stated that the Maritime Museum is the agency authorized to manage the four islands in the Onrust Archaeological Park. However, in practice, the Bidadari Island is managed separately by the Thousand Island Department of Tourism through PT. Seabreeze. Both of these stakeholders aggressively developed Bidadari Island into a tourism destination by building resorts and attractions to accommodate visitors' needs. Although this is beneficial in terms of tourism, on the other hand, there are concerns from conservationists regarding the sustainability of heritage on the island, especially with the plan for revitalizing the island through the 'Soul of Batavia' declared by the provincial government and executed by PT. Pembangunan Jaya Ancol Tbk (Kumparan Travel, April 20, 2018), which is still in progress at the time of writing. From the perspective of archaeology, the Bidadari Island authenticity will be open to serious question by the time the project is finished.

Because the park is managed by groups of stakeholders with different interests, the Maritime Museum seems to be overwhelmed by the task. As decided by Governor Decree No. 323 of 2016, the Maritime Museum not only manages the Onrust Archaeological Park but also Marunda Site and the Maritime Museum itself in the same manner. This places a heavy workload on the agency in terms of human and intellectual resources. Recently, the park has recruited a significant number of workers in response to the need for a cleaning service and in situ protection for the heritage. While this is seen as a positive development, the addition is also criticized because it is considered as not solving the real problem and lacking qualities in the workers, especially their understanding of heritage.

Thus, there are several problems due to the policy of Governor Decree No. 323 of 2016 concerning the management of Onrust Archaeological Park. These problems include the following:

1. The emergence of many stakeholders in the management of the Onrust Archaeological Park, including the Maritime Museum, the Thousand Island Regency Government, PT. Seabreeze, PT. Pembangunan Jaya Ancol, the Cultural Heritage Expert Team, the Jakarta Tourism and Culture Office, and the DKI Jakarta provincial government itself (Governor or Deputy Governor), who sometimes take unilateral decisions.
2. The impact of so many stakeholders is that the occurrence of partial management in certain islands and the authority of the Maritime Museum, as site manager, is very limited and pressurized.
3. The site manager bears a very heavy task, as the Maritime Museum must manage three different sites with limited human resources.
4. Stagnation in Onrust Archaeological Park management, especially the development of interpretation and communication to the public.

3.2 *Area development*

As stated in Regional Regulation No. 1 of 2012 concerning 2030 Regional Spatial Plans and Regional Regulation No. 1 of 2014 concerning Detailed Spatial Planning and Zoning Regulations, the Onrust Archaeological Park is designated as an archaeological park area or cultural heritage that has functions in line with tourism functions and contains elements of activities, research and archaeological tourism. Meanwhile, economic and social development is one of the threats to cultural resources, and in some cases, decisions that must be taken are at the expense of archaeological sites.[7] Based on observations on the site and interviews with

7. Cleere, H. (1984). *Approaches to the archaeological heritage*. Cambridge, UK: Cambridge University Press.

informants, there are at least two aspects that have the potential to threaten the existence of the Onrust Archaeological Park, both physically and non-physically. The first threat is the Jakarta Giant Sea Wall (JGSW) development project which has the potential to cause physical damage to the islands in the Onrust Archaeological Park region, while the second threat is the pace of tourism development that is too fast and could threaten the authenticity and important value of the Onrust Archaeological Park region.

The government of the Republic of Indonesia, through the National Capital Integrated Coastal Development (NCICD) Program in January 2013, made plans to continue the work of the Jakarta Coastal Defense Strategy (JCDS) in order to formulate a strategy to overcome the Jakarta flood problem. The problem of flooding in Jakarta causes losses to four million people living in vulnerable areas and causes economic losses of 104 trillion dollars.[8] Several factors that are taken into consideration in the formulation of the strategic plan are: sea level rise by 7.3 mm/year; land subsidence which reaches an average of 15 cm/year; and the sediment supply from the rivers that flow into the Jakarta Bay, which is 42 tons/year.[9]

One of the strategic plans prepared is the building of the JGSW. In a study of the ecological and physical hydrodynamic aspects of the JGSW development, especially in aspects of current movement patterns with mathematical/numerical modeling, Poernomo et al. (2015) conveyed the impact of the JGSW development on the islands in Jakarta Bay. The JGSW development impact analysis model was formulated according to the 2030 Regional Spatial Plan of the DKI Jakarta Government, stipulated by DKI Jakarta Regional Government Regulation No. 1 of 2012. Based on the analysis, the following impacts were identified:

1. There are two regimes of current circulation patterns, namely the pattern of flow circulation outside the JGSW sea dike and current circulation patterns in the pond formed by the JGSW sea dike.
2. The pattern of circulation of ocean currents outside the JGSW embankment remains dynamic, following the natural pattern of tidal propagation.
3. The current circulation pattern in the JGSW sea dike-pond is very small and decreases its dynamic level.
4. The current circulation pattern outside the sea dike erodes small islands in the western part (Onrust Archaeological Park area).
5. The less dynamic pattern of circulation of currents in a pond formed by sea dikes has the potential to cause material accumulation (waste, freshwater sediment), which causes an increase in the frequency of eutrophication and mass mortality of fish.

If the construction of the JGSW is in accordance with the Regional Spatial Plan of 2030 of the DKI Jakarta Government, then Cipir Island as the southernmost island of Onrust Archaeological Park will be very close to Reclamation Island, which it is planned to build. As a member of the Restoration Assembly Team, Attahiyat (in an interview, February 9, 2018) requested the provincial government of DKI Jakarta to at least place a distance of 300 meters between Cipir Island and the reclamation island, while on the development map, the distance was less than 100 meters. The same thing was conveyed by the Head of the Maritime Museum (in an interview, February 20, 2018), who stated that the buffer zone in Onrust Archaeological Park should be 500 meters from Cipir Island, but as a compromise to the JGSW plan, the area of the buffer zone was reduced to 300 meters.

JGSW's development not only threatens the existence of Onrust Archaeological Park physically but also changes the overall cultural landscape in Jakarta Bay. In Article 1 of the Burra Charter, regarding the definition of cultural significance, it is stated that cultural significance is embedded not only in place, but also material (fabric) and layout. The setting itself is defined as the extension environment of a protected place and contributes to cultural significance and forms a distinctive character. Settings include structure, space, land, water, sky,

8. Poernomo, A. et al. (2015). *Prakiraan Dampak Giant Sea Wall Teluk Jakarta*. Jakarta, Indonesia: Kementerian Kelautan dan Perikanan.
9. Ibid.

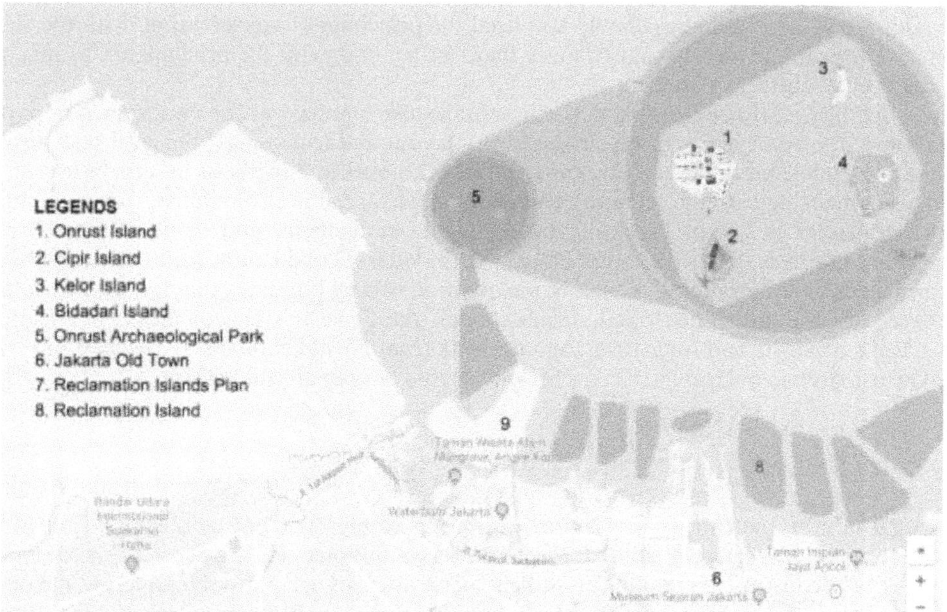

Figure 2. Onrust Archaeological Park in the reclamation blueprint.
(Source: maps.google.co.id, 2018 & Poernomo et al., 2014 with modification)[10]

including view from and to the place. Thus, the changes that will be made with the construction of the JGSW will also threaten the important value of the Onrust Archaeological Park region as a whole. The position of the DKI Jakarta government itself is not consistent in addressing the issue of reclamation in Jakarta Bay. Having previously stated that it would stop the reclamation and seal the islands that had been built, recently with the stipulation of the Governor Regulation No. 58 of 2018 concerning the Establishment of the Organization and Work Procedure of the North Coast Reclamation Coordinating and Management Board of the Jakarta government, the opposite position has been adopted. The institution in charge of managing reclamation is BKP Pantura Jakarta, which is led by the Secretary of DKI Jakarta and is domiciled and responsible to the Governor. According to Article 4, BKP Pantura Jakarta has the task of coordinating the planning, implementation and supervision of the Jakarta and North Coast of Java Reclamation, the management of reclamation results, and the rearrangement of the north coast area of Jakarta, as well as providing policy recommendations in the context of organizing the reclamation and realignment of the north coast of Jakarta.

Another impact of reclamation is the withdrawal of Jakarta Old Town from UNESCO's World Heritage Site Tentative List. UNESCO itself has placed constraints on several projects in establishing Jakarta's Old Town and four islands in Onrust Archaeological Park as world heritage, by saying that they have deficiencies in authenticity and integrity (Jakarta Post, July 9, 2018), which is both the result of development that does not pay attention to the rules of sustainability, and planning that is carried out without in-depth study. The statement is proven by the irreversible development in the Jakarta Old Town and the plan of islets in reclamation. The significance and authenticity of the Onrust Archaeological Park region are also increasingly threatened with the building of new amenities for tourism on these islands. Onrust Island and Bidadari Island are two islands with the greatest addition of new buildings.

10. Poernomo, A. et al. (2014). *Dinamika Teluk Jakarta, Analisis Prediksi Dampak Pembangunan Tanggul Laut Jakarta (Jakarta Giant Sea Wall)*. Jakarta, Indonesia: Kementerian Kelautan dan Perikanan.

The addition of new buildings should still heed the principles of conservation, with the Burra Charter, for example, saying that changes that can be done with the principle of 'as much as necessary but as little as possible'.

Law No. 11 of 2010 concerning cultural heritage also emphasizes the importance of paying attention to the authenticity of materials, forms, layout and technology; the level of change as small as possible; and the use of non-destructive techniques and methods in refurbishment. At the development stage of the economy and people's welfare, it is also required to pay attention to the principles of benefit, security, maintenance, authenticity and values attached to it. Thus, what has been done on Onrust Island and Bidadari Island can be said to be contrary to the principles of conservation, including the addition of new buildings that ignore and tend to interfere with the authenticity and significance of the Onrust Archaeological Park. Careful plans, clear concepts and long-term commitments from all stakeholders are needed to realize that Onrust Archaeological Park can provide benefits but remain sustainable.

4 CONCLUSION

As a legal subject, the Onrust Archaeological Park is certainly bound by the applicable provisions. However, it is unfortunate that these provisions are precisely the cause of the decline in the value of the historical region. The stakeholders' interests are not only hindering the development of the Onrust Archaeological Park but also threaten the authenticity and integrity of the park as a whole. The heavy burden borne by the site manager should also not occur if the management merger is not carried out according to the policy of Governor Decree No. 323 of 2016 concerning the management of Onrust Archaeological Park. As a cultural heritage area, the Onrust Archaeological Park should have a special management body, considering the character of the area that is distinctive and requires its own handling. In addition, it is also necessary to have a clear management vision from the manager to determine the type of utilization and appropriate utilization strategies and to maintain the sustainability of the Onrust Archaeological Park. On the other hand, the development of housing and disaster prevention necessary due to floods and land subsidence has led to the establishment of the JGSW. From an archaeological point of view, the existence of the JGSW will eliminate a very important cultural landscape in the Jakarta Bay. However, for the sake of greater national interest, negotiations must be carried out and the best solution for all parties sought.

ACKNOWLEDGMENTS

We would like to thank PITTA UI 2018 for the support given to make this research possible. We were also greatly helped by the willingness of Candrian Attahiyat and Husnison Nizar to provide the information and discussions needed for the writing of this article.

REFERENCES

Cleere, H. (1984). *Approaches to the archaeological heritage.* Cambridge, UK: Cambridge University Press.

Fitri, I., Ahmad, Y. & Ratna, (2016). Cultural heritage and its legal protection in Indonesia since the Dutch East Indies government period. *Advances in Social Science, Education and Humanities Research, 81*, 127.

Francioni, F. & Gordley, J. (2013). *Enforcing international cultural heritage law.* Oxford, UK: Oxford University Press.

Poernomo, A., et al. (2014). *Dinamika Teluk Jakarta, Analisis Prediksi Dampak Pembangunan Tanggul Laut Jakarta (Jakarta Giant Sea Wall).* Jakarta, Indonesia: Kementerian Kelautan dan Perikanan.

Poernomo, A., et al. (2015). *Prakiraan Dampak Giant Sea Wall Teluk Jakarta.* Jakarta, Indonesia: Kementerian Kelautan dan Perikanan.

Tanudirjo, D.A. (2010). Undang-Undang Cagar Budaya 2010 Dalam Perspektif Arkeologi. In *Diskusi Pembahasan Undang-Undang tentang Cagar Budaya.*
Governor Decree No. 134 of 2002
Governor Decree No. 2209 of 2015 concerning Designated Of Onrust Island, Cipir Island, Kelor Island, And Bidadari Island As A Cultural Heritage Area
Governor Decree No. policy. 323 of 2016 concerning The Management Of Onrust Archaeological Park
Law on Cultural Heritage Items No. 5 of 1992
Law on Cultural Heritage Items No. 11 of 2010
Monumenten Ordonnantie Staatsblad 238 No. 19 in 1931
Regional Regulation No. 1 of 2012 concerning 2030 Regional Spatial Plans
Regional Regulation No. 1 of 2014 concerning Detailed Spatial Planning and Zoning Regulations
UNESCO Convention on Protection of the Underwater Cultural Heritage, 2001

Culture and International Law - Juwana et al. (Eds)
© 2019 Taylor & Francis Group, London, ISBN 978-1-138-38766-9

Author Index

www.ingramcontent.com/pod-product-compliance
Ingram Content Group UK Ltd.
Pitfield, Milton Keynes, MK11 3LW, UK
UKHW050052200926
475702UK00019B/2792
* 9 7 8 0 3 6 7 7 7 6 6 2 6 *